A Grammar of Makasar

Grammars and Sketches of the World's Languages

Mainland and Insular South East Asia

Editor

Paul Sidwell (*Australian National University*)

Co-editor

Mathias Jenny (*University of Zurich*)

Advisory Board

Mark Donohue (*Australian National University*)
Arthur Holmer (*Lund University*)
Joe Pittayaporn (*Chulalongkorn University*)
Antonia Soriente (*University of Naples "L'Orientale"*)

The titles published in this series are listed at *brill.com/gswl*

A Grammar of Makasar

A Language of South Sulawesi, Indonesia

By

Anthony Jukes

Edited by

Paul James Sidwell

BRILL

LEIDEN | BOSTON

Library of Congress Cataloging-in-Publication Data

Names: Jukes, Anthony (Anthony Robert), author. | Sidwell, Paul, editor.
Title: A grammar of Makasar : a language of South Sulawesi, Indonesia / by
    Anthony Jukes ; edited by Paul James Sidwell.
Description: Leiden ; Boston : Brill, [2020] | Series: Grammars and sketches of the
    world's languages. Mainland and insular South East Asia | Includes
    bibliographical references and index.
Identifiers: LCCN 2019046163 (print) | LCCN 2019046164 (ebook) |
    ISBN 9789004363687 (hardback) | ISBN 9789004412668 (ebook)
Subjects: LCSH: Makasar language–Grammar.
Classification: LCC PL5366 .J85 2020 (print) | LCC PL5366 (ebook) |
    DDC 499/.2264–dc23
LC record available at https://lccn.loc.gov/2019046163
LC ebook record available at https://lccn.loc.gov/2019046164

Typeface for the Latin, Greek, and Cyrillic scripts: "Brill". See and download: brill.com/brill-typeface.

ISSN 2352-9342
ISBN 978-90-04-36368-7 (hardback)
ISBN 978-90-04-41266-8 (e-book)

Copyright 2020 by Koninklijke Brill NV, Leiden, The Netherlands.
Koninklijke Brill NV incorporates the imprints Brill, Brill Hes & De Graaf, Brill Nijhoff, Brill Rodopi,
Brill Sense, Hotei Publishing, mentis Verlag, Verlag Ferdinand Schöningh and Wilhelm Fink Verlag.
All rights reserved. No part of this publication may be reproduced, translated, stored in a retrieval system,
or transmitted in any form or by any means, electronic, mechanical, photocopying, recording or otherwise,
without prior written permission from the publisher.
Authorization to photocopy items for internal or personal use is granted by Koninklijke Brill NV provided
that the appropriate fees are paid directly to The Copyright Clearance Center, 222 Rosewood Drive,
Suite 910, Danvers, MA 01923, USA. Fees are subject to change.

This book is printed on acid-free paper and produced in a sustainable manner.

Printed by Printforce, the Netherlands

Contents

List of Figures and Tables XIII
Abbreviations of Grammatical Terms XVI
A Note on Spelling Conventions XIX
Abbreviations of Sources for Example Sentences XX

1 **Introduction** 1
  1.1   The Area and Inhabitants 2
      1.1.1 *Geography* 2
      1.1.2 *Demography* 4
      1.1.3 *Economy* 5
  1.2   Historical Background 6
      1.2.1 *Prehistory* 6
      1.2.2 *Early Kingdoms* 7
      1.2.3 *The Rise and Fall of Gowa* 10
      1.2.4 *Colonialism and Independence* 15
  1.3   Religion and Culture 17
  1.4   Comparative and Historical Data 19
      1.4.1 *The Makassar Family* 20
      1.4.2 *The South Sulawesi Subgroup* 22
      1.4.3 *Homeland and Migration Hypotheses* 26
  1.5   Linguistic Ecology 30
      1.5.1 *Language Status* 30
      1.5.2 *Other Languages of Importance* 30
  1.6   Previous Studies of Makasar 34
      1.6.1 *Colonial Dutch Scholars* 34
      1.6.2 *Indonesian Scholars* 36
      1.6.3 *English Language Scholars* 37
  1.7   Work on Related Languages 38
      1.7.1 *Konjo* 38
      1.7.2 *Selayarese* 38
      1.7.3 *Bugis* 39
  1.8   Sources of Data 39
      1.8.1 *Fieldwork* 39
      1.8.2 *Written Sources* 40
      1.8.3 *The Corpus* 41

2	**Makasar Writing and Literature**	**44**
	2.1 Makasar and Bugis Scripts	44
	2.1.1 *History*	46
	2.1.2 *Problems with the Scripts*	50
	2.1.3 *Punctuation*	50
	2.1.4 *Script Reform Proposals*	51
	2.1.5 *Reading* lontara'	52
	2.2 Arabic Script (*serang*)	54
	2.3 Romanised Orthography	54
	2.3.1 *Matthes' System*	55
	2.3.2 *Cense's System*	55
	2.3.3 *Indonesian Based System*	56
	2.3.4 *Locally Preferred Option*	58
	2.4 Literature	59
	2.4.1 *Orality and Literacy in Makasar*	60
	2.4.2 Lontara'	61
	2.4.3 *Published Works in Bugis Script*	63
	2.4.4 *Oral Genres*	63
3	**Phonetics & Phonology**	**65**
	3.1 Phoneme Inventory	65
	3.1.1 *Phoneme Contrasts*	65
	3.1.2 *Consonants*	68
	3.1.3 *Vowels*	85
	3.2 Phonotactics	93
	3.2.1 *Syllable Structure*	93
	3.2.2 *Word Structure*	97
	3.2.3 *Stress*	100
	3.3 Morphophonological Processes	102
	3.3.1 *Vowel Degemination*	102
	3.3.2 *Nasal Substitution*	104
	3.3.3 *Glottal Strengthening*	106
	3.3.4 *Echo–VC*	107
	3.3.5 *Aphesis of Initial /a/*	111
	3.3.6 *Determiner Glide Insertion*	112
	3.3.7 *Reduplication*	112
	3.3.8 *Compounding*	117

CONTENTS

4   Morphological Units   119

4.1   Roots   119

4.1.1   *Bases*   120

4.1.2   *Stems*   120

4.2   Affixes   120

4.3   Clitics   122

4.3.1   *Properties of Clitics*   123

4.3.2   *Clitic Pronouns*   125

4.3.3   *Aspectual/Modal Clitics*   126

4.4   Affixal Clitics   133

4.4.1   *The Definite Marker* ≡a   134

4.4.2   *Possessives*   137

4.5   Particles   139

4.5.1   *Preposed Particles*   140

4.5.2   *Postposed Particles*   141

4.6   Words   142

5   Word Classes   143

5.1   Root Class and Word Class   143

5.2   Nouns   147

5.3   Verbs   148

5.3.1   *Subcategories of Verbs*   148

5.4   Adjectives   151

5.4.1   *Adjective Morphology*   153

5.5   Adverbs   158

5.5.1   *Preposed Adverbs*   159

5.5.2   *Postposed Adverbial Particles*   160

5.5.3   *Temporal Adverbs*   168

5.6   Pronouns   169

5.6.1   *Personal Pronouns*   169

5.6.2   *Reflexive Constructions*   171

5.6.3   *Demonstratives*   172

5.6.4   *Interrogatives*   173

5.6.5   *Indefinite Pronouns*   173

5.7   Locatives   177

5.7.1   *Relative* (ri) *Locatives*   177

5.7.2   *Absolute* (i) *Locatives*   178

5.7.3   *Deictic Adverbs*   180

5.8   Numerals   181

5.8.1   *Numeral Derivations*   185

	5.8.2	*Fractions* 188
	5.8.3	*Indefinite Quantifiers* 189
5.9	Classifiers, Partitives and Measures 189	
5.10	Prepositions 190	
	5.10.1	*Prepositional Verb* 192
5.11	Conjunctions 193	
5.12	Discourse Particles 194	
5.13	Interjections 194	

6 Nouns and Noun Phrases 196

6.1	Subclasses of Noun 196	
	6.1.1	*Common Nouns* 197
	6.1.2	*Proper Nouns* 200
	6.1.3	*Temporal Nominals* 203
6.2	Nominal Derivation 208	
	6.2.1	*Reduplication* 208
	6.2.2	pa– *Nominal Derivation* 209
	6.2.3	ka⟩⟨ang *Nominal Derivation* 217
	6.2.4	–ang *Nominal Derivation* 221
6.3	The Noun Phrase 222	
	6.3.1	*Specifiers* 223
	6.3.2	*Modifiers* 224
	6.3.3	*Relative Clauses* 226

7 Basic Clause Structure 231

7.1	Word Order 231	
7.2	Clitic Pronouns 232	
	7.2.1	*2P Behaviour* 234
	7.2.2	*Clitic Fronting* 236
	7.2.3	*Agreement or Cross-Reference?* 240
	7.2.4	*Definiteness and Cross-Referencing* 242
7.3	Ambient Clauses 245	
7.4	Intransitive Clauses 246	
	7.4.1	*Verbal Predicates* 246
	7.4.2	*Adjectival Predicates* 247
	7.4.3	*Nominal Predicates* 248
	7.4.4	*Numeral Predicates* 249
	7.4.5	*Locative Predicates* 249
7.5	Semi-transitive Clauses 250	
	7.5.1	*The Intransitive Analysis* 251

CONTENTS IX

	7.5.2	*The Antipassive Analysis* 251
	7.5.3	*The 'Actor Focus' Analysis* 252
7.6	Transitive Clauses 252	
	7.6.1	*Reflexives* 253
7.7	Ditransitive Clauses 254	

8 Voice/Valence-Signalling Prefixes 255

8.1 The Verb Prefixes 256
    8.1.1 aC– *Verbs* 259
    8.1.2 aN(N)– *Verbs* 263
    8.1.3 *Verbs with Either* aC– *or* aN(N)– 265
    8.1.4 amm– *Verbs* 266
    8.1.5 *Adjectival/Stative* ma– 268
8.2 Actor Focus *aN–* 269
8.3 Passive *ni–* 270
8.4 Involuntary/Accidental *taC–* 273
8.5 Other Accounts of South Sulawesi Prefixes 276
    8.5.1 *Makasar* 276
    8.5.2 *Selayarese* 279
    8.5.3 *Konjo* 281
8.6 Voice 282

9 Causative *pa–* and Related Forms 287

9.1 Causative *pa–* 287
    9.1.1 pa– *on Verb Roots* 288
    9.1.2 pa– *on Prefixed Bases* 291
    9.1.3 pa– *on Other Derived Bases* 294
    9.1.4 pa– *on PPs* 295
    9.1.5 pa–*VERB*–i 295
    9.1.6 pa–*VERB*–ang 296
    9.1.7 pa–*VERB*–xi–ang 297
9.2 Causative *paka–* 297
9.3 Experiencer-Oriented *pi–* 299
    9.3.1 pi– 299
    9.3.2 pi––i 301
    9.3.3 pi––ang 303
    9.3.4 pi––i–ang 304
    9.3.5 pi––ang *in Causative Passive Derivations* 304

x CONTENTS

10 Applicative Suffixes 306
  10.1 The Suffix Form *–i* 306
    10.1.1 *Transitiviser* –i 307
    10.1.2 *Locative Applicative* –i 310
    10.1.3 *Extended* –i 311
  10.2 The Suffix Form *–ang* 312
    10.2.1 *Benefactive/Applicative –ang* 312
    10.2.2 *'Afflicted with'* 316
  10.3 *–i* and *–ang* Together 317

11 Other Verbal Affixes 319
  11.1 Unitary/Mutual/Reciprocal *si–* 319
    11.1.1 si– *+ Numeral or Classifier 'One NOUN'* 319
    11.1.2 si– *+ NOUN 'Share One NOUN'* 320
    11.1.3 si–*ADJ*–i *'Be ADJ Together'* 321
    11.1.4 si–*VERB 'Do VERB Together' or 'Do VERB*
      Reciprocally' 321
    11.1.5 *Misc. Uses of* si– 324
  11.2 Erratic *piti*⟩RDP–V⟨*i* 327
  11.3 Subjunctive *–a* 328

12 Grammatical Relations 330
  12.1 Grammatical Relations 330
  12.2 Focus and Topic Marking 334
    12.2.1 *Focus* 334
    12.2.2 *Topicalisation* 338

13 Other Clause Types 340
  13.1 Imperatives 340
  13.2 Questions 342
    13.2.1 *Yes/No Questions* 342
    13.2.2 *Content Questions* 344
  13.3 Negation 354
    13.3.1 ta= *'NEG'* 354
    13.3.2 t(a)ena *'Not'* 355
    13.3.3 tea *'Don't'* 356
    13.3.4 teá *'Not Be'* 357
    13.3.5 iang 358
  13.4 Existentials 359
  13.5 Ascriptives/Presentatives 361

Appendix A: Excerpt of the Gowa Chronicle from Manuscript KIT 668–216   365

Appendix B: Karaeng Ammanaka Bembe: The Karaeng Who Gave Birth to a Goat   391

Appendix C: A'jappa–jappa ri Bulukumba: A Trip to Bulukumba   418

Bibliography   424

Index   435

Figures and Tables

Figures

1	South Sulawesi within Indonesia 2
2	Sulawesi showing current provincial boundaries 3
3	Austronesian family tree 19
4	Detail of the Bungaya Treaty (from Tol 1996) 47
5	Later Makasar script 48
6	*Serang* script (from Cummings 2002:45) 54
7	Single & geminate /p/ 69
8	Single and post-glottal stop /b/ 70
9	Single & geminate /c/ 72
10	Voiced palatal stops with strong and weak fricative release 72
11	Single and geminate palatal nasal 74
12	Single & geminate /l/ 77
13	Single and geminate /r/ 78
14	Nasal + /r/ & tapped /r/ 78
15	Comparison of vowel occurrences 87
16	Normal and lowered mid-vowels 93
17	Non-lowered mid-vowels 93
18	Formation of complex onsets 111
19	Derivation path for nouns 145
20	Derivation path for verbs 146
21	Derivation path for adjectives 146
22	Kinship terms (ego is shaded) 200

Tables

1	Makassar subfamily (Grimes & Grimes 1987) 21
2	Makassar family (Friberg & Laskowske 1989) 21
3	Taxonomy of subgrouping levels (Grimes and Grimes 1987:12–13) 23
4	Functor statistics (Sirk 1989:73) 25
5	The Bugis and Makasar scripts 45
6	Comparison of late and early Makasar aksara 49
7	Phoneme inventory 66
8	Distribution of /w/ 79
9	Distribution of /j/ (Shaded cells show the environment of epenthetic /j/) 80

10	Consonant sequences	85
11	Vowels	86
12	Vowel sequences	88
13	CV patterns	98
14	Roots subject to nasal substitution	105
15	Reduplication of mono- and disyllabic roots	113
16	Reduplication of trisyllabic roots	113
17	Affixes	123
18	Clitics	125
19	Paradigms of pronominal elements	126
20	TAM and pronominal enclitics	127
21	Properties of major word classes	144
22	Heads and modifiers	145
23	Differences between verb prefixes	149
24	Basic verbs	151
25	Adjectives	153
26	Modifiers of degree	153
27	Preposed adverbs	159
28	Postposed adverbs	161
29	to(do)ng postposed adverbs	161
30	Temporal adverbs	168
31	Pronominal elements	170
32	Interrogatives	173
33	Relative locatives	177
34	Absolute locatives	179
35	Basic numerals	182
36	Compound and complex numerals	182
37	Classifiers, partitives and measures	190
38	Conjunctions	193
39	Interjections	195
40	Common nouns	198
41	Generic nouns	199
42	Clock times	204
43	Times of day	205
44	Days of the week	206
45	Month names	207
46	*pa*–root → person who does X	210
47	*pa*–verb base → instrument nominal	211
48	*pa*–verb base → non-instrumental nominal	213
49	*pa*–verb base on basic verbs	214

FIGURES AND TABLES

50 *pa*–inf exceptions 214
51 *pa*>verb base<*ang* → place or time 215
52 *pa*>verb base<*ang* exceptions 216
53 paC>adj<ang → person inclined to be adj 216
54 *ka*>adj<*ang* → 'adj-ness' 217
55 nouns derived with *ka*>basic verb<*ang* 219
56 nouns derived with –*ang* 222
57 NPs with modifying nouns 224
58 Clitics and free NP placement 233
59 Verb prefixes 256
60 Verb types by prefix 258
61 Verbs derived with *aC*– 261
62 Verbs with nasal substituting *aN(N)*– 263
63 Verbs without nasal substitution 264
64 Vowel-initial verbs with *aN(N)*– 264
65 Intransitive/transitive verbs with *aC*– and *aN(N)*– 266
66 Homophonous roots with *aC*– and *aN(N)*– 266
67 Roots with interchangeable *aC*– and *aN(N)*– 266
68 *amm*– verbs 267
69 Verbs with *taC*– 274
70 *pa*–root → CAUS 288
71 Verbs derived with *pi*– 300
72 Verbs with *pi*––*i* 302
73 Grammatical relations 333

Abbreviations of Grammatical Terms

The abbreviations used for grammatical terms are based on the Leipzig Glossing Rules (http://www.eva.mpg.de/lingua/files/morpheme.html) with a few modifications.

1	first person
2	second person
3	third person
A	agent-like argument of trans. verb
ABS	absolutive
ADJ	adjective
AF	actor focus
AFFL	afflicted with
APPL	applicative
BCS	because
BEN	benefactive
BV	bivalent
CAUS	causative
CLF	classifier
COM	comitative
COMP	complementiser
COMPR	comparative
DEF	definite
DEM	demonstrative
DIST	distal
DISTR	distributive
DUR	durative
EC	echo VC (epenthetic syllable)
EQ.COMPR	equal comparative
ERG	ergative
EXCL	exclusive
EXP	experiencer-oriented
F	familiar
FOC	focus
FUT	future
HORT	hortative
INCL	inclusive
INDF	indefinite (pronoun)

ABBREVIATIONS OF GRAMMATICAL TERMS

INF	infinitive
INTR	intransitive
IPF	imperfective
LK	linker
MULT	multiplier
MUT	mutual
MV	monovalent
NEG	negation, negative
NR	nominaliser/nominalisation
NVOL	non-volitional
OBL	oblique
ORD	ordinal
P	polite
P	patient-like argument of trans. verb
P^{INDF}	patient-like arg. of semi-trans. verb
PASS	passive
PERS	personal
PFV	perfective
PL	plural
POSS	possessive
PRO	full pronoun
PROH	prohibitive
PROX	proximal/proximate
PURP	purposive
Q	question particle/marker
QUOT	quotative
RDP	reduplication
RECP	reciprocal
REFL	reflexive
REL	relative
S	singular
S	single argument of intrans. verb
S^{A}	agent-like arg. of semi-trans. verb
SBJV	subjunctive
SG	singular
ST	stative
TOP	topic
TOT	in totality, completely
TR	transitive
TRS	transitiviser
VET	vetative

–	affix
=	clitic
≡	affixal clitic (see § 4.4)

Clitic pronouns are minimally labelled for person, e.g.:

1=	1st person proclitic ('ergative')
=3	3rd person enclitic ('absolutive')

A Note on Spelling Conventions

There is significant confusion about the best way to represent orthographically the name of this language, the ethnic group who speak it, and the city which dominates the region (renamed Makassar in 1999 after 28 years as Ujung Pandang). In the language itself they are respectively *basa Mangkasara'*, *tau Mangkasara'* and *Mangkasara'* (previously *Jumpandang*). In modern Indonesian they are *bahasa Makassar, orang Makassar* and *Makassar*. At various times in English the forms *Makassarese, Macassarese* and *Macassan* (among others) have been found.[1] Recently scholars working on South Sulawesi have come to favour the forms *Makasarese* (e.g. Noorduyn 1991b) or just *Makasar* (e.g. Macknight & Caldwell 2001), to differentiate the language/ethnic name from the name of the city, and also to correct the Indonesian spelling (Indonesian has no geminate /s/ sound so evidently the form has been taken from Dutch). Although in previous work (e.g. 2006) I used the form *Makassarese*, in this and other recent work I have elected to use *Makasar* mainly to avoid perpetuating a confusing schism in South Sulawesi scholarship.

As for orthographic conventions for representing language data, I have largely followed those of the Makasar–Dutch dictionary (Cense & Abdoerrahim 1979), with a few minor alterations, along the lines of those in Chabot (1996), to make the script more compatible with modern Indonesian spelling. Briefly:

> *'* is a glottal stop [ʔ]
> *ng* is a velar nasal [ŋ]
> *ny* is a palatal nasal [ɲ]
> *c* is a voiceless palatal stop [c]
> *j* is a voiced palatal stop [ɟ]

The whole question of orthographic standards is examined in much more detail in Chapter 2.

---

1 The term Macassan (as used in Macknight 1976) is intended as a catch-all term for the people (mostly but not all Makasar) who travelled to northern Australia in search of trepang. Many nowadays fail to draw the distinction.

Abbreviations of Sources for Example Sentences

The following is a list of abbreviations for the most commonly used sources of example sentences. Those left unspecified are generally from my fieldnotes.

C:pp   (Cense & Abdoerrahim 1979)
Cgn:pp   Grammar notes by A.A. Cense, KITLV Or545.43
KIT:ref   Shoeboxed excerpt of the Gowa Chronicle in ms 668–216, Koninklijk Instituut voor de Tropen (see Appendix A)
Maros:ref   Shoeboxed text of the Maros Chronicle (from Cummings 2000)
PT:ref   Shoeboxed folktale Caritana Pung Tedong (Jukes 1998:Appendix B; Zainuddin Hakim 1991)
SKT:ref   Shoeboxed excerpt of Sinrili'na Kappala' Tallumbatua (Aburaerah Arief and Zainuddin Hakim 1993)
bembe:ref   Shoeboxed folktale Caritana Karaeng Ammanaka Bembe, KITLV Or545 .55f (see Appendix B)

CHAPTER 1

Introduction

This is a description of the Makasar language, which is spoken by about 2 million people in the province of South Sulawesi in Indonesia. It is typically placed in a South Sulawesi subgroup within the Western-Malayo-Polynesian branch of the Austronesian language family. Typologically it is a head-marking language which marks arguments on the predicate with a system of pronominal clitics, which canonically follow an ergative/absolutive pattern, while full NPs are relatively free in order. There is a pre-predicate focus position which is widely used. In Himmelmann's (2005) terminology, Makasar (along with other South Sulawesi languages and some from other parts of Indonesia) is a **transitional language**, being neither a **symmetrical voice language** like the majority of Austronesian languages, nor a **preposed possessor language** such as languages of the Moluccas and Timor. The phonology is notable for the large number of geminate and pre-glottalised consonant sequences, while the morphology is characterised by highly productive affixation and pervasive encliticisation of pronominal and aspectual elements. Over the centuries the language has been represented orthographically in many ways: with two indigenous Indic or *aksara* based scripts, a system based on Arabic script, and a variety of Romanised conventions.

This description differs from many modern grammars of living languages in that it draws heavily upon literary sources reaching back more than three centuries. This is partly due to circumstances—various problems throughout my doctoral candidacy prevented me from spending as much time in South Sulawesi as I would have liked, restricting my access to the lively speech community. But it is also due to a conscious decision—Makasar is rare among languages of eastern Indonesia in possessing a literary heritage of moderate antiquity which allows us to see snapshots of the language of the past, and ignoring this source of data seems short-sighted. The older material has been balanced by use of modern written data, either published material or from online chat fora, and also by work with speakers both in Makassar and in Melbourne.

© KONINKLIJKE BRILL NV, LEIDEN, 2020 | DOI:10.1163/9789004412668_002

FIGURE 1   South Sulawesi within Indonesia

1.1   The Area and Inhabitants

Here follows an introduction to the neighbourhood of South Sulawesi: its physical geography and some human geographic information about the major ethnic groups which inhabit it, followed by some background history of the Makasar people and cultural observations.

1.1.1   *Geography*

Sulawesi (also known as Celebes) is an unusually shaped island straddling the equator between Borneo (Kalimantan) and the Moluccas (Maluku), south of the Philippines. Its distinctive shape and mountainous nature are the result of the collision of four major island fragments associated with Eurasian and Australian continental margins; this is also reflected in the island's inclusion in Wallacea, the transitional zone between the Asian and Australian biogeographic regions (Hall 2001).

Sulawesi is part of the Republic of Indonesia, and is divided into six provinces: these are Sulawesi Utara (North Sulawesi), Gorontalo (split off from North Sulawesi in 2000), Sulawesi Tengah (Central Sulawesi), Sulawesi Tenggara (South-East Sulawesi), Sulawesi Selatan (South Sulawesi), and Sulawesi Barat (West Sulawesi, which split off from South Sulawesi in October 2004). South Sulawesi (excluding the string of islands to the south) extends roughly between 2° and 5°5 south of the equator, a length of approximately 400 km. The province, at its widest, stretches over 200 km east to west, but the peninsula proper is about 150 km wide in the north and 80–100 km wide in the south. The area of the province is 62,482 km².

The northern half of South Sulawesi (including the relatively well-known and touristed Tana Toraja region) is mountainous with several peaks over 3000

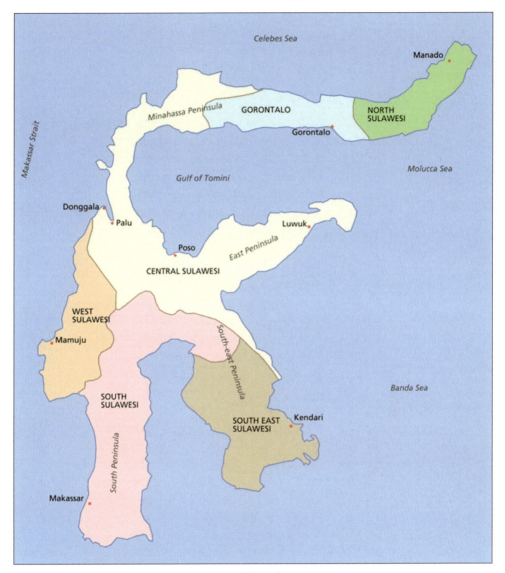

FIGURE 2   Sulawesi showing current provincial boundaries

metres. The southern half of the peninsula is divided by a cordillera into two main parts—a narrow strip of fertile plains on the west coast which becomes wider in the south west corner; and a wider area of plains and lowlands on the east coast and in the centre, including the two shallow lakes Tempe and Sidenreng. These correspond roughly to areas of Makasar and Bugis settlement respectively. The southern tip of the peninsula is dominated by two peaks over 2500 metres, Bawakaraeng and Lompobattang. The south coast is somewhat

4   CHAPTER 1

arid, as is the island of Selayar off the south-east cape. Otherwise, the climate is
tropical and monsoonal, with the west monsoon bringing rain predominantly
to the west coast from November to March, and the east monsoon bringing rain
to the other coast from April to October.

1.1.2 *Demography*

South Sulawesi with more than eight million inhabitants is the most populous
of Sulawesi's provinces, with almost half of the island's population.[1] Of these,
80% live in the southern half of the peninsula (Pelras 1996:7), the mountainous northern half is by comparison sparsely populated by many language/eth-
nic groups concentrated along the coast and in river valleys. Of the 29 South
Sulawesi languages listed in the Summer Institute of Linguistics' Ethnologue
(www.ethnologue.com), 22 are spoken in this northern half and in the part
which is now West Sulawesi. Those with the most speakers are Sa'dan (750,000),
Tae' (340,000) and Mandar (475,000).

The southern half is dominated by speakers of the two largest languages:
Bugis and Makasar and their dialects, together with some closely related languages. The Makasar live in the south-west corner of the peninsula. Most of
them are concentrated in the fertile coastal plain around the city of Makassar and to the south; these are the *kabupatens* (administrative districts) of
Gowa and Takalar, considered the Makasar heartland. Gowa also extends into
the mountains which occupy the centre of the peninsula, but these are more
sparsely populated. To the north of Makassar are the kabupatens of Maros and
Pangkajene Kepulauan (Pangkep), which are densely populated with a mixture of Bugis and Makasar. On the south coast are the kabupatens of Jeneponto
and Bantaeng, whose inhabitants identify as Makasar though their dialects are
substantially different from that of Gowa and Takalar (see §1.4.3). Kabupaten
Bulukumba in the south-east corner of the peninsula is inhabited by a mixture
of Bugis and Konjo (or Kajang) people, while the Selayar people occupy the
island of Selayar to the south. The remainder of the southern part of the peninsula is inhabited by Bugis, including the east coast and the inland plains which
extend roughly from the Sinjai area in the south-east to Pare–pare in the west.

It is difficult to ascertain exactly the number of Makasar speakers, as Indonesian census data does not reliably include language or ethnic data. SIL Ethnologue gives a figure of 2.13 million, similar to Pelras's (1996:12) estimate of
about 2 million. A back-of-the-envelope calculation made by adding together
the populations of the kabupatens which are almost entirely populated by

---

1 8,032,551 in South Sulawesi, around 17 million for Sulawesi as a whole in the 2010 census
   (Badan Pusat Statistik: http://sp2010.bps.go.id/).

INTRODUCTION

Makasar speakers (Maros, Gowa, Takalar, Jeneponto and Bantaeng), together with at least one-third of Makassar city's population and half of the population of kabupaten Pangkep, gives a similar figure of around 2.2 million. This makes it the second largest language in Sulawesi, after Bugis with about 5 million speakers.

1.1.3 *Economy*

There is an obvious economic division between urban and rural Makasar. I would estimate that at least 500,000 Makasar live in urban Makassar, the remainder living in smaller towns, villages and hamlets. The majority of rural Makasar are engaged in farming or fishing. There is extensive wet rice cultivation on the west side and the interior of the peninsula, largely relying on rainfall rather than complex irrigation systems. There are also cash crops such as cacao and vanilla, and fruit such as passionfruit—syrup made from this is one of the more famous local products. On the south coast the kabupatens of Jeneponto and Bantaeng are drier and poorer. Jeneponto in particular is notorious for its poverty and many of its young men work in Makassar or other towns driving taxis or *becak* (bicycle rickshaws). Income from relatively poor agriculture in parts of this region is supplemented by fish farming and evaporating seawater for salt. Shipbuilding used to be an important activity in communities along the south coast, but this is now largely dominated by the Bugis in Bulukumba and the Mandar people in the north-west of the peninsula.

Makassar itself has a complex economy—as a city of over a million inhabitants (with 2.2 million in the greater metropolitan area) it is beyond simple characterisation. As the largest city in eastern Indonesia it attracts large numbers of immigrants, including resettled refugees from intermittently strife-torn Maluku and Central Sulawesi, and also large numbers of students from Sulawesi and all over the eastern part of the archipelago. As an administrative, educational, and commercial centre it supports a sizeable middle class. There are also some modern industrial facilities such as a large paper mill and cement plant, as well as an important port handling produce and primary resources. Within the city of Makassar the Makasar form something of an underclass, though they are still (to the best of my knowledge) the largest single ethnic group in the city, followed closely by the Bugis, and then Torajans and other ethnic groups from the rest of Sulawesi and Indonesia. There is also a sizeable Makassar Chinese population. However, as with many Indonesian centres underemployment is a large problem and many urban Makasar are employed in the informal sector as *becak* drivers and small-scale pedlars.[2]

---

2 See Forbes (1979) for a brief description of the informal sector and some insights into the lives

6   CHAPTER 1

1.2   Historical Background

This section briefly covers the historical background of the peninsula from prehistory to present, drawing on archaeological and linguistic research for the
earliest part, and written history (both indigenous and external) for the last
800 years or so.

1.2.1   *Prehistory*

South Sulawesi was inhabited by humans by at least 40,000 years ago as shown
by dating of cave paintings in Maros (Aubert et al. 2014). Other than these
paintings, the best known pre-Austronesian material culture indicated by the
archaeological record is known as Toalean (or Toalian),[3] 'the most important
industry of the flake and blade technocomplex ... with an array of microliths
(small-backed flakes and geometrics) of types seemingly unique in the Indo-
Malaysian archipelago' (Bellwood 1997:193). These were produced from about
8000 BP until 1500 BP (Bulbeck et al. 2000:71) across the south-west of the peninsula, an area which 'corresponds closely to the area where the Makasar languages (Austronesian) are spoken today' (Bulbeck et al. 2000:74).

The close fit between the Toalean and Makasar areas has led Bulbeck (Bulbeck 1992:512–513) to speculate that there could be a Toalean linguistic substratum in Makasar—an appealing notion but one for which there is no apparent evidence. However, the dates certainly suggest that the hunter–gatherer
Toalean culture survived for some time after the arrival of Austronesian speakers—this is also indicated by the presence of pottery (believed to have been
acquired by trading with Austronesians) in Toalean sites from between 2500–
1500 BC (Bellwood 1997:229). The evidence has led Bulbeck et al. to surmise
that the Toaleans were quite able to coexist and trade with their new neighbours: 'Far from being in peril of rapid replacement, the Toaleans must have
been a dense hunter–gatherer population who evidently tolerated immigrant
Austronesian farmers for the benefits they brought' (Bulbeck et al. 2000:102).

According to Bellwood's generally accepted model, the spread of Austronesian languages throughout the archipelago is associated with the spread of
ceramics and agriculture, starting from a putative proto-Austronesian homeland in Taiwan around 3000 BCE, through the Philippines and into Sulawesi

---

of those who work in it. Although based on data which is now over twenty years old, most of
the general observations are pertinent today.

3   The term 'Toalean' itself is a misnomer, from the Bugis *toale'* 'forest people', who lived in rock
shelters in Lamoncong and appear to have been Bugis exiles (Bulbeck et al. 2000:74; Pelras
1996:37).

INTRODUCTION

by about 2000 BCE (Bellwood 1997:119). The first Austronesians into South Sulawesi may have been speakers of proto-South Sulawesi (PSS), or there may have been earlier incursions by speakers of other groups (see §1.4.3 for a discussion of the historical linguistic evidence). It is worth noting here that for some or all of this period seawater would have covered some of the lowland area between Pare–Pare on the west coast and the Cenrana river valley on the east coast (including the present lakes Tempe and Sidenreng), to a greater or lesser extent separating the southern part of the peninsula from the north. The dating, extent, and ramifications of the saline intrusion remain a matter of ongoing debate. Mills (1975a:513–534), Pelras (1996:41) and Sirk (1994) all assume that the southern part of the peninsula was virtually an island, that the ancestors of the Makasar moved to this island from a PSS homeland to the north, and that the isolation resulting from dwelling on the island in part explains the divergence of Makasar from the other South Sulawesi languages. More recent work by Caldwell & Lillie (2004) has determined that there was seawater as far as the western side of Lake Tempe from 7000–2600 BP, but that it is unlikely that it ever extended all the way across the peninsula (Caldwell pers.comm). I have nothing to add to this debate, but will simply note that a narrow channel would pose little obstacle to a seafaring people, while the cordillera which forms the spine of the peninsula would in all likelihood prove more effective at isolating the Makasar from the rest of South Sulawesi.

The exact pattern of expansion will likely never become clear (again, see §1.4.3)—but for the purposes of this work I will simply assume that at least by the end of the 13th century CE (which is as far back as locally recorded history can be projected) the major ethnic groups of South Sulawesi had occupied their present locations and were divided into small kingdoms.

1.2.2 *Early Kingdoms*

For the purposes of this work, the history of the Makasar people from the early modern period will be conflated with the history of Gowa, the most successful Makasar kingdom; and the port city of Makassar which grew up inside it and its smaller neighbour and ally, Tallo'. This is not only because this grammar is mainly concerned with the language and literature of Gowa, especially its *patturioloang* ('ancestor tale' or Chronicle), but also because this region became the heartland of the Makasar by virtue of the preeminence of Gowa in its heyday of the 16th and 17th centuries.[4] This is not to deny the histories of other Makasar realms such as Bantaeng or Maros, but from a purely linguistic

---

4   Similarly the heartland of the Buginese—and supposedly the oldest kingdom—is considered to be Luwu, in the very north-east of South Sulawesi at the top of the Gulf of Bone. This folk

8   CHAPTER 1

view, the written sources coming from minor realms have either been passed through the filter of the Gowa court or derive from relatively recent oral versions.

Because local histories give sparse and rather mythic information about periods prior to the 16th century, most of what we know about the early Makasar states comes from archaeology or external sources. The most detailed source of archaeological analysis for the Gowa area is Bulbeck's (1992) PhD thesis, which uses archaeological evidence to confirm and augment information given in the Gowa and Tallo' Chronicles. His analysis of ceramic tradeware sherds show that several sites around Gowa were occupied and trading by at least the 13th century.

The influence of Gowa at these early times was probably local and limited. External sources tell us that Gowa is not the oldest identifiable Makasar kingdom—this was probably Bantaeng on the south coast, which was known to Javanese spice traders in the 14th century. The 1365 Javanese poem *Deśawarṇana* (also known as *Nāgarakṛtāgama*) names 'Bantayan' as one of the subjects of the Javanese Majapahit empire in a passage which reads:

> As well as the land of Bantayan, led by Bantayan and Luwuk,
> Including Uḍa, these being the three foremost places on the island
> Taking them island by island: Makasar, Butun and Banggawi,
> Kunir, Galiyahu and Salaya, Sumba, Solot and Muwar ...[5]
>
> PRAPAÑCA 1995

'Luwuk' is probably the Bugis kingdom of Luwu, 'Uḍa' has not been identified (Pelras 1996:66; Reid 2000:107). Another intriguing indication of early Javanese influence in the area is that several local placenames later mentioned in the Gowa Chronicle seem to be based on Javanese names—Sorobaya (Surabaya), Jipang and Garassi' (Grisek)—'all names of north Java cities likely to have sent merchants in this direction' (Reid 2000:107).

The next recorded mention of the Makasar and their kingdoms comes from the Portuguese, who were active in the archipelago from the early 16th cen-

---

  belief has been challenged by research by Bulbeck and Caldwell (2000), suggesting that Luwu is younger than tradition would suggest.

5 This passage is to my knowledge the first recorded mention of the name 'Makasar', however it is confusingly listed as an island separate from Bantayan, along with Buton, Selayar, and others less easily identified. Pelras explains this away by saying that the name Makassar is first and foremost an ethnic name which "could apply to any settlement of Makassar people, even away from mainland South Sulawesi" (Pelras 1996:67).

INTRODUCTION

tury. Their interest in Sulawesi was only peripheral—their real areas of influence were westwards in Malacca (which they conquered in 1511), and the Spice Islands of Maluku to the east. Again, rather confusingly, the early sources talk about the Makassar 'islands'. A passage written by the apothecary Tomé Pires not long after the conquest of Malacca reads in part:

> The islands of Macaçar are four or five days journey beyond the islands we have described ... The islands are numerous. It is a large country. One side goes up to Buton and Madura[6] and the other extends far up north. They are all heathens. They say that these islands have more than fifty kings. These islands trade with Malacca and with Java and with Borneo and with Siam and with all the places between Pahang and Siam. They are men more like the Siamese than other races. Their language is on its own, different from the others. They are heathens, robust, great warriors.[7]
>
> PIRES and RODRIGUES 1944:226

According to Portuguese reports the most prominent of the Makasar kingdoms on the west coast was Siang, which was located in the area of Pangkajene north of modern Makassar. Muslim Malay traders had been established in Siang since before 1500 (Reid 2000:117), and Siang appears (along with Tallo' and Garassi', but not Gowa) on a Portuguese map from 1534 (Pelras 1996:115). The trader Antonio de Paiva visited Siang several times in the 1540s, and even baptised its leader into Catholicism in 1544 (Jacobs 1966). However, Siang appears to have declined rapidly from that point—de Paiva himself moved his ships south to Tallo' due to Siang's inadequate harbour (Pelras 1996:129), and historians have also speculated that the Christianisation of the ruler may have led the Muslim

---

6 This possibly refers to Mandar.
7 The passage mentions that the Javanese call these people the 'BaJuus' (interpreted as 'Bugis' in the English translation): this has led Reid (2000:109–112) to surmise that there must have been a close connection between the Makasar and the Bajau people (also known as Sama, 'Orang Laut', or in Makasar *Bayo* or *tau ri je'ne'* 'people of the water'); and further, that the 'islands of Macacar' might refer to the islands of the Spermonde Archipelago to the west and north of Makassar, which could have been settled by Bajau under Makasar rule. Reid further discusses evidence from folklore of close ties between the two peoples. It must be noted however that these coral islands, though numerous, are small and today sporadically inhabited by Makasar people (rather than Bajau), and that there is no significant Bajau component in the Makasar lexicon nor, to my knowledge, vice versa. Another explanation put forward by Campbell Macknight (p.c) is that the passage is talking about two distinct peoples, the Bajau and the Makasar, who became conflated either by Pires himself (relying as he was on whatever information he could get from traders in Malacca), or simply through unintended ambiguity in the passage.

10   CHAPTER 1

traders to seek opportunities elsewhere (Pelras 1996:129; Reid 2000:114). Not
long afterwards Siang became a vassal state of the rising kingdom of Gowa.

1.2.3 The Rise and Fall of Gowa

The exact date of the founding of the kingdom of Gowa is unknown, but the
first external source who mentions it is Antonio de Paiva, who called it a 'great
city' which had recently been under the dominion of one of Siang's vassals but
was now free. Pelras speculates that this may have been Tallo' (Pelras 1996:115),
though this seems unlikely, given that according to both the Gowa and Tallo'
Chronicles, Tallo' had only recently been established as an offshoot of the Gowa
dynasty. Looking at local sources, Bulbeck (1992) has shown by counting back
the rulers in the Gowa Chronicle that that dynasty probably began in the 13th
century.

The earliest parts of the Gowa Chronicle have a mythological element which
is quite different from the matter-of-fact tone of the later sections. A controversial preface (which does not appear in all versions) may list rulers of Gowa
who predate the dynasty (Noorduyn 1991b:457–462), but the chronicle proper
begins with a female *tumanurung* ('descended one'), who married a certain
Karaeng Bayo. Some versions of the chronicle state that the latter's place of
origin was Bantaeng (Blok 1817:5; Reid 2000:100), which is supported by histories from Bantaeng itself (Cummings 2003), though other versions (perhaps in
an attempt to erase evidence of Bantaeng's precedence over Gowa) simply say
that 'his country is also not known' [*taniassengtongangngai pa'rasanganna*]
(Matthes 1883:146). It is interesting to note also that *Bayo* is Makasar for Bajau,
suggesting another possible link with the seafaring people mentioned in footnote 7.

The son of the *tumanurung* and Karaeng Bayo was known as Tumassalangga
Barayang ('the one with sloping shoulders'),[8] and the chronicle lists the kings
that follow, but with little information about their actions: Puang Loe Lembang,
Tuniatabanri, Karampang ri Gowa, Tunatangkalopi, Batara Gowa, Tunijallo' ri
Passuki'—the latter of whom died around 1510. Meanwhile a feud between
Batara Gowa and his brother, Karaeng Loe ri Sero, resulted in the latter founding
the neighbouring kingdom of Tallo', which would remain closely linked with
Gowa, though not always in friendly circumstances.[9]

---

8 Most karaengs are referred to here by their posthumous names, which often describe some
   characteristic of the individual or the circumstances of their death (see §6.1.2.3). In this case
   the word *barayang* apparently refers to a kind of tree with uneven branches (Cense & Abdoerrahim 1979:78), thus 'the one with uneven/sloping shoulders'.
9 For the hidden turbulent history of Gowa-Tallo' relations see Cummings (1999). It is worth

INTRODUCTION   11

Most scholars agree, however, that it was in the reign of Tumapa'risi' Kallonna ('the one with a sore neck'), who reigned from c. 1510 until c. 1546 that Gowa really started to become powerful. This can be seen partly as a result of strong leadership, and partly because of favourable economic and social conditions. Macknight (1993) has argued that around 1400 CE there was a pronounced increase both in the area and productivity of wet rice agriculture throughout the peninsula, allowing a significant rise in population densities and producing a surplus available for export. Gowa, having control of some of the most fertile land in the peninsula, was in a strong position—particularly so after trading activity became centred there in the mid–16th century—and so it was able to use both economic and military means to subjugate smaller states.

From the reign of Tumapa'risi' Kallonna onwards the Gowa Chronicle contains frequent lists of kingdoms (including Siang) being defeated and/or forced to pay tribute [*sa'bu kati*—literally '1000 catties']. It also recounts the story of a war between Gowa and its smaller neighbour Tallo', possibly in response to the abduction of the daughter of the king of Tallo' by Tumapa'risi' Kallonna's son (Cummings 1999), which ended in a peace treaty and alliance. This was probably around 1535 (Bulbeck 1992:117–127). The relationship between the two states was later characterised as 'only one people but two rulers' [*se'reji ata na rua karaeng*], and often involved the king of Tallo' becoming the *tuma'bicarabutta* ('one who speaks the land') of Gowa, the highest official after the king.

Another important development during Tumapa'risi' Kallonna's rule is described in the Gowa Chronicle as the 'making of Makasar *lontara''* [*ampareki lontara' Mangkasara'*] by the harbourmaster [*sabannara'*] I Daeng Pamatte'. This probably refers to the beginning of the keeping of detailed records and possibly the inception of the Chronicle itself (Cummings 2002:42). Certainly the Chronicle becomes much more detailed about non-genealogical matters from Tumapa'risi' Kallonna onwards.

Tumapa'risi' Kallonna was succeeded upon his death by his son Tunipalangga, who ruled from approximately 1546 until 1565. He was also considered a great king, and the Gowa Chronicle lists many of his achievements. An especially noteworthy event during his reign was the arrival and settling in Makassar of a group of Malay traders under Anakoda Bonang in 1561, a signal of Gowa's growing importance as an entrepôt.

Tunipalangga died in 1565 during a war against the Bugis kingdom of Bone and was succeeded by his brother Tunibatta, who reigned for only 40 days

---

noting here that the story of the founding of Tallo' by Karaeng Loe ri Sero is well supported by archaeological evidence (Bulbeck 1992; Macknight 1993).

before being captured and beheaded in the same war (*tunibatta* = 'the one who was beheaded'). He in turn was succeeded by his son Tunijallo', who reigned until 1590 but was murdered on a ship by a kinsman who had run amok (*tunijallo'* = 'the one who was killed by an amok').

Tunipasulu' (1590–1593) was the son of Tunijallo' and was only fifteen when he ascended the throne. His mother had been ruler of Tallo' so he also took the Tallo' throne (as well as that of Maros to the north, see Cummings (2000)), however he was not a good king and was deposed after two years on the throne [*tunipasulu'* = 'the one who was deposed']. He was forced into exile on Buton where he died in 1617. The Gowa chronicle is frank about his arbitrary behaviour: he killed people who had done no wrong [*manna taena salanna taua niasseng ti'ring nibunoji*], but ultimately concludes that it is better not talked about [*tasitabaji' nikana–kana*].

Tunipasulu' was replaced by his brother Tumamenang ri Gaukanna (ruled 1593–1639), who was only seven at the time of his accession. Because of his young age, the kingdom was put under the regency of the new king of Tallo', Karaeng Matoaya (ruled 1593–1623), and it was during his period of influence (he died in 1636) that Gowa entered its Golden Age. A non-exhaustive list of his achievements from the Gowa and Tallo' Chronicles includes:
– the construction of brick fortifications
– the digging of canals
– improvements in ship design
– the manufacture of firearms
– the minting of currency (Andaya 1981:36; Reid 2000:133–138).
There was also a marked increase in the number of merchants and envoys from other regional powers; and Dutch, Danes and English joined the Portuguese as representatives of Europe, adding to Makassar's increasingly cosmopolitan nature.

Another event symbolic of increasing Makasar interaction with the wider world was Karaeng Matoaya's conversion to Islam around 1605 (he took the Islamic name Sultan Abdullah). He was followed soon thereafter by Tumamenang ri Gaukanna (who became Sultan Alauddin). They then embarked on a campaign of Islamisation which conquered and converted all the major kingdoms south of Tana Toraja by 1611. The speed with which this was achieved seems remarkable, but as Cummings reminds us, we should regard it as 'an ongoing process rather than a single transformative event' (Cummings 2002: 32).[10] The campaigns of Islamisation and/or conquest were not confined to

---

10   See also Cummings (2001b, 2003) for more on this.

INTRODUCTION

South Sulawesi: 'By the time of Matoaya's death in 1636 Makasar's hegemony had extended in this way to embrace almost the whole coast of Sulawesi, the east coast of Borneo, and the Lesser Sundas from eastern Lombok to parts of Timor' (Reid 2000:144).[11]

Matoaya's sons were Karaeng Kanjilo (ruled Tallo' 1623–1641) and Karaeng Pattingalloang (ruled Tallo' 1641–1654). The latter was a particular favourite of European visitors, and he was renowned for his intellectual curiosity and fluency in several European languages. He was also adept at negotiating with the increasingly influential and threatening Dutch East Indies Company (*Verenigde Oostindische Compagnie* or VOC) which was attempting to gain a monopoly on the trade of spices from the Moluccas and did not take kindly to Gowa's role in this trade, nor its friendliness to merchants from other foreign powers.

Meanwhile, following the death of Sultan Alauddin in 1639, the throne of Gowa passed to Alauddin's son Sultan Muhammad Said (Tumamenang ri Papambatua, ruled 1639–1653). Strangely (as Andaya points out), although the Gowa Chronicle praises him as a ruler under whose reign no disaster befell the kingdom, it adds that 'he was loved by the common people, but as for the princes, such as the Tumailalang, they loved Tumamenang ri Gaukanna (Sultan Alauddin) more' [*ningai ri tau ta'balaka, na ponna ri ana' karaenga kammaya Tumailalanga, ningaiangngiji Tumenanga ri Gaukanna*] (Andaya 1981:38–39; Wolhoff and Abdurrahim 1959:70). This rather underwhelming vote of confidence notwithstanding, he seems to have been an effective king, and the partnership between him and Pattingalloang parallels that of their respective fathers Alauddin and Matoaya.

However, the reign of the next king of Gowa was to see the fall of the kingdom at the hands of its rival, the Bugis kingdom of Bone, in alliance with the VOC. Sultan Hasanuddin (Tumamenang ri Balla' Pangkana), ruled from 1653 to 1669 with his *tuma'bicarabutta*, Karaeng Karunrung (the son of Pattingalloang). The chain of events leading to the fall of Gowa is complex and is dealt with very comprehensively by Andaya (1981), but basically involves a series of misjudgements and bad dealings with Bone—resulting in resentment and feelings of *siri'* (§1.3) on the part of the Bone nobility, notably the prince Arung Palakka— and underestimation on Gowa's part of VOC military power.

---

11 It was probably in the 18th century, after the fall of Makassar, that Makasar influence reached its furthest southern extent: the north coast of Australia (*Marege'*), where they went to collect sea-cucumber (*taripang*). These voyages still feature in some Aboriginal ceremonies, and there are still significant numbers of Makasar loan words in languages of northern Australia. See Macknight (1976) for a history of these contacts; there are also several papers discussing the linguistic evidence (Evans 1992, 1997; Walker and Zorc 1981).

There were several minor incidents and skirmishes in the years leading to the Makassar war of 1666–1669—notable being the Dutch occupation of Gowa's fort of Pa'nakkukang in 1660 (Andaya 1981:45). A treaty agreed between Gowa and the VOC at the end of that year stipulated that Portuguese merchants should be expelled from Makassar, but Gowa made no move to do so and instead concentrated on shoring up its defences. It also ignored other treaty requirements that it give up claims to the island of Buton and other territories in favour of the Sultan of Ternate, Sultan Mandar Syah, who was virtually a puppet of the VOC (Ricklefs 2001:71). Further tension was created by Gowa's seizure of goods from shipwrecked VOC ships on Makasar territories, and the murder of a party sent to investigate one of these incidents in 1664 (Andaya 1981:62–63).

In November 1666 the Dutch sent a fleet out from Batavia commanded by Admiral Speelman. In addition to the VOC troops there was a party of Bugis led by Arung Palakka, who had been in exile in Java and elsewhere, fighting as a mercenary on behalf of the VOC. This alliance of Dutch and Bone forces inflicted major military defeats on the Makasar, leading to the 1667 Treaty of Bungaya which gave effective control of trade to the Dutch,[12] and political control to Bone. However Sultan Hasanuddin again failed to observe the terms of the treaty and fighting continued until June 1669, when the royal citadel of Somba Opu was destroyed by the Bone army and Dutch navy, and Sultan Hasanuddin abdicated in favour of his son Sultan Amir Hamzah (Tumammaliang ri Allu', reigned 1669–1674).

Makassar was gradually rebuilt as a Dutch colonial city and became the centre of colonial administration, though Arung Palakka and his heirs retained significant influence for some time. The Makasar rebelled a number of times in the 18th century, but were defeated each time. During this period many Makasar (and Bugis who had sided against Arung Palakka) fled South Sulawesi, spreading throughout the archipelago and as far as the Siamese kingdom of Ayutthaya (Andaya 1981:209).

---

12   For an in-depth examination of Gowa's heyday and its fall see Andaya (1981). The significance of these events in world history is underlined by Fernández-Armesto:

> The fall of Makassar ... did change the world. It completed the Dutch ring of force around the spice islands: now the Dutch could control supply at the source of production and the first level of distribution ... a valuable slice of the gorgeous east really was held in fee, and the economy of part of the Orient was impoverished for the benefit of the stockholders of the Dutch East India Company. This was a reversal of the aeons-old balance of trade, which had enriched the east at western expense (Fernández-Armesto 1995:326–327).

INTRODUCTION 15

In some respects this was seen as the end of Makasar history, and indeed the Gowa Chronicle does not mention the war at all—the final paragraphs contain only genealogical information concerning Sultan Hasanuddin and his successors up until Sultan Abdul Jalil (1677–1709)—while the Tallo' Chronicle finishes in the mid-17th century. In 1759 the Dutch governor of Makassar, Roelof Blok, noted that 'the manuscripts of the Maccassars have, since the conquest of their kingdom, been discontinued, and they have no intention to resume them, until their much wished for restoration be realized' (Blok 1817:iii).

Interestingly, although he had been instrumental in Gowa's defeat, Arung Palakka became a heroic figure in Makasar folklore as the protagonist of the epic tale *Sinrili'na Kappala' Tallumbatua* ('the tale of three ships')—a paradox which is examined in detail by Andaya (1980) and Cummings (2001a), but in a nutshell relies on the folk perception that he had been humiliated by the Gowa court and was therefore entitled to revenge.

1.2.4 *Colonialism and Independence*

The 18th and 19th centuries saw the Dutch consolidating and extending their power throughout South Sulawesi. The victories of the 17th century had resulted in direct Company rule in Makassar itself and, at least in theory, over considerable areas in the southern half of the peninsula, but the previous kingdoms, and Gowa in particular, were still powers to be reckoned with. At the end of the 18th century the VOC was dissolved and the Dutch state took direct control of the Dutch East Indies (with the exception of a brief loss of power to Britain, which occupied Makassar and other Dutch controlled areas from 1812 to 1816 during the Napoleonic Wars). Eventually the Dutch found it necessary to subdue their former Bugis allies, attacking Bone in 1824, 1859–1860, and finally in 1905; a year that also saw the final uprising by Gowa under Sultan Husen, which was once again put down and ended with his death. Following this was a period of more or less complete Dutch control that ended with Japanese invasion in 1942.[13]

Following Japanese occupation and liberation by Australian troops the Dutch attempted to re-establish their rule, and nationalist insurgents were brutally put down by Captain Raymond 'Turk' Westerling. Even when it was obvious that most of the former Dutch East Indies were lost, the Dutch attempted to form a State of East Indonesia (*Negara Indonesia Timur*) with

---

13   The history of this period is briefly recounted by Anthony Reid in Volkman and Caldwell (1995), the story is told more comprehensively in Reid (1981, 1988, 1993).

Makassar as its capital; however this was not viable and in August 1950 it was merged with the Republic of Indonesia.

This did not mean the end of conflict, however, as groups of disgruntled former guerrillas led by the Bugis Kahar Muzakkar rebelled over the new Republic's refusal to automatically absorb them into the army. In itself this may not seem sufficient grounds for armed insurrection, but as Andaya (1976) and Errington (1989:17) note, it should be seen as a typically South Sulawesi manifestation of besmirched honour or *siri'* (see §1.3). In 1952 Kahar Muzakkar joined his rebellion to the broader Darul Islam movement seeking an Islamic republic, then in 1958 attached himself to the Permesta rebellion which sought greater regional autonomy. For a time his forces had control of large parts of South and Southeast Sulawesi (one of the consequences being large-scale migrations of people from the kampongs to Makassar in search of relative tranquility), but gradually he was deserted by his deputies and eventually killed by Republican troops on February 3rd 1965 (Dijk 1981:155–217).

Since becoming part of the Republic of Indonesia South Sulawesi has suffered, like many other peripheral regions of Indonesia, from marginalisation and economic colonialism. It has been widely felt that much of the economic and administrative power is wielded by Chinese and Javanese immigrants respectively, with low-level resentment as a result. Occasionally there are outbreaks of religious or ethnic violence, though not to the extent of those in Central Sulawesi or North Maluku (which is not to deny that groups and individuals from South Sulawesi have been involved in the troubles of neighbouring areas).

One of the high points for South Sulawesi on the national stage came in May 1998, when B.J. Habibie, of Bugis-Makasar descent, took over the presidency after Suharto's fall. His tenure as president was brief but eventful, seeing the referendum which resulted in the independence of East Timor, and (of primarily local interest) the resumption of the name Makassar for the city which had for 29 years been known as Ujung Pandang. Habibie and the ruling party Golkar enjoyed tremendous support within Sulawesi, but the rest of the nation did not feel the same and he lost power to Abdurrahim Wahid in June 1999.

The Bugis businessman and politician Muhammad Jusuf Kalla has also been prominent in national politics. He became vice-president of Indonesia (under President Susilo Bambang Yudhoyono) in October 2004, failed in a presidential bid in 2009, and became vice-president again under President Joko Widodo in 2014.

In 2001 a meeting was held (chaired by Jusuf Kalla) to discuss the possibility of redrawing South Sulawesi's boundaries. Of the five potential breakaway provinces discussed in that meeting, as of this writing only one has as yet

INTRODUCTION   17

become reality: West Sulawesi. However it remains possible that Luwu and
Tana Toraja will also leave South Sulawesi to become the province of Luwu Raya
(Morrell 2005). Further developments are likely.

1.3   Religion and Culture

In this section I will simply outline some of the most salient points of Makasar
religion and culture—this is not the place for a detailed ethnography, a difficult project given the kinds of dichotomies (e.g. urban vs rural, commoner vs
nobility, Islam vs *ada'*, seafarer vs farmer, etc.) which obtain in Makasar society.
Instead the reader is directed to the ethnographic literature, when available.
There are many aspects of culture which are shared by Makasar and Bugis,
which is reflected in the tendency to refer to both ethnic groups by the joint
name 'Bugis-Makasar'—in fact, in my experience, Indonesians from outside
South Sulawesi are often surprised to learn that Bugis and Makasar are distinct
groups with languages that are mutually unintelligible. These similarities mean
that general studies of Bugis culture and society (e.g. Errington 1989; Pelras
1996) contain many observations which are also applicable to the Makasar—
one of the major differences being that the Makasar do not share the La Galigo
literary tradition (§ 2.4).

Both Makasar and Bugis are overwhelmingly orthodox Sunni Muslim,[14]
though as elsewhere in Indonesia Islam is overlaid on an older belief system. Bugis and Makasar are known as quite staunch Muslims, and indeed the
Muslim saint, Sheikh Yusuf, was of Makasar royal blood.[15] There are mosques
all over Makassar and in every village, and the volume of the muezzins' call
is apparently not limited by law as it is in other parts of Indonesia (Hanson
2003:31).

Pre-Islamic traditions (*ada'*) are evident in the stories of royal ancestors of
divine origin coming from the sky (*tumanurung* or 'descended ones'), and in
the reverence for *gaukang* (sacred stones symbolising the centre of a country)

---

14   A search of various evangelical websites produced estimates of the number of Makasar
Christians from "approximately 800" (http://www.calebproject.org/makas.htm) to "less
than 3500" (http://www.bethany.com/profiles/p_code/801.html). Whatever the actual
number, it is extremely small, and many are likely to be Makassar Chinese.

15   Sheikh Yusuf (1626–1699) is famous as a leader of Islamic resistance against the Dutch in
Java, and later in exile in South Africa, as spiritual leader of the Cape Muslim community.
The area where he lived, Zandvliet, is near the modern town of Macassar, near Cape Town;
in 1705 his body was returned to Lakiung in Gowa.

and *kalompoang* (literally 'greatness', usually manufactured regalia or weapons believed to have been left behind by *tumanurung*). Work by the anthropologists Martin Rössler and Birgitt Röttger-Rössler has concentrated on the role of ritual and sacred items in rural Makasar communities in modern times (Rössler 1987, 1990, 2000; Röttger-Rössler 1988, 2000).

Other items considered important—sometimes verging on the sacred—are texts (*lontara'*) of various genres. The cultural importance of texts and histories will be discussed in § 2.4 and is also the subject of much of the work by the American historian William Cummings (1999, 2000, 2001a, 2001b, 2002, 2003). The ethnomusicologist R. Anderson Sutton has also written on the value of both traditional and popular music forms, including the epic poetry genre *sinrili'* discussed here in § 2.4.4.1 (Sutton 1995, 2002).

The kinship system, social hierarchies and gender roles of a Gowa village in the periods before and after WW2 are the subject of Chabot's 'Verwantschap, stand en sexe in Zuid-Celebes' (Chabot 1950), which was published in an English translation as 'Kinship, status and gender in South Celebes' (Chabot 1996). A notable feature of Bugis-Makasar society which he describes has come to be called the 'patron-client' relationship, which is further examined by Pelras (1996:181–186; 2000) for the Bugis. These fluid ties of reciprocal obligation seem to permeate Bugis-Makasar culture, from agriculture through business and trade to marriage arrangements, and it can also be helpful to see political relationships, particularly the shifting patterns of allegiance between kingdoms during the Makassar War, through the perspective of these kinds of relationships. Also central to Makasar society are bilateral kinship and ascriptive status, which explain the local obsession with genealogy.

Any discussion of Makasar culture must address the important cultural keywords of *pacce* and *siri'*, both concepts also found in Bugis (*pessé* and *siri'*). *Pacce*, literally 'to feel a stinging or biting pain' (Cense & Abdoerrahim 1979:534), refers roughly to empathy and sense of loyalty to place and community. *Siri'* has complex semantics which refer to a sense of honour and dignity, and also to the feeling of having been deprived of this by insult to one's person or family, which can result in revenge killings and blood feuds. These two notions go a long way towards explaining the perception across Indonesia of Makasar and Bugis as being proud, loyal and rather hot-headed.[16]

---

16 Detailed discussion of *siri'* and *pacce* (*pessé* in Bugis) can be found in Chabot (1996:234–260), Andaya (1981:15–17), and Pelras (Pelras 1996:206–209). A criminological perspective on *siri'* as a cause of violent crime can be found in Mustofa (1992).

INTRODUCTION

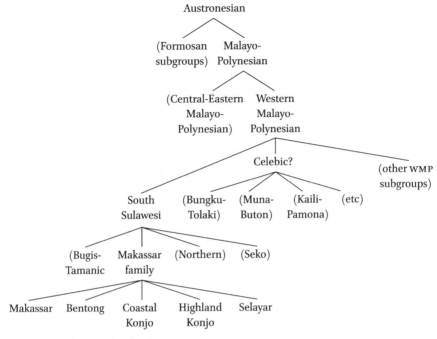

FIGURE 3 Austronesian family tree

1.4 Comparative and Historical Data

Makasar is an Austronesian language which is usually placed in the Western Malayo-Polynesian (WMP) branch. Figure 3 shows its genetic affiliation, extrapolated from Adelaar (2005) and other sources.

The upper levels of this classification are based largely on Blust (1977), though he has acknowledged that WMP is defined largely as a subgroup of the Malayo-Polynesian languages left over after the subtraction of the Central-Eastern Malayo-Polynesian subgroup—that is to say there are no innovations which distinguish proto-WMP from proto-MP (Blust 1999:68). The middle levels are based on Adelaar (2005) and incorporate evidence from Mead (2003) and others that exclude the South Sulawesi subgroup from a 'Celebic' macrogroup which contains most of the other Sulawesi subgroups. The lower levels are based on Grimes & Grimes (1987), as revised by Friberg & Laskowske (1989), and are as they appear in SIL's Ethnologue (www.ethnologue.com). This puts 29 of the 35-odd languages spoken in (geographical) South Sulawesi into one South Sulawesi subgroup (or stock in Grimes & Grimes terminology), the remainder belonging to either the Central Sulawesi or Muna-Buton subgroups.

1.4.1 The Makassar Family

A dialect chain stretches from Gowa through Takalar, Jeneponto (also known as Turatea, literally 'the above people'), Bantaeng and Konjo to Selayar. Most linguists now accept that Konjo and Selayarese are separate languages from Makassar, but the dialect/language boundary is no easier to define here than it is anywhere else. Most of the Gowa Makasar whom I asked considered Konjo and Selayarese to be (substandard) dialects of Makassar, but speakers of those languages would probably disagree.

The Gowa dialect (also called Lakiung, the name of a district of Gowa which is now in urban Makassar) is considered a prestige variety, and it is this dialect which is described here (in fact this can be considered the default reading of 'Makasar'). To the best of my knowledge there are only minor lexical differences between it and the dialect of Takalar to the south. The differences between these two and the dialect of the Jeneponto region are greater, and Gowa speakers readily recognise (and stigmatise) speakers of this variety. Travelling further around the south coast of the peninsula, I have observed that people from Gowa will tend to use Bahasa Indonesia to speak to people from Bantaeng and vice versa (though it is likely the issue has as much to do with group identification as with intelligibility). This also applies to Konjo and Selayarese, although it should also be noted that many speakers of these languages are also reasonably fluent in Gowa Makasar (the same observation can be made for speakers of the Jeneponto and Bantaeng dialects) owing to the city's importance as a regional centre. The town of Malino, though within the Highland Konjo area, is also Gowa Makasar speaking.

There are a few different sources for percentages of shared vocabulary within the Makassar family. Table 1 below shows figures from Grimes & Grimes (1987, based on Kaseng 1978). Since the percentages are all above 60 % (indeed above 70 %) Grimes & Grimes call the group a subfamily rather than a family (see §1.4.2).

A later study by Friberg & Laskowske (1989), though providing no data on Jeneponto and Bantaeng dialects, presents quite a different picture of the five members of the Makassar family for which they provide figures. Most notably, they add the language Bentong (or Dentong),[17] divide the Konjo language into two varieties, and reduce the percentage of shared vocabulary between

---

17   The name of this language, spoken in the inland regions of Kabupatens Pangkep and Maros, is supposedly derived from Makasar and Bugis words for 'non-fluent' (Friberg & Laskowske 1989:3). I was not personally able to confirm the existence of this language— most people from Makassar whom I asked had never heard of it, while others just said it was the same as Konjo.

INTRODUCTION

21

TABLE 1   Makassar subfamily

Gowa				
89	Jeneponto			
77	86	Bantaeng		
70	78	81	Konjo	
70	73	71	78	Selayarese

GRIMES & GRIMES 1987

TABLE 2   Makassar family

Lakiung				
75	Bentong			
68	77	Highland Konjo		
70	73	79	Lowland Konjo	
63	65	71	79	Selayar

FRIBERG & LASKOWSKE 1989

Makasar and Selayarese to 63 % (using data from the southern part of the island rather than the north). The lower figures (shown in Table 2) lead them to call the group a family rather than subfamily (although strictly speaking they are still above the 60 % cutoff which Grimes & Grimes used).

Most of the differences between the dialects/languages are lexical—superficially the grammars seem very similar, and their low percentages of shared vocabulary may give a rather exaggerated impression of the differences. As one would expect, Selayarese seems to be the most unlike Makasar grammatically; for example it has verbal marking for plurality of arguments (Hasan Basri 1998) which is not found in any of the others to my knowledge. Both Konjo and Selayarese use a different relativisation strategy than Gowa Makasar (see footnote 23, this chapter), and while the unmarked word order for Makasar and Konjo seems to be VSO (Friberg 1996), Finer (1994) argues that Selayarese has VOS. For other observations of the differences between Makasar and Selayarese see Hasan Basri (1999:50–54), for differences between Makasar and Konjo see Friberg (2002).

1.4.2 *The South Sulawesi Subgroup*

The existence of the South Sulawesi subgroup, first identified by Esser (1938), has been supported by a reconstruction of elements of proto-South Sulawesi in Mills (1975a), by a lexicostatistical survey in Grimes & Grimes (1987), and with qualitative evidence by Sirk (1989). It consists of the Makassar, Bugis, Northern and Seko families—to these may be added the Tamanic languages of western Kalimantan which Adelaar (1994, 2005) has shown to be linked to the South Sulawesi languages, probably in a subgroup with Bugis.

1.4.2.1 Quantitative Studies

There are a number of studies which consider the South Sulawesi languages from a predominantly or completely lexicostatistical approach. Of these the most significant is Grimes & Grimes (1987)—this forms the basis of the ree-valuation by Bulbeck (1992), and refinements by Friberg & Laskowske (1989) are mostly confined to changes within families. Mills (1975a) also contains some lexicostatistical analysis, but is not especially detailed.

Grimes & Grimes used a 202 item wordlist, basically a modified Swadesh list, and collected data from 39 speech communities across South Sulawesi. Then each wordlist was compared with each other wordlist to derive a matrix showing percentages of lexical similarity between any pair of languages in the study. The languages were then divided into groups and classified according to the taxonomy in Table 3.

According to their analysis, the languages in the study are representative of three stocks within the West Austronesian Superstock (or WMP) of the Austronesian Phylum, these stocks being South Sulawesi, Central Sulawesi, and Muna-Buton.[18] Within the South Sulawesi Stock there are 'five divisions: the Makassar Family-level Subfamily, the Bugis Family, the Northern South Sulawesi family, the Seko Family, and the Lemolang Family-level Isolate' (Grimes and Grimes 1987:23). The Makassar Family-level Subfamily in their analysis consisted of (Gowa) Makasar, Konjo and Selayarese (or more precisely,

---

18 The (presumed) Muna-Buton languages in the study were Laiyolo, Wotu, Kalaotoa and Bonerate. Recent work by Donohue, Mead, and Van den Berg suggests that at least the first two of these are not Muna-Buton languages, though there are competing theories for the actual configuration of subgroups (Adelaar 2005).

INTRODUCTION

TABLE 3   Taxonomy of subgrouping levels

% Lexical similarity	Level of division
>80%	dialect
>75%	language
>60%	subfamily
>45%	family
>25%	stock
>15%	superstock
>0%	phylum

GRIMES AND GRIMES 1987:12–13

a dialect/language chain which includes these languages); as already mentioned more detailed work by Friberg & Laskowske (1989) added the language Bentong, divided Konjo into Highland and Coastal varieties, and revised the group from subfamily down to family level due to a lower percentage spread.

All sources agree that the Makassar family is highly lexically divergent—Grimes & Grimes give the figure of only 43% average lexical similarity to the South Sulawesi stock as a whole (1987:25). This makes its inclusion in the stock rather marginal in strict lexicostatistical terms—the definition used above requires families to show 45% to 60% lexical similarity to the other families within a stock. Grimes & Grimes point out however that within the Makassar family, (Gowa) Makasar diverges the most from the other South Sulawesi languages, while Konjo and Selayarese relate 5 to 10 percentage points higher in lexical similarity and conclude that 'as this subfamily consists of a chain of languages, it would be wrong to include Konjo and Selayar in the South Sulawesi Stock while excluding the Gowa dialect' (1987:25).

The Australian archaeologist David Bulbeck reevaluated the data from Grimes & Grimes in his PhD thesis on the archaeology of Gowa and Tallo' (Bulbeck 1992:Appendix A), and tried various permutations of languages with different statistical methods to derive a number of seriated dendrograms. He shows again that the lexicostatistical evidence alone does not justify the Makassar subfamily's inclusion in the South Sulawesi Stock, instead suggesting that the languages of the peninsula be split into two stocks, namely the Makassar Stock and the 'whimsically' named Remainder Stock. However I view this more as a criticism of inflexibly using lexicostatistics to determine language family trees, than an actual dismantling of the South Sulawesi subgroup. In other respects his findings are not directly relevant to the Makassar languages.

1.4.2.2 Qualitative Studies

As well as the quantitative studies mentioned above there are two scholars who have used more traditional methods of historical linguistics to examine the South Sulawesi languages. One is the American linguist Roger Mills who wrote a PhD thesis on proto-South Sulawesi phonology (Mills 1975a), as well as a short paper summarising the main points (Mills 1975b). The other is the Russian/Estonian linguist Ülo Sirk, who wrote two important papers (Sirk 1988; Sirk 1989).

Mills' thesis is basically a reconstruction of the proto-South Sulawesi sound system, using information from the modern languages Bugis, Makasar, Mandar, Saqdan Toraja, Masenrempulu, Pitu-Ulunna-Salo, Seko, and Mamuju. It also contains some (rather fanciful) hypotheses about homelands and migration scenarios, which will be discussed below.

Mills' work has been strongly criticised for the poor quality of his word-lists and his lexicostatistics (Bulbeck 1992:510), for his failure to adequately identify shared innovations defining the South Sulawesi languages, for 'unexplained and incompletely (or unconvincingly) explained exceptions and cases of idiosyncratic development', and for generally failing to show the basis for why the languages should be grouped together in the first place (Sirk 1989:55–56). That said, however, his phonological reconstruction has not been shown to be substantially in error. One obvious shortcoming is that he was not sufficiently aware of the link between the South Sulawesi languages and Tamanic languages of Borneo (Adelaar 1994), thus languages which should have been included in his comparison were left out.

Sirk (1989) explicitly makes the case for the existence (and composition) of the South Sulawesi group, using several kinds of evidence. The most fundamental is considered to be exclusively shared innovations, though non-exclusive innovations and 'non-trivial retentions' are also mentioned. Significant here are pre-nasalised allomorphs of possessive suffixes as a vestige of a nasal ligature (e.g. ≡ku/≡ngku, see §4.4.2, also the subject of Sirk (1988)); the reflex of proto-Austronesian *R as /r/; and numerous lexical items.

Sirk also adduces some quantitative evidence: lexicostatistics, etymostatistics, and functor statistics. The latter two are of interest here because they show significantly higher figures for shared lexicon between Makasar and the other languages than simple lexicostatistics does.

Etymostatistics (Sirk 1989:72) is a method which basically involves analysing any text in language A ('text language'), and then searching the dictionary of language B ('vocabulary language') for reflexes of the etyma found in the text. Obviously this method is only possible when language B has an adequate dictionary, for example Makasar (Cense & Abdoerrahim 1979), Bugis (Matthes

INTRODUCTION

TABLE 4   Functor statistics

MAK			
65	BUG		
60	66	SAD	
55	65	66	MDR

SIRK 1989:73

1874), and Sa'dan Toraja or Tae' (van der Veen 1940). The relevant figures show that Makasar as 'text language' has 67% lexical similarity with Bugis and 60% with Sa'dan, while as 'vocabulary language' Makasar shows reflexes for 70% of Bugis words, 60% of Sa'dan, and 64% of Mandar. This is markedly higher than Sirk's lexicostatistics which show Gowa Makasar to compare 45% with Bugis, 42% with Sa'dan, and 37% with Mandar.

Functor statistics (Sirk 1989:73) employs a list of pronouns and pronominal clitics, deictic terms, interrogatives, quantifiers, conjunctions and so forth. Again, the figures for items common to Makasar and the other languages were markedly higher than for simple lexicostatistics. The upshot of Sirk's discussion is that qualitative evidence, and two kinds of quantitative evidence argue strongly for the inclusion of Makasar in the South Sulawesi language group, while lexicostatistics suggests another grouping (excluding the 'Makasaric' languages but possibly including Wotu and some other languages of northern South Sulawesi). However, qualitative evidence cannot be found to back up the latter grouping, thus it cannot be supported.

Finally, it could be said that Makasar's lexical divergence is something of a mystery. Grammatically it has very much in common with Bugis and other members of the South Sulawesi family, and the cultural links between the Makasar and Bugis people especially are strong and undeniable—to the point (as mentioned earlier) that they are considered one people by other Indonesians. There are three obvious possible explanations (not mutually exclusive) for such strong divergence:

- Makasar split off from the other South Sulawesi languages very early
- There was influence from a substratum of indigenous, (possibly pre-Austronesian) origin
- Makassar's position as an entrepôt and cultural crossroads exposed the language to a variety of outside influences, leading it to change rapidly

The first is usually assumed to be the case. The third, while attractive, suffers from the fact that neither Malay nor any other identifiable trade language seem to be the source for aberrant lexical items (Bulbeck 1992:506). The second hypothesis has been proposed in various forms. Mills (1975a:513–514) posited a Central Sulawesi origin for the substratum based on his migration scenario (see § 1.4.3 below). Bulbeck and others (Bulbeck 1992:513; Bulbeck et al. 2000:103) have proposed a 'Toalean' (non-Austronesian) origin for the substratum—this possibility remains to be adequately checked.

1.4.3   *Homeland and Migration Hypotheses*

As was noted earlier (§ 1.2.1), the exact method by which South Sulawesi came to be inhabited by the present ethnic groups will probably never be known. Nevertheless, historical linguists have come up with a number of theories, which I will attempt to summarise here—they can be compared with findings from archaeology which were discussed in § 1.2.1.

Mills (1975a:498–514) suggests that speakers of proto-South Sulawesi arrived by sea from another (unspecified) island, settling in the lower reaches of the Sa'dan river in order to trade with the Austronesian peoples of the interior (he strangely assumes the pre-PSS people would have preferred the mountainous interior to the fertile coastal areas, which is a complete reversal of present demographics). Speakers of proto-Makasar would have been the first group to migrate from there, spreading to the east and south.[19] The early Makasar may well have dispersed throughout much of the southern part of the peninsula. After that the early Mandar moved north to their present location (or they went inland and then back to the coast again). The proto-Bugis then crossed the mountains heading for Luwu', from where they spread out to the south along the east coast and inland, pushing the Makasar into the south-west corner. (The remaining groups then wandered to their present locations in a similar fashion). Makasar acquired aberrant lexicon by virtue of being the first of the PSS people to 'have to contend with the indigenous population. Male indigenes were probably killed or enslaved, women were enslaved or taken as wives, which no doubt led to a certain number of bilingual children' (Mills 1975a:508). These substratum languages were probably related to present day Central Sulawesi languages.

---

19   This may have necessitated a sea crossing—as previously mentioned some believe the peninsula may have been cut by a channel which extended from the delta of the Cenrana River on the Gulf of Bone, through the interior where the present day lakes Tempe and Sidenreng are located, to around the location of the town of Parepare on the Makassar Strait (Pelras 1996:62 ff.).

INTRODUCTION 27

Bulbeck has noted the problems with Mills' scenario, which:

> seems to be unnecessarily defiant of the principle of parsimony ... involving as it does long and complex migrations by proto-Makassar and proto-Bugis, and a succession of language replacements. In addition it is difficult to see how the mouth of the Sungai Sakdang could have held such extraordinary benefits for population growth that it remained the static centre for four successive migratory waves ... Mills' argument further involves the presence of a few Makassar toponyms in the area now inhabited by the Bugis, explaining away the Makassar toponym of Majene which does not fit his scenario (Mills, 1975a:502,534), and ignoring the comparable presence of Bugis toponyms (e.g. Sanrabone, Bone-Bone, Pattiro ...) in the area now inhabited by the Makassar. Finally there is Mills' fanciful conflation of isolated statements in the Bugis chronicles and local origin myths into an undated scenario—at least one of these folk stories, Luwuk's reputation as the oldest Bugis kingdom, is almost certainly false.
>
> BULBECK 1992:514–515

To which I can only add: if the Sa'dan delta was in that time such an attractive location, why does it not support any sizeable population today? Bulbeck also notes that there is no lexicostatistical support for a Central Sulawesi substratum in Makasar, which is lexically aberrant from these languages as well as from the other South Sulawesi ones (Bulbeck 1992:513), though it would perhaps be more accurate to say that we simply don't know enough to make substrata claims of this kind.

Sirk (1994), responding to Mills' immigrant scenario (echoed by van den Berg (1996)), debates whether proto-South Sulawesi was indigenous to Sulawesi or migrated from another island. He concludes that 'the common traits the SSul languages share with the 'indigenous' languages of Sulawesi, especially the Badaic group, Rampi and the B(ungku-To)L(aki) languages, are too numerous and weighty to be exclusively ascribed to the contacts between immigrants and former inhabitants of the country' (Sirk 1994:2–3). He posits the following scenario (because this paper is not widely available I quote from it at length):

> Sometime, perhaps during the second half of the first millennium BC, there existed a network of dialects that included the ancestors of the later SSul and Badaic groups, and at least partly, those of the K(aili-)P(amona) and BL groups. [...] (W)e may surmise that what is now the SW peninsula was earlier separated from the main body of Sulawesi by a deeply incised

bay or even by a strait. Let us call the bay or strait in question Tamparan and the island or 'almost-island' south of it—Libukan (both words are PSS reconstructions: *tamparan "sea, great lake", *libukan "island").

The above mentioned network of dialects was probably spread along the north coast of Tamparan but had several branchings towards the interior, perhaps along rivers. It is probably in these branchings where the Proto-Badaic, Proto-Rampi, and Proto-Mori dialects were placed. Most likely the early SSul dialects were spread on the very seashore. [...] Tentatively we may think of the following sequence (from the west to the east): Proto-Mandar, Proto-Makasaric, Proto-Sa'danic, Proto-Bugis (Proto-Seko may have been connected with Proto-Sa'danic).

[...] It is probable that some time, maybe ca. 2000 years ago, the Proto-Makasaric speakers left this chain and went to Libukan—either by crossing Tamparan, provided it was incised from the west, or along the land bridge on the place of the present day watershed (supposing it had not moved considerably, and Tamparan was incised from the east).

On Libukan ... the Proto-Makasaric speakers probably met with Proto-Laiolic speakers who had not belonged to the above mentioned network ... the latter were pressed more and more to the south, at last to the Selayar island. It was either from there or already from Libukan that part of proto-Laiolic speakers undertook a sea voyage to Luwu' where they gave rise to a new language—Wotu ...

Considerably later than the Proto-Makasaric, the early Bugis also appeared in ex-Libukan (their movement to the south, well in the Christian era, and certainly already by dry land, is apparently reflected in the mythology). Especially the eastern groups of the Makasaric linkage— namely early Konjo—were subject to Bugis linguistic influence. A few centuries of contacts in ex-Libukan may be responsible for several Makasaric(incl. Makasar, Konjo, Selayar)-Bugis isoglosses, e.g. the emergence of the post-positional article (it would be difficult to explain these convergences from the initial chain on the north coast of Tamparan where judging by various isoglosses Proto-Makasaric and Proto-Bugis speakers were not immediate neighbours).

SIRK 1994:5–6

Sirk's scenario is attractive in that it does not resort to convoluted migration scenarios and also manages to explain the location of the Laiyolo and Wotu languages. However, as he admits, it is highly speculative.

Bulbeck (1992:513), while allowing ample scope for competing hypotheses, has a strikingly different scenario reflecting the modern rural population stat-

INTRODUCTION

istics which show the highest densities in the Makasar territories, intermediate densities in Bugis lands, and much lower densities to the north. He proposes that the proto-South Sulawesi homeland could have been 'on or near the peninsula's south coast, followed by a northwards colonisation as population densities built up'. He concludes that:

> From the point of view of the present thesis, the fugitive status which Mills would ascribe to the Bugis and especially the Makassar can be safely ignored. The linguistic line leading to modern Bugis would appear to have been based in the present Bugis heartland for several thousand years, and the counterpart proposition for the Makassar is even more certain.
>
> BULBECK 1992:514–515

So this scenario paints the Makasar as the 'stay-at-home' group. In many ways this also seems appealing. Using a narrow channel as a supposed barrier to habitation, as Sirk does, makes little sense when we are talking about seafaring people for whom crossing a narrow strait would be less trouble than crossing a mountain range. So from this point of view the present location in the south-west is a good candidate for the isolation necessary to explain the divergence of the Makassar languages. Recall also (§1.2.1) that Bulbeck has proposed a possible pre-Austronesian 'Toalean' substrate as another partial explanation for this divergence.

Unfortunately however, this scenario also has a number of problems. One is that it runs counter to the usual assumption that a homeland would be in a place of linguistic genetic diversity—instead this puts it in the heart of Makasar territory. Another is that it does not explain the closer relationship between members of the northern South Sulawesi languages and their neighbours from other subgroups in Central and South-East Sulawesi, unless we are to assume it is simply due to convergence.

I am inclined to remain agnostic about these theories. Clearly much remains to be done before we can confidently adopt a scenario as being the 'right' one, and it may well be that we will simply never know.

1.5 Linguistic Ecology

This section contains a discussion of the 'linguistic ecology' of the Makasar areas, including the health of the language, and examines the use of other languages in the area.

1.5.1 *Language Status*

By the standards of eastern Indonesia Makasar seems in fairly good health. In rural areas and poorer sections of Makassar city the language is still widely used, and although in upwardly mobile sections of Makasar society it competes with Indonesian, command of the Makasar language is an important part of ethnic identification. Code-switching and mixing of Makasar and Indonesian is pervasive in the urban setting, less so in rural ones.

Some urban Makasar, especially if they are middle-class and/or in a mixed marriage (for example, marriage between Bugis and Makasar people is common), now speak Indonesian at home, and children born into this situation will not be fluent in Makasar. However my observations suggest that this is still a minority situation and Makasar will be spoken for generations to come even if it does not remain the first language of Makassar city. Literacy is another matter. No-one can read the defunct Makasar script, while few are becoming fluent readers of the Bugis script, and at the same time people are generally prevented from gaining literacy in romanised Makasar by competing standards and a paucity of available texts. In this respect the rise of text-based informal communication (generally SMS and social media) may have an effect. I have already seen a rise in the use of both Makasar and Makassar Indonesian in these contexts.

1.5.2 *Other Languages of Importance*

In this section I discuss other languages which are of relevance, either through genetic or geographical proximity (such as Bugis), or by virtue of their importance within Makasar culture—this group includes Malay/Indonesian as the national language, Arabic as the language of religion, and languages of past or present influence through colonialism (Dutch, Japanese) or global importance (English). They are discussed roughly in descending order of importance.

INTRODUCTION   31

1.5.2.1   Malay/Indonesian

The Gowa chronicle (see Appendix A) records the arrival of Malay traders[20] during the reign of Tunipalangga (c. 1547–1565). The year was probably 1561. Their captain, Anakoda Bonang, asked for a place to dwell and the freedom to trade, which was granted. There must of course have been contact with Malay traders before this, but this event seems to mark the beginning of large-scale Malay involvement with Gowa.[21] This had a bi-directional effect on the languages: Makasar absorbed many Malay loanwords, and a local variety of Malay arose, which has been termed Makassar Malay or Makasar Malay.

Unfortunately the label 'Makassar Malay' and its variants have been used to denote three different things:

- the Malay community in Makassar, and also possibly peranakan Chinese (Sutherland 2001).
- the Malay language as used as a lingua franca between Makasar and non-Makasar, and also used within the non-Makasar population. According to Cense (1978), Makassar Malay was not the language of the Malay community itself (which stopped using Malay in the 19th century), but rather of the 'European' population. (Why this should have been the case is not immediately clear).
- the modern variety of Bahasa Indonesia spoken in Makassar, influenced by Makasar and other local languages, and subject to code-switching/mixing (Aburaerah Arief 2001; Steinhauer 1988; Tadmor 2003). I prefer the label Makassar Indonesian for this variety (Jukes 2014).

In modern Makassar it is not clear that historical Makassar Malay as such can adequately be differentiated from code-switching and code-mixing between Malay/Indonesian and Makasar. According to Tadmor (2003) 'many bilingual speakers possess basically one grammatical structure, and when speaking Malay/Indonesian, they simply 'graft' Malay morphemes onto the Makasar structure, and produce them with Makassarese phonology. In the speech of some younger speakers, who do not speak Makassarese, this strong interference has now become a substratum'.

Makassar Indonesian and its variants in South Sulawesi have not yet been thoroughly investigated. But in general, Makasar influence on local Indonesian can be seen in the following tendencies:

- replacement of all final nasals with velar nasal
- (some speakers) replacement of schwa with /a/[22]

---

20   Identified in the Chronicle as being from Java—the distinction is not clear in these texts.
21   For a history of the Makassar Malays, see Sutherland (2001).
22   Steinhauer remarks that Malay schwa can be represented in Makassar Malay as /a/, /e/,

32   CHAPTER 1

- Makasar stress patterns (strong penultimate stress)—this is the most obvious characteristic of the Makasar or South Sulawesi accent of Indonesian
- the use of Makasar aspectual clitics, usually in 3rd person portmanteau forms =*mi*, =*pi*, =*ji* (§ 4.3.3, Jukes 2014)
- the extension of the Indonesian pronoun *kita* (1st person plural inclusive, or 1pl.incl) to also function as a 2nd person polite form (2p), by analogy with the Makasar pronoun *katte*
- Makasar adverbial particles such as *kodong* 'unfortunately', *paleng* 'in that case' (§ 5.5.2)
- pervasive use of Makasar lexicon generally (e.g. *sekke'* 'stingy', *daeng* 'uncle')

In the other direction, the influence of Malay on Makasar was historically largely lexical (note for example the high proportion of Malay loanwords in the dictionary (Cense & Abdoerrahim 1979)) but with the increased importance of Indonesian as the national language and associated phenomena of bilingualism and diglossia, the situation has become considerably more complex and is a matter for worthy study in its own right. Because I have been concerned predominantly with older text materials, I simply do not have information about this.

1.5.2.2 Arabic

Since the coming of Islam in the early 17th century Arabic has been a high status language in the region, and most Makasar today have at least some facility in it, at the very least being able to produce and preferably understand necessary formulae. Fluency in Arabic is entirely connected with religious belief—there is no particular economic or other secular advantage in comprehensive knowledge of the language.

It is worth noting here that the phonotactics of Makasar are not especially suitable for producing Arabic utterances, often deforming them beyond recognition. In many cases only the formulaic character of much Arabic used within the Makasar context allows it to be interpreted. This is even more the case if Arabic words or passages of text are written in Makasar or Bugis script—an excellent example is given in Cummings (2002:37), where a section of text on a lontar roll in Bugis script translates as:

> Following the words [undecipherable] makes very great the prosperity of all the communities above the winds and below the winds. He makes rul-

---

or /o/—for example with the Malay prefix *məN*– corresponding to *maN*–, *meN*– or *moN*– (Steinhauer 1988:131). This seems very unlikely and I could find no evidence of it, instead Malay schwa will be realized as schwa, or for some speakers /a/.

INTRODUCTION   33

ing decisions with the justness of Allah ta'ala. Whoever reads or hears and
then acts on them, the words of this document will be advantageous to
him. He is called a wise person.

The actual Arabic phrase in question has resisted identification from its representation: 'a/u ta u/a pa la la la ta ra ja sa ha ma ra da' (Cummings 2001b:582).
Probably to avoid that kind of circumstance, but also to show erudition, most
Arabic names and formulae within any but the earliest Makasar texts are written in the Arabic script.

1.5.2.3   Bugis
Given that many Makasar lands border Bugis lands, and that these borders are
quite porous (especially in the case of the city of Makassar which has a very
large Bugis population), one would expect that many Makasar would have good
knowledge of Bugis. However, in my experience though many Makasar have
some partial or passive knowledge, few are truly fluent in Bugis, and within
the city Bugis people are more likely to know Makasar than vice versa. This is
because Makasar, although somewhat low-status, is for precisely this reason
important as a language for daily transactions in the marketplace, on public
transport, and so forth.

1.5.2.4   English
English is widely learned, if less widely spoken. As all travellers to Indonesia will
be aware, seemingly every Indonesian knows at least the words 'Hello Mister',
and Makasar are no exception. Beyond this, most younger people at least have
awareness of English through school, and the (often meaningless) slogans on
clothing and the usual channels of pop music and Hollywood movies. Increasingly young educated Makasar follow the trend found elsewhere in Indonesia
of using English amongst themselves in certain contexts (such as in social
media).

1.5.2.5   Dutch
People of over 80 years can usually remember a little Dutch from the colonial
period, and in fact often expect that this will be readily understood by all white
people (*balanda*). Few people younger than this have any knowledge of the language. Both Makasar and Indonesian are full of Dutch loanwords, however, so
it must be counted as one of the most important influences on the lexicons of
these languages.

1.5.2.6 Japanese

When I first went to Makassar in 1994 there were still people who remembered the Japanese occupation and could often recall a few words or phrases of Japanese, usually in the form of shouted commands. On a more positive note, Japanese tourists and businessmen are among the more numerous of foreign visitors to the province, and Japanese people are also involved in the local coffee industry because Torajan coffee beans are highly regarded in Japan. However, to my knowledge this has not resulted in more than a handful of Japanese-speaking tourist guides.

1.6 Previous Studies of Makasar

The following section is a summary of relevant publications by scholars working on Makasar. For the purposes of this work the scholars have been divided roughly into three broad types:
- (mostly) Dutch scholars from the colonial period and early post-colonial period
- Indonesian scholars in the post-colonial period, writing in Indonesian
- scholars from the post-colonial period, writing in English

Each of these three main groups will be outlined in turn, concentrating first on works which are specifically concerned with Makasar language or literature, then on those which approach Makasar studies from a different discipline such as anthropology or history. For a more thorough evaluation, especially of pre-1990 works, see Noorduyn (1991a).

1.6.1 *Colonial Dutch Scholars*

Much of the early descriptive work on Makasar was carried out by Dutch colonial administrators, though there had already been a brief description of both the Makasar and Bugis writing systems in English by Raffles (1817), and of the Bugis system alone by Crawfurd (1820) and others (see Noorduyn 1993).

1.6.1.1 Matthes

The first major linguistic work on Makasar was carried out by the Dutch bible translator B.F. Matthes (1818–1908), who arrived in Makassar in 1848. His publications include a grammar (1858), a dictionary (1859, 1885), and a chrestomathy (Matthes 1860, 1883), as well as a Bible translation and other assorted texts. He also collected and copied many manuscripts, thus forming an extensive collection of texts, the body of which are now held in the Oriental Manuscripts section of the University Library in Leiden. In addition to this he had printing

INTRODUCTION   35

types for the Bugis syllabary cast in the Netherlands, thus allowing mass production of Makasar and Bugis texts.

Matthes' linguistic work suffers from a number of shortcomings—Noorduyn writes that he 'cannot be called a great linguist, nor an exemplary translator' (1991a:140). As was common with missionary grammarians of the period, Matthes relied heavily on the terminology and framework of traditional European grammar, or failing that, Greek or Hebrew. This led him to some rather clumsy analyses: for example, he proposes a class of adverbs (*bijwoorden*), which includes some freestanding words, some affixed elements, and the phenomenon of reduplication. His discomfort with this category is perhaps shown in this remark: '*Vele andere rededeelen, en zelfs geheele zinnen worden dikwijls als bijwoorden gebezigd*' ('many other parts of speech, and even whole sentences are often used as adverbs' (Matthes 1858:118)). For these reasons and others little use has been made in this work of Matthes' grammatical descriptions.

He was also not immune to condescending colonial attitudes, which could and did affect his linguistics. While complaining about confusion of the nominalising function of the prefix *pa-*, which can form a noun representing the actor or the action of a verb, he stated: '*Trouwens bij een volk, nog zoo achterlijk in verstandelijke ontwikkeling, verwachte men evenmin eene naauwkeurige onderscheiding, als men dit bij onze kinderen doen zoude*' ('Indeed from a people, still so backward in intellectual development, one should expect no more accurate a distinction than from our children' (Matthes 1858:25)). It is worth remembering that he was primarily a missionary and Bible translator, and one who had very little success in converting staunchly Muslim South Sulawesi. His major achievement must be considered the dictionary (Matthes 1859, 1885), and the collection, preservation and publication of historical and literary texts.

1.6.1.2   Cense

A.A. Cense (1901–1977) was the government linguist in South Sulawesi from 1930 until 1941, and continued his work after Indonesian independence with the *Koninklijk Instituut voor Taal-, Land- en Volkenkunde* (KITLV) in the Netherlands. In 1933 he set up the Matthes Foundation in Makassar which collected a large number of manuscripts—unfortunately many were lost during Japanese occupation. His major undertaking was lexicography, and his major publication the Makasar-Dutch dictionary (Cense & Abdoerrahim 1979), with which he was assisted by Abdurrahim Daeng Mone.

Without a doubt the single most useful resource on the Makasar language, this volume of nearly a thousand pages contains a large amount of grammatical and ethnographic information, and a vast number of illustrative sentences. It was Cense's life-work, and was still unfinished at his death—it was prepared for publication by J. Noorduyn and appeared posthumously. Its major drawback is the orthography chosen, which represents a rather uncomfortable compromise between a Dutch-based system of transcription, and a more phonemic one (see § 2.3.2). It should also be noted that in spite of its 1979 publication date the dictionary is based largely on material collected before the Second World War, and also on entries from Matthes' dictionary (the entries of which reappear virtually in their entirety). Nevertheless, it has stood up to the passage of time well, and the proportion of entries and examples rejected by modern speakers as archaic is surprisingly small.

On his death Cense left a large quantity of notes and manuscripts (including several which remain virtually unstudied). These are to be found in the historical documents section (HISDOC) at KITLV, with the catalogue prefix Or. 545. A summary of the collection's contents (prepared by Noorduyn) is available in HISDOC.

1.6.1.3 Noorduyn
Jacobus (Koos) Noorduyn (1926–1993) was another KITLV based scholar who worked predominantly on Bugis and also on Sundanese, but published some important papers on Makasar historiography (Noorduyn 1961, 1965, 1991, 1993). He also prepared an indispensable bibliography of linguistic work on Sulawesi (Noorduyn 1991a).

1.6.1.4 Others
Other scholars of the 19th and early 20th centuries who published works on Makasar literature include G.K. Niemann, the Swiss philologist R. Brandstetter, and R.A. Kern. The latter published some articles on grammatical topics, which were unfortunately based on unreliable data from Matthes (Noorduyn 1991a:145).

Also of some relevance here are some major Dutch ethnographic works. Friedericy (1933) is a study of Makasar and Bugis social structures, while Chabot (1950) is an in-depth study of social and gender relationships in a village in Gowa, which also contains useful language data in the form of kinship terms and several stories and ritual texts. It is also available in English translation (Chabot 1996).

1.6.2 *Indonesian Scholars*
There are several local linguists who have undertaken work on Makasar. Chief among these are Djirong Basang Daeng Ngewa, Abdul Kadir Manyambeang, and Aburaerah Arief, but there have also been many others, because most Indonesian publications on Makasar grammar have been compiled by teams

INTRODUCTION 37

of researchers (e.g. Abdul Azis Syarif et al. 1979; Abdul Kadir Manyambeang et al. 1979; Abdul Muthalib et al. 1995). For the most part these works concentrate on providing lists of forms—some of which are extremely useful, though they tend to overemphasise parallels with Bahasa Indonesia. A major difficulty with using these publications is that due to printing and proofing problems they are riddled with misprints and misspellings. The Makasar-Indonesian dictionary (Aburaerah Arief 1995) is a case in point—many pages are missing, blank, or bound out of order, so it is rather frustrating to use and in any case generally provides only short translations into Bahasa Indonesia which give little idea of the range of senses of words.

Containing more analysis, but also not without shortcomings, are the studies by Indiyah Imran (1976) and the Malaysian linguist Asmah Haji Omar (1979) on morphology. The former also wrote a PhD thesis at Hasanuddin University (Indiyah Imran 1984) on morphological processes in various word classes in Makasar, which Noorduyn praises as a 'major and mature grammatical work' (Noorduyn 1991a:149). Regrettably I have been unable to find a copy of this. In the 1990s there was a study of oblique constructions using a generative grammar framework (Zainab 1996), and also a study of lexemes relating to tense (Nursiah Tupa 1995). There was also a grammar, *Tatabahasa Makassar* (Abdul Kadir Manyambeang et al. 1996), which contains some useful material, and another short description of affixes (Djirong Basang Daeng Ngewa 1997).

From a more literary perspective, there are numerous publications of Makasar poetry (*kelong*) and epic tales (*sinrili'*), along with Indonesian translations of mixed quality (Aburaerah Arief & Zainuddin Hakim 1993; Gani et al. 1987; Parewansa et al. 1992; Sahabuddin Nappu 1986; Sahabuddin Nappu & Sande 1991; Syamsul Rizal & Sahabuddin Nappu 1993; Zainuddin Hakim 1991). Some of these are discussed more completely in § 2.4.4. There is also a collection of 1128 Makasar proverbs (Zainuddin Hakim 1995).

1.6.3 English Language Scholars

There has been little linguistic work on Makasar from the viewpoint of modern linguistics—with the notable exception of the phonological phenomena of Echo–VC and reduplication (see § 3.3.4, § 3.3.7) which have been discussed numerous times from various theoretical perspectives (Aronoff et al. 1987; Hasan Basri et al. 1999; McCarthy 1998; McCarthy and Prince 1994; Nelson 2003). There has been considerably more written on the neighbouring languages Konjo and Selayarese (see § 1.7), and a few papers by the group of linguists from State University of New York Stony Brook who usually work on Selayarese have been concerned with Makasar as well, or instead (e.g. Finer 1997a).

There are also many non-linguists who have written about Makasar culture or history—many have already been mentioned in §1.2 and §1.3. Notable for my purposes are the historian William Cummings and the ethnomusicologist R. Anderson Sutton, because they have both published work with large sections of Makasar text—the former from manuscripts, the latter from oral performances and recordings.

1.7 Work on Related Languages

1.7.1 *Konjo*
From the mid-1980s Barbara and Timothy Friberg from the Summer Institute of Linguistics have been working on Konjo. Among their publications are: a book of sample conversations (Friberg & Karda 1987), a phonological sketch (Friberg & Friberg 1991a), and an examination of verbal morphology (Friberg & Friberg 1991b). Most interesting are two studies of person marking and its interaction with a postulated focus system by Barbara Friberg (Friberg 1988, 1996), who also wrote a short paper on grammatical differences between Makasar and Konjo (Friberg 2002).

1.7.2 *Selayarese*
There has also been a fair amount written in the United States about the nearby language Selayarese—mostly involving the Selayarese linguist Hasan Basri as either author or linguistic informant. Mithun and Basri (1987) is a thorough examination of the phonology, and many of the points raised there are discussed or re-evaluated by Goldsmith (1990:131–136). Basri also collaborated with Mark Aronoff, Ellen Broselow and another student from South Sulawesi, Azhar Arsyad, on an autosegmental analysis of reduplication in Makasar (Aronoff et al. 1987). Yet another native speaker of Selayarese, Mohammad Asfah Rahman, provided the data for an MA paper on verbal morphology by Veronica Ceria at the University of Pittsburgh (Ceria 1993).

In the 1990s several papers on Selayarese syntax were written by Daniel Finer from SUNY Stony Brook (Finer 1994, 1996, 1997a, 1997b, 1998, 1999). They are mostly written from a Principles and Parameters viewpoint, some from an Optimality Theory perspective. Occasionally he presents data purportedly from Makasar, sometimes this data seems incorrect,[23] probably due to using a native speaker of Selayarese (Hasan Basri) as linguistic consultant. He also

---

23 See §5.6.5.2 (Indefinite pronouns) for an example.

INTRODUCTION

collaborated with Basri and Broselow (Hasan Basri et al. 1999) on an interesting Optimality Theory account of the morphophonological behaviour of the determiner in Makasar. Another study using OT is Bhandari (Bhandari 1997) which attempts to explain the behaviour of the nasal substituting verbal prefix which I notate as $aN(N)-$ (§ 7.1.2). This paper seems to be largely based on a paper by Pater (2001) which examines similar nasalising prefixes in other Austronesian languages, including Konjo.

Hasan Basri has also been responsible for a number of interesting works as sole author. Hasan Basri (1998) is a description of an interesting kind of verbal number-marking in Selayarese using the suffix $-i$, which is marginal in Makasar. His doctoral thesis (1999) is a detailed examination of the interaction between phonology and morphosyntax—much of it is relevant for this work and it will often be cited for comparison.

1.7.3 *Bugis*
Bugis has also been the subject of some study. A PhD thesis consisting of a grammar of the Soppeng dialect of Bugis was submitted at LaTrobe University (Hanson 2003). The same author also wrote an article on basic clause structure (Hanson 2001). From the University of Melbourne, Brotchie (1992) is an Honours thesis describing constituent order and its interaction with the agreement system, though it is based on highly unnatural elicited data. From a different perspective, and focussing on the literary register is Sirk (1996), and there is also a grammatical sketch from Noorduyn's thesis (1955) which was translated by Campbell Macknight (2012). For other sources see Noorduyn's bibliography (Noorduyn 1991a). Much more has been written from anthropological or philological perspectives: for an overview see Pelras (1996). Here could also be mentioned the KITLV scholars Roger Tol and Sirtjo Koolhof, experts in Bugis literature (Koolhof 1999; Tol 1990, 1992, 1993, 1996, 2000).

1.8   Sources of Data

Data for this study can be divided into two main types: spoken data collected on fieldwork or from speakers resident in Melbourne or the Netherlands; and written data collected from a variety of published or unpublished sources.

1.8.1 *Fieldwork*
During the course of researching my MA Thesis (Jukes 1998), I conducted two short fieldtrips to South Sulawesi, staying largely in the city of Makassar

(then called Ujung Pandang) with short trips to the mountain area of Malino and around the coast to Bira.

For various reasons, including ongoing political and social instability in the region, I was unable to conduct a lengthy fieldtrip during my PhD candidature, however in the years 2000 and 2001 I was fortunate to find a Makasar speaker studying for a PhD at the University of Melbourne. Asmuddin, a native of Makassar, helped me with interpretations of previously collected material, and also with understanding some of the published texts. In 2003 I met another Makasar speaker studying in Melbourne, Isnawati Osman, who helped with comprehension of texts and grammatical structures, continuing to help via email after her return to Makassar.

In November–December 2003 I was able to have another short fieldtrip where I worked with Haji Djirong Basang Daeng Ngewa on some of the older and more opaque manuscripts, as well as general elicitation/instruction with a number of local people, notably Hasanuddin Salli Daeng Sikki and his family in Makassar and Malino.

1.8.2 *Written Sources*

The written sources are either in the form of published materials in Roman or Bugis script, or handwritten *lontara'* which may be in either the Bugis script or the obsolete Makassar script (also known as *jangang-jangang* or 'bird'-writing, see § 2.1). Most of the manuscript material was studied during a four month stay in Leiden. There are also some informal examples which came from emails or letters from friends in Makassar, augmented by material seen in the online chat room of the local Makassar newspaper, Fajar.[24]

I have relied heavily on the Makasar–Dutch dictionary (Cense & Abdoerrahim 1979) for sentence examples, rather less so for grammatical explanation. The sheer quantity of the example sentences, and the quality of Cense's scholarship, combine to make this an incredibly useful resource, and one which I would be foolish to underutilise. However, I have been cautious about grammatical constructions and explanations which are only found in the dictionary and cannot be found elsewhere in my corpus or confirmed by modern speakers. Where this is the case (e.g. for some derivational possibilities) I have explicitly noted it.

---

24   http://www.fajar.co.id/bukutamu.cfm.

INTRODUCTION   41

1.8.3   *The Corpus*

Over the years I have amassed a large collection of texts from various sources, and I have attempted to bring as much as possible into a database built using SIL's Shoebox program.

1.8.3.1   Manuscripts

The manuscripts which I have examined in some detail are:

– KIT 668–216 from the Koninklijk Instituut voor de Tropen in Amsterdam. This manuscript from c. 1750 is described in detail in §2.1.1, p. 46. The first 33 pages contain a version of the Gowa chronicle (§2.4.2.1) and approximately 10 pages of this were interlinearised and analysed with Shoebox, with an English translation by William Cummings (2007) and myself. A little over 4 manuscript pages is given as Appendix A of this work. A later section of the same manuscript contains a copy of the 1667 Treaty of Bungaya (see §1.2.3), and several articles of the treaty were also analysed with Shoebox.

– Or545.232 (origin unknown) from HISDOC at KITLV in Leiden. This comes from Cense's collection and is a manuscript of 13 double-sided pages in rather poor condition. Its date and provenance are unknown. Pages 1–12 are in the Makasar script and appear to be the story of a certain Karaeng I La Padara, though they seem to be bound out of order (the remainder of the manuscript is in the Bugis script and contains some Makasar poetry and also some Malay fragments in Bugis script). Much of the vocabulary was not comprehensible to me and some passages do not appear to be Makasar at all; as a result this manuscript awaits proper analysis and translation, however a variant use of the epistemic adverb *bedeng* was noted and is discussed in §5.5.2.

– Katalog Naskah Buton LL/27/AMZ. Photographs of this manuscript from the collection of the Sultan of Buton were provided courtesy of Sirtjo Koolhof at KITLV in Leiden. It contains 10 pages in the Makasar script which give a description of Islamic practice, and also appears to contain a list of people, presumably in Buton, who were versed in these matters at the time. To my knowledge the manuscript has not been dated and it awaits detailed analysis, but at a glance it contains a large number of presentative clauses of the type noted in §12.5.

1.8.3.2   Published Material

I have made heavy use of published works on or in the Makasar language. In the vast majority of cases, texts taken from these sources have been discussed with native speakers, and where a translation (into English, Dutch, or Indonesian) was provided, this has been checked for accuracy. The main sources are listed below.

As previously noted, the largest single source of language data for this work is the Makasar–Dutch dictionary (Cense & Abdoerrahim 1979). I scanned and imported several hundred lexical entries (with several thousand example sentences) in their entirety, while many others were incorporated individually.

Various excerpts from Makasar *lontara'* have been published in papers by Bill Cummings. Notable among them are the Maros Chronicle (Cummings 2000), and the oath between Gowa and Tallo' (Cummings 1999). Both were imported into the Shoebox corpus.

There are several large selections of folklore and ritual text with English translations which were published in Chabot (1996). The largest is the *pakkio' bunting* ('call to the bride'). It and other smaller texts were imported and analysed.

Caritana Pung Tedong, a long *rupama* (folktale), was excerpted from a published collection (Zainuddin Hakim 1991) and analysed in detail. It appears as an Appendix to my MA Thesis (Jukes 1998).

Two published *sinrili'* (epic poems) were partially analysed. *Sinrili'na Kappala' Tallumbatua* (Aburaerah Arief & Zainuddin Hakim 1993), and *Sinrili'na iMa'di' Daeng ri Makka* (Parewansa et al. 1992).

Finally, the first 200 of the collection of 1128 Makasar proverbs (Zainuddin Hakim 1995) were analysed.

There is a small number of examples which were taken from local linguistic publications (Abdul Kadir Manyambeang et al. 1996; Nursiah Tupa 1995; Zainab 1996). These have been noted individually.

1.8.3.3 Unpublished Material

KITLV in Leiden had in its collection some unpublished material in or about Makasar. Of particular interest were:

Grammar notes by A.A. Cense, KITLV Or545.43. Although not touching on syntax, these notes included several interesting examples. The notes were imported and analysed in their entirety.

Caritana Karaeng Ammanaka Bembe ('the karaeng who gave birth to a goat'), KITLV Or545.55f. This typewritten folktale (probably collected by Abdurrahim) was analysed in its entirety and appears as Appendix B.

1.8.3.4 Recorded Narratives

Two short (3–4 minutes) narratives were recorded in the field and fully transcribed and analysed. They are 'prompted narratives', by which I mean that I asked people to tell the story of some activity we had both engaged in. The

INTRODUCTION

advantage of this approach in initial fieldwork is that it is naturally easier to work out what is happening in a narrative if one was involved in the activity being described.

Pammekangngang ('fishing time') by Muyazdlala was recorded in April 1996. It appears as Appendix 3 to my MA Thesis (Jukes 1998).

A'jappa-jappa ri Bulukumba ('daytrip to Bulukumba') by Alimuddin was recorded in July 1997. It is included as Appendix C to this grammar.

1.8.3.5 Elicited Examples

Finally, there are elicited data which are included in my Shoebox corpus. In general elicitation was used to draw out fine distinctions or construction types which did not occur in the other data. Some types of construction were only found through elicitation. In cases like this it has been explicitly noted, but if elicited examples are generally acceptable and were not felt to be odd by speakers they have been included without further comment.

Speakers who provided elicited data were:

- Hasanuddin Salli: male, tour guide, born 1965. Native of Malino, family from Gowa and Takalar.
- †Haji Salli: male, losmen owner, born 1928. Childhood in Takalar, and Makassar, later life in Malino.
- †Haji Djirong Basang Daeng Ngewa: male, scholar, born 1932. Childhood in Takalar, then Makassar.
- Muyazdlala: male, tour guide, born 1966. Makasar, Selayarese background.
- Alimuddin: male, student, born 1978. Native of Bontonompo (20 km south of Makassar).
- Asmuddin: male, agricultural scientist, born 1964. Native of Makassar.
- Isnawati Osman: female, student of administration, born 1974. Native of Makassar.

CHAPTER 2

Makasar Writing and Literature

Because this study is based largely on written sources, in this chapter I give an introduction to the different writing systems used for Makasar, consisting of the two indigenous writing systems, an Arabic based script, and a variety of romanisation methods. Significantly more attention will be paid to the Makasar script, because it has not been previously described in detail, whereas the Bugis script is much better known: as well as appearing in standard reference works, it has been the subject of an in-depth article by Noorduyn (1993). I will also give a brief introduction to Makasar literature.

2.1 Makasar and Bugis Scripts

South Sulawesi has two indigenous writing systems: the old Makasar or *jangang-jangang* script which was used exclusively for Makasar until it fell into disuse in the 19th century, and the Bugis-Makassar script, which is still in marginal use today for both Bugis and Makasar, and possibly Mandar. To avoid confusion these will be referred to simply as Makasar and Bugis scripts respectively— other terms which can be found are *ukiri' jangang-jangang* (Bugis *uki' manu'-manu'*) 'bird writing' for the Makasar script, and *lontara' beru* 'new lontare" or simply *lontara'* for the Bugis script.[1] Both are Indic type scripts: syllabic systems in which sequences of (C)V are represented by single characters (referred to as *aksara* by paleographers) where V is inherently /a/ or is modified by vowel diacritics.[2] The two scripts have virtually identical systems, but differ significantly in the actual forms.

---

1 Some advocate the use of the term *lontara'* as the preferred name for the Bugis script, for example in a proposed Unicode revision (Everson 2003). In my opinion *lontara'* refers more properly to manuscripts in general rather than the script itself. To the best of my knowledge the earlier (and preferable) Unicode designation of 'Buginese' remains official; it currently occupies positions 1A00–1A1F. The Makasar script does not currently have a Unicode block, though Miller (2011) has proposed that it be given one.

2 Macknight and Caldwell (2001) have suggested the term **aksary** for this kind of script, while other proposed terms include **neosyllabary** (Daniels 1990) and **abugida** (Daniels and Bright 1996).

© KONINKLIJKE BRILL NV, LEIDEN, 2020 | DOI:10.1163/9789004412668_003

MAKASAR WRITING AND LITERATURE

TABLE 5   The Bugis and Makasar scripts

	ka	ga	nga	ngka	pa	ba	ma	mpa
BUG	〃	〰	⋋	⋏	〰	𝄪	⋁	〰
MAK	ᵱ	⋍	∿		⌁	⌣	⌃	

	ta	da	na	nra	ca	ja	nya	nca
BUG	⋀	⋎	⋀	〰	〰	⌒	⌇	⋀⋀
MAK	⌒	℧	⋀		⌒	⌣	⌇	

	ya	ra	la	wa	sa	a	ha	
BUG	⋀⋀	⌃	⌒⌒	⋀⋀	○	⋀⋀	∞	
MAK	⌁	⌉	⌣	⌣	⌁	⌂		

	ka	ki	ku	ke	ko	kə	
BUG	〃	⁒	〃	〃	〃⋀	⁒	
MAK	ᵱ	ᵱ̇	ᵱ̣	⌐ᵱ	ᵱ⌐		

Table 5 shows instances of the two scripts side by side for comparison.[3] Shaded cells show aksara used only for representing the Bugis language, while the aksara ∞ for /ha/, used primarily in Arabic and Malay loans, never had a counterpart in the Makasar script. The similarity in the systems can clearly be seen, as can the differences in the aksara themselves—the only close matches being Bugis *ta* = Makasar *na*, Bugis *nya* = Makasar *ba*, and both have a (more or less) similar *wa*. In Makasar the aksara themselves are called *anrong lontara'* 'mother of writing', while the vowel modifiers are *ana' lontara'* 'child of writing', specifically: *ana' i rate* 'child above' (ᵱ̇), *ana' i rawa* 'child below' (ᵱ̣), *ana' ri boko* 'child behind' (rᵱ), and *ana' ri olo* 'child in front' (ᵱ1).

Both scripts share the major deficiency that syllable codas are not shown, meaning that the reader must fill in the gaps at the time of reading a text. This

---

3 It should be noted that the Makasar script was never standardised and there was significant variation. The font used here was created by Jason Glavy, based on the handwriting from one particular manuscript: KIT 668/216.

46   CHAPTER 2

obviously requires a high level of fluency, and preferably prior knowledge of
the text matter (see § 2.1.2).

2.1.1   *History*

Little is known for certain about the source of either of the scripts, or when
they first began to be used. They are obviously Indic in origin, descendants like
other South and South-East Asian scripts of the Brahmi script developed in
India by the 5th century BCE. This can be seen both by the syllabic nature of
the system and from the general appearance of the aksaras, however the exact
line of descent for the scripts is far from clear. There is no single obvious pre-
cursor from which either the Makasar or Bugis script was derived, though most
sources agree that Kawi (the script used in Java and its satellites) or something
close to it was a likely ancestor, possibly via a Sumatran intermediary (Hunter
1996; Kozok 1996; Noorduyn 1991b).

For some time it was believed that the Bugis script was derived from the
Makasar, however given their dissimilarity to each other this seems unlikely.
Instead it is now believed that they are both derived from the same ancestor
(Tol 1996:214), but this cannot be identified. There is no evidence suggesting
that the Makasar script is older than the Bugis, or vice versa—speculation on
this subject being hampered by the fact that there are few verifiably antique
examples of either script. The damp tropical climate of South Sulawesi is not
ideal for the preservation of manuscripts written on palm leaves or paper, and
there is no evidence that there was ever any carving on stone, wood or bamboo.[4] It seems fair to assume that the two scripts developed somewhat inde-
pendently in Makasar and Bugis areas respectively, and both coexisted for some
time, with texts written on lontar leaves or paper which simply have not survived the tropical climate or South Sulawesi's turbulent history.

Caldwell (1988, 1998), writing about Bugis, has argued that the desire to
record genealogical information was the impetus for developing a script some-
time in the 14th century, and Macknight (1993:34) concurs. Cummings (2002)
does not speculate on the date of origin of either of the scripts but only says
that they predate the arrival of Islam in 1605. This makes sense—as Noorduyn
(1961) has pointed out, had there not already been a writing system in place at
that time, the new converts would have simply adopted the Arabic script.

---

4   Noorduyn (1993:563–564) reports Kern's speculation that the simplified 'palm-leaf' style of
    writing the Bugis script could have been carried over from carving vertically onto bamboo
    tubes in the manner found in the Philippines and Sumatra. As indicated though, there is no
    evidence for this.

FIGURE 4   Detail of the Bungaya Treaty
            FROM TOL 1996

As for media, Macknight has argued that paper was unlikely to have been available before the 16th century, and that prior to this the medium for writing would have been the strip-roll, in which 'narrow strips of palm-leaf are sewn end to end to form a very long ribbon just wide enough for one line of script. This ribbon is then wound around two spools to form a device very similar to a modern tape cassette and providing the reader with a continuous line of text' (Macknight 1993:11–12). Some of these types of manuscript (in the simplified 'palm-leaf' style of Bugis script) are still preserved, but I am unaware of any in either Makasar script or language.

A frequently cited passage from the Gowa Chronicle records that a certain Daeng Pamatte', the harbourmaster of Gowa in the early 16th century, 'made Makasar *lontara"* (*ampareki lontara' Mangkasaraka'*), and there is also a cryptic comment in the Tallo' Chronicle that 'writing first became good' (*nauru mabaji' ukirika*) at around the same time (Cummings 2002:42). This probably refers to the same event. However, there is agreement among scholars that this means that Daeng Pamatte' instituted the keeping of historical records rather than inventing the script *per se* (Cummings 2002:42; Noorduyn 1993:567). Thus, though we can assume that there must have been writing before this time, it was during the 16th century that it really took off. For discussion of the subject matter of these early manuscripts, see §2.4.

To my knowledge the oldest extant and verifiable specimen of any South Sulawesi orthography is on a copy of the 1667 Treaty of Bungaya which is held in the Arsip Nasional Republic Indonesia in Jakarta (reproduced in Tol 1996:216). Although the articles of the treaty themselves are in Dutch and Malay in Arabic (Jawi) script, the names of the Makasar noble signatories were in Makasar script. They are reproduced in Figure 4.

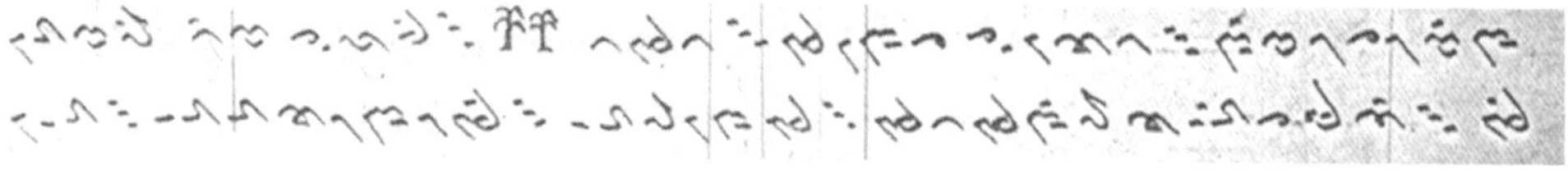

CHAPTER 2

FIGURE 5 Later Makasar script
Note: The text transliterates (without the addition of unrepresented syllable codas) as: *lebapi nibatuwangi. nakana. karenatumena. ribotobira | e. alamoroki. apareka. kanakaripamaitayaji. ki* ('before arriving there, their Kar(a)eng Who Rests in Bontobiraeng spoke, "it is easy to do, because it is only in our nature" ').

The names read: ꦫꦫꦫ (Lengkese'), ꦫꦫ (Popo'), ꦫꦫꦫ (Katampa), ꦫꦫ (Ballo'), ꦫꦫꦫꦫ (Bontosunggu), ꦫꦫ (Karunrung), and ꦫꦫꦫ (Garassi'). (The reader is directed to Andaya (1981) for the story behind the treaty and the parts that the signatories played in the Makassar War).

Some other examples of treaties and similar documents dating from the early 18th century are still extant and are listed by Noorduyn (1991b:472–473). However the oldest surviving large manuscript from South Sulawesi is in the collection of the Koninklijk Instituut voor de Tropen (KIT) in Amsterdam. Known by its catalogue number KIT 668/216, it is a large bound paper volume of 77 leaves (154 pages) written almost entirely in Makasar script. About one-third of the manuscript consists of the Chronicles of Gowa and Tallo' (pp. 1–33 and 33–56 respectively), and the remainder consists of various smaller texts. Noorduyn (1991b:470–472) describes the history of the manuscript and deduces (from the watermark on the paper and the fact that the latest event described in the manuscript is 1739) that it dates from the mid-18th century.

The most recent large manuscript written in Makasar script to my knowledge is a copy of a daily register (§ 2.4.2.3) from a *lontara'* owned by a *tumailalang* (prime minister) of Gowa. The original *lontara'* is probably lost, the copy was presumably commissioned by Cense in the 1930s, and this copy was photographed in the 1970s by Campbell Macknight and forms part of the microfilm collection which is kept at the Australian National University.[5] The register itself covers dates between 1834 and 1858.

The script in this copy is quite unusual. Although it is clearly a variant of the Makasar script, many of the aksara are almost unrecognisable when compared to those in earlier manuscripts. As an example, consider the short extract in Figure 5 above.

Table 6 below gives some isolated forms for comparison with the aksara as seen in the earlier manuscript KIT 668/216. At a superficial glance the script

---

5 Item 4, DS646.4.S6 reel 1 in the Menzies library.

TABLE 6   Comparison of late and early
           Makasar aksara

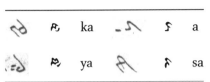

looks quite similar to the Bugis script—this is most likely due to the copyist being much more familiar with the latter and imposing its style on what could have been a more 'authentic' Makasar original. I simply note in passing the use of images of palm trees as punctuation, not seen in any other manuscript to my knowledge.

The process by which the Makasar script became obsolete and was replaced by the Bugis was probably gradual, and may have been influenced by several factors, among them the decline of the power of Gowa and subsequent demoralisation of Makasar chroniclers;[6] the concomitant increase in Bugis power and influence; and the simpler (though less attractive to my eye) nature of the Bugis script. Cummings has speculated that for some time the Makasar script was viewed as 'more arcane, rarified, and hence more spiritually powerful than the (Bugis) script' and also that Makasar used it 'in certain texts to distinguish themselves and their past from Bugis' (Cummings 2002:44). This could explain the script's continued existence for some time after the fall of Gowa, but the fact remains that there are now no Makasar who can read it—my experience tallies with Cummings' (pers. comm.) that Makasar people, even those well versed in reading *lontara'* in Bugis script, need to have old Makasar *lontara'* transliterated for them before attempting to interpret them.

The position of the Bugis script is somewhat better. Although it is rare to find young people who are fluent in reading, at least they are aware of its existence (having been taught it in school). And though it is difficult to gauge actual demand for it, there is a proposal to encode the script (with a few additions) in the Unicode character encoding standard (Everson 2003). This proposal has apparently (and somewhat unexpectedly given the relative smallness of the speech community) been particularly backed by speakers of Mandar (Ka'ōnohi Kai, pers.comm).

---

6 It is worth repeating here Blok's 1759 comment: 'the manuscripts of the Maccassars have, since the conquest of their kingdom, been discontinued, and they have no intention to resume them, until their much wished for restoration be realized' (Blok 1817:iii).

50   CHAPTER 2

2.1.2   *Problems with the Scripts*

I can only agree wholeheartedly with Cummings' lament that '(r)eading Makasar is difficult and requires patience and persistence' (Cummings 2002:xii). As mentioned earlier, both scripts share a major drawback in that they fail to represent any syllable codas, which leads to numerous possible ambiguities and makes it difficult to read texts whose content is not already reasonably well known. Because of this, the scripts have been called 'defective' (Noorduyn 1993:533).

As an example, consider the 9 possible pronunciations of the sequence ✌✌ or ⋏⋏: **baba**, *babang*, **baba'**, *ba'ba*, *ba'bang*, *ba'ba'*, **bamba**, *bambang*, *bamba'*. (Boldface shows words which actually occur in the language). Even if Makasar used the Bugis symbols for prenasalised syllables (such as ⅄ *mpa*), that is no help in this instance because there is still no symbol for *mba*.)[7] When one considers also that in the older *lontara'* there are no gaps between words, while the main element of punctuation, the *passimbang* (∴), is used between chunks of text of no fixed size, the potential for confusion becomes obvious. Cummings (2002:xii) gives the (invented) example ⋏⟋⋏⋏⋏⋏⋎⋏⋏ ⋏⋏⋎⋏⟋, which can be read as either *nakanrei pepe' balla' datoka* 'fire consumed the Chinese temple' or *nakanrei pepe' balanda tokka'* 'fire consumed the bald Dutchman'. Clearly even the most fluent reader will have to pause frequently to work out by context what the intended word is.

2.1.3   *Punctuation*

Punctuation varies widely across documents. The basic unit of punctuation is the *passimbang* (Bugis *pallawa*), three dots, usually vertical ⦂ in the Makasar script rather than the slanted one ∴ normally used in the Bugis script. This is used between units of quite varying size depending on the individual style of the scribe and the nature of the text, but generally either the word or the phrase. In some instances a *passimbang* occurs within words: an example is from Article 16 of the Treaty of Bungaya in KIT 668/216: ⋏⋏⋎⋏⋎⋏⋉⋎⦂⋏⋎ (*napoteranga.sengi* 'he (must) return them all') where the *passimbang* is in the middle of the presumably monomorphemic plural marker *ngaseng*. Whether this is intentional or merely scribal error is impossible to determine, but given that

---

7   Even in Bugis the use of these symbols is inconsistent (Noorduyn 1993:545–549). Note that the failure of Makasar to adopt these Bugis symbols suggests either (a) that the Bugis script was adopted simply as a replacement for the Makasar rather than on its own merits, or (b) that those symbols were a more recent innovation. It certainly cannot be said that Bugis requires these symbols while Makasar can get by without them, as the phonologies of the languages are quite similar in this respect.

MAKASAR WRITING AND LITERATURE

the *passimbang* are in a different colour ink (and would therefore probably have been added after the rest of the page had been written), the latter seems likely.

There are also some idiosyncratic variations of punctuation: both KIT 668/216 and Or.545.232 contain the symbol ⫶, which is clearly used to separate larger chunks of text, such as to signal the end of one king's reign and the beginning of another's (this is equivalent to ◊ found in the Bugis script). The *Lontara' bilang tumailalang Gowa* manuscript uses the more usual slanted *passimbang* ∴, but also uniquely uses small images of palm trees (see Figure 5 above). These can occur singly or up to three at a time. Their purpose is unclear.

After the creation of Bugis printing types in 1856, Matthes introduced the convention of leaving spaces between words in printed Makasar texts and using the *passimbang* more consistently as a clause delimiter. These innovations are also found in some later handwritten manuscripts, though by no means all (Noorduyn 1993:553).

2.1.4 *Script Reform Proposals*

Given the deficiencies of the system it is no surprise that there have been several proposals for modifying the Bugis script (none are known for the Makasar script). Actually the system only needs the addition of two symbols (or diacritics) to become a near perfect way to represent the language. These symbols only need represent the opposition between syllable-final nasal (N) and stop (C); the phonetic realisation is entirely predictable (with the single exception of geminate *rr*, see § 3.2.1.3). Thus, the 9 possibilities for ⫻ given above: *kaka, kakang, kaka', kakka, kakkang, kakka', kangka, kangkang, kangka'*; would be represented by ⫻, ⫻N, ⫻C, ⫻C⫻, ⫻C⫻N, ⫻C⫻C, ⫻N⫻, ⫻N⫻N, ⫻N⫻C respectively.

However, attempts to improve the Bugis script have not always been sensible, nor have they become popular. One modification of the script is to use a caron-like symbol ŏ above an aksara as a *virama* or vowel-killer, to show that the symbol represents a consonant without a vowel, thus representing syllable codas. In this system no allowance is made for predictable assimilation, so nasal codas must be represented by the relevant choice of ∨̆ ∧̆ ∧̆̆ ⋋̆ (*m, n, ny, ng*), and geminates must be represented by sequences of two symbols, with the first carrying the diacritic (e.g. o∧̆∧∧ *salangga* 'shoulder', ∧̆⫷⫻ *nakku'* 'yearning'). This system adds greatly to the length of documents while still only providing a partial solution—there is no conventional way to represent syllable-final glottal stops so these are omitted. Some recommend using ⫻̆ (*k-virama*) for glottal stops, so *nakku'* = ∧̆⫷⫻̆ but this is clearly not an ideal solution. In practice people are generally aware of the virama option but do not seem to use it, though it is provided for in the Unicode proposal (Everson 2003), but with different symbols—either a trailing dot or underlining, thus ∧⫽ ⫽⫽ or ∧⫽⫽ for *nakku'*.

Matthes in his grammar (1858:11) describes the use of the diacritic ȯ (known as *anca'* in Makasar) to represent a syllable ending with a nasal, e.g. ○ᴧᴧ salangga 'shoulder'. This symbol is called *ecce'* in Bugis and represents schwa, so the above would read [saləga] to a Buginese. Matthes remarks that this usage is for beginning readers, although it was also found in a small number of ordinary texts (Noorduyn 1993:549). The Unicode proposal (Everson 2003) includes provision for something similar labelled *anusvara* after Sanskrit tradition. Although this addition is quite sensible, confusingly the proposal is for the caron-like modifier ˇ which has previously been used as virama (see above) though in the proposal ˇ is placed 'before [rather than over—AJ] a consonant which is pre-nasalised', so *salangga* = ○ᴧ ˇ ᴧ. The most recent font for the Bugis script, Xenotype Lontara,[8] includes this provision but the anusvara is placed above the post-nasalised consonant (which was the convention for *anca'*, thus *salangga* = ○ᴧ ˇ ᴧ).

The Unicode proposal also includes provision for representing final stops or glottal stops with a circumflex-like character ˆ, thus *nakku'* = ∧ˆ⫽ˆ. This modification is quite sensible but to the best of my knowledge its use is unattested.

2.1.5 *Reading* lontara'

Cummings describes his experience of reading Makasar as follows:

> Often the meaning of a word or phrase becomes clear only later as the context unfolds, demanding that the reader turn back the page and re-read in this new light. Reading Makasar—scanning, deliberating, choosing, and remaining open to possibilities—involves actively reworking material to achieve a satisfactory, if always tentative, sense. Furthermore, Makasar composers assumed a whole world of associations and knowledge that future readers would bring to the text. Defining a word is never a matter of a simple one-to-one unvarying correspondence between languages. Words are read and gain meaning from the web of implications, allusions, and contrasts they have not only with other words in that language, but with the world to which that language refers. Reading the archaic words that have passed out of use in contemporary spoken Makasar is often a matter of assumption and inference ... In my transla-

---

8 www.xenotypetech.com.

MAKASAR WRITING AND LITERATURE

> tions I have been guided by the desire to reproduce on paper the rhythm of reading Makasar texts I first encountered in Makassar. To do so I have used commas and semicolons liberally to structure the text. Only rarely do I follow strictly the breaks (∴) the Makasar composer placed within his text. Instead, I use commas and semicolons to mark out what I believe are read as coherent units of meaning, a process that is, of course, a matter of judgment. In my experience, Makasar reading *lontaraq* read one statement at a time, scanning, deciding, and then interpreting each such unit as a whole before moving to the next. Makasar reading has both a staccato rhythm and what can only be described as a declarative confidence in each statement. Texts are composed of these typically short declarations.
>
> CUMMINGS 2002:xii–xiii

Leaving aside the difficulty in identifying words, especially those which are archaic and unlikely to be in the dictionary, some of the most difficult (grammatical) aspects of interpreting texts from *lontara'* are:

- given the lack of spaces between words it is often unclear whether any given *na* should be identified as the conjunction *na* 'and', the 3rd person proclitic *na=*, or the 3rd person possessive suffix ≡na
- similarly, it is often difficult to determine whether a *ku* should be attached to the previous element as the 1st person possessive suffix, or the following element as the 1st person proclitic pronoun.
- it is impossible to distinguish between the 1st person absolute enclitic =a', and the article ≡a, so ꦫꦏꦿꦺꦁ could be interpreted as *karaenga'* 'I am king' or *karaenga* 'the king'.
- it is often not clear whether a verb prefix is *aC*– or *aN*– (§7.1), as in ꦄꦧꦺꦇ *a'betai* 'he won' (intransitive) or *ambetai* 'he defeated ...' (transitive).

The last point raises an important problem with using *lontara'* as sources of information about the language's state at a particular historical period: Texts are necessarily filtered through the contemporary language—that is to say that the modern reader unavoidably reconstructs missing elements using knowledge of the language as spoken today. For example, a reader's choice of *aC*– or *aN*– in *a(?)betai* is based on what the choice would be by a modern speaker, or on what one knows of the grammar in general. However there does not seem to be any solution to this particular problem, and it is not in itself an excuse to give up using manuscript data altogether. It simply means we must exercise caution, remembering that some details have been added by the reader.

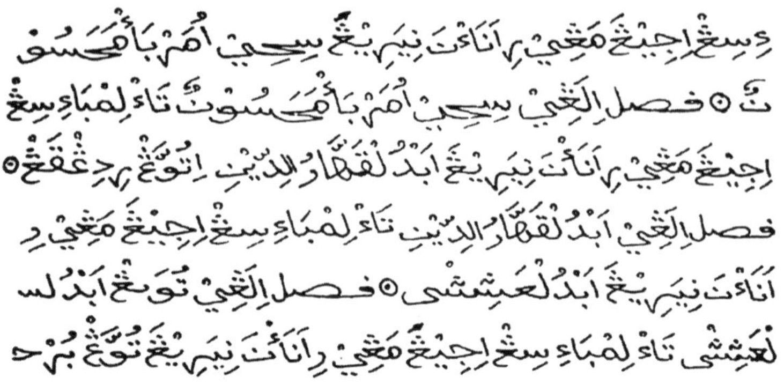

FIGURE 6 *Serang* script
FROM CUMMINGS 2002:45

2.2 Arabic Script (*serang*)

The influence of Arabic following Islamisation in 1605, and also the presence of a Malay trading community using the Arabic-derived Jawi script, gave the option of using the Arabic script to represent Makasar. This script was known as *serang*. It is a more complete way of representing the spoken language than the indigenous scripts, because it allows the representation of syllable-final consonants, but it never became widespread, with only a few manuscripts in such a script represented in collections. One of the major examples is the diary of the courts of Gowa and Tallo', which was transliterated and translated into Dutch by Ligtvoet (1880). However, the use of Arabic script (writing the Arabic language) is common in manuscripts to represent Islamic names, dates, and religious concepts.

2.3 Romanised Orthography

There have been numerous methods of writing Makasar in roman script. Some only appeared in short word lists or explanations of the writing system, such as Raffles (1817), Crawfurd (1820), and Thomsen (1832) (see Noorduyn 1993). Only those which became more common or are used in particularly significant works are examined here.

Not surprisingly, attempts to write Makasar in roman script have been heavily influenced by colonial languages, namely Dutch and Indonesian. At present there is no generally accepted standard—or more accurately, there are several competing romanisation methods.

2.3.1 Matthes' System

There are two main Dutch based orthographies. One, developed by Matthes, was in use until the Second World War. It consisted of the following single letters:

Oral stops: p, b, t, d, k, g
  Nasals: m, n
  Fricatives: s, h
  Liquids: l, r
  Glides: w, y
  Vowels: e, i, a, o

There were also a number of digraphs, with tildes used to tie the two letters together. The palatal stops /c/ and /ɟ/ were represented as *tj̃* and *dj̃*. The palatal and velar nasals /ɲ/ and /ŋ/ were represented by *nj̃* and *ñg̃*. The vowel /u/ was represented by *oe*—since this is considered a single letter in Dutch there was no need to tie the two letters together. Stress was consistently represented by circumflexes on stressed vowels, e.g.: *sikâmma* [siˈkamma]. Geminates were shown as sequences of two identical letters, e.g. *pasaribattañg̃ânna*. The glottal stop was shown by an acute accent on the preceding vowel, e.g.: *kâmbará* [ˈkambaraʔ], *lêleñg̃* [ˈleʔleŋ]. (Actually it appears that Matthes misanalysed the glottal stop as a change in vowel quality, referring to 'scherpe' (sharp) vowels (Matthes 1858:9)). Stressed syllables with final glottal required two diacritics on the vowel.

Matthes generally included affixes and clitic pronouns as part of words, but hyphenated between stems and other bound and semi-bound elements such as the aspect and negation clitics and the particles *na, ka* and *ri*.

An example of text, from the beginning of the story *I Ma'di'* (Matthes 1883: 141).

> *Âpa oerênna? âpa pakâramoelânna?—Kêre pokôna, kêre âká málan-rânna?*

> What is the root? What does it grow from?—Where is the trunk, where does it branch from?

2.3.2 Cense's System

This is found only in Cense's dictionary of 1979. In most respects it is similar to Matthes' system, with the following differences:
– The velar nasal is represented by an unusual symbol rather like the German ß, except when capitalised, in which case it is a large ŋ.

- The digraph *oe* was replaced with *u*.
- The digraphs *tj* and *dj* are no longer tied together with tildes.
- The glottal stop is shown with an apostrophe, e.g.: *balla'*.
- Stress is only shown occasionally, usually when it is deviant, by means of a grave accent, e.g. *pàsara'*.

It is difficult to understand what led Cense to use this particular system. There are a number of inconsistencies—for example he showed predictable assimilation of a nasal to following bilabial, alveolar or velar consonants (*amp-*, *ant-*, *aßk-*), but not palatal consonants (*antj–* rather than *anjtj-*). It is also hard to understand why he consolidated two of the digraphs (*oe* and *ng* → *u* and *ß*), but not the others (*tj, dj, nj*); furthermore the symbol he used for the velar nasal is neither a recognised IPA symbol nor a convenient one for ordinary keyboards.

Of all the various romanised orthographies, Cense's makes Makasar look the most agglutinative—because he not only always attached particles to the following words, but stuck adverbs such as *dudu* 'very' and *tong* 'also' to preceding words and generally joined supposed elements of 'compounds' (really phrases) together with hyphens. Thus, where the local orthography (see below) would write *taena dudu tommo* or *taena–dudu–tommo* Cense wrote *taenadudutommo* 'also not very much anymore'.

In the archive of Cense's papers which is kept in the Historical Documents section of KITLV in Leiden there are some typewritten pages by Cense's friend and co-worker Abdurrahim outlining his preferences for writing Makasar. This document is only a curio as his recommendations never became official, but it is worth outlining here for completeness. In terms of sound values for graphs his system is similar to Cense's, with the exceptions that /ŋ/ = *ng*, /ʒ/ = *j* (not *y*) and /ɲ/ = *nj* (not *ny*)—in this he was following the version of Indonesian orthography prior to the 1972 reforms. He was also in favour of a rather agglutinative looking standard, recommending not only that affixes and clitics be attached to stems, but also particles and adverbs, and he also favoured writing compounds as one word. He also proposed the use of the numeral 2 for reduplication, e.g. *a'jappa2* (*a'jappa-jappa* 'walk for fun'), which reflected contemporary Indonesian usage but is no longer favoured.

2.3.3 *Indonesian Based System*

In 1975 a seminar and workshops on standardising the writing of regional languages were held in the Language Institute in Ujung Pandang, in which a method of romanisation was proposed. This is found in academic publications about the Makasar language, such as the Makasar–Indonesian dictionary (Aburaerah Arief 1995) and various collections of folk texts published by the *Balai Pustaka* and the *Departemen Pendidikan dan Kebudayaan* (e.g. Aburaerah

MAKASAR WRITING AND LITERATURE

Arief & Zainuddin Hakim 1993; Parewansa et al. 1992; Sahabuddin Nappu 1986; Sahabuddin Nappu & Sande 1991; Syamsul Rizal & Sahabuddin Nappu 1993; Zainuddin Hakim 1991). It is also used in school teaching materials.

It uses the orthography of modern Bahasa Indonesia, which is for the most part reasonably adequate. The palatal stops are represented by *c* and *j*, and the only remaining digraphs are the palatal and velar nasals—*ny* and *ng* respectively. These nasals when geminated are inconsistently represented as *nny* or *nyny* [ɲɲ] and *nng* or *ngng* [ŋŋ]. The palatal nasal which arises from assimilation is just shown as *n* (e.g. *moncong*). Geminate consonants are represented as such, but sequences of glottal and voiced stops, for example [ʔb] are variously shown as *kb* and *bb*. This is how the same text from *I Ma'di'* illustrated above (p. 55) appears using this system:

> *Apa uruna apa pakaramulanna, kere pokokna kere akak maklanranna.*
> PAREWANSA et al. 1992:37

The main problem with this system is the representation of the glottal stop as *k*. Usually this is easily understood: syllable-final *k* = [ʔ], so that *lekleng* = [leʔleŋ], for example. However, when a glottal stop is syllable-initial, as when the *a* has been dropped from verbs such as [aʔlampa] 'go', leaving [ʔlampa], this would have to be written as *klampa* (or *'klampa* showing the space left by the *a*). Although this can be understood, because [kl] is not a possible sequence in Makasar, it is misleading. More seriously, when a glottal stop is intervocalic, such as when the verbal prefix *aC–* is attached to a vowel-initial root like [anaʔ] 'child', resulting in [aʔanaʔ], the result is either the misleading *akanak* (as in Imran 1976), or some way must be found to show that this glottal stop does not become *k*. For example, Arief (1995) writes *ak-agang* [aʔagaŋ] 'have friends', showing the morpheme boundary, though this is never otherwise indicated.

But the most compelling argument against using *k* to represent the glottal stop is that they are not the same consonant. Many native speakers seem to agree with this—three different people, when asked to read texts written using this system out aloud, began by pronouncing the *k*s, stopped in confusion, and started again pronouncing them as glottal stops. In my experience, most people prefer to use an apostrophe ', or leave out the glottal stops altogether (a shop in the centre of Makassar has a large sign reading BAJI PAMAI, which is pronounced [baɟiʔ paʔmaiʔ]).

Another drawback is that stress is never shown, and stress is the only way to distinguish between words with the applicative suffix *–i* and the enclitic *=i*.

A quirk of the system is that it often uses an apostrophe to mark 'missing' (elided) letters in verb prefixes and encliticised demonstratives (much as it is used in English words such as *don't*). This can result in constructions such as *iaminne* ⟨ia=mo=i(a)nne⟩ 'this is' being represented as *iami'njo* or *iami 'njo*. Since most Makasar use the apostrophe to represent the glottal stop *iami'njo* looks like [iamiʔɲɟo].

2.3.4   Locally Preferred Option

Makasar who are not scholars use a variant of the above system when writing Makasar. As such, it is found in handwritten notes, on the occasional sign, and in the lyrics sheets included with cassettes of popular songs by artists such as Iwan Tompo and Ismail Wahid, and more recently in subtitled lyrics on Karaoke Video CDs by the same artists. It is identical to the above 'Indonesian' system except that the glottal stop is usually represented by an apostrophe, e.g.: [ciniʔ] 'see' → *cini'*, and is often omitted altogether. Again, stress is never shown.

A similar system (though without the obvious inconsistencies) is used by the Fribergs in their work on Konjo (e.g. Friberg 1996), and is also basically the method proposed by Rössler in the introduction to Chabot (1996:55–56). Noorduyn (e.g. 1991b) and Cummings (2002 etc.) use one which is identical except for showing the glottal stop with a *q*.

It is basically the system described above which is used as a practical orthography for presenting examples in this work. Thus the inventory of letters is as follows:

Oral stops:	p, b, t, d, c, j, k, g, '
Nasals:	m, n, ny, ng
Fricatives:	s, h
Liquids:	l, r
Glides:	w, y
Vowels:	i, e, a, o, u

This system still has a number of shortcomings and redundancies which I have not attempted to resolve—the main being the use of digraphs *ng* and *ny* for single segments, which results in the unaesthetic *ngng* and *nyny* for geminates. Other shortcomings only become apparent when a little is known about the phonotactics of the language (for example, it is redundant to specify anything other than NASAL for syllable final nasals, since their realisation depends on assimilation, with a default velar articulation). However I have adopted the following conventions for clarity and regularity:

- the glottal stop is shown with a straight apostrophe ' to distinguish it from single quote marks ''. The use of *q* to represent glottal stop is com-

MAKASAR WRITING AND LITERATURE

pletely unknown locally, so although it is reasonable I have not attempted
to impose it.

– stress is shown with an acute accent on the vowel (*á é í ó ú*) when it is not fully
predictable. Basically, the accent is used to distinguish between words with
the applicative –*i* and words with the pronominal clitic =*i* (*ciníki / ciniki*), and
also to distinguish trisyllabic words including Echo–VC (§ 3.3.4) from words
which are underlyingly trisyllabic and thus have regular stress (e.g.: *bótolo'*
'bottle' vs *kalúru'* 'tobacco').

– glides which occur automatically between high/mid and low vowels have
not been represented, even if this is usual when using Makasar or Bugis
script, thus *rua* 'two', *mea* 'urine', *riolo* 'before', *siagáng* 'with'; not *ruwa*, *meya*,
riyolo, *siyagang*. An exception is the place name *Gowa*, which has become
reasonably standard.

– conjunctions *na* 'and', *ka* 'because' (§ 5.11), and the preposition *ri* (§ 5.10),
although usually phonologically bound to the following word, are transcribed as separate words to help distinguish them from homophonous
affixes or clitics.

Encliticised adverbs such as *dudu* 'very' and *tong* 'also' (§ 5.5.2), are attached to
their hosts with an en-dash, thus *taena–dudu–tommo* ⟨taena dudu tong=mo |
NEG very also=PFV⟩ 'also not very much anymore', simply because this was the
option preferred by most people whom I asked.

2.4 Literature

In this section I outline the main types of literary genre which are found in
Makasar, from both written and oral traditions.[9] The distinction is important,
because the manuscripts (*lontara'*) which comprise the corpus of pre-modern
indigenous writings represent only a few major types: namely *patturioloang*
(chronicles); *rapang* and *parakara* (expositions of *ada'* or traditional law); texts
of religious instruction, and *lontara' bilang* (diaries or datebooks); while other
genres such as *sinrili'* (epic chanted tales), *kelong* (poems) and *rupama* or *pau-
pau* (folk tales) were transmitted through oral traditions.

It is instructive in fact to examine what sort of manuscripts are not found
in Makasar. For example, the Bugis creation myth/epic tale *I La Galigo*, written in a refined literary register[10] and contained in innumerable manuscripts

---

9   More detailed discussions of Makasar literary genres can be found elsewhere (see especially Cummings 2002, 2003; Noorduyn 1991a).

10   This literary register forms the basis of Sirk's (1996) grammatical description.

60   CHAPTER 2

found throughout the Bugis speaking area, is often reported to form one of the largest single works of literature in the world (Pelras 1996:34). It has also been described as 'the most encompassing, encyclopaedic work regarding the knowledge important to Bugis society' (Koolhof 1999:384). But it has no parallel in Makasar culture. Neither do the epic works of Bugis written poetry known as *tolo'*. Indeed there does not appear to have been a tradition of putting down myth or literature in writing until the colonial era, with a few notable exceptions such as translations of legendary or religious texts from Malay or Islamic tradition.[11]

2.4.1   *Orality and Literacy in Makasar*

Much has been written about the relationship and lack of a clear boundary between oral and written genres in South Sulawesi. Pelras (1979), writing about Bugis literature, claimed that the two genres could not be separated and each borrowed from the other; while Macknight (1993:29) has surmised that the 'writing in an oral style' seen in La Galigo manuscripts could be explained by being the work of a 'writing composer'—a scribe who uses oral composition techniques to create a written work. More recently Cummings (2002, 2003) has written about the complex relationship between Makasar oral and written histories, in which, for example, oral histories from polities outside Gowa may mimic the style of the Gowa Chronicle (which itself borrows from oral traditions) in order to promote their own region's history and deny central claims about Gowa's primacy; in essence using the authority of the Chronicle in order to deny its authority.

However, while the ongoing debate about orality and literacy is important, in some ways it diverts attention from the point, crucial for the present work, that in Makasar certain genres were obviously intended primarily for entertainment or aesthetic pleasure, while others were intended for recording information considered important. The former, such as *sinrili'*, *kelong* and *rupama*, were exclusively oral; the latter, such as *patturioloang*, *rapang* and *lontara' bilang*, may have features of oral composition but, unlike the Bugis examples, there is no indication that they were ever considered as performance genres[12]—

---

11   According to Matthes (1858:xi): *'De meeste, zoo niet alle vertellingen en romantische ver-
      halen ... hebben hunnen oorsprong aan de Maleijers te danken; terwijl die Makassaarsche
      godsdienstige geschriften ... niets dan vertalingen en vrije omwerkingen van Arabische
      stukken te noemen zijn.'* (Most, if not all stories and romantic tales have the Malays to
      thank for their origin; whereas Makasar religious writings ... can be called nothing more
      than translations and free reworkings of Arabic pieces). A similar observation was made
      by Niemann (1863).
12   I have been unable to get conclusive information about this. Although it is likely that

MAKASAR WRITING AND LITERATURE

indeed, in the case of *lontara' bilang* the genre seems to have been designed *not* to be entertaining. When looking at the characteristics of language in various genres this division is important: the 'oral' genres contain a more literary or poetic style, and above all in the case of *sinrili'* are more obviously products of an oral compositional tradition.

2.4.2 Lontara'

In this section I summarise the genres that tend to appear in manuscripts that are referred to as *lontara'*, but first I will discuss the nature of *lontara'* themselves. The word (in origin referring to leaves of the *lontar* palm, as used for Javanese and Balinese literary traditions) in general is used to denote a physical handwritten manuscript, usually in the Bugis or Makasar script, comprising 'a more or less disparate miscellany of items' (Macknight 1984:105). They vary in length from single sheets to hundreds of pages in bound codices, and may contain a fragment of a large work, or a collection of entire texts, or something in between. For example, the *lontara'* believed to be the oldest (KIT 668–216) has 154 surviving pages and contains versions of the Chronicles of Gowa, Tallo', Sanrabone, Bangkala', Maros, and Cenrana as far as p. 62; and from then a variety of different types of text, including treaties, tellings of particular events or reigns of *karaeng, rapang*, Islamic texts including the story of *Noong* (Noah), and so forth.

In both Bugis and Makasar culture certain *lontara'* are believed to have sacred and mystical qualities (see for example Koolhof 1999), and in Makasar they are included in the larger category of *kalompoang* (regalia, lit. 'greatness'). To this day certain *lontara'* are believed to be so powerful that they must not be read by the wrong person (or in some cases even read at all). This of course can result in the knowledge of the substance of the *lontara'* being lost, as Cummings (2002:55) recounts: 'In one case, the carefully handled manuscript of a family who no longer dared to open the case but who generations ago had been instructed to preserve its contents turned out to be only the receipt for the sale of a horse'. Many *lontara'* have however found their way into institutional collections in Indonesia or abroad, or been made available for copying or photographing.

---

lontara' need to be read aloud in order to be properly interpreted (see Saenger 1997 about the difficulty of reading text without word spacing; also Cummings 2002:xii, 41), it is not known if *patturioloang* were ever ceremonially read aloud for education or entertainment.

2.4.2.1 Patturioloang

The main indigenous written text genre in Makasar is the *patturioloang* or Chronicle. (*Patturioloang* is a *pa⟩⟨ang* nominal derivation (see § 6.2.2.3) based on *tu-ri-olo* ⟨person-PREP-front⟩ 'ancestor'.) Of these, by far the best known are the Chronicles of Gowa and Tallo', which exist in many different manuscript copies (for a listing of those known to exist in public collections see Noorduyn (1991b)—many more undoubtedly exist in private collections). Both chronicles were published by Matthes in the Chrestomathie (Matthes 1883), and later translated into Indonesian (Abdul Kadir Manyambeang and Abdul Rahim Daeng Mone 1979; Wolhoff and Abdurrahim 1959), and recently English (Cummings to appear). There are also several recent works that examine particular chronicles or the genre in general (Cummings 1999, 2000, 2002; Noorduyn 1991b).

Cummings (2002:77–88) has discussed the features typical of oral compositions which are found in *patturioloang*. These include paired phrases and the constant use of formulae and conventional phrasings. He goes so far as to list the most common phrases found in the Chronicles:

> *anne karaeng uru* ... 'this was the first ruler to ...'
> *sitau pole bainenna/ana'na* ... 'another wife/child of ...'
> *angnganakkangi* ... 'he had a child ...'
> *anne karaenga (ta)nipuji(jai)* ... 'this ruler was (not) (only) praised as ...'
> *anne karaenga ambetai* ... 'this ruler conquered ...'

To which might be added the constant use of the archaic formulae *iang kumabassung* 'may I not swell up', and *iang kumaweke-weke* 'may I not be destroyed', preceding the naming of members of the royal class. While their superstitious use in warding away misfortune associated with breaking naming taboos should not be underestimated, they have an obvious filler function whose use can be appreciated when it is remembered that most royal personages had at least three sets of names: posthumous names (*areng mate*), personal names (*areng kale*), and family or *daeng* names (*areng pamana'* or *pa'daengang*). With the addition of Islamic names in the 17th century one can understand that the dredging of names from memory was not an inconsiderable part of the oral performance and the formulae would have added valuable thinking time, but then found their way into written texts as well.

2.4.2.2 Rapang and Parakara

Rapang are statements of customary law (*adat*) and guides for correct behaviour based on the pronouncements of ancestors, who may or may not be

MAKASAR WRITING AND LITERATURE   63

named specifically. *Parakara* are similar to *rapang* but from a legal perspective, relating to criminal and inheritance laws, and so forth (Cummings 2002:47,147). Manuscripts consisting of compiled *rapang* and/or *parakara* are common, and there is also a collection of them in the Chrestomathie (Matthes 1883), which were romanised and translated into Indonesian in a publication by the Proyek Penerbitan Buku Sastra Indonesia dan Daerah (Matthes 1985).

2.4.2.3   *Lontara' bilang*

These daily registers, also known as diaries, were records of important events associated with particular kingdoms. The genre has been discussed thoroughly in a paper by Cense (1966). The best known of these is the diary of the courts of Gowa and Tallo', which was transliterated from a *serang* copy and translated into Dutch (Ligtvoet 1880).

2.4.3   *Published Works in Bugis Script*

As has earlier been mentioned, in the mid-19th century Matthes had printing types created for the Bugis script, which made mass production of texts possible for the first time. The largest scale work is Matthes' Chrestomathie of 1860 (revised 1883), which contains a variety of texts based on copied *lontara'*.[13] Also at this time previously oral traditions such as *pau-pau* and *kelong* began to be written and published (see Noorduyn 1991a:143 ff.).

2.4.4   *Oral Genres*

2.4.4.1   *Sinrili'*

This is probably the best known of Makasar literary forms today—most recent local works on *sastra Makassar* (Indonesian: 'Makasar literature') are devoted to it (Cummings 2002:42)—but in origin it was exclusively an oral tradition of epic prose, intended for chanted performance by professional *pasinrili'*, who were customarily blind, to the accompaniment of a two-stringed spike fiddle known as the *keso'-keso'* (Sutton 2002:105). To my knowledge *sinrili'* were first written down at the instigation of Matthes, and several were included in his Chrestomathy (Matthes 1883): these include *Datu Museng*, and *I Ma'di'*. These, together with some others were later published in roman script with Indonesian translation (Parewansa et al. 1992). Others available in published form include the *Sinrili'na Kappala' Tallumbatua* (Aburaerah Arief & Zainuddin Hakim 1993), which tells a fictionalised account of the Bugis prince Arung

---

13   In some cases this book or sections of it have in fact become *lontara'* in their own right and are treated as valued heirlooms (Cummings 2002:54).

Palakka (called Andi Patunru in the *sinrili'*) and his alliance with the Dutch which permitted the defeat of Gowa (see §1.2.3).[14] Some *sinrili'* are (or at least were) also commercially available in abridged versions as recorded performances on cassette tape.

There are a number of *pasinrili'* (*sinrili'* performers) still active, and in fact some *sinrili'* have been composed in recent decades in both Makasar and Indonesian, including one on family planning (*Sinrili' Keluarga Berencana*). However despite (or perhaps because of) the co-option of the *sinrili'* genre as the official exemplar of Makasar literature, it does not seem especially popular today (see Sutton 2002:105–133).

2.4.4.2 Kelong

Kelong are a genre of short chanted or sung poems, similar to Malay *pantun*, with an 8–8–5–8 metre,[15] and free rhyme. The Chrestomathy (Matthes 1883) contains 8 pages of them, many reappearing among 634 romanised *kelong* with Indonesian translations (Sahabuddin Nappu 1986). A later publication (Sahabuddin Nappu & Sande 1991), although not describing them as *kelong*, merely *puisi*, contains nearly 400 of them, as well as some wedding poems with different metres. Another collection contains several hundred (Gani et al. 1987). There are also several hundred *kelong* which were collected by Abdurrahim and can be found in Cense's archives at KITLV (Or.545.55g, 56b).

2.4.4.3 Rupama and Pau-pau

These are folk tales, often recognisable as similar or identical to stories from other Indonesian cultures, for example stories containing the *pulando'* or mouse-deer (not found on Sulawesi) which are from a Malay tradition. There are a number of collections of these, the results of projects in the 1980s and 90s.[16] It does not seem that these were written down until collected by teams working for the Pusat Bahasa or Departemen Pendidikan dan Kebudayaan (DepDikBud). *Pau-pau* are also folk tales but tend to be longer than *rupama*— one early published example is *I Kukang* ('the orphan') (Intje Nanggong Siradjoedin 1940).

14　Andaya (1980) examines the paradox that the person who arguably did most to destroy Makasar political power also became a Makasar folk hero.

15　Incidentally, many Makasar pop songs use this metre, or 8–8–8–8.

16　Two are word for word almost exactly the same, despite having different authors (Syamsul Rizal and Sahabuddin Nappu 1993; Zainuddin Hakim 1991).

CHAPTER 3

Phonetics & Phonology

This chapter contains an overview of the phonological system of the language, based necessarily on the modern spoken language, though there is also some reference to historical differences suggested by manuscript data. Some parts of the chapter are revisions of material presented in Jukes (1998; 2005).

3.1 Phoneme Inventory

This section presents the segment inventory of Makasar, followed by lists of minimal or sub-minimal pairs as evidence for phonemic status. § 3.1.2 gives a more complete description of each consonant phoneme. Spectrograms are given to illustrate some contrasts, particularly length contrasts for single and geminate consonants. For each phoneme there is a list of words illustrating distribution, given in both practical orthography (in italics) and narrow IPA transcription showing stress ['], and syllabification [.]. In § 3.1.2.7 some issues of loan phonology are briefly discussed, particularly with regard to names. § 3.1.2.8 describes the possible consonant sequences. § 3.1.3 describes vowels, and § 3.1.3.1 describes the possible vowel sequences. In Table 7 above bracketed graphs in ⟨*italics*⟩ show practical orthography where this differs from IPA. The glottal stop is discussed briefly in § 3.2.1.1 and also in § 3.1.2.6. Some other consonants which occur only in unadapted loans are discussed in § 3.1.2.7.

3.1.1 *Phoneme Contrasts*
This section briefly presents examples of minimal or near-minimal pairs to illustrate phoneme contrasts. The examples are given in practical orthography—more phonetic detail is given in the next section.

Each pair of voiced and voiceless stops can be contrasted in onset position:

p/b	*palu*	k.o sweet
	balu	widow
t/d	*taeng*	tree species
	daeng	uncle
c/j	*cappa*	contract
	jappa	walk
k/g	*kongkong*	dog
	gonggong	card game

© KONINKLIJKE BRILL NV, LEIDEN, 2020 | DOI:10.1163/9789004412668_004

66 CHAPTER 3

TABLE 7 Phoneme inventory

Consonants	Bilabial	Dental/alveolar	Palatal	Velar	Glottal
voiceless stop	p	t	c	k	ʔ ⟨'⟩
voiced stop	b	d	ɟ ⟨j⟩	g ⟨g⟩	
nasal	m	n	ɲ ⟨ny⟩	ŋ ⟨ng⟩	
fricative		s			h
lateral		l			
trill		r			
glide			j ⟨y⟩	w	

Vowels	Front	Central	Back
high	i		u
mid	e		o
low		a	

Each nasal can be contrasted with the others:

m	*moa'*	crawl
n	*noa'*	gasp
ny	*nyoa'-nyoa'*	reflux
ng	*ngoa'*	gape (e.g. wound)

The liquids *r* and *l* can be contrasted:

l	lamba'	creeper
r	ramba'	luxurious

The fricatives *s* and *h*, and affricated stops *c* and *j* can be contrasted:

s	sala	wrong, miss
h	hala	(call to move buffalo)
c	cala'	put next to
j	jala	fish net

PHONETICS & PHONOLOGY

The glides *w* and *y* can be contrasted between like vowels:

bawang ordinary
bayang shadow

In some environments glides can also be contrasted with sequences of vowels with no intervening glide:

VyV kayu wood VwV bawi pig
VV   kau   you   VV   bai   straddle

The restricted distribution of glides is discussed on p. 78.

An important set of contrasts to establish is those between single consonants and geminate sequences. Single and geminate nasals contrast, as do the continuants *s, l,* and *r*:

m/mm	lama'	handspan		l/ll	bali	face, oppose
	lamma'	liquid from a corpse			balli	price, buy
n/nn	tanang	plant rice		r/rr	sare	give
	tannang	posture, bearing			sarre	k.o grass
ny/nyny	lanya'	strike repeatedly		s/ss	pasu	knot (in wood)
	lanynya'	gone, vanished			passu	snort
ng/ngng	bangi	fragrant				
	bangngi	night				

Single and geminate voiceless stops contrast:[1]

| p/pp | rapo | unlucky | | c/cc | ace | Aceh |
| | rappo | fruit | | | acce' | grab by the throat |

---

1 It can be noted that most of these examples show geminate consonants after /a/. The explanation seems to lie in historical phonology: geminate consonants were at one time conditioned by preceding /*ə/ (see Mills (1975a:208) for a discussion of this). With the disappearance of /*ə/ from the vowel system and its replacement by /a/, Makasar ended up with a large number of minimal pairs which can be distinguished only by the single/geminate contrast. There are of course exceptions, as shown by *leko'/lekko'*.

t/tt	ata	slave	k/kk	leko'	leaf
	atta	take possession		lekko'	put up a sail

There are no examples of geminate voiced stops. Instead there are sequences of glottal stop and voiced stop:

'b	le'ba'	already
'd	ta'do'do'	tired
'j	a'ji	Haji
'g	gari'gi'	notch

The glottal stop can be contrasted with its absence in coda position, though this contrast can be extremely difficult to hear, especially in word-final position (see § 3.1.2.6):

V'#	balla'	house
V#	balla	warm in the fire
V'C	ba'ba'	wrap up
VC	baba'	Chinese
V'C	ba'ba	father

Finally, each of the five vowels contrasts with the others in both closed and open syllables:

a	bambang	hot	bala	misfortune
e	bembeng	way to offer food	bale	tasty
i	bimbang	worried	bali	face, oppose
o	bombong	leaf sprout	balo	k.o.bean
u	bumbung	ridge	balu	widow(er)

3.1.2 *Consonants*

There are corresponding sets of voiceless, voiced, and nasal stops in the four major places of articulation, but only two fricatives, /s/ and /h/; two glides, /w/ and /y/; and two liquids, /r/ and /l/. All consonants except the glottal stop may occur in onset position, but coda position is restricted to the glottal stop, any of the nasals (preceding a homorganic consonant), and voiceless stops as part of a geminate sequence. All the nasals, /l/, /s/, /r/ and the glides /w/ and /j/ appear in lengthened forms which are also analysed as geminated; thus, these also may appear syllable finally. Only two consonants are possible word-finally: the glottal stop /ʔ/ and the velar nasal /ŋ/.

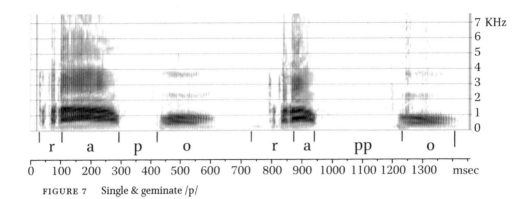

FIGURE 7   Single & geminate /p/

3.1.2.1   Oral Stops

All oral stops may appear in onset position: word-initially, intervocalically, and following homorganic nasals (abbreviated as #_, V_V, and N_). Voiceless stops may occur in geminate sequences, while voiced stops can occur after the glottal stop. Morpho-phonological evidence shows that these are sequences involving an underspecified stop coda and the onset of the following syllable (abbreviated as C_), rather than phonemic geminates or preglottalised stops.[2]

p is a voiceless bilabial stop. There is a small amount of aspiration, with a VOT lag of between 20 to 40 milliseconds. Since aspiration is not contrastive it is only marked in this section which is using fairly narrow IPA transcription.

#_	*palu* [ˈpʰa.lu] 'a kind of sweet'
V_V	*apa* [ˈa.pʰa] 'what'
N_	*lampa* [ˈlam.pʰa] 'go'
C_	*appasara'* [ap.ˈpʰa.sa.raʔ] 'go to market'

The length contrast between single and geminate /p/ is shown in the spectrogram below, with the words *rapo* 'unlucky' and *rappo* 'fruit'. The spectrogram is taken from a field recording of a 24 year old male, and represents careful speech. The single /p/ has a duration of about 150 ms, while the geminate is about 260 ms. This token is considerably above the average of 100 ms (min 70, max 150) and 170 ms (150 to 260) respectively.[3] Post-nasal /p/ tends to be shorter than single /p/, with an average of 70ms, which shows (as do geminate

---

2   With the possible exception of geminate /r/, see §3.2.1.3.
3   The averages were taken from a sample of ten occurences of each in the casual speech of the same speaker and another speaker, a male in his early thirties. There was no significant variation between the speakers.

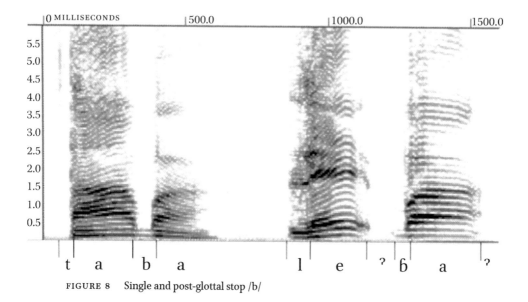

FIGURE 8   Single and post-glottal stop /b/

examples) that stops which occur in a sequence are of shorter duration than single consonants.

b is a voiced bilabial stop. It has the implosive allophone [ɓ] in word-initial position or following a glottal stop.

#_	*balu* [ˈɓa.lu] 'widow'
V_V	*taba* [ˈt̪ʰa.ba] 'hit, succeed'
N_	*bambang* [ˈɓam.bãŋ] 'hot'
C_	*leˈba'* [ˈleʔ.ɓaʔ] 'already'

The spectrogram in Figure 8 shows the words *taba* 'fit' and *leˈba'* 'already'. The single stop is of about 60 ms duration, while the [ʔɓ] sequence is about 125, of which the [ɓ] is about 50 ms, showing that the voiced stop is considerably shorter than the voiceless, which is also the case with /d/ and /g/, though not always with /ɟ/. On average voiced stops have a little more than half the duration of voiceless stops.

t is a voiceless apico-dental aspirated stop. It is the only dental consonant— /d/, /n/, /l/, /s/, and /r/ are alveolar. As with the aspiration, because this dental articulation has no contrastive function it is only mentioned in this section.[4]

---

4 Interestingly the place contrast between /t/ and /d/ is preserved in Makasar loans into Iwaidjan languages of Northern Australia. The correspondence is generally MAK [t̪] → IWJ [t̪],

PHONETICS & PHONOLOGY 71

#_	*tinggi* ['t̪ʰĩŋ.gi] 'high'
V_V	*tata'* ['t̪ʰa. t̪ʰaʔ] 'father'
N_	*benteng* ['ɓẽn.t̪ʰẽŋ] 'fort'
C_	*katte* ['kat̪.t̪ʰɛ] 'we (incl)'

The length of the single and geminate stops is roughly the same as for /p/ as shown in Figure 7—up to 160/280 ms respectively in careful speech, with an average of about 100/180 ms in casual speech. The aspiration can be seen as noise above 4 kHz in the word *taba* (Figure 8).

d is a voiced alveolar stop. It has an implosive allophone [ɗ] following a glottal stop. Length details are roughly as for /b/.

#_	*dinging* ['di.ɲĩŋ] 'cold'
V_V	*dudu* ['du.du] 'very'
N_	*andi'* ['an.diʔ] 'younger sibling'
C_	*a'doleng* [aʔ.'ɗo.lẽŋ] 'hang beneath'

c is a voiceless lamino-palatal stop, often with strongly fricative release. Even one individual can show considerable variation in the pronunciation of this segment, thus it can be realised as the affricate [cç] or even [tʃ]. This concurs with the remarks in Ladefoged & Maddieson (1996:31), that laminal consonants are likely to be affricated, and that 'it is often hard to decide whether a given sound should be classified as a palato-alveolar or a palatal'.

I have analysed this phone as a stop to fit in with the general pattern of oral and nasal stops, and because morphophonological evidence shows that there is a correspondence with the palatal nasal /ɲ/ just as the other oral stops have corresponding nasals. All the palatal consonants trigger palatal on and offgliding in adjoining vowels.

#_	*ca'di'* ['cçaʔ.diʔ] 'small'
V_V	*bicara* [bi.'cça.ra] 'speak'
N_	*moncong* ['mõɲ.cçõŋ] 'mountain'
C_	*pacce* ['pʰac.cçe] 'empathic pain'

Figure 9 shows the words *ace* 'Aceh' and *acce'* 'strangle'. The duration of the single stop is about 150 ms, of which about 30 ms is fricated release, while the

---

MAK [d] → IWJ [t], but some languages such as Maung even show an (unusual) dental phoneme in words such as [kaṯaŋ] ← MAK *gattang* 'carpenter's plane'. See Evans (1992, 1997) for more details.

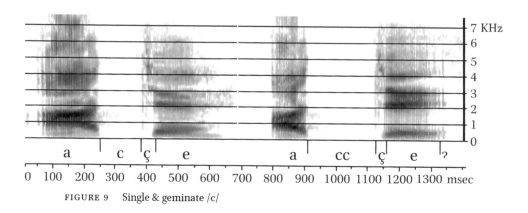

FIGURE 9 Single & geminate /c/

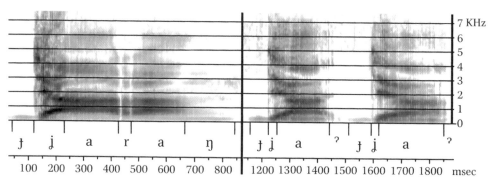

FIGURE 10 Voiced palatal stops with strong and weak fricative release

geminate is 210 ms, also with about 30 ms of frication. The on and off glides in the vowels are seen as raising and lowering of the formants, which co-occurs with the frication in the case of the off-glide.

ɟ (j) is a voiced lamino-palatal stop. It also can also have fricative release, so it can be realised as [ɟʝ]. Unlike /b/ and /d/ it does not have an implosive allophone.

#_	*jarang* [ˈɟʝa.rãŋ] 'horse'
V_V	*baji'* [ˈba.ɟʝiʔ] 'good'
N_	*anjo* [ˈaɲ.ɟʝo] 'that'
C_	*ja'jala'* [ˈɟʝaʔ.ɟʝa.laʔ] 'lean'

Figure 10 is a spectrogram of the two words *jarang* 'horse' and *ja'ja'* 'upright'. *Jarang* shows strongly fricated release of the palatal stop, with about 100 ms of frication, which together with prevoicing gives a length of 200 ms, much longer than most voiced stops. *Ja'ja'* shows only 20≡30 ms of frication, with

PHONETICS & PHONOLOGY

slightly more in the initial occurrence of the stop than in the second. The off-glide from the palatal stop into the vowel is seen clearly in each case.

k is a voiceless aspirated velar stop. It is similar in length and aspiration details to /p/ and /t/.

#_	*kana* [ˈkʰa.nã] 'word'
V_V	*kukang* [ˈkʰu.kʰãŋ] 'orphan'
N_	*dongko'* [ˈdõŋ.kʰoʔ] 'back, ride'
C_	*sakke* [ˈsak.kʰɛ] 'have a cold'

g (*g*) is a voiced velar stop. Unlike /b/ and /d/ it does not have an implosive allophone.

#_	*gana* [ˈga.nã] 'female animal'
V_V	*gaga'* [ˈga.gaʔ] 'stutter'
N_	*mangge* [ˈmãŋ.gɛ] 'father'
C_	*ga'ga* [ˈgaʔ.ga] 'well-chosen'

3.1.2.2 Nasals

All nasals can occur in onset position, either word-initially or intervocalically: in coda position only nasals homorganic with the onset of the following syllable may occur, this results in geminate nasals if the following consonant is a nasal. Word-finally only the velar nasal /ŋ/ is possible. Nasal onsets trigger nasalisation of following vowels, and a nasal coda will trigger nasalisation of the preceding vowel (§ 3.1.3.2).

m is a voiced bilabial nasal. Unlike the stops, geminate /m/ is more than twice as long as single /m/, with an average of 210 and 80 ms respectively. This is also the case with the other nasals and continuants.

#_	*mate* [ˈmã.tʰɛ]	'dead'
V_V	*lame* [ˈla.mẽ]	'root vegetable'
_N	*kamma* [ˈkʰam.mã]	'thus, so'
C_	*pa'mai'* [pʰaʔ.ˈmã.ĩʔ]	'character'
_C[–voice]	*lampa* [ˈlam.pʰa]	'go'
_C[+voice]	*lambu* [ˈlam.bu]	'child's game'

n is a voiced apico-alveolar nasal. Before the dental stop /t/ it has a dental allophone. It can occur in sequences with the stops /t/ and /d/, and also the consonants /s/ and /r/.

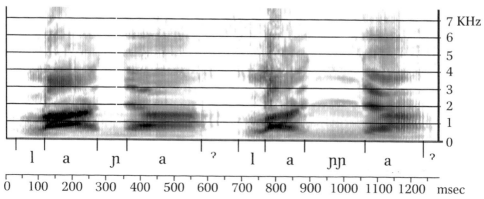

FIGURE 11   Single and geminate palatal nasal

#_	nia' [ˈnĩ.ã ʔ]	'be'
V_V	kana [ˈkʰa.nã]	'word'
_N	anne [ˈan.nẽ]	'this'
C_	ni'ni' [ˈnĩʔ.nĩ]	'fine, delicate'
_C[-voice]	antu [ˈan̪.t̪u]	'that'
	bansa' [ˈban.saʔ]	'rascal'
_C[+voice]	andi' [ˈan.diʔ]	'younger sibling'
	kanre [ˈkan.drɛ][5]	'food, eat'

ɲ (*ny*) is a voiced lamino-palatal nasal.

#_	nyamang [ˈɲã.mãŋ]	'delicious'
V_V	lanya' [ˈla.ɲãʔ]	'hit hard'
_N	lanynying [ˈlaɲ.ɲĩŋ]	'holy, pure'
C_	bi'nyara' [ˈbiʔ.ɲã.raʔ]	'make an oath'
_C[-voice]	moncong [ˈmõɲ.cʃõŋ]	'mountain'
_C[+voice]	anjo [ˈaɲ.ɟɟo]	'that'

The spectrogram in Figure 11 shows the words *lanya'* 'hit hard', and *lanynya'* 'vanished'. The single /ɲ/ is about 80 ms, while the geminate is almost 200 ms. The geminate nasal is louder than the single, and this is clearly seen in the spectrogram. Nasal formants at about 2 and 3 kHz can be seen in the second vowels of both words, but they fade rather quickly. Note also the strong on and off-glides in both words, which reach a peak in the nasals.

---

5   See discussion of /r/ for an explanation of intrusive [d] in the sequence /nr/.

PHONETICS & PHONOLOGY

ŋ is a voiced velar nasal. It appears syllable-initally or finally where it may be followed by a velar consonant, /h/, or nothing. It is the only nasal which may appear in word-final position, indicating that it is the default realisation of a nasal coda.[6]

#_	ngoro' ['ŋõ.roʔ]	'snore'
V_V	jangang ['ɟa.ŋãŋ]	'chicken'
_N	bangngi ['baŋ.ŋĩ]	'night'
C_	bi'ngasa' ['biʔ.ŋã.saʔ]	'split'
_C[-voice]	bangkeng ['bãŋ.kẽŋ]	'leg'
	anghukkung [ãŋ.'huk.kũŋ]	'law'
_C[+voice]	mangge ['mãŋ.gɛ]	'father'
_#	le'leng [leʔ.leŋ]	'black'

3.1.2.3   Fricatives

There is one fricative /s/ which I consider indigenous, and another, /h/, which is probably a loan, but is at least partially nativised. (For a discussion of this, and some other loan fricatives, see § 3.1.2.7). Both may occur in onset position at the beginning of a word or inter-vocalically. /s/ may appear geminated or preceded by the alveolar nasal /n/; and /h/ may follow the velar nasal or glottal stop.

s is a voiceless alveolar fricative. Single /s/ has an average duration of about 100 ms, while the geminate is about 220 ms. Morphophonological evidence shows that geminate /s/ can be the result of an underspecified coda and /s/, for example aC- sura' 'write a letter' [as.'su.raʔ]. This is also the case across word boundaries, e.g. nia' se're 'there's one' → ['ni.as.'sɛʔ.rɛ]. The phonetic sequence [ʔs] is not found.

A velar nasal /ŋ/ also tends to assimilate almost entirely to /s/, thus the name Daeng Sikki' → ['dẽs.'sik.kiʔ], though nasalisation is apparent on the preceding vowel. However when alveolar /n/ precedes /s/ it maintains its nasality, for example in forms with the verbal prefix aN– (§ 7.2) such as ansuro [an.'su.ro] 'order'. Interestingly though, root-internally the sequence /ns/ seems to be found only in loans, especially from Malay, where it corresponds to the sequence /ŋs/ (as in bansa' ← Malay bangsat 'rascal').

---

6   Mills (1975a; 1975b) and Sneddon (1993) both posit a historical process of loss of contrasts in final nasals in South Sulawesi languages; Sneddon arguing that it is part of a tendency to lose final consonants generally in Sulawesi languages.

#_	*se're* ['seʔ.rɛ]	'one'
V_V	*basa* ['ba.sa]	'language'
(N_)	(*bansa'*) ['ɓãn.saʔ]	'rascal'
C_	*kassi'* ['kas.siʔ]	'sand'

h is a voiceless glottal fricative. It is quite rare[7] and, with the exception of some interjections, is seen exclusively in borrowings, generally from Arabic, Malay, or Dutch. I have included /h/ in this list while excluding other loan fricatives such as [f], [z] and [ʃ] because /h/ appears in words which are otherwise adapted to Makasar phonology such as *hukkung* 'law', and also in some interjections, whereas [f], [z] and [ʃ] are not. Consonant sequences involving /h/ are only found across morpheme boundaries.

#_	*harusu'* ['ha.ru.suʔ]	'must'
		(←Malay *harus*)
V_V	*aha'* ['a.haʔ]	'Sunday'
		(←Arabic via Malay *ahad*)
N_	*anghukkung* [ãŋ.'huk.kũŋ]	'punish'
		(←Ar. via Mal. *hukum*)
C_	a'haramanika	'play the harmonica'
	[aʔ.ha.ra.mã.'niÞ.ka]	(←Dutch harmonica)

3.1.2.4 Liquids

There is a lateral /l/and a trill /r/. Both may occur in onset position; word-initially and intervocalically, in geminate sequences and after the glottal stop. Only /r/ can be preceded by a nasal.

l is a voiced alveolar lateral approximant. It occurs syllable-initially (where it may follow a glottal stop) or as a geminate.

#_	*larro* ['lar.ro]	'angry'
V_V	*sala* ['sa.la]	'wrong'
N_	*balla'* ['bal.laʔ]	'house'
C_	*le'leng* ['leʔ.lẽŋ]	'black'

---

7   It can be noted here that /h/ is common in both Selayarese and Konjo (Friberg & Friberg 1991a; Mithun & Basri 1987), where it takes the place of Makasar /w/, which does not occur in either language, and also sometimes /b/. For example, Makasar *bawi* 'pig' → Selayarese and Konjo *bahi*, and Makasar *bari* 'spoiled' → Selayarese *hari*.

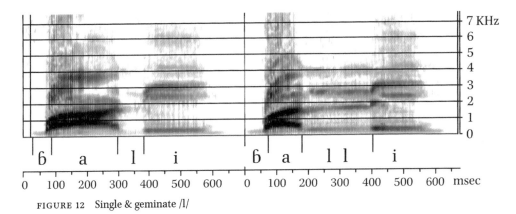

FIGURE 12 Single & geminate /l/

Single /l/ is on average 80 ms duration while the geminate is often over 200 ms. In the spectrogram in Figure 12 it is 240 ms. Note that there appears to be suppression of high frequency sound in the vowels preceding the lateral, lasting for over 100 ms (about half the total length of the vowel) in the open stressed syllable in *bali* 'oppose', but less than 30 ms in the shorter vowel in the closed syllable of *balli* 'price'.

Morphophonological evidence shows that a nasal coda assimilates to a following /l/, for example the word *allanna'* [al.'lan.naʔ] 'kick s.t.' consists of the verbal prefix *aN–* and the root *lanna'*. This also happens across word boundaries, thus *daeng Lala* 'uncle Lala' → ['děl.'la.la]. The phonetic sequence [nl] is not found.

r is a voiced alveolar trill. In very fast speech it may be realised as a single tap [ɾ], but it is usually composed of two taps. It can follow a glottal stop or an alveolar nasal; the sequence /nr/ sounds rather like [ndɾ]. There is a geminate trill which contrasts with the single trill. The single and geminate trills are very similar to those in Italian described in Ladefoged and Maddieson (1996:219–221).

#_	*rua* ['ru.a]	'two'
V_V	*paru* ['pa.ru]	'lung'
N_	*anrong* ['an.drõŋ]	'mother'
CV	*pa'rang* ['paʔ.raŋ]	'calmed'
V_V	*larro* ['lar.ro]	'angry'

Geminate /r/ is the only geminated consonant where the first element (the coda of one syllable) cannot be seen as an underspecified stop or nasal coda given, since both 'r [ʔr] and nr are found as well. It is also the only geminate which only occurs root-internally and not across morpheme boundaries (see §3.2.1.3) for more discussion of this).

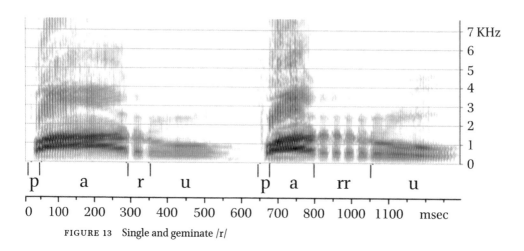

FIGURE 13   Single and geminate /r/

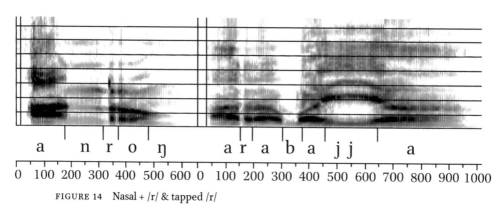

FIGURE 14   Nasal + /r/ & tapped /r/

Figure 13 shows the difference between single and geminate /r/ in the words *paru* 'lung' and *parru'* 'intestine', the former consisting clearly of two taps (two closed phases of about 15 ms and an open vowel-like phase, totalling about 60 ms), and the latter of five taps (about 160 ms). The longest geminate /r/ in my field recordings was six taps (200ms), the shortest was four (120 ms). Single /r/ was realised as a tap on less than a third of the examples, however, even the single taps show one or two 'ghost' taps where the tongue is still vibrating but does not achieve closure. Figure 14 shows this in the word *arabayya* 'Wednesday' and also shows the sequence nasal + /r/ in the word *anrong* 'mother'.

3.1.2.5   Glides

w is a voiced labial-velar glide. It has a somewhat limited distribution, and in some environments should be considered epenthetic. Contrastively it is found in word-initial position before non-back vowels /a/, /e/ and /i/, or intervocalic-

PHONETICS & PHONOLOGY   79

TABLE 8   Distribution of /w/

	_i	_e	_a	_o	_u
#_	*wittiri'* 'k.o.ritual' (†A)	*wedede* 'ouch!'	*wara'* 'north'		
i_			*piwali* 'reply'		
e_	*dewi* 'goddess' (S)	*kewe'* 'sparkle'	*ewa* 'stand next'		
a_	*bawi* 'pig'	*rawe* 'fishing line'	*bawa* 'mouth'		
o_		*loe* 'great'	*Gowa* 'Gowa'		
u_		*pue* 'split'	*rua* 'two'		

ally between two non-back vowels. Most words which begin with /w/ are loans
from Arabic. Interestingly, there are no examples of /w/-initial roots hosting
verb prefixes, so there are no consonant sequences involving /w/ other than
surface geminates formed from underlying /aua/ (see below).

#_	*wara'* ['wa.raʔ]	'north'
V_V	*bawa* ['ɓa.wa]	'mouth'
	bawi ['ɓa.wi]	'pig'
V__V	*paúang* ['paw.waŋ]	'tell someone something'
		⟨*pau–ang* | story-BEN⟩

Epenthetic or non-contrastive [w] appears between back vowels (/o/,/u/) and
–high, –back vowels (/a/,/e/). Examples of this are *Gowa* '(kingdom of) Gowa'
['go.wa] and *rua* 'two' ['ru.wa]. This is indicated inconsistently in local texts
whether in indigenous or romanised orthography,[8] but is only written here
when it can be considered standard (i.e. *Gowa*). Table 8 illustrates the distribution of /w/. (Shaded cells show the environment of epenthetic *w*. † = possibly
archaic, A = Arabic, S = Sanskrit).

A surface geminate *w* occurs when a stressed /u/ appears in the environ-
ment /a_a/, as in the word *taúa* ⟨tau≡a \| person≡DEF⟩ 'the person' ['taw.wa],
which is in contrast with the word *tawa* 'share, lot' ['ta.wa]. This gemination
only occurs at morpheme boundaries; specifically when /u/-final roots host the
affixal clitic ≡a (see see § 3.3.6 and § 4.4.1) or the suffix –*ang* (§ 9.2). Locally this

---

8 For example the Makasar–Indonesian dictionary (Aburaerah Arief 1995) lists both *suarak* and
   suwarak 'bustling'. Both would be transcribed as *suara'* here, since they are clearly the same
   word.

80 CHAPTER 3

TABLE 9 Distribution of /j/ (Shaded cells show the environment of epenthetic
/j/)

_i _e _a	_o	_u
#_		
yako 'hyacinth' (A)		
i_		
nia' 'be'	_io'_ 'yes'	_liu_ 'full'
e_		
mea 'urine'	_meong_ 'cat'	
a_		
bayao 'egg'	_bayo_ 'Bajau'	_kayu_ 'wood'
o_		
boya 'search'	_boyo'_ 'cucumber'	
u_		
		ruyung 'dugong'

is transcribed inconsistently as –_aua_ or –_awwa_; the former spelling is used here.
On average, a single /w/ is about 70 ms, while a geminate is about 130 ms.

j (_y_) is a voiced palatal glide. Like /w/ its distribution as a contrastive element
is somewhat limited. Word-initially its appearance is limited to some Arabic
loans, and only in front of /a/. Intervocalically it can occur between non-front
vowels. As with /w/, there are no /j/-initial roots which host verb prefixes, so it
is not found in consonant sequences other than false geminates (§ 2.2.1.3).

#_	_yako'_ ['ja.koʔ]	'hyacinth' (←Arabic _yākūt_)
V_V	_kayu_ ['ka.ju]	'wood'
	mayang ['ma.jaŋ]	'palm blossom'
V__V	_matayya_ [ma.'taj.ja]	'the eye' ⟨mata≡a ǀ eye≡DEF⟩

At a phonetic level /j/ occurs between front vowels and non-front vowels (in
which case it is irregularly represented in local orthography, but is not shown
in this work). In addition, unstressed /i/ is often reduced to [j] in fast speech
if it is the first element in a vowel sequence (e.g. _ió_ 'yes' → ['jɔ]). Table 9 below
shows the distribution of /j/.

Parallel to /w/, surface geminate /j/ occurs if an underlying stressed /i/
appears in the environment /a_a/, e.g. _taía_ ⟨tai≡a ǀ shit≡DEF⟩ 'the shit' → ['taj.ja].

Interestingly, geminate /j/ also occurs epenthetically between /a/ final roots
and the definite marker ≡a, e.g. _binangayya_ ⟨binanga≡a⟩ [bi.na.'ŋaj.ja] 'the
river' (see § 3.3.6 for more detail). This phenomenon can be seen graphically
in _arabayya_ ⟨araba≡a⟩ 'Wednesday' (Figure 14, p. 78). It is almost always transcribed locally as _yy_, however in the dictionary it is represented by single _y_, e.g.
buttáya 'the land'. The former convention has been followed here.

PHONETICS & PHONOLOGY   81

3.1.2.6   Glottal Stop

ʔ (') is a glottal stop. It can occur before a voiced consonant as the initial element of a complex onset (this only happens when the initial vowel of the verbal prefix *aC–* has been deleted, see § 3.3.5), but it is much more common as a coda. Consonant sequences with glottal stop as first element are realised with increased tension and more forceful release of the oral stop.

The glottal stop is the only word-final obstruent, though it can be realised rather weakly, and it can be difficult to tell if it is there at all. Careful comparison of recorded glottal-final and vowel-final words revealed that the closed syllables always had a slight click of glottal closure lacking in the open ones, and anticipatory creaky voice in the preceding vowels (this can be seen clearly in all spectrograms which include this phone, for example *lanya'* and *lanynya'*, Figure 11, p. 74). It is probably due to its weak articulation that people often neglect to mark the glottal stop in final position when writing (i.e. *saba* for *saba'* 'reason'), though they will usually mark it when it is part of a sequence (*saba'na* 'because', lit. 'its reason').

V_#	*balla'* [ˈbal.laʔ]	'house'
V_CV	*le'ba'* [ˈleʔ.baʔ]	'ready'
V_V	*a'anrong* [aʔ.ˈan.drõŋ]	'have a mother' ⟨aC- anrong⟩
	a'io' [aʔ.ˈi.oʔ]	'say *yes*' ⟨aC- io'⟩
	u'-u' [ˈuʔ.uʔ]	'wig/a kind of sweet' ⟨RDP– u'⟩
		'hair'
#_C	*'jarang* [ˈʔɟ͡ʝa.rãŋ]	'ride a horse' ← ⟨aC- jarang⟩

The glottal stop occurs before all voiced consonants, and /h/. With the remaining voiceless consonants its parallel is the first element of a geminate sequence. Apart from some loans such as *ma'apa* 'sorry' (← Malay *maaf*), intervocalic glottal stop is only found between morphemes—specifically between the verb prefix *aC–* and some vowel-initial stems, or between vowel-initial/glottal-final reduplications.

When a root which ends in a glottal stop is followed by a vowel-initial suffixal element such as the applicatives *–i* and *–ang*, the determiner ≡*a*, and the pronominal enclitics =*a'* 'I' and =*i* 's/he', the glottal stop will be realised as [k]. For example:

(1)   *ballaka*
       balla' ≡*a*
       house ≡DEF
       the house

82   CHAPTER 3

(2) *kuciniki*
     ku= cini' =i
     1=   see =3
     I see her

This glottal strengthening (§ 3.3.3) does not occur between prefixes and stems
(as seen with *a'anrong* above), nor between reduplicated forms (as seen with
u'-u').

Traditionally the glottal stop is seen as an allophone of /k/.[9] However there
is no evidence for this other than the above-mentioned process realising root-
final glottal stop as [k] in a limited set of environments, and it requires some
rather implausible phonological rules to explain why a presumed /k/ should
assimilate completely to consonants such as /p/ and /s/.

The comparison of words in related languages is instructive. For example,
we find [ʔ] appearing in positions corresponding not only to /k/, but also /t/
and /p/ in Malay counterparts.

Malay   adat   →   ada'   'tradition, law'
Malay   adap   →   ada'   'side'

Considering loans from other languages is also instructive. Consider the four
homonyms *ha'*, all of which are loans (Cense & Abdoerrahim 1979:242):

Arabic   ḥakk   →   ha'   'right, law'
Arabic   ḥadd   →   ha'   'punishment'
Dutch   haak   →   ha'   'hook'
English   half   →   ha'   'half'

Here we can see the glottal stop corresponding to a wide range of sounds, which
all have in common the fact that they are not acceptable as word codas in
Makasar.

---

9   This is how it is treated in all local (scholarly) publications without exception, and also in
    the work of Asmah Haji Omar (1979) and Mills (1975a:72). The Dutch scholars Matthes (1858),
    Noorduyn (1991b; Noorduyn 1993), and Cense (1979) were not explicit about phonology, but
    each used a different convention—Matthes regarded the glottal stop as an attribute of the
    preceding vowel ('*scherpe*' vowels) (1858:9) and marked the vowel with a grave accent, Cense
    used an apostrophe ', and Noorduyn used either an apostrophe or *q*. Mithun & Basri (1987) on
    Selayarese and the Fribergs (1991a) on Konjo consider the glottal stop a separate phoneme,
    but its distribution in those languages is slightly different.

PHONETICS & PHONOLOGY   83

I prefer to analyse the glottal stop as the default realisation of a stop (C) in
coda position, where the only other possibilities are nasal (N), and no specification at all (see § 3.2.1 for discussion of the syllabic template). Sneddon (1993)
shows that Sulawesi languages have tended to lose final consonants, and this
reduction of contrasts can be seen as an instantiation of this process.[10]

3.1.2.7   Loan Consonants

Although the phones listed above are those that can be considered indigenous,
it should be remembered that nearly all Makasar people are fluent in Bahasa
Indonesia, and are also part of the Islamic world which requires the use of
Islamic names and other Arabic expressions and formulae. Thus there is frequent use of sounds and combinations of sounds which do not exist in the
Makasar language. Indeed, the vast majority of Makasar people have names
which not only violate the phonotactics of the Makasar language, but include
sounds which do/did not exist in the language.[11] There are many commonly
used expressions which do the same. Just a few examples are given here, with
brief explanations:
- the popular name Hasanuddin has a final [n], where Makasar allows only
  [ŋ]
- the name Syarif has the sounds [ʃ] and [f], neither of which exist in Makasar
- the name Syahrir has the cluster [hr], and final [r]
- the name Zainal has the sound [z]
- the greeting *assalam alaikum* has a final [m]
- the expression *bismillah* ('in the name of Allah') has the cluster [sm] and
  final [h]

The major loan consonants used in names are [f], [ʃ] and [z]. Earlier I mentioned that /h/ is a somewhat marginal phoneme since it appears only in
loans and in some interjections. However, it is somewhat different from the
other non-native sounds mentioned above because it is more frequent, appears
in words which are neither names nor formulaic foreign phrases and, most
importantly, appears in loans which are otherwise adapted to Makasar phonotactics such as *horoloji* 'clock' (← Dutch *horloge*) and *hurupu'* 'letter' (← Arabic
ḥurūf, note that [f] in adapted loans → /p/). Additionally, /h/ is represented
in the Bugis script (though not the Makasar one, see § 3.1.1) with the aksara

---

10   In Sneddon's terminology this is an example of Final Consonant Reduction (FCR). A
     timetable for the reduction of final stops is proposed by Mills (1975a).
11   Note though that most Makasar also have a *pa'daengang* or *daeng* name which is usually
     a descriptive Makasar word following the title *daeng* 'uncle'. An example is Hasanuddin
     Daeng Sikki' 'success'.

∞. Similar things could be said for /w/ and /y/, which have unusually limited distribution and are also seen often in loans (but also in uncontroversial indigenous words). They too are represented in not only the Bugis script (with ∿ and ⋀ respectively), but also the Makasar script (with ⋎ and ⋈). The consonants [f], [ʃ] and [z] have no representation in the local scripts and they tend to be adapted (as seen in *hurupu* above), or the words are written in Arabic script.

There are many examples of loanwords in the Makasar–Dutch dictionary which have been modified to conform to the Makasar phonological system. Some are rather esoteric—such as *ma'arupolo-karahi'* (← Ar. *Ma'rūf* (*ibn Firuz*) *al-Karkhī*, a ninth century saint from Baghdad)—but many are in current use such as *ma'apa'* 'sorry' (← Ar. via Malay *maaf*), *hukkung* 'law' (← Ar. via Malay *hukum*), *garapu* 'fork' (← Portuguese *garfo*) and *hitára'* 'guitar' (← Dutch). However there is no doubt that it is becoming more common to use the Malay equivalents of terms such as these (*maaf, hukum, garpu, gitar*), as Bahasa Indonesia becomes more and more the language of daily use (see § 1.3.1).

3.1.2.8   Consonant Sequences

A limited number of consonant sequences are possible at syllable boundaries—generally they are not possible within a single syllable, note however that complex onsets may remain when the initial /a/ has been deleted from a verbal prefix (see § 3.3.5 for further details).

Table 10 above shows all possible consonant sequences. **C** here is taken to mean plosive, **N** nasal, and **Co** is a convenience label for the non-nasal continuants which seem to form a natural class in this language (/s/,/l/, and /r/, see § 3.3.4). The marginal phoneme /h/ does not seem to belong in any of these groups, and the glides /w/ and /j/ do not appear in sequences other than 'false' geminates as was shown in the discussion of those phonemes and will be discussed in § 2.2.1.3.

Each of these sequences is possible both intra- and intermorphemically, with the exception of [rr], which is only possible morpheme-internally, and [ʔh] and [ŋh], which are formed by attaching the verbal prefixes *a'*- and *ang*- to (rare) [h]-initial roots, e.g.: *a'haramanika* 'play the harmonica' and *anghukkung* 'punish'.

Even a cursory examination of the above chart shows that all consonant sequences either involve a homorganic sequence or a glottal stop + voiced consonant sequence (with the exception of [ŋh], which is simply because there is no nasal homorganic with [h]). Notably missing are the sequences [ʔs] and [nl]—recall that underlying **Cs** and **Nl** sequences surface as [ss] and [ll] respectively (§ 3.1.2.3, § 3.1.2.4).

PHONETICS & PHONOLOGY

TABLE 10   Consonant sequences

$C^{[-voice]} + C^{[-voice]}$	pp	tt	cc	kk
$N + C^{[-voice]}$	mp	nt	ɲc	ŋk
$ʔ + C^{[+voice]}$	ʔb	ʔd	ʔɟ	ʔg
$N + C^{[+voice]}$	mb	nd	ɲɟ	ŋg
$N + N$	mm	nn	ɲɲ	ŋŋ
$ʔ + N$	ʔm	ʔn	ʔɲ	ʔŋ
Co + Co		ss		
		rr		
		ll		
N + Co		nr		
		ns		
ʔ + Co		ʔr		
		ʔl		
N + /h/				ŋh
ʔ + /h/				ʔh

3.1.3   *Vowels*

There are five vowel phonemes, and each can occur as the initial, medial, or final of a syllable.

Each vowel is short in closed and unstressed syllables, and long in open stressed syllables (see, for example, the spectrogram in Figure 8, p. 70).

i is a high front unrounded vowel.

#_	*iru'* [ˈi.ruʔ]	'slurp'
C_C	*dinging* [ˈdi.ŋiŋ]	'cold'
_#	*pocci* [ˈpoc.ci]	'navel'

e is a high-mid front unrounded vowel. It has an allophone [ɛ] which tends to occur word-finally, or to the left of another [ɛ] (see §3.1.3.3).

#_	*ero'* [ˈe.roʔ]	'want'
C_C	*le'ba'* [ˈleʔ.baʔ]	'ready'
_#	*mange* [ˈma.ŋɛ]	'go towards'

TABLE 11   Vowels

	front	central	back
high	i		u
mid	e		o
low		a	

a is a low central unrounded vowel.

#_	*árusu'* [ˈa.ru.suʔ]	'stream'
C_C	*bambang* [ˈbam.baŋ]	'hot'
_#	*tena* [ˈt̪e.na]	'no, not'

In casual speech /a/ in the verb prefixes *aC-*, *aN(N)–* and *aN–* is subject to aphesis, leaving initial geminates, pre-glottalised voiced stops, or pre-nasalised stops, e.g.:

kkanre	'cook, burn'	⟨aC- kanre⟩	→ [ˈkkan.drɛ]
'baji'	'mend'	⟨aC- baji'⟩	→ [ˈʔɓa.ɟiʔ]
ngnganre	'eat'	⟨aN(N)- kanre⟩	→ [ˈŋŋan.drɛ]
mbajíki	'fix something'	⟨aN- baji' -i⟩	→ [mba.ˈɟi.ki]

See §3.3.5 for a discussion of this process. This aphesis is not apparent in /a/-initial roots.

o is a high-mid back rounded vowel. It has the allophone [ɔ] in certain envir-onments, notably word-finally, or to the left of another [ɔ] (§3.1.3.3).

#_	*órasa'* [ˈo.ra.saʔ]	'laden'
C_C	*moncong* [ˈmõɲ.cõŋ]	'mountain'
_#	*lompo* [ˈlõm.pɔ]	'big'

u is a high back rounded vowel.

#_	*úrusu'* [ˈu.ru.suʔ]	'snot'
C_C	*rurung* [ˈru.rũŋ]	'together'
_#	*tallu* [ˈt̪al.lu]	'three'

a   392   (50.5 %)

e   83   (10.7 %)

i   121   (15.6 %)

o   97   (12.5 %)

u   83   (10.7 %)

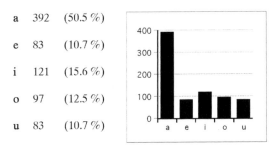

FIGURE 15   Comparison of vowel occurrences

Unlike its neighbour Bugis, Makasar lacks the phoneme /ə/ (schwa). The explanation for this can be surmised by examining vowel distribution—the vowel /a/ occurs between 3 and 5 times more frequently than the others. As an illustration, Figure 15 shows the breakdown of 776 vowels which occurred in a short text of 284 words.

This assymmetry, as well as evidence from neighbouring languages such as Bugis and from comparative-historical linguistics, shows that earlier phonemes /*a/ and /*ə/ have merged into modern /a/. For a detailed discussion of proto-South Sulawesi phonology see Mills (1975a; 1975b).

3.1.3.1   Vowel Sequences

Certain combinations of vowels may occur in sequences of monophthongs. These sequences can be distinguished from diphthongs (contra Rössler in Chabot 1996:55) because each vowel is syllabic; this can be observed from stress patterns and is also evident from songs and poetry requiring a fixed number of syllables per line (see § 3.2.4.2). The combinatory possibilities of vowels are less restricted across morpheme boundaries than morpheme-internally. Table 12 below illustrates the possible vowel combinations,[12] and gives examples of morpheme internal sequences.

Shading of cells in the table denotes that sequences of adjacent identical vowels are prohibited within morphemes in the modern language (though manuscript data suggests they may have been permissible in the 18th century, see § 3.3.1). Sequences involving mid-vowels and their neighbouring high vowels are also not found within morphemes, though between morphemes such sequences may occur. Sequences of like vowels remain somewhat marginal, as is discussed below. Cells left blank show unexplained or perhaps coincidental absences.

---

12   Found in the lexical database built using Shoebox.

TABLE 12   Vowel sequences

Intra-morpheme						Inter-morpheme				
i										u
i										√
e										
a	√									√
o	√									
u	√									√

Examples of intra-morpheme vowel sequences

i	e	a	o	u
		pia 'heal'	*kio'* 'call'	*liu* 'full'
		meang 'stretch'	*meong* 'cat'	
mai' 'breath'	*daeng* title		*bayao* 'egg'	*tau* 'person'
roili' 'bunch'	*doe'* 'money'	*noa'* 'gasp'		
kui 'whistle'	*pue* 'be split'	*rua* 'two'		

Within morphemes there are no more than two adjacent vowels, but with affixes and reduplication there may be six vowels in sequence. An example of this is *kaio-ióang* consisting of reduplicated *ió* 'yes' and the nominalising circumfix *ka*⟨*ang*, meaning roughly 'the propensity to agree with anything'.

Some words which have canonical forms containing the vowel sequence /ae/ have variants in which this is reduced to a single /e/, as can be seen in *daeng*

PHONETICS & PHONOLOGY

→ [deŋ] 'uncle' and *taena* → [tena] 'no'. This is not universal, in fact these two high frequency words are the only examples I am aware of; thus it is considered allomorphy rather than a productive process.

As noted above, sequences of identical vowels do not occur within roots,[13] but can sometimes be found between prefixes/proclitics and roots, or bases and reduplicants. The situation is different between roots and suffixes/enclitics, in which environment vowel degemination takes place (as shown with =*i* in (4), see § 3.3.1). In artificially careful speech ('instructor' speech) identical vowels are sometimes separated by a glottal stop, but this is not the case in normal speech. Instead, both vowels occur in sequence. If the second vowel is stressed intonation sets it apart although there is still no intervening segment. Note that if the second vowel in the sequence belongs to a verb prefix as in (7), it will be deleted (see § 3.3.5 for the rule).

(3) *naallei* [na.ˈal.le.i]
     na= alle =i
     3= take =3
     'she catches it'

(4) *kuuʼrangi* [ku.ˈuʔ.ra.ŋi]
     ku= uʼrangi   =i
     1= remember =3
     'I remember her'

(5) *niioi* [ni.i.ˈjo.i]
     ni–   ió =i
     PASS– yes =3
     'it's agreed'

(6) *eke-eke* [e.ke.ˈe.ke]
     'work slowly'

(7) *nantama* [nan.ˈta.ma]
     na= aN– tama
     3= AF– enter
     'she enters'

---

13   At least not in the modern language. See § 3.3.1 however for an historical counter-example.

90   CHAPTER 3

3.1.3.2   Vowel Nasalisation
Nasal vowels are conditioned by the presence of nasal stops in the vicinity.
There are at least two levels of nasalisation, which can be called light and heavy
nasalisation. Regressive light nasalisation can be seen on vowels in syllables
which are closed by nasals, but which are not utterance final (_N).

> *kanre* 'food' [kãn.dre]
> *anjo* 'that' [ãɲ.ɟjo]

Regressive heavy nasalisation is seen on vowels which precede an utterance
final nasal (_N#), which is by default a velar nasal. Progressive heavy nasalisation is present on vowels which follow any nasal (N_). Nasalisation will further
spread to at least the next vowel if there is no intervening consonant. There
are no examples in my field recordings of more than two vowels following a
nasal so I cannot determine the limits of progressive nasalisation, but even over
the duration of a single vowel spectrograms show that the nasal formants fade
quite rapidly (see e.g. Figure 11) and it seems unlikely that nasalisation could
continue indefinitely.[14] In the following examples only, heavy nasalisation is
shown by a double tilde, e.g. [ã̃].

> *dinging* [di.ŋĩŋ] 'cold'
> *moncong* [mõ̃ɲ.cʃõ̃ŋ] 'mountain'
> *bambang* [bã̃m.bã̃ŋ] 'hot'
> *nia'* [nĩ̃.ã̃ʔ] 'be'

The nasalisation of the first vowel in *nia'* spreads to the second, but is already
weakened. Note that the first vowel in *dinging* is not nasalised. This is because
the word syllabifies so that the first nasal is the onset of the second syllable
rather than the coda of the first.

3.1.3.3   Mid-vowel Lowering
This refers to lowering/laxing of the mid-vowels /e/ and /o/ to [ɛ] and [ɔ]
respectively. Although this seems a relatively minor process, it is given such
prominence in Mithun and Basri's (1987) phonology of the closely related language Selayar, and also in more recent work on Makasar and Selayarese by
Hasan Basri and others (Hasan Basri 1999; Hasan Basri and Chen 1999; Hasan
Basri et al. 1999), that it requires some discussion. The reason this process is

---

14   Though Mithun & Basri (1987:226) report that in Selayar vowel nasalisation spreads to all
      adjacent vowels in the intonation unit, even across glottal stops, giving the example [lam-
      Nẽãĩʔĩ ã:su] 'a dog urinated on him'.

PHONETICS & PHONOLOGY   91

considered important by these authors is that in some cases it can be considered diagnostic for determining the boundaries of the prosodic word. The
findings from the most recent studies are summarised here, and contrasted
with my own observations.

According to Hasan Basri et al. (1999), mid-vowels are laxed word-finally,
before clitics (including for this purpose the determiner =a), and to the left of
an already laxed mid-vowel. Contrary to the analysis in Mithun and Basri (1987),
the vowel /a/ is no longer explicitly mentioned as a trigger for mid-vowel laxing,
and in fact is specifically counter-exemplified with the suffix –*ang*, as illustrated
with the following affix/clitic contrast:

[lɔmpɔ] 'big'   + comparative [-aŋ]   →   [lomˈpoʷaŋ]   'bigger'
                + 1st person enclitic [=aʔ]   →   [ˈlɔmpɔʷaʔ]   'I'm big'

Thus the position before a clitic is phonologically similar to word final position,
and different from the position before an affix. However clitics containing /i/
do not cause laxing.

Vowel laxing is accounted for by a constraint against tense mid-vowels at the
right edge of the prosodic word, *[-hi,tns]$_{PWD}$. The prosodic word is considered
to include affixes but not clitics, explaining why laxing is seen before the latter
but not the former.

Hasan Basri devotes a sizeable section of his 1999 thesis to an OT analysis of
this phenomenon (Hasan Basri 1999:121–151). He describes it as a phenomenon
of vowel harmony in terms of tongue root position: +ATR (Advanced Tongue
Root) for tense mid-vowels [e] and [o], and –ATR for lax mid-vowels [ɛ] and
[ɔ]. High vowels /i/ and /u/ are also +ATR, while low vowel /a/ is +RTR (Retrac-
ted Tongue Root). To summarise the environments in which –ATR mid-vowels
appear:

stem-finally	✓	[ˈtinrɔ]	'sleep'
	✗	[ˈbarroʔ]	'hawk'
to the left of another –ATR mid-vowel	✓	[ˈgɔlɔ]	'ball'
	✗	[ˈsodi]	'next time'
immediately adjacent to /a/ inside a root	✓	[ˈtɔa]	'old'
	✗	[ˈgora]	'shout'
immediately adjacent to /a/ in a suffix	✓	[balˈlɔ-aŋ]	'prettier'
– or enclitic	✓	[ˈballɔ=a]	'I am pretty'
preceding non-adjacent /a/ in an enclitic	✓	[asˈsulɔ=kaŋ]	'we used a torch'
– but not in a suffix	✗	[suˈlo-ba]	'our torch'
and never preceding /i/ or /u/,			

92   CHAPTER 3

– whether adjacent   ✗ ['koi]   'bed'
– or non-adjacent   ✗ ['dolu]   'roll'
– or in a suffix   ✗ [sar'ro-i]   'make intensive'
– or an enclitic   ✗ ['tinro=ki]   'we (incl) sleep'

It is interesting to note that one of these examples, [ballɔ-aŋ] 'prettier', directly contradicts data given in the earlier paper (Hasan Basri et al. 1999), showing that the comparative suffix *–ang* does *not* trigger laxing, thus [lom'powaŋ] 'bigger'. Whether this is due to a difference between the systems of Makasar and Selayarese is difficult to say, given that all the data comes from the same speaker.

My field recordings show data rather different from these accounts. For a start, I would have to describe this as a tendency rather than a process. It is usually slight, and often hardly noticeable. While Mithun and Basri (1987) show that the presence of a following /a/ will lower a preceding mid-vowel, my observation is that mid-vowels are *never* lowered in this environment, whether preceding a clitic or an affix. Furthermore, it seems somewhat implausible to juxtapose a laxed mid-vowel with the epenthetic glides described by Hasan Basri et al. (1999)

In many of my examples, when words ending in mid-vowels were pronounced twice, the second utterance would show lowering while the first would not. This seems to indicate that lowering is associated with utterance-final falling intonation, and in my corpus of narratives it turned out that this was one of the two environments where lowering could confidently be expected to occur, the other such environment being to the left of a lowered mid-vowel, as described in both the papers.

Figure 16 shows the most marked difference between lowered and normal mid-vowels which occurred in my field recordings, in the phrase *tette' sampulo asse're* 'eleven o'clock' as spoken by Alimuddin from the village of Bontonompo. Both /e/s in *tette'* are unaffected, both /e/s in *asse're* are lowered because of the open final syllable. The difference can be seen most clearly in the higher formants, which are about 500 Hz lower in the lowered mid-vowels.

Figure 9 (p. 72), with the words *ace* and *acce'* shows mid-vowel lowering to a lesser degree. By contrast, Figure 17, a spectrogram of the interjection *e'-e'* and the pronoun *inakke* 'I', shows mid-vowels which are actually slightly lower in the closed syllables (*e'-e'*) than the open one (*inakke*). This is due to the utterance-final falling intonation of *e'-e'*.

I would have to conclude that this process must be more marked in Selayarese, and this also explains the data in all the papers (co-)authored by Hasan

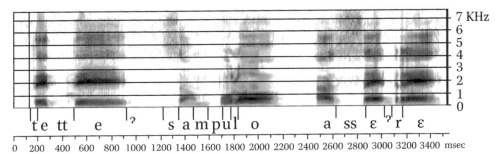

FIGURE 16   Normal and lowered mid-vowels

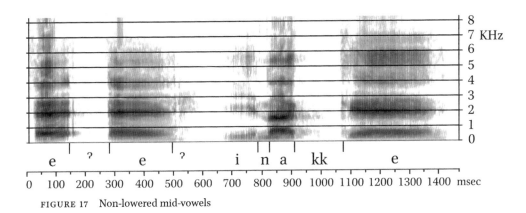

FIGURE 17   Non-lowered mid-vowels

Basri, who is a native speaker of Selayarese and not Makasar. Also, in view of the rather limited (and subjective) nature of the data, I am hesitant to use it as evidence of any prosodic or syntactic phenomena.

3.2   Phonotactics

This section attempts to define phonological and prosodic characteristics of words, and discusses constraints on syllable and word formation. While it attempts to be largely theory-neutral, some use will be made of the basic terminology of autosegmental phonology (Goldsmith 1990). There is also some use of Optimality Theory terms when evaluating previous work done using this framework.

3.2.1   *Syllable Structure*
Basic syllable structure is $(C_1)V(C_2)$. C_1 is largely unrestricted, but C_2 is highly constrained as we will see. C_2 also has slightly different possibilities depend-

ing on whether the syllable occurs within a lexical root, or morpheme-finally. Because the latter environment is somewhat simpler it will be examined first.

3.2.1.1   Syllables at Morpheme Boundaries

A syllable at a morpheme boundary has the basic structure $(C_1)V(C_2)$, where C_1 = any consonant phoneme, V = any vowel, and C_2 = any nasal ([m, n, ɲ, ŋ]), any voiceless stop ([p, t, c, k]), or [s], [l], [ʔ]. A closer look shows that a final nasal is always homorganic with a following stop or nasal, with a default velar articulation if there is no following consonant. Similarly, a voiceless stop will only occur before an identical voiceless stop in a geminate consonant, while the glottal stop occurs before all voiced consonants and word-finally.

These restrictions on distribution allow us to hypothesise that the underlying contrast of C_2 is between stop (C) and nasal (N), with phonetic realisation determined by assimilation. Thus:

C assimilates to a following voiceless consonant (with the exception of the loan consonant /h/). So C is realised as [p] before /p/, [t] before /t/, [s] before /s/, etc. In all other environments it is realised as [ʔ].

N is realised as [m] before a labial consonant, [n] before an alveolar consonant, and so forth. It also assimilates to [l] preceding /l/, and [s] preceding /s/. Otherwise it will be realised as [ŋ].

3.2.1.2   Syllables within Lexical Roots

The syllable structure within lexical roots is slightly different. Although it can still be characterised as $(C_1)V(C_2)$, C_2 in this case has three possibilities rather than two—it may be an underspecified stop (C), underspecified nasal (N), or it may be /r/ (as part of geminate /r/). This differs slightly from Goldsmith's (1990:132) analysis of Selayarese (based on data in Mithun & Basri 1987). He posits only two possibilities for codas; either completely unspecified, or nasal, with all other information coming later through assimilation processes. This is not adequate for Makasar (nor is it for Selayarese), simply because of the case of /r/. As we have seen, /r/ is the only segment which can occur in three different clusters: [ʔr], [nr], and [rr]. While [nr] is obviously a nasal coda followed by /r/, we are still left with [rr] and [ʔr], with no clear indication which of these is to be considered to illustrate the unspecified coda.

It is for the above reason that I propose a three way contrast in coda specification: (1) stop coda, (2) nasal coda, and (3) /r/. Alternatively (3) could be analysed as an unspecified coda or empty timing slot (see discussion of geminates below).

3.2.1.3 Geminates

Geminate consonants are one of the more characteristic features of Makasar, and thus merit some detailed discussion.

A distinction has been drawn between 'true' geminates and 'apparent' or 'fake' geminates (Goldsmith 1990:80). True geminates are those which occur within a morpheme and are taken to be a single element corresponding to two timing slots, while fake geminates occur across morpheme boundaries and each element is a separate slot. Thus the geminates in the two words *appa'* 'four' and *appada* 'do together' would be treated differently—*appa'* is real and *appada* is fake:

```
a)  X  X  X  X       b)  X  X  X  X  X  X
    |  \/  |  |           |  |  |  |  |  |
    a  p   a  ?           a  p  p  a  d  a
```

According to Goldsmith (1990:81) all morpheme-internal geminates are assumed to be true geminates, as a consequence of the Obligatory Contour Principle banning adjacent identical segments at the melodic level. However, we have already seen that most geminates in Makasar can be accounted for as a sequence of underspecified nasal or stop coda and the onset of the following syllable. These need not violate OCP because the principle does not assume them to be identical at an underlying level. Thus, the above examples can also be analysed as follows, where C stands for an underspecified stop coda:

```
c)  X  X  X  X  X    d)  X  X  X  X  X  X
    |  |  |  |  |        |  |  |  |  |  |
    a  C  p  a  C        a  C  p  a  d  a
```

So in most cases it makes no difference whether morpheme-internal geminates are assumed to be true geminates, or sequences as described above. However, the notion of true geminates does help to account for geminate /r/. Recall that this is the only geminate consonant which cannot be analysed as an underlying stop or nasal + /r/ (/Cr/ or /Nr/), since these are realised as the sequences [ʔr] and [nr] respectively. If geminate /r/ is assumed to be a true geminate all possibilities are accounted for. Examples (e) and (f) show a true geminate in *karru'* 'creak' and the sequence /Cr/ in *ka'ru'* 'furrow':

96   CHAPTER 3

Of course, invoking true geminates allows us to analyse all morpheme-internal geminates as true geminates if we so desire—an over-generation which cannot be avoided.

3.2.1.3.1 Post-lexical Geminates

Another layer of complexity is added here when we consider a phenomenon which I will term post-lexical gemination. Until now most of the discussion has focussed on geminates which can contrast with single consonants, and which are not due to any particular environmental conditioning. But there are some environments which condition geminate consonants somewhat irregularly. Typically, a consonant which occurs morpheme-finally (in a root or affix) in the position V_V will be geminated. Some examples are:

(8) *pammekangngang*
     pa– aN(N)– pekang –ang
     NR– BV–   hook   –NR
     fishing time

(9) *angnginung-nginung*
     aN(N)– inung– inung
     BV–   RDP– drink
     drink for fun

(10) *kale'bakkang*
     ka⟩ le'ba' ⟨ang
     NR⟩ finished ⟨NR
     the end

(11) *tawarri*
     tawar –i
     bargain –trs
     haggle the price down on something

Most examples of this phenomenon occur after /a/, and in fact Mills (1975a:76) deduces that this is gemination conditioned by reflexes of proto-South Sulawesi /*ə/, but it does also occur after other vowels (e.g. *gassíngngi* ⟨gassing –i⟩ 'make strong'), and since /a/ is by far the most common vowel it is hardly surprising that examples with it would predominate.

Stress seems to be a factor here. If the benefactive *–ang* is also affixed to *tawárri* so that stress is now after the consonant rather than before, the gem-

PHONETICS & PHONOLOGY

ination does not occur; e.g. *tawaríang* ⟨tawar-i–ang⟩ 'haggle for someone'. But this does not account for the gemination in *angnginung-nginung*. Additionally, there are many cases where although the environment would seemingly condition it, the gemination does not occur. Examples from the dictionary are *balláki* and *ballakang*: ⟨balla' –i⟩ 'have (something) at home' and ⟨balla' –ang⟩ 'reside in' (Cense & Abdoerrahim 1979:57). However on the same page there is also the form *pa'ballakkang* ⟨pa- aC- balla' –ang⟩ 'place to build a house'. It is quite possible that Cense was rather irregular in transcribing this gemination, but I do not have enough data in my own field recordings to make a definitive statement about this. From my questioning on this matter it seemed that words were generally acceptable with or without the gemination (e.g. *gassíngi* or *gassíngngi*).

3.2.2 Word Structure

Defining the word in Makasar is not unproblematic. For a start, clearly the phonological word and prosodic word need not necessarily align—this is evident because clitics are outside the prosodic domain but still part of the phonological word (§ 3.2.2.2). It is also often hard to decide whether a unit should be considered a freestanding word, a clitic, or something in between: examples include the particles *ka* 'because' and *ri* PREP and reduced adverbial particles such as *tong* 'also' (§ 5.5.2.4). There are also the problems of reduplication and compounding, where it must be decided if the result should be considered one word or two (§ 3.3.7, § 3.3.8). Some idea of the difficulty in defining the word can be gained by considering some of the different ways words are written in various orthographies and where word boundaries have been drawn (§ 3.1.3).

3.2.2.1 Root Structure

The majority of Makasar roots (see § 4.1) are bisyllabic—more precisely they are bisyllabic trochee. Stress falls regularly on the penult (§ 3.2.3). A significant subset of roots are trisyllabic with antepenultimate stress: these are roots which have been subject to Echo–VC (§ 3.3.4). There is a smaller number of true trisyllabic roots with regular penultimate stress. Four syllable roots tend to look suspicious, as though they are derived from former compounds or other polymorphemic forms (for example in Table 13 *balakebo'* 'herring' looks like a compound including *kebo'* 'white', though the first element *bala* is not meaningful in this context).[15] Monosyllabic roots are extremely rare, though there are several monosyllabic interjections and particles (such as *o* and *ri* below).

---

15   It could come from *balao* 'mouse'.

98   CHAPTER 3

TABLE 13   CV patterns

V	o	'oh' (interjection)
CV	ri	PREP (particle)
VC	u'	'hair'
CVC	pi'	'birdlime'
VV	io	'yes'
VVC	aeng	'father'
CVV	tau	'person'
CVVC	taung	'year'
VCVC	ulu'	'head'
CVCV	sala	'wrong'
CVCVC	saba'	'reason'
CVCCVC	le'ba'	'already'
CVCVCV	binánga	'river'
CVCVCVC	pásara'	'market'
CVCVCCV	kalúppa	'forget'
CVCCVCVC	ka'lúrung	'palm wood'
CVCVCVCVC	balakebo'	'herring'
CVCVCVCCVC	kalumanynyang	'rich'

Table 13 gives some examples of syllable patterns within morphemes. The list is exhaustive for permutations of mono- and bisyllabic forms, but since CV patterns do not change according to the length of the word only a few illustrative examples are given beyond two syllables. The first two are shaded because they are not roots.

3.2.2.2   Phonological Word vs Prosodic Word

There are two main methods used here to determine wordhood, and for the most part they come up with the same results. The first relies on metrics, defining the word as a prosodic unit which contains a syllable carrying primary stress (see § 3.2.1.3.1). The second considers separability, i.e. whether units can constitute an entire utterance, be moved around within a sentence, or be separated from other units by pauses. Generally these phonological methods also agree with the morphosyntactic definition of a word as a root with or without affixes and clitics.

PHONETICS & PHONOLOGY

There are a few cases where the two methods used above do not match up. For example, while the preposition *ri* does not fulfil the criteria for the minimal prosodic unit and can never take stress, it can be pronounced with a pause or it can be drawn out (while attempting to remember the name of the place or person which follows).[16] It may also be pronounced with no pause at all between it and the following element. This is also seen with the conjunctions *na* and *ka*, but with no other prefixes or proclitics, neither is it possible to pause between roots and suffixes. For example the phrase *na aC- lampa =a'* (CNJ MV–go=1) 'and ... I went' can be realised as *na'lámpa'* or *na ... a'lámpa'* but not **na'... lampa'* or **na'lampa ... a'*.

Similarly in the phrase *ka la= tinro =a'* (BCS FUT= sleep =1S/O) 'because I'm about to go to sleep' a pause may be inserted after *ka* but at no other point. There can be no pause between the homonymic nominalising affix *ka–* and its host, as in *katinroang* 'bed' (**ka ... tinroang*).

I posit these three elements *ri, na and ka* as particles somewhere between clitics and words—grammatical elements which cannot occur in isolation and do not take stress, but which have a degree of phonological independence (see § 4.5). For this reason (and to avoid ambiguity with homophonous affix or clitic forms in the cases of *na* and *ka*) I have transcribed them as separate words.

3.2.2.3 Word Formation

Words can consist of between one and eight or more syllables. The vast majority of roots are two or three syllables, but Makasar is agglutinative and the concatenation of morphemes, especially in combination with reduplication, can produce words of some length.

3.2.2.3.1 *The Minimal Word*

Since a word consists of a root with or without affixed material, the minimal word is a monosyllabic root without affixes. I know of only four definite examples of monosyllabic lexemes which are not obviously loans—there may well be others, but they are clearly uncommon. They are *bu* 'fish trap', *u'* 'hair', *pi'* 'birdlime' and *pa'* 'chisel'. This shows that the bare minimum for a root is CV or VC. Other examples of monosyllabic words are loans, some interjections (which may be simply V, as in *e!* and *o!*), and the aforementioned grammatical elements *ri, na,* and *ka*.

---

16   If it seems that this is taking too long, the pro-noun *anu* 'somewhere/thing/one' is added and the process begins again (e.g. *ri ... anu, riMalino* 'from umm ... Malino').

100   CHAPTER 3

3.2.2.3.2   *The Maximal Word*

It is impossible to give a maximum length because in theory something could always be added, but while six and seven syllable words are common, words above this length get exponentially rarer and always contain reduplications. To illustrate, take the eight syllable word *kagassing-gassingánnami*, which is formed in the following way:

> the root *gássing* 'strong'
> reduplication → *gassing-gássing* (this would normally mean 'strong-ish', but it has a different meaning in combination with the next stage)
> the nominalising confix *ka*⟩⟨*ang* → *kagassing-gassíngang* 'peak of strength'
> the 3rd person possessive suffix ≡*na* → *kagassing-gassingánna* 'peak of his strength'
> the perfective clitic =*mo* → *kagassing-gassingánnamo* 'already the peak of his strength'
> the 3rd person pronominal enclitic =*i* → *kagassing-gassingánnami* 'he's already at the peak of his strength'

This construction is a single phonological word because it only has one syllable carrying primary stress, and also because there is no point within it in which it is possible to pause or insert something else. The affixes *ka*⟩⟨*ang*, ≡*na*, =*mo* and =*i* are all bound elements which must occur in the order given.

It is clear that the results of reduplication are to be considered single words because of the single stressed syllable, and because they can host affixes such as the confix *ka*⟩⟨*ang*. The hyphen between constituents of a reduplication is an orthographic convention with no phonological basis. For more on reduplication see §3.3.7. Compounds (actually collocations) such as *balla'-lompo* ('house' + 'big' = 'palace') are *not* held to be a single phonological word (see §3.3.8).

3.2.3   *Stress*

Stressed syllables differ from unstressed syllables in a number of ways: pitch is normally significantly higher, and they are noticeably louder. There is also a requirement that stressed syllables be heavy—which means that open syllables become long. Not all stressed syllables are equal, however—this is because, unsurprisingly, as well as being assigned regularly by word-level phonological rule, stress is important for marking syntactic units larger than the word, and is also important for emphasis.

PHONETICS & PHONOLOGY   101

Stress is typically on the penultimate syllable of the word, which may be a reduplicated form (plus affixes) of eight or more syllables. Secondary stress only occurs if the word is a reduplication—in these cases the first element will take secondary stress where primary stress would have been assigned if it was a free-standing word. For example the reduplication *ammekang–mekang* receives stress in the pattern *ammèkang–mékang*, where the grave represents secondary stress.

Suffixes are counted for stress, while enclitics are not (because stress is assigned from the right edge of the word it is a moot point whether prefixes and proclitics are counted for stress or not). For example: *tedóng≡ku* (buffalo≡1.POSS) 'my buffalo' but *tédong=a'* (buffalo=1) 'I'm a buffalo'. Thus a word with a suffix (or affixal clitic, see §4.4) will generally retain penultimate stress, while a word with a clitic will have antepenultimate or even preantepenultimate stress—the latter occurring when a word hosts a disyllabic clitic combination such as *=mako* ⟨*=ma* PFV *=ko* 2s⟩ as in *nái'mako* 'climb up!'. The suffixes which are counted for stress are the applicatives *–ang* and *–i* (see §9); and the possessives ≡*ku*, ≡*nu*, ≡*ta*, and ≡*na* (see §4.4.2). The enclitics which do not affect stress placement are the enclitic pronouns *=a'*, *=ko*, *=ki'*, and *=i* (see §4.3.2) and the aspectuals *=mo*, *=ja*, and *=pa* and variants (see §4.3.3). The definite marker ≡*a* shows both behaviours, but in different environments as is discussed in §3.3.6.

Words may have deviant stress because of vowel degemination or echo–VC (see §3.3.1, §3.3.4), and there is a small number of words, mostly loans, which have idiosyncratic stress patterns which mimic the stress in the source language, such as *goboranaméng* 'government' (from Dutch *gouvernemént*) and *ampaló'* 'envelope' (from Dutch *envelóppe*).

Monosyllabic words can behave in two different ways with regard to stress: they can host stress (thus forming a degenerate foot), or they can attach to a neighbouring word much as a clitic would and not host stress. Both can be illustrated with the monosyllabic form of the word *dáeng* 'uncle' which is realised as ['deŋ].[17] If the monosyllabic form precedes a name it will not carry stress, while the full disyllabic form will carry normal penultimate stress. Thus *Daeng Nakku'* can be realised as ['da.en.'nak.ku] or more often [den.'nak.ku]. However, if *daeng* is used without a following name (*daeng* being the most common form of address), it will take stress even if it is a monosyllable, for example in *ammémpoki', déng* 'please sit down, brother'.

---

17   The reduced form is less formal, however, the longer form is always used in writing (it is never written *deng*).

102   CHAPTER 3

The same thing can be seen with the word *u'* 'hair'. Normally constituents of a supposed compound (see §3.3.8) each normally carry stress, as in *bálla'-gárring* 'house' + 'sick' = 'hospital'. In compounds where *u'* is the first element it does not carry stress, as in *u'-céra'* 'blood' + 'hair' = 'lanugo'. If it is the only possible candidate for stress, however, *u'* will carry it, as in the utterance *ri ú'* 'in the hair' (the preposition *ri* never takes stress).

I believe this shows that a monosyllabic word will attach prosodically to the following word in the same phrase if there is one, and the two words will be treated metrically as a single word. If this is not possible, however, the monosyllabic word will form a degenerate foot and take stress.

A small group of common words has stress on the final syllable, or words with normally penultimate stress can have it moved there for emphasis. This is typical in one word utterances, such as *ío'* → *ió'* 'yes!'. Notably there is a difference in social meaning here—*ió'* is quite familiar and may not be used to social superiors.

3.3   Morphophonological Processes

This section discusses the major morphophonological processes.

3.3.1   *Vowel Degemination*
This refers to a process in which sequences of identical vowels are collapsed into a single syllable, for example when a vowel-final root hosts a vowel-initial suffix or enclitic. In the case of the suffixes *–ang* and *–i* this results in ultimate stress, e.g.:

(12) *jappáng*
      jappa –ang
      walk –BEN
      walk with

(13) *attaí*
      aC– tai –i
      MV– shit –APPL
      shit on

The first person pronominal enclitic =*a'* is realised as only a glottal stop on an /a/-final root, while the third person enclitic =*i* has no audible realisation (not even stress-shifting) when hosted by an /i/-final root:

PHONETICS & PHONOLOGY   103

(14) *a'lampa'*
      aC– lampa =a'
      MV– go   =1
      I go

(15) *lari*
      lari =i
      run =3
      s/he runs

This process, following a tendency towards deletion of intervocalic /d/, may also be historically responsible for the allomorphy of the adverbial elements *tódong/tóng, bédeng/béng*, etc. (§ 5.5.2).

I shall note here that evidence from manuscripts suggests that vowel degemination was less prevalent in the Makasar of a few centuries ago. For example, the 18th century manuscript KIT 668–216 (see § 3.1.1.1) alternates between ꦱꦑ (*agang*) and ꦱꦑꦱ (*agaang*) in representing the word which is *agáng* 'do with' in modern Makasar (page 1, line 10). Another example is the representation of ⟨jama –ang⟩ 'work' as ꦛꦛꦱ (*jamaang*), where the modern equivalent is always *jamáng* (page 6, line19). It is possible that at this period long vowels were only just becoming stressed vowels. Of course, it is also possible that this was a particular scribe's method of denoting stressed vowels.[18]

In an earlier work (Jukes 1998) I described a process in which a sequence of non-deletable identical vowels (i.e. between a proclitic and vowel-initial root, as in *naallei* ⟨na= alle =i⟩ 's/he took it' were separated by a glottal stop (thus [naʔallei]). Further exposure to the spoken language in everyday contexts has suggested that, rather than a phenomenon of normal speech, this was either an artifact of 'instructor speak', or more likely an ideolectal variation of one of my main informants at that time, Muyazdlala. The latter, as I discovered later, had been a childhood speaker of Selayarese, in which language a glottal stop is inserted between like vowels at clitic-stem boundaries (Hasan Basri 1999:14). The usual result in Makasar is simply two vowels in sequence, [naallei].

---

18   It is also interesting to note that in the dialect of Bontonompo (southern coastal Gowa) the root *agáng* has a variant form *agádang*.

3.3.2 *Nasal Substitution*

Nasal substitution refers to the process whereby a stem-initial consonant becomes the equivalent nasal when a prefix is added. A well known example of this kind of process is that seen in Malay/Indonesian, where the transitivising nasal prefix *meN–* added to verb stems with initial voiceless consonants will result in those consonants being substituted by nasals in the same place of articulation (for example *meN- pilih* → *memilih* 'to choose'). (See for example Sneddon (1996); for an Optimality Theory based description see Pater (2001); for a survey of the phenomenon across Austronesian languages see Blust (2004)).

The process in Makasar has broad similarities to that described for Malay, but rather than the nasal prefix (see §7.1.2) substituting a single nasal for the voiceless segment, the result is a geminate nasal, for which reason I notate the prefix with the form *aN(N)-*. Furthermore, the process is seen not only with voiceless stops (/p/, /t/, /k/); but also with stems beginning with /b/ (e.g. ⟨aN(N)-balli⟩ → *ammalli* 'buy'), though not with any other voiced stops (/d/, /g/). Lastly, *aN(N)–* contrasts with another nasal prefix *aN–* (§7.2) which does not cause nasal substitution.

Some examples of C-initial roots which take this prefix are:

p	pekang	'hook'	→	ammekang	'fish'
b	balli	'price'	→	ammalli	'buy'
t	tunrung	'be hit'	→	annunrung	'hit s.t'
s	sanggara'	'fried'	→	anynyanggara'	'fry s.t'
c	cokko	'secret'	→	anynyokko	'hide s.t'
k	kanre	'cooked rice'	→	angnganre	'eat'

With V-initial roots the prefix is realised as *angng-*, as in *angnginung* 'drink'.

The phenomenon can be viewed as two processes of spreading: manner (nasal) spreading to the right, and place spreading to the left. For example, the process for the relevent segments of ⟨aN(N)- polong⟩ → *ammolong* 'cut' is shown in the figure below:

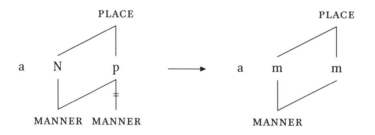

PHONETICS & PHONOLOGY

TABLE 14   Roots subject to nasal substitution

	p	b	t	s	c	k
/20	13	6	13	16	1	8
%	65	30	65	80	5	40

It should be noted that not all eligible consonants are equally likely to be affected by nasal substitution. For example, nearly all /s/-initial roots can host the nasal substituting prefix (usually becoming palatal in the process), but hardly any /c/-initial roots. The latter tend to be derived with the prefix *aC–* (§7.1.1) even if the meaning is transitive, for example *cukkuru'* 'shave' → *accukkuru'* (**anynyukkuru'*) in both intransitive and transitive examples:

(16) *accukuruka'*
    aC– cukur =a'
    MV– shave =1
    I shave

(17) *accukuruka' bulu*
    aC– cukur =a' bulu
    MV– shave =1 body/face.hair
    I shave my body/face hair

Using Cense (1979) as a corpus, and randomly taking 20 roots in each of the above consonants, the ratio with listed forms showing nasal substitution is shown in Table 14. This is not to suggest that the choice between *aC–* and *aN(N)–* is made predominantly on phonological grounds, but it does seem that there is a dispreference for *aN(N)–* on roots beginning with /c/ and to a lesser extent /b/ and /k/, which may partly account for some of the examples of of transitive verbs which are marked with *aC–* (§7.1.1.1).[19]

This process is the subject of an Optimality Theory based account by Bhandari (1997). Basically, she compares the process of nasal substitution in Malay/Indonesian with the process in Makasar, and concludes that the differences are due to the ranking of two of four constraints:

---

19   In his survey of Austronesian nasal substitution, Blust (2004) states that /c/ does not undergo substitution at all, which is not quite correct.

- ***NÇ** (sequences of nasals and voiceless consonants are disallowed)
- **Align word** (the left edge of the root must align with the left edge of the prosodic word)
- ***Double link** (a constraint against gemination)
- **Prefix=σ** (the edges of a prefix must be aligned with syllable edges)

Indonesian ranks ***Double link** above **Prefix=σ**, which allows *me.mi.lih* (violating **Prefix=σ**, because the nasal is no longer in the same syllable as the rest of the prefix) while banning *mem.mi.lih* (fatally violating ***Double link** with a geminate); while Makasar ranks **Prefix=σ** above ***Double link**, licensing ⟨aN(N)-polong⟩ → *am.mo.long* 'to cut' (violating ***Double link**) but banning *a.molong* (which fatally violates **Prefix=σ**).

To account for the fact that a geminate nasal prefix is added to V-initial stems such as ⟨aN(N)- alle⟩ → *angngalle* 'take', Bhandari invokes two further constraints:

- **Onset** (a syllable must have an onset)
- **Dep** (an anti-epenthesis constraint)

Makasar ranks the **Onset** requirement above **Prefix=σ**, **Dep** and ***Double link** in that order, licensing *ang.ngal.le* (violating **Dep** and ***Double link**) but prohibiting *ang.al.le* (fatally violating **Onset**) and *a.ngal.le* (fatally violating **Prefix=σ**). The **Onset** constraint is also invoked to account for a proposed reduplicated form *ang.ngalle.ngalle*.

Unfortunately Bhandari's paper does not account for some problematic facts about Makasar nasal substitution:

- it ignores the nasal substitution of /b/, which is not covered by ***NÇ**.
- it does not account for the non-substituting Actor Focus prefix *aN–* (§ 7.2), which results in violations of ***NÇ** in forms such as *ampolong*. This need not invalidate the analysis but does raise the question of whether these constraints are generally part of the phonology or are morpheme specific.
- the constraint **Prefix=σ** is regularly violated when the initial /a/ of the prefix is elided making the prefix non-syllabic (e.g. *mmolong*, see § 3.3.5).
- the reduplication data are inaccurate, since the reduplicated form of *angngalle* is *angngalle-alle*, not *angngalle-ngalle* (§ 3.3.7.2).

3.3.3   *Glottal Strengthening*

This label (Friberg & Friberg 1991a) refers to the process whereby a root-final glottal stop is realised as [k] in onset position. This happens when the root hosts a vowel-initial suffix or enclitic, either the applicatives *–i* or *–ang*, the determiner ≡*a*, or the pronominal clitics =*a'* or =*i*.

PHONETICS & PHONOLOGY 107

(18) *kuparékangi*
    ku= pare' –ang =i
    1=   make –BEN =3
    I made it for him/her

(19) *nacinika'*
    na= cini' =a'
    3=   see =1
    s/he sees me

This process only occurs between roots and suffixes or enclitics—it is not seen
with the intransitive verbal prefix *aC–*, nor with reduplication or compounding.
For example *aC– anrong → a'anrong* 'have a mother' (**akanrong*), and reduplicated *ana'* 'child' → *ana'–ana'* 'children' (**anakana'*). This indicates that only
suffixing elements are able to recruit a coda from a syllable in another morpheme to act as an onset; that is, they have an onset requirement which ranks
higher than the root's requirement to retain its structure unaltered.

3.3.4 *Echo–VC*

There is a large group of (typically) three syllable roots, in which the final syllable begins with one of /s/, /l/, or /r/. These words contain antepenultimate
stress (unlike the vast majority of (uninflected) words which have penultimate
stress), the final vowel is always the same as the preceding vowel, and they all
end in a glottal stop. The list below shows some examples:

pásara'	'market'	Mangkásara'	'Makassar'
bótoro'	'gamble'	pa'risi'	'pain'
bótolo'	'bottle'	lápisi'	'layer'

Some of these are obviously loan words, but they are by no means the majority,
and since this group of words includes the ethnonym *Mangkásara'* it must be
seen as more than a phenomenon of loan phonology. However it is instructive to look at some of the loans, and also to compare some of the words with
their Malay counterparts. For example, the word *bótolo'* is a loan, probably
from Dutch *bottel*, while *pásara'* and *lápisi'* have Malay counterparts *pasar* and
lapis.

    These echo syllables are absent if the root hosts a stress-shifting affix (*–i* or
–ang). For example:

(20) *botórang*
     botor   **o' –ang*
     gamble   –BEN
     wager something

(21) *sipa'rísi*
     si–   *pa'ris *i' –i*
     RECP– pain   –APPL
     hurt each other

They are, however, present when the roots host pronominal clitics or the determiner (the glottal stop is realised as [k] due to glottal strengthening as described in § 3.3.3):

(22) *appásaraka'*
     aC– pasar   *=a' =a'*
     MV– market =EC =1
     I (go to) market

(23) *pásaraka*
     pasar   *=a' ≡a*
     market =EC ≡DEF
     the market

The echo syllables are also present when the stress-shifting possessive suffixes are added.

(24) *botoló'na*
     botol   *=o' ≡na*
     bottle =EC ≡3.POSS
     his bottle

However, since all the possessive suffixes are C-initial, this is not so surprising, because the consonant sequences which would result if the echo VC was not inserted are all forbidden (**sk, *sn, *lk, *ln, *rk, *rn*).

It is apparent that /s/, /l/, or /r/—which can be grouped for the sake of convenience into a class of non-nasal continuants—are not allowed in coda position except as the first element of geminates. Unless these consonants can be used as onsets for following syllables within the metrical word (therefore excluding extrametrical clitics), an empty VC slot is appended, which is filled by

PHONETICS & PHONOLOGY

spreading of the previous vowel and then closed with a glottal stop by default. This VC is extrametrical, resulting in antepenultimate stress.

This phenomenon (and its counterpart in the Selayar language—which differs in that the echo syllable is only V rather than VC) has been relatively well discussed in the literature. Goldsmith (1990:131–136) gives an autosegmental account based on the description of Selayarese in Mithun & Basri (1987), while Aronoff, Arsyad, Basri & Broselow (1987) mention the phenomenon in their paper on reduplication.[20] Data from the latter paper is used for Optimality Theoretic accounts by McCarthy and Prince (1994) and McCarthy (1998).

The OT analysis of McCarthy and Prince (1994) can be exemplified with the tableau for the word *jamala'* 'naughty' (p. 24), reproduced here:

	Coda-Cond	Align-Stem-Right	Final-C	Fill
jamal‖a'		*		**
jamal‖a		*	*!	*
jamal‖	*!			

CODA-COND stipulates that a coda cannot be specified for place (thus limiting it to [ʔ] and [ŋ]). ALIGN-STEM-RIGHT requires that a stem ends at a syllable edge, which is violated in this instance but is necessary to preserve vowel-final stems from epenthesis via FINAL-C (requiring a coda), which in turn dominates FILL (prohibiting epenthesis). All else being equal, the glottal stop [ʔ] rather than [ŋ] is chosen as the coda of the epenthetic VC because it conforms to a lower ranked constraint NO-NAS favouring oral stops over nasals (p. 32).

McCarthy (1998) uses some of the same data to argue that the distinction between licit and illicit surface forms in Makasar can be explained in terms of paradigm occultation rather than morpheme structure constraints (MSC). The paper's main focus is explaining why Makasar allows roots such as /jamal/ to emerge as *jamala'*, but does not allow putative roots such as /katop/ to emerge as, say *katop, *katopo', or *katopi', concluding that various constraints combine to allow one paradigm which 'occults' any others.

---

20   Unfortunately, as already pointed out, much of the data in this paper seems to describe Selayarese rather than Makasar. For example, comparative forms are given using the suffix *–ang* rather than the more usual *–angngang*. The reduplication data are also rather different to my findings, as will be discussed in § 3.3.7.

The analysis relevant to Echo–VC proposes that VCV spreading is compelled by a faithfulness constraint IO-Max-C (an input segment should have a corresponding output segment). The order of ranking constraints pertaining to vowel-spreading across specific types of segments is what licenses *jamala'* but prohibits *katopo'* et al., as seen in the tableaux below (McCarthy 1998:21).

/jamal/	OO-Dep-C	IO-Dep-VPl	Coda-Cond	IO-Max-C	No-VL-Link	*Pl/Cor+VPl
jáma				*!		
jáma.li'		*!				
jámal			*!			
☞ jáma.la'					*	*

/katop/	OO-Dep-C	IO-Dep-VPl	Coda-Cond	No-VS-Link	*Pl/Lab+VPl	IO-Max-C
☞ káto						*
káto.pi'		*!				
kátop			*!			
káto.po'				*!	*!	

As in McCarthy and Prince (1994), Coda-Cond prohibits *jamal, while IO-Dep-VPl safeguards against the insertion of random vowels (*jamali'). A constraint against the spreading of vocalic place is ranked below IO-Max-C in the case of coronals (*Pl/Cor+VPl), as is a similar constraint against spreading across liquids (No-VL-Link). In the case of /katop/, however, constraints against vowel-spreading across labials (*Pl/Lab+VPl) and obstruents (No-VS-Link) outrank IO-Max-C, leading to deletion of the /p/.[21]

---

21   Actually, in my opinion *kato* is the wrong candidate, and the most obvious candidate, *kato'*, is not considered. This is rather odd because one would assume that *kato'* would violate fewer constraints (actually it appears to violate no constraints at all). If we look at McCarthy's tableau we can see that the candidate *kato* beats the others because it only violates a faithfulness constraint IO-Max-C (an input segment should have a corresponding output segment), while conforming to the higher-ranked constraint Coda-Cond. However, a glottal stop in Makasar is a placeless coda, as stated in McCarthy & Prince (1994:355), so *kato'* conforms to all constraints, including IO-Max-C. More compellingly, if we leave the realm of possible roots thrown out by GEN and look at actual evidence from the language, we find that there are numerous examples in which /p/-final loans have entered the language and had /p/ replaced with /ʔ/. Malay *adap* 'side' and *harap* 'hope' are two obvious examples, which become *ada'* and *(h)ara'* respectively.

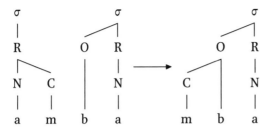

FIGURE 18 Formation of complex onsets

For a broader look at final vowels in Sulawesi languages see Sneddon (1993), who notes that there has been a general tendency for Sulawesi languages to lose final consonants. This process of Echo–VC in Makasar both exemplifies and defies this, because it adds a vowel to prevent a final consonant, but then paradoxically closes the syllable.

3.3.5 Aphesis of Initial /a/

This refers to the fact that the three verb prefixes aC–, aN(N)– and aN– (§ 8.1), as well as the demonstrative set *anne*, *anjo* and *antu*, are all subject to a process of optional deletion which removes the initial vowel in fast speech. This leaves surface forms with initial consonant clusters—*pp, tt, cc, kk, mp, nt, nc, ngk, 'b, 'd, 'j, 'g, mb, nd, nj, ngg, mm, nn, nyny, ngng, ss, ns, 'l, ll, 'r, nr* and *'h*. For example, the word *ambajíki* 'fix something' can be realised as *mbajíki*. This can be explained as follows. With the vowel gone there is no syllable nucleus for the prefix, so the stranded coda attaches itself to the following syllable. The process is shown for the relevant segments in Figure 18.

Note however that the stranded coda will attach itself to a preceding open syllable if there is one, as in the following example:

(25) *lanuápaíntu untia*
     la–   nu= apa =i antu unti   ≡a
     FUT– 2S= what =3 that banana ≡DEF
     what are you going to do with those bananas?

An interesting point in the above example is that the deleted vowel retains its stress contour, which is then assigned to the new syllable nucleus (in this case an extra-metrical enclitic =*i*).

3.3.6 *Determiner Glide Insertion*

The determiner ≡a behaves rather differently from the other suffixes, showing a mixture of clitic and suffix behaviours. When affixed to a C-final stem it behaves as one of the enclitics; it is not visible to stress, and when affixed to one of the s/l/r words the epenthetic VC will be added. Thus *bálla'≡a → bállaka* 'the house', *pásara'≡a → pásaraka* 'the market'.

When affixed to a stem ending in a vowel other than *a*, the determiner is visible to stress. Thus *báwi≡a → bawía* 'the pig', *tape≡a→ tapéa* 'the *tape*' (a fermented rice sweet), *ráppo≡a → rappóa* 'the fruit', *bátu≡a → batúa* 'the stone'. There is a low level glide insertion: *y* between front vowels and ≡a, and *w* between back vowels and ≡a. This is no different to the process seen ordinarily between these sequences of vowels. In addition to this, as was described in the discussion of glides, underlying stressed high vowels in the position *a_a* are realised as geminate glides: *táu≡a → taúa* or *tawwa* ['tawwa] 'the person', *tái≡a → taía* or *tayya* ['tajja] 'the shit'.

Surface geminate *y* also appears when the determiner is affixed to an *a*-final stem, as in *mata≡a → matáyya* 'the eye', *binanga≡a → binangáyya* 'the river'. I analyse this as an insertion of an epenthetic high front vowel *i* because this will result in the surface form with the insertion of only one segment. It is possible that the form of the determiner derives from that of the third person pronoun *ia* and its realisation in *a_a* position is a reflection of that, but this is merely speculation.

Hasan Basri et al. (1999) explain the behaviour of the determiner using Optimality Theory, but in the end resort to using a constraint specific to this morpheme, **Align Det-L, Glide**, which requires a determiner to be left-aligned with a glide.

3.3.7 *Reduplication*

Reduplication is a common phenomenon in Makasar, with a range of semantic functions including diminution, non-specificity, and repetition—the semantics are particular to word classes and are discussed in the relevant sections. This section deals strictly with reduplication as a phonological phenomenon, which has also been the subject of an autolexical study (Aronoff et al. 1987), and more recent Optimality Theoretic accounts (McCarthy and Prince 1994; Nelson 2003) of the same data. Hasan Basri's OT account of Selayarese reduplication (1999:162–190) is largely based on McCarthy & Prince's analysis. In addition there is a local publication (Said Mursalin 1984), which is basically a listing of different kinds and combinations of reduplicated forms. In this section I will first describe the basics of reduplication as seen in my data, then discuss some of the issues which arise from the aforementioned publications.

PHONETICS & PHONOLOGY

TABLE 15   Reduplication of mono- and disyllabic roots

u'	'hair'	→	u'–u'	'a kind of sweet'	['uʔ.uʔ]
ana'	'child'	→	ana'–ana'	'children'	[a.naʔ.'a.naʔ]
le'leng	'black'	→	le'leng–le'leng	'blackish'	[leʔ.lel.'leʔ.leŋ]
bambang	'hot'	→	bambang–bambang	'hottish'.	[bam.bam.'bam.baŋ]

TABLE 16   Reduplication of trisyllabic roots

tettere'	'fast'	→	tette'–tettere'	'quite fast'	[tet.tet.'tet.te.reʔ]
baine	'woman'	→	bai'–baine	'women'	[ba.iʔ.ba.'i.ne]
			*bai–baine		
barumbung	'grey'	→	baru'–barumbung	'greyish'	[ba.ruʔ.ba.'rumbuŋ]
			*barum-barumbung		
balao	'rat'	→	bala'-balao	'toy rat'.	[ba.laʔ.ba.'la.o]
			*bala–balao		

In this discussion I shall focus on reduplication as a productive phenomenon; thus I wish to exclude from the outset forms which appear reduplicated, but where the apparent base is not in itself a lexical item. By this I mean primarily disyllabic forms such as *kongkong* 'dog', *bambang* 'hot', and *rinring* 'ceiling'. These kinds of words (reduplicated monosyllables) are common in many Austronesian languages and Makasar is no exception (Mills 1975a:370 ff.). Said Mursalin (1984) gives a partial listing of these forms.

3.3.7.1   Reduplication of Roots

The basic facts are as follows: mono- or disyllabic roots are copied in their entirety, and the reduplicative prefix is prefixed to the root. All usual processes of assimilation take place, and the entire form is treated as one word for the purposes of stress (though in careful speech the penult of the reduplicative prefix can carry secondary stress). Note that glottal strengthening (§ 3.3.3) does not apply between reduplicant and root. Some examples are provided in Table 15.

For roots of three or more syllables only the first two syllables are copied. The reduplicative prefix will always end in a glottal stop (subject to assimilation), whether the corresponding syllable in the base was open or closed, and even if the original syllable was closed with an acceptable coda consonant such as a nasal. Some examples are provided in Table 16.

114 CHAPTER 3

3.3.7.2 Reduplication of Prefixed Forms

When morphologically complex words are reduplicated, generally the root alone forms the base, and the entire reduplicated form then forms the stem for affixation. Thus, prefixed elements are attached to the reduplicant, and suffixed elements to the base, as in the following examples:

(26) *a'jappa-jappa*
aC– *jappa– jappa*
MV– RDP– walk
stroll

(27) *kaio-ioang*
ka⟩ io– io ⟨ang
NR⟩ RDP– yes ⟨NR
s.o who always agrees

(28) *sitaba-tabai*
si– taba– taba =i
MUT– RDP match =3
they're about the same

When a base containing the nasal substituting verbal prefix *aN(N)–* is reduplicated, it is the nasalised form which is copied, thus:

(29) *ammekang-mekang*
aN(N)– pekang pekang
BV– RDP– hook
fishing (for fun)

This shows that prefixed material can have an effect on both the base and the reduplicant. However, note that V-initial stems with the prefix *aN(N)–* do not show a nasal on the base (e.g. *alle* 'take' → *angngalle-alle* 'take a direction'), unless they are *–ng* final and subject to post-lexical gemination (e.g. *inung* 'drink' → *angnginung-nginung* 'drink for fun', see § 3.2.1.3.1). In contrast, forms with the prefix *amm–* (§ 7.1.4) do show *m–* on the base (*empo* 'sit' → *ammempo-mempo* 'sit awhile').

Said Mursalin (1984:22) reports that in some cases reduplication can include more prefixed material, such as in *pana-panai'* (presumably this should be *pana'-panai'*) 'raise a little' (*naikan sedikit*), from the causative *pa–* and *nai'* 'ascend'. According to Mursalin this can contrast in meaning with replica-

PHONETICS & PHONOLOGY   115

tion of the root alone, for example *panai'-nai'* 'raise more' (*naikan lebih ban-yak*). Examples are also given (p. 30) with the nominaliser *ka*⟩⟨*ang*, such as *kako-kakodiang* 'a bit of badness' (*keburukan sedikit*), contrasting with *kakodi-kodianna* 'his worst (time), the time of his greatest evil' (*masa buruk-buruknya*), which consists of the same circumfix and the 3rd person possessive suffix ≡*na*. I must add here that although I have encountered the latter construction (*kakodi-kodianna*), speakers generally rejected *pana-panai'* and *kako-kako-diang* and stated them to be invented forms.

3.3.7.3   Reduplication of Suffixed Forms

Suffixed forms require some detailed discussion, especially when one considers differences in the data in Aronoff et al. (1987) and the other papers based on it; and examples from some other publications (Cense & Abdoerrahim 1979; Said Mursalin 1984), and my own field data.

Looking first at suffixed bases: according to the data in Aronoff et al. (1987), a consonant final disyllabic root with a suffix attached is counted as a trisyllabic base and conforms to the rule seen earlier for ⟩ disyllabic roots (reduplicant coda → glottal stop), as seen in (30), while a vowel-final suffixed root does not (31). Clitics are not counted as part of the base, so reduplication takes place as though the clitic was not there—thus the contrast between (30) and (32).

(30) *gassi'-gassíngi* (**gassing-gassíngi*)
      RDP– gassing –*i*
      DIM– strong   –trs
      make somewhat strong

(31) *lompo-lompói* (**lompo'-lompói*)
      RDP– lompo –*i*
      DIM– big   –TRS
      make somewhat big

(32) *gassing-gássingi* (**gassi'-gássingi*)
      RDP– gassing =*i*
      DIM– strong   =3
      he is somewhat strong (Aronoff et al. 1987:6–7)

The explanation for the loss of the final nasal of the reduplicant in (30) is that its correspondent in the base is no longer the coda of the 2nd syllable, but has been recruited as onset for the 3rd syllable, and reduplication takes place as normal for a tri-syllabic base.

116   CHAPTER 3

The same data are given an OT analysis in McCarthy & Prince (1994). They posit a number of constraints which apply to reduplication, beginning with R=ROOT (the reduplicant is identical to the root). This is outranked by a cluster of constraints on reduplicant size, namely PARSE-SYLL (every syllable belongs to a foot), ALIGN-FT-RIGHT (every foot stands in final position in the prosodic word), and R=PRWD (the reduplicant is a prosodic word). These three constraints require that the reduplicant be disyllabic, resulting in violation of R=ROOT (due to inexact copying) for roots longer than this. When a root is copied inexactly a further constraint, FINAL-C (every prosodic word is consonant final) applies, giving a reduplicant with the default glottal stop coda as seen in Table 16 above. (R=ROOT dominates FINAL-C, so reduplicated disyllabic vowel-final stems do not gain final consonants). The reason that [ŋ] → [ʔ] in (30) is that R=ROOT is dominated by STROLE (a segment in R(eduplicant) and its correspondent in B(ase) must have identical syllabic roles, so when the [ŋ] in B becomes the onset of [ɲi] rather than the coda of [siŋ], its counterpart in R becomes the default coda [ʔ]).

It is an elegant analysis, and quite plausible. However it differs somewhat from the facts of spoken Makasar as I have observed them. Instead speakers say that the realisation of RDP-*gassing*-TRS is either *gassing-gassíngi* (the supposedly unacceptable example from (30)),[22] or *gassing-gassíngngi* (with post-lexical gemination as described in § 3.2.1.3.1). They explicitly reject **gassi'-gassíngi*. This accords with data from the dictionary, which gives forms such as the *ka*⟨*ang* nominalisation *kagassing-gassingang* 'time of greatest strength', and the verbal form *a'gassing-gassingang* 'find which is the strongest' (Cense & Abdoerrahim 1979:229). Given Cense's normally careful transcription it seems probable that he would have indicated if the realisations were **kagassi'-gassingang* and **a'gassi'-gassingang*.

The reason for the anomalous data in Aronoff et al. (1987) and the other papers is simple: the data do not represent Makasar. Or rather, they represent a version of Makasar spoken by the (Selayarese) co-authors, which differs in several respects from the speech of native speakers of the Gowa variety which is commonly accepted as a standard. This does not cause any real problems for McCarthy & Prince's (1994) analysis: in Gowa Makasar STROLE is simply ranked lower than in Selayarese and does not dominate R=ROOT. Examples which show post-lexical gemination (*gassing-gassíngngi*) are unproblematic in any event as B retains its nasal coda rather than losing it to the following syllable, so the syllabic role is unchanged.

---

22   In actuality, *gassing-gassing* translates as 'healthy' rather than 'somewhat strong', though this has no bearing on the phonological analysis.

PHONETICS & PHONOLOGY

3.3.7.4   Exceptions

A few three syllable words have the whole form copied: e.g. the adverbials *sin-ampe'* 'later' → *sinampe'-sinampe'* 'some time', and *sike'de'* 'a bit' → *sike'de'-sike'de'* 'a tiny bit'. These could be considered repetition rather than reduplication, because each element carries stress.

The demonstratives also behave rather differently from the pattern described above. Instead of the entire form being reduplicated and prefixed to the base, the reduced form is affixed: thus *anne* 'this' → *anne-nne* or even *anne-nne-nne* 'this one! this one!'. The same happens with *anjo* → *anjo-njo* and *antu* → *antu-ntu* 'that one!' ('over there' and 'over by you' respectively).

3.3.8   *Compounding*

There is no compelling evidence that compounding should be considered a phonological process in Makasar. That is to say that supposed compounds such as *balla'-garring* ⟨house sick⟩ 'hospital' or *je'ne-mata* ⟨water eye⟩ 'tears' do not seem to be single phonological words. This differs from the analysis of Bugis in Hanson (2003:150–171), who lists numerous forms, and gives three criteria by which compounds should be defined:

– phonological unity: the compound is a single phonological word with only one stressed syllable
– semantic criteria: the meaning cannot necessarily be considered the sum of its parts
– immutability: the constituent parts cannot be moved around and no other morphemes can be inserted without changing the meaning

The Makasar examples given above do not satisfy the first criterion—instead each constituent word carries stress, although the penult of the entire compound will be more heavily stressed than any single constituent (see § 3.2.3). Neither do they always obey criterion three, as compounds may be interrupted by affixes, for example *mata-allo* ⟨eye day⟩ 'sun' is made definite not just with the determiner ≡*a* but also the 3.POSS suffix ≡*na*, to give *matanna-alloa* (literally 'the day's eye'). Further, there are no examples of entire compounds hosting circumfixes such as *ka*⟩⟨*ang*.[23] The second criterion is not especially helpful

---

23   This is in contrast with Bahasa Indonesia where the comparable *ke*⟩⟨*an* can be placed around entire compounds as in *kesalah-pahaman* 'misunderstanding' (Sneddon 1996:23). Note though that in Makasar there are words which resemble compounds (and could well be derived from compounds historically), which are now indisputably a single lexeme. An example is *balakebo'* 'herring'. *Kebo'* means 'white' and *bala–* also appears in some other fish names but does not now exist as a word (except as a loan *bala* from Arabic 'disaster'). Another is *kalumanynyang* 'rich' which certainly looks like a compound, but

since its application is subjective (one language's 'sick house' is another's 'hospital'), and in any case there are clearly numerous idioms and collocations in which the meaning cannot necessarily be considered the sum of the parts, but which cannot be considered compounds in any phonological sense.

Hasan Basri (1999:33–36) also identifies compounding as a process in Selayarese, giving nominal-headed examples such as *ere-inung* ⟨water- drink⟩ 'drinking water' (Makasar *je'ne'-inung*); verbs with incorporated locatives such as *attolong-kadera* ⟨MV– sit- chair⟩ 'sit on chair'; and verbs where the second element functions as a manner adverb such as *tinro-t-tolong* ⟨sleep- MV– sit⟩ 'sleep while sitting', and *lingka-bonting* ⟨walk-bride⟩ 'walk like a bride'. However, he also points out (1999:143) that mid-vowel lowering (§ 3.1.3.3) does not apply across elements of compounds, thus they should be considered two separate prosodic words.

I would go further, and argue that these 'compounds' are simply collocations at phrase level. *Je'ne-inung* 'drinking water' is not different in structure from *je'ne bambang* 'hot water' or indeed any modified nominal such as *miong le'leng* ⟨cat black⟩ 'black cat'. And while it is true that clitics and affixal clitics typically do not intervene between elements of these supposed compounds (evidence for compound status given by Hasan Basri (1999:33)), the same could also be said of most phrasal constituents which include post-head modifiers. For example a supposed compound hosting the definite marker ≡*a*, such as *balla' garringa* 'the hospital' is formally identical to an ordinary NP containing a modifier such as *miong le'lenga* ⟨cat black ≡DEF⟩ 'the black cat' or *tau ruayya* ⟨person two ≡DEF⟩ 'the two people'. So this evidence is not useful unless one is willing to postulate that most cases of word+postmodifier are compounds.

Incorporated locatives (less common in Makasar than Selayarese) are simply locatives which appear within the nuclear phrase rather than as prepositional adjuncts. Verb phrases may productively contain modifiers from various word classes resulting in meanings which rely on idiom to a lesser or greater degree (e.g. *a'jappa-bunting* ⟨MV– walk bride⟩ 'walk like a bride', i.e. slowly; *a'jappa-balanda* ⟨MV– walk Holland⟩ 'walk like a Dutchman' i.e. swagger). The fact that suffixes and enclitics will occur after the modifier (e.g. *miong le'leng≡ku* 'my black cat', *a'jappa-balanda=i* 'he swaggers') is a feature of phrasal syntax rather than an indication of wordhood.

neither *kalu* nor *manynyang* can be traced now. The latter word can host the circumfix *ka*⟨*ang* → *kakalumanynyángang* 'wealth'.

CHAPTER 4

Morphological Units

This chapter outlines the types of units which are found in Makasar morphosyntax. There are several different types of morphological unit, showing a progression from more lexical to more grammatical. Looking at the major types first, at the lexical end of the scale are lexical **roots**, then there are **clitics** and **affixes**—each being distinguished by clear morphological criteria. Then there are some types of unit which do not fit neatly into those three major types and can be considered to occupy areas between the major types. At the boundary of affixes and clitics there is a group of morphemes which share certain qualities of both and are termed **affixal clitics**, while at the boundary of roots and clitics there are different types of **particle**. Roots combine with clitics, affixal clitics and affixes to form **words**, while the status of particles with regard to wordhood is somewhat debatable.

4.1   Roots

Roots are non-dependent lexical units, meaning they are typically free morphemes which carry lexical meaning and form the basis for words (which may also contain bound morphemes but must have a root as morphological head, see §4.6). Note that being *non-dependent* need not mean that they are *independent* as there are roots which do not occur without apparent derivational morphology—for example the root *do'do'* appears in the derived intransititive verb *a'do'do'* 'trudge' and the non-volitional verb *ta'do'do'* 'be exhausted', but does not appear in isolation. This leads to the practical if inelegant definition that a root is what is left when all identifiable affixes and clitics have been removed, and as such they are the forms which are listed in the dictionary (Cense & Abdoerrahim 1979).

Roots can generally be categorised into various open or closed word classes (see Chapter 5), though it is not always clear that a root belongs unambiguously to any particular word class. Similarly it is not always clear that any particular reading of a root is more 'basic' than another. Prosodically the vast majority of roots can be basically characterised as disyllabic trochee—including the large number of (surface) trisyllabic forms which have been subject to Echo–VC due to an illicit coda (§2.3.4).

© KONINKLIJKE BRILL NV, LEIDEN, 2020 | DOI:10.1163/9789004412668_005

120 CHAPTER 4

4.1.1 *Bases*

The term **base** is used to mean a unit to which affixes are added—in other words the basis of a morphological derivation. This may be a simple root, or it may be a form which is already derived, thus this stage is recursive. An example of recursive combining of derivational affixes can be seen in the word *napap-pikanreangi* in the following sentence:

(33) *napappikanreangi jukuka ri mionga*
    na= *pa–* *aC–* *pi–* *kanre* *–ang* *=i* *juku'* *≡a* *ri* *miong*
    3= CAUS– MV– EXP– eat   –BEN =3 fish ≡DEF PREP cat
    ≡a
    ≡DEF
    he let the fish be eaten by the cat (because of him the cat ate the fish)
    (C:291)

There are a number of possible orderings of the derivations, but it is probably as follows: the root *kanre* means 'food' or 'eat', the addition of *pi–* forms a special passive verbal base *pikanre* 'be eaten',[1] which with the addition of applicative *–ang* makes *pikanreang* 'let something be eaten'. Further derivation with the verb prefix *aC–* and then causative *pa–* forms *pappikanreang (ri)*, which means roughly 'cause/let be eaten (by)'. This last form is the **stem** to which clitic pronouns are added, giving it an argument structure by cross-referencing the core arguments 'he' and 'it' (the fish).

4.1.2 *Stems*

The label **stem** refers to a form to which inflectional morphology in the form of clitics or affixal clitics is added: this may be derived (as in *pappikanreang* in 33), or simple as in *lompo=i* 'he's big'. Given that most clitics are extrametrical, the stem could be characterised as the prosodic word (with the stem + clitics constituting the phonological word); however, the fact that affixal clitics are sometimes metrical confuses the situation somewhat.

4.2 Affixes

Affixes are units of derivational morphology—which is to say they affect the base to which they are attached in some way by changing its word class, semantics, or valence. Affixes have the following properties:

---

1 Regular passives are formed with *ni–*, *pi–* is used within causative derivations to derive a causative passive (see § 8.3.5).

MORPHOLOGICAL UNITS   121

- they attach only to roots or bases formed out of roots and other affixes, i.e. they cannot attach to a word which has already had clitics (§ 4.3) attached.
- they are counted as part of the prosodic word when stress is assigned (see § 3.2.3). (This can only be diagnostic for suffixes, not prefixes, because stress is assigned from the end of a word.)
- when suffixes (*–ang*, *–i*, and *–a*) attach to roots ending in *s*, *l* or *r* (normally subject to Echo–VC, see § 3.3.4) the echo syllable does not appear; in other words, affixes are attached before Echo–VC is applied.

There are **prefixes** and **suffixes**, the former being more numerous (the only true suffix forms are *–i*, *–ang*, and *–a*, but the first two are multifunctional). The most productive/commonly used affixes are the verb prefixes *aC–* and *aN(N)–*, and other affixes relating to voice and valence such as passive *ni–*, causative *pa–*, and the applicatives *–i* and *–ang*.

There are a number of polysyllabic affixes which interestingly appear superficially to be constructed out of monosyllabic affixes, but whose grammatical function cannot be considered to be the sum of the apparent parts. For example the prefix *maka–* (which attaches to numeral stems to denote ordinal numerals) cannot be analysed as consisting of the (unproductive) stative prefix *ma–* and the (rare) nominaliser *ka–*. The same could be said about the prefix *paka–* which forms causative adjectives.[2]

There are also **confixes**: combinations of prefix and suffix forms which occur together and have a function which again cannot be considered a sum of their parts. These could also be regarded as circumfixes, but I find the label confix more apt as it captures the fact that both the prefix and suffix forms also occur as independent affixes. In interlinear examples confixes are shown with angle brackets, thus *pa*⟩BASE⟨*ang*.

There is evidence of former **infixes**, notably ⟨*im*⟩ and ⟨*um*⟩ which are no longer productive but occur in a number of /s/-initial fossilised forms such as:

sorong	'sit' (dial.)	→ simorong	'be seated' (ceremonially)
sengka	'division'	→ sumengka	'be divided'
selang	'dive'	→ sumelang	'dive'
saya'	'hover'	→ sumaya'	'glide'
sombala'	'sail' (n)	→ simombala' / sumombala'	'sail' (vi)

---

2 Although there has been discussion about the likelihood of *paka–* descending from *pa-ka–* at an early stage of Austronesian (Blust 2003).

It is probable that ⟨*um*⟩ is also the ancestor of the variant verb prefix *amm–* (§ 7.1.4), which is seen on some vowel-initial roots such as *ana'* 'child' in *ammana'* 'have a child' (← †⟨*um*⟩*ana'*). Cense also argues that the root *empo* (→ *ammempo* 'sit') comes from an earlier form such as †*t*⟨*um*⟩*empo*, with subsequent loss of the initial syllable *tu* (1979:900).

The dictionary entries state that ⟨*im*⟩ and ⟨*um*⟩ are variants of the same form, or at least that they have the same meaning (Cense & Abdoerrahim 1979:250, 900), whereas Djirong Basang Daeng Ngewa claims that ⟨*im*⟩ forms verbs, while ⟨*um*⟩ makes the word more refined ('menyatakan lebih halus') (Djirong Basang Daeng Ngewa 1997:19). The reasoning for the latter claim is unclear, but I would surmise that it stems from the fact that some ⟨*um*⟩ forms such as *sumengka* and *sumelang* can be replaced by regular *aC–* derived forms *assengka, asselang*, with the older forms being more formal. It seems likely that both are reflexes of proto-Malayo-Polynesian *⟨*um*⟩ which marked agent voice or actor focus (Blust 2003).

Other postulated infix forms are more questionable. The forms ⟨*al*⟩ and ⟨*ar*⟩ are suggested by a small number of words such as *gala'ru'* 'stumble about' (cf. *ga'ru'–ga'ru'* 'move with difficulty'), and *karangkang* 'handful' (cf. *kangkang* 'id.'). Both infix forms are reconstructed as verb infixes for proto-Malayo-Polynesian, but no remnant of their function can be seen in Makasar. Djirong Basang Daeng Ngewa (1997:19) also lists the forms ⟨*in*⟩ and ⟨*an*⟩, but the examples given do not appear to correspond to any uninfixed forms and cannot be substantiated.

Table 17 is a list of the most productive or common affixes, with descriptive labels and abbreviations. Note however that the labels are in some cases only very rough indicators, as some of the affixes appear to have extraordinarily diverse functions—this applies especially to *pa–, –ang*, and *–i*.

4.3 Clitics

Makasar has a siseable inventory of **clitics** (denoted in examples by the use of the equals sign =), which are used pervasively for pronominal cross-referencing of arguments (they are in fact the main way of indicating grammatical relations), and also for coding a range of tense/aspect and modal meanings. In this section the set of clitic pronouns will be introduced, and the functions of the other clitics will be described in detail. Affixal clitics which combine qualities of both affixes and clitics are discussed in § 4.4.

MORPHOLOGICAL UNITS   123

TABLE 17   Affixes

aC–	mv	monovalent
aN(N)–	bv	bivalent
aN–	af	Actor focus
ma–	adj	adjective/stative (archaic)
ni–	pass	passive
pa–	caus	causative (verb base)
pi–	exp	experiencer oriented
paka–	caus.adj	causative (adj. base)
pa–	nr	nominaliser (agent or instrument)
paC⟩⟨ang	nr	nominaliser (someone prone to ADJ)
pa⟩⟨ang	nr	nominaliser (place or time of action)
ka⟩⟨ang	nr	adjective nominaliser
taC–	nvol	non-volitional
sa–	tot	totality, unity
si–	mut	mutual, reciprocal
siN–/saN–	eq.cmpr	equal comparative
piN–	mult	multiplier
maka–	ord	ordinal
–a	sbjv	subjunctive marker
–i	appl	locative applicative
–i	trs	transitiviser
–ang	ben	benefactive
–ang	nr	nominaliser

4.3.1 *Properties of Clitics*

The formal properties of clitics are:
- they attach further from the root than affixes
- they are not counted for stress (because they are not part of the prosodic word, § 3.2.3)
- they attach after Echo–VC (§ 3.3.4)
- they have a tendency to appear in 2nd position (abbreviated as 2P, also known as the Wackernagel position), as will be discussed in § 11.2
- they attach at phrase rather than word level. For example an adverb or other modifier such as an incorporated noun can come between a verb and the clitic pronoun, as in (34) and (35), or the negator may precede an entire PP (36).

124   CHAPTER 4

(34) *naung todonga'*
    naung   todong =a'
    descend also   =1
    I also climbed down

(35) *a'jappa bangkengi*
    aC– jappa bangkeng =i
    MV– walk foot   =3
    he's going on foot

(36) *laisi' ta–ri–nakkena*
    laisi'   ta=   ri   nakke ≡na
    slenderness NEG= PREP 1.sing ≡3.POSS
    her slenderness which is not for me

There are proclitics and enclitics: the proclitics are the pronominal set which canonically cross-reference the actor (the ERG 'ergative'[3] clitics), the future tense marker *la=* and the negator *ta=*. The enclitics include the pronominal set which canonically cross-reference the subject of an intransitive clause or the undergoer of a transitive clause (the ABS 'absolutive' clitics), the aspectual/ modal markers *=mo, =pa, =ja*, and the question marker *=ka*. The stable of clitics is given in Table 18 below.

4.3.1.1   Clitic Ordering

The clitics generally appear in a fixed order which can be exemplified briefly with the following:

(37) **lakuapamako**
    la=   ku= apa =ma =ko
    FUT= 1=   what =PFV =2f
    now what will I do with you?

(38) **takuassengapi**
    ta=   ku= asseng –a   =pa =i
    NEG= 1=   know   –SBJV =IPF =3
    I don't know it/him/her yet

---

3 The use of scare quotes around the terms 'ergative' and 'absolutive' is due to the fact that the clitics do not always conform to ergative-absolutive patterning—often a proclitic represents

MORPHOLOGICAL UNITS 125

TABLE 18   Clitics

Clitic pronouns			TAM clitics	
ku=	=a'	1	la=	fut
nu=	=ko	2f	ta=	neg
ki=	=ki'	2p/1pl.inc	=mo	pfv
	=kang	1pl.exc	=pa	ipf
na=	=i	3	=ja	lim
			=ka	or

These examples show that on both sides of the stem modal and aspectual clitics precede clitic pronouns, which can be illustrated as follows:

$$\left\{\begin{array}{c}\text{aspect/modal}\\\text{proclitic}\end{array}\right\}=\left\{\begin{array}{c}\text{'ERG'}\\\text{clitic pronoun}\end{array}\right\}=\text{STEM}=\left\{\begin{array}{c}\text{aspect/modal}\\\text{enclitic}\end{array}\right\}=\left\{\begin{array}{c}\text{'ABS'}\\\text{clitic pronoun}\end{array}\right\}$$

It appears that each slot may only contain one clitic—which is to say there are (for instance) no examples in which negator *ta=* and future *la=* appear together, or in which perfective *=mo* co-occurs with limitative *=ja*. The exception to this observation is that there may in some circumstances be two 'ERG' clitic pronouns—this and other exceptions to the canonical patterning are examined in detail in § 11.2.

4.3.2   *Clitic Pronouns*
Grammatical relations in Makasar are principally signified by clitic pronouns which are attached to the predicate. The paradigm of the clitic pronoun system, as well as the associated free pronouns and possessive suffixes, appears in Table 19. The 1st person plural exclusive row is missing a proclitic, the remaining forms are marked with † because they are archaic, found for example in the Gowa Chronicle but not in the modern language, with the unusual exception of the enclitic form *=kang*, which is however only found in combination with aspect/modal enclitics (§ 4.3.3).

The enclitics are generally used to cross-reference the subject of an intransitive clause (S) and the patient of a transitive clause (P), while the proclitics

---

S, and in some cases there are two proclitics representing P and A respectively. This is discussed in detail in § 11.2.

126 CHAPTER 4

TABLE 19 Paradigms of pronominal elements

	Pronoun	Proclitic (ERG)	Enclitic (ABS)	Possessive suffix (POSS)
1 sing	inakke	ku=	=a'	=ku
2 fam	ikau	nu=	=ko	=nu
2 pol/1pl inc.	ikatte	ki=	=ki'	=ta
1 pl exc.	†ikambe		†=kang	†=mang
3	ia	na=	=i	=na

are used to cross-reference the agent of a transitive clause (A). For this reason they are, with some caveats, given the labels absolutive and ergative respectively, and Makasar can be described at least superficially as a morphologically ergative language. However, there is a great deal of complexity and many exceptions to this generalisation—these issues are discussed in detail in Chapter 11, as is the question of whether these clitics are arguments in their own right, or agreement affixes (I prefer the former analysis).

4.3.3 *Aspectual/Modal Clitics*

This section deals with the clitics which are associated with tense, aspect, mood, modality and polarity (referred to for convenience as TAM). These consist of two proclitics: *ta=* (NEG negator) and *la=* (FUT future); and four enclitics: *=mo* (PFV perfective), *=pa* (IPF imperfective), *=ja* (LIM limitative), and *=ka* (OR 'or', and also question tag).

The TAM enclitics all behave similarly in that they encliticise onto predicates, following the applicatives *–i* and *–ang*, and preceding enclitic pronouns. The TAM enclitics will lose their final vowel if followed by *=a'* or *=i*.[4] The results of the combination of TAM and pronominal enclitics are shown in Table 20.

The clitic pronoun *=kang* for the first person plural exclusive occurs only in combination with the TAM enclitics and not in isolation. It should also be pointed out there are numerous lexical ways of denoting TAM related meanings— these are not examined here.

Out of the six clitics, *=mo* is by far the most commonly used. Using Shoebox to make a wordlist and concordance from a subset of my corpus (2948 clauses)

---

4 With the exception that *=ka=i* → *=kai*. Vowel-degemination still applies in the case of *=ka=a'* → *=ka'*.

MORPHOLOGICAL UNITS 127

TABLE 20   TAM and pronominal enclitics

		1	1pl.inc/2pol	1pl.exc	2fam	3
	+	=a'	=ki'	=kang	=ko	=i
=mo	→	=ma'	=maki'	=makang	=mako	=mi
=pa	→	=pa'	=paki'	=pakang	=pako	=pi
=ja	→	=ja'	=jaki'	=jakang	=jako	=ji
=ka	→	=ka'	=kaki'	=kakang	=kako	=kai

showed that *=mo* appeared 917 times, *=ja* 134 times, *ta=* 96 times, *=pa* 62 times, *la=* 39 times and *=ka* just 17 times.

4.3.3.1   Negative *ta=*

This proclitic is the most basic (i.e. monomorphemic) of the set of negators, which also includes *tea, teá, tena* and *taena*. The behaviour of this clitic is described in the discussion of negation (§ 12.3).

4.3.3.2   Future *la=*

This is typically attached to a verb stem before all other preposed elements, including the proclitic pronouns. In most cases *la=* is a marker of future tense, in which the time can be left open or specified, ranging from the imminent to the remote or potential.

(39) *la'lampa'*
     la=   lampa =a'
     FUT= go   =1
     I'll go, I'm going (time unspecified)

(40) *tanaasseng lanajappáia*
     ta=   na= asseng la=   na= jappa –i   ≡a
     NEG= 3=   know   FUT= 3=   walk –APPL ≡DEF
     he doesn't know where he's going (Or545.48)

(41) *lamangea' ri pasaraka ammuko*
     la=   mange =a' ri   pasar =a' ≡a   ammuko
     FUT= go   =1 PREP market =EC ≡DEF tomorrow
     I'll go to the market tomorrow

128   CHAPTER 4

The meaning of the above sentence can also be expressed with a verb derived from *pasar* 'market':

(42) *lappasaraka' ammuko*
    la=   *aC–* *pasar*   *=a'* *=a' ammuko*
    FUT= MV– market =EC =1 tomorrow

La= is also often found on wh-words such as *apa* 'what?' and *kere* 'where?' (§5.6.4). (43) is the most common greeting formula, although it is usually shortened to *lakeko mae*.

(43) *lakereko mae*
    la=   *kere*   *=ko mae*
    FUT= where =2f be
    where are you going? (lit. where will you be?)

(44) *lakuapako*
    la=   *ku=* *apa* *=ko*
    FUT= 1=   what =2f
    what will I do with you?

The combination of *la=* and the perfective enclitic *=mo* (see below) means that an action is imminent.

(45) *lakusaremako pa'arengang*
    la=   *ku= sare* *=mo* *=ko pa⟩ aC–* *areng ⟨ang*
    FUT= 1=   give =PFV =2f NR⟩ MV– name ⟨NR
    I will give you a naming (right now) (PT:033)

(46) *tena kuntama ri ballatta ri bangngia ka latinromaki' kucini'*
    tena ku= aN– tama ri   *balla' ≡ta*   *ri*   *bangngi ≡a*
    NEG 1= AF– enter PREP house ≡2p.POSS PREP night   ≡DEF
    ka   *la=*   *tinro =mo =ki' ku= cini'*
    BECAUSE FUT= sleep =PFV =2p 1=   see
    I didn't come in to your house yesterday evening, because I saw that you were about to go to sleep (C:257)

La= is not found in the mid-C18 manuscript KIT 668–216. Matthes noted it in his grammar (Matthes 1858:116)—his examples fit quite well with its current usage, but he associates it with the particle *ala*, which is a marker of deontic

MORPHOLOGICAL UNITS

modality and unlike *la=* requires the subjunctive suffix on the predicate (§10.3). It may be that there is a historical connection, but there is no deontic content to *la=* in the modern language.

4.3.3.3   Perfective *=mo*

This clitic (which is irregular in that its vowel is /o/ rather than /a/ when unaffected by a following enclitic pronoun) has a wide range of functions, the main one of which is to mark completion of an action or event, or attainment of a state. In this way it is the most frequent marker of past tense, but is also used for fine aspectual distinctions, as well as some more obviously discourse/mood related functions such as forming imperatives and expressing certainty. The following examples illustrate the core meaning of completion or attainment.

(47) *angnganrema'*
    aN(N)– kanre =mo =a'
    BV–   eat   =PFV =1
    I've already eaten

(48) *pirambulammi battanta? sibulamma' taccini' cera'*
    piraN–   bulang =mo =i battang ≡ta   si–   bulang =mo =a'
    how.many month =PFV =3 belly   ≡2p.POSS one– month =PFV =1
    ta=   aC– cini' cera'
    NEG= MV– see   blood
    How many months have you been pregnant? (lit: how many months your belly?) It's already a month since I saw any blood (C:840)

In addition, *=mo* is commonly used to form imperatives. This could be viewed as projecting the speaker's certainty that an action will be performed.

(49) *tunrummi*
    tunrung =mo =i
    hit   =PFV =3
    go and hit him (C:459)

(50) *ammempomaki'*
    amm– empo =mo =ki'
    MV–   sit   =PFV =2p
    please sit yourself down (C:459)

On questions, *=mo* is used when an explicit or certain answer is required. Compare the following:

(51) *kerei mae pammantangannu*
　　 kere　 =i　mae pa⟩　amm– antang ⟨ang ≡nu
　　 where =3　be　 NR⟩ MV–　live　　 ⟨NR　≡2F.POSS
　　 where is your home? (C:459)

(52) *keremi mae pammantangannu*
　　 kere　 =mo =i　mae pa⟩　amm– antang ⟨ang ≡nu
　　 where =PFV =3　be　 NR⟩ MV–　live　　 ⟨NR　≡2F.POSS
　　 where exactly is your home? (C:459)

The combination of *ta=* and *=mo* means 'already not ...', and requires the predicate to be marked with subjunctive *–a* (see §10.3).

(53) *takuassengami*
　　 ta=　 ku= asseng –a　　 =mo =i
　　 NEG= 1=　know　 –SBJV =PFV =3
　　 I don't know it anymore, I already forgot it

When *=mo* is attached to the negator *taena* or *tena* the result is a word meaning 'no more' which has scope over the following clause. The presence of *tenamo* in clause-initial position causes clitic fronting (§11.2.2).

(54) *tenamo nakkulle accini'*
　　 tena =mo　na= aC– kulle aC– cini'
　　 NEG =PFV 3=　 MV– can　 MV– see
　　 he can't see any more

If the clause contains no other elements capable of hosting a fronted clitic pronoun, *tenamo* may host an enclitic pronoun. In the following example the clause consists solely of a prepositional phrase which cannot host a proclitic.

(55) *taenami ri barugaya*
　　 taena =mo =i ri　　 baruga ≡a
　　 neg　 =PFV =3 PREP baruga ≡DEF
　　 he isn't in the baruga (hall) any more

MORPHOLOGICAL UNITS 131

The combination of *tinang* 'never' and *=mo* means 'never again'. (*Tinang* also requires subjunctive *–a*).

(56) *tinang niákkamo nasikatinrong karaeng–bainea*
    tinang nia' *–a* *=mo na= si–* *ka⟩ tinro ⟨ang karaeng baine*
    never EXIST –SBJV =PFV 3= one– NR⟩ sleep ⟨NR king   woman
    ≡*a*
    ≡DEF
    it never happened again that he slept with the queen (lit: there was never again him one-bedding the queen) (C:459)

4.3.3.4   Imperfective *=pa*

The converse of *=mo* is expressed by *=pa* which marks incompletion or remainder.

(57) *ingka se'repi kuboya*
    ingka se're =pa =i ku= boya
    but   one =IPF =3 1= search
    but there's still one thing I seek (SKT:0001:007)

(58) *mmantampi tallu*
    amm– antang =pa =i tallu
    MV–   stay   =IPF =3 three
    there's still three left

Note that remainder (with the emphasis on scarcity, 'only X left') may also be expressed with the adverbial particle *mamo* (§5.5.2).

The combination of *=pa* with a negator means 'not yet':

(59) *tenapa kutianang*
    tena =pa ku= tianang
    NEG =IPF 1=   pregnant
    I'm not yet pregnant (bembe009)

(60) *takuassengapi*
    ta= ku= asseng –a   =pa =i
    NEG= 1=   know –SBJV =IPF =3
    I don't know it yet (cf. (53))

132   CHAPTER 4

4.3.3.5   Limitative =ja

The enclitic =ja means 'only' in the sense 'nothing more than' or 'nothing other than'.

(61) *la'lampaja'*
     la=   aC–   lampa =ja   =a'
     FUT= MV– go   =LIM =1
     I'm just going to go

(62) *mannantu lompo, lompo bannanji*
     manna   antu lompo lompo bannang =ja   =i
     although MED big   big   thread   =LIM =3
     even if that's thick, it's only a thick thread (i.e. it may be big, but it's only big for a small thing)

(63) *manna le'leng ka i katte angkana buleng, bulenji*
     manna   le'leng ka   i   katte aN– kana buleng buleng =ja
     although black because PERS you AF– word white white =LIM
     =i
     =3
     although black, since you say 'white', it's nothing but white

4.3.3.6   'Either/Or' =ka

This clitic groups with the aspectual/modal enclitics largely because it fits into the same morphosyntactic slot (between the stem and the pronominal enclitic), and because it is neither counted for stress has a stress contour of its own (unlike the otherwise similar hortative particle *sá*, see § 5.5.2). However its function is somewhat removed from the other members of the group and it has a significant formal difference in that its vowel is not subject to replacement by a pronominal enclitic's vowel, thus =ka +=i → kai (*ki).

Cense describes it has having a 'questioning' (*vragende*) meaning, as did one of my informants who compared it to the Japanese question particle (which is also coincidentally *ka*).[5] However the fact that the vast majority of questions are not marked with =ka makes this explanation somewhat dubious. There seem to be two major functions: one is as a means of seeking confirmation or clarification similar to question tags in English:

---

5 Most Makasar people do not speak Japanese, however this person is a guide for Japanese tourists.

MORPHOLOGICAL UNITS   133

(64) *lanaungkako?*
     la=   naung   =ka =ko
     FUT= descend =or =2f
     will you really go down? (C:257)

The other major function of *=ka*, although less common in spoken Makasar
than the 'questioning' function, could perhaps be considered more primary. In
this, *=ka* marks options or possibilities in an either/or construction, with each
of the alternatives marked with *=ka*. Cense gives the partial example *tedongka
jarangka* ⟨buffalo=or horse=or⟩ 'either buffalo or horses' (C:257) but a larger
example comes from the preamble to the Gowa Chronicle (Wolhoff and Abdurrahim 1959:9):

(65) *Ka punna taniassenga ruai kodina kisa'ringkai kalenta karaeng–dudu na
     kanaka tau ipantaraka tau bawang– dudu.*
     ka   punna ta=   ni–   asseng ≡a   rua =i kodi ≡na   ki=
     BCS if   NEG= PASS– know ≡DEF two =3 bad ≡3.POSS 2p=
     sa'ring =ka =i kale ≡nta   karaeng dudu na   kana =ka tau
     feel   =or =3 self ≡2p.POSS king   very and word =or person
     i   pantara' ≡a   tau   bawang dudu
     PREP outside ≡DEF person ordinary very

Because if it is not known, there are two dangers: either we will feel ourselves
to be kings too, or outsiders will call us common people.

In view of the latter function, it is tempting to compare the use of *=ka* on a
single predicate to the use of leading *or* in English, as in *Do you want to come, or
...* Note though that 'or' in Makasar is in most cases the lexicalised construction
iareka ⟨ia are=ka | 3PRO perhaps=Q⟩.

4.4   Affixal Clitics

There is a small set of units whose behaviour is between that of affixes and
clitics. These units are called **affixal clitics**, after Hasan Basri et al.'s (1999)
account.[6] They are the class of determiners, consisting of the definite marker

---

6 An alternative (and perhaps more felicitous) label is **phrasal affix** (Kroeger 2005:322). I retain
   the label affixal clitic to make plain the debt to Basri et al.'s work. I use the symbol ≡ to differentiate them from affixes (–) and clitics (=).

134   CHAPTER 4

≡*a* and the possessive pronouns. They are marked with a triple-hyphen (≡) to distinguish them from affixes (–) and clitics (=).

They behave like affixes because:
– they are counted for stress (only after a vowel in the case of ≡*a*, see §2.3.6)
They behave like clitics because:
– they attach to phrases rather than words. For example in the phrase *balla' lompóa* 'the big house', the determiner attaches to the adjective *lompo* 'big' rather than the head of the NP *balla'* 'house'.
– they attach after echo–VC (§2.3.4), unlike the true suffixes *–ang* and *–i*. Thus *botolo'na* ⟨botol≡na | bottle 3.POSS⟩ 'his bottle' rather than **botolna*.

4.4.1   *The Definite Marker* ≡a

This affixal clitic marks definiteness, and is also used to mark relative clauses. Phonologically it behaves like an affix (i.e. it is counted for stress) following a vowel-final base, as in *batúa* 'the stone'; and like a clitic (not counted for stress) following a consonant-final base, as in *kóngkonga* 'the dog', *júkuka* 'the fish'. Another way in which it behaves like a clitic is that it attaches after Echo–VC (§2.3.4) on roots which are subject to that process, e.g. *pasaraka* ⟨pasar–EC≡a⟩ 'the market'. A geminate palatal glide *–yy–* is inserted when ≡*a* is suffixed to bases ending in *a*, as in *matáyya* 'the eye'. It seems likely that there is a historical connection between ≡*a* and the 3rd person pronoun *ia*, and the geminate *yy* is in fact a remnant of underlying *i*, i.e. *mataía*.

In its most basic use ≡*a* marks a noun as definite or specific, for example after being introduced by the existential verb *nia'*:

(66) *Nia' se're romang, anjo romanga tanikana–kanayai lompona siagáng luara'na ...*
      nia' se're romang anjo romang ≡a   ta= ni–   kana– kana
      exist one forest that forest ≡DEF NEG= PASS– RDP– word
      –a   =i lompo ≡na   siagáng luar =a' ≡na
      –SBJV =3 big   ≡3.POSS with   wide =EC 3.POSS
      There was a forest, that forest's size and width cannot be described ...
      (PT:002)

Once marked as definite, NPs participate in the agreement system, which is to say that they are cross-referenced with pronominal clitics, as shown by the difference between a sentence with P^INDEF and one with P:

MORPHOLOGICAL UNITS   135

(67) *Angnganrea' unti*
     aN(N)– kanre =a' unti
     BV–   eat   =1 banana
     I eat bananas

(68) *Kukanrei untia*
     ku= kanre =i unti   ≡a
     1=   eat   =3 banana ≡DEF
     I eat the bananas

The interaction between definiteness and cross-referencing is examined further in § 11.2.4.

4.4.1.1   Miscellaneous Uses of ≡a
There are some uses of ≡a which are not easily analysed as marking definiteness, though they are not unrelated.

Demonstratives may sometimes be marked with ≡a to add emphasis, e.g. *annea* 'this one':

(69) *Annea kusuro–alle na maraeng nualle*
     anne ≡a   ku= suro alle na   maraeng nu= alle
     this ≡DEF 1= order take and other   2f= take
     I told you to take this and you took another

There are also some rare examples in which pronouns host ≡a for strong emphasis:

(70) *IAli nakana kodi, iSattu nakana baji' na inakkea tena nakulle kupattantu
     baji'na kodina.*
     i–   Ali na= kana kodi i–   Sattu na= kana baji' na i–
     PERS– Ali 3=   word bad PERS– Sattu 3=   word good and PERS–
     nakke ≡a   tena na= kulle ku= pa–   aC– tantu   baji' ≡na
     1PRO ≡DEF NEG 3=   can 1=   CAUS– MV– certainty good ≡3.POSS
     kodi ≡na
     bad ≡3.POSS
     Ali says 'bad' and Sattu says 'good', I for myself can't be sure whether it's good or bad (Or.545.43:10).

(71) *Iaya kusuro na tau maraeng tosseng nasuro.*

ia	≡a	ku=	suro	na	tau	maraeng	tong	seng	na=	suro
3PRO	≡DEF	1=	order	and	person	other	also	again	3=	order

He was the one I ordered and he ordered someone else again (Or.545 .43:10).

There are also some examples in which ≡*a* is attached to nouns which already host possessive suffixes—usually in itself enough to mark a noun as definite:

(72) *Napatojengi tumalompoa antekamma ri kanantaya, karaeng*

na=	pa–	tojeng	=i	tu–	ma–	lompo	≡a	antekamma	ri
3=	CAUS–	true	=3	person–	STV–	big	≡DEF	how	PREP

kana	≡nta	≡a	karaeng
word	≡2p.POSS	≡DEF	king

The Governor believes it is according to your words, karaeng

≡*a* can be attached to *se're* 'one' when used as a specifier, with the meaning 'a certain X, a particular X':

(73) *Ri se'rea kampong ammantangi se'rea tu–kalabini.*

ri	se're	≡a	kampong	amm–	antang	=i	se're	≡a	tu
PREP	one	≡DEF	village	MV–	stay	=3	one	≡DEF	person

kalabini
couple

In a certain village lived a certain couple (Zainuddin Hakim 1991:126)

And finally, ≡*a* can be used to nominalise verbs, in statements such as the following:

(74) *Angnganrea bawi harangi*

aN(N)–	kanre	≡a	bawi	harang	=i
BV–	eat	≡DEF	pig	forbidden	=3

The eating of pork is forbidden

The definite marker ≡*a* can be distinguished from the homophonous subjunctive suffix –*a* (§10.3) because the latter is invariably counted for stress and attaches before Echo–VC is applied.

MORPHOLOGICAL UNITS 137

4.4.2 *Possessives*

The possessive affixal clitics ≡*ku* (1.POSS), ≡*ta* (1pl.incl.POSS), †≡*mang* (1pl.excl
.POSS, but archaic), ≡*nu* (2f.POSS), and ≡*na* (3.POSS), are suffixed to the possessed NP. The possessor NP, if present, always follows the possessed NP. Some
examples are *ballá'na* ⟨house≡3.POSS⟩ 'his/her/their house', *miong le'léngku*
⟨cat black≡1.POSS⟩ 'my black cat', *bonena gucia* ⟨contents≡3.POSS pot≡DEF⟩
'the pot's contents', *tedonna i Ali* ⟨buffalo≡3.POSS Ali⟩ 'Ali's buffalo'. They can
also be used directly on adjectives to show possessed attributes, as in *luara'na*
⟨wide≡3.POSS⟩ 'its width'. It is very common to have multiple possessive
markers within an NP, for example *tuka'na balla'na ana'na* ⟨ladder≡3.POSS
house≡3.POSS child≡3.POSS⟩ 'her children's house's stairs'.

Each of the possessives has a prenasalised allomorph which appears on
some vowel-final roots, for example *limangku* 'my hand' (**limaku*). There
are also some glottal-final roots which show these prenasalised forms instead
of the expected geminate stops, such as *kaka'* → *kakangku* 'my elder sibling'
(**kakakku*) or the archaic example from the Gowa Chronicle *balla'* → †*ballammang* 'our house'. No obvious pattern for this has been found/ (cf.
andi' → *andikku* 'my younger sibling' (**andingku*)). According to Cense (1979:xi)
in some cases both the regular and prenasalised forms can be used on the
same root with different semantics, and gives the example *bainengku*
⟨woman≡1.POSS⟩ 'my wife' as opposed to *baineku* 'my maid'. However, this pattern (and the use of *baineku*) was not confirmed by modern speakers and it
seems likely that the present usage is irregular and conventionalised.

Unlike the definite marker ≡*a*, possessives may be followed by aspectual/
modal and pronominal enclitics.

(75) *ri wattunnamo nai' ri biseanga Bruce tepokki anjo tuka'na biseanga*

ri	*wattu*	≡*nna*	=*mo*	*nai'*	*ri*	*biseang*	≡*a*	*Bruce tepo'*
PREP	time	≡3.POSS	=PFV	climb	PREP	boat	≡DEF	Bruce broken

–*i*	*anjo*	*tuka'*	≡*na*	*biseang*	≡*a*		
–TRS	that	ladder	≡3.POSS	boat	≡DEF		

When Bruce climbed back on the boat he broke the boat's ladder (lit. on
his climbing onto the boat time Bruce broke that ship's ladder)

(76) *ana'nai karaenga*

ana'	≡*na*	=*i*	*karaeng*	≡*a*
child	≡3.POSS	=3	karaeng	≡DEF

he is the karaeng's son

In some complex constructions more than one may be suffixed:

138   CHAPTER 4

(77) *pa'ja ta–ri–kalengkuna*
      [*pa'ja*   [*ta=   ri   kale ≡ngku*] ≡*na*]
      [good.complexion [NEG= PREP self 1POSS] 3.POSS]
      her beautiful complexion which is not for myself (Cgn:7)

The latter sentence also illustrates an interesting phenomenon: relative clause-
like possessive constructions. Unfortunately, I have only three examples of
these, all from Cense's grammar notes in the archives at KITLV in Leiden
(Cgn:7). The other two follow:

(78) *kalimbu'–ta–tassungkeku*
      kalimbu'   *ta=   taC–   sungke* ≡*ku*
      mosquito.net NEG= NVOL– open   ≡1.POSS
      my mosquito net which is unopened

(79) *laisi'–ta–ri–nakkena*
      laisi'   *ta=   ri   nakke* ≡*na*
      slenderness NEG= PREP 1PRO   ≡3.POSS
      her slenderness which is not for me

A possessive suffix can be placed on a predicate in place of an enclitic, in which
case it forms a subordinate temporal clause. Example (80) shows this on an
intransitive clause.

(80) *Antamaku ri balla'na aganna akkuta'nammi Anthony ri aganna angkana
      '...'*
      aN– tama ≡*ku*   *ri   balla'* ≡*na*   *agang* ≡*na*   *aC–*
      AF– enter ≡1.POSS PREP house ≡3.POSS friend ≡3.POSS MV–
      kuta'nang =*mo* =*i Antoni   ri   agang* ≡*na*   *aN– kana*
      question =PFV =3 Anthony PREP friend ≡3.POSS AF– word
      When we entered his friend's house Anthony asked his friend '...'

And (81) shows it on a transitive clause, in which ≡*na* is co-referent with the
goal Malino.

(81) *Kurapi'na Malino sengka angnganre ri warunga*
      ku= rapi' ≡*na*   *Malino sengka*   *aN(N)– kanre ri   warung*
      1=   reach ≡3.POSS Malino on.the.way BV–   eat   PREP stall

MORPHOLOGICAL UNITS 139

≡*a*
≡DEF
On reaching Malino we stopped to eat at the *warung*

If two consecutive clauses show verbs with possessive markers instead of enclitics there is a strong inference that the second clause is a result of the first, as seen in the following examples.

(82) *Kucini'na, a'lampana*
    ku= cini' ≡na   aC– lampa ≡na
    1=   see ≡3.POSS MV– go   ≡3.POSS
    When I looked at him, he left (he was afraid of me)

(83) *Kucini'na, a'lampaku*
    ku= cini' ≡na   aC– lampa ≡na
    1=   see ≡3.POSS MV– go   ≡3.POSS
    When I saw him, I left (I was afraid of him)

Compare a parallel example with enclitics, where there is a sequential reading but no inference of causation:

(84) *Kuciniki, a'lampai*
    ku= cini' =i aC– lampa =i
    1=   see =3 MV– go   =3
    I saw him, he left

4.5   Particles

The term **particle** is used here to describe units which are not quite clitics but not quite roots. Particles generally carry grammatical rather than lexical meaning but phonologically they do not attach *closely* to words—meaning that it is possible to pause at particle-word boundaries, but the particle is for some reason not generally agreed to be a word in its own right. This can be seen most clearly in the fact that there is no agreement in published sources about whether these elements should be represented orthographically as free or bound. For example, in the convention adopted by Cense (Cense & Abdoerrahim 1979) and the almost identical one recommended by Abdurrahim (KITLV Or.545.46), all the elements discussed in this section are represented as bound forms; whereas in the Indonesianised version more current today

140   CHAPTER 4

(§ 3.1.3.3) they are nearly always represented as free. In the unofficial standard (found in non-scholarly sources, § 3.1.3.4), whether any given particle is represented as free or bound varies on a case-by-case basis.

There are two quite distinct types: preposed particles which are generally conjunctions or prepositions, and postposed particles which are adverbial elements of varying nature, often reduced forms of adverbial roots.

4.5.1 *Preposed Particles*

The six most common preposed particles are the preposition *ri*, the restricted locative preposition *i*, the homophonous personal prefix *i*, the reduced form *tu* of the noun *tau* 'person', and the conjunctions *na* 'and', *de'* 'or', and *ka* 'because'. They all have a degree of phonological independence but are less than the minimal prosodic word and are never assigned stress. They do not form the basis for any derivations, though *ri* and *tu* may be included in lexicalised compounds which may then be derived, as in *turiolo* 'ancestor' → *patturioloang* 'chronicle'.

That they have some phonological independence (compared to clitics) can be illustrated by the fact that it is possible to pause after uttering them, that is to say the gap between a particle and the following word is a 'resting place' while the speaker recalls or formulates what is to follow. This is most often heard when speakers produce *ri* ... or *i* ... before having recalled the name of the place or person in question, often inserting the word *anu* 'whatsit' and starting again. For example, an extremely distracted speaker could produce something like this:

(85) *a'lampai i ... anu, i Ali ri ... Marusu', ka ... nia' aganna*
    aC- lampa =i i   anu   i   Ali ri   Marus ka   nia'
    MV- go   =3 PERS whatsit PERS Ali PREP Maros because EXIST
    agang ≡*na*
    friend ≡3.POSS
    he went, um, whatsisname, Ali, to ... Maros, because ... his friend was there

The boundary between clitics and their hosts is not subject to this phenomenon—for example in the following example only the junctions marked with # allow a pause:

(86) *ka# latinromaki'# kucini'*
    ka   la=   tinro =mo =ki' ku= cini'
    BECAUSE FUT= sleep =PFV =2p 1=   see
    because I saw that you were about to go to sleep (C:257)

MORPHOLOGICAL UNITS 141

If there is a pause between clitics and their host, or between clitics in a cluster, e.g. *la ... tinromaki or *latinroma ... ki, it sounds highly unnatural and disfluent.

4.5.2 Postposed Particles

There are several elements which superficially resemble the modal/aspectual enclitics in that they are closely attached phonologically to a phrasal constituent, usually appearing between the phrase and any enclitics. Examples include the intensifier *dudu*, emphatic imperfective *ija*, hortative *sá*, and a group of formally similar adverbial and epistemic modifiers such as *todong* 'also' and *sedeng* 'again' (which also have reduced forms *tong* and *seng* as seen in (91)).

(87) *lómpo–dúdui tena nakkulle antama ri pattia*
lompo dudu =i tena na= aC– kulle aN– tama ri patti ≡a
big very =3 NEG 3= MV– can AF– enter PREP coffin ≡DEF
he was very big (and) he couldn't fit in the coffin (C:198)

(88) *tállasa'–íjapi anrong–manggeku*
tallas =a' ija =pa =i anrong mangge ≡ku
alive =EC still =IPF =3 mother father ≡1.POSS
my parents are still alive

(89) *ballían–sá' sapatu*
balli –ang sá =a' sapatu
buy –BEN HORT =1 shoe
buy me shoes!

(90) *tena nalompo, tena todong naca'di*
tena na= lompo tena todong na= ca'di
NEG 3= big NEG also 3= small
it wasn't big, neither was it small

(91) *antekámma–tóssengi i Udin?*
antekamma tong seng =i i Udin
how also again =3 PERS Udin
how also was Udin going? (i.e., returning to Udin, how was he going?)

However, these elements differ from the set of clitics in the following ways:
– although like clitics they do not affect stress on the 'host', unlike clitics they

142   CHAPTER 4

have their own stress contour, even if they are monosyllabic such as *sá* or *tóng*.

– unlike the case with enclitics, postposed *ija* on glottal-final roots does not cause glottal strengthening (/ʔ/ → /k/, see §2.3.3), e.g. (88) *tallasa'–ijapi* (**tallasak–ijapi*, cf. *tallasak=i* 'he's alive') (this is only applicable to *ija* because it is the only vowel-initial postposed particle)

It is apparent that these elements are separate prosodic words which are within the phrase as delimited by the enclitics, following and modifying phrasal heads in the same way that, for example, adjectives follow and modify nominal heads. The difference is that these adverbial particles are not lexical roots in their own right—they cannot act as head for any word or phrase, nor do they form the basis for derivations. They are examined in more detail in §5.5.

Another group of postposed particles are the discourse particles *to'* 'don't you think?', *de* 'bah!', and *di* 'isn't it?'. They differ from the adverbial particles because they are utterance final and do not host clitics. These are discussed in §5.12.

4.6   Words

Word is canonically taken to mean a single root, possibly reduplicated, which includes any attached affixes, and/or clitics, and/or affixal clitics. Thus the minimal word consists of a root alone (for example *gassing* 'strong'), while the maximal word would be a reduplicated form with both affixes and clitics, such as the following:

(92) *kagassing–gassingannami*
       ka⟩ RDP– gassing ⟨ang ≡na   =mo =i
       NR⟩ RDP– strong   ⟨NR ≡3.POSS =PFV =3
       he's already at his strongest (C:228)

In my opinion there is no morphosyntactic evidence for word-level compounds, i.e. words which include more than one lexical root—although there are numerous collocations which are often assumed to be compounds, such as *mata allo* 'eye day' = 'sun', *je'ne' inung* 'water + drink' = 'drinking water'; *balla' garring* 'house + sick' = 'hospital'. My reasons for rejecting compounds were presented in §2.3.8.

CHAPTER 5

Word Classes

Words in Makasar can broadly be divided into a number of classes, of which the open ones are nouns, verbs, and adjectives. Nouns and verbs can be subdivided into a number of subclasses for a variety of distributional and structural reasons, while the class of adjectives is more homogeneous in nature. The minor word classes are pronouns (of various types such as personal pronouns, demonstratives and interrogatives), adverbs, locatives, numerals, classifiers, prepositions, conjunctions, discourse particles, and interjections. Two of the minor classes, interrogatives and locatives, are functionally defined classes which transect categories defined on strictly morphological and syntactic grounds, but their members have obvious commonalities justifying their being grouped together in this fashion (Evans 2000). This chapter introduces the major classes and discusses their properties with some representative examples while pointing to chapters where they are discussed in more detail, while the minor classes are detailed more exhaustively.

5.1 Root Class and Word Class

Some roots can be unambiguously assigned a default word class. For example, the root *tedong* 'buffalo' has the potential to head an NP, can function as an argument in a clause, and denotes an entity. It may be called a noun root, and a verb derived from it, *attedong* 'have a buffalo', is clearly secondary to the nominal meaning. Similarly, the root *cini'* 'see' is most likely to occur as a predicate, and takes the morphology associated with intransitive or transitive verbs depending on context—it may be called a verb root, and a nominal derivation such as *pacini'* 'seer' is again clearly secondary to the verbal meaning. And the root *lompo* 'big' can function as an attribute or predicate and denotes a quality—it may be called an adjective root.

Many roots, however, are not so easily analysed. Some have no obvious default interpretation without derivational morphology, others show heterosemy between (usually) nominal or verbal realisations, while still others have an underived meaning which is not primary. The root *jappa*, for example, has an underived nominal interpretation 'foot(length)', but if one asks a speaker what the 'basic' meaning of *jappa* is, they will reply 'walk' (BI *berjalan*); yet for this interpretation it needs to be formally derived with the verb prefix *aC–* →

© KONINKLIJKE BRILL NV, LEIDEN, 2020 | DOI:10.1163/9789004412668_006

144   CHAPTER 5

TABLE 21   Properties of major word classes

Nouns	main function: heads of argument NPs
	can be specified by determiners and/or demonstratives
	may also be predicates
	tend to denote entities
Verbs	main function: head of predicate
	host verb prefixes and/or clitic pronouns
	tend to denote actions or states
Adjectives	function equally as predicates or attributes
	tend to denote qualities

a'jappa 'to walk'. So in cases like these we can see that a default interpretation of a root can in fact refer to the function of a derived form. In any event, ultimately it is a word's function in a clause which is diagnostic for determining word class.

The major distinguishing properties of each word class will be detailed in the relevant sections, but can be summarised as in Table 21.

On a general level there are several similarities and overlaps between the major classes. Nouns, verbs, and adjectives can all function predicatively, though the latter two are more obviously associated with this role. Adjectives and nouns may function attributively to modify nouns; verbs may also function in this way, but usually as relative clauses—direct attributional modification occurs but is not common. Nouns and adjectives can modify verbs adverbially. Adjectives may be modified by nouns or adjectives. Some examples of the possibilities are shown in Table 22.

In addition to the multifunctional nature of the major word classes, there is productive derivation. Most nominal roots with the addition of the verb prefix *aC–* can derive verbs which mean one of 'become-have-use-make NOUN'— this is in addition to the possibility of simply functioning as a nominal predicate without the prefix. To illustrate, the noun root *karaeng* 'king' can act as a nominal predicate in *karaeng=a'* ⟨king=1⟩ 'I am king' or derive a verbal predicate in *ak–karaeng=a'* ⟨MV–king=1⟩ 'I became king'. Conversely, verb roots such as *lampa* 'go', normally appearing with verb morphology as in *a'–lampa=i* ⟨MV–go=3⟩ 'he left' can also host possessive morphology prototypically associated with nouns and thus derive a nominal interpretation, as in *lampa≡na* ⟨go≡3.POSS⟩ 'his departure'. The same observation is true of adjectival roots, e.g. *lompo≡na* ⟨big≡3.POSS⟩ 'its size'. And beyond that there is more overt morphological derivation of causatives, mutuals, instrument nominalisations

WORD CLASSES   145

TABLE 22   Heads and modifiers

Head	Modifier	Phrase	Morphemes	Gloss
Noun	nominal	tanru' tedong≡a	⟨horn buffalo≡DEF⟩	the buffalo horn
	verbal	tedong attanru≡a	⟨buffalo MV–horn≡DEF⟩	the horned buffalo
	adjectival	tedong lompo≡a	⟨buffalo big≡DEF⟩	the big buffalo
Verb	nominal	a'jappa tedong=ko	⟨MV–walk buffalo=2f⟩	you walk like a buffalo
	adjectival	a'jappa kodi=ko	⟨MV–walk bad=2f⟩	you walk badly
Adjective	nominal	baji' pa'maik=i	⟨good character=3⟩	he has good character
	adjectival	baji' tojeng=i	⟨good true=3⟩	he is truly good

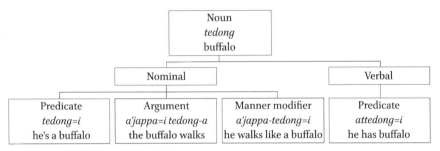

FIGURE 19   Derivation path for nouns

and so forth, which are detailed in chapters specific to nominal and verbal morphology.

Figures 19, 20, 21 show only the main and most regular derivational possibilities for the open word classes.

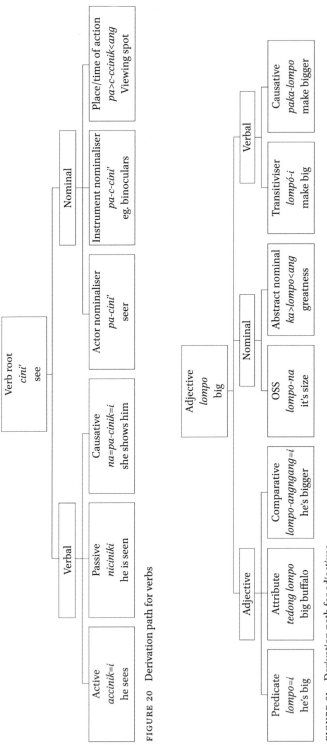

FIGURE 20 Derivation path for verbs

FIGURE 21 Derivation path for adjectives

WORD CLASSES   147

5.2 Nouns

Nouns can be defined syntactically as words with the potential to form or head
noun phrases (including relative clauses), and act as arguments in a predicate
and thus be cross-referenced with clitic pronouns. They have the potential to be
both possessor or possessed (head and modifier) in possessive constructions,
with this relationship being marked morphologically with affixal enclitics on
the possessed NP. They may also be marked for definiteness with the affixal
enclitic ≡a.[1] Like the other major classes they may also function as predicates.
Ex. (93) below illustrates all of these major points:

(93) *ana'nai karaenga*
      ana' ≡na   =i *karaeng* ≡a
      child ≡3.POSS =3 king   ≡DEF
      he is the son of the king

Other typical nominal properties are:
– they can be specified by demonstratives (§ 5.6.3)
– they can be modified by adjectives (§ 5.4)
– they can be quantified with numerals (§ 5.8) or other quantifiers, this process usually also involving a classifier (§ 5.9)
– they can be complements of PPs marked with the preposition *ri* (§ 5.10)
– when prefixed with *aC–*, they will typically derive a verb meaning 'have/use
  NOUN' (§ 5.3.1.1)
Note that the above features are generally true of common nouns, but are not
shared by all subclasses of noun. Nouns can be subdivided a number of ways:
morphologically, combinatorically, and semantically.

  Morphologically the main division is between simple and derived nouns,
with simple nouns tending to refer to entities; such as *tau* 'person', *juku'* 'fish',
tamparang 'ocean', *berang* 'cleaver'; and derived nouns tending to be more
abstract, such as *kakalumanynyangang* 'wealth' (a *ka*⟨*ang* nominalisation of
the adjective *kalumanynyang* 'rich').

---

1   Note though that it cannot be assumed that a word hosting a possessive or definite marker
    is a noun; firstly because these attach at phrase level so may be directly attached to a
    modifying element within the NP rather than the head noun itself (§ 6.3); and secondly
    because the definite marker also marks relative clauses, in which case it may appear on
    the RC-internal verb (§ 6.3.3), while the possessive markers may themselves nominalise
    adjectives (§ 5.4.1.1) and are also seen on verbal predicates in a temporal/causal construction
    (§ 4.4.2).

148   CHAPTER 5

The most obvious division which can be drawn on the grounds of combinatorics is between the majority of common nouns which can take the definite marker ≡a, and names and titles (excluding kin terms) which are unlikely to host ≡a but group together with the class of pronouns in taking the personal prefix *i–*.

Semantically of course nouns may be divided into any number of classes—animals, body parts, artefacts, and so forth. In general these types of division do not appear to be reflected structurally in the language, with the exception that the system of numeral classifiers divides common nouns by shape and/or type (see § 5.6.2). Another possible exception is that the alternation of plain and pre-nasalised possessive markers (≡*ku*/≡*ngku* and so forth) *may* reflect an archaic alienable-inalienable distinction (§ 4.4.2).

More detail on types of nouns and the structure of the noun phrase is given in Chapter 6.

5.3   Verbs

The large open class of verbs expresses actions, processes, achievements, and to a certain extent states, though the latter may also be expressed by adjectives (see § 5.4). Verbs typically function as the heads of verb phrases. They may occur as attributes of nouns (§ 6.3.2.3), but this is relatively rare except within relative clauses (§ 6.3.3). Verbs are distinguished morphologically from other word classes largely by the presence of distinctively verbal affixes encoding voice and valence (§ 7). Furthermore, although other predicates may host clitic pronouns indexing S, only (transitive) verbs may host clitic pronouns indexing both A and P, which is to say that only (a subset of) verbs may take more than one argument.

Some other morphosyntactic features of verbs are:
– licensing of a beneficiary by the applicative *–ang* (§ 9.2)
– licensing of a local by the applicative *–i* (§ 9.1)
– derivation of a passive with *ni–* (§ 7.3)
– derivation of a causative verb by *pa–* (§ 8.1)
– derivation of a mutual/reciprocal verb by *si–* (§ 10.1)
– derivation of occupation/habitual nouns by *pa–* (§ 6.2.2.2)
– derivation of place/time nouns by *pa⟩⟨ang* (§ 6.2.2.5)

5.3.1   *Subcategories of Verbs*
The class of verbs can be subdivided using two main methods. One is syntactic and depends on valence, basically dividing verbs into intransitive and

WORD CLASSES

149

TABLE 23   Differences between verb prefixes

(a)	aC–	*jarang*	'horse'	→	a'jarang	'have/ride a horse'
(b)	amm–	*ana'*	'child'	→	ammana'	'have a child'
(c)	aN(N)–	*tunrung*	'hit'	→	annunrung	'hit'
(d)	aC–	*cokko*	'secret'	→	accokko	'be hidden'
	aN(N)–			→	anynyokko	'hide something'
(e)	aC–	*kanre*	'food'	→	akkanre	'burn, be consumed'
	aN(N)–			→	angnganre	'eat'

transitive classes. The other is morphological and depends on which (if any) verb prefix appears on infinitive forms.[2] Although there are many exceptions, the two methods coincide often enough that it can be generally said that the choice of prefix is related to the inherent valence of the verb. These topics will be examined in detail in § 7.1.1, but the basic facts are summarised below.

5.3.1.1   Regular (Prefixed) Verbs

All verbs (with the exception of the small group of basic verbs) can be said to have an infinitive or citation form consisting of the verb base (simple or derived) plus a verb prefix.[3] These forms, with the addition of enclitic pronouns indexing S, are also found in intransitive or semi-transitive clauses (semantically transitive clauses with indefinite P). Verbs in fully transitive clauses do not have verb prefixes, but rather the base directly hosts a proclitic pronoun indexing A, as well as the enclitic indexing P.

The two most common verb prefixes are *aC–* and *aN(N)–* (for detail on the phonological behaviour see § 2.3.2). A less common prefix found only on some vowel-initial roots is *amm–* (§ 7.1.1.4).[4] As illustrated in Table 23 and put very roughly, *aC–* and *amm–* mark intransitive verbs, often derived from noun roots, (a, b); and *aN(N)–* marks transitive verbs whose roots are often inherently verbal (c). Some roots can be seen with both *aC–* and *aN(N)–*, usually with a difference in transitivity (d) or a broader change in meaning (e).

---

2 There is also the logical possibility of subdividing verbs by their cooccurrence with applicative suffixes (Chapter 9), however there are no obvious paradigms formed in this way.

3 The label **infinitive** is not ideal but tries to capture the fact that once a verb prefix has been attached the word is unambiguously a verb, but has no information about grammatical functions or aspect, these coming from clitics. In an earlier work (Jukes 2005) I used the label **citation form** for the same thing.

4 A further prefix *aN–* (without nasal substitution, § 7.2) is found only in clauses where A is an NP in the pre-predicate Focus position (§ 11.9), and there is a definite P.

As has been stated, there are several exceptions to the above generalisations, which are discussed in § 7.1.1. It should also be noted that verbs derived using the causative or mutual/reciprocal prefixes (*pa–* or *paka–*, and *si–*) always have infinitives with *aC–* even though they may be transitive.

5.3.1.2 Basic Verbs

There is a small group of common intransitive verbs which do not take verb prefixes (though they are all subject to other kinds of derivational morphology). These are labelled basic verbs and are listed in Table 24.

They are not an especially homogeneous group.[5] As can be seen, they can roughly be divided into a group denoting movement or location and another group with more stative meanings, but each has some idiosyncracies, with the exception of the antonym pair *naung* and *nai'* which appear to be identical to each other in distribution and behaviour, Generally speaking though basic verbs have some similarities to the class of adjectives (§ 5.4), notably:

Some of them can take the comparative *–angngang* or *–ang* (§ 5.4.1.3.2; e.g. *naungang(ngang)* 'lower down', *naikang(ngang)* 'higher up', *mangeangngang* 'be more/stronger than ...', *niakkangngang* 'to have more', *erokangngang* 'prefer').

Some can be used attributively quite naturally without needing to be in a relative clause, e.g. *tau mate* 'dead person', *bembe battu* 'a goat (that) came' (i.e. wandered in by itself).

They are often nominalised by the distinctive adjectival nominalising circumfix *ka⟩⟨ang* (§ 6.2.3).

However, their distributional and derivational possibilities are somewhat different from the class of adjectives in the following ways:

They all take the verbal causative prefix *pa–* (§ 8.1) rather than the adjectival causative *paka–* (§ 8.2; e.g. *palari* 'make run', *pakamma* 'make so', *patinro* 'make sleep', *patu'guru'* 'make fall').

The *ka⟩⟨ang* nominalisations are quite different from those derived from adjectives proper. While *ka)*ADJ*⟨ang* derives an abstract noun denoting a quality (e.g. *kagassingang* 'strength'), equivalent derivations of basic verbs either denote an event nominal (*kamateang* 'time of death', *kabattuang* 'arrival') or

---

5 Neighbouring languages have a similar class of basic verbs, but the members are somewhat different. For example Selayarese (Ceria 1993; Hasan Basri 1999) has 8 basic verbs, four of which correspond to basic verbs in Makasar (*mate* 'die', *uru'* 'fall', *tinro* 'sleep', *nae'* 'go up'), and four of which do not (*gege* 'laugh', *sa'ra'* 'set (sun)', *simbara* 'stop (rain)', *kua* 'say'). Bugis (Hanson 2003) has a larger set, many of which have equivalent regular verbs in Makasar (e.g. 'vomit', 'stand', 'cry'). Indonesian (Sneddon 1996) has a much larger set.

WORD CLASSES   151

TABLE 24   Basic verbs

naung	go down	tinro[a]	sleep
nai'	go up	mate	die
battu	come	nia'	exist
mange	go	kamma[b]	be like, be so
mae	be in a place	ero'	want
lari	run	tu'guru'[c]	be fallen
anrai'	go east	bangka	be breached
kalau'	go west[d]	tuli	continue
antama	enter[e]	tulusu'	be straight/upright
		lalo	pass
		le'ba'	be ready, finished

a Although *tinro* always appears without a prefix in manuscripts and published sources, in my field recordings and notes there are some examples of *tinro* with the prefix *aC*– (→ *attinro*). This may indicate that it is becoming a regular (i.e. prefixed) intransitive verb.

b In older texts the form *kontu* is found with the same meaning.

c As with *tinro*, some younger speakers attach *aC*– (→ *attu'guru'*).

d *Kalau'* and *anrai'* are obviously connected with the locatives *lau'* and *raya* (§5.7.2), but are not derived by any regular method and are best treated as basic verbs. Interestingly, *timboro'* 'south' and *wara'* 'north' do not have corresponding verb forms.

e Historically this was probably ⟨aN-tama | AF-tama⟩, however the combination is now lexicalised as can be shown by the fact the the 'prefix' remains when negated (e.g. *tena ku=ntama* ⟨NEG 1=enter⟩ 'I didn't enter'), which is unusual. Its antonym *assulu'* can still be considered *aN-sulu'*.

have irregular meanings (*katinroang* 'bed', *kamangeang* 'miscarriage'). See §6.2.3 for more detail on these forms.

Some of the basic verbs (*tuli, lalo, ero'* and *mange*), are often involved in serial constructions (such as *ero' a'lampa* 'will go' and *mange assikola* lit. 'go schooling') and could perhaps be considered auxiliaries.

5.4   Adjectives

Unlike in many other Austronesian languages (see e.g. Bowden, 2001; Durie, 1985; Klamer, 1998) in Makasar there are clear distributional differences between a class of words which generally denote attributes and qualities, and the other major word classes. Here I shall follow local instincts and label this class **adjectives**, although they could arguably be termed 'stative verbs'.[6] I have avoided labelling them as verbs largely because this class of words does not enter into many of the types of morphosyntactic behaviour which can be characterised as 'verbal', such as the *ni–* passive or *pa–* causative; instead having its own unique behaviour such as the *–i* transitive (§ 9.1.1) and *paka–* causative (§ 5.4.1.2), and *ka*⟨*ang* nominalisation (§ 5.4.1.1). Also unlike verbs, adjectives may be nominalised simply using the possessive markers.[7] However, the main feature that sets this class apart from verbs is that these roots can function predicatively without any verb prefix—a quality they share with nouns and the small group of basic verbs (§ 5.3.1.2).

Historically this word class was marked in both predicative and attributive functions by the prefix *ma–* as part of the paradigm of verb prefixes (§ 5.3.1.1).[8] This is now only found in older texts or in conventionalized forms such as *tu malompo* ⟨person ST–big⟩ 'governor' and in Makasar descriptive names (*pa'daengang*, e.g. Daeng Mabaji' 'Ms Good', for which see § 6.1.2.2). The prefix *ma–* was also used to derive a particular type of attributive nominal predicate, e.g. *tena ku=ma–kopi* ⟨NEG 1=ST–coffee⟩ 'I'm not a coffee-drinker' (C:429), but this use is at best dubious today (see § 7.1.5).

The group of adjectives covers a variety of meanings: colour terms, evaluations, physical characteristics, and the like. A selection is given in Table 25.

As mentioned above, adjectives function predicatively without any derivation other than the attachment of clitic pronouns, e.g.: *garringi taua* ⟨sick=3 person≡DEF⟩ 'the person is sick'. For more detail see § 11.5.2.

In attributive function the adjective is placed after the head of the phrase, which is typically a noun, e.g. *tau garring* ⟨person sick⟩ 'sick person'. Enclitics or affixal enclitics which apply to the phrase are then attached, e.g. *tau garringa* ⟨person sick≡DEF⟩ 'the sick person'. (For more detail on noun phrase structure see § 6.3). Adjectives may also modify verbs, e.g. *a'jappa kodi* ⟨MV–walk bad⟩ 'walk the wrong way', though this is less common.

Adjective phrases may also contain a variety of basic or derived adverbs, most obviously degree modifiers such as those presented below. Most of them precede the adjective; a selection of adjective forms is provided at Table 25.

---

6 Hyslop (2004:264) describes a similar dilemma when she refers to 'stative-inchoative verbs ... (which) could equally well be called adjectival verbs, verb-like adjectives, or simply adjectives'.

7 Possessive markers on verbs do not nominalise the verbs, but instead result in a temporal/ causal construction (§ 4.4.2).

8 A reflex of pMP *ma- 'stative verb prefix (realis)' (Blust 2003:37).

WORD CLASSES

153

TABLE 25   Adjectives

baji'	good	cara'de'	clever
kodi	bad	dangngala'	stupid
le'leng	black	tojeng	true
kebo'	white/silver	sala	false
eja	red	larro	angry
lolo	young	rannu	happy
toa	old	lambusu'	straight
battala'	heavy	jeko	crooked
nipisi'	light	tu'guru'	fallen
gassing	strong/healthy	reppe'	broken
garring	sick	kalumanynyang	rich
pongoro'	mad	kasiasi	poor

TABLE 26   Modifiers of degree

Preposed modifiers

kurang	less
lebe	more (Indonesian or Bugis influence, usually –*angngang*, see § 5.4.1.3.2)
kaminang	the most
sanga'	very
ta'lalo	exceedingly, too
ta'liwa'	surpassingly, too

Postposed modifiers

sikali	a bit
tojeng	truly
dudu	very

5.4.1   *Adjective Morphology*

There are a number of morphological derivational processes which may act upon adjectives. The processes which affect valence or result in a different word class are dealt with in other chapters and will be discussed only briefly here, but processes that modify the semantics of adjectival roots while still resulting in adjectives are dealt with in detail in this section. There do not seem to be any

154 CHAPTER 5

derivational processes which derive adjectives as such from other word classes, given that other word classes can function attributively without modification.

5.4.1.1 Derivation of Nouns

There are four distinct ways of deriving nominals from adjectives. Three use dedicated nominalising morphology, the other simply attaches possessive affixal clitics.

– ka⟩ADJ⟨ang

Adjectives can be nominalised with the confix *ka*⟩⟨*ang*, resulting in abstract nouns meaning 'ADJ-ness' e.g. *kagassingang* 'strength' (← *gassing* 'strong') This is discussed in §6.2.3.1.

– paC⟩ADJ⟨ang

This confix derives a noun meaning 'someone who is easily ADJ', e.g. *pa'mallakang* 'scaredy-cat' (← *malla'* 'afraid'). It is discussed in §6.2.2.6.

– *ka*⟩RDP–ADJ⟨*ang*

The confix *ka*⟩⟨*ang* when attached to a reduplicated adjectival base results in a nominal with the meaning 'peak of ADJ-ness', e.g. *kagassing–gassingang* 'peak of strength', see §6.2.3.2.

– ADJ≡poss

It is also possible to nominalise adjectives simply by adding possessive markers:

(94) *bajiki lompona*
    baji' =i *lompo* ≡*na*
    good =3 big   ≡3.POSS
    it's a good size

(95) *anjo romanga tanikana–kanayai lompona siagáng luara'na*
    anjo romang ≡*a* *ta=* *ni–* *kana– kana –a* =*i lompo*
    that forest ≡DEF NEG= PASS– RDP– word –SBJV =3 big
    ≡*na*   *siagáng luar* =*a'* ≡*na*
    ≡3.POSS with   wide =EC ≡3.POSS
    that forest's size and depth can't be described (PT:002)

We can see that the adjectives have been nominalised because they are arguments and thus are cross-referenced with clitic pronouns, and furthermore in (95) they are conjoined with the nominal conjunction *siagáng* (§5.10.1). Possessed adjectives are functionally equivalent to *ka*⟩⟨*ang* nominalisations but are less formal and also less abstract. In some cases they must be used because the equivalent *ka*⟩⟨*ang* form has a specialised meaning (i.e. *kalompoang* 'regalia').

WORD CLASSES

5.4.1.2 Derivation of Verbs

There are two main ways of deriving verbs from adjectives, both involving valence increasing morphology, and both resulting in verbal bases which are then subject to verb prefixation and other morphosyntactic processes characteristic of verbs.

– Causative *paka*–

The prefix *paka*– is unique to the class of adjectives (the main causative prefix being *pa*–, see § 8.1). It derives causative verb bases which mean 'to make more ADJ, to ADJ-en'. By nature these are transitive, though like *pa*– derived verbs the infinitive forms of these verbs are formed with the (normally) intransitive verb prefix *aC*–, e.g. *appakalompo* ⟨aC–paka–lompo⟩ 'to enlarge' (← *lompo* 'big'). This prefix is discussed in detail in § 8.2.

– Applicative/transitiviser –*i*

Among the many uses of the suffix –*i* is the derivation of transitive verb bases from adjectival roots—the resulting base may then take the transitive verb prefix *aN(N)*– and/or clitic pronouns, e.g. *ammajíki* ⟨aN(N)–baji'–i⟩ 'to improve, to fix' (← *baji'* 'good'). For detailed discussion see § 9.1.1.

Derivations with –*i* differ from those with *paka*– because with the latter it can be assumed that the undergoer already has the quality to some degree, e.g. *kupakabambangi je'neka* ⟨ku=paka–bambang=i je'ne'≡a | 1=CAUS.ADJ–hot=3 water≡DEF⟩ 'I heat the water' implies that the water is already warm (but not hot enough), whereas *kubambángi je'neka* ⟨ku=bambang–i=i je'ne'≡a | 1=hot–TRS=3 water≡DEF⟩ does not have this implication.

5.4.1.3 Derivation of Adjectives

5.4.1.3.1 *Reduplication*

Reduplication of adjectives weakens or moderates the meaning in a similar way to English '-ish', without changing the word class or distributional possibilities, e.g. *lompo–lompo* 'large-ish', *baji'–baji'* 'pretty good, OK', *kebo'–kebo'* 'white-ish'.

5.4.1.3.2 *Comparative* –angngang

A feature that adjectives share with locatives (§ 5.7) is that they can be modified by the comparative suffix –*angngang*, which has the somewhat archaic variant –*ang*. It appears that –*angngang* is a fairly recent development from –*ang*, as only –*ang* is described by Matthes (1858:43), and to my knowledge there are no examples of –*angngang* in old manuscripts. Cense, who collected most of his data in the 1930s, merely states that –*ang* is sometimes found alongside the more usual –*angngang*, especially in dialect and poetry (Cense & Abdoerrahim, 1979:24, 27). As for the reason why such a development

156   CHAPTER 5

would have taken place, it could possibly be because simple *–ang* was felt to have too many functions.

In comparative constructions, the comparative element (the thing being compared) is the S argument and is cross-referenced with an enclitic pronoun, while the standard of comparison is in a conjoined NP marked with the conjunction *na*:

(96) *lompoangngangi balla'nu na ballakku*
     lompo –angngang =i balla' ≡nu   na balla' ≡ku
     big   –COMPR   =3 PERS ≡2f.POSS and PERS ≡1.POSS
     your house is bigger than mine

(97) *cara'dekangngangko na inakke*
     cara'de' –angngang =ko na i   nakke
     clever   –COMPR   =2f and PERS 1PRO
     you are smarter than me

(98) *gassingangngangi angnganre na inakke*
     gassing –angngang =i aN(N)– kanre na i   nakke
     strong –COMPR   =3 BV–   food and PERS 1PRO
     his appetite is bigger than mine (lit. he's stronger eating than me)

Superlatives are expressed with the preposed adverb *kaminang* 'most', e.g. *tedong kaminang lompoa* ⟨buffalo most big≡DEF⟩ 'the biggest buffalo'.

5.4.1.3.3   *Equal-Comparative* siN–/saN–

Unlike verbs and the majority of nouns, adjectives can host the equal-comparative prefix *siN–/saN–*; the two forms seem to be interchangeable according to any source which mentions them (Abdul Azis Syarif et al., 1979; Abdul Kadir Manyambeang et al., 1996; Cense & Abdoerrahim, 1979).

Equal comparative constructions are similar to the comparatives described above, with two minor differences. The first is that the use of *na* 'and' to conjoin the standard of comparison NP is optional rather than obligatory if the comparative element is only denoted by a clitic pronoun:

(99) *sintinggia' (na) bainennu*
     siN–   tinggi =a' (na) baine   ≡nnu
     EQ.COMPR– high   =1 (and) woman ≡2f.POSS
     I'm the same height as your wife

WORD CLASSES 157

The second is that if both the comparative element and the standard of comparison are full NPs, they may be conjoined with *siagáng* 'with' instead of *na*:

(100) *sallompoi ballakku na/siagáng balla'na*

saN–		*lompo*	*=i*	*balla'*	*≡ku*	*na*	/	*siagáng*	*balla'*
EQ.COMPR–	big		=3	house	≡1.POSS	and	/	with	house

≡na
≡3.POSS
my house is as big as his

The comparative element may also appear clause-initially. The following example from the Gowa chronicle describes the feet of the misshapen Karaeng Tumassalangga Barayang (§1.1.4.3):

(101) *pala' bangkenna salla'bui katulu'na mange ri olo*

pala'	*bangkeng*	*≡na*	*saN–*		*la'bu*	*=i*	*katulu'*	*≡na*
span	foot	≡3.POSS	EQ.COMPR–	long	=3	heel		≡3.POSS

mange	*ri*	*olo*
go	PREP	front

the span of his foot was the same length as from its heel forwards (Wolhoff and Abdurrahim, 1959:10)

The other roots which may be modified by *siN/saN–* are nouns denoting type or value, such as *rupa* 'type' (→ *sanrupa* 'the same type'), and the adverb *kamma* (and its archaic variant *kontu*) 'so, thus'. These latter forms (*singkamma/sangkamma* 'the same') may themselves be used for equal comparative constructions:

(102) *singkammai lompona ballakku na balla'na*

siN–		*kamma*	*=i*	*lompo*	*≡na*	*balla'*	*≡ku*	*na*	*balla'*
EQ.COMPR–	thus		=3	big	≡3.POSS	house	≡1.POSS	and	house

≡na
≡3.POSS
my house is as big as his (the size of my house is the same as his)

5.4.1.3.4 si/sa– + RDP-ADJ ≡POSS 'Always ADJ'

There is a construction in which *si–* or *sa–* (in free variation) are prefixed to possessed reduplicated bases to derive the meaning 'always doing X'. It is most common on verb bases, but is also possible with adjectival bases:

158   CHAPTER 5

(103)   *sagarring–garrinna*
        sa–   garring– garring ≡na
        TOT–   RDP–   sick   ≡3.POSS
        he's always sick

Note that these forms can be identical to those derived via the process
described below.

5.4.1.3.5   si/sa– + *RDP– ADJ* ≡*POSS 'as ADJ as Possible'*
This construction has the dictionary definition 'in the highest degree',[9] though
it seems to be closer in meaning to the Indonesian construction seen in forms
such as *sebaik–baiknya* 'as well as possible':

(104)   *sibella–bellana; sisallo–sallona*
        si–   bella– bella ≡na   si–   sallo– sallo ≡na
        TOT–   RDP–   far   ≡3.POSS TOT– RDP–   long   ≡3.POSS
        as far as possible; as long as possible (C:692)

The example in (105) seems to show this construction without possessive ≡*na*,
however the string *sajarre'–jarre' tena sangkamma* may be considered a phrasal
constituent, with the allomorph ≡*nna* attached:

(105)   *"Jarre'mi sajarre'–jarre' tena sangkammanna."*
        jarre' =mo =i sa–   jarre'– jarre' tena saN–   kamma
        strong =PFV =3 TOT– RDP– strong NEG EQ.CMPR– thus
        ≡*nna*
        ≡3.POSS
        'It's strong, strong as strong can be with no equal.' (SKT 129)

5.5   **Adverbs**

There is a heterogeneous class of predicate and clause modifiers which can
be labelled adverbs. Their main common feature is that they cannot function as heads of arguments or as predicates in their own right. In general they

---

9   *in de hoogste mate* (Cense & Abdoerrahim 1979:692). Cense only discusses this construction
    with the prefix form *si–*, but I observed that actually it is also possible with *sa–*, confirmed in
    a locally published description (Abdul Kadir Manyambeang et al. 1996:180,188).

WORD CLASSES 159

TABLE 27 Preposed adverbs

maka	surely, be expected to
poro	may well (negative sense)
barang	maybe
ti'ring	by chance
pila'	the more (correlative)
kaminang	the most (superlative)

have restricted derivational possibilities, and many of them are particles (§ 4.5) rather than full words. They can be divided formally into preposed or postposed elements—in general the preposed adverbs modify clauses while postposed elements modify just the immediately preceding constituent. The postposed adverbs can be further subcategorised into those which are internal to the phrase as delimited by enclitics, and those which are external to it. There are also temporal adverbs whose distribution is less constrained.

Many words with adverbial types of meaning and/or function belong formally to other word classes. For example, the set of basic verbs (§ 5.3.1.2) includes words such as *tuli* 'continually', *le'ba* 'already', and *kamma* 'be like so, thus', which modify verbal or clausal constituents. Nouns and adjectives can modify verbs for manner, and the majority of temporal expressions are nouns (§ 6.1.3).

5.5.1 Preposed Adverbs
This type of adverb precedes the modified constituent (generally a clause, except in the case of the superlative marker *kaminang*). They do not host clitics nor cause clitic-fronting (§ 11.2), and are not subject to any derivational processes.

(106) *maka mateki' punna nia'lukinne pakua*
    maka   mate   =ki'   punna   ni–   a'lu'   =i   (a)nne   paku   ≡a
    should   death   =2p   if   PASS–   swallow   =3   this   nail   ≡DEF
    you'll surely die if you swallow this nail (C:432)

(107) *poro angngarru'nu*
    poro   aN(N)–   karru'   ≡nu
    may.well   BV–   cry   ≡2f.POSS
    may well you cry (but it won't help) (C:561)[10]

---

10   Predicates preceded by *poro* usually take possessive markers rather than clitic pronouns.

160   CHAPTER 5

(108) *barang iUdin angngassengi, kuta'nangi*
       barang i   Udin aN(N)– asseng =i kuta'nang =i
       maybe PERS Udin BV–   know =3 ask   =3
       maybe Udin knows, ask him

Pila' 'the more' introduces correlative clauses:

(109) *pila' lompoi pila' ja'dalaki*
       pila'   lompo =i **pila'**   ja'dal   =a' =i
       the.more big   =3 the.more naughty =EC =3
       the bigger he is the naughtier he gets

The superlative adverb *kaminang* (also sometimes *minang*) modifies adjectives
and absolute locatives (§ 5.7.2):

(110) *Nakanamo ana'na kaminang toaya 'Inai paleng kiarenganga' amma'?'*
       na= kana =mo ana' ≡na   **kaminang** *toa ≡a   i–   nai*
       3= word =PFV child ≡3.POSS the.most   old ≡DEF PERS– who
       paleng   *ki= areng –ang =a' amma'*
       in.that.case 2p= name –BEN =1 mother
       Her oldest child said 'What, then, will you call me, mother?' (PT:034)

5.5.2 *Postposed Adverbial Particles*
The postposed adverbial particles (see also § 4.5.2) vary somewhat in function
and distribution. Some modify nominals as well as other categories, but they
share enough features that they should be grouped together.

The last eight postposed adverbs in Table 28 share a phonological peculiar-
ity: the consonant in the middle (/d/ or /l/) is often deleted, and if the vowels
are identical vowel degemination (§ 2.3.1) will take place and delete one syllable, the result being that these words all have reduced allomorphs. The choice
between the full and reduced forms seems to be largely stylistic.

I have represented the postposed adverbs orthographically as being attached
to the preceding word by an en-dash (–) if they are the kind that are usually
phrase-internal and host enclitics (i.e. they intervene between the phrase-head
and enclitics), and as separate words if they are external. This is a compromise
between the approach taken by Cense (1979), who always joined them to the
preceding word, and the ad hoc nature of later publications (e.g. Abdul Kadir
Manyambeang et al., 1996; Aburaerah Arief & Zainuddin Hakim, 1993; Djirong
Basang Daeng Ngewa & Aburaerah Arief, 1981; Parewansa et al., 1992) in which
they are sometimes attached and sometimes separate.

WORD CLASSES   161

TABLE 28   Postposed adverbs

Adverb	Meaning	Modifies	Phrase-internal
sá	HORTative	V	yes
mamo	only	N, V	yes
i(n)ja	still	Adj, V	yes
dudu	very	Adj, †N	yes
are	perhaps	wh-, N, V	yes
memang	immediately	V, N	yes
pole	even	N	no
todong	also	V, N, Adj, wh-	yes
sedeng	again	V, N, Adj, wh-	yes
bedeng	hearsay	S	no
kodong	what a pity	N	no
rolong	first	V	no
paleng	in that case	X	no
poleng	do again	Pred	yes
kutadeng	perhaps	wh-, S	no

TABLE 29   to(do)ng postposed
           adverbs

Full form	Reduced form
todong	*tong*
sedeng	*seng*
bedeng	*beng*
kodong	*kong*
rolong	*rong*
paleng	*paeng*
poleng	*poeng*
kutadeng	*kutaeng*

Only the most common of the postposed adverbs will be discussed in detail
here.

162   CHAPTER 5

5.5.2.1   *sa, mamo, ija*

The first three items in Table 28 show some similarities to the set of aspectual/
modal enclitics =*mo* etc., (§ 4.3.3) and are in fact analysed as enclitics by Cense
(1979). *Sá* resembles the TAM enclitics in form because it is monosyllabic, but
differs from them because its vowel is not subject to elision by the vowel of the
3rd person enclitic =*i*; thus ⟨sá=i⟩ → *sái* (*si, compare ⟨=pa=i⟩ → *pi*). The final
vowels of *mamo* and *ija will* elide if followed by =*a'* or =*i*, e.g. *mami, iji*. However,
unlike TAM enclitics *sá, mamo* and *ija* have their own stress contour, showing
that they are prosodic words in their own right.

(111)   *mánge–sáko*
         mange sá   =ko
         go   HORT =2S
         go, get a move on (C:626)

(112)   *Bembea–mami naboli' kale–kalenna najoli pakke'bu'.*
         bembe ≡a   mamo =i na= boli'   kale– kale ≡nna   na= joli
         goat   ≡DEF only   =3 3= hidden RDP– self ≡3.POSS 3=   bolt
         pakke'bu'
         door
         Only the goat was still there, she hid herself, locked the door. (bembe:
         030)

(113)   *battu–mami bosi lompoa*
         battu mamo =i bosi lompo ≡a
         come only =3 rain big   ≡DEF
         there's nothing but heavy showers coming

The adverb *inja* 'still' modifies adjectives and verbs—it has a variant *ija* in
which form it can be found in the dictionary (1979:248):

(114)   *ca'di–inji ana'na*
         ca'di inja =i ana' ≡na
         small still =3 child ≡3.POSS
         his child is still small

(115)   *Nakanamo manggena: "Angngapa nummantang–inja na bangngimo".*
         na= kana =mo mangge ≡na   angngapa nu= amm– antang
         3= word =PFV father ≡3.POSS why   2f= MV– stay

WORD CLASSES   163

> *inja* na   *bangngi* =mo
> still CMP night   =PFV
> His father said: 'Why are you still here and it's already night?' (bembe: 086)

In many examples where *inja* somewhat redundantly co-occurs with =*pi* (the combination of the imperfective clitic =*pa* and the 3rd person enclitic =*i*), the form *i(n)ji* appears instead of *i(n)ja*. This could be a result of vowel harmony, but it seems more likely that the combination ⟨ija=i⟩ → *iji* has become lexicalised, resulting in what appears to be two 3rd person clitic pronouns:

(116)   *jai–ijipi*
      jai   *ija*   =i   =pa   =i
      many   still   =3   =IPF   =3
      there are still many (C:248)

5.5.2.2   *dudu*
dudu is an intensifier which in the modern language modifies adjectives and the basic verb *ero'* 'want':

(117)   *ero'–dudui angnginung.*
      ero'   **dudu**   =i   aN(N)–   *inung*
      want   very   =3   BV–   drink
      they really wanted to drink (PT:224)

(118)   *Bella–dudu–ijipi na nacini'mo balla'na andi'na*
      bella **dudu** *iji*   =pa   =i   na   na= *cini'* =mo *balla'* ≡na
      far   very   still   =IPF   =3   and   3=   see   =PFV house ≡3.POSS
      andi'   ≡na
      ↓sibling ≡3.POSS
      They were still very far away and they saw their sister's house (PT:217)

In the Gowa chronicle there is one example of *dudu* following a noun, *karaeng* 'king':

(119)   *kisa'ringkai kalenta karaeng–dudu, nakanaka tau i pantaraka tau bawang–dudu.*
      ki=   *sa'ring* =ka   =i *kale* ≡nta   *karaeng* **dudu** na= *kana* =ka
      2p= feel   =or   =3 self ≡2p.POSS karaeng very   3=   word =or

> tau   i   pantara' ≡a   tau   bawang **dudu**
> person PREP outside ≡DEF person ordinary very
> either we feel ourselves to be too much like kings, or outsiders will say
> we are very common people (Matthes, 1883:146).

5.5.2.3   *are*

The particle *are* 'perhaps' is typically used on interrogatives in rhetorical questions:

(120)   *Siapa–arei sallona attayang anne ana' karaeng tallua*
  siapa ***are*** =*i* *sallo* ≡*na* *aC–* *tayang anne ana'*
  how.many **perhaps** =3 long ≡3.POSS MV– wait this child
  karaeng tallu ≡*a*
  king three ≡DEF
  how long was it that the three princes waited? (PT:097)

It is also used on nouns where it expresses uncertainty, similar to questions with 'surely':

(121)   *Juku'–are nuballi*
  juku' ***are*** *nu=* *balli*
  fish **perhaps** 2f= buy
  Surely you bought fish?

Are can also be placed on both parts of correlative structures with the meaning 'whether ... or ...':

(122)   *Taenapa kuasseng akkulle–are taena–are*
  taena =*pa* *ku=* *asseng aC–* *kulle* ***are*** *taena* ***are***
  NEG =IPF 1= know MV– can **perhaps** NEG **perhaps**
  I don't know yet whether it's possible or not (C:31)

5.5.2.4   *to(do)ng*

To(do)ng means 'also'. It is usually placed between the head of the predicate and the enclitic pronoun, if present:

(123)   *Nia'– tommonjo joa' sitau ampangngapási*
  nia' tong =*mo anjo joa'* *si–* *tau* *aN– pa–* *aN(N)–*
  be   also =PFV that followers one– person AF– CAUS– BV–

WORD CLASSES   165

> apas   –i
> take.care.of –TRS
> There was also one servant who took care of it (bembe:19)

(124) *Ero'–tongi ammekang–mekang*
       ero' tong =i aN(N)– pekang– pekang
       want also =3 BV–   RDP–   hook
       They also wanted to go fishing

To(do)ng often appears in presentative clauses (see §12.5) in discourses where
numerous entities or events are being introduced using these constructions.

(125) *ia–tommi anne. uru angngallei. pa'rasangang. Bontomanai'.*
       ia   tong =mo =i anne uru   aN(N)– alle =i
       3PRO also =PFV =3 this beginning BV–   take =3
       pa'rasangang Bontomanai'
       land   Bontomanai'
       He was also the first to take the land of Bontomanai'

       ia–tonji nikana. Gallarang Loaya.
       ia   tong =ja =i ni–   kana gallarang loa   ≡a
       3PRO also =LIM =3 PASS– word chief   ill-favoured ≡DEF
       He was also just called Gallarang Loaya (KIT:1.04)

In environments where there is clitic fronting (§11.2.2), *to(do)ng* will move with
the clitic:

(126) *Taena nalompo, taena todong naca'di'*
       tena na= lompo tena todong na= ca'di
       NEG 3= big   NEG also   3= small
       It wasn't big, it also wasn't small (cf. *ca'di'–todong=i* 'it was also small')

Unlike most of the other adverbial particles, *to(do)ng* can be the base for a
verbal derivation, *atto(do)ng* 'to say "me too"'.

5.5.2.5   *se(de)ng*
Se(de)ng means 'again'. In contrast to *to(do)ng* it does not usually intervene
between the predicate head and enclitics.

166   CHAPTER 5

(127) *Ma'gilingi seng Karaeng Tunisombaya*
       maC– giling   =i seng karaeng tu–   ni–   somba ≡a
       MV–   other.side =3 again karaeng person– PASS– homage ≡DEF
       Karaeng Tunisombaya turned around again (SKT:095)

(128) *Le'baki anjo mangei sedeng ri romanga angngalle rea naparekangi*
       sedeng pattongko' balla'na ana'na.
       le'ba'   =i anjo mange =i sedeng ri   romang ≡a   aN(N)–
       finished =3 that go   =3 again PREP forest ≡DEF BV–
       alle rea na= pare' –ang =i sedeng pa–   aC– tongko' balla'
       take reed 3= make –NR =3 again CAUS– MV– cover   house
       ≡na   ana' ≡na
       ≡3.POSS child ≡3.POSS
       After that she went again to the forest to get thatch to make a roof for
       her children's house (PT:049)

Seng often appears in combination with *tong* (see above), in which case they
form a portmanteau *tosseng*. In this combination they may in fact appear
before the enclitic:

(129) *Antekamma–tossengi i Udin?*
       antekamma tong seng =i i   Udin
       how   also again =3 PERS Udin
       How also was Udin going? (i.e., returning to Udin, how was he going?)

5.5.2.6   *ko(do)ng*
Ko(do)ng is an attitudinal modifier, showing that the speaker feels bad about
the events reported, or sorry for the person involved:

(130) *Gassingka nia'– inja nucokko–cokko?*
       gassing =ka nia' inja nu= cokko– cokko
       sure   =or be still 2f= RDP– hide
       Maybe there's still (some) you've hidden away?

       Tenamo kodong. Ia–maminne sibatua.
       tena =mo kodong ia   mamo =i =nne si–   batu   ≡a
       NEG =PFV pity   3PRO only =3 =this one– CLF.misc ≡DEF
       No more, unfortunately. There's only this one.

WORD CLASSES 167

(131) *O amma' nabuntulu'– tonga' kodong ammakku*
    o   amma' na= buntul =u' tong =a' kodong amma' ≡ku
    oh mother 3= find   =EC also =1 pity   mother ≡1.POSS
    Oh mother, you finally found me, my poor mother (PT:203)

5.5.2.7   *ro(lo)ng*

This means 'first', in the sense 'do (something) first (before doing something else)', similar to Indonesian *dulu*.

(132) *Angnganre rong*
    aN(N)– kanre rong
    BV–   eat   first
    Eat first (then we'll talk)

This is most likely a lexicalisation of *ri olo–ang* ⟨PREP before–COMPR⟩ 'further forward than ...'

5.5.2.8   *be(de)ng*

Be(de)ng is a epistemic marker showing that the information is second-hand or based on hearsay, or alternatively is an indirect quotation:

(133) *nikanaja bedeng assari'battangi Lakipadada*
    ni–   kana =ja   bedeng aC– sari'battang =i Lakipadada
    PASS– word =LIM QUOT MV– sibling   =3 Lakipadada
    it is only said that he (Karaeng Bayo) was brother to Lakipadada (from the preamble to the Gowa Chronicle (Wolhoff and Abdurrahim 1959))

(134) *Kupauangko tena tau ri balla'na bedeng*
    ku= pau –ang =ko tena tau   ri   balla' ≡na   bedeng
    1= story –BEN =2f NEG person PREP house ≡3.POSS QUOT
    I tell you there was no-one at home (someone told me, e.g. a neighbour)

Be(de)ng can also be used as an intensifier similar to 'I say' in English:

(135) *Mange–sáko beng!*
    mange sa   =ko beng
    go   HORT =2f QUOT
    I say, get a move on!

168 CHAPTER 5

TABLE 30   Temporal adverbs

ammempo	tomorrow	sumpa(d/l)eng	earlier
ammembara	day after tomorrow	nampa	just then
subangngi	yesterday	sinampe	soon
subangngiangngang	day before yesterday	sallang	later
subangngiangangngang	three days ago		

In an old manuscript found in Cense's archives at KITLV in Leiden,[11] *bedeng* is used frequently as a textual device to mark the story as a myth or legend:

(136)   *le'baki bedeng, makkana karaeng i La Padara "kusomba–guruki'"*
         le'ba'   =i bedeng maC– kana karaeng i   La   Padara ku=
         already =3 QUOT MV– word king   PERS HON Padara 1=
         somba   guru   =ki'
         homage teacher =2p
         then, so it's said, Karaeng I La Padara said 'I pay you homage'

5.5.3   *Temporal Adverbs*

This class consists of words used to situate a clause in time which do not have nominal characteristics, which is to say they do not require prepositions or allow determiners unlike temporal nominals such as *allo* 'day', *wattu* 'time' (§ 6.1.3). A list of temporal adverbs is given in Table 30.

Subangngiangangngang 'three days ago' is unique in apparently being a doubly comparativised form ⟨subangngi–ang–angngang | yesterday–COMPR–COMPR⟩ 'more than more than yesterday'. Note that its root, *bangngi* 'night' is a temporal noun. 'Earlier' appears in the forms *sumpadeng, sumpaleng*, and *sumpaeng* in seemingly free variation, similar to the phenomenon seen with the *to(do)ng* adverbs discussed in § 5.5.2.

Other ways of referring to tense and aspect are the aspectual clitics (§ 4.3.3), and temporal uses of the locatives (§ 5.7.1).

---

11   KITLV HISDOC Or.545.232. Oud-Makass. HS (fragment).

WORD CLASSES   169

5.6   Pronouns

This section discusses the small but important classes which have pronominal characteristics: personal pronouns, the reflexive pronoun, demonstratives, and interrogatives.

5.6.1 *Personal Pronouns*

There are four types of personal pronominal element: (1) free pronouns, (2) enclitic pronouns marking S and P ('absolutive' or =ABS), (3) proclitic pronouns marking A ('ergative' or ERG=), and (4) possessive affixal clitics. This section discusses the free pronouns, as the clitic pronouns were introduced in § 4.3.2 and cross-referencing will be discussed in § 11.2.

The 1st person inclusive is also used for the 2nd person plural, and is in addition the polite form for 2nd person singular. In the modern spoken language the 1st person plural exclusive is expressed by the 1st person '*ku=*' set—the pronoun *kambe* and the possessive ≡*mang* are archaic, while the enclitic =*kang* is only found in combinations with modal enclitics (e.g. =*pakang* ⟨=pa=kang | =IPF=1pl.excl⟩) and there is no proclitic counterpart. The *i* in front of the free pronouns is a personal prefix which also appears before proper names and can be omitted (with the exception of *ia*).

Free pronouns and enclitics can be quantified by the particle *ngaseng* 'all', which appears after free pronouns (*ia–ngaseng* 'they all'), but before enclitics (*ngaseng=i* 'they all'). *Ngaseng* is not found attached to proclitics or indeed any other part of speech.

Clitic pronouns do most of the work of identifying and tracking referents in discourse as shall be discussed in § 11.2. The free pronouns are used relatively rarely, usually in the following circumstances:

– presentatives (§ 12.5)
– for **emphasis**, including where the pronoun is in Topic or Focus position (11.9)
– in **PP** arguments and adjuncts
– when the pronoun itself is the **predicate.**

In **presentative** clauses the 3rd person pronoun *ia* often appears in combination with demonstratives and a modal/aspectual clitic; as in *iaminne* ⟨ia=mo=i (a)nne | 3PRO=PFV=3 this⟩ 'this is …', *iapinne* ⟨ia=pa=i (a)njo | 3PRO=IPF=3 that⟩ 'that's still …' and so forth.

(137)   *iaminjo allo makaruaya*
          ia   *=mo* *=i* (a)njo allo maka– rua ≡a
          3PRO =PFV =3 that   day ORD– two ≡DEF
          that was the second day

170   CHAPTER 5

TABLE 31   Pronominal elements

	Free pronoun (PRO)	Proclitic (ERG)	Enclitic (ABS)	Possessive (POSS)
1	(i)nakke	ku=	=a'	≡ku
1pl.incl/2pol	(i)katte	ki=	=ki'	≡ta
1pl.excl	†(i)kambe	*	*=kang	†≡mang
2fam	(i)kau	nu=	=ko	≡nu
3	ia	na=	=i	≡na

These constructions are discussed in detail in § 12.5.

Sentences (138) and (139) show **emphatic** use, in topic and focus position respectively (§ 11.9):

(138)   *... lompo–lompoi ana'na, na inakke, tenapa kutianang.*
       lompo– lompo =i ana' ≡na   na i–   nakke tena =pa ku=
       RDP– big   =3 child ≡3.POSS and PERS– 1PRO NEG =IPF 1=
       tianang
       pregnant
       ... his child is growing, and me, I'm not yet pregnant (bembe:009)

(139)   *ikambe sipammanakang*
       i–   kambe si– pa⟩ amm– ana' ⟨ang
       PERS– 1pl.excl one NR⟩ MV– child ⟨NR
       we are one family

Sentences (140) and (141) show **personal pronouns in PPs**:

(140)   *amminawanga' ri katte*
       aN(N)– pinawang =a' ri   katte
       BV–   follow   =1 PREP 2fPRO
       I'm following you

(141)   *mallaki ri nakke*
       malla' =i ri   nakke
       afraid =3 prep 1PRO
       he's afraid of me

WORD CLASSES 171

Finally, sentence (142) gives an example of a **pronoun as a predicate**, with clitics attached to it:

(142) *inakkeji*
　　　i–　　nakke =ja　=i
　　　PERS– 1PRO　=LIM　=3
　　　it's only me[12]

5.6.2　*Reflexive Constructions*

Reflexives are formed by combining the noun *kale* 'body, self' with a possessive affixal clitic (always from the prenasalised set, § 4.4.2). Its most common use is as a nominal modifier in terms such as *areng kalenna* ⟨name self≡POSS⟩ 'personal name', but it is also used as an argument in sentences such as (143), where it is cross-referenced with the enclitic =*i*:

(143) *naciniki kalenna lalang ri televisia*
　　　na= cini' =i kale　≡nna　　lalang ri　　televisi　≡a
　　　3=　see　=3　REFL　≡3.POSS　inside PREP television ≡DEF
　　　she saw herself on the television

Sometimes *kale* can be ambiguous between its reflexive meaning and its 'personal' interpretation:

(144) *nitunrungi ri kalenna*
　　　ni–　tunrung =i ri　　kale　≡nna
　　　pass– hit　　=3 PREP REFL　≡3.POSS
　　　he was hit by himself / he was hit in his self (he was deeply affected)

The reduplicated form *kale–kale≡POSS* has an adverbial meaning 'alone, by oneself'.

(145) *'Inai kiagáng battu anrinni?' 'Kale–kalengku'*
　　　i　　nai ki= agáng　battu anrinni kale– kale ≡ngku
　　　PERS who 2p= do.with　come　here　　RDP– self ≡1.POSS
　　　'Who did you come here with?' 'I'm alone'

12　The 3rd person enclitic pronoun shows that such examples in Makasar have similar agreement patterns to English and French (*c'est moi*), rather than Dutch *ik ben het*, for example.

172   CHAPTER 5

There is no reciprocal pronoun, but rather a mutual/reciprocal marker *si*–
(§10.1).

5.6.3   *Demonstratives*

The set of demonstratives and the corresponding deictic adverbial set (see §5.7.3) show a three-way deictic contrast: 'this' (near speaker), 'that' (near hearer), and 'that' (far from both, not present): they are *anne, antu,* and *anjo* respectively.

The primary function of demonstratives is to modify (specify) the head of an NP; they generally precede the nouns which they specify, as in *anjo tedong≡a* ⟨that buffalo≡DEF⟩ 'that buffalo'; the reverse order, *tedonga (a)njo*, is also found but is much less common and is associated with western dialects and Selayarese.[13] Demonstratives can co-occur with the definite marker ≡a, and in most cases do. They may also be used as emphatic pronouns, e.g.: *garringa'anne* ⟨garring=a' anne | sick=1 here⟩ 'me here, I'm sick'.

The initial /a/ of the demonstratives is subject to aphesis (§2.3.5) if there is a preceding vowel-final word, and as a result the demonstratives are often phonologically attached to words which are structurally external to the NP, as in the following example:

(146)   *lanuapai[**ntu** taipayya]?*
     la=   *nu=* *apa* *=i* [*(a)ntu taipa* *≡a*]
     FUT= 2f= what =3 [that   mango ≡DEF]
     what are you going to do with those mangoes? (C:841)

This phenomenon is most often seen in the presentative constructions (§12.5) based on the 3rd person pronoun *ia* and various enclitics, such as *iaminne* ⟨ia=mo=i (a)nne| 3.PRO=PFV=3 this⟩ 'this is/was' …, *iapinne* ⟨ia=pa=i (a)nne| 3.PRO=IPF=3 this⟩ 'this (still here) is …' and so forth.

(147)   *Iaminne Patturioloang Gowa.*
     ia   *=mo* *=i* *(a)nne pa*⟩ *tu*   *ri*   *olo* ⟨*ang Gowa*
     3.PRO =PFV =3 this   NR⟩ person PREP front ⟨NR Gowa
     This is the Chronicle of Gowa

---

13   Selayarese, lacking the definite marker –*a*, attaches enclitic forms of the demonstratives to the NP with a similar function, e.g. *lokanjo* ⟨loka=njo | banana=that⟩ 'that/the banana' (Makasar *untia*). In Makasar demonstratives often attach phonologically to preceding elements (see ex. (146)), but these are usually not the specified noun, so this is quite different from the Selayarese phenomenon.

WORD CLASSES   173

TABLE 32   Interrogatives

apa	what
angngapa	why
ringngapanna	when
siapa	how much, to what extent
inai	who
pirang	how many (days)
kere	where
antekamma	how

(148)   *Iapinne anunnu?*
        ia   =pa =i =nne anu   ≡nnu
        3PRO =IPF =3 =this INDF ≡2f.POSS
        Is this here your thing?

5.6.4   *Interrogatives*

The interrogative proforms are examined in detail in the section on questions,
§12.2. Table 32 is simply a listing of them. They are not considered to form a
cohesive word class as they are formally considered members of the class about
which information is sought: i.e. *siapa* 'how many' behaves morphosyntactic-
ally like a numeral, but it is useful to present them together as they obviously
share functional properties. (Evans, 2000)

5.6.5   *Indefinite Pronouns*
5.6.5.1   *anu*
There is an all-purpose indefinite pronoun *anu* 'someone, something'.

(149)   *punna anunta anunna na punna anunna apantai ikatte*
        punna anu ≡nta   anu ≡nna   na punna anu ≡nna
        if   thing ≡2p.POSS thing ≡3.POSS and if   thing ≡3.POSS
        apa ≡nta   =i i–   katte
        what ≡2p.POSS =3 PERS– 2pPRO
        if something's ours it's his, and if something's his, what's ours for us?
        (C:23)

Anu has a discourse function as a hesitation marker 'um'; and also as a 'recog-
nitional expression' (Enfield 2003) like English 'whatsit', 'thingummyjig', which
is used when a speaker temporarily forgets or does not wish to say the name

174   CHAPTER 5

in question. The hearer must share the knowledge for communication to be
successful.

(150)   *daeng Anu ri anu*
        daeng anu   ri   anu
        title thing pref thing
        Mr Whosit from where-is-it

5.6.5.2   *tu*

In addition to *anu* there is a more restricted indefinite pronoun: *tu* 'the one
who', a reduced form of *tau* 'person'. It most often occurs in lexicalised con-
structions such as *turiolo* ⟨tu–ri–olo | person–PREP–front⟩ 'ancestor', and other
conventionalised forms such as posthumous names (§ 6.1.2.3, e.g. *Tunibatta* 'the
one who was beheaded'), government positions (e.g. *Tuma'bicara–butta* 'Prime
Minister', lit. 'the one who speaks the land'), and ethnic or locational identifi-
ers (e.g. *tu–Balandaya* 'the Dutch', *tu–Marusuka* 'the people of Maros'). It also
heads NPs in certain clauses with *kamma* 'thus' (§ 5.6.5.2.1).

In a paper by Finer (1997), Makasar *tu* is analysed as a 'relativising affix' for
humans, with *nu* its parallel for non-humans, e.g.:

(151)   **anakana' tuambunoai bawia*
        anakana' tu–   aN–   buno ≡a   =i   bawi ≡a
        boy   REL PREF– kill ≡DEF =3A pig ≡DEF
        the boy who killed the pig

(152)   **bawi nunabunoa anakanaka*
        bawi nu–   na= buno ≡a   anakanak ≡a
        pig REL– 3E= kill ≡DEF boy   ≡DEF
        the pig that the boy killed

I have starred these sentences because in Makasar they are ungrammatical in
several ways:

– the glottal stop in *ana'* does not become [k] in reduplication, → *ana'–ana'*.
  Also, *ana'–ana'* does not mean 'boy' or even 'child', except as a sort of
  job title, e.g. *ana'–ana' palukka'* 'child-thief' (cf. English *stable-boy, paper-
  boy*).

– there is no 'relativising affix *nu*–'. In Makasar *nu=* is the proclitic for 2nd person familiar, so sentence (152) would more accurately be glossed as 'the pig
  that the boy killed you', which makes no more sense in Makasar than in English. Selayarese has *nu* (presumably ← *anu*), but Makasar does not. *Anu* can

WORD CLASSES   175

head relative clauses itself, where it means 'the thing that'. In this context it behaves no differently to any other relativised nominal.

- although Makasar has *tu*, it is not a relativiser *per se*, and in fact is not productively available to head relative clauses (with the exception of *kamma* clauses, see §5.6.5.2.1), being restricted to the names and lexicalised constructions noted above. The full form *tau* often heads relative clauses, where it means 'the person who' (relativisation itself is one of the functions of the definite marker =*a*, see §6.3.3). But *tau* and *anu* do not appear where the RC already has a head, as it does in both these examples.

The corrected sentences should read:

(153)   *ana' ambunoai bawia*
        ana'   aN–   buno =a   =i bawi =a
        child PREF– kill =DEF =3 pig   =DEF
        the child who killed the pig

(154)   *bawi nabunoa anaka*
        bawi na= buno =a   ana' =a
        pig   3=   kill =DEF child =DEF
        the pig that the child killed

The sentences in the paper are anomalous because the informant was a native speaker of Selayarese, in which language it appears that *tau* and *anu* have grammaticised more completely than in Makasar.

5.6.5.2.1   tu *in* kamma *Clauses*

There is an environment in which *tu* productively heads NPs, including relative clauses. This is as subject of clauses headed by the basic verbs *kamma* or *kontu* 'thus, like so' or derivations thereof such as *singkamma* ('the same as').

(155)   *kammai tu–pongoroka gio'na*
        kamma =i tu   pongor =o'   =a   gio'   =na
        thus   =3 INDF   mad   =EC =DEF manner =3.POSS
        he acts like a madman

This construction is most often seen in idioms such as the following, which have roughly synonymous interpretations, i.e. 'he's clearly not comfortable with his situation':

176 CHAPTER 5

(156) *kammai tu–niaka saleang ri pajana*
    kamma =i tu   nia' ≡a   saleang ri   paja ≡na
    thus   =3 INDF exist ≡DEF bedbug PREP rump ≡3.POSS
    he's like someone with bedbugs on his bum

(157) *sangkammai tu–puru–puruanga pajana tammari ri pakkangkang*
    saN–   kamma =i tu   puru– puru –ang ≡a   paja
    EQ.COMPR– thus   =3 INDF RDP– pustule –AFFL ≡DEF rump
    ≡na   ta= amm– ari ri   pa– aC– kangkang
    ≡3.POSS NEG= MV–   stop PREP CAUS– MV– handful
    he's just like someone who has sores on his bum and can't stop scratching

Although one would expect *tu* to be confined to human NPs, this is not always the case, as is shown by these unusual examples from Cense's grammar notes (Or.545.43:9–10):

(158) *kammai tu–la–reppeka ulungku napakamma pa'risi'*
    kamma =i tu   la=   reppe' ≡a   ulu ≡ngku na= pa–
    thus   =3 INDF FUT= broken ≡DEF head ≡1.POSS 3= CAUS–
    kamma pa'ris =i'
    thus   pain =EC
    my head (is like something that) will break because of the pain

(159) *cini'–sái anjo lamaria kammai tu–tattilinga nicini'*
    cini' sá   =i anjo lamari ≡a   kamma =i tu   taC–
    see HORT =3 that cupboard ≡DEF thus   =3 INDF NVOL–
    tiling   ≡a   ni– cini'
    crooked ≡DEF PASS– see
    look at that cupboard, it looks (like something that is) crooked

(160) *kamma tu–tiananga anjo kongkonga kucini'*
    kamma tu   tianang ≡a   anjo kongkong ≡a   ku= cini'
    thus   INDF pregnant ≡DEF that dog   ≡DEF 1= see
    that dog looks to me (like something that is) pregnant

It may be that *tu* represents a conflation of reduced forms of *tau* 'person' and the demonstrative *antu* 'that (near you)', however this is merely speculation.

WORD CLASSES 177

TABLE 33 Relative locatives

boko	back, behind
olo	front, before
kairi	left
kanang	right
dallekang	in front of, facing

5.7 Locatives

This is a functional class comprising three subclasses, arguably members of different formal word classes. They are grouped together because they share fundamental morphosyntactic and semantic features. The most obvious similarity is that they are all terms of spatial deixis which situate entities or events in space (and in some cases, in time). They also share derivational possibilities; namely the comparative *–ang* 'further in a direction' (usually seen on adjectives, § 5.4.1.3.2), and causative *pa–* 'put something in a location' (§ 8.1.4).

5.7.1 *Relative* (ri) *Locatives*
This class consists of five directional terms which are relative—they are based on the orientation of the speaker .

They are nouns which refer to planes inherent to objects and the space directly in front. They are often marked for possession; e.g. *bokona tedong* 〈back≡3.POSS buffalo〉 'buffalo's back', *kairinna biseanga* 〈left≡3.POSS ship≡ DEF〉 'the ship's port side'. As locative terms they take the preposition *ri*:

(161) *a'lampa' ri olo mae a'boya kaluku*
       aC– lampa =a' mae   ri   olo aC– boya   kaluku
       MV– go   =1 be.in.aplace PREP front MV– search coconut
       I went forward to look for coconuts

Ri boko and *ri olo* are also used for temporal reference, in which *ri olo* = past, and *ri boko* = future, e.g. *bulang ri boko* 'next month' (lit. 'month at back'), *taung ri olo* 'last year'. This 'past to the front' method of referring to time is different from the Indonesian way, in which the past is generally (*yang*) *lalu* 'passed' and the future is *depan* 'facing' or (*yang*) *akan datang* 'to come'. Perhaps influenced by this, younger Makasar people use what appear to be calques of the Indonesian constructions, to the point of making equivalent relative clauses. Makasar and Indonesian expressions are shown side by side in (162) and (163):

(162) *minggu allaloa / minggu yang lalu*
    minggu aN(N)– lalo ≡a   minggu yang lalu
    week BV–   pass ≡DEF week REL PASS
    last week (lit. week that has passed)

(163) *taung labattua / tahun yang akan datang*
    taung la=   battu ≡a   tahun yang akan datang
    year FUT= come ≡DEF year REL FUT come
    next year (lit. year that will come)

These usages do not appear in my literary corpus, nor were they apparently known to Cense as they do not appear under the relevant dictionary entries.

5.7.2 *Absolute* (i) *Locatives*

This subclass has nine members: five general locatives and four cardinal directions based on the topography of the area. Table 34 shows them as they are used in Gowa on the west coast of the peninsula.

In contrast to the relative set, they can be regarded as 'absolute'—the sea is usually west, up is always up, regardless of speaker or hearer's orientation.[14] Unlike the relative set, these are associated with a variant preposition *i* (rather than *ri*) which is not found in any other environment. It may be instructive that the Bugis parallel for *i rawa* is *ri awa* (Ide Said DM, 1977).[15] It seems likely that the variant form of the preposition comes from metathesis of **ri ate → i rate* and by extension from there to the entire class. Further evidence from this comes from the fact that causatives of *i rate* and *i rawa* can still be realised as either *pairate* and *pairawa*, or *pariate* and *pariawa* ('put up' and 'put down' respectively).

---

14   This is only true up to a point—in fact along the south coast of the peninsula the cardinal directions are rotated anti-clockwise, because the sea (*lau'*) lies to the south rather than to the west as in Gowa. Thus in Bantaeng *lau'* means 'south', *timboro'* 'east', *raya* 'north' and *wara'* 'west'. But as a general rule it holds true and is a useful generalisation.

        Interestingly, Makasar has kept variant forms of *timboro'* and *wara'*—*timoro'* and *bara'* respectively—as names for the eastern and western winds and monsoon seasons (§ 6.1.3.6).

15   The Bugis equivalent of *i rate* 'above' is *ri ase'*. Other related languages do seem to share the *ri/i* alternation, though apparently not as systematically as Makasar. For example, Tae' has *i*, at least in conjunction with *lan* 'in' and *lo'* 'south', *di* elsewhere (van der Veen 1940). Apparently some Bugis dialects use *i* rather than *ri* but they are not noted as coexisting (Sirk 1996:112).

WORD CLASSES   179

TABLE 34 Absolute locatives

i rate	up	i lau'	west (seawards)
i rawa	down	i timboro'	south
i lalang	in	i raya	east (inland)
i pantara'	out	i wara'	north
i ba'le	across		

The absolute terms are used more commonly than the relative ones in
Makasar, however their use does not translate well into Indonesian (which
favours relative terms), and some people report a decline in the use of the absolute system by young semi-fluent speakers.

Raya and *lau'* have corresponding irregular verbal forms, *anrai'* and *kalau'*,
which are used to refer to movement in those directions, especially in the following idiomatic phrase used to describe someone going everywhere (looking
for something):

(164) *a'lampami timboro' wara', anrai' kalau'.*
      aC– lampa =mo =i timbor wara' anrai' kalau'
      MV– go   =PFV =3 south north go.east go.west
      she went south and north, east and west (PT:016)

(165) *kalau'ma' ri Jakarta minggu ri olo*
      kalau' =mo =a' ri Jakarta minggu ri   olo
      go.west =PFV =1 PREP Jakarta week   PREP front
      I went to Jakarta last week

The absolute locatives are often modified by the comparative *–angngang*,
or more commonly the older form *–ang* (§ 5.4.1.3.2). These constructions are
found in even quite small scale settings, as seen in (167):

(166) *A'limbammi anta'le ri binangaya laukanna Tammamaung,*
      aC– limbang =mo =i aN– ta'le ri   binanga ≡a   lau'
      MV– cross =PFV =3 AF– cross PREP river   ≡DEF west
      –ang   ≡na   Tammamaung
      –COMPR ≡3.POSS tammamaung
      They crossed the river westwards of Tammamaung,

180   CHAPTER 5

(167)   *alleanga' piringa rayangnganna*
        alle –ang =a' piring ≡a   raya –angngang ≡na
        take –BEN =1 plate ≡DEF east –COMPR   ≡3.POSS
        bring me the eastward plate (i.e. the one furthest east on the shelf)

5.7.3   *Deictic Adverbs*

The deictic adverbs show similarities with demonstratives (§ 5.6.3) in that
the forms are clearly related and they share the same three-way deictic contrast. The difference is that the deictic adverbs refer to the spatial location
of events rather than entities. In distribution and derivational potential the
deictic adverbs are similar to the other locatives, however, unlike those and
other terms of spatial reference the deictic adverbs do not require prepositions
ri or *i*.

The set is: *anrinni* 'here' (near speaker), *antureng* 'there' (near hearer), and
anjoreng 'there' (remote). *Anjoreng* occurs much more frequently in my corpus than *anrinni*, while the only sentential example with *antureng* comes from
Cense's grammar notes (KITLV Or.545.43).

Deictic adverbs may appear in post-verbal (168) or pre-verbal position (169)
within the predicate. In initial position, the deictic adverbial hosts the (absolutive) enclitic pronoun (see § 11.2 on clitic placement):

(168)   *ammantangi anjoreng*
        amm– antang =i anjoreng
        MV   live   =3 there
        he lives there

(169)   *anjorengi ammantang*
        anjoreng =i amm– antang
        there   =3 MV   live
        there he lives

Unlike demonstratives the deictic adverbials are subject to derivational processes, identical to those seen on the other locatives (§ 5.7). These are the comparative (with the suffix *–ang* rather than *–angngang* as seen on adjectives),
and the causative (with the affix *pa–*, associated with verbs, rather than the
adjectival causative *paka–*).

The comparative form *anjorengang* means roughly 'beyond', and metaphor-
ically 'the hereafter':[16]

---

16   There are no comparative derivations of the other two deictic adverbials in the corpus.

WORD CLASSES 181

(170) *punna tanucinika ri lino anjorengampi nucini'*

punna	*ta=*	*nu=*	*cini'*	*-a*	*ri*	*lino*	*anjoreng*	*-ang*	*=pa*
if	NEG=	2f=	see	-SBJV	PREP	world	there	-COMPR	=IPF

=i	*nu=*	*cini'*
=3	2f=	see

if you don't see it in this world you'll see it later in the hereafter (C:18)

The causative derivations are predicative, and mean 'put here/there':

(171) *kupanjorengi anunna ri balla'na*

ku=	*pa-*	*anjoreng*	*=i*	*anu*	*≡nna*	*ri*	*balla'*	*≡na*
1=	CAUS–	there	=3	INDF	≡3.POSS	PREP	house	≡3.POSS

I put his stuff there in his house

5.8 Numerals

Numerals form a cohesive word class because as well as denoting the natural class of numbers, they can be distinguished morphologically by association with the prefixes *piN–* 'MULTiplier', *maka–* 'ORDinal', and *taC–* 'DISTributive' (see § 5.8.1). The corresponding interrogative pro-form *siapa* 'how much/many' is also subject to the same derivational processes. The other interrogative *piraN–* behaves somewhat differently (12.2.2.8).

The set of basic numerals is given in Table 35. The word for seven is evidently from Malay *tujuh* where most South Sulawesi languages use *pitu*. The word for eight, *sagantuju*, derives from *sa–agáng–tuju* 'one with seven'. *Salapang* is also evidently from Malay, as etymologically it can be analysed as **sa–alap–ang* 'one taken (from ten)' (cf. Malay *d–elap–an* 'two taken (from ten)'). *Bilangngang* is derived from *bilang* 'to count', probably with the old form *–ang* of the comparative suffix (§ 5.4.1.3.2). All other numerals are formed by combining the above basic numerals, with a few irregularities.

'Ten' is shown by combining *pulo* with an irregular form for 'one', *saN–*, thus *sampulo*, while the other numbers use *si–*, thus *sibilangngang* '100', *sisa'bu* '1000'. As a modifier of a compound numeral *appa'* 'four' is substituted by *pata*, thus *patassa'bu* '4000'.

In order to explain some morphosyntactic peculiarities it is necessary to distinguish between compound and complex numerals. **Compound numerals** are those consisting of a basic numeral and a single order of magnitude of base ten, i.e. two ten = 20, three hundred = 300. In these, a nasal linker *–N–* 'LK' is inserted after the basic numerals which end in open syllables, (i.e.: *rua, tallu, lima*),

TABLE 35   Basic numerals

1	se're	6	annang	0	*nolo'* (← Indon. *nol*)
2	rua	7	tuju	10	–pulo
3	tallu	8	sagantuju	100	–bilangngang
4	appa'	9	salapang	1000	–sa'bu[a]
5	lima	10	sampulo	10000	–lassa

a   Chronicles such as the Maros Chronicle (Cummings 2000) show an archaic form for 'thousand', *cokkoang*.

TABLE 36   Compound and complex numerals

Compound numerals		Complex numerals	
10	sampulo	11	sampulo–asse're
20	ruampulo	12	sampulo–anrua
30	tallumpulo	13	sampulo–antallu
40	patampulo	14	sampulo–angngappa'
50	limampulo	15	sampulo–allima
60	annampulo	16	sampulo–angngannang
70	tujupulo	17	sampulo–antuju
80	sagantujupulo	18	sampulo–assagantuju
90	salapampulo	19	sampulo–assalapang
100	sibilangngang		
200	ruambilangngang	21	ruampulo–asse're
400	patambilangngang	32	tallumpulo–anrua
700	tujubilangngang	43	patampulo–antallu
1000	sisa'bu	54	limampulo–angngappa'
2000	ruassa'bu	65	annampulo–allima
4000	patassa'bu	76	tujupulo–angngannang
7000	tujusa'bu	87	sagantujupulo–antuju
10000	silassa	98	salapampulo–assagantuju

though not after the loans *tuju* and *sagantuju*. **Complex numerals** are those which draw numbers from more than one base level, i.e. one ten and one = 11. In these numerals a different linker –*aN*– is placed at each order of magnitude, i.e. between thousands and hundreds, between tens and ones. Compound numerals form a single word, while complex numerals are multi-word and are likely

WORD CLASSES

183

to be interrupted by a 2P clitic (see below). And (finally), *bilangngang* usually hosts the possessive marker ≡na:[17]

(172) *ruassa'bu–allimambillangnganna–ntallumpulo–anrua*
 rua –N– sa'bu –(a)N– lima –N– bilangngang –(a)N– tallu
 two –LK– ooo –LK– five –LK– oo –LK– three
 –N– pulo –(a)N– rua
 –LK– o –LK– two
 2532

In NPs numerals tend to precede the head noun if it is indefinite, as in (173), but follow it if it is definite, in which case the numeral hosts the definite marker, as in (174).

(173) *assibuntulu'ma' rua tau Parancisi'*
 aC– si– buntulu' =ma =a' rua tau Parancisi'
 MV– RCP– meet =PFV =1 two person France
 I met with two French people

(174) *assibuntulu'ma' tau ruayya*
 aC– si– buntulu' =ma =a' tau rua ≡a
 MV– RCP– meet =PFV =1 person two ≡DEF
 I met with the two people

Complex numerals are multi-word. This can be shown by the fact that in definite NPs containing complex numerals the definite marker appears after the first complete word of the numeral:

(175) *taung sisa'bua salapambilangnganna–mpatampulo–assagantuju*
 taung si– sa'bu ≡a salapang– bilangngang ≡na –aN–
 year one – ooo ≡DEF 9 oo ≡3.POSS –LK–
 pata –N– pulo –aN– sagantuju
 four –LK– o –LK– eight
 the year 1948

---

17 In this respect *bilangngang* behaves similarly to spatial adverbs when similarly derived with comparative *–ang* (§5.7.2). The possessive marker does not appear to have any function here other than a stylistic one.

184   CHAPTER 5

The order of constituents within NPs will be discussed more comprehensively in Chapter 6, but here I shall simply note that this behaviour parallels the placement of ≡*a* in relative clauses (§6.3.3), and also the placement of clitic pronouns when numerals occur predicatively as in (176), (177) and (178):

(176)   *ruai bainenna*
        rua =i baine   ≡nna
        two =3 woman ≡3.POSS
        he has two wives (lit. two are his wives)

(177)   *tallumpulomi angngannang (taung) umurukku*
        tallu –N– pulo =mo =i –aN– annang taung umuru' ≡ku
        three –LK– o   =PFV =3 –LK– six   year   age   ≡1.POSS
        I'm already 36 years old (36 is my age)

(178)   *Nikanai Patanna Langkana ka iami ampareki langkanaya, **sampuloi***
        ***anrua** pa'daseranna.*
        ni–   kana =i pata   ≡nna   langkana ka   ia   =mo =i
        PASS– word =3 owner ≡3.POSS palace   because 3PRO =PFV =3
        aN– pare' =i langkana ≡a   sampulo =i aN– rua pa⟩ aC–
        AF– make =3 palace   ≡DEF ten   =3 LK– two NR⟩ MV–
        daser   ⟨ang ≡na
        floorboard ⟨NR ≡3.POSS
        He was called 'Patanna Langkana' because he built a palace, it had twelve sections. (Maroso61)

In the archaic style of the Gowa chronicle, the constituent order of sentences such as (177) is somewhat different in that not only the enclitic pronoun but also the quantified element is found in 2nd position:

(179)   *tallumpulo taungi. angngannang. ma'gau'*
        tallu –N– pulo taung =i –aN– annang maC– gau'
        three –LK– ten year =3 –LK– six   MV– action
        For thirty-six years he ruled (KIT:refi2)

This constituent order is anachronistic in the modern language.

WORD CLASSES   185

5.8.1 *Numeral Derivations*

Numerals and the associated interrogative proform *siapa* 'how many' are subject to three derivational processes which are unique to this class.

5.8.1.1 Prefix *piN–* MULT

The prefix *piN–* is derives numerals with an adverbial function meaning 'X times', thus *pinruang* 'twice', *pissiapa* ⟨piN– siapa⟩ 'how many times'. The nasal linker after the numeral (*pinruang*) is seen on numerals which end in an open syllable except for *tuju, sagantuju,* and *pulo*; thus *rua, tallu, lima* → *pinruang, pintallung, pillimang* (see discussion of the linker 181). It is not seen in any compound numerals, e.g. *pimpatampulo(*ng)* '14 times'. This prefix is not used for 'once' which takes the form *sikali* 'one time'.

Forms with *piN–* generally modify verbs, either following them as in (180), or preceding them as in (181):

(180) *nainrói–seng pintallung.*
 na= inro   –i   seng piN–   tallu –N
 3=   circumnavigate –APPL again MULT– three – LK
 and they went round it (the wall) three times again (SKT:082).

(181) *battua' mange ri balla'na, a'rinra–iji kanjolika na kupintallung akkio' na*
 tena tau appiwali
 battu =a' mange ri   balla' ≡na   aC– rinra ija =i kanjoli'
 come =1   go   PREP house ≡3.POSS MV– light still =3 candle
 ≡a   na ku= piN–   tallu –N aC– kio' na tena tau   aC–
 ≡DEF and 1= MULT– three – LK MV– call and NEG person MV–
 piwali
 reply
 I came to his house, still the candle burned, three times I called and nobody answered (Cgn:5)

In the latter sentence the numeral hosts the clitic pronoun, which appears as a proclitic rather than enclitic (i.e.: it has been fronted) due to the presence of the conjunction *na*. See §11.2.2 for more discussion of this phenomenon.

PiN– numerals may also themselves head predicates where the repeated action is understood to refer to the preceding verb. These may even be transitive as in (183):

186   CHAPTER 5

(182)   *anjo ulunna Karaeng Marusu' tulu nabokoi Arumpone pissiapangi*
        anjo ulu   ≡nna   Karaeng Marusu' tulu na= boko =i
        that head ≡3.POSS king   Maros   keep 3=   back =3
        Arumpone piN–   siapa   –N =i
        Arumpone MULT– how.many – LK =3
        Karaeng Maros' head kept turning away from the Arumpone again and
        again (i.e. who knows how many times? Maros:190)

(183)   *Kipinruangi amma', kipintallungi*
        ki= piN–   rua –N =i amma' ki= piN–   tallu –N =i
        2p= MULT– two – LK =3 mother 2p= MULT– three – LK =3
        (call) twice mother, (call) three times (antecedent verb = *akkio'* 'call',
        PT:066)

Another common use of *piN–* is in kin terms such as *sampu–pinruang* '2nd
cousin', which are often seen in verbal form, e.g.:

(184)   *assampu–pinruanga' katte*
        aC– sampu piN–   rua –N =a' katte
        MV– cousin MULT– two – LK =1 2fPRO
        I'm your second cousin (see § 6.1.1.2 on kin terms).

PiN– can also be prefixed with the intransitive verb marker *aC–* to derive the
verb *apping* 'sign with a cross' (i.e. of illiterate people), as in *nipingi arenna*
⟨ni–ping=i areng≡na | PASS–cross=3 name≡3.POSS⟩ 'his name was signed with
a cross' (C:547).

5.8.1.2   Prefix *maka–* ORD

Ordinal numerals are formed with the prefix *maka–*, thus *makarua* 'second',
makatallu 'third'. 'First' can be *makase're* but is more often *uru–uru* ⟨RDP–
beginning⟩ As is usual with NP internal modifiers, if the head noun is definite,
the ordinal numeral will host the definite marker, e.g. *allo makaruayya* ⟨allo
maka–rua≡a | day ORD–two≡DEF⟩ 'the second day'; or more often they are
marked with possessive affixal clitics referencing the context for the series—
that is, the sequence of which they are a member. For example, in *parakara
makatallunna* ⟨article ORD–three≡3.POSS⟩ 'its third article', the possessive suffix refers to the document, usually a treaty or similar legal document.
    If the numeral is complex, the affixal clitic will be hosted by the first com-
plete word of the complex, as was discussed on p. 183:

WORD CLASSES 187

(185) *allo makaruampuloa–anrua*
allo maka– rua –N– pulo ≡a   –aN– rua
day ORD– two –LK– ten ≡DEF –LK– two
the 22nd day

(186) *parakara makasampulona–angngannang*
parakara maka– sampulo ≡na   –aN– annang
article   ORD– ten   ≡3.POSS –LK– six
article 16 (of the treaty of Bungaya) (KIT668–216)

The combination of *maka–* and *piN–* means 'the Xth time', e.g. *makapinruang* 'the second time'. The prefix *maka–* does not appear to be related to the adverb *maka* 'certainly' (§ 5.5.1).

5.8.1.3   Prefix *taC–* DISTR
The prefix *taC–* has a distributive meaning, e.g.:

(187) *tattallung–kayu jangang*
taC–   tallu –N– kayu jangang
DISTR– three –LK– CLF chicken
three chickens each

There does not seem to be any semantic connection to the non-volitional verb prefix *taC–* (§ 7.4).

5.8.1.4   Numerals Deriving Verbs
Numerals can also derive verbs—the most commonly seen is *asse're* ⟨aC–se're | MV–one⟩ 'be one, gather', which can be seen in that form and also further derived into a passive causative in the sentences below:

(188) *Tallu allo tallu bangngi asse're ngasemmi Karaenga ...*
tallu allo tallu bangngi aC– se're ngaseng =mo =i karaeng
three day three night   MV– one all   =PFV =3 king
≡a
≡DEF
After three days and nights all the karaengs gathered ... (SKT:032)

(189) *"Apa saba'na nipasse're ngasengki' ..."*
apa saba' ≡na   ni– pa– aC– se're ngaseng =ki'
what reason ≡3.POSS PASS– CAUS– MV– one all   =1pl
'Why were we all made to gather ...?' (SKT:034)

188   CHAPTER 5

The only other example of a numeral derived into a verb in my corpus comes from a song, *Pangngu'rangimami* 'Only memories remain' by the singer Iwan Tompo:

(190) *Sarenta tosseng sipa'rua*
       sare ≡*nta*   =*tong* =*seng* *si*–   *pa*–   *aC*– *rua*
       give ≡2p.POSS =also =again MUT– CAUS– MV– two
       we were 'given' to be made two again (i.e. we were forced to separate)

Note that numerals do not need to be verbalised in order to be predicates.

5.8.2   Fractions

The basic fractions are *tangnga* 'half' and *parapa'* 'quarter', e.g. *sitangnga* 'one half', *tallu parapa'* 'three quarters'. Notice there is no nasal linker between numerals and the basic fractions. Other fractions are formed by using *tawa* 'divided by' (*tawa* is also a noun, 'portion, share') in the following way:

(191) *se're tawa tallu*
       se're tawa   tallu
       one   divide three
       one third

(192) *rua tawa lima*
       rua   tawa   lima
       two   divide five
       two fifths

(193) *lima tawa sampulo–angngannang*
       lima tawa   saN–   pulo –aN– annang
       five   divide one– ten   –LK– six
       five sixteenths

These forms are as they have been taught in the post-colonial school system and are greatly simplified from the two different permutations found in older texts and described by Cense in his grammar notes (KITLV Or.545.43):

(194) *rua ri tawa tallunna / rua ri tallu–ntawanga*
       rua ri   tawa   tallunna ≡*nna   rua ri   tallu –N– tawa*
       two PREP divide three   ≡3.POSS two PREP three –LK– divide

WORD CLASSES   189

> *–ang* ≡*a*
> –NR ≡DEF
> two thirds (two by its three divided / two by the three divisions)

5.8.3   *Indefinite Quantifiers*

There are a few indefinite quantifiers, which come from a number of different word classes, specifically the adjective *jai* 'many' (e.g. *jai tau* 'many people'); the classifier-like nominal *ke'de* or *ka'de* 'bit' (e.g. *sike'de' golla* 'a bit of sugar'); and the pronominal plural marker *ngaseng* 'all' (p. 169), e.g. *ia–ngaseng* 'all of them'. Other ways of denoting the meaning 'all' or 'whole' are formed with the prefix *si–* as discussed in (§10.1.5.1), e.g. *siGowa* 'everyone in Gowa', *sibaine* 'all women'.

5.9   Classifiers, Partitives and Measures

Like other Southeast Asian languages, including Indonesian (Sneddon 1996: 134 ff.), Makasar has an extensive system of nominal classifiers which describe various types or shapes of noun when they are enumerated. Many of the classifiers are derived from (and still function as) regular nouns. Measure nouns and partitives are formally indistinguishable from classifiers and so they are included here as well. The classifier for humans, *tau*, is an incomplete member of the class, being optional and limited to the number one (e.g. *se're karaeng*, *sitau karaeng*, 'a king' but *rua karaeng*, **ruantau karaeng*).

Other measures which were used historically but are no longer current include *katti* (≅ 625 grams), *gantang* (five *katti*), *pikulu'* (20 *gantang*), and *lontang* 'shedful' (16 *pikulu'*, ≅ 1 tonne).

Classifiers, partitives and measures behave morphophonologically like higher order numerals (see §5.8), thus 'one' is denoted by the bound form *si–* instead of the full form *se're*, likewise 'four' is *pata* rather than *appa'*. Vowel-final numerals require insertion of a nasal linker between the numeral and the classifier (see discussion of the linker 181), again with the exception of *tuju* and *sagantuju* as can be seen with *bollo*.

TABLE 37   Classifiers, partitives and measures

Classifier/measure		Example	
bakkarang	folded flat things	sibakkarang jali'	one folded rattan mat
balle'	can, container	siballe'mantega	a container of margarine
barrisi'	line	sibarrisi' tulísang	a line of writing
batu	misc. (lit. stone)	annambatu balla'	six houses
bollo	flowers	tujubollo bunga	seven flowers
botolo'	bottle	ruambotolo' minynya'	two bottles of oil
bukuang	words	tallumbukuang kana	three words
dotere'	bunch (of fruit)	sidotere' taipa–lolo	a bunch of young mangoes
gompo	pile (of small goods)	sigompo markisa	a pile of passionfruit
gulung	spool	sigulung bannang	a spool of thread
kaca	glass	sikaca kopi	a glass of coffee
kalabini	pair, couple	sikalabini jangang	a breeding pair of fowl
kangkang	fistful	sikangkang doe'	a fistful of dollars
karanjeng	wide basket	sikaranjeng tude	a basket of scallops
kayu	animals[a]	ruangkayu tedong	two buffalo
ke'de'/ka'de'	a bit (adverbial use)	sike'de' cipuru'	a bit hungry
kodi	score	tallungkodi lipa'	three score of sarongs
la'la'	hand (of bananas)	sila'la' unti	a hand of bananas
lawara'	flat things	ruallawara' baju	two shirts
leo'	quids (for chewing)	sileo' pangngajai	one quid of betel
lisere'	small round things	tallullisere' kalereng	three marbles
litere'	litre (esp. of rice, sugar)	tallullitere' minnya'	three litres of oil
losi	dozen	tallullosi piring	three dozen plates
pappa'	rings and cylinders (inc. stalks)	ruampappa' ta'bu	two pieces of sugarcane
pasang	pair	sipasang bunting beru	a pair of newlyweds
poko'	trees and branches (also of rivers)	limampoko' kaluku	five coconut palms
pusa	narrow basket	sipusa ce'la'	a basket of salt
roili'	bunch	siroili' taipa	a bunch of mangoes
roko'	packets	patanroko' te	four packets of tea
sikko'	bunch (of long things, tied with string)	ruassikko' bine	two bunches of rice seedlings
tau	people	sitau ana'	a child
te'ngala'	piece (broken off from a larger piece)	site'ngala' golla eja	a chunk of palm sugar
ujung	bundle	tallungujung ta'bu	three bundles of sugarcane

a   Interestingly *kayu* itself means 'wood'. It is also of note that in the Gowa Chronicle *kayu* is used to count *soongang* ('headfuls', a load carried on a woman's head) of fabric (KIT:4:18).

WORD CLASSES 191

5.10 Prepositions

There is one main preposition, *ri*, and another form *i* which has extremely limited distribution, occurring only before absolute locatives such as *i rate* 'above', and *i lalang* 'inside' (see § 5.7.2), whereas *ri* is found in all other environments. *Ri* heads prepositional phrases with the following kinds of semantic roles:

spatial location, source, or goal

(195) *ri Mangkasaraka' ammantang*
 ri Mangkasar =a' =a' aC– antang
 PREP Makassar =EC =1 MV– stay
 I live in Makassar

(196) *sura' battu ri kakangku*
 sura' battu ri kaka' ≡ku
 letter come PREP ↑sibling ≡1.POSS
 a letter from my elder brother

(197) *a'lampa' ri pasaraka*
 aC– lampa =a' ri pasar =a' ≡a
 MV– go =1 PREP market =EC ≡DEF
 I go to the market

Given the wide semantic range of the preposition, combinations with movement/location basic verbs (§ 5.3.1.2) are understandably common to avoid ambiguity. Most frequent are *mange ri* GOAL ⟨go PREP⟩ 'go to', and *battu ri* SOURCE ⟨come PREP⟩ 'come from'.

In addition to purely spatial reference, *ri* also marks temporal location:

(198) *ri subangngi ammekanga' juku'*
 ri subangngi aN(N)– pekang =a' juku'
 PREP yesterday BV– hook =1 fish
 yesterday I was fishing

(199) *tette' sampulo ri bari'basa'*
 tette' sampulo ri bari'bas =a'
 o'clock ten PREP morning =EC
 ten o'clock in the morning

192   CHAPTER 5

In passive sentences (those with the prefix *ni–*, see §7.3) *ri* marks the (optional) agent.

(200)   *nimeái bangkengku (ri kongkong)*
        ni–   mea –i   bangkeng ≡ku   (ri   kongkong)
        PASS– urine –APPL leg   ≡1.POSS (PREP dog)
        my leg was pissed on (by a dog)

There are some examples of lexicalised prepositional phrases being incorporated into derived forms. One example is the word *patturioloang* 'chronicle', which is a *pa*⟩⟨*ang* nominalisation (§6.2.2.4) based on *turiolo* ⟨person PREP front⟩ 'those who came before, ancestors'. There are also verbal examples, e.g. the following causative verbal derivations with *i*:

(201)   *paipantara'ma' inakke*
        pa–   i   pantara' =mo =a' i   nakke
        CAUS– PREP outside =PFV =1 PERS 1.PRO
        leave me out, don't count on me

(202)   *kupailalangi*
        ku= pa–   i   lalang =i
        1= CAUS– PREP inside =3
        I enclose it

5.10.1   *Prepositional Verb*

There is a lexicalised construction *siagáng* (based on *si–* 'one' or 'mutual' with the verb *agáng* 'accompany'), which has become common as both a conjunction for NPs 'and', and as a comitative marker 'with', e.g.:

(203)   *battua' ri Mangkasara' siagáng bainengku*
        battu =a' ri   Mangkasar =a' siagáng baine   ≡ngku
        come =1 PREP Makassar   =EC with   woman   ≡1.POSS
        I came to Makassar with my wife

This latter use could be considered prepositional.

WORD CLASSES   193

TABLE 38   Conjunctions

na	and
siagáng	and, together with
de'	or
iareka	or
(m)ingka	but
ka	because
saba'na/nasaba'	because
lanri	because
napakamma	because
jari	so
punna/ponna	if/when
manna	although
sanggenna	until

5.11   Conjunctions

There is a substantial set of conjunctions, listed in Table 38.

As discussed in § 4.5.1, *na*, *de'* and *ka* are considered to be preposed particles, while the other conjunctions are of various morphological types. The ones whose etymologies are clear are listed below:

- *siagáng* is a grammaticised mutual verb ⟨si–agáng | MUT–accompany⟩
- *iareka* is probably a grammaticised construction ⟨ia are=ka | 3PRO perhaps=Q⟩, roughly 'or it could be ...' (see *are* § 5.5.2, *=ka* § 4.3.3.6)
- *saba'* is a noun root meaning 'reason'
- *napakamma* is literally ⟨na=pa–kamma | 3=CAUS–thus⟩ 'made so'
- *jari* is also the root of the verb *anjari* 'become'
- *punna* is lexicalised from ⟨pung=na | if≡3.POSS⟩ 'if s/he'. The corresponding forms *pungku* ⟨if≡1.POSS⟩ 'if I' and so forth are still found in poetry.
- the above is also the case for *manna* ⟨mang=na | although≡3.POSS⟩
- *sangge* is also an adverb 'as far as'

194   CHAPTER 5

5.12 Discourse Particles

Discourse particles are clause-final elements with pragmatic or phatic rather than lexical meanings. Unlike interjections (§ 5.13) they cannot form complete utterances in isolation. They are distinct from adverbial particles (§ 5.5.2) because they are not integrated into clauses or the agreement system, but like the other particles they do not form the basis of derivations.

de 'bah! bugger it!'
di 'isn't it?' (checking information)
to' 'isn't it? true? right?' (demanding agreement)

(204)   *mange–sáko de!*
       mange sá   =ko de
       go   HORT =2f EMPH
       oh, just piss off!

(205)   *le'ba'mako bunting di?*
       le'ba'   =mo =ko bunting di
       already =PFV =2f wedding TAG
       you're already married, aren't you?

(206)   *pongoroki to'?*
       pongoro' =i to'
       crazy   =3 TAG
       he's crazy, right?

5.13 Interjections

Interjections are usually complete utterances in their own right, at the very least being extra-clausal, separated by a pause from other elements of a sentence. Their meanings are often not strictly lexical but emotive or attitudinal, being used to attract attention, express surprise, happiness, pain and so forth. A selection is given in Table 39.

(207)   *ce, teamako de!*
       ce tea =mo =ko de
       hey NEG =PFV =2f EMPH
       Hey, don't do that!

WORD CLASSES   195

TABLE 39   Interjections

ae	hey (attract attention)
ba	yeah, sure
ce	hey (annoyed)
o	oh
wa	gosh
(w)adada	ouch
(w)edede	ouch, wow, what the ...
ididi	ouch
aulé	oh my God! (how sad, how beautiful, etc.)

(208)   *edede, ga'gana sapatunu*
         edede ga'ga ≡na   sapatu ≡nu
         wow   nifty ≡3.POSS shoe   ≡2f.POSS
         Wow, cool shoes!

In addition to the Makasar interjections there are numerous borrowed interjections and formulae which play the same sort of role in the language. As part of the Islamic world, naturally Makasar people use a variety of Arabic words and formulae as interjections, generally filtered through either Indonesian or Makasar phonotactics, though obviously the extent of this filtering depends on the level of education of the speaker. Some examples are: *Allahú* 'oh God!', *alahandulilla* (← al-ḥamdu li'llāh) 'praise be to God'; *assalamu alaikung* (← as-salāmu 'alaikum) 'peace be unto you' (greeting formula), and so forth.

Going further into cultural literacy, there are many native Makasar formulae, without knowledge of which one's knowledge of the language is embarrassingly incomplete. These include proverbs, phrases from *kelong* and other poetic genres, and the like; however this aspect of the language requires further investigation beyond the scope of this work.

CHAPTER 6

Nouns and Noun Phrases

This chapter describes both nouns and the structure of noun phrases. The basic features of nouns in opposition to other parts of speech were described briefly in § 5.2, but this chapter looks in more detail at different types of noun, and at the morphological processes which derive nouns. The first section discusses subtypes of nouns including proper nouns and other referential terms, and temporal nominals. The second section discusses derivational processes which result in nouns. The third section discusses the noun phrase, including morphology typically associated with noun phrases, and the structure of various types of NP, including relative clauses.

6.1 Subclasses of Noun

In § 5.2 nouns were defined primarily syntactically as words with the potential to form or head noun phrases, and act as arguments in a predicate and thus enter into the system of cross-referencing. All nouns share at least these properties, but other syntactic properties such as the ability to enter into a possessor/possessed relationship are more restricted. Semantically nouns tend to refer to entities such as people, animals or objects in the world, though there are also of course nouns which refer to abstract or intangible things. Morphologically, common nouns at least are associated with the affixal enclitic ≡a which marks definiteness, and the possessive affixal enclitics. Other typical nominal properties were listed in § 5.2 and are repeated here:
- they can be specified by demonstratives (§ 5.6.3)
- they can be modified by adjectives (§ 5.4)
- they can be quantified with numerals (§ 5.8) or other quantifiers, this process usually also involving a classifier (§ 5.9)
- they can be complements of PPs marked with the preposition *ri* (§ 5.10)
- when prefixed with *aC–*, they will typically derive a verb meaning 'have/use NOUN' (§ 5.3.1.1)

For the purposes of this section, nouns will be divided into types according to broad differences in morphosyntactic behaviour and to a lesser degree semantic differences. One major such division is between **common nouns** which can take the definite marker ≡a and possessive markers ≡*ku* etc.; and **proper nouns** such as names and titles (excluding kin terms) which are unlikely

© KONINKLIJKE BRILL NV, LEIDEN, 2020 | DOI:10.1163/9789004412668_007

NOUNS AND NOUN PHRASES

to host such markers but instead group together with the class of pronouns in taking the personal prefix *i–*. Semantically this group is of course distinct because they tend to refer to unique referents, and for this reason place names are included within it. **Kin terms** themselves are a subset of common nouns which are distinct because they are used as address terms and form a self-contained system. The other major subgroup is the set of **temporal nominals** which are distinct both semantically because they refer to time, and syntactically because they occur in PPs which are temporal adjuncts.

The purely morphological division between simple and derived nouns is not reflected in differences in morphosyntax, and only superficially in semantics—although simple nouns tend to be more concrete (e.g. *juku'* 'fish') and derived nouns tend to be more abstract (e.g. *kakalumanynyangang* 'wealth' ← *kalumanynyang* 'rich'), this is not always the case (cf. *rasa* 'scent/taste/feel' and *katinroang* 'bed' ← *tinro* 'sleep'). Thus, the division simple/derived is not reflected in this section.

6.1.1 *Common Nouns*

It is difficult to define the class of common nouns other than to refer to the list of nominal properties above and note that it applies most universally to this class, and excludes proper nouns and certain nominals. Semantically common nouns may be divided into any number of classes—animals, body parts, artefacts, and so forth. Although these types of division are not reflected in the morphosyntax, they are used here just to organise the representative examples which are of course only a tiny selection—for comprehensive coverage refer to either the Makasar–Dutch or Makasar–Indonesian dictionaries.

6.1.1.1 Generic Nouns

There are some common nouns which are notable for occurring in large numbers of compounds in which the head supplies a general meaning, which is then given a specific meaning by a nominal or adjectival modifier.[1] Although this is not a unique process, as virtually any noun may be modified in the same sort of way, it is simply worth noting that these compounds make up a large part of the Makasar lexicon. The nouns most commonly used as heads of these kinds of compounds are: *je'ne'* 'water', *kanre* 'cooked rice, food', *tai* 'shit', *ana'* 'child', *rappo* 'fruit', *juku'* 'fish' and *tau* 'person'. Some examples of common nouns are given in Table 40.

---

1 Note that this is not phonological compounding, as was discussed in § 2.3.8.

198   CHAPTER 6

TABLE 40   Common nouns

Animals		Geographical features	
olo'–olo'	animal[a]	tamparang	ocean
olo'	worm	binanga	river
lamu'	mosquito	moncong	mountain
jarang	horse	liukang	island
tedong	buffalo	parang	field
kongkong	dog		
tumpang	frog	Physical phenomena	
jangang–jangang	bird	bosi	rain
jangang	chicken	gunturu'	thunder
kiti'	duck	bintoeng	star
juku'	fish	anging	wind
balakebo'	herring	bombang	wave
Body parts		Tools, weapons	
ulu'	head	berang	cleaver
u'	hair	badi'	sword
mata	eye	pande'de'	hammer[b]
lima	hand/arm	uring	saucepan
bangkeng	foot/leg	guci	jar
Trees, fruit		Clothing	
poko'	tree	lipa'	sarong
rappo	pinang, fruit	baju	shirt
kaluku'	coconut	sapatu	shoe
unti	banana	songko'	cap
taipa	mango	saluara'	trousers
Buildings, furniture		People, occupations	
balla'	house	tau	person
baruga	hall	karaeng	king
kadera	chair	ata	slave
lamari	cupboard	guru	teacher
katinroang	bed[c]	pakoko	gardener[d]

a   Interestingly, the general term for animal is a reduplication of
    olo' 'worm'. It includes insects and mammals, but excludes fish
    (*juku'*) and birds (*jangang-jangang*).
b   A *pa*-INF instrument nominalisation, see § 6.2.2.2.
c   An irregular *ka*⟩⟨*ang* nominalisation, see § 6.2.3.3.
d   A pa-ROOT occupation nominalisation, see § 6.2.2.1.

NOUNS AND NOUN PHRASES

TABLE 41   Generic nouns

je'ne'	inung	water+drink	drinking water
je'ne'	mata	water+eye	tears
je'ne'	uring	water+pot	bean mush
je'ne'	bawa	water+mouth	prattle
tai	bani	shit+bee	wax
tai	bassi	shit+iron	rust
tai	anging	shit+wind	medicinal moss
tai	ka'muru	shit+nose	snot
tai	roda	shit+wheel	grease
tai	toli	shit+ear	earwax
ana'	baine	child+woman	daughter
ana'	bura'ne	child+man	son
ana'	jarang	child+horse	foal
ana'	irate	child+above	diacritic for vowel i (see Ch. 3)

6.1.1.2   Kin Terms

Kin terms merit a discussion of their own because they are pervasively used as terms of address, though not always accurately if the link is distant or obscure. Otherwise they are not notably different from common nouns. The major kin-terms are shown (greatly simplified) in Figure 22.[2] Only for the central married pairs (husband and wife, father and mother) is there a gender difference in the terminology, for the rest of the kin relationships the terms are ambisexual (and also extend to spouses of the actual blood relation), so this is reflected in the use of semicircles rather than the usual gender specific symbols.

Other terms which should be mentioned are *daeng*, which as well as being a general respectful address term between non-intimates (§ 6.1.2.2), is also used by a wife to her husband, and *andi'*, which as well as meaning 'younger sibling' is used by a husband to his wife. *Cikali*, the shortened form of *samposikali* ('1st cousin'), is also commonly used between friends. There is also a complex system of referring to kin-in-law which awaits further investigation.

---

2   For more detailed discussion see anthropological studies, e.g. Chabot 1996; Röttger-Rössler 1988.

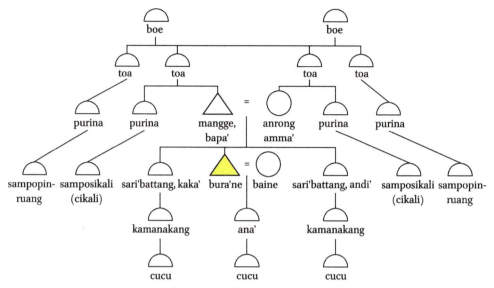

FIGURE 22   Kinship terms (ego is shaded)

Like other nouns, kinship terms can derive verbs meaning 'have an X', such as *a'baine* 'have a wife, get married', *assari'battang* 'have a sibling'; while reciprocal relationships can be marked attributively with the mutual prefix *si–* (see §10.1), as in *sisari'battang* 'siblings'.

6.1.2   *Proper Nouns*

Proper nouns include the names of people and places. They have unique referents, or at least are intended to within the contexts of a discourse. They include personal names and local customary variants *pa'daengang* and other noble names, and place names.

6.1.2.1   Personal Names

On the surface modern Makasar naming practices are not unlike those of other Islamic parts of Indonesia. Men use one or more Arabic based names (those very popular in South Sulawesi include Hasanuddin, Asmuddin, Sirajuddin), while women have Arabic names such as Fatima or other Indonesian names such as Isnawati or Dewi. Most people nowadays go almost exclusively by these 'Indonesian' names or a nickname variant thereof (e.g. Udin, Isna). Names are usually preceded by the personal prefix *i–* in speech, e.g. *iUdin, iBaso'*.

NOUNS AND NOUN PHRASES

6.1.2.2   Pa'daengang (Daeng Names)

Depending on age, social circumstance, or personal preference, traditional Makasar names may also be used. Most Makasar have a *pa'daengang* or *daeng*-name, which can be used as both an address and reference term. *Pa'daengang* consist of the title *Daeng* followed by a word, usually an adjective (with the archaic *ma–* adjectival prefix), though nominals or verbs (with the archaic *maC–* form of the verb prefix) are also found. *Daeng* itself is a gender neutral term of address which was formerly used as a term of respect for semi-nobility but is now in general use—in fact the same observation could be made for the practice of giving *pa'daengang* generally.[3] *Pa'daengang* are given in infancy and are usually positive descriptions of character or appearance. Names for men typically emphasise strength or ability (e.g. *Daeng Makkulle* ⟨MV–can⟩ 'Capability'; *Daeng Magassing* ⟨ADJ–strong⟩ 'Strong'; *Daeng Manai'* ⟨ADJ–ascend⟩ 'Climbing'); while names for women emphasise good character or beauty (e.g. *Daeng Baji'* 'Good'; *Daeng Bollo* 'Flower').

The place of *pa'daengang* in modern Makasar society is complex. Elderly rural people use them almost exclusively, but there are also urban middle-aged or young people who have elected to use them, though others find them backward and embarrassing and rarely use them. Educational level is certainly a factor here, but there is also a complicated dynamic of Makasar pride and ethnic or national identity. Purely on a practical level they can be used to help in differentiating between people with the same Islamic name, such as the numerous Hasanuddins; but they are also a mark of 'Makasar-ness' in an increasingly multi-ethnic city, though they are also bestowed on outsiders as a general token of acceptance.

An extension of the *pa'daengang* system is used when addressing tradespeople or others who are referred to by their occupation rather than by name, e.g. *Daeng Beca'* 'pedicab driver', *Daeng Paballi* ⟨NR–sell⟩ 'stallholder'.

6.1.2.3   Noble and Royal Names

Other types of names which are worth mentioning briefly here are those which were given to royalty: *areng kale* or *Mangkasara'* (personal or Makasar names), *areng pamana'* (royal or birth names, equivalent to *pa'daengang*), *pakkaraeng-gang* (*karaeng*-titles), *areng mate* (posthumous names), and (following Islamisation) *areng ara'* (Arabic names). These can be illustrated by the names held by the ill-fated Sultan Hasanuddin of Gowa (ruled 1653–1669, see §1.1.4.3), as listed in the Gowa Chronicle (KIT:p. 30).

---

3 Bugis also use *pa'daengang* but the practice is less widespread and still somewhat restricted to the nobility (Sirtjo Koolhof pers.comm.).

202 CHAPTER 6

(209) *Tumamenang. ri Balla' Pangkana. ansossorangi. ma'gau' ... anne kara-*
enga. areng ara'na. nikana. Sultan Hasanuddin. areng Mangkasara'na.
iangku mabassung. nikana I Mallombasi. kana pamana'na. nikana. I
Daeng Mattawang. pakaraenganna. ri tama'gau'na. nikana. Karaenga
ri Bontomangngape.

tu	*ma–*	*menang*	*ri*	*Balla' Pangka*	*≡na*	*aN–*
person	ADJ–	rest	PREP	house well.made	≡3.POSS	AF–

sossorang =i maC– gau'
inherit =3 MV– action
Tumamenang ri Balla' Pangkana ('one who rests in his sturdy house',
his posthumous name) inherited the throne.

anne	*karaeng*	*≡a*	*areng ara'*	*≡na*	*ni–*	*kana*	*Sultan*
this	karaeng	≡DEF	name Arab	≡3.POSS	PASS–	word	Sultan

Hasanuddin
Hasanuddin
This karaeng, his Arab name was Sultan Hasanuddin.

areng	*Mangkasara'*	*≡na*	*iang*	*ku=*	*ma–*	*bassung*	*ni–*
name	Makassar	≡3.POSS	VET	1=	STV–	swollen.belly	PASS–

kana I Mallombasi
word PERS Mallombasi
His Makasar name, may I not be cursed, was I Mallombasi.

kana	*pa–*	*amm–*	*ana'*	*≡na*	*ni–*	*kana*	*I*	*daeng bonto*
word	NR–	MV–	child	≡3.POSS	PASS–	word	PERS	daeng shore

His royal name was I Daeng Mattawang.

pa⟩	*karaeng*	*⟨ang*	*≡na*	*ri*	*ta=*	*maC–*	*gau'*	*≡na*
NR⟩	karaeng	⟨NR	≡3.POSS	PREP	NEG=	MV–	action	≡3.POSS

ni– kana karaeng ri Bontomangngape
PASS– word karaeng PREP Bontomangngape
His *karaeng*-title before he became ruler was the Karaeng of Bonto-
mangngape.

Deceased members of the nobility are referred to after their death by posthumous names, which usually describe something about the manner or location of
their death or alternatively their place or manner of burial. Posthumous names
take the form *tu* 'person' followed by a modifying phrase, such as Tunibatta ⟨tu
ni–batta | person PASS–sever⟩ 'beheaded one', who ruled Gowa for a short time
in 1565. Some other examples of posthumous names are:

NOUNS AND NOUN PHRASES

(210)   *Tumapa'risi'–kallonna*
        tu   ma– pa'ris =i'   kallong ≡na
        person ADJ– pain =EC neck   ≡3.POSS
        sore necked one (ruled Gowa 1510–1546)

(211)   *Tumamenang ri Agamana*
        tu   ma– menang ri   agama ≡na
        person ADJ– rest   PREP religion ≡3.POSS
        one resting in his religion (ruled Tallo' 1593–1623)

(212)   *Tumamenang ri Kala'biranna*
        tu   ma– menang ri   ka⟩ la'bir   ⟨ang ≡na
        person ADJ– rest   PREP NR⟩ exalted ⟨NR ≡3.POSS
        one resting in his majesty (ruled Gowa 1742–1753)

Although these names are similar to relative clauses (§ 6.3.3), the absence of the definite marker ≡*a* marks them as distinct.

6.1.2.4   Place Names
Many Makasar place names are etymologically transparent and descriptive, e.g. *Bontomanai'* 'shore going up'; others can be decomposed but are not immediately interpretable, e.g. *Je'ne'ponto* 'water bracelet'; while still others have no obvious meaning, e.g. *Marusu'*, *Takalara'*. A small number of place names in South Sulawesi appear to have been borrowed from Javanese, e.g. *Jipang* and *Garassi'* (← Jipang, Grisek) (Reid 2000:107). However, a detailed study of Makasar toponyms has yet to be performed.

6.1.3   *Temporal Nominals*
The words referring to specific times are formally nouns, including *wattu* 'time' itself. They typically occur in temporal adjuncts which are prepositional phrases formally identical to spatial adjuncts, and with the exception of the clock times they tend to take determiners, either the definite article or the possessives. They can be specified with demonstratives.

A subset of temporal expressions do not fit clearly into this category because they do not usually appear in prepositional phrases. These are words such as *subangngi* 'yesterday', *ammempo* 'tomorrow', *kamma–kammanne* 'now', *sumpaeng* 'earlier', and *nampa* 'then, after that'. These are analysed as temporal adverbs and were discussed in § 5.5.3.

TABLE 42   Clock times

5.00	tette' lima
9.30	tette' sampulo sitangnga
5.50	tette' annang kurang sampulo mani'
12.05	tette' sampulo–anrua la'bi lima mani'

6.1.3.1   Clock Times

Clock times are designated by the word *tette'*, using the Dutch/Indonesian system in which half-hours refer forward, i.e. 'half ten' = 9.30.

(213) *Tette' siapa kamma–kammanne? Tette' limami*
       tette'   siapa   kamma– kamma (a)nne tette' lima =mo =i
       o'clock how.much RDP–   thus   this   o'clock five =PFV =3
       What time is it now? It's already five o'clock.

(214) *tayanga' ri dallekannna balla' ri tette' sampulo*
       tayang =a' ri   dallekang ≡na   balla' ri   tette'   sampulo
       wait   =1 PREP in.front ≡3.POSS house PREP o'clock ten
       wait for me in front of the house at ten o'clock

The Malay loan *jang* (← *jam*) is also used, but it refers to hours of duration rather than absolute time, and behaves like a classifier or measure noun (§ 5.9), in that it follows the numeral (with a linker), and when it occurs in questions it takes the interrogative *piraN–* rather than *siapa* (§ 12.2.2.8):

(215) *tallun–jang kutayammi*
       tallu –N– jang ku= tayang =mo =i
       three –LK– hour 1= wait   =PFV =3
       three hours I've waited for him

6.1.3.2   Time of Day

As well as the more exact clock times, Makasar also has a set of general terms referring to parts of the day, from the more general *allo* and *bangngi* to more specific times, including the Islamic prayer times whose origins are obviously Arabic:

NOUNS AND NOUN PHRASES

TABLE 43   Times of day

day	allo	
evening, night	bangngi	
pre-dawn	subu	← Ar. ṣubḥ
dawn (prayer)	pa'jara'	← Ar. fajr
morning	bari'basa'	
midday	tangngallo	
midday (prayer)	lohoro'	← Ar. ẓuhr
afternoon	karueng	
late afternoon (prayer)	asara'	← Ar. 'aṣr
sunset	(tallang) bayang	
sunset (prayer)	mangngaribi	← Ar. maghrib
evening (prayer)	isa	← Ar. 'isjā'
between 2 and 4 am	danniari	

(216) *tena kutinro ri bangngia napakamma lamu'*
       tena ku= tinro ri   bangngi ≡a   na= pa–   kamma lamu'
       neg   1=   sleep PREP night   ≡DEF 3=   CAUS– thus   mosquito
       I didn't sleep last night because of mosquitoes

(217) *anne karuenga eroka' anjama*
       anne karueng   ≡a   ero' =a' aN– jama
       this afternoon ≡DEF want =1   BV– work
       this afternoon I want to work

6.1.3.3   Days of the Week
The names for days of the week derive from Arabic, probably via Malay, and
co-occur with *allo* 'day', or *bangngi* 'night'; see Table 44.

When a narrative begins with the name of a day it is usually in the frame ⟨ri
allo≡nna DAY≡a | PREP day≡3.POSS DAY≡DEF⟩, as follows:

(218) *Ri allonna Arabayya ku'lampa ri Sungguminasa*
       ri   allo ≡nna   Araba   ≡a   ku= aC– lampa ri
       PREP day ≡3.POSS Wednesday ≡DEF 1=   MV– go   PREP
       Sungguminasa
       Sungguminasa
       On Wednesday I went to Sungguminasa

206   CHAPTER 6

TABLE 44   Days of the week

Sunday	Aha'	← Mal. ahad	← Ar. aḥad
Monday	Sanneng	← Mal. senin	← Ar. ithnain
Tuesday	Salasa	← Mal. selasa	← Ar. thalāthā'
Wednesday	Arabá	← Mal. rabu	← Ar. arba'ā'
Thursday	Kammisi'	← Mal. kamis	← Ar. khamīs
Friday	Jumá'	← Mal. jumat	← Ar. juma'
Saturday	Sattu	← Mal. sabtu	← Ar. sabt

In other contexts the above frame is not required:

(219) *Allo apa anne alloa? Allo Salasa.*
       allo apa   anne allo ≡a   allo Salasa
       day what this   day ≡DEF day Tuesday
       'What day is it today?' 'Tuesday.'

6.1.3.4   Dates

Dates are designated with the word *tanggala'*, which behaves in a similar fashion to *tette'* (§6.1.3.1), e.g.:

(220) *Tanggala' siapa tammu taunnu? Tanggala' ruampulona–angngannang*
       bulang Juni.
       tanggal siapa   tammu   taung ≡nu   tanggal rua –N–
       date   how.many go.around year ≡2f.POSS date   two –LK–
       pulo –aN– annang bulang Juni
       ten –LK– six   month June
       What date is your birthday? The 26th of June.

There was previously a complex system of pre-Islamic dates, generally referring to specific times for planting or fishing. Regrettably information about these is elusive and may be lost. There are also numerous special names for various days taken from the Islamic calendar.

6.1.3.5   Months

The names of the months are taken from either Portuguese or Dutch in the case of the Western calendar, or Arabic in the case of the Islamic lunar calendar. They are shown in Table 45. In all cases they are preceded by the word *bulang* 'month'. For some of the month names both Portuguese- and Dutch-derived

NOUNS AND NOUN PHRASES

TABLE 45 Month names

Western calendar (← Portuguese, Dutch)		Islamic calendar (← Arabic)	
January	Janeru, Januari	Muharram	Muharrang
February	Pareru, Peberiwari	Safar	Sappara'
March	Marusu', Mara'	Rabi al-awwal	Ra'bele'–auala'
April	Parelu	Rabi al-thani	Ra'bele'–ahera'
May	Mayong, Mei	Jumada l-ula	Jumadele'–auala'
June	Juni, June	Jumada l-akhira	Jumadele'–ahera'
July	Juli	Rajab	Ra'ja'
August	Aguttu, Guttusu'	Sha'ban	Sabang
September	Sepetembere', Sitembere'	Ramadan	Ramalang
October	Katuburu'	Shawwal	Sauala'
November	Nombere', Nobere'	Dhu al-Qa'da	Dolokae'da
December	Demberu', Semberu'	Dhu al-Hijja	Doloa'ji

forms exist side-by-side, in which case the Portuguese-derived form is sometimes believed to be indigenous. For both the Western and Islamic calendars the Makasar adapted forms are giving way to Indonesian forms.

It is likely that there was an indigenous method of naming the months as there was in Bugis (*Naagai, Palagunai*, and so forth[4]), but I am not aware of any record of it.

6.1.3.6 Times of Year

There are a variety of ways to describe times of year or seasons. The most fundamental are the terms *bara'* and *timoro'* (optionally preceded by *museng* 'monsoon' or *wattu* 'time'), which refer to the west and east monsoons respectively.[5] *Museng bara'* (also called *wattu bosi* ⟨time rain⟩ 'rainy season') lasts from approximately November until April. The dry season or *museng timoro'* lasts from approximately May until September. The driest time of year, around July, is called *timoro' karring* ⟨east.monsoon dry⟩. There are also innumerable terms referring to planting and harvest times, but for the most part these are no longer known by urban Makasar, with the exception of *museng taipa* 'mango season'.

---

4   These names are painted on a board near the museum of Benteng Somba Opu south of Makassar. At present I am unaware of any published information regarding this topic.

5   Cf. the cardinal directions *wara'* 'north' and *timboro'* 'south' (§ 5.7.2).

208   CHAPTER 6

(221) *Tale'baki nabattu musing baraka.*
       ta=   le'ba'   =i na= battu musing bara' ≡a
       NEG= finished =3 3=   come season west ≡DEF
       Good weather never came (Maros:015)

(222) *la'bui baraka anne taunga*
       la'bu =i bara'   ≡a   *anne taung* ≡a
       long =3 west.monsoon ≡DEF this   year   ≡DEF
       the rainy season is long this year

6.2   Nominal Derivation

Makasar has very productive nominalising derivational morphology which
mainly involves reduplication, the prefixes *pa–* and *ka–*, and the suffix *–ang*,
either in isolation or in combinations which are considered confixes (§ 4.2).
This section examines noun derivation in detail, concentrating on the most
productive processes. Some processes were described in the dictionary but
were not otherwise found in the corpus; where this is the case it has been
noted.

6.2.1   *Reduplication*
Reduplication as a phonological phenomenon was discussed in § 2.3.7 (in essence, disyllabic roots are copied exactly, while trisyllabic (or longer) bases
have the first two syllables copied and then closed with a glottal stop). This
section deals with its effect on nominal bases, the results being nouns with
altered semantics. The most common productive meanings are of diminution
and imitation, for example a toy or NOUN-like object:

tau	person	→	tau–tau	statue, doll
kappala'	ship	→	kappa'–kappala'	toy ship
oto	car	→	oto–oto	toy car
jarang	horse	→	jarang–jarang	model horse, rocking horse
kiti'	duck	→	kiti'–kiti'	rubber ducky

This is quite productive, so even where there is no obvious expectation that a
toy or model thing would exist this is nevertheless the default interpretation,
e.g. *miong–miong* 'toy cat'. Sometimes however the interpretation will be one
of imitation or similarity alone, e.g.:

NOUNS AND NOUN PHRASES

kaluara ant → kalu'–kaluara something like an ant (but not an ant)
lima hand → lima–lima hand-like object (such as a stick with twigs looking like fingers).

In some cases the diminution does not imply imitation at all, but simply a small (or young) NOUN:

baine woman → bai'–baine girl
bura'ne man → bura'–bura'ne boy
balla' house → balla'–balla' hut

In a few other cases reduplication expands from a specific kind of referent to a more general term:

olo' worm → olo'–olo' animal
jangang chicken → jangang–jangang bird

Finally, in some cases reduplication indicates metaphorical extension used in insults, e.g. *tai* 'shit' and *mea* 'piss' when reduplicated and possessed both have the meaning 'descendant, offspring, spawn':

(223) *toanu lagi tangngewa' apapa seng ikauntu mea–meanaya*
     toa ≡*nu*   *lagi* *ta=*   *aN(N)–* *ewa*   *=a'* *apa* *=pa* *seng*
     old ≡2f.POSS even NEG= BV–   oppose =1 what =IPF again
     i–   *kau*   *=ntu* *mea–* *mea* ≡*na*   ≡*a*
     PERS– 2fPRO =that RDP– urine ≡3.POSS ≡DEF
     even your grandfather didn't dare oppose me, what (compared to him) are you who is his piss (C:453)

6.2.2   pa– *Nominal Derivation*

This section covers nouns which are derived with prefixation of *pa–* on various kinds of base, ranging from bare roots to bases which are already derivations themselves.

6.2.2.1   *pa*–ROOT

On the majority of nominal or verbal roots, *pa–* derives a noun: 'person who makes/does/uses X habitually or as occupation'. Some examples are listed in Table 46.

The following sentence is from the Gowa chronicle and lists occupations which were organised under supervisors appointed by Karaeng Tunipalangga (ruled 1546–1565):

TABLE 46   *pa*-ROOT → person who does X

Nominal root

kelong	song	→	pakelong	singer of *kelong*
sinrili'	epic poem	→	pasinrili'	performer of *sinrili'*
jarang	horse	→	pajarang	rider
lukka'	stolen goods	→	palukka'	thief
koko	garden	→	pakoko	gardener
ballo'	palm wine	→	paballo'	maker of *ballo'*
teke'	load (for animal)	→	pateke'	muleteer, driver of pack buffalo, etc.

Verbal root

inung	drink	→	painung	drunkard
balu'	sell	→	pabalu'	seller (e.g. *pabalu' juku'* 'fishmonger')
botoro'	gamble	→	pabotoro'	gambler
cini'	see	→	pacini'	spectator, seer
de'de'	smelt, smith	→	pade'de'	smith (e.g. *pade'de' bassi* 'ironsmith', *pade'de' bulaeng* 'goldsmith')

(224)   *pade'de' bassi. pade'de' bulaeng. panrita balla'. panrita biseang. parau'*
        sappu'. patiri'. pagurinda. palari'. paotere'.

    pa– de'de'   bassi pa– de'de'   bulaeng panrita balla' panrita
    NR– smithing iron NR– smithing gold   expert house expert
    bise   –ang pa– rau'   sappu'   pa– tiri' pa– gurinda
    paddle –NR NR– whittle blowpipe NR– pour NR– grindstone
    pa– lari'   pa– oter =e'
    NR– turn.on.lathe NR– rope =EC
    ... ironsmiths, goldsmiths, builders, shipwrights, blowpipe makers,
    weaponsmiths, sharpeners, turners, ropemakers. (KIT:4.08, ref083)

Adjectives and adverbs are not subject to this process, while basic verbs
(§ 5.3.1.2) with *pa–* do not result in occupation/habitual nominals but instead in
event nominals—these forms should be considered instances of *pa*–INF derivation (see § 6.2.2.4 below). Note that *pa–* derived nouns are often identical in
form to causative verbs, e.g. *painung* 'drunkard', or 'cause/allow to drink', see
§ 8.1.

NOUNS AND NOUN PHRASES 211

TABLE 47   *pa*–VERB BASE → instrument nominal

aC– verbs

barrasa'	→	a'barrasa'	sweep	→	pa'barrasa'	broom
ke'bu'	→	akke'bu'	shut door	→	pakke'bu'	door
keso'	→	akkeso'	scrape	→	pakkeso'	bow (e.g. for violin etc.)
kuta'nang	→	akkuta'nang	ask	→	pakkuta'nang	question
sare	→	assare	give	→	passare	gift

aN(N)– VERBS

balli	→	ammalli	sell	→	pammalli	goods for sale
de'de'	→	ande'de'	forge metal	→	pande'de'	smith's hammer
jo'jo'	→	anjo'jo'	point	→	panjo'jo'	index finger, pointer
pasa'	→	ammasa'	split	→	pammasa'	wedge
pa'rang	→	amma'rang	calm s.t or s.o	→	pamma'rang	s.t soothing (medicine, drink)

6.2.2.2   *pa*–VERB BASE

This refers to the prefixation of *pa*– on infinitival verb forms marked with *aC*–
or *aN(N)*– (§ 7.1). An alternative way of analysing this is as individual morphemes *paC*– and *paN(N)*– (Djirong Basang Daeng Ngewa 1997; Abdul Kadir Manyambeang et al. 1996). I believe an infinitival analysis is a more elegant solution,
as it keeps the morpheme inventory down and avoids the need to explain that
paC– is found on verbs which are normally derived with *aC*–, and *paN(N)*– on
verbs which are normally derived with *aN(N)*–.[6] The derived meaning is (usually) instrumental—'thing with which X is done', as can be seen in Table 47.

A few examples are given in sentences below:

(225)   *apa passarena ri katte?*
      apa *pa*– *aC*– *sare* ≡*na*   *ri*   *katte*
      what NR– MV– give ≡3.POSS PREP 2p
      what was his gift to you?

---

6   There is a very small number of exceptions to this, see Table 50; note also that there *is* a morpheme found on adjectives which is better analysed as *paC*– than the combination *pa*–*aC*– (see
§ 5.4.1.1).

212   CHAPTER 6

(226) *kocci pajanu ara'-ara' panjo'jo'nu*

kocci	*paja*	≡*nu*	*ara'-*	*ara'*	*pa-*	*aN(N)-*	*jo'jo'*
insert.finger	bottom	≡2f.POSS	RDP-	sniff	NR-	BV-	point

≡*nu*
≡2f.POSS

stick it in your arse and then sniff your index finger! (C:338)

6.2.2.3   *pa–* + Derived Verbal Bases

Complex verb bases such as causatives derived from verbs with *pa–* (§ 8.1) or adjectives with *paka–* (§ 8.2) can also host verb prefixes and then undergo instrument nominalisation with *pa–*. Some examples are given below:

(227) *pappaturung*

pa–	*aC–*	*pa–*	*turung*
NR–	MV–	CAUS–	descend

alarm (lit. thing that makes you come down, e.g. a drum to call people down from their houses)

(228) *pappakagassing*

pa–	*aC–*	*paka–*	*gassing*
NR–	MV–	CAUS.ADJ–	strong

tonic, fortifying medicine or drink (lit. thing that makes you strong)

(229) *pappiu'rangi*

pa–	*aC–*	*pi–*	*u'rangi*
NR–	MV–	EXP–	remember

reminder (lit. thing that makes you remember, see § 8.3 on *pi–*)

6.2.2.4   *pa–*VERB BASE: Irregularities and Exceptions

In some cases the meaning of *pa–*VERB BASE forms is slightly different from the examples above, denoting different kinds of concrete or abstract nominal, but the principle can still be seen, as in the examples in Table 48.

Some examples, including a proverb (232):

(230) *nia'mi pa'boyata battu*

nia'	=*mo*	=*i*	*pa–*	*aC–*	*boya*	≡*ta*	*battu*
exist	=PRF	=3	NR–	MV–	search	≡2p.POSS	come

here comes the one you were looking for (C:132)

NOUNS AND NOUN PHRASES
213

TABLE 48 *pa*–VERB BASE → non-instrumental nominal

aC– verbs

kio'	→	akkio'	call	→	pakkio'	a calling (i.e. ceremony)
boya	→	a'boya	search	→	pa'boya	goal of search
mai'	→	a'mai'	breathe	→	pa'mai'	breath, character

aN(N)– VERBS

asseng	→	angngasseng	know	→	pangngasseng	knowledge
ali'	→	angngali'	feel shame	→	pangngali'	shame
u'rangi	→	angngu'rangi	think of	→	pangngu'rangi	memories

(231) *tena pangngassengku ri anjo parakarayya*
tena pa– aN(N)– asseng ≡ku   ri   anjo parakara ≡a
NEG NR– BV–   know ≡1.POSS PREP that matter   ≡DEF
I have no knowledge of that matter (C:35)

(232) *Punna taena pangngali'nu angnginrang–inrangko pangngali' na nia'*
nupake– pake
punna   taena pa– aN(N)– ali'   ≡nu   aN(N)– inrang–
if/when NEG NR– BV–   shame ≡2f.poss BV–   RDP–
inrang =ko pa– aN(N)– ali'   na nia' nu= pake pake
debt   =2f NR– BV–   shame and be 2f= wear wear
If you don't have shame, borrow some shame and wear it (Zainuddin
Hakim 1995:2)

As mentioned earlier, words derived with *pa*– from basic verbs appear to
belong to a subset of *pa*–VERB BASE nominals in which the result means either
the event or process itself, or the time at which it takes place. Cense gives the
examples at Table 49.

However, these derivations appear to be rare—there are no examples with
these kinds of meaning in my corpus, although there are numerous homophonous causative examples such as *panaung* 'drop' (§ 8.1).

In a very few cases the actual infinitive form is derived with a different prefix
from that used in the base for the *pa*–VERB BASE form, as seen in the first two
examples in Table 50, where *aN(N)*– infinitives correspond to *pa–aC*– derived
instruments. There are also some *pa*–VERB BASE forms whose corresponding
prefixed verb is not found, as seen in the final example.

214 CHAPTER 6

TABLE 49 *pa*–VERB BASE on basic verbs

nai'	go up	→	panai'	the (moment of) going up
naung	go down	→	panaung	the going down, the going northwards
mange	go	→	pamange	the going

TABLE 50 *pa*–INF exceptions

tongko'	→	(n/a)	annongko'	cover, close	→	pattongko'	lid
sambila	→	(n/a)	anynyambila	throw	→	passambila	throwing tool
balle	→	k.o plant	*a'balle	(n/a)	→	pa'balle	medicine

6.2.2.5 *pa*⟩VERB BASE⟨*ang*

The confix *pa*⟩⟨*ang* when attached to a prefixed verb base typically results in nouns meaning either 'place for doing X', or less commonly 'time for doing X'. With some bases there are both possibilities, as can be seen in Table 51.

(233) *baji'mi pammentengangku anrinni*
    baji' =mo =i *pa*⟩ *amm*– *enteng* ⟨*ang* ≡*ku*   *anrinni*
    good =PRF =3 NR⟩ MV– stand ⟨NR ≡1.POSS here
    I've got a good spot here (C:206)

(234) *angngalleko pammempoang akkullea nipammempói*
    aN(N)– *alle* =*ko* *pa*⟩ *amm*– *empo* ⟨*ang* *aC*– *kulle* ≡*a*   *ni*–
    BV– take =2f NR⟩ MV– sit ⟨NR MV– can ≡DEF PASS–
    pa– *amm*– *empo* –*i*
    CAUS– MV– sit –APPL
    take a seat where there's a spot (lit. a sitting place that can be sat on, C:204)

(235) *pabattuang toanami nutinro–ija*
    pa⟩ *battu* ⟨*ang* *toana* =*mo* =*i* *nu*= *tinro* *ija*
    NR⟩ come ⟨NR guest =PRF =3 2f= sleep still
    it's already the time for guests to arrive and you're still asleep (C:91)

NOUNS AND NOUN PHRASES

TABLE 51 *pa*⟩VERB BASE⟨*ang* → place or time

aC– verbs

je'ne'	→ a'je'ne'	bathe	→ pa'je'nekang	bathing place, bathtime
pilajara'	→ appilajara'	study	→ pappilajarang	lesson
bunting	→ a'bunting	get married	→ pa'buntingang	wedding

aN(N)– VERBS

pekang	→ ammekang	fish with a hook	→ pammekangang	fishing time/place
polong	→ ammolong	cut	→ pammolongang	abbatoir
sanggara'	→ anynyanggara'	fry, roast	→ panynyanggarang	roasting/frying pan
kanre	→ angnganre	eat	→ pangnganreang	plate

amm– verbs

| enteng | → ammenteng | stand | → pammentengang | standing place, spot |
| empo | → ammempo | sit | → pammempoang | place to sit |

basic verbs

| battu | → battu | come | → pabattuang | place or time s.t/s.o comes |

The base may also be a previously derived form such as a causative, e.g.:

(236) *pappajappáng* (*jangang*)
        pa⟩ aC– pa–   *jappa* ⟨*ang jangang*
        NR⟩ MV– CAUS– walk ⟨NR chicken
        place where fighting cocks are made to walk, so that onlookers can
        examine them before betting

As always, there are some derivations whose meaning does not conform to the usual pattern, see the examples in Table 52.

Pammanakang is perhaps a metaphorical extension from 'place to have children', while *pangnginungang* has a meaning comparable to a *pa*–INF instrumental derivation (6.2.2.2), as does *pakkaraengang* at a stretch (in the sense 'thing (i.e. name) used for *karaeng*-ing'). *Pangngarrukang* is comparable to a *paC*⟩ADJ⟨*ang* derivation (6.2.2.6).

216   CHAPTER 6

TABLE 52   *pa*⟩VERB BASE⟨*ang* exceptions

ana'	→	ammana'	have child	→	pammanakang	family
inung	→	angnginung	drink	→	pangnginungang	drinking vessel
karaeng	→	akkaraeng	be king	→	pakkaraengang	royal name
karru'	→	angngarru'	cry	→	pangngarrukang	crybaby
asseng	→	angngasseng	know	→	pangngassengang	mystical knowledge

TABLE 53   paC⟩ADJ⟨ang → person inclined to be ADJ

garring	sick	→	pa'garringang	sickly person
malla'	scared	→	pa'mallakang	scaredycat
cipuru'	hungry	→	paccipurang	greedyguts
nakku'	longing	→	pa'nakkukang	melancholic
tinro[a]	asleep	→	pattinroang	sleepyhead, narcoleptic

a   *Tinro*, a basic verb (§ 5.3.1.2), behaves like an adjective in this case.

Another rather irregular example is *patturioloang* 'chronicle', which is derived from the lexicalised NP *turiolo* ⟨tu ri olo | person PREP front⟩ 'ancestor', presumably via the verb *atturiolo* 'be an ancestor', thus *patturioloang* 'place or time for ancestors' → 'chronicle'.

Note that there are identical forms derived with the two affixes *pa*– and –*ang* as the combination CAUS––BEN 'do something for someone' (§ 8.1.6).

6.2.2.6   *paC*⟩ADJ⟨*ang*

This confix is attached to an adjectival base to derive a noun meaning 'someone who is easily ADJ, inclined to be ADJ'. The prefix part of the confix should be analysed as *paC*–, rather than the combination of *pa*– and the verb prefix *aC*–, because adjectives do not have infinitival forms and can stand as predicates without further derivation.[7] For example, *pa'larroang* means 's.o prone to anger' (← *larro* 'angry'), but there is no form **a'larro*. Other examples are given in Table 53.

This confix only appears to be used to derive nouns with somewhat negative connotations—although speakers would more or less accept made-up forms

---

7   The alternative to this analysis is to postulate a medial stage of infinive adjective bases, which exist solely as bases for these kinds of derivation and are not in themselves well-formed.

NOUNS AND NOUN PHRASES

TABLE 54 *ka*⟩ADJ⟨*ang* → 'ADJ-ness'

gassing	strong	→	kagassingang	strength
kodi	bad	→	kakodiang	badness
kalumanynyang	rich	→	kakalumanynyangang	wealth
malla'	scared	→	kamallakang	fear

such as *pa'rannuang* '?someone who is easily happy' or *pa'la'birang* '?someone who is easily splendid', it was obvious that these are not idiomatic. An exception is *pa'bajikang* (← *baji'* 'good'), the name of a ceremony which takes place after a wedding and symbolises the beginning of a couple's sexual relationship (Chabot 1996:221).

6.2.3 ka⟩⟨ang *Nominal Derivation*
This section describes the nominalising functions of the *ka*⟩⟨*ang* confix, which is found productively on adjectives, somewhat irregularly on basic verbs, and less commonly on nominal and adverbial bases.

6.2.3.1 *ka*⟩ADJ⟨*ang* → ADJ-ness
Most if not all adjective roots can take the confix *ka*⟩⟨*ang*[8] (it is one of the defining features of the word class), and in most cases it derives abstract nouns meaning roughly 'ADJ-ness', with occasional more concrete or idiomatic exceptions. Some examples are provided in Table 54.

(237) *Siapa todong kagassinganna balla'nu?*
     siapa   *todong ka*⟩ *gassing* ⟨*ang* ≡*na*   *balla'* ≡*nu*
     how.many also   NR⟩ strong ⟨NR ≡3.POSS house ≡2f.POSS
     Anyway, how much strength does your house have? (*Caritana Pung Tedong*) (Zainuddin Hakim 1991:72)

(238) *tenamo assauruki kakodianna balia*
     tena ≡*mo aC–* *sauru'*   ≡*i ka*⟩ *kodi* ⟨*ang* ≡*na*   *bali*
     NEG ≡PRF MV– be.defeated ≡3 NR⟩ bad ⟨NR ≡3.POSS enemy
     ≡*a*
     ≡DEF
     the wickedness of the enemy cannot be surpassed (C:54)

---

8 A reflex of pMP *ka- -en 'abstract nouns (nonlocative)' (Blust 2003).

218 CHAPTER 6

One of the more concrete nominal derivations is *kala'busang* 'end' (← *la'busu* 'finished'):

(239) *Nipauammi ri pakaramulanna sanggenna mange ri kala'busanna.*
   ni–   pau –ang =mo =i ri   pakaramula ≡nna   sangge
   PASS– story –BEN =PRF =3 PREP beginning ≡3.POSS until
   ≡nna   mange ri   ka⟩ la'bus ⟨ang ≡na
   ≡3.POSS go   PREP NR⟩ finished ⟨NR ≡3.POSS
   They were told the story from the beginning right until the end (*Caritana Pung Tedong*) (Zainuddin Hakim 1991:76)

There is also an idiomatic reading of *kalompoang* (← *lompo* 'big'), which as well as the regular meaning 'greatness' (as seen in *kalompoanna Alla Ta'ala* 'the greatness of God'), has the special meaning of 'regalia' or 'ornament'.[9]

It is not always necessary to use *ka⟩⟨ang* to derive a nominal interpretation of an adjective—there are many examples in which possessive affixal clitics appear to be sufficient to derive the same sort of meaning:

(240) *Ikau tojemmi gassingku*
   i   kau   tojeng =mo =i gassing ≡ku
   PERS 2f.sing true   =PRF =3 strong ≡1.POSS
   You are truly my strength (SKT:ref052)

6.2.3.2   *ka⟩RDP–ADJ⟨ang* → 'Peak of ...'
The confix *ka⟩⟨ang* when attached to a reduplicated adjectival base results in a nominal with the meaning 'the peak of ADJ-ness', e.g. *kagassing–gassingang* 'greatest strength' in the following example:

(241) *kagassing–gassingannami*
   ka⟩ gassing– gassing ⟨ang ≡na   =mo =i
   NR⟩ RDP–   strong ⟨NR ≡3.POSS =PRF =3
         strong:peak.of
   he's already at the peak of his strength (C:228)

These are assumed to be nominal derivations not only because of the general nominalising function of *ka⟩⟨ang*, but also because they must be specified with a possessive affixal clitic, and can furthermore occur within a PP, as in (242):

---

9 See e.g. Cummings (2002:55–57) for a discussion of *kalompoang* and their cultural meaning.

NOUNS AND NOUN PHRASES 219

TABLE 55 nouns derived with *ka*⟩BASIC VERB⟨*ang*

nia'	exist	→	kaniakkang	existence, presence
nai'	go up	→	kanaikang	ascent, rise in standing
naung	go down	→	kanaungang	descend, fall in standing
battu	come	→	kabattuang	arrival
mate	die	→	kamateang	death

(242) *ri kabaji'–bajikanna iji gajia nanjama*

ri	ka⟩ baji'– baji' ⟨ang	=na	ija	=i	gaji	≡a	na=	aN–
PREP	NR⟩ RDP– good ⟨NR	≡3.POSS	still	=3	wage	≡DEF	3=	BV–
	<u>good:peak.of</u>							

jama
work
he worked at the time when the wages were still at their best (C:44)

Note that these are not superlative forms (singling out the entity showing the
highest degree of some quality) which are marked by *kaminang* (§ 5.4.1.3.2), but
rather denote that an entity has reached its individual zenith in that particular
quality.

6.2.3.3 *ka*⟩BASIC VERB⟨*ang*

In the majority of cases, basic verbs with *ka*⟩⟨*ang* become nominals meaning
roughly 'the state (or process) of V-ing', such as we see in Table 55.

For example, the following is from the Maros Chronicle (Cummings 2000):

(243) *ka taena nangai kaniakanna Balandaya ri Marusu'.*

| ka | taena | na= | ngai | ka⟩ nia' ⟨ang | =na | Balanda | ≡a | ri |
| BCS | NEG | 3= | love | NR⟩ be ⟨NR | ≡3.POSS | Holland | ≡DEF | PREP |

Marus =u'
Maros =EC
because he did not like the Dutch presence in Maros (Maros:175)

while the following example appears early in the Gowa chronicle (Wolhoff and
Abdurrahim 1959:9):

(244) *ka taniassengai kabattuanna siagáng kamateanna*

| ka | ta= | ni– | asseng | –a | =i | ka⟩ battu ⟨ang | =na |
| because | NEG= | PASS– | know | –SBJV | =3 | NR⟩ come ⟨NR | ≡3.POSS |

iagáng ka⟩   mate   ⟨ang ≡na
with   NR⟩ death ⟨NR ≡3.POSS
because nothing is known of her arrival or her death

As with the adjective examples, there are numerous examples of basic verbs taking nominal readings simply through attachment of a possessive affixal clitic, with no obvious difference in meaning from the *ka⟩⟨ang* derived forms. For example the death of Karaeng Tumapa'risi' Kallonna (in 1546) is described in the Gowa chronicle as follows:

(245)   *matena mate magarringji.*
        mate ≡na   mate ma– garring =ja   =i
        death ≡3.POSS death ADJ– sick   =LIM =3
        his death was just a death of illness (KIT:2.15)

When I asked speakers about the difference between the use of *mate* and *kamateang*, the difference was explained as one of stylistics—*mate* is more stark and effective in this context, whereas *kamateang* sounds more refined but a little euphemistic.

Again, there are some irregular derived meanings. A concrete exception is *katinroang* (← *tinro* 'sleep') which means 'bed'. Other exceptions are derived from *ero'* 'want' and *mange* 'go': *kaerokang* means 'luck, fortune, happenstance' (either good or bad); while *kamangeang* means 'miscarriage'.

(246)   *anne sapedayya kaerokanna kuballi ka battu–mamo nia' i Ali assare doe'*
        anne sapeda ≡a   ka⟩ ero' ⟨ang ≡na   ku= balli ka
        this bicycle ≡DEF NR⟩ want ⟨NR ≡3.POSS 1= buy because
        battu mamo nia' i   Ali aC– sare doe'
        come only exist PERS Ali MV give money
        this bicycle, by good fortune I bought it, only because Ali happened to give me money (C:209)

6.2.3.4   ka⟩N⟨ang

Cense (1979:257) gives some examples of *ka⟩⟨ang* on nominal bases, with the meaning 'the being ...' (*het ... zijn*), e.g. *katuGowáng* 'the being someone from Gowa' (*het iemand van Gowa zijn*). I was unable to confirm these constructions with modern speakers, and the only examples I have in context come from the Maros chronicle (Cummings 2000:18), e.g. *kakaraengang* '*karaeng*-ship, being *karaeng*' in (247):

NOUNS AND NOUN PHRASES 221

(247) *tena– todong nawarisi' ri kakaraenganna ri Marusu'.*
       tena todong na= waris =i' ri   ka⟩ karaeng ⟨ang ≡na
       NEG also   3= inherit =EC PREP NR⟩ king   ⟨NR ≡3.POSS
       ri   Marus
       PREP Maros
       ... he could not inherit the *karaeng*-ship of Maros either.

An idiomatic (and exceptional) token of this derivational process is *katauang* 'genitals' (← *tau* 'person'), comparable to English 'manhood'.

6.2.3.5   ka⟩ADV⟨ang

To my knowledge there is one adverb, the negator *taena*, which can undergo *ka⟩⟨ang* nominalisation to form *kataenáng* 'lack':

(248) *jai kataenangku*
       jai   ka⟩ taena ⟨ang ≡ku
       many NR⟩ NEG   ⟨NR ≡1.POSS
       I'm lacking many things (lit. many are my lacks)

6.2.4   –ang *Nominal Derivation*

A small (but common) group of nouns is derived with just *–ang* from bare roots. In some cases these are noun roots (they have a default nominal interpretation), but the derived *–ang* forms have meanings more obviously related to verbs derived from those nouns, as illustrated in the first two examples of Table 56. In the remaining examples the roots are verb roots (the bare root does not normally appear without verbal morphology), but they appear in this construction without the usual prefix. In essence the derived meanings appear similar to those of the *pa⟩*VERB BASE⟨*ang* instrumental derivations (6.2.2.2).

An exception to this rule is the common word *kanreang* (← *kanre* 'food'), which means something like 'edibility':

(249) *bajiki kanreanna*
       baji' =i kanre –ang ≡na
       good =3 food –NR ≡3.POSS
       it is good to eat (cf. *bajiki kanrena* 'her food is good')

TABLE 56 Nouns derived with *–ang*

dongko'	back	→	dongkokang	vehicle
→a'dongko	ride			
bise	oar	→	biseang	ship
→ammise	row			
kokko'	*	→	kokkokang	bit (for a horse)
→angngokko'	bite			
bule'	*	→	bulekang	sedan chair
→a'bule'	carry on shoulders			
ta'gala'	*	→	ta'gallang	handle
→anna'gala'	grasp			
inung	*	→	inungang	drink
→angnginung	drink			
jama	*	→	jamáng	job
→anjama	work			

Another exception is *battuang* 'meaning' from the basic verb *battu* 'come':

(250) *tena kuassengi battuanna*
       tena ku= asseng =i battu –ang ≡na
       NEG 1= know =3 come –NR ≡3.POSS
       I don't know what it means

6.3   The Noun Phrase

This section discusses the structure of noun phrases, including the ordering of elements within the phrase, and the placement of morphological markers characteristic of noun phrases. Most of the interesting phenomena relate to the placement of the definite marker ≡*a*, whose general properties and functions were discussed in § 4.4.

The minimal NP is simply a noun such as *tau* 'person' or *berang* 'cleaver'. The maximal NP is rather harder to determine as it is unclear to what extent an NP may contain multiple modifiers.

Noun phrase constituents can basically be divided into the following types: heads, specifiers, and modifiers. Heads are nouns by definition, specifiers are demonstratives or numerals, and modifiers may be nouns, adjectives, verbs or relative clauses. There are also morphological determiners in the form of the definite marker ≡*a* and/or the possessive markers.

NOUNS AND NOUN PHRASES

6.3.1 *Specifiers*

Specifiers are the demonstratives and numerals (including classifiers). They can be distinguished from modifiers because they may appear before the head noun. The demonstratives (§ 5.6.3) generally precede the head noun, as in *anjo kongkong≡a* (that dog≡DEF) 'that dog'; the reverse order, *kongkong≡a (a)njo*, is also found but is much less common and is associated with western dialects and Selayarese. Even if the demonstrative appears after the noun, it cannot host the definite marker.

Numerals almost always precede the head noun if it is indefinite, as in (251), (253) and (255), but follow it if it is definite, in which case the numeral hosts the definite marker, as in (252), (254) and (256). In this respect, numerals in definite noun phrases behave like post-head modifiers (see below):

(251)　*assibuntulu'ma' rua tau Parancisi'*
　　　　aC- si- buntulu' =ma =a' rua tau Parancis =i'
　　　　MV– MUT– meet　=PFV =1 two person France　=EC
　　　　I met with two French people

(252)　*assibuntulu'ma' tau ruayya Parancisi'*
　　　　aC- si- buntulu' =ma =a' tau rua ≡a Parancis =i'
　　　　MV– MUT– meet　=PFV =1 person two ≡DEF France　=EC
　　　　I met with the two French people

(253)　*nia' tallu ana'na*
　　　　nia' tallu ana' ≡na
　　　　exist three child ≡3.POSS
　　　　he had three children (lit. there were three of his children)

(254)　*cara'deki anjo ana'na tallua*
　　　　cara'de' =i anjo ana' ≡na tallu ≡a
　　　　clever　=3 that child ≡3.POSS three ≡DEF
　　　　those three children of his are clever

(255)　*nia' ruang–kayu miong anjoreng*
　　　　nia' rua –N kayu miong anjoreng
　　　　exist two –LK CLASS cat　there
　　　　there are two cats there

224   CHAPTER 6

TABLE 57   NPs with modifying nouns

balla' kayu	⟨house wood⟩	wooden house
kayu kaluku	⟨wood coconut⟩	coconut-palm wood
je'ne' golla	⟨water sugar⟩	syrup
kongkong je'ne'	⟨dog water⟩	otter
tau Mangkasara'	⟨person Makassar⟩	Makasar
jangang Balanda	⟨chicken Holland⟩	turkey
badi' Bugisi'	⟨knife Bugis⟩	Bugis knife
bawi romang	⟨pig forest⟩	wild boar
tukang bulaeng	⟨smith gold⟩	goldsmith
je'ne' mata	⟨water eye⟩	tears
lisere' mata	⟨seed eye⟩	pupil
kappala' pepe'	⟨ship fire⟩	steamship

(256)   *kubunoi anjo miong ruayya*
        ku= buno =i anjo miong rua ≡a
        1=   kill =3 that cat   two ≡DEF
        I killed those two cats

6.3.2   *Modifiers*

Modifying elements always follow the head noun—they may be of various
types:

– modifying nouns
– adjectives, such as *balla' garring* ⟨house sick⟩ 'hospital'; *juku' lompo* ⟨fish big⟩
  'big fish'
– modifying verbs
– possessors
– relative clauses.

Relative clauses will be discussed in detail in § 6.3.3, and the structure of possessives was discussed in § 4.4.2; the other types will be discussed briefly here.

6.3.2.1   Modifying Nouns

Modifying nouns always follow the head noun. They can have a range of meanings, giving detail about the head noun in terms of its material, origin, location,
habitat, occupation, type, and so forth. Some examples are given in Table 57.

   When NPs with modifying nouns are marked for definiteness or possession,
the marker is attached at the end (i.e. the right edge) of the NP, thus *balla'
kayu≡a* 'the wooden house', *je'ne' mata≡ngku* 'my tears'.

NOUNS AND NOUN PHRASES · 225

NPs may contain more than one modifying noun—or more accurately, the modifying noun may itself be an NP with a modifying noun, e.g. *kadera kayu kaluku* ⟨chair wood coconut⟩ 'chair made of coconut wood'. However, modifying nouns may not be conjoined to denote different types of head noun, e.g. **tukang bulaeng na kayu* ⟨smith gold and wood⟩—instead they must be separate NPs, e.g. *tukang bulaeng na tukang kayu* 'goldsmiths and carpenters'.

6.3.2.2   Adjectives

As attributive modifiers adjectives also always follow the head noun, e.g. *juku' lompo* ⟨fish big⟩ 'big fish'; *balla' garring* ⟨house sick⟩ 'hospital'. Adjectival modifiers such as the intensifier *sanna'* may precede the adjective, or the intensifier *dudu* may follow it e.g. *songko' sanna' baji'* ⟨hat very good⟩ 'a really good hat'; *tau pongoro'–dudu* ⟨person crazy very⟩ 'a very crazy person'. Affixal enclitics which apply to the whole phrase are then attached at the right edge, e.g. *miong le'lengku* ⟨cat black≡1.POSS⟩ 'my black cat'; *anjo tau garring–dudua* ⟨that person sick very≡DEF⟩ 'that very sick person'.

In indefinite NPs adjectives may be conjoined with *na*, e.g. *moncong lompo na tinggi* ⟨mountain big and tall⟩ 'a big and tall mountain'; *tau garring na pongoro'* ⟨person sick and mad⟩ 'a sick and mad person'. However, in definite NPs conjoined adjectives are dispreferred. They do not occur in my corpus, and though they can be elicited, there is confusion about where the definite marker should go in these cases, i.e. it is unclear whether ≡*a* should behave like a 2P clitic as it does in relative clauses (see § 6.3.3) and be placed on the first adjective, e.g. *tau garring≡a na pongoro'*; or at the end of the NP, e.g. *tau garring na pongorok≡a* 'the sick and mad person'.

6.3.2.3   Modifying Verbs

These are verbs used attributively to describe what the head noun does, such as *kappala' anri'ba'* ⟨ship fly⟩ 'airplane'; *bembe battu* ⟨goat come⟩ 'a goat which just wandered in', *tau tinro* ⟨person sleep⟩ 'sleeping person'. Affixal clitics attach to the right edge, e.g. *tedong angnganrea* ⟨buffalo BV–eat≡DEF⟩ 'the eating buffalo'.

There is a fuzzy boundary between NPs with modifying verbs and relative clauses. For the sake of analysis I have assumed that NPs with a single verb marking an attribute contain modifying verbs, while anything more complex than that is a relative clause, especially if it contains any cross-referencing clitic pronouns.

226   CHAPTER 6

6.3.3 *Relative Clauses*

Relative clauses are clausal modifiers of nominal heads. Makasar does not have
a dedicated relative clause marker, unlike Indonesian *yang* and Selayarese and
Konjo *tu* and *nu* (see § 5.6.5), but instead the clausal modifier simply follows
the head.

6.3.3.1   Relative Clauses on Definite Core Arguments

In the the vast majority of examples the NP is definite, and there is a distinctive
use of the definite affixal clitic ≡*a*, which attaches to the verb inside the relative
clause, as follows:

(257)   *tau battua ri Jepang*
     tau   battu ≡a   ri   Jepang
     person come ≡DEF PREP Japan
     the person who came from Japan (head = S)

(258)   *tau nabunoa sorodadu*
     tau   na= buno ≡a   sorodadu
     person 3= kill ≡DEF soldier
     the person killed by a soldier (head = P)

(259)   *sorodadu ammunoa tau*
     sorodadu aN(N)– buno ≡a   tau
     soldier BV–   kill ≡DEF person
     the soldier who killed a person (head = A)

If P in an A-headed relative clause is indefinite, as exemplified in (259), it is not
cross-referenced within the relative clause by an =ABS clitic pronoun (§ 11.2).
However, if P is definite, as exemplified in (260), it is cross-referenced, as indicated by the enclitic =*i after* the definite marker. The verb is also marked with
the Actor Focus prefix *aN*– (§ 7.2).

(260)   *sorodadu ambunoai taua*
     sorodadu aN– buno ≡a   =i tau   ≡a
     soldier   AF– kill ≡DEF =3 person ≡DEF
     the soldier who killed the person

Relative clauses which host the 1st person enclitic =*a'* have no overt realisation
of the definite marker due to vowel degemination (§ 2.3.1). Compare (261) and
(262):

NOUNS AND NOUN PHRASES

(261)   *tau ansarea' baju*
       tau   *aN– sare* (≡*a*)   =*a' baju*
       person AF– give (≡DEF) =1 shirt
       the person who gave me a shirt

(262)   *tau ansareako baju*
       tau   *aN– sare* ≡*a*   =*ko baju*
       person AF– give ≡DEF =2f shirt
       the person who gave you a shirt

Sentences (263) and (264) relative clauses modifying A and P respectively within simple matrix clauses.

(263)   *tau ambunoai tedonga ammotere'mi*
       tau   *aN– buno* ≡*a*   =*i tedong* ≡*a*   *amm– oter*   =*e'* =*mo*
       person AF– kill ≡DEF =3 buffalo ≡DEF MV–   return =EC =PFV
       =*i*
       =3
       the man who killed the buffalo went home

(264)   *tedong nabunoa i Baso' lompoi*
       tedong na= buno ≡*a*   *i*   *Baso' lompo* =*i*
       buffalo 3= kill ≡DEF PERS Baso' big   =3
       the buffalo that Baso' killed was big

Note that although NPs containing relative clauses appear in pre-predicate position (i.e. in Focus position, see §11.9), nevertheless they are cross-referenced with clitic pronouns in the matrix clause as shown by =*i* on *lompo* in (264), unlike simple NPs in the same position (e.g. *tedonna lompo* ⟨tedong ≡na lompo | buffalo ≡3.POSS big⟩ 'his buffalo is big').

As in main clauses, a definite secondary object is licensed by the use of the benefactive suffix *–ang*, and the definite marker is placed between it and the enclitic pronoun:

(265)   *tau ansareangako anjo baju*
       tau   *aN– sare –ang* ≡*a*   =*ko anjo baju*
       person AF– give –BEN ≡DEF =2f that shirt
       the person who gave you that shirt

228   CHAPTER 6

Relative clauses may themselves contain verbal complements; the following shows an Undergoer-headed relative clause with an infinitival complement *a'bicara* 'speak', the whole modified by a temporal adverb:

(266)   *bura'ne kuagánga a'bicara sumpaeng nakana mae ri nakke nia' bawi*
        romang anrinni punna bangngi
        bura'ne ku= agáng   ≡a   aC– bicara sumpaeng na= kana
        man   1=   accompany ≡DEF MV– speak   earlier   3=   word
        mae   ri   nakke nia' bawi romang anrinni punna   bangngi
        toward PREP 1PRO be   pig   forest here   if/when night
        the man I talked with earlier said to me there are wild pigs here at night

6.3.3.2   Relative Clauses on Indefinite Core Arguments

There are some cases of RCs modifying indefinite heads, such as in the following examples with relatives on indefinite S, P and A respectively:

(267)   *tau battu ri Jepang*
        tau   battu ri   Jepang
        person come   PREP Japan
        a person who came from Japan

(268)   *tau nabuno sorodadu*
        tau   na= buno sorodadu
        person 3=   kill soldier
        a person killed by a soldier

(269)   *sorodadu ammuno tau*
        sorodadu aN(N)– buno tau
        soldier   BV–   kill person
        a soldier who killed a person

However, these are extremely rare—in my corpus they only arise through elicitation and there are also some examples in Cense's grammar notes (KITLV HISDOC Or545.43). There may be discourse-related reasons for this rarity, on the assumption that generally an entity which is discourse-prominent enough to have a relative clause attached to it, is also prominent enough to be considered definite. Alternatively these constructions might be avoided because they are formally identical to clauses containing focused indefinite arguments (§11.9.1)[10] and can legitimately be understood as independent clauses with the

---

10   Relative clauses are constructed like focused clauses in that they always follow the head

NOUNS AND NOUN PHRASES

following meanings: (267) *a person* came from Japan, (269) *a soldier* killed a person, (268) *someone* was killed by a soldier.

6.3.3.3 Relative Clause on Goal

A goal (normally an oblique in a prepositional phrase) may become the head of a relative clause, but the preposition is omitted and the locative applicative *–i* is used (see §9.1.2). It does not appear possible to relativise on a source.

(270) *sikola namangéia agangku bajiki*
  sikola na= mange –i   ≡a   agang ≡ku   baji' =i
  school 3= go   –APPL ≡DEF friend ≡1.POSS good =3
  the school my friend goes to is good (cf. *mangei agangku ri sikola* 'my friend goes to school')

(271) *tau kubuntúlia anne karuénga napauanga' nia' bawi romang anrinni*
  punna bangngi
  tau   ku= buntul –i   ≡a   anne karuéng –a   na= pau
  person 1= find   –APPL ≡DEF this afternoon ≡DEF 3= story
  –ang =a' nia' bawi romang anrinni punna   bangngi
  –BEN =1 be pig forest here   if/when night
  the person I met this afternoon, he told me there are wild pigs here at night (cf. *a'buntuluka' ri tau* 'I met a person')

6.3.3.4 Relative Clause on Instrument

An instrument may be relativised upon in two ways. One is to use the suffix *–ang* in its function of licensing an instrument (§9.2.1.4):

(272) *sele' nibunoangai tarangi*
  sele' ni–   buno –ang ≡a   =i tarang =i
  kris PASS– kill –BEN ≡DEF =3 sharp =3
  the kris he was killed with was sharp

Alternatively instruments may simply be expressed by using the verb *pake* 'use', with a VP complement:

---

noun (equivalent to the focused argument), which is obligatorily gapped (in the same way that a focused argument is not cross-referenced).

230   CHAPTER 6

(273) *lading kupakea ammolong juku' lading pokkolo'*
lading ku= pake ≡a   aN(N)– polong juku' lading pokkol =o'
knife 1= wear ≡DEF BV–   cut   fish knife blunt =EC
the knife that I used to cut fish was a blunt knife

6.3.3.5   Headless Relative Clauses

Headless relative clauses are relatively rare—instead *anu* 'thing', *tau* 'person', or a demonstrative will usually act as head.

(274) *anjo/anu kukanrea juku'*
anjo/anu ku= kanre ≡a   juku'
DIST/thing 1= eat   ≡DEF fish
that which I ate was fish

That said, there are occasional examples of headless relatives, such as the following from the Gowa Chronicle:

(275) *ma'gauka. ri Marusu'. nikana. Patanna Langkana.*
maC– gau' ≡a   ri   Marus =u' ni–   kana pata ≡nna
MV–   action ≡REL PREP Maros =EC PASS– word owner ≡3.POSS
langkana
palace
(He) who ruled in Maros was called Patanna Langkana (KIT:1.12)

or this one from Cense's grammar notes, which again uses *–i* to denote a goal:

(276) *tanaasseng lanajappáia*
ta=   na= asseng la= na= jappa –i   ≡a
NEG= 3= know FUT= 3= walk –APPL ≡DEF
he doesn't know (where) he's going (Or545.48)

CHAPTER 7

Basic Clause Structure

7.1   Word Order

A discussion of word order in Makasar needs to distinguish between the order of full NPs denoting arguments with respect to the predicate head, and the order of cross-referencing clitic pronouns on the predicate itself. Both show some variation for reasons which will be the subject of detailed discussion (§ 7.2.1, § 7.2.2, § 12.2), but are summarised very briefly below.

The order of core argument NPs in relation to a predicate head is fairly free, and it is unclear that there is in fact a 'basic' order. It has been argued that Selayarese has VPA (VOS) as basic order (Finer 1997b; Hasan Basri 1999), and that Konjo has VAP (VSO) (Friberg 1988; 1996), but I am hesitant to make either claim for Makasar, based on the fact that neither of these orders shows up in my entire corpus of actual non-elicited texts.[1] They can certainly be elicited, are quite acceptable (and thus need to be accounted for), but rarely if ever are produced. This is because full NPs representing core arguments are only used to introduce, disambiguate, or emphasise those arguments; and within the context of a narrative it is unlikely that both arguments of a transitive clause would need to be introduced, disambiguated, or emphasised at the same time (and in any case, an argument being emphasised will most likely appear in the pre-predicate focus position, see § 12.2). The clitic pronouns do the actual work of marking grammatical functions on the predicate.[2]

That said, in Makasar VPA seems to be the most likely ordering when simple, context-free transitive clauses are elicited, and is likewise the order preferred when such clauses are interpreted by hearers—all else being equal. However pragmatics will readily override an anomalous VPA interpretation and suggest VAP instead. For example, the Makasar translation of the English sentence 'the buffalo eats the grass' will most likely be given as:

---

1   Friberg acknowledges that 'a clause with VSO word order is rarely found in texts or conversations' (Friberg 1996:140).
2   This makes it tempting to analyse full NPs of core arguments as adjuncts, as Klamer does for the Kambera language, spoken on Sumba (Klamer 1998). See § 11.2.3 for more discussion of this.

© KONINKLIJKE BRILL NV, LEIDEN, 2020 | DOI:10.1163/9789004412668_008

232 CHAPTER 7

(277) *Nakanrei rukuka tedonga*
    na= kanre =i ruku' ≡a   tedong ≡a
    3= eat   =3 grass ≡DEF buffalo ≡DEF
    The buffalo eats the grass

But switching the order of the NPs (*nakanrei tedonga rukuka*) will in no way result in the interpretation 'the grass is eating the buffalo'. If one is determined to force this meaning (in order to warn of the dangers of carnivorous grass), the focus position must be used. This may be either Actor focus (*rukuka angkanrei tedonga*), or Undergoer focus (*tedonga nakanre rukuka*). See §12.2 for details of this.

When A and P are of equal animacy and there is no prior information about the nature of their participation in an event, clauses are genuinely ambiguous:

(278) *Naciniki iAli iUdin*
    na= cini' =i i   Ali i   Udin
    3= see =3 PERS Ali PERS Udn
    Udin saw Ali / Ali saw Udin

The preference for VPA is slim. When there are ambiguous clauses such as the one above, most speakers will proffer the VPA interpretation first most of the time, but will always add that it could well be interpreted the other way around.

It would be a mistake, however, to analyse Makasar as predominantly non-configurational, since configuration plays an important role in other types of clause, especially for marking information structure, as opposed to argument structure. For example, there is a pre-predicate **focus** position (§12.2) which is extensively used for both A and P, thus AVP and PVA are also commonly found. In addition to focus, there is a left-dislocated **topic** position (§12.2.2), which means that A,PV and P,AV are also possible.

7.2 Clitic Pronouns

Clitic pronouns cross-reference definite core arguments on the predicate (see §11.3 for discussion of core argument status, and §7.2.4 for discussion of definiteness and cross-reference). In simple clauses the clitic pronouns pattern according to an ergative/absolutive system—the enclitic which markes S in an intransitive clause also marks P in a transitive clause (absolutive), while A is marked with a proclitic (ergative). P[INDEF] is not cross-referenced, but A

BASIC CLAUSE STRUCTURE

TABLE 58 Clitics and free NP placement

Focus	erg=	Prefix	HEAD	=abs	NP 1	NP 2	Gloss
		Intransitive					
		aC–	lampa	=i (S)	miong (S[INDEF])		?a cat goes
		aC–	lampa	=i (S)	i Ali (S)		Ali goes
miong (S[INDEF])		aC–	lampa				a cat goes
i Ali (S)		aC–	lampa				Ali goes
		Semi-transitive					
		aN(N)–	kanre	=i (S[A])	miong (A[INDEF])	juku' (P[INDEF])	cats eat fish
		aN(N)–	kanre	=i (S[A])	i Ali (S[A])	unti (P[INDEF])	Ali eats bananas
miong (A[indef])		aN(N)–	kanre		juku' (P[INDEF])		a cat eats fish
i Ali (A)		aN(N)–	kanre		unti (P[INDEF])		Ali eats bananas
		Transitive					
	na= (A)		kanre	=i (P)	i Ali (A)	untiku (P)	Ali eats my banana
i Ali (A)		aN–	kanre	=i (P)	untiku (P)		Ali eats my banana
untiku (P)	na= (A)		kanre		i Ali (A)		Ali eats my banana
juku' (P[INDEF])	na= (A)		kanre		miong (A[INDEF])		cats eat fish
unti (P[INDEF])	na= (A)		kanre		i Ali (A)		Ali eats bananas
	na= (A)		kokko'	=i (P)	miongku (A)	mionnu (P)	my cat bit your cat
	na= (A)		kokko'	=i (P)	miongku (P)	mionnu (A)	your cat bit my cat
miongku (A)		aN–	kokko'	=i (P)	mionnu (A)		my cat bit your cat
mionnu (P)	na= (A)		kokko'		miongku (A)		my cat bit your cat

is cross-referenced whether definite or not,[3] as is S in the majority of cases. Furthermore, focused arguments are not cross-referenced, whereas topicalised arguments are (see §12.2.2).

Table 58 below summarises the permutations of clitic and core argument NP placement in simple verbal clauses. (Because topicalised arguments are external to the clause, they are not included).

Not all permutations are equally acceptable. While it is difficult to judge on context-free examples, in Table 58 I have attempted to roughly represents degrees of acceptability with shading. Light shading shows that it is more or less acceptable, but odd, because of ambiguity which could be avoided by use of

---

3 Clauses with indefinite A can be elicited, but are unnatural.

the focus position, passivisation, or through a more developed context. Darker shading shows constructions which are acceptable in some circumstances, but generally dispreferred in discourse because S and especially A should be definite.[4] Note that in clauses with P^{INDEF}, A is cross-referenced with an =ABS enclitic if P^{INDEF} is a postverbal NP, but by an ERG= proclitic if P^{INDEF} is a focused NP. In other words, the morphosyntactic contrast between semi-transitive and transitive clauses is lost if P^{INDEF} is focused.

7.2.1 2P Behaviour

The =ABS enclitic tends to appear in second position (the Wackernagel position, or 2P). The host may be of various categories; for example, in (279) it is a verb derived from the noun *sikola* 'school', in (280) it is a deictic adverb, in (281) it is a locative prepositional adjunct, in (282) it is a quantified nominal expressing duration, in (283) an adverbial derived numeral 'twice', and in (284) an adjective modifying the verb:

(279) *Assikolai anjoreng ri Balanda*
     aC– sikola =i anjoreng ri   Balanda
     MV– school =3 there   PREP Holland
     He studies there in Holland

(280) *Anjorengi ri Balanda assikola*
     anjoreng =i ri   Balanda aC– sikola
     there   =3 PREP Holland MV– study
     There in Holland he studies

(281) *Ri Balandai assikola*
     ri   Balanda =i aC– sikola
     PREP Holland =3 MV– study
     In Holland he studies

(282) *Tallun–taungi ammantang anjoreng*
     tallu –N– taung =i amm– antang anjoreng
     three –LK– year =3 MV–   stay   there
     He's been there three years

---

4 It is possible that indefinite S (as in *a'lampa=i miong* 'cats go') is cross-referenced because *a'lampa miong* could in fact equally be interpreted as containing a manner modifier: 'go in a cat-like manner'.

BASIC CLAUSE STRUCTURE 235

(283) *Pinruama' mange anjoreng*
piN– rua =mo =a' mange anjoreng
MULT– two =PFV =1 go   there
I've gone there twice

(284) *Salloa' attayang*
sallo =a' aC– tayang
long =1 MV– wait
I waited a long time

This 2P phenomenon is also found in transitive clauses, in which case the =ABS enclitic and the ERG= proclitic may be found on different words, if the verb is not the first constituent. Compare (285), where the verb hosts both, with (286), in which the =ABS enclitic indexing *sura'nu* appears on the secondary verb *le'ba'*:

(285) *Kubacai sura'nu*
ku= baca =i sura' ≡nu
1= read =3 letter ≡2f.POSS
I read your letter

(286) *Le'baki kubaca sura'nu*
le'ba'   =i ku= baca sura' ≡nu
finished =3 1=   read letter ≡2f.POSS
I already read your letter

Other examples are (287), in which =ABS is hosted by a (comparativised) deictic adverb, and (288) and (289), in both of which it is hosted by adjectives modifying verbs:

(287) *Anjorengampi nucini'*
anjoreng –ang   =pa =i nu= cini'
there   –COMPR =IPF =3 2f= see
You'll see it further on

(288) *Salloko kutayang*
sallo =ko ku= tayang
long =2f 1= wait
I waited a long time for you

236   CHAPTER 7

(289) *Bajiki' kupasialle siagáng i Anu*
       baji' =ki' ku= pa–   si–   alle siagáng i   anu
       good   =2p   1=   CAUS– MUT– take with   PERS thingy
       It's good that I let you marry with whatshisname (Cgn:3)

Example (288) may also be compared with the intransitive counterpart seen
earlier in (284).

   Not all types of clause-initial element count for the purposes of defining
'second position'. For example, for example prepositional adjuncts containing
temporal expressions do not tend to host an =ABS enclitic:

(290) *Ri subangngi ammekanga' juku'*
       ri   subangngi aN(N)– pekang =a' juku'
       PREP   yesterday   BV–   hook   =1   fish
       Yesterday I was fishing

Additionally, some pre-verbal elements do seem to draw 2P clitics to them, but
may not host enclitics directly, in which case 2P is manifested by ERG= forms
rather than =ABS. This is referred to as clitic fronting and is discussed below.

7.2.2   Clitic Fronting

Although clitics are normally patterned according to an ergative/absolutive
system, in several environments S is cross-referenced by an ERG= proclitic
instead of the expected =ABS enclitic. One such environment is following the
free negator *t(a)ena* (§12.3.2). For example:

(291) *Tena kutinro*
       tena ku= tinro
       NEG   1=   sleep
       I don't/didn't sleep

(292) *Tena na'lampa*
       tena na= aC– lampa
       NEG   3=   MV– go
       He doesn't/didn't go

Compare the positive examples *tinroa'* ⟨sleep=1⟩; *a'lampai* ⟨MV–go=3⟩.
   The same pattern can be seen with semi-transitive clauses, e.g.:

BASIC CLAUSE STRUCTURE 237

(293) *Tena nungngerang jarang*
       tena nu= aN(N)– erang jarang
       NEG 2f= BV–   bring horse
       You didn't bring a horse (Cgn:4)

(294) *Tena kungnganre duriang*
       tena ku= aN(N)– kanre duriang
       NEG 1= BV–   eat   durian
       I don't eat durian

Examples such as (292), (293) and (294) show proclitics and verb prefixes co-occurring. Clitic fronting is the main circumstance in which this will happen, and note that the vowel of the prefix is deleted as discussed in § 2.3.5.

At first glance this could be taken to be a split-S phenomenon triggered by negation, however it seems more likely that it is another manifestation of the =ABS enclitic being drawn to 2nd position as described above. Clearly there is a constraint against certain elements (such as the negator) hosting enclitics, and so the clitic spells out as an ERG= proclitic.[5]

In transitive clauses where both clitic slots are filled the presence of one of these preverbal elements can result in two major possibilities: either the clitics can stay in their original place, or more interestingly the P can be represented by a proclitic from the A series (!) placed before the regular A proclitic, such as the form *ki=* in (297) which represents the P despite being in proclitic position. Thus both (296) and (297) are possible negations of (295):

(295) *Kubuntulukki'*
       ku= buntul =u' =ki'
       1= meet   =EC =2p
       I met you

(296) *Tena kubuntulukki'*
       tena ku= buntul =u' =ki'
       NEG 1= meet   =EC =2p
       I didn't meet you

---

5 It should be noted here that passive clauses are not subject to clitic fronting (see § 7.3).

238   CHAPTER 7

(297)   *Tena kikubuntulu'*
    tena ki= ku= buntul =u'
    NEG 2p= 1= meet =EC
    I didn't meet you

Finally, for some speakers the following is possible, where the absolutive enclitic is in fact hosted by the negator itself:

(298)   *Taenaki' kubuntulu'*
    tena =ki' ku= buntul =u'
    NEG =2p 1= meet =EC
    I didn't meet you (C:145)

However, the last option is not universally permissible. It is at the very least held to be characteristic of southern/eastern dialects or Selayarese.[6]

In most of these constructions the complementiser *na* may optionally appear, with no change to the ordering possibilities of the other elements:

(299)   *Tena (na) kubuntulukki'*
    tena (na)   ku= buntul =u' =ki'
    NEG (COMP) 1= meet =EC =2p
    I didn't meet you

(300)   *Tena (na) kikubuntulu'*
    tena (na)   ki= ku= buntul =u'
    NEG (COMP) 2p= 1= meet =EC
    I didn't meet you

There are several preverbal elements which are associated with this phenomenon; others include discourse connectives such as *apaji* 'what but ...' *naia* 'and it's ...', the conjunction and complementiser *na*, and preposed temporal adjuncts in general:[7]

(301)   *Apaji na kusulu'mo ri balla'nu na nukucini'*
    apa =ja =i na   ku= sulu' =mo ri   balla' ≡nu   na
    what =LIM =3 COMP 1= exit =PFV PREP house ≡2f,POSS and

---

6 Selayarese has no restriction on the negator (or other preverbal elements) hosting enclitics.
7 Preposed locative constructions may host the =ABS enclitic themselves, so do not trigger clitic fronting.

BASIC CLAUSE STRUCTURE 239

> *nu= ku= cini'*
> 2f= 1= see
> I had only just left your house when I saw you

(302) *Se're taung namange Karaenga ri Kuri assingara' sima.*
se're taung na= mange karaeng ≡a ri Kuri aC– singar
one year 3= go karaeng ≡DEF PREP Kuri MV– collect.debt
=a' sima
=EC tax
One year the Karaeng [I Malalakang Daeng Pawello] went to Kuri to collect taxes (Maros:244)

(303) *16.VI.1673 kinapilarí karaeng Tu–ammenang–ri–lampana i ba'le ri Sambawa*
16.VI.1673 ki= na= pi– lari –i karaeng tu amm– enang
16/6/1673 1pl= 3= EXP– run –APPL karaeng person MV– lie
ri lampa ≡na i ba'le ri Sambawa
PREP go ≡3.POSS PREP across PREP Sumbawa
On the 16/6/1673 Karaeng Tu–ammenang–ri–lampana left us to go across (the sea) to Sumbawa (C:380)

Sometimes even clauses not containing any of these elements (but still constituting a temporal expression) may trigger this phenomenon:

(304) *Numaloko ri dallekang ballaku kunucini' ammempo ri tontonganga*
numalo =ko ri dallekang balla' ≡ku ku= nu= cini' amm–
pass.by =2f PREP front house ≡1.POSS 1= 2f= see MV–
empo ri tontongang ≡a
sit PREP window ≡DEF
You came in front of my house and you saw me sitting in the window

The optional presence of the complementiser/conjunction *na* seems to be the clue to what is common to the environments which trigger clitic fronting—put informally, it appears that an enclitic cannot adjoin to *na*, nor to a node where *na* may occur, even if *na* is not in fact present. This explanation is further strengthened by the probability that the negator *taena* in fact contains *na*, albeit incorporated in a lexicalised construction ⟨ta=ia na | NEG=3PRO COMP⟩.

As a last comment on this phenomenon I will add that in the speech of one of my consultants in particular there is yet another configuration associated with the complementiser/conjunction *na*—namely, attaching a proclitic form *after na* (preceding and separate from a prefixed verb), in effect *en*cliticising the proclitic onto the conjunction, as seen in (305) and (306):

(305) *Ri allonna arabaia tette' sampulo–asse're **naku** ... a'lampa ammekang ri Bulukumba.*

ri	allo	≡nna	arabaia	tette'	sampulo	aN–	se're	**na**
PREP	day	≡3.POSS	Wednesday	o'clock	ten	LK–	one	COMP

=**ku**=	aC–	lampa	aN(N)–	pekang	ri	Bulukumba
=1=	MV–	go	BV–	hook	PREP	Bulukumba

On Wednesday at 11 o'clock I went fishing at Bulukumba

(306) *... ammotere'ma' mange ri biseanga **naku** ... a'lampamo mange ri Tanjung Bira ri anjo tampa' kupammantang nia'.*

amm–	oter	=e'	=mo	=a'	mange	ri	bise	–ang	≡a	**na**
MV–	return	=EC	=PFV	=1	go	PREP	paddle	–NR	≡DEF	**and**

=**ku**=	aC–	lampa	=mo	mange	ri	Tanjung	Bira	ri	anjo
=1=	MV–	go	=PFV	go	PREP	peninsula	Bira	PREP	that

tampa'	ku=	pa–	amm–	antang	nia'
place	1=	NR–	MV–	stay	exist

... we went back to the boat and went to Tanjung Bira to the place we were staying.

Note that unlike examples (292), (293) and (294) above, the vowel of the prefix remains (we would normally expect to see *na ku'lampa*), and there is a pause between the proclitic form and the verb, where this would not typically be allowed. Whether this is a generational change (the speaker is younger than most of my other consultants), dialectal (he is from Bontonompo, 20 km south of Makassar), ideolectal, or merely a repeated speech error, requires further investigation. See Appendix C for the complete text.

7.2.3 *Agreement or Cross-Reference?*

The status of clitic pronouns such as these (and indeed the entire phenomenon of pronominal affixes) is somewhat controversial or 'problematic, since some treat them as agreement, while others claim they are pronouns' (Corbett 2003: 168). For example, Finer (e.g. 1996) describes the Makasar and Selayarese phenomenon as **verbal agreement** (but given that the clitics are not restricted to appearing on verbs this term does not seem especially apt); while Klamer has analysed a similar phenomenon in Kambera (Sumba) as being one of **cross-reference**:

BASIC CLAUSE STRUCTURE 241

> *Agreement* is the indexing of one or two clause actants on the head in a generally dependent-marking language. So-called 'head-marking' languages have rich pronominal marking on the head of the clause, the verb, and poor case marking on the NPs. In such languages *crossreference* is used to mark the arguments on the verb, where the verb (plus its pronominal markers) itself normally constitutes a complete sentence and the full NPs are included only for emphasis, focus, disambiguation, etc. ... They (the NPs) are in essence optional, the verb plus the pronominal markers already constituting a complete clause. In crossreference languages the relation between the head and its dependent is normally unilateral: the dependent NP requires the pronominal marker on the head, whereas the head plus the pronominal marker can occur without the dependent NP. In Kambera crossreference is used as the means to mark verbal arguments on the verb. The pronominal clitics are markers of crossreference and not of agreement.
>
> KLAMER 1998:61

Klamer's position is probably too strong, as cross-reference can arguably be considered an agreement phenomenon according to the set of features laid out in Corbett (2003). At the very least, the clitic pronouns agree with antecedents beyond the clause in the same way that other pronouns do—this is the base level justification for including pronominal elements in the Surrey Agreement Database (Corbett 2003:183).

However, ultimately I feel that describing the Makasar case as agreement is somewhat misleading, as it is clearly a far-from-canonical example of the phenomenon, and is well on the pronominal side of the agreement—pronoun scale. Applying some of the relevant heuristics given by Corbett makes this clear.

Case roles: only the clitic pronouns carry any information about case roles, grammatical relations and argument structure. Full NPs (including free pronouns) do not signal anything about the grammatical relations of their referents through either word order[8] or case marking

Referentiality: clitic pronouns overwhelmingly cross-reference definite, identifiable antecedents

Complementary distribution: full NPs are generally optional if the clitic pronouns will suffice for identification. More cogently, clitic pronouns and free

---

8 A partial exception to this is the use of the pre-predicate Focus position (§11.9), but even in these constructions it is the clitic pronouns which identify the grammatical function of the focused argument.

242   CHAPTER 7

pronouns do not normally co-occur because they are semantically equivalent, so a sentence such as (307) is extremely questionable:[9]

(307)   ??*kucinikko inakke ikau*
        ku= cini' =ko inakke ikau
        1=   see =2f 1PRO 2fPRO
        ??I see you

Free pronouns may appear in the pre-predicate Focus slot (see §12.2), but in that case they are not cross-referenced, as in (308) and (309):

(308)   *ikau kucini'*
        ikau   ku= cini'
        2fPRO 1=   see
        I see *you*

(309)   *inakke ancinikko*
        inakke aN– cini' =ko
        1PRO   AF– see =2f
        I see you

7.2.4   *Definiteness and Cross-Referencing*
For the sake of analysis I have, like other researchers on similar languages (Friberg 1988:108, 1996:139; Hanson 2003:210; Hasan Basri 1999:236) assumed that there is a correlation between definiteness and cross-referencing, that is that certain arguments must be definite in order to be cross-referenced with a clitic pronoun. This is particularly so with respect to the P function, but also applies to S in certain circumstances.

Of the types of argument which are obligatorily referenced, some have this status by default. These are: 1st or 2nd person arguments (which are rarely doubled with full pronouns, see §5.6), and those referred to by proper names and titles. These can be considered inherently definite. Other types of NP are cross-referenced usually only when they meet certain criteria for definiteness or specificity. These include:
– NPs with the definite marker ≡*a* (including relative clauses). These may be concrete or abstract

---

9   It is not completely unacceptable, but this level of redundancy is highly marked and suggests that the listener is obviously failing to pay attention.

BASIC CLAUSE STRUCTURE · 243

- NPs marked with possessive affixal clitics
- NPs which are habitually not cross-referenced are:
- Focused NPs (see §12.2)
- NPs consisting of common nouns, generally not marked with =a or a possessive affixal clitic

Thus, leaving aside the focused NPs, the difference between arguments which are cross-referenced and those which are not can be assumed to be definiteness and/or specificity (we can assume =a to mark definiteness for reasons put forward in §4.4.1, while NPs with possessive markers are self-evidently specific).

Intransitive clauses with indefinite (and un-cross-referenced) S are most commonly existentials (see §12.4), but can also be other basic clauses as in (310):[10]

(310) *Battu jai toana*
       battu   jai   toana
       come   many   guest
       Many guests are coming

The failure to cross-reference indefinite P (P^{INDEF}) is much more pervasive, and is the basis for distinguishing the semi-transitive clause ((311), and see §11.6):

(311) *Ammallia' ballo'*
       aN(N)–   balli =a' ballo'
       BV–   buy   =1   palm.wine
       I buy palm wine

However, there are also some important and suggestive exceptions to the assumed correlation between definiteness and cross-referencing. Consider the following example, a proverb describing an overly critical person (Zainuddin Hakim 1995):

(312) *Tedong lompo mate i rawa ri sirinna na tena naciniki, sama–sama mate*
       ri sirinna taua na nacini'
       tedong lompo mate i   rawa   ri   siring =na   na   tena
       buffalo big   death PREP beneath PREP cellar =3.POSS and   NEG
       na= cini' =i sama– sama mate ri   siring =na   tau
       3=   see   =3 RDP–   louse death PREP cellar =3.POSS person

---

10   Note though that S in passive clauses must be definite (§7.3).

244   CHAPTER 7

≡a   na   na= cini'
≡DEF and 3=   see
A big dead buffalo in his cellar and he doesn't notice it, a dead louse in
someone else's cellar and he notices

Although both of the Undergoers in these two clauses are indefinite, in the first
the buffalo is cross-referenced, and in the second the louse is not. The explanation given to me was that this helps to underscore the fact that the buffalo is
large and unavoidable, whereas the louse is insignificant. This shows that 'definiteness' can be manipulated for discourse purposes.

Conversely, there are some rare examples of clauses in which P bears a possessive or definite marker but is not cross-referenced, as for example in the
complement clause in the following example:

(313) ero'–dudua' appala' je'ne'nu
       ero'   dudu =a' aC– pala' je'ne' ≡nu
       want very =1 MV– ask   water ≡2f.POSS
       we really want to ask for (some of) your water (PT:131)

The interpretation is that the princes in the example (cross-referenced with
=ABS) are only asking for *some* of the princesses' water. Enquiring about the
preceding example led to the following elicited semi-transitive examples,
which are unusual but acceptable with a particular interpretation:

(314) Angnginunga' je'ne'nu
       aN(N)– inung =a' je'ne' ≡nu
       BV–   drink =1 water ≡2f.POSS
       I drank (some of) your water

(315) Ammallia' gollaya
       aN(N)– balli =a' golla ≡a
       BV–   buy =1 sugar ≡DEF
       I bought (some of) the sugar (we mentioned earlier)

This shows that a contrast between definiteness and specificity can be forced
where necessary, but note that this does not mean that the P argument has been
backgrounded in any sense, which is why I do not analyse these as Actor voice
constructions (see §7.5 and §8.6).

There are certain other circumstances in which the connection between definiteness and cross-referencing does not hold. For example, an inherent patient

BASIC CLAUSE STRUCTURE   245

which has been promoted to P by *–ang* (§ 9.2.1.1) need not be definite as seen in
(316), nor does a secondary object in a benefactive construction (also marked
with *–ang*, § 9.2.1.3) as seen in (317):

(316)   *Kuje'nekangi je'ne' kammu*
        ku= je'ne' –ang =i je'ne' kammu
        1=   water –BEN =3 water warm
        I use warm water to bathe in

(317)   *Kuballiangko baju*
        ku= balli –ang =ko baju
        1=   buy –BEN =2f shirt
        I bought you a shirt

7.3   Ambient Clauses

It does not appear that there are zero-valence or ambient clauses in Makasar,
unlike what has been claimed for Bugis (Hanson 2003:188). The example that
Hanson gives, *bosi* 'it's raining' is identical in Makasar, but here it can be argued
that *bosi* 'rain' is in fact a nominal predicate with a dummy subject enclitic
pronoun *=i*, which is invisible due to vowel degemination (§ 3.3.1). The hidden enclitic can be forced to reveal itself by adding an aspectual enclitic, as
in *bosimi* ⟨bosi=mo=i | rain=PFV=3⟩ 'it's already raining', or negating the clause
causing clitic fronting (§ 7.2.2) as in *tena nabosi* ⟨NEG 3=rain⟩ 'it's not raining'.
It also shows up clearly with other weather terms which do not end with *i*, e.g.
gunturuki ⟨guntur=EC=i⟩ 'it's thundering', *kilaki* ⟨kila'=i⟩ 'it's lightning-ing'.

There are instances of clauses which have no cross-referencing clitics and
could thus be considered zero-valent from a certain point-of-view—these
however have overt NP arguments which are not cross-referenced because they
are indefinite or for other reasons. Existential clauses such as (318) are the most
common exemplars of this, but they are not the only ones as illustrated by (319):

(318)   *Nia' sikayu tedong ri romanga*
        nia' si– kayu tedong ri romang ≡a
        exist one– CLASS buffalo PREP forest   ≡DEF
        There's a buffalo in the forest

246   CHAPTER 7

(319)   *Battu jai toana anne minggu*
        battu jai   toana anne minggu
        come many guest this week
        Lots of guests are coming this week

This was discussed in §7.2.4.

7.4   Intransitive Clauses

Intransitive clauses can be of several major types, depending on the category
of the predicate head. What they have in common is that there will be an 'absolutive' (=ABS) enclitic cross-referencing the sole argument S, if S is definite or
otherwise salient in the discourse (see discussion in §7.2.4), and not in focus
(§12.2). The ABS enclitic tends to attach to the first constituent, whatever its
category, resulting in the typologically common second position clitic (2P, see
§11.2.1).

7.4.1   *Verbal Predicates*

Intransitive verbal predicates are headed by intransitive verbs. These may be
unambiguously intransitive as with (320) and (321), intransitive readings of
ambitransitive verbs as with (322), or intransitive verbs which include inherent objects such as (323):

(320)   *Tinroi iAli*
        tinro =i i   Ali
        sleep =3 PERS Ali
        Ali is sleeping

(321)   *A'jappai Balandayya*
        aC– jappa =i balanda ≡a
        MV– walk =3 Dutch   ≡DEF
        The Dutchman is walking

(322)   *Angnganrea'*
        aN(N)– kanre =a'
        BV–   eat   =1
        I'm eating

BASIC CLAUSE STRUCTURE 247

(323) *A'jaranga'*
aC– jarang =a'
MV– horse =1
I ride a horse

Intransitive verbs are typically marked with a verb prefix, usually *aC–* (§ 7.1.1), but basic verbs such as *tinro* 'sleep' do not require these.

VPs may contain incorporated nominals as manner modifiers, in which case the ABS clitic occurs after the incorporated nominal:

(324) *A'jappa–Balandai*
aC– jappa balanda =i
MV– walk Dutch =3
He walks like a Dutchman (i.e. he stomps about with his nose in the air)

If the clause does not begin with the verb but rather with an auxiliary or other verbal modifier, the ABS enclitic will occur after the first constituent, to put it in 2P. For example, (325) has two clauses, the first containing the auxiliary verb *le'ba'* 'already' or 'after':

(325) *Le'bakki a'je'ne–je'ne, naikki ri puloa*
le'ba' =ki' aC– je'ne– je'ne nai' =ki' ri pulo ≡a
finished =1pl MV– RDP– water climb =1pl PREP island ≡DEF
After we'd swum we landed (went up) on the island

This 2P phenomenon was discussed in § 11.2, along with other facts about the permutations of clitic placement and movement.

7.4.2 *Adjectival Predicates*
Adjectives may function directly as either attributes or predicates in Makasar. There is no copula, and the clitic pronoun is placed directly on the adjective phrase, which may contain a modifier such as the degree adverb seen in (327):

(326) *Bambangi alloa*
bambang =i allo ≡a
hot =3 day ≡DEF
The day is hot

(327) *Pongoro'-dudui anjo taua*
    pongor =o' dudu =i anjo tau   ≡a
    mad   =EC very =3 that person ≡DEF
    That person is really crazy

Adjectives may form transitive predicates by using either causative *paka–* (§7.2.2) or transitiviser *–i* (§7.2.5.1).

7.4.3   *Nominal Predicates*

Nominals may function as predicates directly without use of a copula or other morphosyntactic device. Clitics are placed directly on the predicate. Nominal predicates may be distinguished from verbs derived from nouns by the absence of a verb prefix, e.g. compare (328) with (323) earlier, but otherwise nominal predicates may host the same range of cross-referencing and aspectual clitics as other types of predicate. Nominal predicates generally assert (or question) the identity of S.

(328) *Jaranga'*
    jarang =a'
    horse =1
    I am a horse

(329) *Tau–battu–kere–ko*
    tau   battu kere   =ko
    person come where =2f
    Where are you from (lit. a person coming from where you)

(330) *Atangkui anjo taua*
    ata   ≡ngku =i anjo tau   ≡a
    servant ≡1.POSS =3 that person ≡DEF
    That man is my slave

(331) *Ana'naki' karaenga*
    ana' ≡na   =ki' karaeng ≡a
    child ≡3.POSS =2p karaeng ≡DEF
    You are the karaeng's son

(332) *Inakkeji*
    inakke =ja   =i
    1PRO = LIM =3
    It's only me

BASIC CLAUSE STRUCTURE 249

7.4.4 *Numeral Predicates*
An alternative to predicate possession formed with the existential verb *nia'*
(§ 13.4) is a predicate headed by a numeral:

(333) *Ruai bainenna*
      rua =i baine ≡nna
      two =3 woman ≡3.POSS
      He has two wives (lit. 'two (are) his wives')

(334) *Nikanai Patanna Langkana ka iami ampareki langkanaya, sampuloi*
      anrua pa'daseranna.
      ni– kana =i pata ≡nna langkana ka ia =mo =i
      PASS– word =3 owner ≡3.POSS palace because 3PRO =PFV =3
      aN– pare' =i langkana ≡a sampulo =i aN– rua pa⟩ aC–
      AF– make =3 palace ≡DEF ten =3 LK– two NR⟩ MV–
      daser ⟨ang ≡na
      floorboard ⟨NR ≡3.POSS
      He was called 'Patanna Langkana' because he built a palace with twelve
      sections on pillars (lit. 'twelve (were) its sections', Maros061).

7.4.5 *Locative Predicates*
In some clauses the only candidate for predicate head is a locative adverb or
prepositional phrase:

(335) *Ri balla'nai*
      ri balla' ≡na =i
      PREP house ≡3.POSS =3
      He's at home

(336) *Anrinnima'!*
      anrinni =mo =a'
      here =PFV =1
      Here I am!

(337) *Anjorengji*
      anjoreng =ja =i
      there =LIM =3
      It's just there

250   CHAPTER 7

7.5   Semi-transitive Clauses

The term *semi-transitive* refers to clauses which, although clearly describing events involving two participants, only include a clitic pronoun cross-referencing one of those participants—the Actor. This is because as a general rule Undergoers must be definite to be cross-referenced—in other words referred to by name or title (or otherwise pragmatically salient such as 1st and 2nd person), or marked with the determiner ≡*a* or a possessive suffix. Thus, semi-transitive clauses contain verbs which are lexically transitive, but which host only an absolutive enclitic indexing the Actor, while the Undergoer appears only as an NP and is not cross-referenced. The verb is marked with a verb prefix, usually *aN(N)*–.

(338)   *angnganrea' taipa*
         aN(N)– kanre =a' taipa
         BV–   eat   =1   mango
         I eat a mango/mangoes

In some cases, as in the example above, omission of P[INDEF] results in an intransitive clause which is quite well-formed (though obviously it differs in meaning).

(339)   *angnganrea'*
         aN(N)– kanre =a'
         BV–   eat   =1
         I eat, I'm eating

That is because verbs such as *kanre* 'eat' are ambitransitive, equally allowing intransitive and transitive readings. In others however, such as (340), the verb *balli* 'buy' requires an overt Undergoer and there is no possible intransitive interpretation:

(340)   *ammallia' ballo'*
         aN(N)– balli =a' ballo'
         BV–   buy   =1   palm.wine
         I buy palm wine (cf **ammallia'* 'I bought')

I have elected to use the term semi-transitive for these types of clauses. This term captures the fact that these clauses are different from both typical intransitive and transitive clauses, and that they 'exhibit properties that fall in between those of normal intransitive and transitive clauses' (Dryer to appear). They

BASIC CLAUSE STRUCTURE 251

differ from intransitive clauses because of the obvious fact that these clauses contain Undergoers, both in their logical structure and in their syntax. They differ from fully transitive clauses in that the undergoer is not marked with a clitic—signalling that it is not like an ordinary P, if it is a P at all.

Other labels which have been or could be used are actor focus, actor voice, antipassive, or simply intransitive. I don't find compelling evidence for any of these options, as I will explain below.

7.5.1 *The Intransitive Analysis*

Examples such as (340) above, with an indefinite Undergoer which is essential to the clause and cannot be omitted, lead me to consider with suspicion claims such as those by Friberg (1996:144) and Basri (1999:19) that these clauses should be considered 'formally intransitive'—as does the fact that verbs in these types of clauses overwhelmingly host the prefix *aN(N)–*, which in general distinguishes lexically bivalent verbs from monovalent verbs derived with *aC–* (see §7.1).

Furthermore, the fact that these P[INDEF] areguments are available for syntactic operations such as Focus, in which event the clitic cross-referencing the Actor will change from =ABS (S) to ERG= (A), as in (341), suggests that P[INDEF] is at least present in the thematic structure of these clauses (see also discussion in §11.3):

(341)   *ballo' kuballi*
         ballo'   *ku= balli*
         palm.wine 1= buy
         I buy palm wine

Lee (2006) has suggested labelling a parallel construction in the related language Mandar 'extended intransitive'. I have no argument with this—the important thing is to capture the fact that this is more than an ordinary intransitive construction.

7.5.2 *The Antipassive Analysis*

Another possibility is that *aN(N)–* should be analysed as an antipassive marker. This is (for example) Mead's analysis of the function of a similar prefix *poN–* in Mori Bawah (Mead 2005). This may be appropriate in a very general sense in that *aN(N)–* appears in clauses in which an ABS enclitic cross-references the Actor rather than the Undergoer, and *aN(N)–* has thus 'demoted' the Actor, but it is clearly not a prototypical antipassive inasmuch as in these clauses the Undergoer is not oblique. In addition, since the prefix *aN(N)–* also appears in

252 CHAPTER 7

normal intransitive constructions such as *angnganrei* 'he's eating' (see §7.1.2.1), it is difficult to simply call it an antipassive marker.

Less important, but still relevant, the prefix cannot be used simply because the speaker wishes to realign the grammatical functions in a clause, but rather its presence is a given if the Undergoer is indefinite. Finally, an antipassive analysis is made somewhat anomalous by the fact that there is the perfectly regular passive formed by *ni–*.

7.5.3 *The 'Actor Focus' Analysis*

In two papers (1988; 1996), Friberg analyses the verb prefix and cross-referencing systems of the closely related language Konjo as part of a 'focus' system. The use of the label is confusing, since Friberg is using 'focus' in a Philippine-language sense (i.e. **voice** (Himmelmann 2002)). It essentially boils down to an opposition between 'actor' or 'subject focus' (= actor voice), and 'goal' or 'object focus' (= undergoer voice).

In her analysis, fully transitive clauses (with definite P) have 'object focus', while intransitive and semi-transitive clauses (with no P, or P^{INDEF}) have 'subject focus'. Since for any given clause these conditions are given (by the presence or absence, definiteness or indefiniteness of an Undergoer), I find that a 'focus' (= voice) analysis does not fit especially well. Unlike in a prototypical Philippine-type system, or other Indonesian voice systems, in which speakers may use affixes or other marking to realign the mapping of participants on to grammatical functions in a clause,[11] this system is simply marking the valence of the clause—a marking which is also sensitive to the definiteness of the Undergoer and thus distinguishes three levels of transitivity: fully intransitive, semi-transitive, and fully transitive.

Voice was discussed in more detail in §7.6, while the status of the indefinite Undergoer (P^{INDEF}) was examined further in §11.3.

7.6 Transitive Clauses

In transitive clauses both proclitic and enclitic are canonically on the verb, and there is no verb prefix.

---

11   The Makasar passive does exactly this—it promotes the Undergoer of the parallel active transitive clause so that it is S, the only core argument of an intransitive clause. The Actor, if it is expressed, is done so by means of an oblique.

BASIC CLAUSE STRUCTURE 253

(342) *Nakokkoka'miongku*
na= kokko' =a' miong ≡ku
3= bite =1 cat ≡1.POSS
My cat bit me

(343) *Lakuarengko Daeng Nakku'*
la= ku= areng =ko Daeng nakku'
FUT= 1= name =2 (title) yearning
I'll call you 'Daeng Nakku"

When both arguments are 3rd person it can sometimes be unclear which clitic pronoun indexes which argument, and the order of free NPs does not help to clarify this, as can be seen in (344):

(344) *Naciniki tedongku i Ali*
na= cini' =i tedong ≡ku i Ali
3= see =3 buffalo ≡1.POSS PERS Ali
Ali sees my buffalo / my buffalo sees Ali

In these situations context or pragmatics must resolve the ambiguity. See § 11.1 for more discussion about preferred word order.
Exceptions to the normal transitive pattern occur for three main reasons:
(1) either A or P may be in focus position (§ 12.2);
(2) the clitics may appear on separate words as a 2P phenomenon or there may be two proclitics as a result of clitic movement (§ 11.2.2); or
(3) the clause may have an indefinite Undergoer and therefore be semitransitive (see § 7.5).

7.6.1 *Reflexives*
Reflexives are a subtype of transitive clause in which P is the reflexive noun *kale* 'self' plus a possessive marker from the prenasalised set (§ 4.4.2):

(345) *Naciniki kalenna ri kaca*
na= cini' =i kale ≡nna ri kaca
3= see =3 self ≡3.POSS PREP glass
She saw herself in the mirror

(346) *... kisa'ringkai kalenta karaeng–dudu*
ki= sa'ring =ka =i kale ≡nta karaeng dudu
2p= feel =or =3 self ≡1pl.POSS king very
or we will feel ourselves to be kings

254   CHAPTER 7

(347) *Kukaluppai kalengku*
　　　ku= kaluppa =i kale ≡ngku
　　　1=　forget　=3 self ≡1.POSS
　　　I fainted (lit. I forgot myself)

The reflexive pronoun is always cross-referenced with a 3rd person enclitic. It cannot be focused or topicalised, i.e.: **kalenna nacini'* 'she saw **herself**, **kalenna, naciniki* 'herself, she saw it'. For more examples see § 5.6.2.

7.7　Ditransitive Clauses

There is only one unambiguously ditransitive verb: *sare* 'give', though there are productive ways to license three-place predicates with other verbs, for example with the use of benefactive *–ang* (see § 9.2.1.3), or causative *pa–* (§ 8.1). *Sare* itself occurs in clauses of two main types: those in which the secondary object (theme) is indefinite and is not marked on the verb, and those in which the secondary object is definite, this fact being marked by a special use of the applicative *–ang*:

(348) *Lakusareko doe'*
　　　la=　ku= sare =ko doe'
　　　FUT= 1=　give =2f money
　　　I'll give you some money

(349) *Lakusaréangko doekku*
　　　la=　ku= sare –ang =ko doe'　≡ku
　　　FUT= 1=　give –BEN =2f money ≡1.POSS
　　　I'll give you my money

The NP denoting the indefinite secondary object is not omissible (**lakusareko* 'I'll give you'), but may be omitted if definite (*lakusaréangko* 'I'll give you it'). This is reminiscent of the distinction between transitive and semi-transitive clauses, and suggests the label **semi-ditransitive**.[12] However further investigation of these types of clause is needed.

12　Lee (2006) has suggested 'extended transitive' for similar constructions in Mandar.

CHAPTER 8

Voice/Valence-Signalling Prefixes

This chapter is concerned with a particular subset of verbal morphology, specifically the prefixes which signal voice and valence. These occupy a particular slot at the beginning of the verb complex and include the subset of 'verb prefixes'—markers of lexical valence which also mark active voice and can be considered markers of verbhood, along with the Actor Focus prefix, and the passive and non-volitional prefixes.

Altogether there are seven prefixes in this set which are grouped together for the simple reason that they are in complementary distribution—which is to say that they occupy the same morphosyntactic slot. In other words, a verb may be prefixed by only one of these prefixes, which will be decided according to voice, transitivity and the shape of the clause. Table 59 shows the prefixes with their descriptive labels.

Only one is unambiguously a voice marker; namely the passive prefix *ni–* (§ 8.2). Of the others, the prefix *taC–* is a marginally productive marker of non-volitionality (§ 8.4), and *ma–* is an archaic stative or adjectival marker. The prefix *aN–* marks Actor Focus (§ 8.2). The functions of the remaining prefixes, *aC–*, *amm–*, and *aN(N)–*, are somewhat less straightforward to characterise, as discussed in the following section. They are markers of active voice simply by virtue of not marking any other voice—the other default 'marker' of active voice being absence of any prefix at all in fully transitive structures. (For a general discussion of voice see § 7.6).

There are three exceptional cases to the generalisation that there may only be one verb prefix from this series. One is that the prefix *aC–* may be attached to a derived verb base which already contains a verb prefix internal to the derivation, for example *appasse're* ⟨aC–pa–aC–se're | MV–CAUS–MV–one⟩ 'cause to gather together'. The second is that *taC–* is in some sense an imperfect member of this group as there are two verbs, *atta'mea* 'urinate' and *attattai* 'defecate', which contain both *taC–* and *aC–*. This is further illustrated by the third exception, which is that *taC–* derived forms may themselves be passivised with *ni–*, as in *nita'langngere'* 'to be overheard'.

© KONINKLIJKE BRILL NV, LEIDEN, 2020 | DOI:10.1163/9789004412668_009

256   CHAPTER 8

TABLE 59   Verb prefixes

Morpheme	Gloss	Label
aC–	mv–	lexically intransitive (monovalent)
amm–	mv–	lexically intransitive (monovalent)
aN(N)–	bv–	lexically transitive (bivalent)
aN–	af–	Actor focus
ni–	pass–	passive
ma–	stv–	stative
taC–	nvol–	non-volitional

8.1   The Verb Prefixes

The class of verbs is largely defined and subclassified by association with a
paradigm of verb prefixes whose exact functions have been much debated in
the literature but without much consensus having been reached (the various
analyses are summarised later in § 7.5). For lack of a more suitable label this
subgroup will simply be referred to as 'verb prefixes'. This section will begin
with a general introduction to the circumstances in which they are found, and
a discussion of each prefix with lists of sample derived forms.

In an active intransitive or semi-transitive clause, a verbal predicate will be
marked with one of the verb prefixes, usually either *aC–* or *aN(N)–*, and host
an enclitic pronoun referencing S, as in (350), (351) and (352); while in a transitive clause the verb will host both ERG= proclitic and =ABS enclitic pronouns
referencing A and P, but will not be marked with a verb prefix (353):

(350)   *A'jappai*
         aC– jappa =i
         MV– walk =3
         He walks

(351)   *Angnganrea'*
         aN(N)– kanre =a'
         BV–   eat   =1
         I eat

VOICE/VALENCE-SIGNALLING PREFIXES

(352) *Angnganrea' taipa*
    aN(N)– kanre =a' taipa
    BV–   eat   =1 mango
    I eat mangoes

(353) *Kukanrei taipanu*
    ku= kanre =i taipa =nu
    1= eat   =3 mango =2f.POSS
    I eat your mangoes

Thus, at first glance it appears that the function of these verb prefixes is simply to mark verbs as intransitive (or semi-transitive), as opposed to fully transitive, leading some writers on Makasar and similar languages to label them **intransitivisers** (Hasan Basri 1999; Mithun and Basri 1987; Ceria 1993). This is not especially apt since it implies valence reduction, but in fact *aC–* usually appears on verbs which are inherently intransitive already and thus need no such reduction, whereas *aN(N)–* usually occurs on verbs which are lexically transitive, but which appear in clauses as semi-transitive due to an indefinite Undergoer, but are not intransitive as such.

Rather than give the prefixes the misleading label **intransitiviser**, I have elected to analyse these prefixes as (a) markers of verbhood, and (b) markers of lexical valence. I have thus glossed them as either MV– or BV– for monovalent or bivalent, which is to say they subcategorise for one or two arguments respectively. The combination of a verb plus prefix, without further marking, functions as a 'citation form' since it is necessary to know which prefix a given verb root takes. A prefixed verb may also be considered an infinitive form of a verb, for the simple reason that without further morphological marking (in the form of pronominal or aspect clitics) such forms contain no information about argument structure or tense/aspect, and furthermore these are the forms typically found as complements of verbs such as *ero'* 'want', *isseng* 'know', and the like, as seen in (354) and (355):

(354) *Eroka' angnginung*
    ero' =a' aN(N)– inung
    want =1 BV– drink
    I want to drink

(355) *Tanaissengai a'lange*
    ta= na= isseng –a =i aC– lange
    NEG= 3= know –SBJV =3 MV– swim
    He doesn't know how to swim

258 CHAPTER 8

TABLE 60   Verb types by prefix

verb class	basic	aC–	amm–	aN(N)–
example	tinro	a'jappa	ammantang	angnganre
morphemes	⟨tinro⟩	⟨aC–jappa⟩	⟨amm–antang⟩	⟨aN(N)–kanre⟩
	⟨sleep⟩	⟨MV–walk⟩	⟨MV–stay⟩	⟨BV–food⟩
gloss	sleep	walk	stay	eat

The fundamental contrast between the two major verb prefixes *aC–* and *aN(N)–*, is that they denote (roughly) *lexically* intransitive and transitive verbs respectively—by which I mean that the verbs either proscribe or require the presence of an Undergoer, as will be shown in § 8.1.1 and § 8.1.2. Some verb roots can appear with either prefix, usually with a difference in meaning (§ 8.1.3). A smaller class of vowel-initial intransitive verbs take the less common prefix form *amm–* (§ 8.1.4). Some verbs, the so-called 'basic' verbs, do not appear with verb prefixes at all (§ 5.3.1.2).

Thus, verbs can roughly be formally divided into four main groups: basic verbs, *aC–* verbs, *aN(N)–* verbs, and *amm–* verbs, as shown in Table 60.

Basic verbs, *aC–* verbs and *amm–* verbs are overwhelmingly lexically intransitive, while *aN(N)–* verbs are predominantly lexically transitive. In context within a clause the prefixes can be seen as valence-*signalling* (rather than valence-reducing), in that that their very presence identifies a clause as being less than fully transitive (i.e.: intransitive or semi-transitive), because a fully transitive clause will have an ERG= proclitic pronoun rather than a verb prefix.

In many cases the morphological connection between verb prefixes and roots is not part of speakers' metalinguistic awareness and the prefixes are believed to be part of the root—this is particularly the case with some members of the *amm–* class such as *ammotere'* 'return' or *ammempo* 'sit', whose roots are generally explained by speakers as being *motere'* and *mempo* respectively. This can also extend to the nasal-substituting prefix *aN(N)–* and I have had *nganre* offered as the root for *angnganre* 'eat' (← *kanre*) on several occasions. This is despite the fact that there are derived forms which serve as counter-examples, such as passives and causatives, e.g. *niempói* ⟨PASS–sit–APPL⟩ 'be sat upon' or *pakanre* ⟨CAUS–eat⟩ 'make/let eat'.

Historically each of these prefixes was also found with initial *m–*, (*maC–*, *maN(N)–* and *mamm–*), thus conforming to a general paradigm which also included the archaic adjectival marker *ma–* (§ 8.1.5).[1] Examples from the Gowa

---

1   In Konjo this prefix conforms to the other members of the group in appearing as *a–*. This variant is not present in Makasar.

VOICE/VALENCE-SIGNALLING PREFIXES 259

chronicle include *ma'bundu'* ⟨maC–bundu' | MV–war⟩ 'make war', *mammeta*
⟨maN(N)–beta | BV≡DEFeat⟩ 'defeat', and *mammio'* ⟨mamm–io' | MV–yes⟩
'agree'.

Dating of the loss of initial *m–* is difficult, as it was (and is) retained in
some archaic forms and registers to this day, and still occurs in many titles
and *pa'daengang* (§ 6.1.2.2) such as Daeng Makkulle ⟨maC–kulle | MV–can⟩
'Mr Capability'. In the Gowa chronicle forms are found with and without *m–*,
which makes it tempting to assume that it was in the process of disappear-
ing at the time of composition, however this is not conclusive as the chronicle
was routinely recopied and it is thus difficult to precisely date any particular
section. It does not appear that the Actor Focus prefix *aN–* (§ 8.2) ever had a
maN– variant, which implies that it either has a separate historical source or
is a relatively recent innovation from a period when the initial *m–* had already
disappeared (at least productively) from this paradigm of prefixes.[2]

Continuing the trend to reduction seen above, in informal speech the initial *a–* of the prefixes is also often omitted (§ 2.3.5) resulting in forms such as
ngnganre ⟨aN(N)–kanre⟩ 'eat' or *'lampa* ⟨aC–lampa⟩ 'go'.

8.1.1 aC– *Verbs*
One set of verb forms is clearly produced by prefixation of an underlying form
aC–,[3] with assimilation to voiceless consonants and default glottal realisation
before voiced consonants. Table 61 shows how *aC–* is realised in all possible
environments. An asterisk in front of a root gloss means that the root does not
appear underived, but has the meaning suggested.

The most common use of *aC–* is to derive an intransitive verb from a nominal root. The derived verb will mean 'having/using/making X', where X is the
root. They may seem at first glance to be transitive, but the patient is inherent.[4]
Consider the following examples:

jarang	horse	→	a'jarang	ride a horse
tedong	buffalo	→	attedong	keep buffalo
oto	car	→	a'oto	go by car

---

2 The only apparent exception to this observation is that the verb 'enter' (*antama* in the modern language) appears as *mantama* in the KIT manuscript's version of the Gowa chronicle.
However, as noted in § 5.3.1.2, *antama* is better analysed as a basic verb rather than the combination of ⟨aN–tama⟩.

3 A reflex of PMP *maR– 'intransitive verb; relation of parent and child or of siblings' (Blust
2003). Historically this prefix was *maC–* and in fact the form *mar–* appears in one word, *mare-
wangang* 'be armed' (← *ewa* 'oppose'; C:429).

4 The patient may be made explicit using the suffix *–ang*, see § 7.2.6.1.

260 CHAPTER 8

buburu'	rice porridge	→	a'buburu'	make rice porridge
bayao	egg	→	a'bayao	lay an egg
jonga	deer	→	a'jonga	hunt deer
juku'	fish	→	a'juku'	go fishing

(356) *massing eroki antama ri romanga a'jonga.*
massing ero' =*i* antama ri romang ≡a aC– jonga
each want =3 enter PREP forest ≡DEF MV– deer
they all wanted to go into the forest to hunt deer (PT:7)

This contrasts with the use of unaffixed nouns as nominal predicates, as in *olo'–oloka', tedonga'* 'I'm an animal, I'm a buffalo' (PT:29).

If the root is a place, the result means 'go to X':

bonto	shore	→	a'bonto	go to shore
pasara'	market	→	appasara'	go to market
Bantaeng	name of town	→	a'Bantaeng	go to Bantaeng

(357) *Appasaraka' ri bari'basa'*
aC– pasar =a' =a' ri bari'bas =a'
MV– market =EC =1 PREP morning =EC
I go to market in the mornings

If the root is a temporal noun, the result means 'spend X amount of time':

bangngi	night	→	*a'bangngi*	spend the night
bulang	month	→	*a'bulang*	stay for a month

(358) *A'bulangi ri Malino ri timoro' karring*
aC– bulang =i ri Malino ri timor =o' karring
MV– month =3 PREP Malino PREP east.monsoon =EC dry
He stays months in Malino during the dry season

If the root is an interjection, the result means 'say X':

io'	yes	→	*a'io'*	say 'yes'[5]
taena	no	→	*attaena*	say 'no'

---

5 The stylistic variant *io* (without final glottal, and used when speaking to those lower in status)
takes *amm–*, thus *ammio* 'agree'.

VOICE/VALENCE-SIGNALLING PREFIXES

TABLE 61 Verbs derived with *aC*–

	Root	Root gloss		Verb form	Derived verb meaning
Voiceless consonants					
aC–p	*pasara'*	market	→	appasara'	go to market
aC–t	tunu	*grill	→	attunu	grilled
aC–s	sapatu	shoe	→	assapatu	wear shoes
aC–c	cini'	*see	→	accini'	see
aC–k	kelong	song	→	akkelong	sing a *kelong*
aC–h	hitara'	guitar[a]	→	a'hitara'	play the guitar
Voiced consonants					
aC–b	baine	woman	→	a'baine	take a wife
aC–d	dakka	a step	→	a'dakka	step
aC–j	jarang	horse	→	a'jarang	ride a horse
aC–g	gari'gi'	notch	→	a'gari'gi'	be notched/marked
aC–m	moro'	*grunt	→	a'moro'	grunt/snore in sleep
aC–n	noa'	*gasp	→	a'noa'	gasp
aC–ny	nyila	indigo	→	a'nyila	prepare indigo
aC–ng	ngisi	*sneer	→	a'ngisi	sneer
Vowels					
aC–a	angko	cousin[b]	→	a'angko	call someone *angko*
aC–e	enta	mother[c]	→	a'enta	call someone *enta*
aC–i	ingkong	tail	→	a'ingkong	have a tail
aC–o	ongkoso'	price[d]	→	a'ongkoso'	have a price
aC–u	uang	grey hair	→	a'uang	have grey hair

a ← Dutch *gitaar*.
b This word is associated with the Chinese–Makasar community, thus *a'angko* is also a way of saying 'be of Chinese descent'.
c This word is associated with nobility, so it can also be used to mark someone as being of noble ancestry.
d ← Dutch *onkosten*.

(359) *Tangngassengai attaena*
    ta=   aN(N)– asseng –a   =i aC– taena
    NEG= BV–   know –SBJV =3 MV– no
    He doesn't know how to say 'no'

If the root is a kin term or title, the result can mean either 'call someone X', 'become X', or 'have X':

daeng	uncle	→	*a'daeng*	call someone *daeng*[6]
karaeng	king	→	*akkaraeng*	become *karaeng*
mangge	father	→	*a'mange*	have a father[7]
anrong	mother	→	*a'anrong*	have a mother

If the root is a numeral, the verb means 'be X', with metaphorical extensions in some cases:

se're	one	→	*asse're*	be one, gather together
rua	two	→	*a'rua*	be two, be divided
pulo	tens	→	*appulo*	be numbered in tens

(360) *Asse're–ngasengi taua*
   aC– se're ngaseng =i tau   ≡a
   MV– one all   =3 person ≡DEF
   All the people gathered

8.1.1.1 Transitive Examples

A small number of frequently used *aC–* verbs are exceptions in that they may be transitive. For example, although *cini'* 'see' has an infinitive formed with *aC–* (with a possible intransitive interpretation 'have sight'), this is no bar to it appearing in a transitive clause, as can be seen in the following example.

(361) *kucinikko*
   ku= cini' =ko
   1= see =2f
   I see you

Other similar verbs are *a'boya* 'search', *akkana* 'say', *assuro* 'order' and *attayang* 'wait'. These transitive *aC–* verbs may also appear with the Actor Focus prefix *aN–*, e.g.:

(362) *... sari'battanna anciniki ana'na Pung Tedong.*
   sari'battang ≡na   aN– cini' =i ana' ≡na   pung   tedong
   sibling   ≡3.POSS AF– see =3 child ≡3.POSS lord/lady buffalo
   ... (one of) their brothers saw Lady Buffalo's children. (PT:098)

---

6 The person called *daeng* is in a prepositional phrase, e.g. *a'daengi ri bura'nenna* (MV–*daeng*=3 PREP man≡3.POSS) 'she calls her husband *daeng*'.

7 As the antonym of 'be orphaned'.

VOICE/VALENCE-SIGNALLING PREFIXES

TABLE 62   Verbs with nasal substituting *aN(N)*–

	Root	Root gloss		Verb form	Derived verb meaning
aN(N)–p	*pekang*	hook	→	*ammekang*	fish with a hook
aN(N)–b	*balli*	price	→	*ammalli*	buy
aN(N)–t	*tunrung*	*hit	→	*annunrung*	hit
aN(N)–s	*sanggara'*	fried	→	*annyanggara'/annangara'*	fry
aN(N)–c	*cokko*	secret	→	*annyokko*	hide (something)
aN(N)–k	*kanre*	rice/food	→	*angnganre*	eat

In addition to these exceptions, all verbs derived with the causative prefixes *pa*– (§ 9.1) or *paka*– (§ 9.2), which are by nature at least transitive, form infinitives with *aC*–.

8.1.2   aN(N)– *Verbs*
Another set of verbs are derived through prefixation with *aN(N)*–,[8] where the second nasal is formed by nasal substitution of the initial consonant of the stem, at the same place of articulation (see § 2.3.2). This occurs on roots with voiceless initial consonants (excluding marginal /h/), and /b/. With roots in /s/ the nasal may be alveolar or palatal in seemingly free variation. Table 62 shows examples of verbs derived with this prefix. Notice that they all lend themselves to a transitive interpretation—a patient is assumed, though not inherent to the verb as with *aC*– examples such as *a'jarang* 'ride a horse'. Note however that in fully transitive examples with definite P, *aN(N)*– does not appear and instead there is an ERG= clitic pronoun referencing A.

(363)   *Angnganrea' unti*
    aN(N)– kanre =a' unti
    BV–   eat   =1 banana
    I eat bananas

(364)   *Ammalliko golla'?*
    aN(N)– balli =ko golla'
    BV–   buy   =2f sugar
    Did you buy sugar?

---

8   A reflex of PMP *maŋ– 'active verb' (Blust 2003:473).

264 CHAPTER 8

TABLE 63   Verbs without nasal substitution

	Root	Root gloss		Verb form	Derived verb meaning
aN(N)–d	doli'	*tumble	→	andoli'	tumble, somersault
aN(N)–j	jama	*work	→	anjama	work
aN(N)–g	gappa	*reach	→	anggappa	reach
aN(N)–h	hukkung	law	→	anghukkung	punish

TABLE 64   Vowel-initial verbs with aN(N)–

	Root	Root gloss		Verb form	Derived verb meaning
aN(N)–	alle	*take	→	angngalle	take
aN(N)–	erang	belongings	→	angngerang	bring
aN(N)–	inung	*drink	→	angnginung	drink
aN(N)–	ondang	*chase	→	angngondang	chase
aN(N)–	unte	*wring	→	angngunte	wring

(Compare the fully intransitive parallel to (363))

(365)   *kukanrei untia*
        ku= kanre =i   unti   ≡a
        1=   eat   =3 banana ≡DEF
        I eat the bananas

Roots which begin with voiced stops other than /b/, and also with /h/, are
not subject to nasal substitution, so the allomorph *aN–* is found, as shown in
Table 63. This means that the contrast between *aN(N)–* and Actor Focus *aN–* is
neutralised in these environments.

With vowel-initial roots *aN(N)–* is realised as *angng–*, which contrasts with
both *aC–* (realised as [aʔ], see Table 61) and the irregular prefix *amm–* (§8.1.4).

It can be observed here that, compared to *aC–* verbs which often come from
nominal roots, a larger proportion of *aN(N)–* verbs come from roots which do
not appear without verbal morphology.

VOICE/VALENCE-SIGNALLING PREFIXES 265

8.1.2.1 Intransitive Examples

Just as the basically intransitive marker *aC–* appears on some transitive verbs, there are some *aN(N)–* verbs which can appear in intransitive clauses. These are clauses where Undergoers are completely unspecified (not to be confused with semi-transitive clauses, in which any transitive verb has an Undergoer which is specified but indefinite, such as *ammallia' golla'* ⟨aN(N)–balli=a' golla' | BV–buy=1 sugar⟩ 'I bought sugar', see §11.6). The most obvious of these ambitransitive verbs are *angnganre* 'eat' and *angnginung* 'drink', shown in intransitive (366), semi-transitive (367), and fully transitive (368) examples below.

(366) *Angnginunga'*
       aN(N)– inung =a'
       BV–   drink =1
       I drink

(367) *Angnginunga' ballo'*
       aN(N)– inung =a' ballo'
       BV–   drink =1 palm.wine
       I drink palm wine

(368) *Kuinungi ballo'nu*
       ku= inung =i ballo'   ≡nu
       1= drink =3 palm.wine ≡2f.POSS
       I drink your palm wine

Clearly though, although these verbs can appear in intransitive clauses, they are still lexically transitive and obviously at least permit the presence of a specific Undergoer, even if it is not required.

8.1.3 *Verbs with Either* aC– *or* aN(N)–

Generally roots are associated with only one of the major prefixes, but there are also several examples of roots which can take either *aC–* or *aN(N)–* with intransitive and transitive meanings respectively. A small selection of these is seen in Table 65.

In other examples (Table 66), the meanings of the different forms are quite distinct, and we must assume that they are based on separate homophonous roots.

Some verbs may appear with either prefix with no apparent difference in meaning, but this is quite rare, with only two examples found so far.

266　　　　　　　　　　　　　　　　　　　　　　　　　　　　　CHAPTER 8

TABLE 65　Intransitive/transitive verbs with *aC*– and *aN(N)*–

banynyang	*stretch	→	*a'banynyang*	stretch (self)
		→	*ammanynyang*	stretch (something)
kanuku	nail, claw	→	*akkanuku*	have nails/claws
		→	*angnganuku*	scratch with nails/claws
kanyame	taste	→	*akkanyame*	have a flavour
		→	*angnganyame*	try, sample
kokkoro'	crumbling	→	*akkokkoro'*	tumble down
		→	*angngokkoro'*	knock down
cokko	secret	→	*accokko*	hide (self)
		→	*anynyokko*	hide (something)
jari	so	→	*a'jari*	become something
		→	*anjari*	succeed in something
kanre	food	→	*akkanre*	be consumed (e.g. by fire)
		→	*angnganre*	eat
lesang	*move	→	*a'lesang*	move (self)
		→	*allesang*	move (something)

TABLE 66　Homophonous roots with *aC*– and *aN(N)*–

balu'	goods	→	*a'balu'*	sell
balu'	*roll up	→	*ammalu'*	roll up
tunrung	coconut bunch	→	*attunrung*	be in a bunch
tunrung	*hit	→	*annunrung*	hit

TABLE 67　Roots with interchangeable *aC*– and *aN(N)*–

| *soso'* | pass away (i.e. die) | → | *assoso'/ anynyoso'* | pass through (e.g. a forest) |
| *ko'bi'* | pluck | → | *akko'bi'/ angngo'bi'* | play stringed instrument |

8.1.4　amm– *Verbs*

The prefix form *amm*– is clearly associated with intransitivity as it occurs on
verbs such as *ammantang* 'stay', and it could thus be said to serve the same
function as *aC*–.

It is tempting to analyse *amm*– as an allomorph of *aC*– which occurs with
vowel-initial roots, and this analysis has in fact been proposed for Konjo by

VOICE/VALENCE-SIGNALLING PREFIXES

TABLE 68   *amm–* verbs

adang	*lie dying	→	*ammadang*	lie dying
ado	*nod	→	*ammado*	nod, agree
antang	*stay	→	*ammantang*	stay
ana'	child	→	*ammana'*	have a child
e'da'	gait	→	*amme'da'*	walk with a gait
e'jere'	*stand silently	→	*amme'jere'*	stand silently
empo	position	→	*ammempo*	sit
enteng	*stand	→	*ammenteng*	stand
ikkiri'	*shudder	→	*ammikkiri'*	shudder
iri'	*blow	→	*ammiri'*	blow (of wind)
io	yes	→	*ammio*	be agreeable
ontoro'	*be erect	→	*ammontoro'*	be erect (of penis, nipple)
opang	*lie on belly	→	*ammopang*	lie on belly
otere'	rope[a]	→	*ammotere'*	return
ulu	head	→	*ammulu*	hold head straight
umba	appearance[b]	→	*ammumba*	rise into view

a   Perhaps a homophone.
b   For example of a fish coming out of the water, or the sun coming above the horizon.

Friberg & Friberg (1991a:87)—they identify *amm–* as an allomorph of the intransitive prefix *a'–*, and posit an ad hoc rule called Glottal Nasalisation to explain it. Arguing against this analysis for Makasar is the fact that *aC–* does in fact occur as [aʔ] on a variety of vowel-initial roots (see Table 61).

One observation which can be made is that *amm–* is no longer productive; any new words must take *aC–*, such as *a'oto* 'drive a car'. It is also apparent that the forms with *amm–* are more frequently used and thus more likely to retain archaic forms (as with irregular verbs in English).[9]

It seems likely that forms with *amm–* are words which at one point took an historical pre-/infix ⟨*um*⟩[10] and were then reanalysed. An example is *empo* 'sit', which appears with the *amm–* form in *ammempoki'* 'sit down'. This is cognate with *simpuh* 'sit' in Malay. Cense (Cense & Abdoerrahim 1979:900) hypothesises an earlier form †*tempo*, which then became †*t⟨um⟩empo*, †*mm–empo*, and

---

9   Compare 'have a child' with 'have a mother'—whether or not someone has a child is salient information, while the fact of someone having a mother can be taken as given.

10   PMP *–um– 'actor focus/agent voice; inchoative verb' (Blust 2003:473).

then the initial nasal was assigned to the prefix resulting in *amm–empo*. The existence of *um–* as a prefix on vowel-initial roots can account for forms such as *ammana'* 'have a child',[11] and a similar process to this seems to have occurred in Bugis (Sirk 1996:46). Alternatively, forms with *amm–* can be analysed as roots which incorporate the stative prefix *ma–* (§ 8.1.5), so that *antang* becomes *mantang* 'stay', for example. Whichever is the case, the bilabial nasal is clearly not part of the root (contra Asmah Haji Omar 1979; Indiyah Imran 1976) as can be seen in forms such as the causative *paenteng* 'make stand'.

8.1.5   *Adjectival/Stative* ma–

This prefix[12] is included here because it was once part of the stable of verbal prefixes, and it was probably only recently that it became unproductive. Of its parallel in Konjo, Friberg & Friberg write 'the ability of this class of words to take a STV (stative) prefix is one of the features that distinguishes adjectives from verbs as a basic word class' (Friberg & Friberg 1991b). This may well be the case in Konjo, but in Makasar this prefix is seen only in descriptive names; including titles such as *Tu–malompo* ⟨person–STV–big⟩ 'boss'; and nicknames and *pa'daengang* (§ 6.1.2.2) such as *Daeng Matinro* ⟨STV–sleep⟩ 'Mr Sleepy' or *Daeng Mabaji'* ⟨STV–good⟩ 'Ms Good'. Even in the latter case the use of *ma–* is becoming rare and I have witnessed several disputes about whether *pa'daengang* such as *Daeng Nakku'* ⟨yearning⟩ (my own name in Makassar) should include *ma–* or not (i.e. *Daeng Manakku'*).

According to Cense, *ma–* could also be used on nominals to make them into attributes, as can be seen in the following example:

(369)   *tena kumakopi*
    tena ku= ma– kopi
    NEG 1=   STV– coffee
    I don't (really drink) coffee (C:429)

However this use was not universally accepted by speakers when I tested it.

---

11   Imran (1976:90) gives *akanak* (*a'ana'*) as the form of this word. However this was rejected by every native speaker I asked.

12   pMP *ma– 'stative verb prefix (realis)' (Blust 2003:473).

VOICE/VALENCE-SIGNALLING PREFIXES   269

8.2   Actor Focus *aN–*

This prefix is found on verbs in a particular syntactic circumstance: when a transitive verb (with a definite Undergoer) appears without a proclitic referencing the Actor as a result of Actor Focus (this is further discussed in §11.9).[13] The Actor is not cross-referenced, the Undergoer is cross-referenced with an =ABS enclitic.

(370) *Inai angkanrei untiku?*
       i–   nai aN– kanre =i unti   ≡ku
       PERS – who AF– eat   =3 banana ≡1.POSS
       who ate my banana? (cf. *inai angnganre unti* 'who ate bananas?')

(371) *Kongkonga ambunoi miongku*
       kongkong aN– buno =i miong ≡ku
       dog   AF– kill =3 cat   ≡1.POSS
       a dog killed my cat

There is one common exception to the rule that verbs with *aN–* should have definite (cross-referenced) Undergoers as well as focused Actors. This is the verb *angkana* 'say', which precedes a direct quote (the quote itself is the Undergoer):

(372) *Lassu'na assulu' ana'na, ammarranna angkana "mbee'".*
       lassu' ≡na   aC– sulu' ana' ≡na   amm– arrang ≡na
       birth ≡3.POSS MV– exit child ≡3.POSS MV–   shout   ≡3.POSS
       aN– kana mbee'
       AF– word baa!
       When her child came out, it shouted 'baaa!' (bembe:016)[14]

As illustrated, the quoted element is not marked as definite, nor is it cross-referenced on the verb (**angkanai*).

Note that *aN–* can only be distinguished from *aN(N)–* on roots which begin with voiceless consonants or /b/, and further that *aN–s* is only realised as *ans*

---

13   In an earlier work (Jukes 1998) I considered *aN–* to be a syntactically conditioned allomorph of the lexical bivalence marker *aN(N)–*. However, I had overlooked cases in which *aN–* corresponds with verbs whose usual infinitive is derived with *aC–*, such as *accini* 'see'.

14   The possessive markers on *lassu'* and *ammarrang* exemplify the temporal/causal construction mentioned in §4.4.2.

270 CHAPTER 8

(e.g. *ansuro* 'send (AF)') in careful speech. At other times normal assimilation rules result in *assuro* (§ 2.3.3). This can only be distinguished from the *ass* which results from *aC–s* because there may be some nasalisation on the vowel [ãss], however it is unlikely that people generally pay close enough attention to notice.

8.3 Passive *ni–*

The passive prefix *ni–* attaches to bare verb stems, in complementary distribution with the verb prefixes or ERG= proclitics. It functions to promote an Undergoer to the only core argument (S), which is marked with an =ABS enclitic. The demoted Actor may optionally be expressed in an adjunct preceded by the preposition *ri*—this must follow the verb. The contrast between a passive clause and an active transitive clause is shown below:

(373) *Nikokkoka' (ri meongku)*
    ni–   kokko' =a' (ri   meong ≡ku)
    PASS– bite   =1 (PREP cat   ≡1.POSS)
    I was bitten (by my cat)

(374) *Nakokkoka' meongku*
    na= kokko' =a' meong ≡ku
    3= bite   =1 cat   ≡1.POSS
    My cat bit me

Note that passivisation is not the only way to put emphasis on the Undergoer, as Undergoer focus will also do this (see §11.9).

(375) *Inakke nakokko' meongku*
    i–   nakke na= kokko' meong ≡ku
    PERS– 1PRO 3= bite cat   ≡1.POSS
    My cat bit **me**

For this reason it may be more accurate to analyse the passive as a way of taking emphasis off the Actor, rather than putting it on the Undergoer *per se*, however the exact discourse motivations for choosing the passive (and the effects on information structure) require further research.

    The frequency of passive clauses is variable according to the style and genre of texts, with older, more formal, literary texts showing a larger proportion. For

VOICE/VALENCE-SIGNALLING PREFIXES 271

example, the extract from the Gowa chronicle (Appendix A) shows 55 passive clauses in 108 sentences, and the Maros chronicle (Cummings 2000) shows 127 out of 247 (both roughly 51%); while the folktale *Karaeng ammanaka bembe* (Appendix B) has 23 passive clauses out of 123 sentences (18%), and *Caritana Pung Tedong* (Jukes 1998) only 20 out of 248 (8%).

In narrative contexts the most common use of the passive is when the Actor cannot be identified, as in (376) where it is magic, or (377) where it is generic 'they' or people in general:

(376) *Niroko'mi bulaeng balla'na Puttiri Bida Sari.*
    ni-   roko' =mo =i bulaeng balla' ≡na   puttiri Bida Sari
    PASS– pack =PRF =3 gold   house ≡3.POSS princess Bida Sari
    Puttiri Bida Sari's house was filled with gold (by magic, PT:196).

(377) *areng kalenna. iangku mabassung. nikana. I Mangayoaberang.*
    areng kale ≡nna   iang ≡ku   ma– bassung   ni–   kana
    name self ≡3.POSS PROH ≡1.POSS STV– swollen.belly PASS– word
    I   Mangayoaberang
    PERS Mangayoaberang
    His personal name, may I not swell up, was called I Mangayoaberang (KIT:1:10)

The subject of a passive clause may be focused (§ 11.9), in which case there will be no enclitic. Example (378) shows S in focus position, as does (377), albeit with the formulaic expression *iangku mabassung* intruding between it and the verb. (379) is a clause with an ellipsed focused S inherited from a previous clause:

(378) *Meongku nibuno (ri kongkong)*
    meong ni– buno ri   kongkong
    cat   PASS– kill PREP dog
    My cat was killed (by a dog)

(379) *Apaji na nicini'mo ri Puttiri Bida Sari siagang bura'nenna.*
    apa =ja   =i na   ni–   cini' =mo ri   puttiri   Bida Sari
    what =LIM =3 COMP PASS– see =PFV PREP princess Bida Sari
    siagang bura'ne ≡nna
    with   man   ≡3.POSS
    So (she) was seen by Puttiri Bida Sari and her husband (PT:178).

272 CHAPTER 8

S NPs in post-verbal position in passive clauses must be definite—(380) is ungrammatical:

(380) *Nikanre ruku' ri tedong
ni–   kanre ruku' ri   tedong
PASS– eat   grass PREP buffalo
Grass was eaten by the buffalo

However, indefinite S is permitted in focus position:

(381) Ruku' nikanre ri tedong
ruku' ni–   kanre ri   tedong
grass PASS– eat   PREP buffalo
Grass was eaten by the buffalo

Verbs in passive clauses cannot host fronted clitics (§11.2.2), unlike active clauses:

(382) Taena niassengi bainenna (*Taena na=ni–asseng bainenna)
taena ni–   asseng =i baine   ≡nna
neg   PASS– know   =3 woman ≡3.POSS
His wife is not known (Maros:037) (cf. taena na=battu bainenna 'his wife didn't come')

The following sentence from the Gowa chronicle shows a headless relative passive clause nigappaya, which itself has a passive complement clause:

(383) areng kalenna. taena angngassengi. sanggenna. nigappaya nikuta'nang.
areng kale ≡nna   taena aN(N)– asseng =i sangge ≡nna
name self ≡3.POSS NEG   BV–   know   =3 until   ≡3.POSS
ni–   gappa ≡a   ni–   kuta'nang
PASS– result ≡DEF PASS– question
His personal name no one knows; among (those) who were able to be asked none knew (KIT:2:23)

There is no formal way to distinguish between an oblique representing the agent and a locative or temporal prepositional phrase, but in general context will make this clear, as can be seen in examples (384) and (385), where the PP can only be agent, and (386) where it can only be a location:

VOICE/VALENCE-SIGNALLING PREFIXES

(384) *Nikodí ri kaluru'*

ni–	kodi –i	=i	ri	kalur	=u'
PASS–	bad –TRS	=3	PREP	cigarette	=EC

He feels sick because of the smoke

(385) *Battu ri gau'nai[15] na niba'ji ri taua*

battu	ri	gau'	≡na	=i	na	ni–	ba'ji	=i	ri	tau
come	PREP	deed	≡3.POSS	=3	COMP	PASS–	biff	=3	PREP	person

≡a
≡DEF

It comes from his actions (it's his own fault) that he was beaten by the people (C:91)

(386) *Apaji na nipangngalleammi je'ne' ri kaca bulaeng*

apa	=ja	=i	na	ni–	pa–	aN(N)–	alle	–ang	=mo	=i
what	=LIM	=3	COMP	PASS–	CAUS–	BV–	take	–BEN	=PFV	=3

je'ne'	ri	kaca	bulaeng
water	PREP	glass	gold

So they were made to take water (for themselves) in a gold cup (PT:225).

In the event of both Actor and locative PPs occurring in a clause it seems to be preferred for the Actor to come first as in (387), it should be noted however that this is a rather stilted invented example:

(387) *Anjo taua pa'risi' bangkenna nasaba' nikokkoki ri kongkonga ri kokonna*

anjo tau	≡a	pa'ris	=i'	bangkeng	≡na	na= saba'
that person	≡DEF	pain	=EC	leg	≡3.POSS	3= reason

ni–	kokko'	=i	ri	kongkong	≡a	ri	koko	≡nna
PASS–	bite	=3	PREP	dog	≡DEF	PREP	garden	≡3.POSS

That man has a sore leg, because he was bitten by the dog in his garden

8.4 Involuntary/Accidental *taC–*

This prefix (comparable with Malay *ter–*, and appearing on vowel-initial roots as *tar-*)[16] is relatively uncommon and its occurrence with verbs is largely con-

---

15 *Battu ri X* collocations are often lexicalised (see §5.10), which explains why the enclitic pronoun occurs at the end rather than apparent 2P after *battu*.

16 A reflex of PAN *taR– 'spontaneous or accidental action' (Blust 2003).

274 CHAPTER 8

TABLE 69   Verbs with *taC–*

taC– form	Gloss		Equivalent form	Type	Gloss
tappinawang	follow by mistake	←	*amminawang*	Vtr	follow
ta'langngere'	overhear	←	*allangngere'*	Vtr	hear
tassambang	be snagged on s.t	←	*anynyambang*	Vtr	catch (on hook, rope)
tassungke	be opened accidentally	←	*anynyungke*	Vtr	open
(at)ta'mea	piss	←	*mea*	N	piss
(at)tattai	shit	←	*tai*	N	shit
ta'muri	smile	←	*muri–muri*	N	smile
tatti'la'	come to mind	←	*ti'la'*	N	unbidden thought
ta'do'do'	be tired	←	*a'do'do'*	Vi	trudge
ta'langnge	vomit	←	*a'langnge*	Vi	lose colour
ta'bangka	start, shudder	←	*bangka*	Adj	breached
tattiling	be crooked	←	*tilíngi*	Adj–TRS	tilt (head)

ventionalised. Some examples of verbs with *taC–* are given in Table 69, together with a corresponding regular verbal or nominal form if there is one. A clear commonality is that they all refer to actions or states which are non-volitional or accidental, but beyond that there seem to be several subclasses, which are separated in the table with lines. The first subclass consists of actor-oriented 'accidental' verbs derived from transitive verbs. The second is similar but the verbs are undergoer-oriented. The third subclass consists of verbs derived from nouns, which mean roughly 'have NOUN (involuntarily)'. This includes the two 'verbs of excretion' (see Bowden 2001:196) which uniquely take the intransitive prefix *aC–* in addition to *taC–*. The fourth group consists of verbs which are primarily seen in the *taC–* form, and whose connection with the presumed roots is somewhat removed, though still comprehensible.

(388) *Tappinawangi ri otoa baju–bosiku*
       taC– *pinawang* =i ri   oto ≡a   baju bosi ≡ku
       NVOL– follow   =3 PREP car ≡DEF shirt rain ≡1.POSS
       My raincoat went in the car by mistake

VOICE/VALENCE-SIGNALLING PREFIXES

(389) ... *nasaba' tassambangi pekangku anjoreng ri batua*
       na= saba' taC–   sambang =i pekang ≡ku   anjoreng ri
       3= reason NVOL– snag   =3 hook   ≡1.POSS there   PREP
       batu ≡a
       stone ≡DEF
       ... because my hook was snagged there on the rocks

(390) ... *sikalinna massing nabattúi eroka atta'mea.*
       si–   kali ≡nna   massing na= battu –i   ero' ≡a   aC–
       one–   time ≡3.POSS each   3= come –APPL want ≡DEF MV–
       taC–   mea
       NVOL– urine
       ... they each suddenly got the desire to urinate (PT:10)

Verbs with *taC–* can themselves be made passive:

(391) *nita'langngerammi ri sari'battang toana*
       ni–   taC–   langnger –ang =mo =i ri   sari'battang toa
       PASS– NVOL– listen   –BEN =PFV =3 PREP sibling   old
       ≡na
       ≡3.POSS
       it was heard about by her eldest sister (PT:211)

Ceria (1993:101) analyses the counterpart of this prefix in Selayarese as a passive
marker which disallows the presence of the agent, while Hasan Basri analysed
it as an 'intransitivizer for stative verbs' (1999:20) (which seems unusual since
stative verbs are already intransitive). The examples he gives are for the most
part similar to those given above, however he also notes the 'agentless passive'
reading on voluntary verbs, giving the following example:

       ta?–   lette? =i   kadera –ɲjo
       PASS– move =3A chair –the
       The chair was moved (1999:25)

It seems that *taC–* is quite productive in this usage in Selayarese, but there are
very few examples in Makasar which are similar. One is perhaps *taralle* (from
alle 'take'):

(392) *punna nia' pulisi' taralle ngasenginjo pabotoroka*
     punna nia' pulis taC– alle ngaseng =i (a)njo pa– botor
     if   be police NVOL– take all   =3 that NR– gamble
     ≡*a*
     ≡DEF
     when the police come, all those gamblers will get caught (C:10)

However in general *taC*– cannot straightforwardly be called a passive marker in
Makasar because the majority of *taC*– verbs are inherently intransitive with no
possible transitive counterpart, e.g. *ta'do'doka'* 'I'm tired' (**nado'doka'* 'he tired
me'), *ta'muria'* 'I smile' (**kumuriko* 'I smile you'), and so forth.

Some speakers have a variant *tiC*– rather than *taC*– on at least *do'do'*, i.e.
ti'do'do' rather than *ta'do'do'* 'tired' (opinions were mixed as to whether *tiC*– was
allowed on other roots). I noticed this only in the speech of one family from the
Malino area, which is approximately 50 km inland from Makassar, close to an
area where Highland Konjo is spoken. However I have no reason to believe that
this is a feature of Highland Konjo, and the family in question were generally
viewed as speakers of standard Gowa Makasar. To the best of my knowledge,
there is no mention of this variant in any of the literature on Makasar, Konjo,
Selayarese, or Bugis.

There is a homophonous prefix *taC*– which attaches to numerals for a distributive meaning (§ 5.8.1.3).

8.5 Other Accounts of South Sulawesi Prefixes

In order to show the confusion existing in the literature about the functions of
these prefixes, in this section I will summarise the different analyses that have
been proposed for the system in Makasar or closely related languages.

8.5.1 *Makasar*
8.5.1.1 Matthes (1858:83 ff.)
Matthes identified three prefixes:
- *á*– (here *aC*–, see § 3.1.3.1 for an explanation of Matthes' system of transcription)
- nasal (*neusletter*)
- *má*– (*maC*– as above)

According to Matthes, the first was affixed to nouns to derive verbs meaning 'having a ...' and then by extension to other meanings, such as *jarang*
'horse' → *a'jarang* 'riding'. The third was said to be used in the same way, e.g.

VOICE/VALENCE-SIGNALLING PREFIXES   277

anrong 'mother' → *ma'anrong* 'have a mother'. The second was affixed to verb roots, without changing meaning, and could occur variably as either the prefix I notate as *aN(N)–* (with nasal substitution), or *aN–*, in both cases with or without the initial /a/. Thus *pinawang* 'follow' → *minawang, aminawang*, or *ampinawang*.

It is apparent that he conflated the prefixes *aN(N)–* and *aN–* into 'nasal' (he missed the geminate nasals resulting from *aN(N)–*), and divided the prefix *aC–* into the prefixes *a'–* and *ma'–*.[17] The vowel-initial roots which take *amm–* are not mentioned.

8.5.1.2   Imran (1976)

Imran (a native speaker linguist) noted two prefixes *aN–* (with four allomorphs) and *aK–* (with two). (Strangely, she attributed Matthes with only recognising one verbal prefix, *a–*). The allomorphy of *aN–* is based on assimilation, however there are a number of errors in her analysis.

– she misses the geminate nasals in every case, e.g. *polong* → *amolong* (actually *ammolong*) 'cut'.
– the supposed allomorphy between *aN(N)–* and Actor Focus *aN–* (see §7.2) is simply explained as the initial stop of the root being 'usually dropped' or 'sometimes retained' (p. 89).
– vowel-initial roots which take the prefix form *amm–* are assumed to be /m/-initial, e.g. *mantang* instead of *antang* 'stay'. (I discussed this contradiction between speakers' metalinguistic awareness and morphology in §7.1.4).
– She assumes the prefix *aK–* to have the allomorphs *ak–* and *aC–*, where the /k/ is actually a glottal stop (*a'–*), and *aC–* assimilates to voiceless consonants resulting in geminates, e.g. *kiok* → *akkiok* (*akkio'*) 'call'. She further claims that it is common for vowel-initial roots to take *aK–*, and gives *akanak* (*a'ana'*) 'have a child' and *akoto* (*a'oto*) 'go by car' as examples.[18]

She has little to say about the functions of the prefixes, only noting that *aK–* is preferred on noun bases and *aN–* on transitive verbs. She also claimed that *aK–* is more productive than *aN–*, and that loans always get *aK–*. This claim is probably made because most obvious loans are nouns, but it is demonstrably false,

---

17   Each of the prefixes historically began with /m/, now only seen in frozen forms such as *tu–ma'bicara–butta* (literally) 'the one who talks to the land' → 'the kingdom's administrator'.

18   Confusion stemming from the use of *k* to represent the glottal stop aside, my findings are that the combination of the form *a'–* and a vowel-initial root is quite rare, though it does occur. Notably, *a'ana'* was unacceptable to all the speakers I asked, *ammana'* being the only possible form. *A'anrong* 'have a mother' is possible, however.

as can be seen with forms such as *hukkung* → *anghukkung* 'punish' (← Arabic via Malay *hukum*), *sapatu* → *anynyapatu* 'shoe a horse' (← Port. *sapato* 'shoe') or (as I have observed) the more recent *sotting* → *anynyotting* 'to film/video something' (← Eng. *shooting*).

8.5.1.3 Asmah Haji Omar (1979)

The Malaysian linguist Asmah Haji Omar assumes two prefixes, *a*– and *ma*–.

- *a*– will cause gemination of any following voiceless consonant or nasal (again vowel-initial roots which take the prefix form *amm*– are misanalysed as having the nasal as part of the root, e.g. *empo* 'sit' is given as *mempo* to form *ammempo*). Sometimes *a*– is said to be realised with a glottal stop and sometimes with a nasal.
- *ma*– is realised as *ma?*– or *a?*– preceding /l/ or a vowel. Before /s/ it will sometimes cause nasal substitution (which she interprets as a single nasal, e.g. *suro* 'order' → *manuro* or *anuro*),[19] and sometimes it won't (e.g. *susa* 'difficult' → *masusa* 'have trouble'). Before a nasal it will cause gemination identical with *a*–.

Here again an allomorph (with initial /m/) has been interpreted as a separate morpheme, while clear distributional differences between actual morphemes have been overlooked. No mention is made of the functions of the prefixes.

8.5.1.4 Manyambeang et al. (1979)

In this work two prefixes are identified: *aK*– and *aN*–. This is the same as in Imran (1979), however they correctly note the geminates resulting from nasal substitution of voiceless stops and /b/ (e.g. *aN–pelak* → *ammelak* 'throw'). They do not explicitly comment on the distinction between the nasal-substituting prefix (*aN(N)*–) and the non-substituting prefix (Actor Focus *aN*–), although several examples are given which show the contrast (e.g. *ampelaki* 'throw it'). Like Matthes, they completely overlook the vowel-initial roots which take *amm*–.

8.5.1.5 Manyambeang et al. (1996)

This work again identifies *aK*– and *aN*–, both of which are analysed as deriving both intransitive and transitive forms (the 'transitive' *aK*– forms are actually those with inherent objects such as *akjarang* 'ride a horse'). The prefix *amm*– is analysed as an unexplained allomorph of *aN*–, e.g. *aN–anak* → *ammanak* 'have

---

19   This example is strange not only because of the single rather than geminate nasal, but also because in my data the root *suro* never takes the nasal-substituting prefix.

VOICE/VALENCE-SIGNALLING PREFIXES   279

a child' but *aN–aru* → *angngaru* 'take an oath'. The actual *aN(N)–/aN–* contrast
is again not explained, although it shows up in several examples.

8.5.1.6   Cense (1979)
Cense includes definitions for the verb prefix forms in the dictionary. The relevant ones are translated below:

> *ma'–*: prefix, comparable with Malay *ber–*, with very diverse meanings:
> 'provided with', 'working with', 'making', 'making use of' that which is
> indicated by the root; with numerals: 'by Xs'; also with numerous verb
> roots. The full form *ma'–* (with assimilation of the glottal stop to follow-
> ing stops and /s/) is mainly found in old writings and is now more often
> shortened to *a'–* or *'–*; an older form *mar–* is no longer productive and is
> only found in a few forms starting with vowels. Examples: *(m)a'bura'ne*
> or *'bura'ne* 'wed with a man' (← *bura'ne* 'man'); *(m)a'jarang* 'ride a horse'
> (← *jarang* 'horse'); *(m)accini'* 'to see'; *marewanang* 'arm oneself' (← *ewa*
> 'oppose').
>
> p. 429

> *ma–* + nasal: prefix for forming transitive and intransitive verbs—the full
> form *ma–* + nasal is mostly found in old or archaic texts, now more often
> shortened to *a–* + nasal or just the nasalised form. Examples: *(m)annun-*
> *rung* or *nnunrung* 'hit' (← *tunrung*); *(m)anynyungke* or *nynyungke* 'open'
> (← *sungke*); *(m)ande'de'* or *nde'de'* 'forge' (← *de'de'*); *(m)ammolong* or *mmo-*
> *long* 'cut' (← *polong*); *(m)ammu'bu'* or *mmu'bu'* 'pull out' (← *bu'bu'*).
>
> p. 429

> *ang–*: prefix for verb forms with definite objects when emphasis falls on
> preceding subject. Examples: *ia ampareki balla'–lompoa* 'he built the royal
> palace'; *inakke ambetako* 'I beat you'.
>
> p. 24

Of all the analyses summarised, Cense's is by far the most complete and accurate.

8.5.2   *Selayarese*
8.5.2.1   Mithun & Basri (1987)
The authors identify two prefix forms, *a?–* and *aŋ–*, but it is unclear whether
they consider them two different prefixes or allomorphs of one. They are said
to occur with active intransitive verbs—meaning verbs with no object or with

280   CHAPTER 8

an indefinite object, and are thus labelled 'intransitivisers'. The form of the prefix (*a?*- or *aŋ*-) is 'generally not predictable on phonological, syntactic, or semantic grounds' (p. 248). Examples are given where:

- the choice distinguishes between homophonous roots; (*a*)*ŋanre* 'eat' and (*a*)*kkanre* 'burn' (← *kanre*, nasal substitution results in a single nasal in Sela-yarese rather than the geminates seen in Makasar).[20]
- either form is possible with no difference in meaning; (*a*)*njari* ↔ (*a*)*?jari* 'become', or the choice is stylistic.
- a set of verbs will take *a?*- where there is no object, and *aŋ*- if there is an indefinite object; (*a*)*?beso?* 'pull' and (*a*)*mbeso?* 'pull something' (/b/ is not subject to nasal substitution).

A footnote (p. 253) mentions a prefix which does not cause nasal substitution ('merger') of the stem, e.g. (*a*)*ntama?* 'enter' and (*a*)*nsulu?* 'get out'. These forms must be followed by a locative phrase. The authors hint that it should be considered a separate prefix, but this is not followed up.[21]

8.5.2.2   Ceria (1993)

This paper quite exhaustively lists forms which take one or other of the two identified prefixes (*a?*- or *aŋ*-), which the author analyses as valency-reducing affixes, or intransitivisers (p. 82). She also includes the prefix *taC*- as an intransitiviser (a non-volitional marker in Makasar, see §8.4). The non nasal-substituting prefix, as in *antama?* above, appears in examples but is not remarked upon. She uses the choice of prefix as a way of dividing the verbs into classes, but does not identify a principle behind this, noting that 'it seems to be an idiosyncratic process' (p. 82).

8.5.2.3   Hasan Basri (1999)

This work identifies two categories of 'intransitivizer'; those for voluntary verbs (*a?*- or *aŋ*-), and *taC*- for stative verbs (see §8.4) (1999:20). He identifies four possibilities for verbs taking *a?*- and *aŋ*-:

(a) verbs which take *a?*- only, (b) verbs which take *aŋ*- only, (c) verbs which take both *a?*- and *aŋ*-, and (d) verbs which take no intransitivizers. The choice of *a?*- or *aŋ*- is largely lexical.

---

20   Actually, in Makasar at least, it does not seem that there are two roots *kanre* 'eat' and 'burn' but rather a single root with a core meaning 'consume' with divergent interpretations depending on the prefix. This is apparent because exactly the same contrast is seen with the high style variant *ka'do'*.

21   This parallels the situation in Makasar where these verbs appear to have been lexicalised with the prefix attached.

VOICE/VALENCE-SIGNALLING PREFIXES   281

He does however make some generalisations, i.e. that the *aʔ–* group includes
verbs derived from nouns, while the *aŋ–* group includes roots which are vowel-
initial. Within the group that can take both *aʔ–* and *aŋ–* he identifies two
possibilities: (a) free variation, e.g. *aʔriʔbaʔ/anriʔbaʔ* 'fly'; and (b) verbs which
'need no object when used with *aʔ–* and take an indefinite object when used
with *aŋ–*' (1999:24), e.g. *assossoro/aɲossoro* 'scrub' or the following:

> *aʔlesaŋa ri kaderaku*
> *aʔ–   lesaŋ =a ri   kadera –ku*
> INTR– move =1 PREP chair   –1.POSS
> I moved from my chair

> *allesaŋa kadera*
> *aŋ–   lesaŋ =a kadera*
> INTR– move =1 chair
> I moved a chair

There are also verbs in which '*aʔ–* shows a kind of agentless passive while
aŋ– implies an indefinite object' (1999:24), as in *aʔuruʔa* ⟨aʔ–uruʔ=a | INTR–
massage=1⟩ 'I had somebody massage me' versus *aɲurua* ⟨aŋ–uru=a | INTR–
massage=1⟩ 'I massaged somebody'.

Two comments can be made here about the obvious differences between
Selayarese and Makasar. The first is that it appears Selayarese does not have
the productive distinction between *aN(N)–* and Actor Focus *aN–* that Makasar
does, although it has some irregular forms which do not show nasal substitution such as *antamaʔ* 'go in', *antaʔle* 'go across', and *ansuluʔ* 'go out'.[22] The
second is that Selayarese does not appear to have the prefix *amm–* that appears
on some vowel-initial roots in Makasar.

8.5.3   *Konjo*
The papers on Konjo (Friberg 1988; 1996; Friberg & Friberg 1991a; 1991b) describe
either three or four verbal prefixes which they term verbalisers, one of which is
also labelled an adjective marker *a–* (see § 8.1.5). In Friberg & Friberg (1991b:6)
two prefixes other than *a–* are recognised, *a'–* and *ang–*, which are intransitive and transitive verbalisers respectively, and are 'in some sense optional'.
Only one example, *angnganre* 'eat' is given to illustrate that verbs with *ang–* are

---

22   Hasan Basri groups them as 'intransitive verbs which need prepositional temporal ad-
     verbs' (1999:55) which is surely a misprint for 'prepositional complements' as they have
     no particular relationship with temporal adverbs.

transitive. In Friberg & Friberg (1991a:87) they identify *amm–* as an allomorph of the intransitive prefix *a'–*, and posit an ad hoc rule called Glottal Nasalisation to explain it.[23]

In Friberg (1988) two different *ang–* prefixes are identified, the first of which (causing nasal substitution) is labelled Actor Focus Transitive, and the second (without nasal substitution) is labelled Goal Focus Transitive. They are described as follows:

> *a'–* indicates an intransitive verb: there cannot be a syntactic object ... *ang₁–* indicates a semi-transitive verb with actor focus; there may or may not be an object, but it cannot be a definite object ... *ang₂–* indicates a transitive verb with goal focus; i.e. the goal (or object) is fully specified (108).

> ... *ang₁–* attaches to a reduced form of the infinitive, while *ang₂–* attaches to the basic root or derived stem. *a'–* can be viewed as an infinitive marker, which when attached to a bare root indicates an intransitive form, but may also attach to forms which are transitive by virtue of the *pa–* transitivizer (CTV or causative prefix). Thus the combination of *a'–* plus *pa–* has the same function as *ang–* GFT (109).[24]

In Friberg (1996) the analysis has been changed so that *aN–* is no longer seen as a marker of Goal Focus but is more accurately identified as a 'definite verbaliser' which appears when 'the subject is topicalised (i.e. focused—AJ) in a transitive construction' (1996:145). The problems with Friberg's analysis of 'focus' (= voice) will be discussed in the following section.

8.6   Voice

In this section I will discuss the voice system of Makasar, examine analyses which assume a more pervasive voice system than I do, and give justification for the limited use of voice in my analysis.

---

23   It may be that Konjo lacks forms where *aC–V _ a'V*, such as *a'oto*.

24   This is a highly misleading statement(at least for Makasar, and I suspect for Konjo as well). Friberg (1988:109) gives the example *a'pakanrea ana'-ana'* 'I feed children' which according to her discussion should be synonymous with *angkanrea ana'-ana'*. However the latter can only be interpreted as meaning '(it) ate me, children'—assuming a focused but ellipsed Actor from a previous clause.

VOICE/VALENCE-SIGNALLING PREFIXES   283

The major voice alternation in Makasar is between (unmarked) active voice
and (marked) passive voice. Makasar does not have a symmetrical voice system
as found in languages such as Malay/Indonesian, nor anything comparable to
the more complicated voice systems (often referred to as 'focus') seen in Phil-
lippine type languages.[25]

Voice is conventionally understood as being a means whereby the speaker
can realign the mapping of participants onto grammatical functions in a clause.
The Makasar passive prefix *ni–* does exactly this—it promotes the Undergoer
(P in a corresponding transitive clause) so that it is S, the only core argument
of an intransitive clause. The Actor, if it is expressed, is done so by means
of an oblique. The difference between an active and passive clause is seen in
examples (393) and (394):

(393)   *Nakokkoka' meongku*
        na= kokko' =a' meong ≡ku
        3=   bite   =1 cat   ≡1.POSS
        My cat bit me

(394)   *Nikokkoka' (ri meongku)*
        ni– kokko' =a' ri   meong ≡ku
        PASS– bite   =1 PREP cat   ≡1.POSS
        I was bitten (by my cat)

Active voice is associated with the other verb prefixes (which are valence-
signalling rather than voice marking *per se*), or the absence of a prefix altogether. The set of verb prefixes was discussed in detail earlier in this chapter,
but those which are relevant to discussion here mark a clause as being intransitive (*aC–*) or semi-transitive (*aN(N)–*), while the absence of a verb prefix and
presence of an ERG= proclitic marks a clause as being fully transitive.

---

25   Malay/Indonesian, for example, shows alternations such as the following (Himmelmann
     2005:112):
     Anak saya me-lihat orang itu
     child 1s   AV-see person DIST
     My child saw that person.
     Orang itu   di-lihat anak saya
     person DIST UV-see child 1s
     My child saw that person
     The first is in Actor voice, and the second in Undergoer voice. Arguably, neither can be con-
     sidered clearly the 'basic' form, since in both the verbs are marked with voice prefixes and
     both clauses are syntactically equivalent, with only the order of arguments being changed.

This difference between fully transitive and semi-transitive clauses, which turns on whether the Undergoer is definite (P^{DEF}) or indefinite (P^{INDEF}) respectively, has itself been analysed by some writers as a type of voice (or 'focus') phenomenon, in some sense similar to the symmetrical alternation between actor voice and undergoer voice in other West Austronesian languages. (See for example Friberg 1988; Hanson 2003). As is plain by my choice of label, I prefer to view it as a marking of different levels of transitivity: basically there is a type of clause intermediate to intransitive and transitive clauses. My reasoning for this is laid out in §11.6 where I also discuss alternative analyses, but in essence reflects the fact that a speaker cannot select a prefix in order to realign participants and grammatical functions in the way that one might expect of either an Indonesian or Philippine-type voice system, but rather the selection falls out automatically depending on whether there is an Undergoer, and if so, whether it is definite or not.

Voice ('focus') in the closely related language Konjo has been discussed in two articles by Friberg (1988, 1996). Her analysis is entirely different to mine. The most obvious difference is terminological—Friberg is using 'focus' in a Philippine-language sense (i.e. voice (Himmelmann 2002)) whereas I prefer to use focus to describe the fronting of arguments (see §11.9) in a way which is more compatible with syntactic theory (e.g. Bresnan 2000:155 ff.; Van Valin 1999). However, even substituting the term 'voice' for 'focus' leaves Friberg's analysis unclear.

In the earlier article, she analyses focus as being designated by the choice of verb prefixes in transitive clauses, with $aN(N)$– being used for 'actor focus', and aN– being used for 'goal focus ... when the actor is a free form pronoun or a noun' (1988:109). The fact that this noun or pronoun should canonically be in pre-predicate position is not made explicit, though tellingly she later remarks that 'the absolutive suffix is dropped when the object (whether definite or indefinite) is fronted for focus' (1988:117). Thus, by this definition, actors receive focus simply as a result of there being an indefinite goal, while goals receive focus simply by virtue of being definite; on the other hand objects (= goals) may also be focused by being fronted. There are two problems here: the first being that there is no real explanation of what 'focus' is, or what it does (made all the more confusing by the fact that she is clearly using it in two different ways); and the second being that the article misses the point that if arguments can also be 'fronted for focus', then the aN– prefix (marking *goal focus*) appears in clauses where the *actor* has been 'fronted for focus' (see §7.2 and §11.9.1).

In the later article, the terms are changed somewhat. Actor and goal focus have been replaced by subject and object focus, in which:

VOICE/VALENCE-SIGNALLING PREFIXES

> *Subject focus* implies that there is no object, or that the object is not relevant to the action at hand. *Object focus* implies that there is a specifically referred-to object. Subject focus requires an 'absolutive' enclitic referent to the subject. Object focus requires an 'ergative' proclitic referent to the subject while the object is referred to by an 'absolutive' enclitic.
>
> FRIBERG 1996:143

In this article, the phenomenon of 'fronting for focus' (my **focus**, §11.9.1) is analysed as topicalisation.[26] Left-dislocation (my **topicalisation**, see §12.2.2) is not mentioned.

Thus, in the latter article focus was more-or-less defined, but there are problems with the definition. For example, one of Friberg's examples of a sentence with subject focus is the following:

(395)　*Langnginranga berangta*
　　　la=　　aN(N)– inrang　=a　　berang　≡ta
　　　FUT= VRt–　borrow　=1ABS knife　≡2(H)POSS
　　　I want to borrow (one of) your knives (Friberg 1996:144).[27]

I find no obvious way to interpret this clause as having 'no object, or that the object is not relevant to the action at hand' (Friberg 1996:143), as clearly the object is integral to the event. Rather, the point (as made in Friberg's earlier paper (1988:108)), is that there is no **specific** referent. This however seems more relevant to the interaction between specificity/definiteness and cross-referencing (§7.2.4) rather than focus (=voice) as such.

But by far the biggest problem with Friberg's analysis of 'focus' or voice is that it is essentially redundant. What it boils down to, in its 1996 formulation, is that the argument cross-referenced by an =ABS enclitic is focused; i.e. S in intransitive clauses (with or without indefinite P), and P in fully transitive clauses. Thus, by this definition, a clause can be transitive and have 'object focus' (= undergoer voice), or intransitive and have 'subject focus' (= actor voice). Since no other possibilities are permitted, saying that a clause has 'object focus' is the same as saying it is transitive, and vice versa. But if the notions of transitivity and focus are so inextricably linked (and cross-defined), it is difficult to see that they are both necessary.

A similar criticism could be made of Hanson's (2001:159) analysis of focus, in which:

26　I made the same error in my Masters thesis (Jukes 1998).
27　VRt = Transitive verbaliser, H = Honorific.

the unmarked focus being 'Patient focus', the *maC–* construction indicating 'Agent focus' and the benefactive and locative suffixes (*–əŋ* and *–i*) representing 'Benefactive' and 'Locative' focus respectively.

Since *maC–* in Bugis seems to behave much like *aC–* in Makasar (i.e. marking intransitive verbs), the notion that it should also remove focus from the (non-existent) Patient is not especially enlightening. And again, if stating that a clause has a particular argument 'focus' is just a way of saying that there *is* that argument in the clause, it is difficult to reconcile this with a productive voice system.

The error in the approaches presented above is, I believe, in attempting to analyse South Sulawesi languages as having symmetrical voice systems, whereas as Himmelmann has argued (2005), they do not have this characteristic. In any event, I prefer to separate the two issues of valence-signalling and voice. The notion of transitivity in Makasar certainly has degrees, and is sensitive to the definiteness or specificity of the Undergoer (though I do not go so far as to say that clauses with indefinite Undergoers are intransitive, see §7.5). But rather than the speaker realigning the grammatical functions by placing an affix on the verb, the choice of affix is given according to a tripartite distinction in valence: fully intransitive, semi-transitive, and fully transitive.

CHAPTER 9

Causative *pa*– and Related Forms

The following chapter discusses the causative prefix *pa*– and the related forms *paka*– and *pi*–, the former being a causative for adjectives, and the latter being harder to characterise as shall be discussed, but included here because it is often in free variation with *pa*– in some of its more peripheral uses. It can be noted here that bases derived with *pa*–, *paka*– or *pi*– cannot host the prefix *aN(N)*– (§ 7.1.2); which is to say they are not subject to nasal substitution, but rather take the prefix *aC*– (§ 7.1.1) or Actor Focus *aN*– (§ 7.2) if appropriate.

9.1 Causative *pa*–

The prefix *pa*–[1] as a verb prefix can most usefully be characterised as a causative, which adds an argument (the causer) to intransitive or transitive verbs, resulting in a verb meaning 'cause/allow to do X'. (Adjectives are causativised by the prefix *paka*–, see § 9.2). This process is extremely productive and most verbs have an associated causative derivation if this is semantically feasible.[2] *Pa*– is typically found directly on verb roots, but can also be found on certain derived infinitival forms (i.e. the sequence *pa–aC/aN(N)*–ROOT, § 9.1.2); and also on more complex bases such as verbs which are themselves derived with prefixes such as *pi*– or *si*– (§ 9.1.3), and even on some prepositional phrases (§ 9.1.4). It often occurs in combination with the benefactive and locative applicatives – *ang* or –*i*.

---

1 A reflex of PMP **pa*– 'causative of dynamic verbs; divide into X (X = numeral)' (Blust 2003).
2 Basri notes that in Selayarese only a small subset of verbs take *pa*–, only where 'the causee is not able to do the job by himself (herself) because he (she) is physically weak, or because of some disabilities, or because he (she) is not in a position to do it on his (her) own' (Hasan Basri 1999:332). He also notes that Selayarese uses *paka*– (in Makasar used for causativising adjectives) rather than *pa*– where force rather than help or permission is implied. This would appear to be an area of considerable grammatical difference between Selayarese and Makasar.

© KONINKLIJKE BRILL NV, LEIDEN, 2020 | DOI:10.1163/9789004412668_010

TABLE 70   *pa*–ROOT → CAUS

Basic verb base

lari	run	→	*palari*	put to flight
tinro	sleep	→	*patinro*	put to sleep
battu	come	→	*pabattu*	make come, bring
mange	go	→	*pamange*	make go, put, translate, abort
kamma	be thus	→	*pakamma*	make be thus
tu'guru'	fall	→	*patu'guru'*	make fall, lower

Intransitive verb base

| *a'jappa* | walk | → | *pajappa* | make walk, make go, mend |
| *ammantang* | stay | → | *pantang* | make stay, hold still |

Transitive verb base

angnganre	eat	→	*pakanre*	make eat
angnginung	drink	→	*painung*	make drink
accini'	see	→	*pacini'*	show

9.1.1   pa– *on Verb Roots*

Most causative derivations are built on intransitive verbal bases which are in themselves roots. These include the class of basic verbs,[3] most regular intransitive verbs, and ambitransitive verbs in their intransitive interpretations. Transitive verbs may also derive causatives—but these usually require applicative morphology in addition to *pa-*, thus if there is a P[INDEF] present the combination *pa--i* is used (§ 9.1.5), while if there is a definite P *pa--ang* (§ 9.1.6) or even *pa--i-ang* (§ 9.1.7) are used. A selection of causative verbs with *pa–* is shown in Table 70.

Causative verb bases derived with *pa–* will be prefixed with *aC–* in intransitive or semi-transitive clauses (or in other contexts where infinitive forms are found), e.g. *appajappa* ⟨aC–pa–jappa | MV–CAUS–walk⟩ 'make go, fix'. They will host the prefix *aN–* if there is a focused Actor and definite Undergoer (§ 7.2), e.g. *ampajappa* 'fix'. Note that they are not subject to derivation with the prefix *aN(N)–*, so there are no forms such as **ammajappa*.

---

3   All basic verbs can be derived into causative verbs, with the irregularity that the causative of *nia'* 'exist' is *pa'nia'* (rather than *pania'*, see § 9.1.2).

CAUSATIVE PA– AND RELATED FORMS   289

The argument structure of a causative verb is typically realigned so that the (former) S argument of the comparable intransitive clause becomes P (still referenced by an enclitic), and there is an added A argument denoting the causer of the action (which is referenced with a proclitic). For example, (396), (397) and (398) are intransitive clauses which can be compared with their causative counterparts (399), (400) and (401):

(396)   *Tinroi anakku*
        tinro =i   ana' ≡ku
        sleep =3   child ≡1.POSS
        My child sleeps

(397)   *Tu'guruki ballinna*
        tu'gur =u' =i   balli ≡nna
        fall   =EC =3   price ≡3.POSS
        Its price fell

(398)   *A'langea' ri tamparanga'*
        aC– lange =a' ri   tamparang ≡a
        MV– swim   =1   PREP sea   ≡DEF
        I swam in the sea

(399)   *Kupatinroi anakku*
        ku= pa–   tinro =i   ana' ≡ku
        1=   CAUS– sleep =3   child ≡1.POSS
        I put my child to sleep

(400)   *Lakupatu'guruki ballinna*
        la=   ku= pa–   tu'gur =u' =i   balli ≡nna
        FUT= 1=   CAUS– fall   =EC =3   price ≡3.POSS
        I'll lower its price

(401)   *Kupalangei anakku ri tamparanga*
        ku= pa–   lange =i   ana' ≡ku   ri   tamparang ≡a
        1=   CAUS– swim   =3   child ≡1.POSS PREP sea   ≡DEF
        I made/let my child swim in the sea

Derived causative verbs may also be semi-transitive, i.e. with an indefinite P. In these examples, as might be expected, the verbs are marked with the prefix *aC–* and S(=A) is referenced with an enclitic, while P[INDEF] is not referenced. This can

290   CHAPTER 9

be seen in (402) and (403), and also in (404), in which the Undergoer (a fetus)
is not only indefinite but customarily ellipsed:

(402)   *Appatinroi ana'–ana' iRamla*
        aC– tinro =i ana'– ana' i–   Ramla
        MV– sleep =3 RDP– child PERS– Ramla
        Ramla puts children to sleep

(403)   *Appajappai oto*
        aC– pa–   jappa =i oto
        MV– CAUS– walk =3 car
        He fixes cars (lit. makes them go)

(404)   *Appamangei antu*
        aC– pa–   mange =i antu
        MV– CAUS– go   =3 that
        That (drug) will cause an abortion

As will be discussed in § 11.2.4, the contrast between P and P^INDEF can lead to
some interesting alternations, as can be seen in examples (405) and (406), the
latter showing that a 3rd person enclitic pronoun in a transitive clause with
an indefinite NP will be interpreted as referring to a more salient anaphoric or
exophoric argument:

(405)   *Kupakanrei bembeku*
        ku= pa–   kanre =i bembe ≡ku
        1= CAUS– eat   =3 goat   ≡1.POSS
        I fed my goat

(406)   *Kupakanrei bembe*
        ku= pa–   kanre =i bembe
        1= CAUS– eat   =3 goat
        I made/let him eat goat (meat)[4]

Causative verbs are also subject to passivisation (passive causatives):[5]

---

4 If P is definite, the suffix *–ang* is needed to license a definite theme, see § 9.1.6.
5 Causative passives are also found, see § 9.3.5.

CAUSATIVE PA– AND RELATED FORMS   291

(407)   *Nipakanrei bembea (ri Ali)*
        ni–   pa–   kanre =i bembe ≡a   ri   Ali
        PASS–   CAUS–   eat   =3 goat   ≡DEF PREP Ali
        The goat was fed (by Ali)

The form *pa–* is also involved in several other derivational processes. On roots
it is used for deriving actor nominals, and on prefixed verb bases it derives
instrument nominals, while the confix *pa*⟩⟨*ang* on prefixed verb bases derives
place/time-of-action nominals (see § 6.2.2 for these). These are regarded as separate processes involving at least one other homophonous affix.

9.1.2   pa– *on Prefixed Bases*
A small minority of *pa–* causatives are built on derived verbal bases rather than
bare roots—that is, the verb prefix is internal to the causative prefix, resulting
in the sequences *pa–aC–*, *pa–aN(N)–*, *pa–amm–*, which are realised as portmanteau forms *paC–*, *paN(N)–*, and *pamm–*. Of these, the *amm–* verbs seem
to be exceptional in that derived causatives may appear with or without *amm–*
in seemingly free variation, while *aC–* and *aN(N)–* verbs are much more restricted in this regard.

   To my knowledge only one verb contains the sequence *pa–aN–*, namely
pantama 'make enter', which can be explained because the verb and prefix
complex has become lexicalised:

(408)   *Anjo assingku siagáng bone lalangku pantamai ri guci.*
        anjo assi   ≡ngku   siagáng bone   lalang ≡ku   pa–
        that contents ≡1.POSS with   contents inside ≡1.POSS CAUS–
        aN–tama =i ri   guci
        enter   =3 PREP urn
        Put my flesh and my innards in an urn (PT:200)

In Konjo it appears that there is a productive contrast between the sequences
*pa–*ROOT and *pa–aC/aN(N)–*ROOT. This has been explained as a contrast in
directness or intentionality of the action, with pa–ROOT forms being more direct or intentional (Friberg & Friberg 1991b:10), however there is no evidence of
this type of contrast in Gowa Makasar.

9.1.2.1   *pa–aC–*
The examples of *pa–aC–* in the corpus fall into two major types: those regularly built on verbs derived from numerals; and some irregular forms built on
verbs derived from a variety of sources, notably the existential basic verb *nia'*,

the negator *taena*, and then a seemingly random selection whose main commonality is that the *pa–aC–* derived form is in contrast with a more regularly derived form.

Verbs derived with *aC–* from numerals ('be NUMERAL') were mentioned on p. 262, and further derivation with causative *pa–* results in verbs meaning 'make be NUMERAL' which is common as far as 'make be one' = 'gather' and 'make be two' = 'separate', but beyond these does not seem to be idiomatic.

(409) *Apa saba'na nipasse're ngasengki' sikontu kara'–karaenga sanggenna rangka'na Gowa.*

apa   saba' ≡na   ni–   pa–   aC– se're ngaseng =ki' si–
what reason ≡3.POSS PASS– CAUS– MV– one   all   =2p MUT–
kontu kara'– karaeng ≡a   sangge ≡nna   rangka' ≡na
like RDP– karaeng ≡DEF until ≡3.POSS the.whole ≡3.POSS
Gowa
Gowa
Why were we all made to gather like this, all the karaengs from the whole of Gowa? (SKT:034)

(410) *Sarenta tosseng sipa'rua*

sare ≡nta   =tong =seng si–   pa–   aC– rua
give ≡2p.POSS =also =again MUT– CAUS– MV– two
We were made to separate again (from the song *Pangngu'rangimami* by Iwan Tompo)

The irregular derivations of the existential basic verb *nia'* and the negator *taena* mean 'make be' (= create) and 'make not be' respectively:

(411) *ia ampa'niaki lisere' matanna*

aN– pa–   aC– nia' =i liser =e' mata ≡nna
AF– CAUS– MV– be   =3 seed =EC eye ≡3.POSS
she made my pupil (a common metonymic idiom, meaning 'she made me') (PT:203)

(412) *Kupattaenai ri atingku*

ku= pa–   aC– taena =i ri   ati   ≡ngku
1= CAUS– MV– NEG   =3 PREP liver ≡1.POSS
I'll put it out of my heart, I won't think/feel it any more (lit: I'll make it not be in my liver, C:747)

CAUSATIVE PA– AND RELATED FORMS

Of other derivations of this type which I am aware of, some are based on verbs derived from adjectival roots with extended or specialised meaning. For example the form *appa'baji'* ⟨aC–pa–aC–baji' | MV–CAUS–MV–good⟩ means 'cause to be reconciled' (i.e. of estranged spouses or relations). It is in contrast with the regular causativised adjective *appakabaji'* ⟨aC–paka–baji' | MV–CAUS.ADJ–good⟩ 'mend, fix' (see § 9.2).

There is also at least one example where *pa–aC–* is used in contrast with *pa–* alone to distinguish homophonous roots: this is *appakkanre* ⟨aC–pa–aC–kanre | MV–CAUS–MV–burn⟩ 'make burn' (and assorted metaphorical extensions), which contrasts with *appakanre* ⟨aC–pa–kanre | MV–CAUS–eat⟩ 'feed'.

9.1.2.2   *pa–aN(N)–*
There does not appear to be a general statement that can be made about the sequence *pa–aN(N)–* other than to observe that a small minority of *aN(N)–* verbs retain *aN(N)–* in derived causatives, but the majority do not. Several of those retaining *aN(N)–* have roots beginning with *a*—which makes it tempting to analyse *pa–aN(N)–* as a device for avoiding the sequence *pa–a* and subsequent degemination of the two *a*s. Thus, *appangngaji* ⟨aC–pa–aN(N)–aji | MV–CAUS–BV–recite⟩ 'make (someone) recite the Koran' (← *angngaji*) rather than **appaji*, and the same with *appangngalle* 'make/let take' (← *angngalle* 'take') rather than **appalle*, as can be seen on the following passive causative benefactive example:

(413)   *Apaji na nipangngalleammi je'ne' ri kaca bulaeng.*
        apa =ja   =i na   ni–   pa–   aN(N)– alle –ang =mo =i
        what =LIM =3 COMP PASS– CAUS– BV–   take –BEN =PFV =3
        je'ne' ri   kaca bulaeng
        water PREP glass gold
        So they were made to take water (for themselves) in a gold cup (PT: 225)

There are however some odd counter-examples such as *appara'* 'make/let smell' (← *angngara'* 'smell, sniff'), and furthermore some verbs which do not begin with *a* also show this pattern (such as *appangngerangang* ⟨pa–aN(N)–erang–ang | CAUS–BV–carry–BEN⟩ 'bring something for someone') so a purely phonological explanation does not suffice.

9.1.2.3   *pa–amm–*
In contrast with the two preceding cases, verbs whose infinitives are formed with the prefix *amm–* are generally equally acceptable with *pa–* or *pa–amm–*,

294   CHAPTER 9

e.g. *paenteng* or *pammenteng* 'make stand', *paotere'* or *pammotere'* 'make
return', *pao'joro* or *pammo'joro'* 'make stay still'.

9.1.3   pa– *on Other Derived Bases*

Pa– may productively be placed on bases which have already been derived by
other processes apart from those involving the verb prefixes as discussed above.
The major examples of these are causative passives (*pappi––ang*, see §9.3.5),
causative mutual/reciprocals (*pa–si–*), and causative equal comparatives (*pa–siN–*).

(414)   *Punna para nia' anatta andi', kipasiallei*
        punna para nia' ana' ≡*ta*   *andi'*   *ki=* *pa–*   *si–*   *alle*
        when both be child ≡2p.POSS ↓sibling 2p= CAUS– MUT– take
        =*i*
        =3
        When we both have children little sister, let's betroth them (lit. make
        them take each other) (bembe:005)

(415)   *Napasilaga–ngasengi tedonga*
        na= *pa–*   *si–*   *laga ngaseng* =*i* *tedong* ≡*a*
        3= CAUS– MUT– fight all   =3 buffalo ≡DEF
        They make all the buffalo fight

(416)   *ia– iannamo. tau. ampasiewai. Gowa. Tallo'. iamo nacalla. rewata.*
        ia– *ia*   ≡*nna* =*mo tau*   *aN–* *pa–*   *si–*   *ewa*
        RDP– 3PRO ≡3.POSS =PFV person AF– CAUS– MUT– oppose
        ≡*a* =*i Gowa Tallo' ia*   =*mo na=* *calla*   *rewata*
        ≡DEF =3 Gowa Tallo' 3PRO =PFV 3= condemn god(s)
        Any person who sets Gowa and Tallo' against each other, he is cursed
        by the gods (KIT:ref039)[6]

(417)   *Pasinjai doekku na doe'na*
        pa– *siN–*   *jai*   *doe'* ≡*ku*   *na doe'*   ≡*na*
        CAUS– EQ.COMPR– many money ≡1.POSS and money ≡3.POSS
        Make my money the same as his

---

6   There is no enclitic pronoun in the second clause because P is focused (§11.9.1).

CAUSATIVE PA- AND RELATED FORMS   295

Conversely, causative verbs may occur as bases for mutual/reciprocal derivations with *si-* (§ 10.1).

9.1.4 pa– *on PPs*

Pa– derivations can be built on certain prepositional phrases. In most cases these consist of a preposition + a locative of either the *i* or *ri* sets (§ 5.7) such as *pariolo* 'put before' (← *ri olo*), *pariate* 'put above' (← *i rate*), *pariawa* 'put below' (← *i rawa*),[7] *pailalang* 'put inside' (← *i lalang*), *paipantara'* 'put outside' (← *i pantara'*).

(418) *Paipantara'ma' inakke*
       pa–   i   pantara' =mo =a' inakke
       CAUS– PREP outside   =PFV =1 1PRO
       Leave me out, don't count on me

(419) *Kupailalangi ri pattia*
       ku= pa–   i   lalang =i ri   patti ≡a
       1= CAUS– PREP inside =3 PREP box ≡DEF
       I put it in the box

However there are also examples where *pa–* is affixed to prepositional phrases consisting of *ri* and a noun, such as *parilima* ⟨CAUS–PREP–hand⟩ 'take in hand' and *paripatti* ⟨CAUS–PREP–box⟩ 'put in a box'. This only seems to be possible with certain conventional nouns, for example *pariballa'* 'put in a house' was widely accepted while *paripoko'* 'put in a tree' was considered marginal (*pariate ri poko'* being more acceptable). PPs containing place names cannot be derived with *pa–*, e.g. **pariSoppeng* 'put in Soppeng'.

9.1.5 pa–*VERB*–i

Pa– appears to have two quite different functions in these types of derivation. One is straightforwardly causative, and results in ditransitives with indefinite secondary objects.

(420) *Napacinikia' ba'bala'*
       na= pa–   cini' –i   =a' ba'bal =a'
       3= CAUS– see –APPL =1 whip =EC
       He showed me a whip (C:841)

---

7 Note that *pariate* and *pariawa* contain non-metathesised variants of the *i* locatives *irate* and *irawa* (see § 5.7.2).

296   CHAPTER 9

In this function *pa–* appears to be in free variation with *pi–*; in fact *pi––i* is more commonly found than *pa––i* in this sense (see §9.3.2).

The other (and perhaps more common) function of *pa––i* is quite different—and arguably contains a distinct prefix *pa-*. The causative meaning (and thus the causer) is usually not present. Instead, these forms are very like the verbs formed with the locative applicative *–i* alone, in which a goal or other locative argument is taken out of a PP and brought into the clause nucleus, usually for the purpose of focusing or relativising upon it (§10.1.2). The reason for using *pa–* as well as *–i* may be that for these lexemes the form ROOT–*i* has a dominant reading which is distinct. Some examples are: *palarí* 'run to a place' (cf. *larí* 'run to a person'); *panaíki* 'go up to something/someone' (cf. *naíki* 'look up to someone'):

(421)   *Pa'rasangang apa napalarí?*
        pa'rasangang apa na= pa–   lari –i
        land   what 3=   CAUS– run –APPL
        Which land did he run to? (C:379)

(422)   *kupala'–palaki. tanipanaikia. ballammang.*
        ku= pala'– pala'   =i ta=   ni–   pa–   nai'   –i   –a
        1=   RDP– request =3 NEG= PASS– CAUS– go.up –APPL –SBJV
        balla' ≡*mang*
        house ≡1pl.excl.POSS
        We ask that our homes not be climbed up to (KIT:96).

9.1.6   pa–*VERB*-ang

The function of *pa––ang* can be a fairly straightforward combination of certain of the functions of the two suffixes, i.e. most commonly *pa–* derives a causative transitive verb (i.e. a ditransitive), while *–ang* licenses a definite secondary object (theme):

(423)   *kupakanreangi bembea*
        ku= pa–   kanre –ang =i bembe ≡a
        1=   CAUS– eat   –BEN =3 goat   ≡DEF
        I made/let him eat the goat (cf. (405) and (406))

Interestingly, *pa––ang* does not appear to be used to derive causative verbs with beneficiaries, i.e. to cause something to be done on someone's behalf.

Other *pa––ang* derivations appear identical to verbs derived with *–ang* alone in which an instrument or other extra argument is brought into the clause

CAUSATIVE PA– AND RELATED FORMS   297

nucleus (§ 7.2.6.4). The reason for adding *pa–* here may be that the particular
verb + *–ang* has a dominant reading which is different, i.e. *balliang* on its own
has an unambiguous benefactive reading 'buy for (someone)', but *paballiang*
means 'buy with':

(424)   *unti kupaballiangi doekku*
       unti   ku= pa–   balli –ang =i doe'   ≡ku
       banana 1=   CAUS– buy –BEN =3 money ≡1.POSS
       Bananas I bought with my money (C:59)

There are also several derivations which seem to be predicative equivalents of
the place/time nominalisations formed by *pa⟩⟨ang* (§ 6.2.2.5), e.g. *pabattuang*
'come at a particular time' (cf. *pabattuang* 'time or place people/things come');
patinroang 'sleep at a certain time':

(425)   *allo apa napabattuang?*
       allo apa   na= pa–   battu –ang
       day what 3=   CAUS– come –LOC
       On what day did he come?

(426)   *bangngi tena nabaji' nipatinroang*
       bangngi tena na= baji' ni–   pa–   tinro –ang
       night   NEG 3= good PASS– CAUS– sleep –LOC
       a night not good for sleeping

9.1.7   pa–*VERB*–i–ang
To the best of my knowledge these forms are in free variation with the more
common *pi––i–ang* derivations (§ 9.3.4).

9.2   Causative *paka–*

Adjectives can take the prefix *paka–*[8] (not *pa–* as is usual for verb roots) to
form causative verb bases, which are by their nature transitive. In spite of their
inherent bivalent nature, like *pa–* derived causatives (§ 9.1), infinitives of *paka–*
verbs are marked with *aC–* rather than *aN(N)–*. In context they host clitic pronouns and/or the prefixes *aC–* or *aN–* depending on the syntax of the clause.

---

8   A reflex of PMP *pa–ka– 'causative of stative verbs' (Blust 2003).

298　　　　　　　　　　　　　　　　　　　　　　　　　　　　　CHAPTER 9

For example, (427) is imperative, thus has no verb prefix and an enclitic indexing P (*empo*), while (428) is transitive and has both A and P clitics.

(427)　*Pakabaji'mi emponu ana'–ana'*
　　　　paka–　　baji'　=mo　=i　empo　≡nu　　　ana'– ana'
　　　　CAUS.ADJ good　=PFV =3　seat　≡2f.POSS RDP– child
　　　　Sit comfortably, children (lit. improve your seating)

(428)　*Napakabambanga'*
　　　　na= paka–　　　bambang =a'
　　　　3= CAUS.ADJ– hot　　=1
　　　　He provokes me

Sentence (429) has an intransitive clause (the subject is the clause headed by
nicini'), while the clause in (430) shows Actor Focus with the prefix *aN–*.

(429)　*Appakala'bi'–la'biriki nicini' lampunna pasara'–malanga*
　　　　aC– paka–　　la'bi'– la'bir　=i'　=i ni–　cini' lampu ≡nna
　　　　MV– CAUS.ADJ– RDP– exalted =EC =3 PASS– see　lamp　≡3.POSS
　　　　pasar　=a'　malang ≡a
　　　　market =EC night　≡DEF
　　　　The night market lamps make it look quite splendid (lit. it makes exal-
　　　　tation (when) the night market lamps are seen, C:350)

(430)　*Ikau ampakalompoi pa'maikku*
　　　　i　　kau aN– paka–　　lompo =i pa'mai' ≡ku
　　　　PERS 2　AF– CAUS.ADJ– big　=3 breath ≡1.POSS
　　　　You make me happy (you enlarge my heart)

Derivations with *paka–* differ from those with *–i* such as *lompói* 'make big'
(§10.1.1) because it is assumed that the Undergoer already has the quality
to some degree, thus *appakalompo* 'make bigger' (similar to the distinction
between Indonesian *per–* and *–kan* (Sneddon 1996:98)).

　　Interestingly, Basri (1999:337) claims that in Selayarese this prefix means
'force to do something'. There is no hint of this connotation in Gowa Makasar.
Nor is there the possibility of placing the prefix before verb prefixes and even
proclitic pronouns as Basri describes (1999:338).[9]

9　However the prefix *pa–* in Makasar will sometimes have verb prefixes following it (§ 9.1.2.1

CAUSATIVE PA– AND RELATED FORMS   299

9.3   Experiencer-Oriented *pi–*

The prefix *pi–* is relatively uncommon in isolation and should perhaps be analysed as being only in fossilised derivations or at best semi-productive—however in combination with the applicative suffixes it is still quite commonly found. Its cognate in PAn is described by Blust as a 'causative of location' (2003:453), but that interpretation does not seem appropriate in Makasar. Its exact function is difficult to identify and seems to differ according to which root it is placed on, and also whether or not it appears in combinations with the applicative *–i* or the applicative combination *–i–ang*, thus these combinatory possibilities are examined separately in the sections below. Sometimes *pi–* can be characterised as causative (= valence-increasing) but more often it cannot easily be characterised in this way—and indeed often it seems to *decrease* valence. In several contexts *pi–* seems to be interchangeable with *pa–* with no apparent change in meaning. This is especially the case when *pi–* occurs in combination with the applicative suffix *–i* (§ 9.3.2), and also when *pi–* functions to mark verbs as passive within *pa–* causative derivations (§ 9.3.5).

In the absence of any clear single meaning of *pi–* I have elected to gloss it as something like a marker of experiencer-orientation (EXP–). This is because in isolation it derives forms with meanings like '(examine/inspect/listen) carefully or intently'. This is only a label of convenience, however, and it often has other functions.

9.3.1   pi–

Only a very few verbs are formed with affixation by *pi–* alone as opposed to combinations of *pi–* with *–ang* or/and *–i*. Of the four such forms listed by Matthes (1858:97), two are either errors or no longer acceptable; *pipake* and *pirassi* are in fact *pipakéi* ⟨pi–pake–i⟩ and *pirassí* ⟨pi–rassi–i⟩ (see § 9.3.2), and of the other two, *pinana'* has no independent root *nana'* so it is not possible to tell what meaning is added by the prefix, leaving only *pipasu*. However, I was able to find a few more in Cense and elsewhere in my corpus.

---

etc.), whereas Selayarese does not allow this: "*pa–* constructions are more cohesive than *paka–* constructions because *pa–* does not allow any elements to intervene between it and the base, while *paka–* allows intransitivizer, ergative marker, and secondary verb to intervene between it and the base" (Hasan Basri 1999:341).

300   CHAPTER 9

TABLE 71   Verbs derived with *pi–*

nana'	?	→	*pinana'*	take part, be involved
tappa'	entirety	→	*pitappa'*	skilful
pasu	knot, knurl	→	*pipasu*	pay attention to knots, examine carefully
sipa'	quality	→	*pisipa'*	examine qualities, inspect
dandang	sit still	→	*pidandang*	be attentive, notice
ajara'	teach	→	*pilajara'*	study

In the first two the function of *pi–* is opaque, and examining these words in
sentences does not make it any clearer, especially given that the form in (432)
appears to be an adjective, with the archaic prefix *ma–*:

(431)   *Eroka' appinana' ammalli kopi*
        ero'   =a' aC– pi–   nana' aN(N)– balli kopi
        want =1 MV– EXP– ?   BV–   buy   coffee
        I want to take part in the coffee buying (C:470)

(432)   *Mapitappa'–tongi mamma'dili'*
        ma– pi–   tappa'   tong =i maN(N)– ba'dil =i'
        STV– EXP– entirety also =3 BV–   gun   =EC
        He was also an excellent shot (C:779)

The *pi–* forms based on *pasu* and *sipa'* are are roughly synonymous, and
together with *pidandang* share the derived meaning of doing something carefully or intently. They are generally transitive, the exception being (435):

(433)   *ampipasui buloa*
        aN– pi–   pasu   =i bulo   ≡a
        AF– EXP– knot(of.wood) =3 bamboo ≡DEF
        Inspect the knurls of the bamboo (so as to cut it properly) (C:531)

(434)   *Pisipa'– sái jarangku*
        pi–   sipa'   sa   =i jarang ≡ku
        EXP– quality HORT =3 horse ≡1.POSS
        Inspect my horse (C:705)

CAUSATIVE PA– AND RELATED FORMS 301

(435) *Appidandangko kamma jangang*
    aC– pi–   dandang =ko kamma jangang
    MV– EXP– stay.still =2f thus   chicken
    You're listening like a chicken (i.e. with your head tilted to one side)

(436) *Salloinjo akkelong bembea nipidandammi ri karaenga ri Massere'.*
    sallo =i anjo aC– kelong bembe ≡a   ni–   pi–   dandang
    long =3 that MV– song goat ≡DEF PASS– EXP– stay.still
    =mo =i ri   karaeng ≡a   ri   Massere'
    =PFV =3 PREP karaeng ≡DEF PREP Massere'
    The goat sang for a while and was observed closely by Karaeng Massere'
    (bembe:061)

Another interesting example is the verb *appilajara'* 'study, learn' (with an irregular prefix form *pil–*), which is based on the transitive verb *angngajara'* 'teach'. In this case rather than a causer or facilitator being added as an argument the reverse has happened, as can be seen in (437) and (438). Note that in both cases the theme (the thing being studied) is not cross-referenced:

(437) *Kuajaraki anakku basa Anggarisi'*
    ku= ajar =a' =i ana' ≡ku   basa   anggaris =i'
    1=   teach =EC =3 child ≡1.POSS language England =EC
    I teach my child English

(438) *Appilajaraki basa Anggarisi' anakku*
    aC– pilajar =a' =i basa   anggaris =i' ana' ≡ku
    MV– study =EC =3 language England =EC child ≡1.POSS
    My child studies English

9.3.2 pi––i
The combination of the prefix *pi–* and applicative suffix *–i* has several functions: the first and most regular has an obvious similarity with *pa––i* derived causatives (§7.2.1.5) and in fact often these forms are in free variation with *pa––i* forms. These are generally ditransitives with indefinite secondary objects.

(439) *Tallu patti doe'na napita'gáli ngaseng pakkonciang*
    tallu patti doe'   ≡na   na= pi–   ta'gal –i   ngaseng pa⟩
    three chest money ≡3.POSS 3=   EXP– hold –APPL all   NR⟩
    aC– konci ⟨ang
    MV– key ⟨NR
    He has fitted all of his three money chests (UF) with locks (C:749)

302   CHAPTER 9

TABLE 72   Verbs with *pi--i*

ta'gala'	grasp	→	*pita'gáli*	make/let s.o grasp s.t
erang	carry	→	*pierangngi*	make/let s.o carry/bear s.t
balli	buy	→	*piballí*	make/let s.o buy s.t
cini'	see	→	*piciníki*	make/let s.o see s.t
mata	eye	→	*pimatái*	make/let s.o see s.t
pake	use, wear	→	*pipakéi*	make/let s.o wear/use s.t
asoro'	wear a hood	→	*piasóri*	make/let s.o wear s.t as hood
ponto	bracelet	→	*pipontói*	make/let s.o wear s.t as bracelet

(440) *Napierangngi anjo taua anu tanakullea*
       na= pi-   erang -i   =i anjo tau   ≡a   anu   ta=
       3= EXP- carry -APPL =3 that person ≡DEF something NEG=
       na= kulle ≡a
       3= can   ≡DEF
       He made that man carry something that he could not carry (C:209)

(441) *Mangemi bura'nenna anynyonyoki, ampiasóri lipa'.*
       mange =mo =i bura'ne ≡nna   aN- nyonyo' =i aN- pi-   asor
       go   =PFV =3 man   ≡3.POSS AF- comfort =3 AF- EXP- wrap
       -i   =i lipa'
       -APPL =3 sarong
       Her husband came, comforted her, wrapped her with a sarong (bembe:
       104)

(442) *Napimatáia' ba'bala'*
       na= pi-   mata -i   =a' ba'bal =a'
       3= EXP- eye -APPL =1 whip   =EC
       He showed me a whip (C:449)

Note that if there is a definite secondary object, the suffix *-ang* is found as well
as *-i* (§ 9.3.4).

Other derived forms are irregular and do not have a causative interpretation, but rather contrast with causative *pa-* derivations. Example (443) shows
a derivation from the intransitive basic verb *lari* 'run', resulting in a transitive
verb which clearly differs from a straightforward causative derivation:

CAUSATIVE PA– AND RELATED FORMS 303

(443)   *Lanupilaría'*
    la=   nu= pi– lari –i   =a'
    FUT= 2f= EXP– run –APPL =1
    You are going to leave me (C:xi)

(Compare *lanupalaria'* ⟨FUT–2f=CAUS–run=1⟩ 'you will make me run'.)[10] This quasi-passive sort of meaning has some similarity with the causative passive discussed in § 9.3.5. A similar sort of derivation can be seen in (444):

(444)   *Baji'na na kupisangkáiko ammantang*
    baji' ≡na   na   ku= pi–   sangka –i   =ko amm– antang
    good ≡3.POSS CMP 1=   EXP– forbid –APPL =2f MV–   stay
    It's a good thing I forbade you to stay (bembe:123)

Finally, at least one derivational possibility adds the meaning of doing something carefully or intently which was identified for *pi–* in isolation. In this there is no increase in valence when compared to the regular verb *allangngere'* 'hear':

(445)   *... nupilangngéri baji'–baji' bateku akkio' ri kau*
    nu= pi– langnger –i   baji'– baji' bate   ≡ku   aC– kio'
    2f = EXP– listen   –APPL RDP– good method ≡1.POSS MV– call
    ri   kau
    PREP 2fPRO
    listen well to my way of calling to you (PT:067)

9.3.3   pi––ang

Verbs forms derived with *pi–* and the benefactive/applicative *–ang* are uncommon. Of those that I found in Cense, speakers confirmed that they would be equally or more acceptable with *pi––i-ang*.

(446)   *Nipicinik(i)angi salanna nalarro*
    ni–   pi– cini' (–i)   –ang =i sala   ≡nna   na= larro
    PASS– EXP– see (–APPL) –BEN =3 wrong ≡3.POSS 3=   angry
    He was shown his faults and became angry (C:841)

---

10   The exact parallel construction (including the applicative) **lanupalaría'* ⟨FUT-2f=CAUS-run-APPL=1⟩ is not acceptable—*palarí* is somewhat unexpectedly a derivation used when a locative argument is in focus or heading a relative clause, see § 9.1.5.

304 CHAPTER 9

The most common occurrence of this combination is within causative passive forms § 9.3.5.

9.3.4 pi--i-ang

Verbs derived with *pi--i-ang* are for the most part identical to those formed with *pi--i*, with the difference that the secondary object is definite—the licensing of definite Themes or other kinds of secondary argument being one of the regular functions of *–ang* (§ 9.2.1.2).

(447) *Kupicinikiangi jarangku i Ali*
      ku= pi–   cini' –i   –ang =i jarang ≡ku   i   Ali
      1= EXP– see –APPL –BEN =3 horse ≡1.POSS PERS Ali
      I let Ali see my horse (C:841, compare P^{INDEF} example in (442), and also causative passive (455))

(448) *kupita'galiangko anne koncina tokoa*
      ku= pi– ta'gal –i   –ang =ko anne konci ≡na   toko ≡a
      1= EXP– hold –APPL –BEN =2f this key ≡3.POSS shop ≡DEF
      I give you (lit. make you hold) this key to the shop

(449) *Takupiballiangngai antu*
      ta=   ku= pi– balli –ang –i   –a   =i antu
      NEG= 1= EXP– buy –BEN –APPL –SBJV =3 that
      I didn't make him buy that (C:59)

9.3.5 pi--ang *in Causative Passive Derivations*

Another function of *pi–* is to act (in combination with *–ang*) as a passive morpheme *within* a *pa–* causative derivation, resulting in a causative passive. These consist of the combination *pappi--ang* ⟨pa–aC–pi--ang | CAUS–MV–EXP--BEN⟩.

(450) *Napappikanreangi jukuka (ri mionga)*
      na= pa–   aC– pi– kanre –ang =i juku' ≡a   ri   miong
      3= CAUS– MV– EXP– eat   –BEN =3 fish ≡DEF PREP cat
      ≡a
      ≡DEF
      He let/made the fish be eaten (by the cat) (C:291)

This unusual use of *pi–* may be motivated by the fact that the regular passive prefix *ni–* must occur external to other derivational morphology (i.e. *pa–ni–* is

CAUSATIVE PA– AND RELATED FORMS   305

not a permissible ordering), and the alternative ordering *ni–pa–* would have a
passive causative meaning as shown in (451) rather than the intended causative
passive meaning in (450):

(451) *Nipakanreangi jukuka mionga (ri Ali)*
  ni– *pa–* *kanre –ang =i juku' ≡a* *miong ≡a* *ri* *Ali*
  PASS– CAUS– eat –BEN =3 fish ≡DEF cat ≡DEF PREP Ali
  The cat was let/made to eat fish (by Ali)

Looking at it more closely, the clause in (450) is like a combination of a simple
passive in (452), and a causative in (453):

(452) *Nikanrei jukuka (ri mionga)*
  ni– *kanre =i juku' ≡a* *ri* *miong ≡a*
  PASS– eat =3 fish ≡DEF PREP cat ≡DEF
  The fish was eaten (by the cat)

(453) *Napakanreangi jukuka mionga*
  na= pa– *kanre –ang =i juku' ≡a* *miong ≡a*
  3= CAUS– eat –BEN =3 fish ≡DEF cat ≡DEF
  He fed the cat the fish

Some other examples are:

(454) *Napappiassengangi kalenna (ri nakke)*
  na= pa– *aC– pi–* *asseng –ang =i kale ≡nna* *ri* *nakke*
  3= CAUS– MV– EXP– know –BEN =3 self ≡3.POSS PREP 1PRO
  He made himself known (to/by me)

(455) *Kupappicinikangi jarangku (ri Ali)*
  ku= pa– *aC– pi–* *cini' –ang =i jarang ≡ku* *ri* *Ali*
  1= CAUS– MV– EXP– see –BEN =3 horse ≡1.POSS PREP Ali
  I let my horse be seen (by Ali) (C:841)

As Cense notes (1979)\:543\, in the combination *pappi–* it is common for *pi–*
to be replaced by *pa–*, resulting in *pappa–*. This has the result that one of the
apparent functions of *pa–* is as a valence-*reducing* passive marker, in contrast
to its regular function as a valence-*increasing* causative.[11]

---

11 The use of the same morpheme to mark both passives and causatives has been noted (for
  Korean) by Manning (1996:44).

CHAPTER 10

Applicative Suffixes

This chapter discusses the two most productive suffixes in Makasar, *–i* and *–ang*. In their core uses they are most usefully characterised as applicative: *–i* as a locative applicative and *–ang* as a way to promote arguments and also as a benefactive marker. However, there are also other clear (and some not so clear) functions which suggest that each of these suffix forms can be analysed as consisting of more than one distinct morpheme—where I suspect this to be the case I have mentioned it, but without making the identification of discrete morphemes a major part of the description as I believe there are also arguments for a multifunctional analysis.

To my knowledge applicative suffixes can co-occur with verb prefixes (and/or clitic pronouns) without restriction, with a few notable exceptions (such as the monovalent *aC–* prefix not occurring on transitivised adjectives as noted in §9.1.1). In view of this productivity I have not attempted to exhaustively list possible forms—which may in any case be found in the dictionary (Cense & Abdoerahim 1979)—but rather have exemplified the major functions.

10.1 The Suffix Form *–i*

This suffix form serves a variety of purposes—in the dictionary Cense has given it 8 sub-entries (Cense & Abdoerrahim 1979). It seems probable that *–i* consists of at least two different homophonous suffixes: the first derives transitive verbs from adjectives and certain nouns, while the second is an applicative which licenses a goal or other kind of locative argument. There is a third function which is harder to characterise, but basically evokes extended, iterative, or metaphorical meanings. It is most likely no longer productive.

The somewhat different functions of the suffix form can to some extent be unified by assuming a meaning like 'have X-ness applied'. The distinction between this and straightforward transitivising (in the case of adjectives) is not usually apparent, but note for example that the *–i* derivation of *koasa* 'mighty' does not mean 'make mighty', but instead means 'be subjected (by)' (i.e. have might applied to them):

© KONINKLIJKE BRILL NV, LEIDEN, 2020 | DOI:10.1163/9789004412668_011

APPLICATIVE SUFFIXES 307

(456) *Le'ba'namo anjo antama Balandaya naerang bundu'na na nakoasái-*
tommi butta Marusu' ri tau Boneya.

le'ba'	≡*na*	=*mo*	*anjo*	*antama*	*Balanda*	≡*a*	*na*=	*erang*
finished	≡3.POSS	=PFV	that	enter	Holland	≡DEF	3=	bring

bundu'	≡*na*	*na*	*na*=	*koasa*	–*i*	*tong*	=*mo*	=*i*	*butta*	*Marus*
war	≡3.POSS	and	3=	mighty	–TRS	also	=PFV	=3	land	Maros

=*u'*	*ri*	*tau*	*Bone*	≡*a*
=EC	PREP	person	Bone	≡DEF

After the Dutch entered, bringing war, the land of Maros was controlled
by the people of Bone (Maros:160)

It should be noted here that the enclitic pronoun =*i* will not manifest phonologically when attached directly to a stem ending in –*i*, this is due to vowel
degemination (§ 2.3.1).

10.1.1 *Transitiviser* –i

Adjectives and certain nouns may form transitive predicates by using –*i*. The
result can be considered a verbal base, but they do not usually host verb prefixes other than Actor Focus *aN–* or passive *ni–*. This may be because these
transitivised forms usually occur in fully transitive clauses or in imperatives,
environments in which verb prefixes are rarely seen.

10.1.1.1 Adjectives

All adjectives may be transitivised with –*i*—it is one of the defining characteristics of the class.

(457) *Lakubambángi je'neka*

la=	*ku*=	*bambang*	–*i*	*je'ne'*	≡*a*
FUT=	1=	hot	–TRS	water	≡DEF

I'll heat up the water

(458) *Nalompói pa'maikku*

na=	*lompo*	–*i*	=*i*	*pa'mai'*	≡*ku*
3=	big	–TRS	=3	breath	≡1.POSS

He encourages me (lit: he enlarges my breath)[1]

---

1 *Pa'mai'* literally means 'breath' (← *a'mai'* 'breathe'), but also means 'nature' or 'character'.

308   CHAPTER 10

(459)   *Lanubattalijintu jaranga*
        la=   nu= battal –i   =ja   =i (a)ntu jarang ≡a
        FUT= 2f= heavy –TRS =LIM =3 that horse ≡DEF
        You'll make the horse too heavy (i.e. by loading too much onto it, C:89)

(460)   *Numanynyéri otoku!*
        nu= manynyer   –i   =i oto ≡ku
        2f= smell.of.fish –TRS =3 car ≡1.POSS
        You made my car stink of fish!

The following examples show passive and actor focus constructions on transitivised adjectives:

(461)   *Nibodói paua, nita'langngerangmi ri sari'battang toana siagáng ri*
        sari'battang tangngana.
        ni–   bodo –i   pau ≡a   ni–   taC–   langnger –ang =mo
        PASS– short –TRS story ≡DEF PASS– NVOL– listen   –BEN =PFV
        =i ri   sari'battang toa ≡na   siagáng ri   sari'battang
        =3 PREP sibling   old ≡3.POSS with   PREP sibling
        tangnga ≡na
        middle ≡3.POSS
        To cut the story short, her eldest sister and middle sister heard about it
        (PT:211).

(462)   *Jaimi pa'balle le'ba' napaballe mingka iapanne anggassíngi*
        jai   =mo =i pa'balle le'ba' na= pa–   balle mingka ia
        many =PFV =3 medicine already 3= CAUS– spill but   3PRO
        =pa (a)nne aN– gassing –i
        =IPF this AF– strong –TRS
        He already took a lot of medicine but it hasn't made him strong yet
        (C:229)

As mentioned in § 9.2, adjectives transitivised by –*i* differ from those made
causative by *paka*–, because the latter implies that the quality is already present
to some degree, while –*i* has no such implicature.[2]

---

2   Friberg & Friberg (1991b:8–11) analyse a similar contrast in Konjo as being between 'focus on
    process' (–*i*) and 'focus on the result of an action' (*paka-*).

APPLICATIVE SUFFIXES   309

10.1.1.2   Nouns

Certain nouns may be transitivised by *–i*, resulting in verbs meaning 'put X in/on something'. The most commonly seen derivations come from nouns denoting substances which can be added to something else, especially ingredients or condiments added to foodstuffs:

(463)   *Tenapa kugollái kopia*
         tena =pa ku= golla –i   kopi   ≡a
         NEG =IPF 1=   sugar –TRS coffee ≡DEF
         I haven't sugared the coffee yet

(464)   *Nasantangngi sara'bayya*
         na= santang   –i   sara'ba   ≡a
         3= coconut.cream –TRS ginger.drink ≡DEF
         She put coconut cream in the *sara'ba* (a kind of ginger drink)

There are examples of *–i* used on other types of noun, such as those seen below, but in general this use of *–i* seems to be fairly restricted in Makasar when compared to Konjo (Friberg & Friberg 1991b:8) or Selayarese (Hasan Basri 1999:310).[3]

(465)   *Kammai tu–nikaluaráia pajana*
         kamma =i tu   ni–   kaluara –i   ≡a   paja ≡na
         thus   =3 person PASS– ant   –TRS ≡DEF rump ≡3.POSS
         He's like someone with ants in his pants (C:276; cf. *kaluaráng* 'infested with ants', §10.2.2)

(466)   *Batúi–sai anjo kongkonga*
         batu –i   sa   =i anjo kongkong ≡a
         stone –TRS HORT =3 that dog   ≡DEF
         Throw a stone at that dog

(467)   *Nabosía' ri agánga*
         na= bosi –i   =a' ri   agáng ≡a
         3= rain –TRS =1 PREP road ≡DEF
         Rain got me on the road.

---

3 For example, Selayarese has *–i* derivations on nouns denoting items of clothing, with the derived meaning being 'help to wear (clothing)', or on crops, meaning 'plant a place with crops' (Hasan Basri 1999:316–317). These derivations are not natural in Gowa Makasar.

310   CHAPTER 10

(468)   *Teako ammempói antureng naallóiko!*
        tea   =ko amm– empo –i   antureng na= allo –i   =ko
        NEG =2f MV–   sit   –APPL there   3= sun –TRS =2f
        Don't sit there, go in the sun!

10.1.2   *Locative Applicative* –i

As a locative applicative –*i* is basically used to derive transitive verbs from corresponding intransitive verbs which have goals or other locative kind of arguments in prepositional complements or adjuncts. The arguments are promoted out of the PP into the clause nucleus and are then cross-referenced as is normal for core arguments. For example, clauses such as (469) and (471) have corresponding intransitive clauses with PPs in (470) and (472):

(469)   *Nabattúia' pongoro'*
        na= battu –i   =a' pongor   =o'
        3=   come –APPL =1 madness =EC
        Madness came over me

(470)   *Battui pongoro' ri nakke*
        battu =i pongor   =o' ri   nakke
        come =3 madness =EC PREP 1PRO
        Madness came to me

(471)   *Naempóia' i Ali*
        na= empo –i   =a' i   Ali
        3=   sit   –APPL =1 PERS Ali
        Ali sat on me

(472)   *Ammempoi i Ali ri nakke*
        amm– empo =i i   Ali ri   nakke
        MV–   sit   =3 PERS Ali PREP 1PRO
        Ali sat on me

There are a number of reasons why the locative applicative construction might be preferred to those with arguments in obliques. One is that this construction allows these locative arguments to be focused (§ 11.9) or relativised upon (§ 6.3.3), which is not possible for PPs, e.g.:

APPLICATIVE SUFFIXES 311

(473) *Tappere' kuempói*
       tapper =e' ku= empo –i
       mat   =EC 1= sit   —APPL
       I sit on a mat (also *tappere' kuempoía* ⟨mat 1=sit–APPL≡DEF⟩ 'the mat I
       sit on').

There are also most likely stylistic reasons, such as to avoid the use of free pronouns, as in the examples (469)–(472). The *–i* construction also seems to give
a sense that the location is more immediate, has been more affected, or is generally of more relevance than corresponding PPs. For example, consider the
following clauses:

(474) *A'meai ri lipa'na*
       aC– mea =i ri   lipa' ≡na
       mv– urine =3 PREP sarong ≡3.POSS
       He pissed in his sarong

(475) *Nameái lipa'na*
       na= mea –i   =i lipa' ≡na
       3= urine –APPL =3 sarong ≡3.POSS
       He pissed his sarong

In (474) *lipa'na* is an adjunct—it is simply some extra information about the
event of a child wetting the bed. But (475) is about the sarong, and implies that
it is soaked through in a way that (474) does not convey.

    Another reason for using *–i* is that it allows the goal to be unexpressed or
abstract. For example, (476) has no counterpart with a PP, as there is no possible NP to put inside it:

(476) *Nia' lakumangéi*
       nia' la=   ku= mange –i
       exist FUT= 1= go   —APPL
       There is (somewhere) I'll go (= I need to go to the toilet)

10.1.3 *Extended* –i
In some very rare examples *–i* evokes extended meanings of habituality or iter-
ativity.

(477) *Lakusaréiko bunga–bunga sollanna nuga'ga'*
　　　la= ku= sare –i　　=ko bunga– bunga sollanna nu= ga'ga'
　　　FUT= 1=　give –APPL =2f RDP–　flower so.that　2f= pretty
　　　I'll keep you provided with flowers so that you're beautiful (cf. *lak-usareko bunga–bunga* 'I'll give you flowers')

This is perhaps similar to the 'number marking' on verbs described for Sela-yarese in Basri (1998), in which *–i* can be suffixed to any predicates other than nouns, with the interpretation that either the participants are plural, or the activity is repeated. The same appears to be the case for Konjo (Friberg & Friberg 1991b). Speakers argue about the status of iterative or plural *–i* in Makasar. Tellingly, those who use or allow it have universally (in my exper-ience) had Selayarese (or at least eastern) origins, even if they now identify themselves as Gowa Makasar and otherwise seem to be fluent speakers of that variety. Makasar without Selayarese origins generally reject iterative/plural *–i*.

10.2　The Suffix Form *–ang*

The suffix form *–ang* is used widely for many purposes—as an indication it is given nine distinct senses in the dictionary (Cense 1979). This is not alto-gether surprising when one considers that it most likely represents a coales-cence of several distinct PMP affix forms: these being **–aken* 'benefactive suffix'; **–an* 'locative focus/local voice, deverbal nouns of location, group of X (X = numeral)'; and **–en* 'patient focus/undergoer voice, polite imperative, suffer bodily afflictions; nominalizer, be divided into X (X = numeral)' (Blust 2003:450) Its nominalising functions (both alone and as part of the *pa⟩⟨ang* and *ka⟩⟨ang* confixes) were discussed in § 6.2, and its function as a comparat-ive marker (now usually doubled as *–angngang*) was discussed in § 5.4.1. This section discusses the functions of *–ang* as a verbal applicative suffix, and also the separate homophonous suffix *–ang* which is much less common and marks predicate nominals with the meaning 'afflicted with X' (§ 10.2.2).

10.2.1　*Benefactive/Applicative –ang*
As an applicative suffix *–ang* has two regular functions which are clearly related but can to some degree be distinguished: the first function is to license pro-motion of an argument, i.e. adding one by promoting an inherent patient to a specific P (§ 9.2.1.1), or promoting an indefinite secondary object to a definite one (§ 9.2.1.2). The second function is to give a benefactive reading to transitive clauses by adding a beneficiary as primary object (§ 9.2.1.3). I have elected to

APPLICATIVE SUFFIXES   313

gloss –*ang* consistently as –BEN to differentiate it from the other applicative
suffix –*i*, but it must be remembered that licensing a beneficiary is only one of
its functions.

10.2.1.1 Inherent Patient to P

When attached to an intransitive verb derived from a noun, with the meaning 'have NOUN' (in which the semantic patient is inherent and non-specific),
–*ang* licenses a specific Undergoer, thus promoting an inherent patient into
a core argument P, which is then cross-referenced with an =ABS enclitic. For
example, *a'baine* means 'have a wife' (← *baine* 'woman')—the patient is inherent to the predicate, which is formally intransitive, e.g. *a'bainea'* ⟨aC–baine=a'
| MV–woman=1⟩ 'I am married'. However, it can be given a specific P as fol-
lows:

(478) *Karaengta Barasa', nabaineangi I Basse' Nguakeng.*
       karaeng ≡*ta*   *Barasa'* *na=* *baine* –*ang* =*i* *I*   *Basse'*
       karaeng ≡2p.POSS Barasa' 3=   female –BEN =3 PERS Basse'
       Nguakeng
       Nguakeng
       As for Karaeng Barasa', he married I Base Nguakeng (Maros:145)

Similarly, *atta'mea* means 'urinate' (← *mea* 'urine'), and again the patient is
inherent and the predicate is normally intransitive, e.g. *atta'meai* ⟨aC–taC–
mea=i | MV–NVOL–urine=3⟩ 'he is pissing'. The patient can be made specific
and promoted into an P with –*ang*:

(479) *Nata'meángi cera'*
       na= *taC–*   *mea* –*ang* =*i* *cera'*
       3=   NVOL– urine –BEN =i blood
       He's pissing blood

Verbs derived from nouns in which the meaning is 'use NOUN' are also subject to this process, e.g. *a'je'ne'* 'bathe' (← *je'ne'* 'water') can have the medium of
bathing made explicit as follows:

(480) *Kuje'nekangi je'ne' kammu*
       ku= *je'ne'* –*ang* =*i* *je'ne'* *kammu*
       1=   water –BEN =3 water warm
       I use warm water to bathe in

314 CHAPTER 10

Note that in contrast with the usual rules for cross-referencing of P, the specific P licensed by *–ang* in these constructions need not be definite to be cross-referenced (as shown in (479) and (480) above).

10.2.1.2   Definite Secondary Object

In three-participant constructions such as those with *sare* 'give', *–ang* licenses a definite secondary object (theme) while the =ABS enclitic indexes the primary object (recipient):

(481)   *Lakusaréangko bo'bokku*
      la=   ku= sare –ang =ko bo'bo' ≡ku
      FUT= 1= give –BEN =2f book ≡1.POSS
      I'll give you my book

Compare the construction with an indefinite secondary object in (482). In these types of construction the primary object is still indexed with an =ABS enclitic but the secondary object is not reflected in the morphology by the use of *–ang*:

(482)   *Lakusareko doe'*
      la=   ku= sare =ko doe'
      FUT= 1= give =2f money
      I'll give you some money

These types of construction are examined further in §11.8.

10.2.1.3   Benefactive

The suffix *–ang* is also used to add a benefactive meaning to transitive clauses, in which case the argument with the thematic role of beneficiary is indexed with the =ABS enclitic and can thus be regarded as the primary object. This is in contrast with the parallel transitive (non-benefactive) constructions in which the argument indexed with the =ABS enclitic has the thematic role of theme. Compare the benefactive construction in (483) with the ordinary transitive construction in (484):

(483)   *Kuballiangko baju*
      ku= balli –ang =ko baju
      1= buy –BEN =2f shirt
      I bought you a shirt

APPLICATIVE SUFFIXES   315

(484)   *Kuballi bajua*
        ku= balli =i   baju ≡a
        1=   buy   =3 shirt ≡DEF
        I bought the shirt

These benefactive constructions differ from the *–ang* marked ditransitives seen above, in that they are not sensitive to the definiteness of the secondary object, which may be indefinite (483) or definite (485) with no difference in structure:

(485)   *Naboyánga' anjo pa'ballea*
        na= boya   –ang =a' anjo pa'balle   ≡a
        3= search –BEN =1 that medicine ≡DEF
        he looks for that medicine for me

I have noticed a tendency for some younger speakers to use the preposition *untu'* (from Indonesian *untuk* 'for') to mark beneficiaries (instead of using *–ang* to mark the benefactive relation and an =ABS enclitic to mark the beneficiary):

(486)   *Ammallia' baju untu' anakku*
        aN(N)– balli =a' baju untu' ana'   ≡ku
        BV–   buy   =1 shirt for   child ≡1.POSS
        I bought a shirt for my child

(487)   *Kuballi bajua untu' anakku*
        ku= balli =i baju ≡a   untu' ana'   ≡ku
        1=   buy   =3 shirt ≡DEF   for   child ≡1.POSS
        I bought the shirt for my child

As illustrated above, unlike *–ang* benefactives these constructions are sensitive to the definiteness of the theme—if it is indefinite, it is not cross-referenced and the clause is semi-transitive (486). This is doubtless because the theme is P rather than a secondary object, while the beneficiary is oblique. It is difficult to gauge when the *untu'* construction entered the language, but as there is no entry for *untu'* in the dictionary it seems likely that this is quite recent. There is no structural equivalent in 'pure' Makasar.

10.2.1.4   Other Types of Argument

There are also examples of *–ang* being used to license an instrument or other thematic role. For example, in the following sentence *–ang* licenses a third argument, the kris used for killing:

(488) *anjo seleka nabunoangi balia*

anjo	*sele'*	≡*a*	*na=*	*buno*	*–ang*	*=i*	*bali*	≡*a*
that	kris	≡DEF	3=	kill	–BEN	=3	enemy	≡DEF

he killed the enemy with that kris (Cgn:24)

In other cases the thematic role of the additional argument is less clear. For example *mangeang* ⟨go–BEN⟩ is glossed by Cense as 'go with' (Cense & Abdoerrahim 1979:439), but only in the sense of going with a choice in a game, e.g.:

(489) *apa numangeang*

apa	*nu=*	*mange*	*–ang*
what	2f=	go	–BEN

which card will you play?

Similarly, *jappáng* ⟨jappa–ang⟩ has the gloss 'walk with', and appears in the idiom *jappáng jappana* 'walk with his walk', i.e. do what he usually does, follow his usual behaviour. In addition, the same derived form seen in (488) above may be used in a relative clause, licensing a temporal location:

(490) *allo nibunoangai*

allo	*ni–*	*buno*	*–ang*	≡*a*	*=i*
day	PASS–	kill	–LOC	≡DEF	=i

the day he was killed

10.2.2 'Afflicted with'
A specialised function of *–ang* is found in which it is attached to nouns denoting vermin, illnesses, or other adverse things to create a predicate nominal with the meaning 'afflicted with X'.[4]

(491) *Kaluarángi gollaya*

kaluara	*–ang*	*=i*	*golla*	≡*a*
ant	–AFFL	=3	sugar	≡DEF

The sugar is full of ants

---

4 One of the meanings present in pMP *–en* 'patient focus/undergoer voice; polite imperative; *suffer bodily afflictions*; nominalizer; be divided into X (X = numeral)' (Blust 2003:450).

APPLICATIVE SUFFIXES 317

(492) *Kaluaránga' ri ballakku*
kaluara –ang =a' ri   balla' ≡ku
ant   –AFFL =1 PREP house ≡1.POSS
I've got trouble with ants at my house

(493) *Ca'doangi*
ca'do –ang =i
hiccup –AFFL =3
He has hiccups

(494) *Setangngangi anjo leanga*
setang –ang =i anjo leang ≡a
devil   –AFFL =3 that cave ≡DEF
That cave is haunted

It is tempting to analyse this as an extended reading of benefactive *–ang*, in effect a malefactive, but the structure is quite different in that the affliction is the predicate rather than an argument.

10.3 *–i* and *–ang* Together

The sufixes *–i* and *–ang* can occur in combination, always in that order. All the examples I have found are of two types—the first a combination of transitiviser *–i* (§ 9.1.1) plus benefactive *–ang* (§ 9.2.1.3), as in (495), (496) and (497):

(495) *Nace'laianga'jukuka*
na= ce'la –i   –ang =a' juku' ≡a
3= salt –TRS –BEN =1 fish ≡DEF
She salted the fish for me

(496) *Kuerangngangko sirikku tongkokianga'*
ku= erang –ang =ko siri'   ≡ku   tongko' –i   –ang =a'
1= bring –BEN =2f shame ≡1.POSS lid   –TRS –BEN =1
I brought you my shame, cover it for me (i.e. please sort out this shameful matter, C:707)

318   CHAPTER 10

(497)   *Nabattuangianga'*
        na= battu –ang –i   –ang =a'
        3=   come –NR –TRS –BEN =1
        He explained it for me (*battuang* 'meaning', so lit. 'he 'meaninged' it for
        me')

The second type is a combination of transitiviser *–i* and instrumental *–ang*
(§ 9.2.1.4) as in (498):

(498)   *Batu kubattaliangi rakika*
        batu ku= battal –i   –ang =i raki'   ≡a
        stone 1=   heavy –TRS –BEN =3 fishing.float ≡DEF
        I weigh down the float with stones (C:89)

See also § 8.3.4 on the combination *pi––i–ang.*

CHAPTER 11

Other Verbal Affixes

11.1 Unitary/Mutual/Reciprocal *si*–

This section discusses constructions derived with the prefix *si*–, which is labelled MUT for 'mutual', the label being chosen because the meaning is rather broader than simple reciprocity. This prefix has a number of functions and a range of meanings, but while the different functions can clearly be identified it is not easy to see where a clear line can be drawn between them, thus *si*– is analysed as a single prefix rather than a number of homophonous forms. That said, it seems likely that *si*– reflects two distinct PMP prefixes, namely **sa*– 'prefix of unity' (clitic form of **esa* 'one'), and **si*– 'distributive' (Blust 2003). The reasons for considering this are not only that *si*– covers those sorts of functions, but also that there are some cases where *si*– and *sa*– are interchangeable in the modern language (see §11.1.5.3).

The major functions of *si*– roughly fall within the following list:
– one (classified) NOUN
– (a number of people) sharing one NOUN
– (a number of people) sharing the activity of doing VERB
– (a number of people) doing VERB to each other

Each of the above functions is illustrated in the sections below, followed by some miscellaneous functions which are less common. As with some of the other morphemes, there are a few functions given by Cense which cannot be confirmed by in-context examples from my corpus, which is not to say that they are incorrect or one-offs.

11.1.1 si– + *Numeral or Classifier 'One NOUN'*

This function is outlined in the sections on numerals, classifiers and measures (§5.8, §5.9). In these constructions *si*– is simply a bound form corresponding to the numeral *se're* 'one'. Some examples are: *sisa'bu* 'one thousand', *sikayu tedong* 'one buffalo', *sibatu balla'* 'one house', *sipasang sapatu* 'one pair of shoes', *sikalabini jangang* 'one breeding pair of fowl' (cf. *ruangkayu jangang* 'two hens/cocks'). It is also used in this way on units of time, e.g. *sibulang* 'one month'.

© KONINKLIJKE BRILL NV, LEIDEN, 2020 | DOI:10.1163/9789004412668_012

320   CHAPTER 11

11.1.2 si– + NOUN 'Share One NOUN'

In this usage the prefix functions to derive nominals, usually functioning as intransitive predicates, with meanings ranging from 'be N together', to 'share the state of being (involved with) N'. They are analysed as nominal predicates rather than verbs because although they can host clitic pronouns, they do not bear any verb morphology. Some examples are *siballa'* 'share a house', *sikatinroang* 'share a bed', and *sisari'battang* 'be siblings':

(499) *siballaki mionga juku'–langgaya*
       si–   balla' =i miong ≡a   juku' langga ≡a
       MUT– house =3 cat   ≡DEF fish baked ≡DEF
       the cat and the baked fish are sharing a house (proverb: a single man
       and single woman should not be left together)

(500) *tinang niakkamo nasikatinrong karaeng–bainea*
       tinang nia' –a   =mo na= si–   ka⟨ tinro ⟩ang karaeng
       never   exist –SBJV =PFV 3= MUT– NR⟨ sleep ⟩NR karaeng
       baine   ≡a
       woman ≡DEF
       he never again slept with the queen (C:459)

These may also be used attributively:

(501) *ana' karaeng tallua sisari'battang*
       ana' karaeng tallu ≡a   si–   sari'battang
       child karaeng three ≡DEF MUT– sibling
       the three prince brothers

With event nominals (§ 6.2.2.5) the derived meaning is 'do X at the same time', a logical subclass of co-participation:

(502) *Naumminne ri jaranna Karaeng Botolempangang sipanaungang suro*
       bangkeng bicaraya.
       naung   =mo =i nne ri   jarang ≡na   karaeng
       go.down =PRF =3 this prep horse ≡3.POSS karaeng
       Botolempangang si–   pa⟩ naung   ⟨ang suro   bangkeng bicara
       Botolempangang MUT– NR⟩ go.down ⟨NR order leg   speak
       ≡a
       ≡DEF
       Karaeng Botolempangang got down from his horse at the same time as
       the messenger (SKT:ref224)

OTHER VERBAL AFFIXES   321

11.1.3 si-*ADJ*-i *'Be ADJ Together'*

The combination of *si-* and the applicative *-i* on adjectival bases results in mutual adjectival predicates, rather than equal comparative adjectives which are derived by *siN-* or *saN-* (§ 5.4.1.3.3). The NPs (if present) are simply listed, not conjoined with *na* or any other conjunction:

(503) *Sikebóki bajunna lipa'na*
       si- kebo' -i =i baju ≡nna lipa' ≡na
       MUT– white –TRS =3 shirt ≡3.POSS sarong ≡3.POSS
       His shirt and sarong are both white

(cf: equal comparative *singkeboki* ⟨siN–kebo'=i⟩ *bajunna na lipa'na* 'his shirt and white are equally white')

(504) *Sibodóiki'*
       si- bodo -i =ki'
       MUT– short –TRS =1pl
       We are both short

Given that *-i* usually transitivises adjectives (§ 10.1.1), this is a somewhat irregular derivation—one would expect a meaning more like 'make each other ADJ'. This meaning is instead derived with the combination of *si-* and the adjective causativiser *paka-* (§ 9.2, see e.g. (511)).

11.1.4 si-*VERB 'Do VERB Together'* or *'Do VERB Reciprocally'*

On verbal bases *si-* adds either a comitative/associative meaning: to do something together or simultaneously, or a reciprocal one: to do something to each other. The two readings are not always easy to distinguish—and indeed the distinction is somewhat artificial since clearly the language itself does not make it formally but rather it depends on the valence and semantics of the verbal base. In general intransitive verbs derive comitative meanings, while transitive verbs derive reciprocals, however there are ambiguous cases such as *sibuno* 'kill each other' or 'kill (someone else) together' where the core meaning is simply that both participants were involved in the activity. Structurally they are intransitive in that there is only one clitic pronoun, and there is no reciprocal pronoun corresponding to *saling* in Indonesian. *Si-* derivations sometimes have verb prefixes, but more often do not, and they seem to be optional. One *si-* derivation has grammaticised into a preposition or prepositional verb *siagáng* ⟨MUT–accompany⟩ 'with' (§ 5.10.1).

(505) *Battua' ri Mangkasara' siagáng bainengku*
    battu =a' ri   Mangkasar =a' siagáng baine   ≡ngku
    come =1 PREP Makassar   =EC with   woman ≡1.POSS
    I came to Makassar with my wife

A good selection of both comitative and reciprocal meanings are found in the song *Pangngu'rangi mami* ('Only memories remain') by the popular singer Iwan Tompo:

(506) *Sallota tojeng assingai, Sisayang sika'jalái, Na ki'giling sila'leang, Ka ero'na tutoanu. Sarenta tosseng sipa'rua*
    sallo ≡ta   tojeng aC– si–   ngai si–   sayang si–   ka'jal
    long ≡1pl.POSS true   MV– MUT– love MUT– pity   MUT– hard
    –a   –i   na   ki= aC– giling   si–   la'le   –ang ka
    –SBJV –TRS and 1pl= MV– other.side MUT– faded –BEN because
    ero'   ≡na   tu–   toa ≡nu   sare ≡nta   =tong =seng
    want ≡3.POSS person– old ≡2f.POSS give ≡2p.POSS =also =again
    si–   pa–   aC– rua
    MUT– CAUS– MV– two
    For a long time we truly loved each other, sharing compassion and pain, and we turn away neglecting each other, because of your parents' wishes. (They) made us separate again

This short selection shows *si–* on one transitive verb root (*ngai*); one noun (*sayang*); in one *si–*ADJ*–i* derivation (*ka'jalái*, see §11.1.3[1]); on another adjective (*la'le* 'faded') which has been derived with *–ang* to have an extended meaning (*la'leang* 'not see s.o anymore'); and on a causative verb derived from a numeral (*pa'rua*). Of these, only the first and third (on transitive bases) have clearly reciprocal meanings, while the others denote sharing or undergoing something together rather than reciprocity (i.e. *sipa'rua* because of the relative ordering of the prefixes means 'they made us two' not 'they made each other two').

    An example of a clear simultaneous rather than reciprocal meaning is seen in (507):

(507) *Anne Karaeng Assakayai Binangaya silanynyakangi sikalabinina.*
    anne karaeng aC– saka ≡a   =i binanga ≡a   si–   lanynya'
    this king   MV– split ≡DEF =3 river   ≡DEF MUT– gone

---

1 The placing of the subjunctive suffix *–a* is unusual.

OTHER VERBAL AFFIXES 323

-*ang* =*i* *si*–   *kalabini* ≡*na*
–BEN =3 MUT– couple ≡3.POSS
This Karaeng Assakayai Binangaya disappeared with his wife (lit. 'his couple disappeared together'; Maros:142)

In contrast, the following examples show *si*– deriving reciprocal verbs:

(508) *Assijanjiki' a'lampa ammuko*
       aC– *si*–   *janji*   =*ki' aC*– *lampa ammuko*
       MV– MUT– promise =1pl MV– go   tomorrow
       We promised each other to go tomorrow

(509) *... nasisambe Gowa Bone na Balandaya angngatái Marusu'*
       na= *si*–   *sambe*   *Gowa Bone na Balanda* ≡*a   aN(N)*–
       3=   MUT– exchange Gowa Bone and Holland ≡DEF BV–
       ata   –*i*   *Marus* =*u'*
       servant –TRS Maros =EC
       ... the Dutch exchanged with Gowa and Bone in ruling Maros (Maros: 177)

(510) *taua ri Marusu' sikanre–balei*
       tau   ≡*a*   *ri*   *Marusu' si*–   *kanre bale* =*i*
       person ≡DEF PREP maros   MUT– food fish =3
       (at that time) the people of Maros ate each other like fishes[2] (Maros:10)

As was shown in (506), *si*– may be placed on *pa*– causative verbs such as *pa'rua*, and also causative verbs derived from adjectives with *paka*–:

(511) *nasaba' sipakala'biri' na sirannu–rannu*
       na= *saba' si*–   *paka*– *la'bir* =*i'   na   si*–   *rannu– rannu*
       3=   reason MUT– CAUS– exalted =EC and TOT– RDP– happy
       because (we) made each other feel good, and were as happy as could be[3]

As mentioned earlier (§ 9.1.3), *si*– verbs may themselves form bases for *pa*– causatives, and these are transitive. An example was given earlier in (414), another one is:

---

2 An incorporated nominal generally acts as a manner modifier.
3 See § 11.1.5.2 for *si*–RDP–ADJ.

324   CHAPTER 11

(512)   *Barang bajikki' kupasialle siagáng i Anu*
         barang baji' =ki' ku= pa–   si–   alle siagáng i   anu
         maybe good =2p 1= CAUS– MUT– take with   PERS thingy
         Maybe it's better that I let you marry with whatshisname (Cgn:3)

Note the floating of the P clitic to the preverbal modifier *baji'*.

An unusual example of a construction with two instances of *si–* (on both sides of *pa–* in a headless relative clause) occurs in an old manuscript recording the oath taken by the rulers of the kingdoms of Gowa and Tallo'.[4]

(513)   *manna namaso'naja assipasiewaaki' Gowa Tallo' ia nacalla Rewata.*
         manna na= ma– so'na =ja   aC– si– pa–   si–
         if   3=   ADJ– dream =LIM MV– MUT– CAUS– MUT–
         ewa   ≡a   =ki' Gowa Tallo' ia   na= calla   rewata
         stand.against ≡DEF =2p Gowa Tallo' 3PRO 3= condemn god(s)
         Even if he only dreams of setting us, Gowa and Tallo', against each other, he is cursed by the Gods.

The version of this oath given in the KIT manuscript is somewhat different (it has evidently been 'fixed' by a scribe while recopying), with only one *si–* and an Actor-headed relative clause used instead:

(514)   *ia– iannamo. tau. ampasiewai. Gowa. Tallo'. iamo nacalla. rewata.*
         ia–   ia   ≡nna   =mo tau   aN– pa–   si–   ewa
         RDP– 3PRO ≡3.POSS =PFV person AF– CAUS– MUT– oppose
         ≡a   =i Gowa Tallo' ia   =mo na= calla   rewata
         ≡DEF =3 Gowa Tallo' 3PRO =PFV 3= condemn god(s)
         Any person who sets Gowa and Tallo' against each other, he is cursed by the gods (KIT:refo39)

11.1.5   *Misc. Uses of* si–

A few senses of *si–* are somewhat different to the main ones identified above, though can still generally be seen as connected to senses of unity or entirety. These are listed in the following sub-sections.

---

4   'A rare manuscript written in the old Makasarese script (this manuscript is available on microfilm in the Arsip Nasional Wilayah Sulawesi Selatan in Ujung Pandang, Indonesia. The catalogue number is 26/22. The section quoted here is found on page 37) briefly describes the occasion on which the pronouncement was first made in a little more detail. The text contains the formulaic oath sworn by the rulers of Goa and Talloq, Tunijalloq (r. 1565–1590) and Tumamenang of Makkoayang (r. early 1540s to late 1570s).' (Cummings 1999:110).

OTHER VERBAL AFFIXES

325

11.1.5.1   *si–* + Noun 'All/Whole'
In this usage, *si–* is affixed to nouns denoting place (such as *butta* 'land', *pa'ra-sangang* 'country') and place names (such as Gowa), and results in a noun meaning 'the whole of N, all of N'. Examples of this type are infrequent—the following is from the Maros Chronicle:

(515) *Iaminne Karaenga ampasallangi Mangkasaraka siMangkasara' ampas-allangi Bugisika siBugisi' passangngalinna Luwu'.*

ia	*=mo*	*=i*	*=nne*	*karaeng*	*≡a*	*aN–*	*pa–*	*sallang*	*=i*
s/he	=PRF	=3	=this	king	≡DEF	AF–	CAUS–	Islam	=3

Mangkasar	*=a'*	*≡a*	*si–*	*Mangkasar*	*=a'*	*aN–*	*pa–*	*sallang*
Makassar	=EC	≡DEF	one–	Makassar	=EC	AF–	CAUS–	Islam

=i	*Bugis*	*=i'*	*≡a*	*si–*	*Bugis*	*=i'*	*pa–*	*aC–*	*sangngali*
=3	Bugis	=EC	≡DEF	one–	Bugis	=EC	CAUS–	MV–	except

≡nna	*Luwu'*
≡3.POSS	Luwu'

This Karaeng Islamized [people] throughout the land of Makassar, Islamized [people] throughout the land of the Bugis, except Luwu'. (Cummings 2000:9–10)

Cense also gives an example of the prefix on a common noun *baine* 'woman', with the result meaning 'all women' or women in general:

(516) *antu bura'ne kammaya gau'na sibainentu tangngai*

antu	*bura'ne*	*kamma*	*≡a*	*gau'*	*≡na*	*si–*	*baine*	*=ntu*
that	man	thus	≡DEF	action	≡3.POSS	one–	female	=that

ta=	*aN(N)–*	*ngai*
NEG=	BV–	love

women don't like men who do such things (C:692)

11.1.5.2   *si–* + RDP– ADJ (≡POSS) 'as ADJ as Possible'
This construction (6th sense of *si–*) is defined as having the meaning 'in the highest degree' (*in de hoogste mate*). The semantic link with the other meanings of *si–* is in the sense of unity=totality. It was discussed in §5.4.1.3.5, for convenience the example is repeated below:

(517) *Sibella–bellana; sisallo–sallona*

si–	*bella–*	*bella*	*≡na*	*si–*	*sallo–*	*sallo*	*≡na*
TOT–	RDP–	far	≡3.POSS	TOT–	RDP–	long	≡3.POSS

At its furthest; at its longest (C:692)

326 CHAPTER 11

The possessive suffix is not necessary, though it appears more often than not. (518) is an example of this construction without a possessive, as was (511) earlier:

(518) *"Jarre'mi sajarre'–jarre' tena sangkammanna."*
       jarre' =mo =i sa- jarre'– jarre' tena saN–   kamma
       strong =PRF =3 TOT– RDP– strong NEG EQ.CMPR– thus
       ≡nna
       ≡3.POSS
       'Strong as strong can be, nothing like it.' (SKT 129)

In form this construction is identical to the one described in the following section, especially as seen on an basic verb as in (521).

11.1.5.3   *sa-/si-* + RDP– VERB/ADJ ≡POSS 'Always VERB-ing'
This construction is given under entries for both *sa-* and *si-*, as the 2nd and 7th senses respectively (Cense & Abdoerrahim 1979:626, 692). The reduplicated verb takes a verb prefix (*aC-* in all examples) if the the verb would normally require one, thus the regular verbs in (519) and (520) have them, but not the basic verb in (521). The meaning given is 'always doing nothing but ...', 'only doing this or that':

(519) *Sa'bendi–bendina*
       sa- aC- bendi– bendi ≡na
       TOT– MV– RDP– carriage ≡3.POSS
       He's always riding in *bendis* (C:626)

(520) *Tinang le'bakako kurapikang ri balla'nu sa'lampa–lampanu (si'lampa–lampanu)*
       tinang le'ba'   –a   =ko ku= rapi'   –ang ri   balla'
       never finished –SBJV =2f 1= achieve –BEN PREP house
       ≡nu   sa- aC- lampa– lampa ≡nu   (si– aC- lampa–
       ≡2f.POSS TOT– MV– RDP– go   ≡2f.POSS (TOT– MV– RDP–
       lampa ≡nu)
       go   ≡2f.POSS)
       I never find you at home, you're always on the road (C:626)

(521) *Satinro–tinronamami (sitinro–tinronamami)*
       sa– tinro – tinro ≡na   =mamo =i (si– tinro – tinro
       TOT– RDP– sleep ≡3.POSS =only =3 (TOT– RDP– sleep

OTHER VERBAL AFFIXES 327

≡na   =mamo =i⟩
≡3.POSS =only =3⟩
She sleeps continuously (C:626)

Although Cense does not mention it, this construction is also possible with adjectival bases:

(522) *Sagarring–garrinna*
       sa–   garring– garring ≡na
       TOT– RDP– sick   ≡3.POSS
       He's always sick

There is also a usage of *sa–* on an unprefixed verb, to my knowledge only found on an idiom built on the verb root *lampa* 'go' (usually marked with *aC–*, see (520) above). The meaning is somewhat different, but not unrelated:

(523) *A'lampai salampa–lampana*
       aC– lampa =i sa–   lampa– lampa ≡na
       MV– go   =3 TOT– RDP– go   ≡3.POSS
       She went without deviation (PT:160)

11.2 Erratic *piti*⟩RDP–V⟨*i*

This combination of a confix *piti*⟩⟨*i* (the first part also appearing as *pati–*) and reduplicated verb root means 'do V in a crazy or erratic manner', while with a reduplicated adjective root it means 'be ADJ for no good reason'.

(524) *A'lampami pitilampa–lampái*
       aC– lampa =mo =i piti⟩ lampa– lampa ⟨i
       MV– go   =PFV =3 MAD⟩ RDP– go   ⟨MAD
       She wandered about wildly (PT:148)

(525) *Pitimalla'–mallakiko*
       piti⟩ malla' malla' ⟨i   =ko
       MAD⟩ RDP– angry ⟨MAD =2f
       You're angry for no reason

328   CHAPTER 11

11.3   Subjunctive *–a*

This suffix[5] (glossed SBJV) is placed on verbs and implies that the action might
happen—it is usually used as a warning or admonition.

(526)   *Tu'gúrako*
        tu'gur –a   =ko
        fall   –SBJV =2f
        (Be careful) you might fall (C:1)

(527)   *Naikko mae nakanréako buaja*
        nai' =ko mae   na= kanre –a   =ko buaja
        go.up =2f be.in.a.place 3=   eat – SBJV =2f crocodile
        Come up here, a crocodile might eat you (Or.545.48:11)

There are also some rare examples of it functioning as a more general subjunctive marker of hypotheticality or contingency:

(528)   *Battúako ri Pangkaje'ne' na taena balla' nuasseng mangeko ri karaeng*
        battu –a   =ko ri   Pangkaje'ne' na   taena balla' nu= asseng
        come – SBJV =2f PREP Pangkaje'ne' and NEG   house 2f= know
        mange =ko ri   karaeng
        go   =2f PREP karaeng
        If you go to Pangkaje'ne' and there is no house that you know, go to the
        karaeng (Or.545.48:11)

More often these kinds of contingency clauses are introduced explicitly with
ta'bangkang 'in case' or *ti'ring* 'if by chance':[6]

(529)   *Ti'ring battúako ri Marusu' pammalli–allaloa' berasa'*
        ti'ring   battu –a   =ko ri   Marus pa-   aN(N)– balli
        by.chance come – SBJV =2f PREP Maros CAUS– BV–   buy
        aN(N)– lalo =a' beras
        BV–   PASS =1 rice
        If by chance you come to Maros will you buy me rice? (C:819)

---

5   A reflex of PAN and PMP *–a 'subjunctive' (Blust 2003).
6   Clauses introduced with *punna* 'if/when' do not take the subjunctive.

OTHER VERBAL AFFIXES 329

This suffix is also found in negative constructions formed with *ta=* (but not *taena*), such as *takuasséngai* ⟨NEG=1=know–SBJV=3⟩ 'I don't know it' (see §12.3.1).

Although subjunctive *–a* is superficially identical in form to the definite marking affixal clitic ≡*a* (§4.4.1), it can be distinguished in the following ways:

- it is always stress shifting, unlike the article ≡*a* which is only stress shifting after a vowel; thus *garríngako* ⟨sick–SBJV =2f⟩ 'you might get sick', but *tau gárringa* ⟨person sick≡DEF⟩ 'the sick one'
- it blocks Echo–VC (§2.3.4), thus *tu'gúrako* (**tu'gurukako*), but compare *tau túguruka* ⟨person fall≡DEF⟩ 'the one who fell'

For the above reasons it falls clearly into the class of affixes, at least from a phonological point of view. Note that otherwise tense and aspect are marked either lexically or with clitics (§4.3.3).

CHAPTER 12

Grammatical Relations

In this chapter I will introduce the basic structure of the major types of Makasar clause. The main structural division in clause types is between intransitive, semi-transitive and transitive clauses. Predicates in intransitive clauses can be from any of the major classes (verbal, adjectival, or nominal), or from certain of the minor classes (numeral, adverbial, locative); those in semi-transitive and transitive clauses are verbal. Grammatical relations are marked by clitic pronouns which usually follow an ergative/absolutive pattern, but the appearance and placement of these is conditioned by several factors, some of which will be discussed below. Because there is an inexact match between the labels ERG= and =ABS on the one hand, and the actual grammatical functions of pro- and enclitics in clauses on the other, in general I have avoided using those labels in glosses and use them sparingly in discussion.

In line with general practice I will use the labels S for the sole core argument of an intransitive clause, P for the patient-like argument of a transitive clause, and A for the agent-like argument of a transitive clause. However, the facts of Makasar, as will be discussed later, make it useful to further divide P into P and P^{INDEF}, and S into S, S^{INDEF} and S^A.[1] In addition, sometimes for making general statements I will use the macro-role labels Actor and Undergoer, in which Actor = A and S^A; and Undergoer = P and P^{INDEF}.

12.1 Grammatical Relations

In order to discuss the system of grammatical relations it will first be necessary to identify and define core arguments. This is not entirely unproblematic in Makasar as there are often mismatches between morphological coding of arguments and the syntactic/thematic structure of a clause. This section attempts to summarise the main facts and propose an analysis.

The fact that there are two clitic pronoun slots (ERG= and =ABS) available on predicates for cross-referencing arguments leads to the natural assumption that arguments which are thus cross-referenced are privileged in some way.

---

1 Note that there is no specific marking of S^P, such as one might expect by analogy with some other Austronesian languages, e.g. Acehnese (Durie 1985).

© KONINKLIJKE BRILL NV, LEIDEN, 2020 | DOI:10.1163/9789004412668_013

GRAMMATICAL RELATIONS

Further, the fact that in the majority of cases =ABS corresponds to S and P, while ERG= corresponds to A, suggests that clitics cross-reference core arguments, and that they do this according to an ergative-absolutive pattern. The omissibility of the NPs denoting these arguments suggests that the clitic pronouns in fact are the core arguments, and that any full NPs co-referent with them are in apposition, only present for purposes of disambiguation or emphasis.[2] Thus, at the very least we can identify the grammatical relations S, A and P.

However, when examining the behaviour of certain Makasar clauses it becomes clear (a) that it is not always easy to correlate =ABS or ERG= clitics with particular grammatical relations, and (b) that some arguments which are arguably core are not always cross-referenced.

To illustrate point (a), there is not a one-to-one correspondence between either the form or position of a clitic pronoun and a grammatical function. In brief:

- S is referenced by an =ABS enclitic pronoun in basic clauses, as in (530), but by an ERG= proclitic pronoun in negative clauses and in many other kinds of complement or complement-like clauses, as in (531) (§11.2.2)
- P may in similar circumstances be referenced by an ERG= proclitic pronoun *preceding and in addition to* the ERG= proclitic pronoun referencing A, as in (532) (§11.2.2)
- (semantic) A may be represented by an =ABS enclitic when P is indefinite, as in (533) (§11.5)

(530)   *Tinroi*
        tinro =i
        sleep =3
        He sleeps

(531)   *Tena natinro*
        tena na= tinro
        NEG 3= sleep
        He doesn't sleep

---

2   This is not an entirely uncontroversial position, but is common enough. For example, Van Valin (1993:17) states that 'in head marking languages, the pronominal affixes on the verb are the core arguments of the clause, not the optional independent lexical NPs and pronouns'. See also e.g. Donohue (1999:123–129), Foley (1991:227–228), Klamer (1998:68–71) for relevant discussion in other grammars; while for further theoretical discussion see e.g. Jelinek (1984) and the response in Austin & Bresnan (1996).

332   CHAPTER 12

(532)   *Tena nukucini'*
        tena nu= ku= cini'
        NEG 2f= 1=   see
        I don't see you

(533)   *Angnganrea' unti*
        aN(N)– kanre =a' unti
        BV–   eat   =1 banana
        I eat bananas

To illustrate point (b), arguments are not cross-referenced with clitic pronouns
under certain circumstances. Specifically these are:

– indefinite S in certain clauses—most commonly existentials as in (534) (see
  §12.4) but also other basic clauses as in (310) earlier
– indefinite P in semi-transitive clauses,[3] as in (533) above (§11.6)
– any of S, A or P when denoted by an NP in focus position, as in (535) with
  Actor focus (§11.9)

(534)   *Nia' tau anjoreng*
        nia' tau   anjoreng
        exist person there
        There's someone there

(535)   *Inakke ambetako*
        inakke aN– beta   =ko
        1PRO   AF– defeat =2f
        I defeated you

The alternation in form between =ABS and ERG= for S and P due to clitic fronting can be asumed to be a relatively superficial phenomenon which does not
change the grammatical relation. The lack of cross-referencing of focused NP
arguments could be accounted for by an analysis where focus promotes an NP
to core argument status within the clause, making cross-referencing redundant.[4] However, this leaves the contrast between P and P^{INDEF} (and S and S^{INDEF})
to explain.

What then is the status of these indefinite arguments? They are clearly
important, as can be shown by the fact that they cannot be omitted (unlike NPs

---

3   A is always cross-referenced even if indefinite.
4   This applies equally well to P and P^{INDEF}, see §11.9.

GRAMMATICAL RELATIONS

TABLE 73   Grammatical relations

Label	Function	Clitic pronoun	NP
S	sole argument of intransitive clause	usually =ABS	optional
P	undergoer of transitive clause	usually =ABS	optional
A	actor of transitive clause	ERG=	optional
S^A	actor of semi-transitive clause	usually =ABS	optional
S^INDEF	sole indefinite argument of intransitive clause	o	obligatory
P^INDEF	undergoer of semi-transitive clause	o	obligatory

coreferent with clitics denoting S, A or P). They are not oblique. They are not incorporated. Some have claimed that clauses with P^INDEF are in fact intransitive (see § 11.6 and discussion in § 7.5). However this does not answer the question of what P^INDEF is,[5] nor do these treatments propose an analysis for sentences with S^INDEF such as (310), which by analogy should be zero-transitive.

So it comes down to a tension between morphosyntactic marking (clitic pronouns) on the one hand, versus the non-omissibility of indefinite arguments on the other. I propose that there is a two-way split in the nature of representing core arguments in Makasar. The most common way is with clitic pronouns cross-referencing S, A or P. However there are two circumstances in which NPs themselves serve as core arguments. The first is by being promoted to that status by use of the clause-initial focus position. The other is by virtue of being indefinite. Blocked for cross-referencing because of their indefiniteness or non-specificity, the NPs must bear the referential load themselves. However the difference in the way these arguments are treated suggests that they should not be assumed to fit within the system of grammatical relations as it functions for definite arguments and simply be P or S, but instead can be labelled P^INDEF and S^INDEF. Furthermore, a corollary of recognising the function P^INDEF is its counterpart S^A, an argument marked as S which is agent-like.

In summary, there are arguably six distinct grammatical relations, as laid out in Table 73.

---

5   Lee (2006) is the exception, having proposed that P^INDEF is a 'non-core obligatory extended argument'.

334   CHAPTER 12

12.2   Focus and Topic Marking

In the following sections I discuss overt marking of focus and topic, which
are each associated with particular syntactic positions. The basic facts are
not unlike those described for Tukang Besi (South-East Sulawesi) by Donohue
(2002), and are also similar to those described for Mayan languages by Aissen
(1992), which is that there is a clause-initial focus slot, and a clause-external
(i.e. left-dislocated) topic slot.[6] However the 'basic' characterisation, especially
with regard to focus, misses subtleties and irregularities in complex sentences
which also need to be accounted for. Note that the alternative analysis of 'focus'
(= voice) was discussed in § 7.6.

12.2.1   *Focus*

Alongside the marking of voice and transitivity, there is a phenomenon best
described by the label **focus**, despite the unfortunate overuse of that term in
the Austronesianist literature (Himmelmann 1996; Himmelmann 2002). In its
most basic manifestation, this involves an NP referring to a core argument
being placed in pre-predicate position. There is a prefix *aN–* (§ 7.2) which explicitly marks Actor focus (appearing in the place of the ERG= proclitic), whereas
Undergoer focus is marked by the absence of an =ABS enclitic. (I use the mac-
rorole labels here because both P and P[INDEF] may be focused).

Thus, arguments which occur as full NPs directly preceding the predicate
are not cross-referenced—for example, compare (536) and (537):

(536)   *Tinroi i Ali*
     tinro =i i   Ali
     sleep =3 PERS Ali
     Ali is asleep

(537)   *I Ali tinro*
     i   Ali tinro
     PERS Ali sleep
     Ali is asleep

This pre-predicate slot is a focus position,[7] which performs a variety of pragmatic functions such as disambiguating, emphasizing, adding certainty or

---

6   See also Finer's work on A' positions in Selayarese (Finer 1994).
7   Specifically, it is a slot for marked argument focus (Van Valin 1999). As for the configuration,
    Finer (1994) has analysed the focus position (for Selayarese) as Spec of IP.

GRAMMATICAL RELATIONS   335

uncertainty. So while (536) is just a statement of fact, (537) with S in focus can express such meanings as: 'Are you sure it's Ali who is asleep?', 'I tell you that Ali is asleep', 'I've heard that Ali is asleep'. It is also the answer to the question *inai tinro?* 'who is asleep?' (interrogative pronouns are typically focused, see §12.2). Another example of how focus conveys extended meanings is the following:

(538)   *Ballakku kicini'*
        balla' ≡ku   ki= cini'
        house ≡1.POSS 2p= see
        You see **my house**

This could be given as an answer to the question: what can you give as a guarantee for a loan? (The unmarked way of saying 'you see my house' is *kiciniki ballakku* ⟨ki=cini'=i balla'≡ku | 2f=see=3 house≡1.POSS⟩).

In transitive clauses either A or P can be in focus. The following two sentences show A focus and P focus respectively where both arguments are definite:

(539)   *Kongkonga ambunoi mionga*
        kongkong ≡a   aN– *buno* =i *miong* ≡a
        dog   ≡def AF– kill =3 cat   ≡DEF
        The **dog** killed the cat

(540)   *Mionga nabuno kongkonga*
        miong ≡a   na= *buno kongkong* ≡a
        cat   ≡DEF 3= kill dog   ≡DEF
        The dog killed the **cat**

Thus, in (539) there is no proclitic cross-referencing *kongkonga* (A), while in (540) *mionga* (P) lacks a corresponding enclitic.[8] Also note that in (539) the verb is marked with the Actor Focus prefix *aN–* (found in clauses where A is in focus and P is definite, see §7.2).

If P is indefinite (i.e. if the corresponding non-focused clause is semi-transitive) either argument may still be focused, so sentence (541) shows A focus, while (542) shows P^{INDEF} focus:

---

8   When A is in Focus this has obvious similarities with the phenomenon of 'ergative extraction' as described for Mayan languages (1992)—except that there is a parallel 'absolutive extraction' when O is in Focus.

336 CHAPTER 12

(541) *Inakke angnganre juku'*
       inakke aN(N)– kanre juku'
       1PRO BV–   eat fish
       I'm eating fish

(542) *Juku' kukanre*
       juku' ku= kanre
       fish 1= eat
       I'm eating **fish**

Note that in (541) the verb is marked as semi-transitive with the prefix *aN(N)–* (the missing clitic pronoun being 1st person =*a'*), but in (542) the verb hosts a proclitic, identical to clauses with focused definite P such as (540) above. This suggests that focus promotes P[INDEF] to P (i.e. promotes it from a non-core to a core argument), with concomitant promotion of S[A] to A.[9]

Sentences with indefinite A are marginal as a general rule, and examples (543) and (544) are no exception.

(543) *?Miong ammuno kongkong*
       miong aN(N)– buno kongkong
       cat   BV–   kill dog
       A **cat** killed a dog / **cats** kill dogs

(544) *?Kongkong nabuno miong*
       kongkong na= buno miong
       dog   3= kill cat
       A cat killed a **dog** / cats kill **dogs**

Note however, that to make it even marginally acceptable in (544) *miong* (A) has been cross-referenced with *na=* even though it is indefinite and indefinite arguments are not usually cross-referenced. This could again suggest that focusing P[INDEF] promotes it to P, which further promotes A[INDEF] to A.

Finally, sentences in which A is not only indefinite but lower on the animacy hierarchy than P are unacceptable.[10]

---

9   Basri & Finer (1987) have a different analysis, in which it is the trace (left behind when P[INDEF] is moved) that is definite and which triggers the ERG= marking of S[A]. I prefer an analysis in which focus itself promotes an argument to core status.

10 This appears to be the case whether or not focus is involved.

GRAMMATICAL RELATIONS 337

(545) *Miong angkokkoka'
       miong aN– kokko' =a'
       cat   AF– bite =1
       A cat bit me

(546) *Inakke nakokko' miong
       inakke na= kokko' miong
       1PRO 3= bite   cat
       A cat bit **me**

Complex sentences show focus phenomena which differ somewhat from simple examples. For example, NPs may be be in standard (postverbal) position in one clause, and simultaneously occupy focus position (as can be seen by the use of the Actor focus prefix *aN–*) in a subsequent clause. For example, (547), shows the S NP from one clause serving as focused A in the following clause, and then as A (equi-deleted) in a third clause:

(547) *battu– tommi kongkonga ampasire'bokangi, angkanrei.*
       battu tong =mo =i kongkong ≡a   aN– pa–   si–   re'bo'
       come also =PFV =3 dog   ≡DEF AF– CAUS– MUT– squabble
       –ang =i aN– kanre =i
       –BEN =3 AF– eat   =3
       the dogs came, fought over it, ate it (bembe:100)

Example (548) from the same story shows three clauses with typical focus morphology, but only one in which an NP (*bembea*) actually occupies the focus slot. In the second clause the 1st person (represented by the preposed clitic pronoun on the initial adverbial modifier *dikki'–dikki'*) is marked as focused A by the prefix *aN–* on *ambuangi*, after which the unfocused P of the second clause becomes the focused (but ellipsed) P of the third clause:

(548) *Bembea mange a'je'ne', kudikki'–dikki' mange ambuangi karungkunna*
       naung ri buttaya, napasire'bokang kongkong.
       bembe ≡a   mange aC– je'ne' ku= dikki'– dikki' mange aN–
       goat ≡DEF go   MV– water 1= RDP–   creep go   AF–
       buang =i karungkung ≡na   naung ri   butta ≡a   na=
       fall   =3 disguise   ≡3.POSS go.down PREP land ≡DEF 3=
       pa–   si–   re'bo'   –ang kongkong
       CAUS– MUT– squabble –BEN dog
       The goat went to bathe, I crept to throw her disguise down to the ground, it was torn apart by dogs (bembe:111)

338   CHAPTER 12

In the preceding examples, although focus can be identified according to the structural principles as noted for simple clauses, it is unclear what the pragmatic effects are. This requires further investigation not only of focus but of clause integration phenomena.

12.2.2 *Topicalisation*
There is a further possibility for preposing elements in a clause, which is left-dislocation. In this (unlike with focus) a clear prosodic break occurs between the preposed element and the remainder of the clause, and if the preposed element is a core argument, cross-referencing does occur (again, unlike focus). This can be seen in both (549) and (550)—in the former A is topicalised and both arguments are cross-referenced, in the latter A is topicalised, P is focused and thus only A is cross-referenced with a proclitic:

(549)   *kongkonga, nabunoi mionga*
        kongkong ≡a   *na= buno =i miong* ≡a
        dog   ≡DEF 3= kill =3 cat   ≡DEF
        the dog, it killed the cat

(550)   *kongkonga, mionga nabuno*
        kongkong ≡a   *miong* ≡a   *na= buno*
        dog   ≡DEF cat   ≡DEF 3= kill
        as for the dog, it was the cat that it killed

Example (551) has two clauses illustrating the structural contrast between topic and focus—in the first clause P is topicalised and thus is cross-referenced with an enclitic, while in the second P is in focus and is not cross-referenced:

(551)   *Anjo bainea, nalantiki Karaeng ri Massere'; anjo bura'nea nalanti'*
        Karaeng ri Roong
        anjo baine ≡a   *na= lanti'*   =i *karaeng ri   Massere' anjo*
        that female ≡DEF 3= inaugurate =3 karaeng PREP Massere' that
        bura'ne ≡a   *na= lanti'*   *karaeng ri   Roong*
        man   ≡DEF 3= inaugurate karaeng PREP Roong
        That girl, he made her Karaeng of Massere', that boy he made Karaeng of Roong. (bembe:003)

Topicalisation differs functionally from focus as one would expect. Whereas marked focus is generally used in a contrastive function, topicalisation is most often used when setting a topic either for a whole text (as was the case in (551) as the story is basically about Karaeng Massere'), or for switching between alternative topics. It also clearly differs syntactically. Whereas a focused argument is an argument within the phrase (as indicated by omission of its corresponding clitic pronoun), a topicalised NP is external to the phrase (as indicated by the presence of the clitic pronoun).

CHAPTER 13

Other Clause Types

In this chapter I will examine less 'basic' but still common types of clause.

13.1 Imperatives

Transitive imperative clauses are distinguished from indicative clauses because they lack ERG= proclitic pronouns indexing A. Intransitive imperatives do contain a 2nd person =ABS enclitic pronoun indexing S, which means that in fact they are indistinguishable from indicatives, though context can of course make clear which interpretation is intended. In addition, intransitive imperatives are often marked with the perfective enclitic =mo (this is also considered polite), and/or less commonly the hortative adverb sá:

(552) *Ammempomaki'!*
    amm– empo =mo =ki'
    MV–   sit   =PFV =2p
    Please sit! (lit. 'you sat')

(553) *Angnganre–sámako rong*
    aN(N)– kanre sá   =mo =ko rong
    BV–   eat   HORT =PFV =2f first
    Please eat first!

(554) *A'lampako punna tanungaia!*
    aC– lampa =ko punna ta=   nu= ngai –a
    MV– go   =2f if   NEG= 2f= like –SBJV
    Go if you don't like it!

(555) *Naikko ri balla'!*
    nai'   =ko ri   balla'
    go.up =2f PREP house
    Get in the house!

Intransitive imperatives may also be formed from adjectives (556), and deictic adverbs (557); in such cases the =ABS enclitic pronoun is also employed.

© KONINKLIJKE BRILL NV, LEIDEN, 2020 | DOI:10.1163/9789004412668_014

OTHER CLAUSE TYPES

(556) *Sa'barakko naung antayangi pappidalle'na Alla–ta'ala*
    sa'bar =a' =ko naung aN– tayang =i pa– aC– pi– dalle'
    patient =EC =2f go.up AF– wait =3 NR– MV– EXP– livelihood
    ≡na   A–T
    ≡3.POSS God
    Be patient [upwards], wait for sustenance from God (C:627)

(557) *Anrinnimako! Anjoremmako*
    anrinni =mo =ko anjoreng =mo =ko
    here =PFV =2f there =PFV =2f
    Come here! Go there! (*anturemmako '*go there near you')

It does not appear, however, that nominal predicates may function as imperatives, for example *guruko* can only be interpreted as 'you are a teacher', not 'be a teacher!'.

In contrast, transitive imperatives, as mentioned above, do not mark (2nd person) A, and the =ABS enclitic pronoun indexes P. They are further distinguished by the fact that they also lack verb prefixes:

(558) *Tayamma'*
    tayang =mo =a'
    wait =PFV =1
    Please wait for me

(cf. *attayamma'* 'I waited'; *nutayamma'* 'you waited for me'; *tayammako *'wait for yourself')

(559) *Inungi pa'ballenu!*
    inung =i pa'balle ≡nu
    drink =3 medicine ≡2f,POSS
    Drink your medicine!

(cf. *angnginungko pa'balle* 'he drank medicine'; *nuinungi pa'ballenu* 'you drink your medicine')

Transitivised and causative adjectives may also form imperatives:

(560) *Bajíki sapedanu, reppeki*
    baji' –i =i sapeda ≡nu reppe' =i
    good –APPL =3 bicycle ≡2f broken =3
    Fix your bike, it's broken

342   CHAPTER 13

(561)   *Pakabambammi kopiku*
        paka–   bambang =mo =i kopi   ≡ku
        CAUS.ADJ– hot   =PFV =3 coffee ≡3.POSS
        Heat up my coffee please

Benefactive imperatives and ditransitive imperatives with definite themes are
marked as might be expected with benefactive *–ang* (see § 7.7), and as expected
do not take the ERG= proclitic:

(562)   *Sungkeanga' pakke'bu'nu ana'*
        sungke –ang =a' pakke'bu' ≡nu   ana'
        open   –BEN =1 door   ≡2f,POSS child
        Open the door for me kids (PT:118)

(563)   *Ballian–sá' anjo bajua!*
        balli –ang sá   =a' anjo baju ≡a
        buy   –BEN HORT =1 that shirt ≡DEF
        Buy me that shirt!

Negative imperatives are formed with *tea*, see § 13.3.3.

13.2   Questions

Two main types of question are distinguished: yes/no questions and content
questions. The former are marked by use of some characteristic morphemes
and intonation, or by intonation alone. The latter contain interrogative pro-
forms, which were introduced briefly in § 5.6.4, but are examined more thoroughly here.

13.2.1   *Yes/No Questions*
The most common way of marking yes/no questions in spoken Makasar is with
intonation, which typically rises throughout the question, reaching a peak on
the stressed syllable of the last word, after which it falls and then has a lesser
terminal rise:

(564)   *Le'ba'mako angnganre?*
        le'ba'   =mo =ko aN(N)– kanre
        already =PFV =2f BV–   eat
        Have you eaten already?

An attempt to represent it diagrammatically (albeit impressionistically) follows:

le' ba' ma ko ang ngan re?

Yes/no questions can frequently be identified because they are cast in the negative, e.g.:

(565) *Tenamo nule'ba' angnganre?*
tena =mo nu= le'ba' aN(N)- kanre
NEG =PFV 2f= already BV- eat
Haven't you eaten yet?

In addition to intonation, the either/or clitic =*ka* (§ 4.3.3.6) is sometimes used to mark leading questions, which although still yes/no questions invite the hearer to add more information:

(566) *Tinrokako?*
tinro =ka =ko
sleep =Q =2f
Are you asleep or ...?

(567) *Lanukanrekainjo?*
la= nu= kanre =ka =i (a)njo
FUT= 2f= eat =or =3 that
Are you going to eat that or ...?

The question tag/discourse particle *di* (see § 5.12) is also used on yes/no questions when the answer is anticipated, or to check that a hypothesis or expectation is correct:

(568) *Le'ba'mako angnganre, di?*
le'ba' =mo =ko aN(N)- kanre di
already =PFV =2f BV- eat TAG
You've already eaten, haven't you?

In the traditional scripts there was no punctuation similar to a question mark, and perhaps as a result in writing and in other formal genres, the sentential

344   CHAPTER 13

adverb *maka* which is usually a marker of deontic modality ('should') can be used to explicitly mark a yes/no question:

(569) *Maka inakke lassuro*
       maka i–   nakke la=   aC– suro
       should PERS– 1PRO FUT= MV– order
       Will I give the order? (C:432)

(570) *Maka tenapa nule'ba' nasareang Ali doe' jai?*
       maka   tena =pa nu= le'ba'   na= sare –ang Ali doe' jai
       should NEG =IPF 2f= already 3= give –BEN Ali money many
       Didn't Ali once give you a lot of money? (Friberg 2002:4)

13.2.2 *Content Questions*

Content questions seek specific information, and are formed by using interrogative pro-forms which correspond to the word class of the type of answer being sought. Several of these interrogatives are clearly based on the interrogative pronoun *apa*: namely the question verb *angngapa*, the numeral interrogative *siapa*, and the temporal interrogatives *ringngapanna* and *siapayya*. Of these only *apa* can be used as an indefinite pronoun ('something') or negated to function as a negative pronoun (*tena apa* 'nothing') Other negative pronoun-like meanings are expressed by using a negator and appropriate nominal, e.g. *tena tau* 'no person', *tena tampa* 'no place'.

In general, questioned NPs are not cross-referenced, usually because they are in focus position.

13.2.2.1 *apa* 'What'

The interrogative pronoun *apa* is used when information is sought about a noun other than a human (for which see *inai* 'who' below). *Apa* can appear in any position in which a noun could occur, but it is most often found in focus position (§12.2). The following examples show *apa* in questions about S with verbal (571) and nominal predicates (572), (573); and A (574) and P (575) in verbal predicates:

(571) *Apa angngarru' kamma?*
       apa   aN(N)– karru' kamma
       what BV–   cry   thus
       What's howling like that?

OTHER CLAUSE TYPES 345

(572) *Apa ero'nu?*
apa ero' ≡nu
what want ≡2f
What do you want?

(573) *Apa saba'na nipasse're ngasengki' sikontu kara'–karaenga sanggenna*
rangka'na Gowa?
apa saba' ≡na ni– pa– aC– se're ngaseng =ki' si–
what reason ≡3.POSS PASS– CAUS– MV– one all =2p one-
kontu karaeng– karaeng ≡a sangge ≡nna rangka' ≡na
thus RDP– karaeng ≡DEF until ≡3.POSS the.whole ≡3.POSS
Gowa
Gowa
Why were we all made to gather like this, all the karaengs from the
whole of Gowa? (SKT:034)

(574) *Apa ampakalumanynyangko?*
apa aN– pa– kalumanynyang =ko
what AF– CAUS– rich =2f
What made you rich? (PT:220)

(575) *Apa nukanremo ri bari'basa?*
apa nu= kanre =mo ri bari'basa
what 2f= eat =PFV PREP morning
What did you eat for breakfast?

It may function as an attributive modifier of a noun, meaning 'what, which':

(576) *Agama apa nata'gala' taua ri Bali?*
agama apa na= ta'gal =a' tau ≡a ri Bali
religion what 3= hold =EC person ≡DEF PREP Bali
What religion do people have in Bali? (C:748)

Apa may also occur within predicates, either as the head of a nominal predicate
itself (577), or as an attributive modifier in nominal (578) or adjectival predicates (579):

(577) *Apai?*
apa =i
what =3
What is it?

346   CHAPTER 13

(578)   *Tau apaki'?*
        tau   apa   =ki'
        person what   =2p
        What (kind of) person are you? (i.e. what nationality or ethnicity)

(579)   *Garring apai i Nona?*
        garring apa   =i i   Nona
        sick   what   =3 PERS   Chinese.girl
        What's wrong with Nona? (a song title)

Reduplicated *apa–apa* means 'things, stuff' and is roughly equivalent to the
indefinite pronoun *anu* 'whatsit' (see §5.6.5.1), as in *jai apa–apanna* ⟨many
RDP–what≡3.POSS⟩ 'he has many things' (= *jai anunna*). Other derivations of
apa are interrogatives in their own right, see *angngapa* (§13.2.2.4), *ringngapanna* (§13.2.2.5), *siapayya* (§13.2.2.6), *siapa* (§13.2.2.7).

   Apa is also the base of the lexicalised discourse connective *apaji* ⟨apa=ja=i |
what=LIM=3⟩ 'so, it ended up that …':

(580)   *I Ali antu nisuro anjamai mingka téai apaji na inakke–mamo anjamai*
        i–   Ali antu ni–   suro   aN– jama =i mingka téa   =i
        PERS–   Ali that PASS–   order BV– work =3 but   not.want =3
        apa   =ja   =i na   i–   nakke mamo aN– jama =i
        what   =LIM =3 COMP PERS–   1PRO   only BV– work =3
        Ali was told to do the work but he didn't want to, so in the end I was
        left to do it (C:27)

13.2.2.2   *inai* 'Who'
The pronoun *inai* is used when information is sought about a person. The initial
i– is probably the personal prefix, but the form *nai* is not seen without it. *Inai*
is always clause initial, i.e. in focus position. The following three examples all
show it being used to enquire the identity of S (or the owner of S) with intransitive nominal predicates:

(581)   *Inainjo tau?*
        inai   (a)njo tau
        who   that   person
        Who is that person?

When *inai* is used to ask about a non-human referent, it is assumed to refer to
the owner of that referent, as can be seen in (582) and (583):

OTHER CLAUSE TYPES   347

(582) *Inai arenta?*
       inai   areng ≡ta
       who   name   ≡2p.POSS
       What is your name?

(583) *A: Inainjo bembe? Bembenu? B: Teái, bembe battu*
       inai (a)njo bembe bembe ≡nu   teá   =i bembe battu
       who that   goat   goat ≡2f,POSS NEG.be =3 goat   come
       A: Whose is that goat? Your goat? B: No, it's a goat that just turned up
       (C:90)

Examples (584)-(586) show *inai* with verbal predicates, in reference to S, A, and
P respectively:

(584) *Inai angngarru' kamma?*
       inai aN(N)– karru' kamma
       who BV–   cry   thus
       Who's crying like that? (cf. (571))

(585) *Inai amba'ji i Udin?*
       inai aN– ba'ji =i i   Udin
       who AF– hit   =3 PERS– Udin
       Who hit Udin?

(586) *Inai naba'ji i Ali?*
       inai na= ba'ji i   Ali
       who 3= hit   PERS– Ali
       Who did Ali hit?

Because it must be in focus position (§ 11.9), *inai* cannot be used to ask about
non-core arguments such as agents of passive clauses or complements of the
prepositional verb *siagáng* 'with'. Thus, to ask about the former, the sentence
must be made active with A focus (e.g. (585)); while in the latter circumstance, to avoid the sentence **battuki' anrinni siagáng inai?* 'you came here
with whom?', the following construction may be used:

(587) *Inai kiagáng battu anrinni?*
       inai ki= agáng   battu anrinni
       who 2p= accompany come here
       Who did you come here with? lit. 'who did you accompany here?'

348   CHAPTER 13

13.2.2.3   *kere* 'Where, Which'

This interrogative has two functions. One is to ask 'which' (of a set), while in the
other it usually combines with the basic verb *mae* 'be in a place' to ask 'where'.
In the 'which' usage, *kere* appears in focus position and represents an argument,
similar to the usages of *apa* and *inai*, and thus does not host an enclitic:

(588)   *Kere nungai anne anu ruayya*
         kere   nu= ngai anne anu   rua ≡a
         which 2f= like this thingy two ≡DEF
         Which do you like out of these two? (C:322)

(589)   *Apa uruna, apa pakaramulanna, kere poko'na, kere aka' ma'lanranna.*
         apa   uru ≡na   apa pakaramula ≡nna   kere   poko'
         what first ≡3.POSS what beginning   ≡3.POSS which trunk
         ≡na   kere   aka' ma'lanrang ≡na
         ≡3.POSS which root tap.root   ≡3.POSS
         What is its start, what is its beginning, which is its trunk, which is its
         root. (Sinrili': I Ma'di')

In its 'where' usage, *kere mae* (often reduced to *ke mae*) is itself either a predicate or part thereof, and can host clitic pronouns—the placement of which is
quite variable:

(590)   *Lakereko mae? Lakeko mae? Lake(re) maeko?*
         la=   kere   =ko mae la= ke   =ko mae la= ke   mae
         FUT= where =2f be.at FUT= where =2f be.at FUT= where be.at
         =ko
         =2f
         Where are you going?

(591)   *Battuki' ke(re) mae? Battu ke(re)ki' mae? Battu ke(re) maeki'?*
         battu =ki' kere   mae battu kere   ki' mae battu kere   mae
         come =2p where be.at come where =2p be.at come where be.at
         =ki'
         =2p
         Where have you been? Where are you from?

In practice, inanimate 3rd person arguments are rarely cross-referenced on *kere
mae*, as seen in the following example where there is no 3rd person clitic *=i* on
either *kere* or *mae*:

OTHER CLAUSE TYPES 349

(592) *Kere mae balla'na?*
kere   mae   balla' ≡na
which be.in.a.place house ≡3.POSS
Where is his house? (cf. *kere balla'na* 'which is his house?')

13.2.2.4 *angngapa* '(Do) What', 'Why'

Angngapa is a verb derived with *aN(N)–* from the root *apa* (§ 13.2.2.1). It has two major uses which in English are expressed with a '(do) what', and 'why'. The two uses are quite distinct. In the '(do) what' sense *angngapa* is a main predicate, which can be either intransitive (and rather vague) as in (593), or transitive as in (594) and (595):

(593) *Angngapako?*
aN(N)– apa =ko?
BV–   what =2f
What are you doing? What is it? What do you want? How are you? What's the matter with you?

(594) *Lakuapamako?*
la=   ku= apa   =mo =ko
FUT= 1= what =PFV =2f
What will I do with you now?

(595) A: *Lanuapaintu mionga?* B: *Lakupakanrei.*
la=   nu= apa =i (a)ntu miong ≡a la= ku= pa–   kanre
FUT= 2f= what =3 that   cat   ≡DEF FUT= 1= CAUS– eat
=i
=3
A: What are you going to do with that cat? B: I'm going to feed it.

When it is used to mean 'why', *angngapa* occurs in initial position and takes as a complement a clause expressing the queried state of affairs. This suggests that *angngapa* 'do what' is a genuine verb, whereas the 'why' use has shed its verbal morphosyntax. Like negative clauses with *taena* (§ 13.3.2) and other 'fronting' constructions (§ 11.2.2), *angngapa* does not usually host a clitic itself, but causes clitic fronting on the following clause. The complementiser *na* may optionally be present in all such sentences, but must be present when the complement clause itself begins with an element causing clitic movement such as a negator, as can be seen in (599):

(596) *Angngapa (na) numakkala'?*
aN(N)– apa (na) nu= makkal =a'
BV– what (COMP) 2f= laugh =EC
Why are you laughing?

(597) *Angngapa nummantang inja, nabangngimo.*
aN(N)– apa nu= amm– antang inja na= bangngi =mo
BV– why 2f= MV– stay still 3= night =PFV
Why are you still here? it's already night (bembe:086)

(598) *Angngapa nukalumanynyang kamma?*
aN(N)– apa nu= kalumanynyang kamma
BV– what 2f= rich thus
Why are you rich like this? (PT:220)

(599) *Angngapa na tena kierangi pammanakanta?*
aN(N)– apa na tena ki= erang =i pammanakang ≡ta
BV– what COMP NEG 2p= bring =3 family ≡2p.POSS
Why didn't you bring your family?

13.2.2.5 *ringngapanna* 'When'
Ringngapanna is used to ask about the timing of past events, or habitual events
(601). Morphologically it appears to consist of the interrogative verb *angngapa*
preceded by the preposition *ri* and suffixed with the 3rd person possessive
≡*na*, however it is not obvious how the combination of these parts denotes
the actual meaning. Cense (1979:28) considers the preposition *ri* optional, and
(602) below appears without it in the dictionary, but *angngapanna* without *ri*
was rejected by modern speakers.

Ringngapanna always occurs clause-initially, and like other temporal expressions it causes clitic fronting (i.e. it is followed by a complement clause).

(600) *Ringngapanna nubattu?*
ringngapanna nu= battu
when 2f= come
When did you arrive?

(601) *Ringngapanna nabiasa appasara'?*
ringngapanna na= biasa aC– pasar =a'
when 3= usual MV– market =EC
When does she usually go to market?

OTHER CLAUSE TYPES

(602) *Ringngapanna nanutunrung*
       ringngapanna na= nu= tunrung
       when   3= 2f= hit
       When did you hit him? (C:28)

13.2.2.6   *siapayya* 'When' (FUT)

Siapayya is used to ask about the timing of a future event. In all cases it may optionally be preceded by the preposition *ri*. Morphologically it appears to consist of the numeral interrogative *siapa* and the definite marker ≡*a*, but as with *ringngapanna* it is unclear how this combination could result in the actual meaning.

Like *ringngapanna*, *siapayya* always occurs clause-initally, and causes clitic fronting.

(603) *Ri siapayya nummotere' ri pa'rasangannu?*
       ri   siapayya   nu= amm– oter   =e' ri   pa'rasangang
       PREP when.FUT 2f= MV–   return =EC PREP country
       ≡*nu*
       ≡2f,POSS
       When will you return to your country?

(604) *(Ri) siapayya nanisungke sikolayya?*
       ri   siapayya   na= ni–   sungke sikola ≡a
       PREP when.FUT 3= PASS– open   school ≡DEF
       When will the school open? (C:28)

13.2.2.7   *siapa* 'How Much/ How Many'

Siapa is used for asking about numbers and quantities of things in constructions which do not include classifiers (see *pirang* below). This includes asking the time or date, and the price of items. Morphologically *siapa* appears to be composed of the mutual prefix *si–* and the interrogative pronoun *apa*, though its meaning cannot be predicted clearly from that combination.[1]

(605) *Tette' siapa kamma–kammanne? Tette' lima.*
       tette' siapa   kamma– kamma (a)nne
       o'clock how.much RDP–   thus   this
       What time is it now? Five o'clock.

---

1   The same combination (with different forms) is found in other languages of the region; for example in Muna, Southeast Sulawesi (Berg 1989:218) 'how many' is *se-hae* ⟨one-what⟩.

352   CHAPTER 13

(606)   *Siapa ballinna anjo sapeda?*
        siapa   balli   ≡nna   anjo sapeda
        how.much price ≡3.POSS that bicycle
        How much is that bike?

In examples like those above, the expected answer is a numeral. In other
examples though *siapa* asks about things which are less easily quantified, such
as a hypothetical length of time in (607) and the extent of a house's strength in
(608).

(607)   *Angkana "siapa sallona nala'busu' tau Marusuka punna taena naero'*
        ampinawangi ero'na Arumpone?"
        aN– kana siapa   sallo ≡na   na= la'bus   =u' tau
        AF– word how.much long ≡3.POSS 3= finished =EC person
        Marus =u' ≡a   punna taena na= ero' aN– pinawang =i
        Maros =EC ≡DEF if/when NEG 3= want AF– follow   =3
        ero' ≡na   Arumpone
        want ≡3.POSS Arumpone
        He said [to himself], 'How long [will it be until] all the people of Maros
        are killed if I do not give in to the wish of the Arumpone?' (Maros:186)

(608)   *Siapa todong kagassinganna balla'nu ...*
        siapa   todong ka⟩ gassing ⟨ang ≡na   balla' ≡nu
        how.much also   NR⟩ strong ⟨NR ≡3.POSS house ≡2f,POSS
        How much strength does your house have anyway ... (PT:126)

Siapa is subject to the same major derivational processes as numerals (see
§ 5.8.1): namely the ordinal prefix *maka–* (*makasiapa* 'the how many-th?'), the
multiplier *piN–* (*pissiapa* 'how many times?'), and the distributive prefix *taC–*
(*tassiapa* 'how many each?').

13.2.2.8   *pirang* 'How Many'
The numeral interrogative *pirang* is used where the corresponding numeral
would be attached to a classifier or measure noun, or higher order numeral, or
in other words wherever the numeral linker –*N*– would be found (see § 5.8).[2]

---

2 In fact the final nasal on *pirang* is most likely the linker, but as there is no context in which
   the form *pira* is ever found, I have analysed the nasal as integral.

OTHER CLAUSE TYPES   353

(609)   *Pirangkayu tedong? Pirambatu balla'?*
        pirang   kayu tedong pirang   batu   balla'
        how.many CLASS buffalo how.many CLASS house
        How many buffalo? How many houses?

(610)   *Pirangngallomaki' anrinni?*
        pirang   allo =mo =ki' anrinni
        how.many day =PFV =2p here
        How many days have you been here?

(611)   *Pirambilangngang taungi umuru'na?*
        pirang   bilangngang taung =i umur =u' ≡na
        how.many hundred   year   =3 age   =EC ≡3.POSS
        How many centuries old is it?

13.2.2.9   *antekamma* 'How'

This interrogative appears to be formed from *ante* (a dialectal and archaic variant of *kere* 'which, where', see §13.2.2.3), and *kamma* 'be like so, thus'. It is used to
ask about manners and methods of doing things. *Antekamma* can host enclitics. Cense gives an example in which the enclitic occurs on *ante* (*ante=i kamma*
'how is it'), but in all the examples in my corpus the enclitic is attached to the
compound form.

(612)   *Antekammaminne amma' punna lanaikki' ri balla'?*
        antekamma =mo =i anne amma' punna la=   nai' =ki' ri
        how   =PFV =3 this mother if/when FUT= go.up =2p PREP
        balla'
        house
        How will you climb up to the house, mother? (lit. How this, mother,
        when you'll climb up to the house?) (PT:053)

(613)   *Antekamma–tossengi i Yasuto?*
        antekamma tong seng =i i   Yasuto
        how   also again =3 PERS Yasuto
        How was Yasuto again? (i.e. returning to Yasuto, how was he going?)

In some examples such as (614) *antekamma* asks about a noun relating to manner or method, in which case there is no enclitic. In such examples *antekamma*
could be substituted by *apa* with no change in meaning.

354   CHAPTER 13

(614)   *Antekamma batena akkio' tedonga anjo?*
        antekamma bate   ≡na   aC– kio' tedong ≡a   anjo
        how   method ≡3.POSS MV– call buffalo ≡DEF that
        In what manner is that buffalo calling? (PT:153)

13.3 Negation

There are several related ways of expressing negation, most based either syn-
chronically or etymologically on the negating clitic *ta=*. Apart from *ta=* itself,
those derived from it are: *taena* 'not', *tea* 'not want', and *teá* 'not be'. The prohibitive *iang* is an exception.

13.3.1 ta= 'NEG'
Although *ta=* is not the most common negator, it is the most basic (i.e. unambiguously monomorphemic) whereas the other negators described below can
be analysed as grammaticalised compounds. In isolation *ta=* simply means
'not' and is equivalent to the default negator *taena* (see below), and thus most
clauses with *taena* could be recast with *ta=* instead, e.g. (615) and (616):

(615)   *taena kuássemmi*
        tena ku= asseng =mo =i
        NEG 1=   know   =PFV =3
        I don't know it anymore, I forgot it

(616)   *takuasséngami*
        ta=   ku= asseng –a   =mo =i
        NEG= 1=   know   –SBJV =PRF =3
        I don't know it anymore, I forgot it

In practice, clauses such as (616) are quite marked in the modern language.
This may be partly because the presence of *ta=* on a verb usually requires the
addition of subjunctive *–a* to the verb before any enclitics (see §10.3), and the
subjunctive itself is somewhat archaic. In the modern language *ta=* is most
often found in combination with the free negators in double negative constructions such as (621) below. These do not require subjunctive *–a*.

     The use of *ta=* was much more common in the language of the Gowa chron-
icle, and is also not uncommon in genres which preserve archaic/literary style,
such as folk tales (*rupama*) and epic prose (*sinrili'*). From the KIT manuscript,
example (617) is from the Gowa chronicle, while (618) is from article 16 of the
Bungaya treaty of 1667:

OTHER CLAUSE TYPES 355

(617) *anne Karaenga. tanipujiyai. malambusu'. tanipujiyai. panrita.*
 anne karaeng ≡a ta= ni– puji –a =i ma– lambus
 this karaeng ≡DEF NEG= PASS– praise –SBJV =3 STV– upright
 =u' ta= ni– puji –a =i panrita
 =EC NEG= PASS– praise –SBJV =3 expert
 This karaeng was not praised for being just, was not praised for being learned. (KIT:3.07)

(618) *ka le'ba' naadóimi manna silawara ruku tania' apa nakana anunna*
 ka le'ba' na= ado –i =mo =i manna si– lawar
 because already 3= agree –APPL =PFV =3 even one– blade
 =a' ruku ta= nia' apa na= kana anu ≡nna
 =EC grass NEG= exist what 3= say thingy ≡3.POSS
 because he (Sultan Hasanuddin) already agreed that he has no claim to even one blade of grass (of Buton): lit. there does not exist anything (about which) he says (that is) his thing

There is an additional usage found only in the chronicles, in which the combination of *ri* and *ta=* prefixed to a verb functions as a kind of irrealis marker, with the meaning 'before the time of VERB', literally 'at (the time when) not':

(619) *Areng pakaraengang ri tama'gaukang nikana Karaeng Passi'*
 areng pa⟩ karaeng ⟨ang ri ta= maC– gau' –ang ni–
 name NR⟩ king ⟨NR PREP NEG= MV– action –NR PASS–
 kana karaeng Passi'
 word king Passi'
 His karaeng name before he became ruler (lit: at not ruling) was Karaeng Passi' (Maros:056).

13.3.2 t(a)ena 'Not'

The most common negator is *t(a)ena*; the two variants *taena* and *tena* are distinguished only by level of formality, with *taena* being more formal. It seems likely that *taena* is a grammaticised compound derived from *ta=ia na* ⟨NEG= 3PRO COMP⟩, literally 'it's not that ...'—the presence of *na* would help to explain why it should cause clitic fronting (§11.2.2). This negator does not require subjunctive –*a*:

(620) *tena kuássemmi*
 tena ku= asseng =mo =i
 NEG 1= know =PFV =3
 I don't know it anymore, I forgot it

356 CHAPTER 13

The combination of *taena* and *ta=* forms a negative + negative (= positive) construction. These are quite common, and interestingly, they do not require insertion of *–a* either.

(621) *baju keboka taena tanamangéi*
       baju kebo' ≡a   taena ta=   na= mange –i
       shirt white ≡DEF NEG   NEG= 3= go   –APPL
       the white shirt goes with everything (lit: the white shirt, there's no it not going with)

(622) *tenamo tau tampaui*
       tena =mo tau   ta=   aN– pau =i
       NEG =PFV person NEG= AF– story =3
       everyone says it (lit: there's no longer anyone who doesn't say it)

As the previous example shows, *taena* can host TAM enclitics—the combinations of the negators and TAM enclitics were discussed in § 4.3.3.
    Double *taena* constructions are also found, e.g.:

(623) *Taenamo taena nia' ngasengmako anne*
       taena =mo taena nia' ngaseng =mo =ko anne
       NEG   =PFV NEG   exist all   =PFV =2f this
       No-one isn't, there's everyone here (SKT:76)

13.3.3 tea 'Don't'
The third negative element is *tea* (probably derived from *ta=ia* (NEG=3PRO) 'it's not'), which hosts enclitics itself, rather than causing clitic movement. In 1st and 3rd person it means 'not want'; in the 2nd person the meaning is vetative, 'don't':

(624) *tea' angnganre*
       tea   =a' aN(N)– kanre
       not.want =1 BV–   eat
       I don't want to eat

(625) *teai anjama*
       tea   =i aN– jama
       not.want =3 BV– work
       he doesn't want to work

OTHER CLAUSE TYPES

(626) *teako sungkéi andi' punna teái i amma'*

tea	*=ko*	*sungke*	*–i*	*andi'*	*punna*	*teá*	*=i*	*i*	*amma'*
VET	=2f	open	–APPL	↓sibling	if	not.be	=3	PERS	mother

don't open it (the door), sister, if it's not mother (PT:121)

As with other negatives, in both of its senses *tea* is often found in negative + negative (= positive) constructions:

(627) *teai takicini' kakangku punna kilampa ri Soppeng*

tea	*=i*	*ta=*	*ki=*	*cini'*	*kaka'*	*≡ngku*	*punna*	*ki=*	*lampa*
not.want	=3	NEG=	1pl=	see	↑sibling	≡1.POSS	if	1pl=	go

ri	*Soppeng*
PREP	Soppeng

my sister doesn't want us to not see (her) if we go to Soppeng (= we'd better visit her)

(628) *teako ta'lampa*

tea	*=ko*	*ta=*	*aC–*	*lampa*
VET	=2f	NEG=	MV–	go

don't not go (= you'd better go)

13.3.4 teá 'Not Be'

Teá (with deviant final stress) is a negator of nominals roughly equivalent to Indonesian *bukan*. It can host enclitic pronouns, e.g.: *teái* 's/he/it's not', *teá'* ⟨tea=a'⟩ 'I'm not'. One example was in the second clause of (626) above: *teái i amma'* 'it's not mother', another appears below:

(629) *teái kanangku*

teá	*=i*	*kana*	*≡ngku*
not.be	=3	word	=1.POSS

they are not my words (i.e. I didn't say that)

Cense speculates that *teá* is most likely etymologically ⟨ta=ia–a | NEG=3PRO– SBJV⟩ 'it's not' (C:240), which seems plausible, though older examples which actually contain *taiá* show it with a different function, as seen in the following sentence from the Gowa Chronicle:

(630) *taiái. nipailalang. lontara'. kana–kanaya. ri bundu'na.*

ta=	*ia*	*–a*	*=i*	*ni–*	*pa–*	*i*	*lalang*	*lontar*	*=a'*
NEG=	3PRO	–SBJV	=3	PASS–	CAUS–	PREP	inside	lontar	=EC

358 CHAPTER 13

> kana– kana ≡a   ri   bundu' ≡na
> RDP– word ≡DEF PREP war   ≡3.POSS
> There was not put in the *lontara'* words about their war (KIT:2.13)

13.3.5 iang

Iang is a prohibitive marker found in manuscripts, but quite marked in modern use. Its meaning in manuscripts is 'may I not'. The vast majority of clauses containing *iang* are in the archaic formulae *iangku mabassung* or *iangku mawekeweke* 'may I not swell up', 'may I not be diminished', used in *patturioloang* (chronicles) to ward off bad luck from the writer when personal names of nobility are mentioned.

(631)   *areng kalenna. iangku mabassung. nikana. I Mangayoaberang.*
          areng kale ≡nna   *iang*   ≡ku   ma– bassung   ni–   kana
          name self ≡3.POSS PROH ≡1.POSS STV– swollen.belly PASS– word
          I   *Mangayoaberang*
          PERS Mangayoaberang
          His personal name, may I not swell up, was I Mangayoaberang. (KIT:1)

All the examples which were produced by speakers upon my request were somewhat different, in the 2nd clause of a 'I do X, lest Y' pattern (e.g. (632)).

(632)   *kusareko doe' iannu tau kasi–asi dudu*
          ku= sare *=ko doe'*   *iang*   ≡nu   tau   kasi–asi dudu
          1= give =2f money PROH ≡2f,POSS person poor   very
          I give you money lest you be a pitiful person

Cense (1979:247–248) identifies this as *ia* (homonymic with the 3rd person pronoun), and always suffixed with the prenasalised versions of the possessive markers (≡*ngku*, ≡*nna* and so forth, see §4.4.2). Ultimately there is no way to tell whether the nasal belongs to the prohibitive or the possessives. In fact, initially I assumed that these constructions were in fact showing fronted clitic pronouns as is common after a negator (see *taena* above), thus (631) would be *iang ku=mabassung*. However, a counter-example exists in the form 1pl/2pol form, which is *ianta* rather than **iang ki=* as seen in (633) below:

(633)   *iantamo tu'guru' naung*
          iang   ≡ta   =*mo tu'gur* =*u'* naung
          PROH ≡1pl.POSS =PFV fall   =EC go.down
          may we not fall down (C:248)

OTHER CLAUSE TYPES   359

I have analysed this form as *iang* rather than *ia* partly to distinguish it from
the pronoun, and partly because the form is suggested by the existence of a
similar form *jang* (cf. Indonesian *jangan*) in the mixed Indonesian/Makasar
vernacular used by students and prevalent on the internet. This is a vetative
marker and hosts enclitics rather than possessives, quite similar to the vetative use of *tea* seen in §13.3.3. An example is the following warning posted in
the message board of the newspaper Fajar, not long after acts of terrorism in
Makassar in 2002 (the Indonesian words are in bold):

(634)   *Kubilang jangko pigi di McD*
        ku= **bilang** *jang* *=ko* **pigi di**   *McD*
        1= say   VET =2f go   prep McDonalds
        I say don't go to McDonalds

There is another reason to consider it as *iang*, which is that there is a clear parallel with the sentential adverbs *mang* 'even though' and *pung* 'if'. Being more
productive these have lexicalised with the 3rd person possessive into *manna*
and *punna*, the differently inflected forms *mangku, pungku*, etc., are extremely
archaic.

13.4   Existentials

Existential clauses are are formed with the basic verb *nia'*. They have three main
functions.

The primary one is introductory: to introduce participants into discourse:

(635)   *Nia' se're romang ... i lalanna anjo romanga nia' todong sikayu tedong*
        angnganre ruku'.
        nia' *se're romang i*   *lalang* ≡*na*   *anjo romang* ≡*a*   ***nia'***
        exist one forest PREP inside ≡3.POSS that forest ≡DEF **exist**
        todong si-   *kayu*   *tedong aN(N)- kanre ruku'*
        also   one– animal buffalo BV–   food grass
        There was a forest ... in that forest there was a buffalo eating grass
        (PT:002–003)

The second major function of existential clauses is to signal predicate possession, which is shown by the combination of *nia'* and possessive markers on the
noun:[3]

---

3   There is no verb corresponding easily to English 'have' or Indonesian *punya*—the noun *pata*

360   CHAPTER 13

(636)   *Nia' doe'nu?*
        nia' *doe'*   *≡nu*
        exist money ≡2s.POSS
        Do you have money?

(637)   *Nia' se're karaeng nia' ana'na rua, baine sitau, bura'ne sitau.*
        *nia' se're karaeng **nia'** ana'   ≡na   rua baine   si–   tau*
        be   one karaeng **exist** child ≡3.POSS two female one– person
        bura'ne si–   tau
        man   one– person
        There was a karaeng, he had two children, one girl, one boy (bembe:
        001)

Note that numeral predicates can be an alternative to existential predicate pos-
session, e.g. *ruai ana'na* ⟨rua=i ana'≡na | two=3 child ≡3.POSS⟩ 'he had two
children' rather than *nia' ana'na rua* (see §7.4.4).

    Thirdly, and least commonly, there are some circumstances in which *nia'* is
in fact existential (or at least locative) rather than introductory or possessive,
as in the following examples:

(638)   *Angngapai nunia'?*
        *angngapa =i nu= **nia'***
        why   =3 2s= **exist**
        Why are you here?

(639)   *Gassingka nia'–inja nucokko–cokko?*
        *gassing =ka **nia'** inja nu= cokko– cokko*
        sure   =or **exist** still 2f= RDP– hide
        Maybe there's still (some) that you've hidden away?

Note that in (639) the subject of *nia'* (the potential hidden things) has been
ellipsed.

    Nia' in its introductory or possessive functions does not usually host pro-
nominal clitics, which is generally explicable in the case of introductory uses
because the entity being introduced is not yet definite (see discussion in
§7.2.4). Why this should also be the case in possessive functions is not clear.

    'owner' can be used if ownership is specifically at issue. There are also cases in which *nia'*
    need not be used for predicate possession because there is a verb derived from a noun with
    the meaning 'have NOUN', e.g.: *ammana'* 'have a child'.

OTHER CLAUSE TYPES 361

However, in existential functions pronominal clitics are sometimes found, as was seen in (638), above, and in the following biblical example:

(640) *Mingka niaki koasa malompona Alla-ta'ala a'gio' i rate ri tompo'na je'neka.*

mingka **nia'** =i koasa ma– lompo ≡na   Alla–ta'ala   aC–
but   **exist** =3 mighty STV– big   ≡3.POSS God Almighty MV–

gio' i   rate ri   tompo' ≡na   je'ne' ≡a
act PREP above PREP top   ≡3.POSS water ≡DEF

And the Spirit of God moved upon the face of the waters (lit. but there was God's great might, acting above the surface of the water).

Nia' is subject to a similar range of derivational possibilities as other basic verbs, for example the nominalising confix *ka⟩⟨ang* (§ 6.2.3) forms *kaniakkang* 'existence, presence':

(641) *ka taena nangai kaniakanna Balandaya ri Marusu'*

ka   taena na= ngai ka⟩ nia' ⟨ang ≡na   Balanda ≡a
because NEG 3= love NR⟩ exist ⟨NR ≡3.POSS Holland ≡DEF

ri   Marus =u'
PREP Maros =EC

because he did not like the Dutch presence in Maros. (Maros:175)

13.5 Ascriptives/Presentatives

Ascriptive and presentative clauses are similar to existentials, but rather than simply asserting the existence of something, they assert its identity or nature, roughly 'he/she/it is ...' and the like. They are basically equational clauses, based on predicates formed by the 3rd person pronoun *ia*, with the addition of aspectual and pronominal clitics. They take complements which may be clauses, or NPs.

The combinations are:
– *iami* ⟨ia=mo=i | 3PRO=PFV=3⟩ 'it was ...'
– *iapi* ⟨ia=pa=i | 3PRO=IPF=3⟩ 'it still is ...' or 'it will be ...'
– *iaji* ⟨ia=ja=i | 3PRO=LIM=3⟩ 'it's just ...'

(642) *iami naagaang. situju. tu-Polombangkenga.*

ia   =mo =i na= agáng si–   tuju tu–   Polombangkeng
3PRO =PFV =3 3= do.with MUT– goal person– Polombangkeng

≡*a*
≡DEF
they were united (against) the people of Polombangkeng. (KIT:26)

(643) *Iaji bawang attallasa', maraenganga mate–ngasengi*
ia =*ja* =*i bawang aC– tallas* =*a' maraeng –ang* ≡*a*
3PRO =LIM =3 only MV– life =EC other –COMPR ≡DEF
mate ngaseng =*i*
death all =3
He's the only one still alive, the others all died

The addition of the complementiser *na* gives specialised meanings. For example, *iami na* can be used as a justification: 'that's why ...':

(644) *Iami na kukana katutuko a'dongko' jarang*
ia =*mo* =*i na ku*= *kana ka*– *tutu* =*ko aC*– *dongko'*
3PRO =PFV =3 COMP 1= word NR– look.after =2f MV– back
jarang
horse
So that's why I say, be careful on horseback (after describing a riding accident)

Iapi na is used for conditionals: 'it would be X if Y':

(645) *Iapi na kuppilajara' punna nia' gurungku bai'–baine*
ia =*pa* =*i na ku*= *aC*– *pilajar* =*VC punna nia' guru*
3PRO =IPF =3 COMP 1= MV– study =epen if be teacher
≡*ngku bai'*– *baine*
≡1.POSS RDP– female
I'd study if I had a pretty female teacher

And *iaji na* can be used for clarification or lessening of a previous statement, 'what I meant was ...':

(646) *Iaji na tettere' kalotoro' anjo bajunta, punna bambangi alloa*
ia =*ja* =*i na tetter* =*e' kalotor* =*o' anjo baju*
3PRO =LIM =3 COMP quickly =EC dry =EC that shirt
≡*nta punna bambang* =*i allo* ≡*a*
≡2p.POSS if/when hot =3 day ≡DEF
What I mean is, that shirt of yours will dry quickly, if it's a hot day

OTHER CLAUSE TYPES 363

When the complement is an NP, the *ia*+clitic cluster tends to coalesce with a demonstrative which is syntactically part of the following NP, e.g. *iaminne* ⟨ia=mo=i (a)nne | 3PRO=PFV=3 this⟩ 'this is'; *iajinjo* ⟨ia=ja=i (a)njo | 3PRO=LIM=3 that⟩ 'that's just'. There are nine permutations (3 aspect clitics by 3 demonstratives) of these:

(647) *Iaminne patturioloanga Gowa*
       ia   *=mo* *=i* *(a)nne pa⟩ aC–* *tu*   *ri*   *olo*   *⟨ang* *≡a*
       3PRO =PFV =3 this   NR⟩ MV– person prep front ⟨NR   ≡DEF
       Gowa
       Gowa
       This was the Gowa Chronicle

(648) *Iajinjo anungku*
       ia   *=ja* *=i* *(a)njo anu*   *≡ngku*
       3PRO =LIM =3 that   thingy ≡1.POSS
       Only that thing there is mine

(649) *Iapintu anunna taua*
       ia   *=pa* *=i* *(a)ntu anu*   *≡nna*   *tau*   *≡a*
       3PRO =IPF =3 that   thingy ≡3.POSS person ≡DEF
       There's still someone's thing (left behind) near you

APPENDIX A

Excerpt of the Gowa Chronicle from Manuscript KIT 668–216

Slightly more than 4 pages, covering the rules of Tuma'pa'risi'–kallonna ('the sorenecked one', ruled c. 1510–1546) and Tunipalangga ('the suspended one', ruled c. 1546–1565). Unreadable graphs in the original script are represented with □. References are to the original page and line in the manuscript, i.e. KIT:1.01 is page 1, line 1. The text is broken roughly into sentences and the 'missing' sounds (i.e. syllable codas) were filled in in consultation with Haji Djirong Basang Daeng Ngewa, and by comparison with the published version of the chronicle (Wolhoff and Abdurrahim 1959). The translation is based on Cummings (to appear), modified in places to more accurately reflect this particular version. For background to the historical period see § 1.1.2.3.

KIT:1.01

ᜒᜓᜆᜒ꞉

(1)   ... *ri Bajeng.*
      ... *ri   Bajeng*
      ... PREP Bajeng
      ... of Bajeng

ᜊᜒᜆᜒᜐᜀᜒᜋᜆᜒᜀᜊᜒᜈᜒᜐᜆᜒᜌᜒᜌᜓᜐᜊᜀᜒᜀᜊᜀᜒᜆᜓᜆ ᜊᜒ

(2)   *Karaenna. tu Bonea. naaganga. ma'ulu–kana. nikana. Boteka.*
      karaeng ≡na   tu   Bone ≡a   na= agang ≡a maC- ulu–kana ni-
      karaeng ≡3.POSS person Bone ≡DEF 3= friend ≡rel MV– treaty   PASS-
      kana Boteka
      word Boteka
      The karaeng of the people of Bone that he also made a treaty with was called Boteka

ᜌᜓᜋᜒᜀᜈᜒᜀᜒᜈᜊᜒᜆᜓᜆᜒᜀᜊᜒ

(3)   *iami anne. aenna. Bongkanga.*
      ia   =mo =i anne aeng ≡na   Bongkanga
      3PRO =PFV =3 this father ≡3.POSS Bongkanga
      he was the father of Bongkanga.

© KONINKLIJKE BRILL NV, LEIDEN, 2020 | DOI:10.1163/9789004412668_015

APPENDIX A

KIT:1.02

ᨔᨑᨀᨙᨑᨂ᨞ᨕᨊ᨞ᨄᨙᨍ᨞ᨆᨅᨍᨗ᨞ᨁᨕᨘ᨞ᨆᨒᨅᨘᨔᨘᨀᨗ᨞

(4) *anne Karaenga. nipuji panrita dudu. mabaji' gau'na. malambusuki.*

anne	*karaeng*	*≡a*	*ni–*	*puji*	*panrita*	*dudu*	*ma–*	*baji'*	*gau'*	*≡na*
this	karaeng	≡DEF	PASS–	praise	expert	very	ST–	good	action	≡3.POSS

ma–	*lambus*	*=u'*	*=i*
ST–	upright	=EC	=3

This karaeng was praised as a very learned person, as ruling well and justly.

ᨁᨒᨑᨊ᨞ᨊᨗᨀᨊ᨞ᨕᨗᨀᨔᨘᨕᨂ᨞ᨑᨗᨍᨘᨑᨘ᨞

(5) *gallaranna. nikana. I Kasuiang. ri Juru.*

gallarang	*≡na*	*ni–*	*kana*	*I*	*Kasuiang*	*ri*	*Juru*
Chief	≡3.POSS	PASS–	word	PERS	Kasuiang	PREP	Juru

His gallarang-title was Kasuiang ri Juru.

ᨄᨀᨑᨙᨕᨊ᨞ᨊᨗᨀᨊ᨞ᨕᨗᨀᨑᨙᨆᨂᨘᨈᨘᨂᨗ᨞

(6) *pakkareanna. nikana. I Kare Mangngutungi.*

pa⟩	*aC–*	*kare*	*⟨ang*	*≡na*	*ni–*	*kana*	*I*	*Kare*	*Mangngutungi*
NR⟩	MV–	Kare	⟨NR	≡3.POSS	PASS–	word	PERS	Kare	Mangngutungi

his Kare title was I Kare Mangngutungi

KIT:1.04

ᨕᨗᨈᨚᨆᨗᨕᨊᨙ᨞ᨕᨘᨑᨘᨕᨂᨔᨒᨙᨕᨗ᨞ᨄᨑᨔᨂ᨞ᨅᨚᨈᨚᨆᨊᨕᨗ᨞

(7) *ia tommi anne. uru angngallei. pa'rasangang. Bontomanai'.*

ia	*tong*	*=mo*	*=i*	*anne*	*uru*	*aN(N)–*	*alle*	*=i*	*pa'rasangang*
3PRO	also	=PFV	=3	this	beginning	BV–	take	=3	land

Bontomanai'

Bontomanai'

He was also the first to take the land of Bontomanai'

ᨕᨗᨈᨚᨍᨗᨊᨗᨀᨊ᨞ᨁᨒᨑᨂᨒᨚᨕᨐ᨞

(8) *ia tonji nikana. Gallarang Loaya.*

ia	*tong*	*=ja*	*=i*	*ni–*	*kana*	*gallarang*	*loa*	*≡a*
3PRO	also	=LIM	=3	PASS–	word	chief	ill.favoured	≡DEF

He was also called Gallarang Loaya

EXCERPT OF THE GOWA CHRONICLE FROM MANUSCRIPT KIT 668–216 367

KIT:1.06

ꦱꦷ꦳ꦲꦮꦴꦢꦷꦱꦷꦧꦴꦲꦮꦴꦣꦷꦢꦷꦱꦷꦲꦷꦱꦷꦢꦷꦱꦷꦴꦢꦷꦴ꧈

(9) *anne Karaenga. napanjari ase. lamung–lamunga.*

anne	*karaeng*	*≡a*	*na=*	*pa–*	*aN–*	*jari*	*ase*	*lamung–*	*lamung*	*≡a*
this	karaeng	≡DEF	3=	CAUS–	AF–	become	rice	RDP–	plant	≡DEF

This karaeng, he caused rice, other plants to grow.

ꦲꦴꦢꦶꦧꦴꦴꦢꦷ꧈

(10) *napanraráki juku'.*

na=	*pa–*	*aN–*	*rara'*	*–i*	*juku'*
3=	CAUS–	AF–	be.common	–TRS	fish

He made fish become plentiful.

KIT:1.07

ꦱꦴꦲꦴꦢꦷꦱꦴꦲꦷꦴꦢꦴꦢꦷꦴꦲꦴꦲꦴꦴꦢꦷꦴꦢꦴꦢꦷꦴꦢꦴꦢꦴꦲꦴꦢꦴꦴꦢꦴꦢꦴ꧈

(11) *ia tommi anne. ma'gau'. na battu. Jawa nikanaya. I Galasi. ma'bunduki. ri Pammo-likang.*

ia	*tong*	*=mo*	*=i anne*	*maC–*	*gau'*	*na*	*battu*	*jawa*	*ni–*	*kana*
3PRO	also	=PFV	=3 this	MV–	action	COMP	come	Java	PASS–	word

≡a	*I*	*Galasi*	*maC–*	*bundu'*	*=i*	*ri*	*Pammolikang*
≡REL	PERS	Galasi	MV–	war	=3	PREP	Pammolikang

It was while he was ruling that a Javanese named I Galasi came and warred in Pammolikang.

KIT:1.08

ꦲꦷꦢꦷꦱꦷꦲꦴꦢꦴꦴꦷꦱꦴꦲꦷꦴꦢꦴꦱꦷ

(12) *tallum– pulo taungi. angngannang. ma'gau'*

tallu	*–N*	*pulo*	*taung*	*=i*	*aN–*	*annang*	*maC–*	*gau'*
three	–LK	ten	year	=3	LK–	six	MV–	action

For thirty-six years he ruled.

368 APPENDIX A

KIT:1.09

ᨔᨑᨕᨗᨈᨚᨆᨗᨕᨊᨙᨈᨆᨁᨕᨘᨊᨊᨗᨒᨗᨄᨘᨂᨗᨊᨗᨅᨘᨉᨘᨑᨗᨈᨘᨈᨒᨚᨊᨑᨗᨈᨘᨆᨑᨘᨔᨘᨊᨑᨗᨈᨘᨄᨚᨒᨚᨅᨂᨙᨂ

(13) ia– tommi anne. ma'gau'. na nilipungi. nibundu'. ri tu Talloka. ri tu Marusuka. ri tu
Polombangkenga.
ia   tong =mo =i anne maC– gau'   na   ni–   lipung =i ni–   bundu'
3PRO also =PFV =3 this MV– action CMP PASS– gather =3 PASS– war
ri   tu   Tallo' ≡a   ri   tu   Marus =u' ≡a   ri   tu
PREP person Tallo' ≡DEF PREP person Maros =EC ≡DEF PREP person
Polombangkeng ≡a
Polombangkeng ≡DEF
It was also while he was ruling that he was surrounded and attacked by the people
of Tallo', by the people of Maros, by the people of Polombangkeng.

KIT:1.10

ᨅᨑᨕᨂᨑᨗᨈᨒᨚᨊᨕᨁᨕᨂᨔᨗᨕᨙᨓᨈᨘᨊᨗᨄᨔᨘᨑᨘ

(14) Karaenga. ri Tallo'. naagaanga. siewa. Tunipasuru'.
karaeng ≡a   ri   Tallo' na= agáng ≡a si–   ewa   tu   ni–
karaeng ≡DEF PREP Tallo' 3= do.with ≡rel MUT– oppose person PASS–
pa–   suru'
CAUS– subsided
The karaeng of Tallo' with whom he struggled was called Tunipasuru'.

ᨕᨑᨙᨀᨒᨙᨊᨕᨗᨕᨂᨀᨘᨆᨅᨔᨘᨊᨗᨀᨊᨕᨗᨆᨂᨕᨚᨅᨙᨑ

(15) areng kalenna. iang kumabassung. nikana. I Mangayoaberang.
areng kale ≡nna   iang ku= ma– bassung   ni–   kana I
name self ≡3.POSS VET 1= ST– swollen.belly PASS– word PERS
Mangayoaberang
Mangayoaberang
His personal name, may I not be cursed, was I Mangayoaberang.

KIT:1.12

ᨆᨁᨕᨘᨀᨑᨗᨆᨑᨘᨔᨘᨊᨗᨀᨊᨄᨈᨊᨒᨂᨀᨊ

(16) ma'gauka. ri Marusu'. nikana. Patanna Langkana.
maC– gau' –a   ri   Marus =u' ni–   kana pata   ≡nna   langkana
MV– action ≡REL PREP Maros =EC PASS– word owner ≡3.POSS palace
He who ruled in Maros was called Patanna Langkana.

EXCERPT OF THE GOWA CHRONICLE FROM MANUSCRIPT KIT 668–216

ꦱꦫꦺꦪꦠꦤꦲꦤꦶꦏꦤꦠꦸꦩꦩꦼꦤꦁꦫꦶꦧꦸꦭꦸꦝꦸꦮꦪ꧈

(17) *areng matena. nikana. Tumamenang ri Bulu'duaya.*

areng	*mate*	≡*na*	*ni-*	*kana*	*tu*	*ma-*	*menang*	*ri*	*Bulu'dua*
name	death	≡3.POSS	PASS–	word	person	ST–	resting	PREP	Bulu'dua

≡*a*

≡DEF

His posthumous name was Tumamenang ri Bulu'duaya.

ꦱꦫꦺꦏꦭꦼꦤꦪꦁꦏꦸꦩꦧꦱꦸꦁꦆꦩꦥꦥꦱꦺꦴꦩꦧ꧈

(18) *areng kalenna iang kumabassung. I Mappasomba.*

areng	*kale*	≡*nna*	*iang*	*ku=*	*ma-*	*bassung*	*I*	*maC-*	*pa-*
name	self	≡3.POSS	VET	1=	ST–	swollen.belly	PERS	MV–	CAUS–

somba

homage

His personal name, may I not be cursed, was I Mappasomba.

ꦱꦫꦺꦥꦩꦤꦲꦤꦶꦏꦤꦆꦢꦲꦼꦁ�ꦴꦫꦒ꧈

(19) *areng pamana'na. nikana. I Daeng Nguraga.*

areng	*pa-*	*amm-*	*ana'*	≡*na*	*ni-*	*kana*	*I*	*daeng*	*Uraga*
name	NR–	MV–	child	≡3.POSS	PASS–	word	PERS	daeng	Uraga

His royal name was I Daeng Nguraga.

KIT:1.15

ꦠꦸꦩꦒꦲꦸꦏꦫꦶꦧꦗꦼꦁꦲꦤꦲꦤꦏꦫꦲꦺꦁꦭꦺꦴꦨꦶꦏꦤꦪꦢꦲꦼꦤꦤꦆꦥꦱꦲꦻꦫꦶꦏꦏꦤꦤꦆꦢꦲꦼꦁꦩꦱꦫ꧉

(20) *Tuma'gauka. ri Bajeng. ana'na. Karaeng Loe. nikanaya Daenna I Pasairi. kakanna I Daeng Masarro.*

tu	*maC-*	*gau'*	≡*a*	*ri*	*Bajeng*	*ana'*	≡*na*	*karaeng*	*loe*	*ni-*
person	MV–	action	≡rel	PREP	Bajeng	child	≡3.POSS	karaeng	Great	PASS–

kana	≡*a*	*daeng*	≡*na*	*I*	*Pasairi*	*kaka'*	≡*nna*	*I*	*daeng*	*ma-*
word	≡rel	daeng	≡3.POSS	PERS	Pasairi	↑sibling	≡3.POSS	PERS	daeng	ST–

sarro

strong

He who ruled in Bajeng was the child of Karaeng Loe called (Daenna) I Pasairi.

370 APPENDIX A

[Makasar script line]

ꦫꦴ

(21) *iaminne. sari'battang. Tuma'gauka. ri Sanrabone. ri Lengkese'. ri Katingang. ri Jamarang. ri Jipang. ri Mandalle'.*

ia	=mo	=i	=nne sari'battang	tu	maC– gau'	≡a	ri	Sanrabone
3PRO	=PFV	=3	=this sibling	person	MV– action	≡rel	PREP	Sanrabone

ri Lengkese' ri Katingang ri Jamarang ri Jipang ri
PREP Lengkese' PREP Katingang PREP Jamarang PREP Jipang PREP

Mandalle'
Mandalle'

He was siblings with those who ruled in Sanrabone, in Lengkese', in Katingang, in Jamaraang, in Jipang, in Mandalle'.

[Makasar script line]

(22) *tujui sisari'battang. ma'la'lang sipue– ngaseng.*

tuju	=i	si–	sari'battang	maC– la'lang	si–	pue	ngaseng
seven	=3	MUT–	sibling	MV– shelter	one–	half	all

They were seven siblings; all had royal sunshades.

KIT:1.19

[Makasar script line]

(23) *iaminne Karaeng. nilipungi. ri Gaukang Tallua.*

ia	=mo	=i	=nne karaeng	ni– lipung	=i	ri	gau'	–ang
3PRO	=PFV	=3	=this karaeng	PASS– gather.round	=3	PREP	action	–NR

tallu ≡a
three ≡DEF

This karaeng was supported by the Three Gaukang.

[Makasar script line]

(24) *Karaenga ri Lakiung. angngagangi. Gurudaya. tu Mangngasaya. tu Tomboloka. tu Saomataya.*

karaeng	≡a	ri	Lakiung	aN(N)– agáng	=i	Gurudaya	tu
karaeng	≡DEF	PREP	Lakiung	BV– do.with	=3	Gurudaya	person

Mangngasa	≡a	tu	Tombol	=o'	≡a	tu	Saomata	≡a
Mangngasa	≡DEF	person	Tombolo'	=EC	≡DEF	person	Saomata	≡DEF

Karaeng ri Lakiung and Gurudaya, with the people of Mangngasa, Tombolo', Saomata,

EXCERPT OF THE GOWA CHRONICLE FROM MANUSCRIPT KIT 668-216   371

ᵗᵉˣᵗ *(Lontara script line)*

(25) *anjorengi. kalenna. imamakasi. Baro'boso'. napamménténgi.*

anjoreng	*=i*	*kale*	*≡nna*	*imamakasi*	*Baro'bos*	*=o'*	*na=*	*pa–*	*amm–*
there	=3	centre	≡3.POSS	??		Baro'boso'	=EC	3=	CAUS–	MV–

enteng –i

stand –APPL

there in Baro'boso' they readied their arms,

ᵗᵉˣᵗ *(Lontara script line)*

(26) *iami naagaang. situju. tu Polombangkenga.*

ia	*=mo*	*=i*	*na=*	*agáng*	*si–*	*tuju*	*tu*	*Polombangkeng*	*≡a*
3PRO	=PFV	=3	3=	do.with	MUT–	goal	person	Polombangkeng	≡DEF

they were united (against) the people of Polombangkeng. {and stood against the people of Polombangkeng.}

KIT:1.22

ᵗᵉˣᵗ *(Lontara script line)*

(27) *kalenna Karaenga. siagángi. Sulengkaya.*

kale	*≡nna*	*karaeng*	*≡a*	*siagáng*	*=i*	*sulengka*	*≡a*
self	≡3.POSS	karaeng	≡DEF	with	=3	lap	≡DEF

The karaeng himself and Sulengkaya,

ᵗᵉˣᵗ *(Lontara script line)*

(28) *Rappocini. napamménténgi. siagángi. tu Sudianga. tu Manujua. tu Borisalloa.*

Rappocini	*na=*	*pa–*	*amm–*	*enteng*	*–i*	*siagáng*	*=i*	*tu*	*Sudiang*
Rappocini	3=	CAUS–	MV–	stand	–APPL	with	=3	person	Sudiang

≡a	*tu*	*Manuju*	*≡a*	*tu*	*Borisallo*	*≡a*
≡DEF	person	Manuju	≡DEF	person	Borisallo	≡DEF

poised in Rappocini with the people of Sudiang, the people of Manuju, the people of Borisallo,

ᵗᵉˣᵗ *(Lontara script line)*

(29) *tu Talloka. siagaang. kalenna. I Daeng Masarro. iami naagaang. situju. kalenna Karaenga.*

tu	*Tallo'*	*≡a*	*siagáng*	*kale*	*≡nna*	*I*	*daeng*	*ma–*	*sarro*	*ia*
person	Tallo'	≡DEF	with	self	≡3.POSS	PERS	daeng	ST–	strong	3PRO

=mo	*=i*	*na=*	*agáng*	*si–*	*tuju*	*kale*	*≡nna*	*karaeng*	*≡a*
=PFV	=3	3=	do.with	MUT–	goal	self	≡3.POSS	karaeng	≡DEF

The people of Tallo' with I Daeng Masarro himself, they stood against the karaeng.

(30) *Karaenga ri Data'. siagángi. Cakkuridia. Tamamangung. napammenténgi. siagángi. Paccellekang. Pattallassang. Bontomanai'.*

karaeng	*≡a*	*ri*	*Data'*	*siagáng*	*=i*	*Cakkuridia Tamamangung na=*
karaeng	≡DEF	PREP	Data'	with	=3	Cakkuridia Tamamangung 3=

pa– amm– enteng –i siagáng =i Paccellekang Pattallassang
CAUS– MV– stand –APPL with =3 Paccellekang Pattallassang

Bontomanai'
Bontomanai'

Karaeng ri Data' and Cakkuridia, in Tamamangung he held firm with Paccellek-
kang, Pattallassang, Bontomanai',

(31) *tu Marusuka. naagaang. situju.*

tu	*Marus*	*=u'*	*≡a*	*na=*	*agáng*	*si–*	*tuju*
person	Maros	=EC	≡DEF	3=	do.with	one–	goal

and fought against the people of Maros.

KIT:2.05

(32) *le'baki. ma'bunduki. nipalarimi. tu Talloka tu Marusuka. tu Polombangkenga.*

le'ba'	*=i*	*maC–*	*bundu'*	*=i*	*ni–*	*pa–*	*lari*	*=mo*	*=i*	*tu*	*Tallo'*
finished	=3	MV–	war	=3	PASS–	CAUS–	run	=PFV	=3	person	Tallo'

≡a	*tu*	*Marus*	*=u'*	*≡a*	*tu*	*Polombangkeng*	*≡a*
≡DEF	person	Maros	=EC	≡DEF	person	Polombangkeng	≡DEF

Once the battle raged the people of Tallo', the people of Maros, the people of
Polombangkeng were put to flight.

(33) *tu Marusuka. larina. ri Tamamangung. tulusuki. manaung ri Marusu'.*

tu	*Marus*	*=u'*	*≡a*	*lari*	*≡na*	*ri*	*Tamamangung*	*tulus*	*=u'*	*=i*
person	Maros	=EC	≡DEF	run	≡3.POSS	PREP	Tamamangung	directly	=EC	=3

ma–	*naung*	*ri*	*Marus*	*=u'*
ST–	go.down	PREP	Maros	=EC

The people of Maros fled from Tamamangung straight down to Maros.

EXCERPT OF THE GOWA CHRONICLE FROM MANUSCRIPT KIT 668–216　　373

ᨑᨉᨂᨗᨍᨗᨌᨑᨅᨗᨌᨐᨍᨗᨌᨍᨔᨗᨌᨗᨌᨗᨌᨑᨅᨗᨊᨌᨌᨑᨅᨌᨌᨊᨛᨔᨗᨗ

(34) tu Polombangkenga. mangnguloro'– mami. biseang. na ma'biseang manai'.

tu　　　　Polombangkeng ≡a　　maN(N)– ulor　　=o' mamo =i bise　　–ang
person Polombangkeng ≡DEF BV–　　　　launch =EC only　=3 paddle –NR

na　maC– bise　　–ang ma– nai'
and MV–　paddle –NR ST– go.up

The people of Polombangkeng launched ships and flew up [to Polombangkeng].

ᨑᨊᨔᨑᨅᨗᨌᨔᨛᨌᨊᨌᨛᨔᨗᨗ

(35) tu Talloka. malari mantama ri Tallo'

tu　　　Tallo' ≡a　　ma– lari maN– tama ri　　Tallo'
person Tallo' ≡DEF ST– run AF–　　enter PREP Tallo'

The people of Tallo' fled deep into Tallo'

KIT:2.09

ᨊᨅᨍᨌᨑᨔᨗᨊᨅᨛᨑᨗᨅᨅᨛᨑᨅᨛᨑᨔᨔᨂᨐᨌᨅᨛᨅᨑᨔᨗᨊᨗᨔᨊᨌᨛᨔᨗᨗ

(36) nassulu' mae. nasuro kio'. Karaenga. Tumapa'risi Kallonna. antama ri Tallo'.

na= aC– sulu' mae　　　　na= suro　kio' karaeng ≡a　　tu　　ma–
3=　MV– exit be.in.a.place 3=　order call karaeng ≡DEF person ST–

pa'ris =i'　kallong ≡na　　aN– tama ri　　Tallo'
pain =EC neck　≡3.POSS AF– enter PREP Tallo'

Then an invitation was sent out to Tumapa'risi' Kallonna. He entered Tallo'.

ᨊᨌᨌᨛᨔᨗᨔᨔᨗᨊᨑᨓᨊᨗᨅᨛᨉᨍᨗᨔᨗ

(37) tuju bangngi i. lalang. nitoana. nirappói.

tuju　bangngi i　　lalang ni–　toana ni–　rappo　　–i
seven night　　PREP inside PASS– guest PASS– areca.nut –TRS

For seven [nights] there he was feasted and honoured.

KIT:2.10

ᨔᨅᨌᨕᨑᨗᨊᨅᨊᨔᨌᨗᨑᨅᨛᨑᨔᨌᨛᨈᨓᨑᨅᨛᨑᨔᨌᨛᨛᨊᨔᨗᨔᨔᨌᨛᨔᨅᨌᨑᨅᨛᨌᨕᨈᨌᨊᨑᨅ
ᨔᨓᨗ

(38) iaminjo. nasitalli'mo. Karaenga. ri Gowa. Karaenga. ri Tallo'. gallaranga. ia– ngaseng. ri baruga nikelua.

ia　　　=mo =i =njo na= si–　　talli'　=mo karaeng ≡a　　ri　　Gowa
3PRO =PFV =3 =that 3=　MUT– pledge =PFV karaeng ≡DEF PREP Gowa

karaeng ≡a　　ri　　Tallo' gallarang ≡a　　ia　　ngaseng ri　　baruga
karaeng ≡DEF PREP Tallo' chief　　　　≡DEF 3PRO all　　　　PREP feast.hall

ni–   kelu   ≡a

PASS– roof.beam ≡DEF

They all swore oaths: the karaeng [of Gowa], the karaeng of Tallo', all the gallarrang in the great hall:

ꤷꤢꤷꥁꤰ꤮ꤢ꤭ꤲꤰ꤬ꤢꤷꤢꤱ꤬ꤰꤲꤤꤰꤲ꤬ꤢꤷꤲꤰꤢꤷꤢꤷ꤬ꤲ꤭ꤲꤰꤢꤲ꤮ꤰꤢ꤬ꤲꤪꤲ꤮ꤰ꤭ꤢꤰꤢꤰꤢ꤬ꤢ꤮ꤲ꤬ꤲꤪꤤꤰ꤬ꤢꤰ꤮ꤲꤢ꤮ꤰꤰꤢꤪꤤꤰ꤮ꤲ

(39) ia– iannamo. tau. ampasiewai. Gowa. Tallo'. iamo nacalla. rewata.

ia   ia   ≡nna   =mo tau   aN– pa–   si–   ewa   ≡a =i Gowa

3PRO 3PRO ≡3.POSS =PFV person AF– CAUS– MUT– oppose ≡rel =3 Gowa

Tallo' ia   =mo na= calla rewata

Tallo' 3PRO =PFV 3= reject gods

'Anyone who sets Gowa and Tallo' against each other, he is cursed by the gods.'

KIT:2.13

ꤵꤢ꤮ꤵꤢꤷꤦꤡ꤭ꤲꤰ꤮ꤷꤢ꤭ꤢꤲꤱꤲ꤬ꤢ꤬ꤢ꤭ꤢ꤮ꤲꤰꤲꤵꤢꤵꤢꤵꤢꤦꤲꤲꤪꤢꤰꤲ

(40) kana–kanayaji. taiái. nipailalang. lontara'. kana–kanaya. ri bundu'na.

kana– kana ≡a   =ja   =i ta= ia   –a   =i ni–   pa–   i

RDP– word ≡DEF =LIM =3 NEG= 3PRO –SBJV =3 PASS– CAUS– PREP

lalang lontar =a' kana– kana ≡a   ri   bundu' ≡na

inside lontar =EC RDP– word ≡DEF PREP war   ≡3.POSS

There was not put in the lontara' words about their war.

ꤷꤢꤦꤡꤰꤲꤢꤲ꤬ꤰꤪꤲꤪꤢꤲ

(41) iaji nipailalang. mabundu'na.

ia   =ja   =i ni–   pa–   i   lalang ma– bundu' ≡na

3PRO =LIM =3 PASS– CAUS– PREP inside ST– war   ≡3.POSS

It was only put in that they warred.

KIT:2.15

ꤪꤤꤰꤢꤪꤤꤰꤢꤪꤥꤦꤤ꤭ꤤ꤮ꤤꤰꤢꤵ꤬ꤢ꤮ꤲꤰꤲꤪꤢ꤮ꤥꤵꤢꤵꤲ꤮ꤲ

(42) matena mate magarrinji. anne Karaenga. Tumapa'risi' Kallonna.

mate ≡na   mate ma– garring =ja   =i anne karaeng ≡a   tu

death ≡3.POSS death ST– sick   =LIM =3 this karaeng ≡DEF person

ma– pa'ris =i'   kallong ≡na

ST– pain =EC neck   ≡3.POSS

As for his death, he died of illness, this Karaeng Tumapa'risi' Kallonna.

EXCERPT OF THE GOWA CHRONICLE FROM MANUSCRIPT KIT 668–216

KIT:2.16

ꦱꦺꦫ꦳ꦠꦤꦲꦩ꦳ꦒꦲꦸꦤꦩ꦳ꦭꦸꦭꦏꦤꦭꦸꦮꦸꦏꦢꦠꦸꦩꦠꦶꦤꦿꦺꦴꦮꦗꦺꦴ꧈

(43) *iaminne. ma'gau'. na ma'ulu–kana. Luwuka. Datu Matinroa. ri Wajo.*

    ia   *=mo* *=i* *=nne maC– gau'*   *na*   *maC– ulu–kana Luwu'* ≡*a*   *datu*

    3PRO *=PFV =3 =*this MV– action CMP MV– treaty   Luwu' ≡DEF king

    ma– tinro ≡*a*   *ri*   *Wajo*

    ST– sleep ≡DEF PREP Wajo

    He fought and then made an agreement with Luwu''s Datu' Matinroa ri Wajo'.

KIT:2.17

ꦪꦱꦭꦸꦭꦏꦤꦏꦫꦉꦁꦫꦶꦱꦭꦸꦩꦺꦏꦤꦶꦏꦤꦪꦩꦒꦗꦪ꧈

(44) *ma'ulu–kana. Karaenga. ri Salumeko. nikanaya. Magajaya.*

    maC– ulu–kana karaeng ≡*a*   *ri*   *Salumeko ni–*   *kana* ≡*a*

    MV– treaty   karaeng ≡DEF PREP Salumeko PASS– word ≡DEF

    Magajaya

    Magajaya

    He made an agreement with Karaeng ri Salumeko called Magajaya.

KIT:2.18

ꦱꦺꦫ꦳ꦠꦤꦱꦩꦥꦫꦺꦏꦥꦭꦶꦭꦶꦱꦤꦿꦧꦺꦴꦤꦺꦗꦶꦥꦁꦒꦭꦺꦱꦺꦴꦁꦲꦒꦁꦤꦶꦪꦺꦴꦚꦺꦴꦏꦲꦸꦥꦏꦺꦴꦩꦧꦺꦴꦁ꧈

(45) *iaminne. ampareki palili'. Sanrabone.. Jipang. Galesong. Agang–nionjo'. Kau.*
    Pakombong.

    ia   *=mo* *=i* *=nne aN– pare'* *=i pa–*   *lili'*   *Sanrabone Jipang*

    3PRO *=PFV =3 =*this AF– make *=3* CAUS– vassal Sanrabone Jipang

    Galesong Agang–nionjo' Kau Pakombong

    Galesong Agang–nionjo' Kau Pakombong

    [He made vassals of] Sanrabone, Jipang, Galesong, Agangnionjo', Kawu, Pakombong.

KIT:2.19

ꦱꦺꦫꦤꦠꦺꦴꦚꦶꦉꦸꦫꦸꦤꦱꦺꦴꦉꦶꦥꦫꦁꦒꦶ꧈

(46) *ia– tonji. uru nasorei. Paranggi'.*

    ia   *tong =ja* *=i uru*   *na= sore*   *=i Paranggi'*

    3PRO also *=*LIM *=3* beginning 3= pull.ashore *=3* Portugal

    He was also first to have the Portuguese come ashore.

376 APPENDIX A

ᜆᜐᜈᜦᜑᜒᜒᜊᜆᜈᜌᜊᜈᜑᜇᜒᜒᜌᜊᜐᜇᜒᜒᜈᜒᜌᜌᜊᜒ

(47) *julu taungi. na betana. Garassi'. betana todong. Malaka. ri Paranggika.*

julu	*taung*	*=i*	*na*	*beta*	*≡na*	*Garassi'*	*beta*	*≡na*
life.partner	year	=3	CMP	conquer	≡3.POSS	Garassi'	conquer	≡3.POSS

todong	*Malaka*	*ri*	*Paranggi'*	*≡a*
also	Malacca	PREP	Portugal	≡DEF

In the same year he conquered Garassi', also Melaka was conquered by the Portuguese.

KIT:2.21

ᜐᜈᜊᜇᜐᜇᜒᜒᜌᜅᜐᜈᜐᜈᜐᜊᜒᜒᜇᜊᜐᜐᜒ

(48) *anne Karaenga. ri ma'gau'na. taena palukka'. ri pa'rasanganga.*

anne	*karaeng*	*≡a*	*ri*	*maC-*	*gau'*	*≡na*	*taena*	*pa-*	*lukka'*
this	karaeng	≡DEF	PREP	MV-	action	≡3.POSS	NEG	NR-	stolen.thing

ri	*pa'rasangang*	*≡a*
PREP	land	≡DEF

During this karaeng's reign there were no thieves in the land.

ᜐᜇᜌᜒᜒᜐᜈᜊᜇᜐᜇᜒᜒᜐᜐᜇᜒᜇᜒᜇᜐᜊᜐᜊᜐᜒᜐᜐᜒᜒ

(49) *ia- todong. anne Karaenga. antabángi. pa're nikanaya. patamba' rinring.*

ia	*Todong*	*anne*	*karaeng*	*≡a*	*aN-*	*taba*	*-ang*	*=i*	*pa're*	*ni-*	*kana*
3PRO	Also	this	karaeng	≡DEF	AF-	fit	-BEN	=3	famine	PASS-	word

≡a	*pa-*	*tamba'*	*rinring*
≡rel	NR-	become	wall

Then too a famine struck called Tambarinring.

KIT:2.23

ᜊᜇᜌᜐᜒᜐᜈᜊᜇᜐᜇᜒᜒᜊᜈᜒᜐᜇᜐᜌᜈᜒᜒ

(50) *kana pamana'na. anne Karaenga. nikana. I Daeng Matanre.*

kana	*pa-*	*amm-*	*ana'*	*≡na*	*anne*	*karaeng*	*≡a*	*ni-*	*kana*	*I*
word	NR-	MV-	child	≡3.POSS	this	karaeng	≡DEF	PASS-	word	PERS

daeng	*Matanre*
daeng	Matanre

The royal name of this karaeng was I Daeng Matanre.

EXCERPT OF THE GOWA CHRONICLE FROM MANUSCRIPT KIT 668–216 377

ꦱꦴ...

(51) *areng kalenna. taena angngassengi. sanggenna. nigappaya nikuta'nang.*

areng	kale	=nna	taena	aN(N)–	asseng	=i	sangge	=nna	ni–	gappa
name	self	≡3.POSS	NEG	BV–	know	=3	until	≡3.POSS	PASS–	result

=a	ni–	kuta'nang
≡rel	PASS–	question

His personal name no one knows; among all those who were asked none knew.

KIT:3.02

(52) *anne ana'na. tumapa'risi' kallonna. tunipalangga ...*

anne	ana'	=na	tu	ma–	pa'ris	=i'	kallong	=na	tu	ni–
this	child	≡3.POSS	person	ST–	pain	=EC	neck	≡3.POSS	person	PASS–

pa–	langga
CAUS–	suspend

Tunipalangga, this was the child of Tumapa'risi' Kallonna.

(53) *matei tumapa'risi' kallonna.*

mate	=i	tu	ma–	pa'ris	=i'	kallong	=na
death	=3	person	ST–	pain	=EC	neck	≡3.POSS

Tumapa'risi' Kallonna died.

(54) *tunipalanggamo. ansossorangi. ma'gau'.*

tu	ni–	pa–	langga	=mo	aN–	sossorang	=i	maC–	gau'
person	PASS–	CAUS–	suspend	=PFV	AF–	inheritance	=3	MV–	action

Tunipalangga replaced him as ruler.

KIT:3.03

(55) *iang kumabassung. areng kalenna. nikana. I Mariugau'.*

iang	ku=	ma–	bassung	areng	kale	=nna	ni–	kana	I
VET	1=	ST–	swollen.belly	name	self	≡3.POSS	PASS–	word	PERS

Mariugau'
Mariugau'

May I not be cursed, his personal name was I Mariugau'.

APPENDIX A

ᨑᨊᨍᨐᨂᨊᨈᨛᨐᨑᨊᨛᨔᨘᨑᨘᨔᨗᨐᨑᨂᨛ

(56) *kana pamana'na. nikana. I Daeng Bonto.*

    kana pa- amm- ana' ≡na   ni-   kana I   daeng bonto

    word NR– MV–   child ≡3.POSS PASS– word PERS daeng shore

    His royal name was I Daeng Bonto.

ᨍᨑᨛᨈᨔᨚᨊᨛᨗᨐᨐᨐᨔᨂᨊᨂᨑᨊᨛᨑᨛᨈᨔᨔᨑᨛᨛ

(57) *pakaraenganna. ri tama'gau'na. nikana. Karaeng Lakiung.*

    pa) karaeng ⟨ang ≡na   ri   ta=   maC– gau'   ≡na   ni-   kana

    NR) karaeng ⟨NR ≡3.POSS PREP NEG= MV–   action ≡3.POSS PASS– word

    karaeng Lakiung

    karaeng Lakiung

    His karaeng-title before he became ruler was Karaeng Lakiung.

KIT:3.06

ᨊᨔᨍᨔᨚᨊᨔᨛᨛᨔᨘᨘᨂᨐᨔᨗᨊᨕᨍᨔᨚᨊᨔᨔᨄᨐᨚᨈᨗᨐᨔᨗᨊᨐᨚᨗ

(58) *tallum–pulo taungi. angngannang. na ma'gau'. na sampulo taung assagantuju. ma'gau'. na mate.*

    tallu –N pulo taung =i aN– annang na   maC– gau' na   sampulo

    three –LK ten year =3 LK– six   CMP MV–   action and ten

    taung aN– sagantuju maC– gau'   na mate

    year LK– eight   MV–   action and death

    At age thirty-six he became ruler and ruled eighteen years, then died.

KIT:3.07

ᨔᨗᨊᨑᨛᨈᨔᨚᨗᨊᨕᨍᨛᨑᨛᨗᨐᨔ᨝᨞ᨄᨗᨊᨕᨍᨛᨑᨛᨗᨍᨛᨊᨚᨗ

(59) *anne Karaenga. tanipujiyai. malambusu'. tanipujiyai. panrita.*

    anne karaeng ≡a   ta=   ni-   puji   –a   =i ma– lambus =u' ta=

    this karaeng ≡DEF NEG= PASS– praise –SBJV =3 ST– upright =EC NEG=

    ni-   puji   –a   =i panrita

    PASS– praise –SBJV =3 expert

    This karaeng was not praised for being just, was not praised for being learned.

ᨊᨑᨊᨈᨗᨊᨛᨑᨘᨈᨘᨐᨔᨗᨗᨊᨑᨍᨊᨑᨘᨗᨊᨛᨄᨊᨔᨔᨑᨛᨗ

(60) *nikanaja. tu barani–dudui. tu kapatiangi. tuganna'– aiki.*

    ni-   kana =ja tu   barani dudu =i tu   ka) pati   ⟨ang =i

    PASS– word =LIM person brave very =3 person NR) essence ⟨NR =3

EXCERPT OF THE GOWA CHRONICLE FROM MANUSCRIPT KIT 668–216   379

tu   ganna'   ai'   =i
person complete interior =3
He was just said to be a brave man, renowned, wise.

KIT:3.09

ᨊᨆᨈᨔᨑᨒᨖᨉᨑᨔᨛᨔᨑᨖᨊᨔᨗᨛᨑᨈᨗᨔᨑᨖᨊᨔᨗᨑᨔᨑᨉᨑᨊᨗᨄᨍᨅᨔᨒᨖᨑᨅᨛᨊᨚᨑᨅᨛᨑᨑᨗ

(61) *iami anne. Karaenga. ambetai. Bajeng. ambetai. Lengkese'. tuPolombangkenga. ia
ngaseng.*

ia   =mo =i anne karaeng ≡a   aN- beta   =i Bajeng aN- beta
3PRO =PFV =3 this   karaeng ≡DEF AF- conquer =3 Bajeng AF- conquer
=i Lengkese' tu   Polombangkeng ≡a   ia   ngaseng
=3 Lengkese' person Polombangkeng ≡DEF 3PRO all
This karaeng conquered Bajeng; conquered Lengkese', all the peoples of Polombangkeng;

ᨔᨛᨑᨚᨆᨅᨘᨉᨘᨅᨘᨁᨗᨔᨗᨀᨑᨗᨅᨆᨕᨊᨉᨊᨄᨒᨑᨗᨊᨊᨄᨔᨚᨅᨒᨆᨘᨑᨘᨔᨛᨁᨛᨊᨆᨔᨛᨁᨛᨓᨒᨊᨐᨆᨉᨑ

(62) *uru ma'bundu'. Bugisika. ri Bampangang. na napalari. na napasomba. Lamuru.
sanggenna masangge Walanaya.*

uru   maC- bundu' Bugisi' ≡a   ri   Bampangang na   na= pa-
beginning MV– war   Bugis ≡DEF PREP Bampangang CMP 3=   CAUS–
lari na   na= pa-   somba Lamuru sangge ≡nna   ma- sangge
run CMP 3=   CAUS– homage Lamuru until   ≡3.POSS ST– until
Walanaya
Walanaya
first warred with the Bugis at Bampangang; then mastered Lamuru' right to the
Walanaya.

ᨊᨒᨛᨑᨔᨗᨅᨘᨀᨈᨗᨊ

(63) *naallei. sa'bu katina.*

na= alle =i sa'bu   kati ≡na
3=   take =3 thousand catty ≡3.POSS
He took sa'bu katti[1] from them,

---

1   *Sa'bu katti* (literally 'thousand katti') was a metonym for the act of paying tribute rather than
an actual amount.

(64) *naallei. sonri' turiolona. tuLamurua. nikanaya. I La Pasari*

na=	alle	=i	sonri'	tu	ri	olo	≡na	tu	Lamuru	≡a
3=	take	=3	sword	person	PREP	front	≡3.POSS	person	Lamuru	≡DEF

ni–	kana	≡a	I	La	Pasari
PASS–	word	≡rel	PERS	HON	Pasari

then took the sword of the ancestors of the people of Lamuru named I Lapasari.

KIT:3.14

(65) *antalliki. tuSoppenga. Karaenna. tuSoppenga. nikanaya. Puang ri Jamma'.*

aN–	talli'	=i	tu	Soppeng	≡a	karaeng	≡na	tu	Soppeng
AF–	pledge	=3	person	Soppeng	≡DEF	karaeng	≡3.POSS	person	Soppeng

≡a	ni–	kana	≡a	Puang	ri	Jamma'
≡DEF	PASS–	word	≡rel	parent(royal)	PREP	Jamma'

He then had swear an oath the one from Soppeng named Puang ri Jamma'

(66) *naallei. naallei sonri' turiolona. nikanaya. (I La) Pautuli.*

na=	alle	=i	na=	alle	=i	sonri'	tu	ri	olo	≡na	ni–	kana
3=	take	=3	3=	take	=3	sword	person	PREP	front	≡3.POSS	PASS–	word

≡a	I	La	Pautuli
≡REL	PERS	HON	Pautuli

and took the sword of their ancestors named I Lapattuli

KIT:3.16

(67) *ambetai. Datu baineya. nikanaya. I Daengku. siagaang. palili'na.*

aN–	beta	=i	datu	baine	≡a	ni–	kana	≡a	I	daeng	≡ku
AF–	conquer	=3	king	female	≡DEF	PASS–	word	≡rel	PERS	daeng	≡1.POSS

siagáng	pa–	lili'	≡na
with	NR–	vassal	≡3.POSS

He conquered the female Datu who was called I Daengku and her vassals.

EXCERPT OF THE GOWA CHRONICLE FROM MANUSCRIPT KIT 668–216   381

ᨔᨑᨇᨊᨔᨗᨑᨀᨛᨊᨗᨅᨔᨑᨕᨑᨅᨗᨕᨂᨊᨗᨃᨑᨛᨗᨑᨔᨛᨕᨛᨗᨐᨔᨑᨛᨐᨔᨗᨕᨛᨘᨑᨗᨔᨑᨕᨗ

(68) *ambetai. Cenrana. Salumeko. Cina. Patukung. Kalubimbing. Bulo–Bulo. Raja. Lamatti.*

aN– beta   =i Cenrana Salumeko Cina Patukung Kalubimbing Bulo–Bulo
AF– conquer =3 Cenrana Salumeko Cina Patukung Kalubimbing Bulo–Bulo
Raja Lamatti
Raja Lamatti
He conquered Cenrana, Salu'mekko', Cina, Patukung, Kalubimbing, Bulo–Bulo, Raja, Lamatti.

KIT:3.18

ᨕᨅᨔᨘᨐᨊᨔᨗᨛᨄᨐᨛᨂᨅᨗᨊᨘᨕᨊᨔᨗᨕᨐᨛᨛᨗᨑᨀᨊᨗᨐᨛᨘᨗ

(69) *niagángi. manai'. ri tuMarusuka. nabetai. Samanggi. Cenrana. Bengo.*

ni–   agáng =i ma– nai' ri   tu   Marus =u' ≡a na= beta
PASS– do.with =3 ST– go.up PREP person Maros =EC ≡DEF 3= conquer
=i Samanggi Cenrana Bengo
=3 Samanggi Cenrana Bengo
Accompanied by the people of Maros he advanced and conquered Samanggi, Cenrana, Bengo,

ᨊᨊᨉᨑᨛᨉᨔᨄᨔᨗᨐᨊᨗᨒᨘᨗᨕᨑᨘᨑᨅᨛᨐᨑᨅᨕᨗᨔᨐᨊᨔᨗ

(70) *na napare' palili' Saomata. Camba. nidedeki. lima kati. lima tai'.*

na   na= pare' pa– lili'   Saomata Camba ni–   dede' =i lima kati lima
and 3= make NR– vassal Saomata Camba PASS– fine =3 five catty five
tai'
tahil
made into vassals Saomata and Camba who were charged five katti and five tai.

ᨕᨅᨔᨘᨐᨊᨔᨗᨛᨔᨘᨐᨅᨗᨊᨔᨑᨔᨔᨗᨗᨐᨛᨑᨅᨊᨘᨕᨘᨘᨐᨛᨗᨕᨑᨘᨑᨅᨛᨘᨉᨔᨑᨅᨊᨗ

(71) *niagángi manai' ri Luwuka. naallei. sa'bu katina. Wajo. nidedeki. ruam–pulo. katina.*

ni–   agáng =i ma– nai' ri   Luwu' ≡a   na= alle =i sa'bu
PASS– do.with =3 ST– go.up PREP Luwu' ≡DEF 3= take =3 thousand
kati ≡na   Wajo ni–   dede' =i rua –N pulo kati ≡na
catty ≡3.POSS Wajo PASS– fine =3 two –LK ten catty ≡3.POSS
Accompanied he advanced to Luwu' and took tribute from Wajo', who were charged twenty katti.

382 APPENDIX A

KIT:3.22

ᨕᨅᨑᨁᨗᨆᨊᨕᨗᨑᨗᨈᨘᨔᨗᨉᨙᨑᨙᨁᨗᨊᨅᨙᨈᨕᨗᨒᨈᨗᨕᨒᨘᨌᨛᨊᨑ

(72) *niagangi. manai'. ri tuSidenrengi. nabetai. Otting. Bulu' Cenrana.*

ni–   agang =i ma– nai' ri   tu   Sidenreng =i na= beta   =i
PASS– friend =3 ST– go.up PREP person Sidenreng =3 3=   conquer =3

Otting bulu'   Cenrana
Otting mountain Cenrana

Accompanied by the people of Sidenreng he advanced and conquered Otting,
Bulu' Cenrana,

ᨊᨄᨔᨚᨅᨕᨗᨓᨍᨚᨊᨕᨒᨙᨈᨗᨅᨔᨑᨙᨕᨚᨊᨊᨗᨉᨙᨉᨙᨀᨗᨔᨄᨘᨒᨚᨀᨈᨗᨊ

(73) *na pasombai. Wajo. naallei. timba' sareonna. nidedeki. sampulo katina.*

na pa–   somba =i Wajo na= alle =i timba'
and CAUS– homage =3 Wajo 3=   take =3 open(by.separating)

sareong   ≡na   ni–   dede' =i sampulo kati ≡na
window.shade ≡3.POSS PASS– fine =3 ten   catty ≡3.POSS

then mastered Wajo' and took timba' sareong,[2] charging them ten katti.

KIT:4.01

ᨊᨅᨙᨈᨕᨗᨔᨘᨄᨔᨓᨗᨈᨚᨊᨄᨒᨗᨒᨗᨀᨁᨗᨉᨘᨑᨗᨄᨊᨕᨗᨀᨅᨘᨁᨗᨔᨗᨀᨕᨗᨕᨊᨁᨔᨛ

(74) *nabetai. Suppa'. Sawitto na palilikangi. Duri. Panaikang. Bugisika. ia– ngaseng.*

na= beta   =i Suppa' Sawitto na pa–   lili' –ang =i Duri pa–
3=   conquer =3 Suppa' Sawitto and CAUS– vassal –BEN =3 Duri CAUS–

nai' –ang Bugisi' ≡a ia   ngaseng
go.up –BEN Bugis   ≡DEF 3PRO all

He then conquered Suppa', Sawitto, and made into vassals Letang, Duri, Panaikang, and all the Bugis.

ᨊᨅᨊᨈᨕᨗ

(75) *nia' naatái.*

nia' na= ata   –i
be   3= servant –TRS

Some were made slaves.

---

2 I am unsure of the contextual meaning of this.

EXCERPT OF THE GOWA CHRONICLE FROM MANUSCRIPT KIT 668–216 383

ᨕᨗᨊᨕᨉᨒᨗ

(76) *nia' napalilika.*

nia' na= pa– *lili'* *≡a*

be 3= CAUS– vassal ≡DEF

Some were made vassals.

KIT:4.03

ᨔᨒᨒᨗᨂᨗᨈᨘᨔᨓᨗᨈᨚᨕᨈᨘᨔᨘᨄᨑᨂᨈᨘᨅᨌᨕᨗᨑᨗᨕᨆᨊᨕᨗᨆᨕᨙ

(77) *allalingi. tuSawittoa. tuSuppaka. tuBacukikia manai' mae.*

aN(N)– laling =i tu Sawitto ≡a tu Suppa' ≡a tu

BV– relocate =3 person Sawitto ≡DEF person Suppa' ≡DEF person

Bacukiki ≡a ma– nai' mae

Bacukiki ≡DEF ST– go.up be.in.a.place

He relocated people from Sawitto, people from Suppa', people from Bacukiki up to [Gowa].

KIT:4.04

ᨕᨆᨙᨈᨕᨗᨅᨘᨒᨘᨀᨘᨅᨕᨘᨍᨘᨒᨚᨄᨎᨗᨀᨚᨀ ᨅᨄᨒᨗᨕᨚᨗᨕᨅᨉᨑᨑᨂᨙᨑᨚᨔᨗᨒᨐᨑ

(78) *ambetai. Bulukumba. Ujung Loe. Pannyikkokang Palioi. Gantarang. Wero. Silayara'.*

aN– beta =i Bulukumba ujung loe Pannyikkokang Palioi Gantarang

AF– conquer =3 Bulukumba bundle Great Pannyikkokang Palioi Gantarang

Wero Silayar =a'

Wero Selayar =EC

He conquered Bulukumba, Ujung Loe, Pannyikkokang, Palioi {Pationgi}, Gantarang, Wero, Selayar.

ᨕᨂᨒᨙᨗᨔᨅᨘᨀᨈᨗᨊᨈᨘᨅᨗᨑᨐ

(79) *angngallei. sa'bu katina. tuBiraya.*

aN(N)– alle =i sa'bu kati ≡na tu Bira ≡a

BV– take =3 thousand catty ≡3.POSS person Bira ≡DEF

He took sa'bu katti from the people of Bira

ᨕᨄᨒᨗᨒᨗᨀᨂᨗᨈᨘᨑᨗᨓᨓᨚᨅᨘᨒᨘᨕᨗᨑᨈᨙᨕᨂ

(80) *appalilikangi. tu ri wawo bulu' irateanga.*

aC– pa– lili' –ang =i tu ri wawo bulu' i rate

MV– CAUS– vassal –BEN =3 person PREP ?? mountain PREP above

384 APPENDIX A

–ang ≡*a*
–COMPR ≡DEF

and made into vassals those who lived in the upland mountains.

KIT:4.06

ꦱꦫꦴꦯꦠꦴꦏꦧꦺꦏꦠꦱꦄꦏꦱꦺꦩꦪꦴꦠꦱꦴꦏꦴꦪꦴꦏꦠꦁ

(81) *iapa anne. Karaenga. uru matali. ponna mammeta.*

    ia   =*pa* *anne karaeng* ≡*a*   *uru*   *ma–* *tali ponna maN(N)–*

    3PRO =IPF this karaeng ≡DEF beginning ST– cord if/when BV–

    beta

    conquer

This was the karaeng who first made vassals of those he conquered.

ꦱꦫꦴꦟꦠꦯꦴꦟꦴꦱꦫꦄꦱꦫꦴꦧꦱꦫꦴꦪꦴꦏꦪꦴꦏꦧꦴ

(82) *ia– tompa. ampattallikangi. angkanaya. akkanama'. numammio.*

    ia   *tong* =*pa aN– pa– aC– talli' –ang* =*i aN– kana* ≡*a aC–*

    3PRO also =IPF AF– CAUS– MV– pledge –BEN =3 AF– word ≡rel MV–

    kana =*mo* =*a' nu*= *mamm– io*

    word =PFV =1 2f= MV–   yes(fam)

He also made them swear oaths saying, 'I speak and you agree.'

KIT:4.08

ꦱꦫꦴꦟꦠꦯꦺꦪꦠꦺꦪꦴꦫꦯꦄꦪꦫꦧꦠꦴꦧꦄꦯꦴꦧꦠꦴꦩꦏꦴꦫꦴꦯꦴꦫꦴꦩꦺꦪꦴꦪꦴꦯꦧꦺꦏꦴꦱꦴꦟꦴ
ꦏꦄꦴꦫꦫꦴꦧꦯꦴꦫꦴꦟꦴꦱꦏꦴꦧꦴꦏꦴꦟꦴꦏꦟꦴꦏꦴꦟꦴꦫꦴꦏꦴꦟꦴꦫꦴꦏꦴꦯꦴꦄꦫꦴꦏꦁ

(83) *ia– tompa. uru massuro. mangngalle tu makkajannangngang. ana' bura'ne.*
    pade'de' bassi. pade'de' bulaeng. panrita balla'. panrita biseang. parau' sappu'.
    patiri'. pagurinda. palari'. paotere'.

    ia   *tong* =*pa uru*   *maC– suro maN(N)– alle tu*   *maC– ka*⟩

    3PRO also =IPF beginning MV– order BV–   take person MV– NR⟩

    jannang   ⟨*ang ana' bura'ne pa– de'de'   bassi pa– de'de'   bulaeng*

    functionary ⟨NR child man   NR– smithing iron NR– smithing gold

    panrita balla' panrita bise   –ang pa– rau'   sappu'   pa– tiri' pa–

    expert house expert paddle –NR NR– whittle blowpipe NR– pour NR–

    gurinda   pa– lari'   pa– oter =*e'*

    grindstone NR– turn.on.lathe NR– rope =EC

He too was the first to order established administrators for ana' karaeng, iron-
smiths, goldsmiths, builders, shipwrights, blowpipe makers, weaponsmiths,
sharpeners, turners, ropemakers.

EXCERPT OF THE GOWA CHRONICLE FROM MANUSCRIPT KIT 668–216 385

KIT:4.11

꜌꜌꜌꜌꜌꜌꜌꜌꜌꜌꜌꜌꜌꜌꜌꜌꜌꜌꜌꜌꜌꜌꜌꜌

(84) *ia– tompa. nasisa'la'mo. passabannaranga. patumailalanganga*

ia	*tong*	*=pa*	*na=*	*si–*	*sa'la'*	*=mo*	*pa⟩*	*aC–*	*sabannar*	*⟨ang*
3PRO	also	=IPF	3=	MUT–	divide	=PFV	NR⟩	MV–	harbourmaster	⟨NR

≡a	*pa⟩*	*tu*	*ma– i*	*lalang*	*⟨ang*	*≡a*
≡DEF	NR⟩	person	ST– PREP	inside	⟨NR	≡DEF

He too separated the harbourmaster position from the prime minister position.

꜌꜌꜌꜌꜌꜌꜌꜌꜌꜌꜌꜌꜌꜌꜌

(85) *na I Daeng. ri Mangallekana. sabannara'.*

na	*I*	*daeng*	*ri*	*Mangallekana*	*sabannar*	*=a'*
and	PERS	daeng	PREP	Mangallekana	harbourmaster	=EC

I Daeng ri Mangallekana became harbourmaster.

꜌꜌꜌꜌꜌꜌꜌꜌꜌꜌꜌꜌꜌꜌꜌꜌꜌꜌

(86) *areng pamana'na. nikana. I Kare Mangngaweang.*

areng	*pa–*	*amm–*	*ana'*	*≡na*	*ni–*	*kana*	*I*	*kare*	*Mangngaweang*
name	NR–	MV–	child	≡3.POSS	PASS–	word	PERS	Kare	Mangngaweang

His royal name was I Kare Mangngaweang.

꜌꜌꜌꜌꜌꜌꜌꜌꜌꜌꜌꜌꜌꜌꜌꜌

(87) *areng kalenna. nikana. I Mangngambari.*

areng	*kale*	*≡nna*	*ni–*	*kana*	*I*	*Mangngambari*
name	self	≡3.POSS	PASS–	word	PERS	Mangngambari

His personal name was I Mangngambari.

꜌꜌꜌꜌꜌꜌꜌꜌꜌꜌꜌꜌꜌꜌꜌꜌

(88) *tumailalanna nikana. I Daeng Pamatte'.*

tu	*ma– i*	*lalang*	*≡na*	*ni–*	*kana*	*I*	*daeng*	*Pamatte'*
person	ST– PREP	inside	≡3.POSS	PASS–	word	PERS	daeng	Pamatte'

The prime minister was I Daeng Pamatte'.

KIT:4.14

ꢀ (Makassarese script line - transliterated in example 89)

(89) *ia– tompa. uru mappailalang benteng. appareki. taikanga. dacinga. batua. gantang bannaraka. patam– pulo kakana appa'nassai. nikanaya. patung. akuka. koyanga.*

ia	*tong*	*=pa*	*uru*		*maC–*	*pa–*	*i*	*lalang*	*benteng*	*aC–*	*pare'*
3PRO	also	=IPF	beginning		MV–	CAUS–	PREP	inside	fort		MV– make

=i	*tai'*	*–ang*	*–a*	*dacing*	*–a*	*batu*	*–a*	*gantang*	*bannar*	*=a'*
=3	k.o.coin	–NR	≡DEF	k.o.scale	≡DEF	stone	≡DEF	(20katti)	tonnage?	=EC

–a	*pata*	*–N*	*pulo*	*kakana*		*aC–*	*pa–*	*aC–*	*nassa*	*=i*	*ni–*
≡DEF	four	–LK	ten	cargo.measure?		MV–	CAUS–	MV–	be.certain	=3	PASS–

kana	*–a*	*patung*	*akuka*	*koyang*		*–a*
word	≡rel	20katti	??		unknown.measure	≡DEF

He too was the first to encircle fortifications; to make taikang, dacing, weights; to establish gantang, ship tariffs of forty kakana; to clarify what would be known as a patung, the measure of a koyang.[3]

ꢀ (Makassarese script line - transliterated in example 90)

(90) *ia– tommi. uru. manjijiri'. ba'dili' lompo. ri benteng lompoa.*

ia	*tong*	*=mo*	*=i*	*uru*	*maN–*	*jijir*	*=i'*	*ba'dil*	*=i'*	*lompo*	*ri*
3PRO	also	=PFV	=3	beginning	AF–	row, line	=EC	gun	=EC	big	PREP

benteng	*lompo*	*≡a*
fort	big	≡DEF

He too first placed great cannons in a row on the great fortifications.

ꢀ (Makassarese script line - transliterated in example 91)

(91) *ia– todong. Mangkasara'. uru mangngaseng. mappare' uba'. manynyanga bulaeng. mande'de' bata.*

ia	*todong*	*Mangkasar*	*=a'*	*uru*	*maN(N)–*	*aseng*	*maC–*	*pare'*
3PRO	also	Makassar	=EC	beginning	BV–	all	MV–	make

uba'	*maN(N)–*	*sanga*	*bulaeng*	*maN–*	*de'de'*	*bata*
gunpowder	BV–	refine	gold	AF–	smithing	brick

He also was the Makasar who first knew how to make gunpowder, smelt gold, fire bricks.

---

3 The meaning of many of these terms is not clear.

EXCERPT OF THE GOWA CHRONICLE FROM MANUSCRIPT KIT 668–216   387

KIT:4.18

ᨔᨛᨑᨂᨗᨚᨈᨗᨇᨊᨛᨐᨛᨔᨑᨗᨔᨇᨗᨚᨈᨘᨗᨉᨂᨇᨂᨛᨗᨔᨂᨑᨗᨚᨐᨗᨂᨛ

(92) *ia- tommi. napappaláki empo. Jawa nikanaya. Anakoda Bonang.*

ia	*tong*	*=mo*	*=i*	*na=*	*pa-*	*aC-*	*pala'*	*–i*	*empo*	*jawa*	*ni–*
3PRO	also	=PFV	=3	3=	CAUS-	MV-	request	–APPL	sit	Java	PASS–

kana ≡a anakoda bonang
word ≡rel skipper flooding

He also made an agreement with the Javanese (Malay) who asked for a place to dwell named Anakoda Bonang.

ᨑᨔᨛᨑᨛᨑᨂᨛᨇᨛᨑᨛᨔᨛᨂᨐᨉᨔᨉᨔᨂᨗᨑᨔᨉᨑᨇᨗᨐᨑᨔᨑᨂᨗᨑᨛᨒᨘᨔᨓᨇᨘᨔᨊᨗᨓᨔᨊᨐᨘᨂᨈ
ᨚᨉᨔᨂᨗᨅᨗᨑᨗᨔᨗᨅᨂᨂᨑᨛᨔᨛᨑᨛᨑᨛᨂᨊᨘᨈᨘᨑᨛᨐᨛᨈᨂᨗᨂᨊᨂᨑᨂᨉ

(93) *erang-eranna. ri Karaenga. napala'-pala'na. empo kontua anne. kamaleti sibatu. belo sagantuju-pulona. soonganna. sakalla' sikayu. bilulu' sikayu. cinde sitangnga kodi.*

erang-	*erang*	*≡na*	*ri*	*Karaeng*	*≡a*	*na=*	*pala'-*	*pala'*	*≡na*
RDP-	bring	≡3.POSS	PREP	Karaeng	≡DEF	3=	RDP-	request	≡3.POSS

empo	*kontu*	*≡a*	*anne*	*kamaleti*	*si-*	*batu*	*belo*	*sagantuju*
sit	like	≡DEF	this	blunderbuss	one-	CLS.misc	ornamented	eight

pulo	*≡na*	*soong*	*–ang*	*≡na*	*sakalla'*	*si-*	*kayu*	*bilulu'*
ten	≡3.POSS	carry.on.head	–BEN	≡3.POSS	cloth	one-	CLS.animal	velvet

si-	*kayu*	*cinde*	*si-*	*tangnga*	*kodi*
one-	CLS.animal	fine.cotton	one-	middle	score

He (Anakoda Bonang) brought to the karaeng, when he asked for a place to dwell, these things: eighty blunderbusses, one piece of cloth, one piece of velvet, half a score of silk.[4]

ᨂᨑᨂᨗᨔᨂᨑᨗᨚᨐᨗᨂᨛᨇᨛᨑᨛᨑᨔᨛᨂᨐᨉᨔᨘᨗᨔᨉᨑᨛᨉᨂᨗᨑᨉᨔᨉᨔᨑᨛᨇᨛᨑᨂ

(94) *nakana. Anakoda Bonang. ri Karaenga. Tunipalangga. appaki rupana. kupala'-palaka. ri katte.*

na=	*kana*	*Anakoda Bonang*	*ri*	*karaeng*	*≡a*	*tu*	*ni–*	*pa–*
3=	word	Anakoda Bonang	PREP	karaeng	≡DEF	person	PASS–	CAUS–

---

4 Note the unusual use of the classifier *kayu*, normally used for animals, being used to count cloth. The translation is from Cummings, personally I suspect it is more likely that he brought one ornamented blunderbuss and 80 'headloads' (i.e. bundles) of cloth, perhaps of which half a score each were velvet and fine cotton.

langga appa' =i rupa ≡na ku= pala'– pala' ≡a ri katte
suspend four =3 shape ≡3.POSS 1= RDP– request ≡rel PREP you[p]
Said Anakoda Bonang to Karaeng Tunipalangga, 'There are four things that I ask from you.'

∧ℬ∧ᵞ1ℬℵℐℐ∿ℐℵ⦂

(95) *nakanamo Karaenga apa.*

na= kana =mo karaeng ≡a apa
3= word =PFV karaeng ≡DEF what
Said the karaeng, 'What?'

∧ℬ∧ᵞ⦂ℬℐℐℐℐℐℬ⦂∩∧ℐ∧ℐℬℬ⦂∿ℐᵞ⦂

(96) *nakanamo. kupala'–palaki. tanipanaikia. ballammang.*

na= kana =mo ku= pala'– pala' =i ta= ni– pa– nai' –i
3= word =PFV 1= RDP– request =3 NEG= PASS– CAUS– go.up –APPL
–a balla' ≡mmang
–SBJV house ≡1pl.excl.POSS
He spoke, 'We ask that our homes not be climbed up to,

∩∧ℐ∩ᵞℐℬ⦂ℐℐᵞ⦂

(97) *tanipantamáia. embammang.*

ta= ni– pa– antama –i –a emba ≡mmang
NEG= PASS– CAUS– enter –APPL –SBJV compound ≡1pl.excl.POSS
our compound not be entered,

∩∧ℨℬ∿⦂ℐ1∩∧ℬ⦂ℐ∧ᵞ⦂

(98) *tanigayanga. ponna nia'. anammang.*

ta= ni– gayang   –a ponna nia' ana'
NEG= PASS– payment.for.youngest.child –SBJV if/when be child
≡mmang
≡1pl.excl.POSS
payment not be demanded if we have children,

∩∧ℰℐ∿⦂ℐ1∩∧ℬℐℐᵞ⦂

(99) *tanirappunga. ponna nia'. salammang.*

ta= ni– rappung –a ponna nia' sala ≡mmang
NEG= PASS– pick.up –SBJV if/when be wrong ≡1pl.excl.POSS
our goods not be confiscated if we commit a crime.'

EXCERPT OF THE GOWA CHRONICLE FROM MANUSCRIPT KIT 668–216

KIT:5.03

ᨄᨊᨕᨗᨚᨕᨗᨑᨑᨀᨑᨕᨛ

(100) *naniioi. ri Karaenga.*

    na= ni– io   =i ri   karaeng ≡a

    3= PASS– yes(fam) =3 PREP karaeng ≡DEF

    This was agreed to by the karaeng.

ᨊᨀᨊᨀᨑᨕᨛᨑᨈᨙᨉᨚᨁᨀᨕᨚᨄᨚᨔᨚ

(101) *nakana. Karaenga. tedongku. aposo kuparamme.*

    na= kana karaeng ≡a   tedong ≡ku   a– poso   ku= pa–

    3= word karaeng ≡DEF buffalo ≡1.POSS ST– short.of.breath 1= CAUS–

    ramme

    soak

    The karaeng said, 'If my water buffalo is tired, I will rest him in water.'

ᨆᨅᨈᨒᨀᨈᨑᨚᨕᨗ

(102) *mabattala' kutaroi.*

    ma– battal =a' ku= taro   =i

    ST– heavy =EC 1= set.down =3

    If his burden is heavy, I will set it down.

ᨕᨒᨕᨗᨀᨕᨘᨆᨆᨚᨔᨙᨂᨄᨑᨂᨘᨐᨈᨕᨘ

(103) *ala ikau. mamoseng. parangkuya tau.*

    ala   i–   kau   mamo seng para ≡ngku   ≡a   tau

    what.should? PERS– 2f.sing only   again both ≡1.POSS ≡DEF person

    What then should (I do) for you, my fellow man?

ᨊᨕᨗᨕᨈᨆᨅᨘᨊᨚᨕᨀᨚᨑᨗᨅᨘᨈᨈᨀᨚᨄᨚᨊᨈᨀᨘᨕᨔᨙᨂ

(104) *naia. tamammunoako. ri buttaku. ponna takuassenga.*

    na ia   ta=   maN(N)– buno –a   =ko ri   butta ≡ku   ponna

    CMP 3PRO NEG= BV–   kill   –SBJV =2f PREP land ≡1.POSS if/when

    ta=   ku= asseng –a

    NEG= 1= know –SBJV

    'You may not kill in my land without my knowledge.'

ᨔᨗᨕᨄᨕᨗᨑᨘᨄᨊᨈᨕᨘᨊᨘᨄᨀᨊᨕᨗ

(105) *siapai rupana. tau nupakkanái.*

    siapa   =i rupa ≡na   tau   nu= pa–   aC– kana –i

    how.many =3 shape ≡3.POSS person 2f= CAUS– MV– word –APPL

    'For what peoples do you speak?'

ᜈᜀᜊᜀᜒᜐᜀᜊᜒᜒᜁᜒ᜔ᜒᜁᜈᜒ

(106) *na nakana. Anakoda Bonang.*

na na= kana Anakoda Bonang

and 3= word Anakoda Bonang

and Anakoda Bonang said to the karaeng,

ᜐᜊᜁᜈᜐᜐᜊᜒ᜔ᜒᜁᜐᜈ᜔ᜁᜊᜒ

(107) *sikontui kambe. ma'lipa' baraya.*

si–　kontu =i kambe maC– lipa'　bara ≡a

MUT– like　=3 1pl.excl MV– sarong sash ≡DEF

'All of us who wear sarongs like sashes.'

ᜊᜁᜈᜊᜒᜈᜐᜀᜊᜐᜈᜊᜒᜒ᜔ᜒᜊᜒᜒᜊᜒ᜔ᜒᜁᜊᜁᜈᜐᜒ

(108) *kontuya. Pataniya Campaya. Marangkaboya. Joroka. Paanga.*

kontu ≡a　Patani ≡a　Campa ≡a　Marangkabo　≡a　Joro' ≡a

like　≡DEF Patani ≡DEF Campa ≡DEF Minangkabau ≡DEF Johor ≡DEF

Paang　≡a

Pahang ≡DEF

'such as Patani, Campa, Minangkabau, Johor, Pahang.'

APPENDIX B

Karaeng Ammanaka Bembe: The Karaeng Who Gave Birth to a Goat

A typewritten manuscript containing this story was found in A.A. Cense's archives in the historical document section of KITLV in Leiden (Or545.55f). Its source is unknown, but it is likely that it was typed up by or for Abdurrahim Daeng Mone and sent to Cense after the latter had left Makassar.

(1) *Karaeng Ammanaka Bembe*
     karaeng amm– ana' ≡a   bembe
     karaeng MV–   child ≡DEF goat
     The karaeng who gave birth to a goat

(2) *Nia' se're karaeng nia' ana'na rua, baine sitau, bura'ne sitau.*
     nia' se're karaeng nia' ana' ≡na   rua baine si–   tau   bura'ne si–
     be   one karaeng be   child ≡3.POSS two female one– person man   one–
     tau
     person
     There was a karaeng with two children, one girl, one boy.

(3) *Anjo bainea, nalantiki Karaeng ri Massere'; anjo bura'nea nalanti' Karaeng ri Roong.*
     anjo baine ≡a   na= lanti'   =i karaeng ri   Massere' anjo bura'ne
     that female ≡DEF 3= inaugurate =3 karaeng PREP Massere' that man
     ≡a   na= lanti'   karaeng ri   Roong
     ≡DEF 3= inaugurate karaeng PREP Roong
     The girl he made Karaeng of Massere', the boy he made Karaeng of Roong.

(4) *Para lompoi ana'na para napa'bunting– ngasemmi.*
     para lompo =i ana' ≡na   para na= pa–   aC– bunting ngaseng =mo
     both big   =3 child ≡3.POSS both 3= CAUS– MV– bride   all   =PFV
     =i
     =3
     When both his children were big he made them each get married.

© KONINKLIJKE BRILL NV, LEIDEN, 2020 | DOI:10.1163/9789004412668_016

(5) *Nakanamo karaenga ri Roong:*

na= kana =mo karaeng ≡a ri Roong
3= word =PFV karaeng ≡DEF PREP Roong
The Karaeng of Roong said:

(6) *"Punna para nia' anatta andi', kipasiallei, a'de'nangki' sisari'battang".*

punna para nia' ana' ≡ta andi' ki= pa– si– alle =i aC–
if/when both be child ≡2p.POSS ↓sibling 2p= CAUS– MUT– take =3 MV–
de'nang =ki' si– sari'battang
parent.of.child-in-law =2p MUT– sibling
'When we both have children little sister, let's make them take each other, become parents-in-law to them'.

(7) *Siapai sallona tianammi bainenna karaenga ri Roong.*

siapa =i sallo ≡na tianang =mo =i baine ≡nna karaeng
how.many =3 long ≡3.POSS pregnant =PFV =3 female ≡3.POSS karaeng
≡a ri Roong
≡DEF PREP Roong
A little while later, the wife of the Karaeng Roong was pregnant.

(8) *Salloi tianang, ammana'mi sitau bura'ne.*

sallo =i tianang amm– ana' =mo =I si– tau bura'ne
long =3 pregnant MV– child =PFV =3 one– person man
She was pregnant for a while, she gave birth to a son.

(9) *Lompo–lompoi ana'na karaenga ri Roong, nakanamo karaenga ri Massere':*

lompo– lompo =i ana' ≡na karaeng ≡a ri Roong na= kana
RDP– big =3 child ≡3.POSS karaeng ≡DEF PREP Roong 3= word
=mo karaeng ≡a ri Massere'
=PFV karaeng ≡DEF PREP Massere'
Karaeng Roong's child was getting bigger, Karaeng Massere' said:

(10) *"Anjo taua karaenga ri Roong lompo–lompoi ana'na, na i nakke tenapa kutianang".*

anjo tau ≡a karaeng –a ri Roong lompo– lompo =i ana'
that person ≡DEF karaeng ≡DEF PREP Roong RDP– big =3 child
≡na na inakke tena =pa ku= tianang
≡3.POSS and 1PRO NEG =IPF 1= pregnant
'That person Karaeng Roong his child is growing, and I'm not yet pregnant'.

KARAENG AMMANAKA BEMBE

(11) *Nia'mo se're allo nammempo ri tontonganna, na nia' tau angngembai bembena nia' ruampulo kayunna.*

nia'	*=mo*	*se're*	*allo*	*na=*	*amm–*	*empo*	*ri*	*tontongang* ≡*na na nia'*
be	=PFV	one	day	3=	MV–	sit	PREP	window ≡3.POSS and be

tau aN(N)– emba =i bembe ≡na nia' rua –N pulo kayu
person BV– herd =3 goat ≡3.POSS be two –LK ten CLS.animal

≡*nna*
≡3.POSS

One day she was sitting by her window, and there was a man herding his goats, there were twenty of them

(12) *Na nakanamo karaenga ri Massere':*

na na= kana =mo karaeng ≡*a ri Massere'*
and 3= word =PFV karaeng ≡DEF PREP Massere'

And Karaeng Massere' said:

(13) *"Poro nia' lalo anakku kamma –tong anjo bembea".*

poro nia' lalo ana' ≡*ku kamma tong anjo bembe* ≡*a*
if.only be pass child ≡1.POSS thus also that goat ≡DEF

'If only I could have children like those goats'

(14) *Mingka sala kanai.*

mingka sala kana =i
but wrong word =3

But she spoke badly.

(15) *Nia' sibulang le'ba'na akkana kamma tianang tojemmi karaenga ri Massere'.*

nia' si– bulang le'ba' ≡*na aC– kana kamma tianang tojeng =mo*
be one– month finished ≡3.POSS MV– word thus pregnant true =PFV

=i karaeng ≡*a ri Massere'*
=3 karaeng ≡DEF PREP Massere'

One month after saying that, she was really pregnant.

(16) *Narapiki bulang pammanakanna, mmana'mi.*

na= rapi' =*i bulang pammanakang* ≡*na amm– ana' =mo =i*
3= achieve =3 month family ≡3.POSS MV– child =PFV =3

She reached the month to have her family, and gave birth.

(17) *Lassu'na assulu' ana'na, ammarranna angkana mbee'.*

lassu'	≡*na*		*aC–*	*sulu'*	*ana'*	≡*na*		*amm–*	*arrang*	≡*na*		*aN–*	*kana*

birth ≡3.POSS MV– exit child ≡3.POSS MV– shout ≡3.POSS AF– word

mbee'

baa!

When the child came out, it shouted 'baaa!'

(18) *Nasanna'mo siri'–siri'na karaenga ri Massere' lanri mmana'na sikayu bembe.*

na= *sanna'* *=mo* *siri'–* *siri'* ≡*na* *karaeng* ≡*a* *ri* *Massere'*

3= extremely =PFV RDP– shame ≡3.POSS karaeng ≡DEF PREP Massere'

lanri *amm–* *ana'* ≡*na* *si–* *kayu* *bembe*

reason MV– child ≡3.POSS one– CLS.animal goat

She was very ashamed because she had given birth to a goat.

(19) *Nasuro erangmi mange ri bokona pakke'buka nasuro boli'.*

na= *suro* *erang* *=mo* *=i* *mange* *ri* *boko* ≡*na* *pakke'bu'* ≡*a* *na=*

3= order bring =PFV =3 go PREP back ≡3.POSS door ≡DEF 3=

suro *boli'*

order hidden

She ordered it taken behind the door and hidden.

(20) *Nia'– tommonjo joa' sitau ampangngapási ansi'ruki je'ne' uring, sanggenna akkulle angnganre ruku'.*

nia' *tong* *=mo* *(a)njo* *joa'* *si–* *tau* *aN–* *pa–* *aN(N)–*

be also =PFV that followers one– person AF– CAUS– BV–

apas *–i* *aN–* *si'ru'* *=i* *je'ne'* *uring* *sangge* ≡*nna* *aC–* *kulle*

take.care.of –APPL AF– spoon =3 water cookpot until ≡3.POSS MV– can

aN(N)– *kanre* *ruku'*

BV– food grass

There was also one servant who took care of it, spooned bean mush, until it could eat grass.

(21) *Jari tulusu' naung– tommi angnganre ruku' anjo bembea.*

jari *tulus* *=u'* *naung* *tong* *=mo* *=i* *aN(N)–* *kanre* *ruku'* *anjo* *bembe*

so directly =EC go.down also =PFV =3 BV– food grass that goat

≡*a*

≡DEF

Then it straight away went down to eat grass, that goat.

KARAENG AMMANAKA BEMBE

(22) *Sanggenna kamma tau, anjo bembea akkale ana' rarami.*

sangge	*≡nna*	*kamma*	*tau*	*anjo*	*bembe*	*≡a*	*aC-*	*kale*	*ana'*	*rara*
until	≡3.POSS	thus	person	that	goat	≡DEF	MV-	self	child	young.girl

=mo =i
=PFV =3

As if it were a person, that goat became a young girl.

(23) *Nipa'gau'–gaúkimi ana'na karaenga ri Roong.*

ni-	*pa-*	*aC-*	*gau'-*	*gau'*	*-i*	*=mo*	*=i*	*ana'*	*≡na*	*karaeng*
PASS-	CAUS-	MV-	RDP-	action	-APPL	=PFV	=3	child	≡3.POSS	karaeng

≡a ri Roong
≡DEF PREP Roong

The child of the Karaeng Roong was given a party.

(24) *Kalau'mi mae nipauang sari'battanna angkana:*

kalau'	*=mo*	*=i*	*mae*	*ni-*	*pau*	*-ang*	*sari'battang*	*≡na*	*aN-*	*kana*
go.west	=PFV	=3	go	PASS-	story	-NR	sibling	≡3.POSS	AF-	word

Westward came his sister's invitation, saying:

(25) *"Massing anrai' ngasengki', ka ero'mi nisunna' kamanakanta".*

massing	*aN-*	*rai'*	*ngaseng*	*=ki'*	*ka*	*ero'*	*=mo*	*=i*	*ni-*
each	AF-	(go)east	all	=2p	because	want	=PFV	=3	PASS-

sunna' kamanakang ≡ta
circumcision nephew ≡2p.POSS

'Everyone come east, because your nephew is going to be circumcised'.

(26) *Nakanamo karaenga ri Massere':*

na=	*kana*	*=mo*	*karaeng*	*≡a*	*ri*	*Massere'*
3=	word	=PFV	karaeng	≡DEF	PREP	Massere'

The Karaeng of Massere' said:

(27) *"Pauang baji' mami iraya karaenga ri Roong, a'matapi sallang gauka na anrai' ka tena tau ri ballakku".*

pau	*-ang*	*baji'*	*mamo*	*=i*	*i=*	*raya*	*karaeng*	*≡a*	*ri*	*Roong*	*aC-*
story	-BEN	good	only	=3	PREP=	east	karaeng	≡DEF	PREP	Roong	MV-

mata	*=pa*	*=i*	*sallang*	*gau'*	*≡a*	*na*	*anrai'*	*ka*	*tena*	*tau*
eye	=IPF	=3	probably	action	≡DEF	and	go.east	because	NEG	person

ri balla' ≡ku
PREP house ≡1.POSS

'Tell him well the Karaeng Roong in the east, when it's time for the party (I'll) go east because there's no-one at my house'.

(28) *Ammotere'mi anrai' suroa.*

amm–	oter	=e'	=mo	=i	aN–	rai'		suro	≡a
MV–	return	=EC	=PFV	=3	AF–	(go)east		order	≡DEF

The messenger went back.

(29) *Anjo karaenga ri Roong, tenamo kamma suara'na pa'gaukanna.*

anjo	karaeng	≡a	ri	Roong	tena	=mo	kamma	suar	=a'	≡na	pa–
that	karaeng	≡DEF	PREP	Roong	NEG	=PFV	thus	busy	=EC	≡3.POSS	NR–

aC–	gau'	–ang	≡na
MV–	action	–NR	≡3.POSS

That karaeng of Roong, there was nothing like the sound of his celebration.

(30) *Eroki a'mata gau'na,[1] anrai'mi sari'battanna; a'lampa– ngasengi sibatu balla'.*

ero'	=i	aC–	mata	gau'	≡na		aN–	rai'		=mo	=i	sari'battang
want	=3	MV–	eye	action	≡3.POSS		AF–	(go)east		=PFV	=3	sibling

≡na		aC–	lampa	ngaseng	=i	si–	batu		balla'
≡3.POSS		MV–	go	all	=3	one–	CLF.misc		house

Just before the main day of the celebrations, his sister went east; the whole houseful went.

(31) *Bembea mami naboli' kale–kalenna najoli pakke'bu'.*

bembe	≡a		mamo	=i	na=	boli'		kale–	kale	≡nna		na=	joli	pakke'bu'
goat	≡DEF	only		=3	3=	hidden		RDP–	self	≡3.POSS		3=	bolt	door

Only the goat was there, (someone) hid her (someone) locked the door.

(32) *Na anne bembea naasseng– tommi angkana a'gau'–gauki purinanna.*

na	anne	bembe	≡a		na=	asseng	tong	=mo	=i	aN–	kana	aC–	gau'–
and	this	goat	≡DEF		3=	know	also	=PFV	=3	AF–	word	MV–	RDP–

gau'	=i	purina		≡nna
action	=3	uncle/aunt		≡3.POSS

Now this goat, she also knew about her uncle's party.

(33) *A'mata je'neki tunigauka, assulu'mi ri karungkunna na mange nakonci pattina
amma'na nampa naalle pakeanna amma'na sanggenna pakeang ana' karaenga.*

aC–	mata	je'ne'	=i	tu–		ni–		gau'	≡a		aC–	sulu'	=mo	=i	ri
MV–	eye	water	=3	person–		PASS–		action	≡DEF		MV–	exit	=PFV	=3	PREP

---

1 *A'mata* has an idiomatic meaning 'be at the main/high point of'.

KARAENG AMMANAKA BEMBE 397

karungkung ≡na   na mange na= *konci patti* ≡na   *amma'* ≡na
disguise   ≡3.POSS and go 3= key case ≡3.POSS mother ≡3.POSS
nampa na= alle pake –ang ≡na   *amma'* ≡na   *sangge* ≡nna   pake
then 3= take wear –NR ≡3.POSS mother ≡3.POSS until ≡3.POSS wear
–ang ana' karaeng ≡a
–NR child karaeng ≡DEF
Just at the time of the party, she took off her (goat) disguise and unlocked her mother's trunk to take her mother's clothes until she was dressed as a princess.

(34) *Nampa mange todong ri poko' buloa, angkana:*
nampa mange todong ri   poko' bulo   ≡a   aN– kana
then go also PREP trunk bamboo ≡DEF AF– word
Then she went to a bamboo trunk and said:

(35) *"Ka tojengku ana' panrita ri anrongku ri manggeku, a'jariko bulekang poko' bulo".*
ka   tojeng ≡ku   ana' panrita ri   anrong ≡ku   ri   mangge
because true ≡1.POSS child expert PREP mother ≡1.POSS PREP father
≡ku   aC– jari   =ko bule'   –ang poko' bulo
≡1.POSS MV– become =2f carry.on.pole –NR trunk bamboo
'Because I'm truly the noble child of my mother and father, become a carrying pole, bamboo trunk'.

(36) *A'jarimi bulekang poko' buloa.*
aC– jari   =mo =i bule'   –ang poko' bulo   ≡a
MV– become =PFV =3 carry.on.pole –NR trunk bamboo ≡DEF
The bamboo trunk became a carrying pole.

(37) *Mangéi seng ri ruku'-rukuka, ri bajeng–bajenga angkana:*
mange –i   seng ri   ruku'– ruku' ≡a   ri   bajeng–bajeng ≡a
go   –APPL again PREP RDP– grass ≡DEF PREP k.o.grass   ≡DEF
aN– kana
AF– word
She went again to the grass, to the bajeng–bajeng grass, saying:

(38) *"Ka tojengku ana' panrita ri anrongku ri manggeku, a'jariko tau, na nubuleka' mange ri pa'gaukanna karaenga ri Roong angngióri".*
ka   tojeng ≡ku   ana' pa–   aN– ri   ≡ta   ri   anrong
because true ≡1.POSS child CAUS– AF– PREP ≡2p.POSS PREP mother
≡ku   ri   mangge ≡ku   aC– jari   =ko tau   na nu=
≡1.POSS PREP father ≡1.POSS MV– become =2f person and 2f=

bule'   *=a' mange ri*   *pa⟩ aC– gau'*   ⟨*ang* ≡*na*   *karaeng* ≡*a*
carry.on.pole =1   go   PREP NR⟩ MV– action ⟨NR ≡3.POSS karaeng ≡DEF
ri   *Roong aN(N)– kior*   *–i*
PREP Roong BV–   scatter –APPL

'Because I'm really the noble child of my mother and father, become people, and carry me to the celebration of Karaeng Roong to give an offering'.

(39) *A'jari taumi ruku'–rukuka, anjo buloa a'jari bulekang tommi.*

    aC– jari   *tau*   *=mo =i ruku'– ruku'* ≡*a*   *anjo bulo*   ≡*a*   *aC–*
    MV– become person =PFV =3 RDP– grass ≡DEF that bamboo ≡DEF MV–
    jari   *bule'*   *–ang tong =mo =i*
    become carry.on.pole –NR also =PFV =3

The grass became people, the bamboo became a carrying pole.

(40) *Mangemi apparuru, nampa mange naalle doe'na amma'na, nai'mi ri bulekanna, nibule'mi anrai' ri pa'gaukanna karaenga ri Roong.*

    mange =mo =i aC– paruru   *nampa mange na= alle doe'*   ≡*na*
    go   =PFV =3 MV– get.ready then   go   3= take money ≡3.POSS
    amma' ≡*na*   *nai' =mo =i ri*   *bule'*   *–ang* ≡*na*   *ni–*
    mother ≡3.POSS go.up =PFV =3 PREP carry.on.pole –NR ≡3.POSS PASS–
    bule'   *=mo =i anrai'*   *ri*   *pa⟩ aC– gau'*   ⟨*ang* ≡*na*
    carry.on.pole =PFV =3 (go)east PREP NR⟩ MV– action ⟨NR ≡3.POSS
    karaeng ≡*a*   *ri*   *Roong*
    karaeng ≡DEF PREP Roong

She went to get ready, then went to take her mother's money, went up on the carrying pole and was carried east to the party of the Karaeng of Roong.

(41) *Battui anrai' tettere'mi karaenga ri Roong anruppai toananna, na naerang nai' napaempo antemma ada'na ana'– karaenga.*

    battu =i aN– rai'   *tetter*   *=e' =mo =i karaeng* ≡*a*   *ri*   *Roong*
    come =3 AF– (go)east quickly =EC =PFV =3 karaeng ≡DEF PREP Roong
    aN– ruppa =i toana ≡*nna*   *na na= erang nai'*   *na= pa– empo*
    AF– greet =3 guest ≡3.POSS and 3= bring go.up 3= NR– sit
    antemma ada'   ≡*na*   *ana' karaeng* ≡*a*
    how   customs ≡3.POSS child karaeng ≡DEF

Arriving east quickly the Karaeng of Roong greeted his guest, and brought her up to the seating place like the custom of a princess.

KARAENG AMMANAKA BEMBE 399

(42) *Mangemi ri bainenna angkana:*

mange	*=mo*	*=i*	*ri*	*baine*	*≡nna*	*aN–*	*kana*
go	=PFV	=3	PREP	female	≡3.POSS	AF–	word

He went to his wife saying:

(43) *"Ana' karaeng battu kereareinjo mae na tena kuissengi kabattuanna.*

ana'	*karaeng*	*battu*	*kere*	*=are*	*=i*	*(a)njo*	*mae*	*na*	*tena*	*ku=*	*isseng*	*=i*
child	karaeng	come	where	=ever	=3	that	go	and	NEG	1=	know	=3

ka⟩	*battu*	*⟨ang*	*≡na*
NR⟩	come	⟨NR	≡3.POSS

'A princess came from wherever and I don't know her origin.

(44) *Ana' karaeng baji'–baji' mamo tappana".*

ana'	*karaeng*	*baji'–*	*baji'*	*mamo*	*tappa*	*≡na*
child	karaeng	RDP–	good	only	demeanour	≡3.POSS

A princess only with good demeanour'.

(45) *Nipasilolongammi pattoanana.*

ni–	*pa–*	*silolongang*	*=mo*	*=i*	*pa–*	*aC–*	*toana*	*≡na*
PASS–	CAUS–	ready	=PFV	=3	NR–	MV–	guest	≡3.POSS

Everything was made ready for the guests' food.

(46) *Anjo nitoananamo anjo ana' karaenga mangemi karaenga ri Massere' andalle-kangi.*

anjo	*ni–*	*toana*	*≡na*	*=mo*	*anjo*	*ana'*	*karaeng*	*≡a*	*mange*	*=mo*	*=i*
that	PASS–	guest	≡3.POSS	=PFV	that	child	karaeng	≡DEF	go	=PFV	=3

karaeng	*≡a*	*ri*	*Massere'*	*aN–*	*dallekang*	*=i*
karaeng	≡DEF	PREP	Massere'	AF–	front	=3

Having eaten (lit. having been guested) that princess went to Karaeng Massere' and sat before her.

(47) *Nacini'minjo pakeanna ana' karaenga sangkamma le'baki pakeanna karaenga ri Massere'*

na=	*cini'*	*=mo*	*=i*	*(a)njo*	*pake*	*–ang*	*≡na*	*ana'*	*karaeng*	*≡a*
3=	see	=PFV	=3	that	wear	–NR	≡3.POSS	child	karaeng	≡DEF

saN–	*kamma*	*le'ba'*	*=i*	*pake*	*–ang*	*≡na*	*karaeng*	*≡a*	*ri*
as_adj_as–	thus	finished	=3	wear	–NR	≡3.POSS	karaeng	≡DEF	PREP

Massere'
Massere'

She saw that the clothes of the princess were the same as the clothes of Karaeng Massere'.

(48) *Naallemi nagiling–giling pontona, najama–jama tokenna na nakana pa'mai'na*
karaenga ri Massere':

na= alle	=mo	=i	na= giling– giling		ponto	≡na	na= jama–
3= take	=PFV	=3	3= RDP– changeable armband			≡3.POSS	3= RDP–

jama tokeng	≡na	na	na= kana pa'mai'	≡na	karaeng	≡a	ri
work necklace	≡3.POSS	and	3= word heart	≡3.POSS	karaeng	≡DEF	PREP

Massere'
Massere'

She took to twisting her bracelet and fiddling with her necklace, and Karaeng
Massere' said to herself:

(49) *"Titti'ma' anne kapang nilukkaki i lau', ka bembea maminjo mae kale–kalenna ri*
balla' kuboli'"

titti'	=mo	=a'	anne	kapang	ni– lukka'	=i	i	lau'
cleaned.out	=PFV	=1	this	suppose	PASS– stolen.thing	=3	PREP	sea, west

ka	bembe	≡a	mamo	=i	(a)njo	mae	kale– kale	≡nna
because	goat	≡DEF	only	=3	that	be.in.a.place	RDP– self	≡3.POSS

ri	balla'	ku= boli'
PREP	house	1= hidden

'I'm all cleaned out, this was probably stolen in the west, because only that goat
is there, by herself in the house I hid (her).'

(50) *Nakanamo ri ana' karaenga le'ba'namo nitoana: "Ana' karaeng battu keko mae*
galle'"

na= kana	=mo	ri	ana' karaeng	≡a	le'ba'	≡na	=mo	ni–
3= word	=PFV	PREP	child karaeng	≡DEF	finished	≡3.POSS	=PFV	PASS–

toana	ana' karaeng	battu	ke	=ko	mae	galle'
guest	child karaeng	come	where	=2f	go	young.lady

She said to the princess (after eating something): 'Princess where did you come
from?'.

(51) *Nakanamo anjo ana' karaenga: "Inakke Karaeng, ana' karaeng tuba'leang je'neka".*

na= kana	=mo	anjo	ana' karaeng	≡a	inakke	karaeng	ana'	karaeng
3= word	=PFV	that	child karaeng	≡DEF	1.sing	karaeng	child	karaeng

tu–	ba'le	–ang	je'ne'	=a'
person–	other.side	–COMPR	water	=1

That princess said: 'Me Karaeng, I'm a princess from across the sea'.

KARAENG AMMANAKA BEMBE 401

(52) *Nakana tojemmo pa'mai'na karaenga ri Massere': "Apa–apangku tojemminne kapang nalukka' taua, naerang anta'leang je'ne' nabalukang".*

na= kana tojeng =mo pa'mai' ≡na   karaeng ≡a   ri   Massere' apa–
3=   word true   =PFV heart ≡3.POSS karaeng ≡DEF PREP Massere' RDP–
apa ≡ngku tojeng =mo =i (a)nne kapang na= lukka'   tau
what ≡1.POSS true   =PFV =3 this   suppose 3=   stolen.thing person
≡a   na= erang aN– ta'le –ang je'ne' na= balu'   –ang
≡DEF 3=   bring AF– cross –BEN water 3=   roll.up –BEN

The heart of Karaeng Massere' really spoke: 'This is truly my stuff, probably someone stole it, took (things) to sell across the water'

(53) *Nakanamo anjo pole karaenga ri Massere' ri sari'battanna: "Ero'ma' nakke andi' appala' kana, punna le'ba'mo taua assunna', ka bata–bata', ka bembea mami anjo mae kale–kalenna".*

na= kana =mo anjo pole   karaeng ≡a   ri   Massere' ri
3=   word =PFV that still, yet karaeng ≡DEF PREP Massere' PREP
sari'battang ≡na   ero' =mo =a' nakke andi'   aC– pala'   kana
sibling   ≡3.POSS want =PFV =1 1.sing ↓sibling MV– request word
punna le'ba'   =mo tau   ≡a   aC– sunna'   ka   bata–
if/when finished =PFV person ≡DEF MV– circumcision because RDP–
bata   =a' ka   bembe ≡a   mamo =i anjo mae   kale– kale
uncertain =1 because goat   ≡DEF only   =3 that be.in.a.place RDP– self
≡nna
≡3.POSS

Karaeng Massere' spoke again to her brother: 'I want you to excuse me brother, when the circumcision's finished, because I'm worried, because there's only a goat there alone'.

(54) *Anne ana' karaenga le'ba'na mamo nitoana appala' kana– tommi nammotere'.*

anne ana' karaeng ≡a   le'ba'   mamo ni–   toa ≡na   aC– pala'
this   child karaeng ≡DEF finished only   PASS– old ≡3.POSS MV– request
kana tong =mo =i na= amm– oter   =e'
word also =PFV =3 3=   MV–   return =EC

This princess when she had finished eating also asked leave and went home.

(55) *Battui mange ri balla'na napattasa'–ngasemmi apa–apanna amma'na kamma ri batena.*

battu =i mange ri   balla' ≡na   na= pattas =a' ngaseng =mo =i
come =3 go   PREP house ≡3.POSS 3=   pack   =EC all   =PFV =3

apa– apa ≡nna amma' ≡na kamma ri bate ≡na
RDP– what ≡3.POSS mother ≡3.POSS thus PREP method ≡3.POSS
She came to her mother's house and packed everything of her mother's like so.

(56) *Anjo poko' buloa nasuro– tommi mange ri batena, siagáng ruku'–rukuka, nampa mange napake karungkunna.*

anjo poko' bulo ≡a na= suro tong =mo =i mange ri bate
that trunk bamboo ≡DEF 3= order also =PFV =3 go PREP method
≡na siagáng ruku'– ruku' ≡a nampa mange na= pake karungkung
≡3.POSS with RDP– grass ≡DEF then go 3= wear disguise
≡na
≡3.POSS
That bamboo pole she ordered to its original state with the grass, then she went to wear her disguise.

(57) *Le'baki nisunna' ana'na karaenga ri Roong, ammotere'mi karaenga ri Massere'.*

le'ba' =i ni– sunna' ana' ≡na karaeng ≡a ri Roong
finished =3 PASS– circumcision child ≡3.POSS karaeng ≡DEF PREP Roong
amm– oter =e' =mo =i karaeng ≡a ri Massere'
MV– return =EC =PFV =3 karaeng ≡DEF PREP Massere'
After the child of Karaeng Roong had been circumcised, Karaeng Massere' went home.

(58) *Allantena balla' mangena naparessa apa–apanna.*

aN(N)– lante ≡na balla' mange ≡na na= paressa apa– apa
BV– reach ≡3.POSS house go ≡3.POSS 3= check RDP– what
≡nna
≡3.POSS
When she reached the house she went directly to check things.

(59) *Tenaja apa–apa taena, nia' asengji.*

tena =ja apa– apa taena nia' aseng =ja =i
NEG =LIM RDP– what NEG be all =LIM =3
Nothing wasn't there, everything was there.

(60) *Nakanamo pole ri bonena balla'na: "Tamma'– tommi bateku apparri–parri ammotere', kukana barang titti'ma', na manna sibi'bi' tania' sisalana pakeangku".*

na= kana =mo pole ri bone ≡na balla' ≡na tamma'
3= word =PFV still, yet PREP contents ≡3.POSS house ≡3.POSS end

KARAENG AMMANAKA BEMBE — 403

tong =mo =i bate   ≡ku   aC- parri–parri amm- oter =e' ku=
also =PFV =3 method ≡1.POSS MV- hurry   MV-   return =EC 1=
kana barang titti'   =mo =a' na manna si- bi'bi' ta= nia' si-
word goods cleaned.out =PFV =1 and though one– piece NEG= be one–
sala   ≡na   pake –ang ≡ku
wrong ≡3.POSS wear –NR ≡1.POSS
She said to her household: 'I used up all my strength hurrying back, I thought all
was lost, but not even one little thing is wrong with my clothes'.

(61) *Bangngi kammanjo, sannang ngasemmi taua tinrona akkelomminjo bembea
angkana: "Magiro denre karaenga ri Massere' nagiling–giling pottoku, nakarawa
genokku".*

bangngi kamma (a)njo sannang ngaseng =mo =i tau   ≡a   tinro
night   thus   that content all   =PFV =3 person ≡DEF sleep
≡na   aC- kelong =mo =i (a)njo bembe ≡a   aN- kana magiro denre
≡3.POSS MV- song =PFV =3 that goat ≡DEF AF- word
karaeng ≡a   ri   Massere' na= giling– giling   pottoku nakarawa
karaeng ≡DEF PREP Massere' 3= RDP-   changeable
genokku

That night, while everyone was asleep the goat sang, saying (in Bugis) 'O Karaeng
Massere', why turn your bracelet, why fiddle with necklace'

(62) *Salloinjo akkelong bembea nipidandammi ri karaenga ri Massere'.*
sallo =i (a)njo aC- kelong bembe ≡a   ni- pi-   dandang =mo =i
long =3 that MV- song   goat ≡DEF PASS- EXP- stay.still =PFV =3
ri   karaeng ≡a   ri   Massere'
PREP karaeng ≡DEF PREP Massere'
The goat sang for a while and got the attention of Karaeng Massere'

(63) *Salloi nipidandang, na ronrong ngasemmi tau tinroa nampa nakana: "Inainjo
akkelong gere'".*
sallo =i ni- pi-   dandang na ronrong   ngaseng =mo =i tau
long =3 PASS- EXP- stay.still and earthquake all   =PFV =3 person
tinro ≡a   nampa na= kana inai (a)njo aC- kelong gere'
sleep ≡DEF then   3= word who that MV- song like.that
For a long time they listened, and all the sleeping people woke with a start and
said 'who is singing like that?'

(64) *Nakana ngasemmonjo bonena ballaka.*

na=	kana	ngaseng	=mo	(a)njo	bone	≡na	balla'	≡a
3=	word	all	=PFV	that	contents	≡3.POSS	house	≡DEF

All the household said.

(65) *"Apa nakana kelonna Karaeng".*

apa	na=	kana	kelong	≡na	karaeng
what	3=	word	song	≡3.POSS	karaeng

'What does the song say Karaeng?'

(66) *Nakana kulangngere': "Magiro denre karaenga ri Massere', nagiling–giling pottoku, nakarawa genokku".*

na=	kana	ku=	langnger	=e'	magiro	denre	karaeng	≡a	ri	Massere'
3=	word	1=	listen	=EC			karaeng	≡DEF	PREP	Massere'

na=	giling–	giling	pottoku	nakarawa	genokku
3=	RDP–	changeable			

She said I hear 'O Karaeng Massere', why turn your bracelet, why fiddle with necklace'

(67) *Mangemi nisulói tau akkelonga.*

mange	=mo	=i	ni–	sulo	=i	tau	aC–	kelong	≡a
go	=PFV	=3	PASS–	torch	=3	person	MV–	song	≡DEF

They went to (search for) the singing person with a torch

(68) *Naummi taua ri buttaya ansulói, natena.*

naung	=mo	=i	tau	≡a	ri	butta	≡a	aN–	sulo	–i	na=
go.down	=PFV	=3	person	≡DEF	PREP	land	≡DEF	AF–	torch	–TRS	3=

tena
NEG

The people went down to the ground (with) a torch, but nothing.

(69) *Ka ammotere'mi pole mange tinro.*

ka	amm–	oter	=e'	=mo	=i	pole	mange	tinro
because	MV–	return	=EC	=PFV	=3	still, yet	go	sleep

Because she'd already gone back to sleep.

KARAENG AMMANAKA BEMBE

(70) *Nipalette kiseng pau–paua mange ri karaenga ri Roong, nia'mo se're allo na nakana ri ana'na: "Ri wattungku le'ba' bunting ana', le'ba'–tong bunting purinannu karaenga ri Massere', sijanjia' sisari'battang, kukana, punna para nia' anatta, a'de'nangki' sisari'battang; mannanjo bembe naanakkang purinannu ero'ja' anruppai kanangku, ka saba' janjingku".*

ni–	*pa–*	*lette*	*ki=*	*seng*	*pau – pau*	*≡a*	*mange ri*	*karaeng*
PASS–	CAUS–	be.moved	2p=	again	RDP– story	≡DEF	go	PREP karaeng

≡a	*ri*	*Roong nia'*	*=mo*	*se're allo na*	*na=*	*kana ri*	*ana'*	*≡na*
≡DEF	PREP	Roong be	=PFV	one day and	3=	word PREP	child	≡3.POSS

ri	*wattu*	*≡ngku*	*le'ba'*	*bunting ana'*	*le'ba'*	*tong bunting*
PREP	time	≡1.POSS	finished	bride child	finished	also bride

purina	*≡nnu*	*karaeng*	*≡a*	*ri*	*Massere' si–*	*janji*	*=a'*
uncle/aunt	≡2f.POSS	karaeng	≡DEF	PREP	Massere' MUT–	promise	=1

si–	*sari'battang*	*ku=*	*kana*	*punna*	*para nia' ana'*	*≡ta*		*aC–*
MUT–	sibling	1=	word	if/when	both be child	≡2p.POSS		MV–

de'nang	*=ki'*	*si–*	*sari'battang*	*manna*	*(a)njo bembe*	*na=*
parent.of.child-in-law	=2p	MUT–	sibling	though	that goat	3=

ana'	*–ang purina*	*≡nnu*	*ero'*	*=ja*	*=a' aN–*	*ruppa*	*=i kana*
child	–BEN uncle/aunt	≡2f.POSS	want	=LIM	=1 AF–	greet	=3 word

≡ngku	*ka*	*saba' janji*	*≡ngku*	
≡1.POSS	because	reason promise	≡1.POSS	

Let's move the story back to the Karaeng of Roong, there was a day and he said to his son: 'When I got married, also your aunt got married, we promised each other, we said, when we both have children, we'd become (parents-in-law of each other's children), even though your aunt has a goat for a daughter, I nevertheless want my words to be followed, because it's my promise'.

(71) *Nakanamo anjo ana'na: "Punna ikatte Karaeng angkana le'lengi, le'lengi; punna ikatte bulengi, bulengi".*

na=	*kana*	*=mo*	*anjo ana'*	*≡na*	*punna ikatte*	*karaeng aN–*	*kana*	
3=	word	=PFV	that child	≡3.POSS	if 2pPRO	karaeng AF–	word	

le'leng	*=i*	*le'leng*	*=i*	*punna ikatte*	*buleng*	*=i buleng*	*=i*
black	=3	black	=3	if 2pPRO	white(haired)	=3 white(haired)	=3

His son said: 'If you Karaeng say it's black, it's black, if you (say) it's white, it's white'.

(72) *Jari mangemi nipasurói ana'na karaenga ri Massere', anjo bembea.*

jari mange	*=mo*	*=i*	*ni–*	*pa–*	*suro*	*–i*	*ana'*	*≡na*	*karaeng* *≡a*
so go	=PFV	=3	PASS–	CAUS–	order	–TRS	child	≡3.POSS	karaeng ≡DEF

ri   Massere' anjo bembe ≡a
PREP Massere' that goat   ≡DEF
So he went to propose to the child of Karaeng Massere', that goat.

(73) *Nakanamo karaenga ri Massere': "Sanna'mintu rannuku andi', mingka apa lanu-tujuangi bembea?"*

na= kana =mo karaeng ≡a   ri   Massere' sanna'   =mo =i (a)ntu
3= word =PFV karaeng ≡DEF PREP Massere' extremely =PFV =3 that
rannu ≡ku   andi'   mingka apa la= nu= tuju –ang =i bembe ≡a
happy ≡1.POSS ↓sibling but   what FUT= 2f= goal –BEN =3 goat   ≡DEF
Kareng Massere' said: 'I'm so happy brother, but what do you want the goat for?'

(74) *Nakanamo karaenga ri Roong: "Apa paeng ka le'ba' kananta."*

na= kana =mo karaeng ≡a   ri   Roong apa paeng ka   le'ba'
3= word =PFV karaeng ≡DEF PREP Roong what then because finished
kana ≡nta
word ≡2p.POSS
Karaeng Roong spoke: 'What else, because we already said'

(75) *Jari tenamo naisseng nakanáng karaenga ri Massere'.*

jari tena =mo na= isseng na= kana –ang karaeng ≡a   ri   Massere'
SO NEG =PFV 3= know 3= word –BEN karaeng ≡DEF PREP Massere'
So she didn't know what to say about it, Karaeng Massere'.

(76) *Karaeng ri Roong ammotere' tommi mange ri pa'rasanganna appassilolongang.*

karaeng ri   Roong amm– oter   =e' tong =mo =i mange ri
karaeng PREP Roong MV–   return =EC also =PFV =3 go   PREP
pa'rasangang ≡na   aC– pa–   aC– silolongang
land   ≡3.POSS MV– CAUS– MV– ready
Karaeng Roong went back to his country to make everything ready.

(77) *Karaeng ri Massere' appassilolongang tommi bone balla'na.*

karaeng ri   Massere' aC– pa–   aC– silolongang tong =mo =i
karaeng PREP Massere' MV– CAUS– MV– ready   also =PFV =3
bone   balla' ≡na
contents house ≡3.POSS
Karaeng Massere' also prepared her household.

KARAENG AMMANAKA BEMBE

(78) *Silolongangi appa'buntimmi.*

silolongang	=i	aC–	pa–	aC–	bunting	=mo	=i
ready	=3	MV–	NR–	MV–	bride	=PFV	=3

They were ready to have a wedding.

(79) *Anjo nai'namo buntinga a'rurung memammi tappu' kananna.*

anjo nai'	≡na	=mo	bunting	≡a	aC–	rurung	memang	=mo	=i
that go.up	≡3.POSS	=PFV	bride	≡DEF	MV–	walk.with	actually	=PFV	=3

tappu'	kana	≡nna
snapped	word	≡3.POSS

The ascension of the groom was at the same time as the marriage negotiations.

(80) *Anjo bembea a'lumpa'–lumpa' tommi angkanrei erang–eranna.*

anjo bembe	≡a	aC–	lumpa'–	lumpa'	tong	=mo	=i	aN–	kanre	=i	erang–
that goat	≡DEF	MV–	RDP–		jump	also	=PFV	=3	AF–	food	=3	RDP–

erang	≡na
bring	≡3.POSS

The goat jumped for joy and ate the gifts.

(81) *Anne Karaeng ri Massere' tenamo nasulu'–sulu' ri ga'donna napakamma siri'–siri'.*

anne	karaeng	ri	Massere'	tena	=mo	na=	sulu'–	sulu'	ri	ga'dong
this	karaeng	PREP	Massere'	NEG	=PFV	3=	RDP–	exit	PREP	storeroom

≡na	na=	pa–	kamma	siri'–	siri'
≡3.POSS	3=	CAUS–	thus	RDP–	shame

This Karaeng Massere' didn't come out of her storeroom because she was ashamed.

(82) *Le'baki nitoana paerang bunting bura'nea tenamo nammotere', ammantammi ri balla'na purinanna.*

le'ba'	=i	ni–	toa	≡na	pa–	erang	bunting	bura'ne	≡a	tena	=mo
finished	=3	PASS–	old	≡3.POSS	NR–	bring	bride	man	≡DEF	NEG	=PFV

na=	amm–	oter	=e'	amm–	antang	=mo	=i	ri	balla'	≡na
3=	MV–	return	=EC	MV–	stay	=PFV	=3	PREP	house	≡3.POSS

purina	≡nna
uncle/aunt	≡3.POSS

After the groom had eaten he didn't go home, he stayed at his aunt's house.

(83) *Nia'mo sibulang sallona le'ba'na bunting, nakanamo ri purinanna: "Eroka' rong ammotere' mange ri ballakku Karaeng ka a'bangngi–bangngima' ilau' mae".*

nia'	=mo	si–	bulang	sallo	≡na	le'ba'	≡na	bunting na= kana
be	=PFV	one–	month	long	≡3.POSS	finished	≡3.POSS	bride 3= word

=mo	ri	purina	≡nna	ero'	=a' rong	amm–	oter	=e' mange
=PFV	PREP	uncle/aunt	≡3.POSS	want	=1 first	MV–	return	=EC go

ri	balla'	≡ku	karaeng ka	aC–	bangngi–	bangngi =mo	=a'
PREP	house	≡1.POSS	karaeng because	MV–	RDP–	night	=PFV =1

i=	lau'	mae
PREP=	sea, west	be.in.a.place

A month after he'd been married, he said to his aunt: 'Now I want to go back to my house because I've slept in the west already'.

(84) *Nakanamo Karaeng ri Massere': "Mangemako ana'".*

na=	kana	=mo	karaeng ri	Massere'	mange	=mo	=ko	ana'
3=	word	=PFV	karaeng PREP	Massere'	go	=PFV	=2f	child

Kareang Massere' said 'Go child'.

(85) *A'lampami mange ri balla'na manggena.*

aC–	lampa	=mo	=i	mange ri	balla'	≡na	mangge	≡na
MV–	go	=PFV	=3	go PREP	house	≡3.POSS	father	≡3.POSS

He went to his father's house.

(86) *Battui mange, le'ba' nisare kanre, bangngi tommi.*

battu	=i	mange le'ba'	ni–	sare	kanre	bangngi	tong	=mo	=i
come	=3	go finished	PASS–	give	food	night	also	=PFV	=3

He came there, was given food, and it was night.

(87) *Nakanamo manggena: "Angngapa nummantang inja nabangngimo".*

na=	kana	=mo	mangge	≡na	angngapa	nu=	amm–	antang inja	na=
3=	word	=PFV	father	≡3.POSS	why	2f=	MV–	stay still	3=

bangngi	=mo
night	=PFV

His father said: 'Why are you still here staying the night?'

(88) *Nakanamo ana'na: "Na ammantang–mantanga' rong Karaeng, ka le'ba'ji kupau-ang ilau' Karaeng ri Massere'"*

na=	kana	=mo	ana'	≡na	na	amm–	antang– antang	=a' rong
3=	word	=PFV	child	≡3.POSS	and	MV–	RDP– stay	=1 first

KARAENG AMMANAKA BEMBE   409

karaeng ka   le'ba'   =ja =i ku= pau −ang i=   lau'
karaeng because finished =LIM =3 1= story −BEN PREP= sea, west
karaeng ri   Massere'
karaeng PREP Massere'
His child said: 'I'll stay here first Karaeng, because I already said so to Karaeng Massere' in the west'.

(89) *Nakanamo Karaeng ri Roong: "Teako ana' a'bangngí, ammotere'ko kalau', ri purinannu, manna teai mamo tau bainennu.*

na= kana =mo karaeng ri   Roong tea   =ko ana' aC− bangngi
3= word =PFV karaeng PREP Roong not.want =2f child MV− night
−i   amm− oter =e' =ko kalau' ri   purina   ≡nnu   manna
−TRS MV− return =EC =2f go.west PREP uncle/aunt ≡2f.POSS though
tea   =i mamo tau   baine ≡nnu
not.want =3 only   person female ≡2f.POSS
Karaeng Roong said: 'Don't spend the night here child, go back west, to your aunt, even though your wife isn't human.

(90) *Tenajantu najule ammantang ilau' angkusiangi purinannu, ka purinannu tonji".*

tena =ja (a)ntu na= jule   amm− antang i=   lau'   aN− kusiang
NEG =LIM that   3= strange MV− stay   PREP= sea, west AF− homage
=i purina   ≡nnu   ka   purina   ≡nnu   tong =ja =i
=3 uncle/aunt ≡2f.POSS because uncle/aunt ≡2f.POSS also =LIM =3
It's not strange to stay west to pay respect to your aunt, because she's your aunt'.

(91) *Ammotere'mi kalau' ri purinanna.*

amm− oter =e' =mo =i kalau' ri   purina   ≡nna
MV− return =EC =PFV =3 go.west PREP uncle/aunt ≡3.POSS
He went west to his aunt.

(92) *Anjo ana'na karaenga ri Roong punna karuéng nipirassi−rassí nai' gumbang pa'je'nekanna.*

anjo ana' ≡na   karaeng ≡a ri   Roong punna karuéng ni−
that child ≡3.POSS karaeng ≡DEF PREP Roong when afternoon PASS−
pi−   rassi− rassi −i   nai' gumbang pa) aC− je'ne' ⟨ang ≡na
EXP− RDP− full −APPL go.up water.pot NR⟩ MV− water ⟨NR ≡3.POSS
That son of Karaeng Roong, when it was afternoon (he) had his bathing pot filled up.

(93) *Na punna bari'basa' naero' mange appira'nyu', tenamo seng je'ne'na.*

na   punna   bari'bas   =a'   na=   ero'   mange   aC–   pira'nyu'   tena   =mo
and if/when morning =EC   3=   want   go   MV– bathwater   NEG   =PFV
seng   je'ne'   ≡na
again   water   ≡3.POSS
In the morning when he wanted to wash, there was no water left.

(94) *Nakanamo pa'mai'na: "Apanjo nipala'búsi je'neka.*

na=   kana   =mo   pa'mai'   ≡na   apa   (a)njo ni–   pa–   la'bus   –i
3=   word   =PFV   heart   ≡3.POSS   what   that   PASS–   CAUS–   finished   –TRS
je'ne'   ≡a
water   ≡DEF
He said to himself: 'What used up the water?

(95) *Punna karuéng napirassi–rassí paalle je'neka; na punna bari'basa' eroka' appira'nyu', tenamo."*

punna   karuéng   na=   pi–   rassi–   rassi   –i   pa–   alle   je'ne'   ≡a
if/when   afternoon   3=   CAUS?–   RDP–   full   –TRS   NR–   take   water   ≡DEF
na   punna   bari'bas   =a'   ero'   =a'   aC–   pira'nyu'   tena   =mo
and   if/when   morning   =EC   want   =1   MV–   bathwater   NEG   =PFV
In the afternoon the water carriers filled it, and in the morning when I want to wash there isn't any.'

(96) *Nia'mo se're bangngi, na nakana pa'mai'na: "Kualle sai beng kujagái ampela'-pelakai je'nekku"*

nia'   =mo   se're   bangngi   na   na=   kana   pa'mai'   ≡na   ku=   alle   sa   =i
be   =PFV   one   night   and   3=   word   heart   ≡3.POSS   1=   take   HORT   =3
beng   ku=   jaga   –i   aN–   pela'–   pela'   ≡a   =i   je'ne'   ≡ku
QUOT   1=   watch   –APPL   AF–   RDP–   throw.out   ≡DEF   =3   water   ≡1.POSS
There was one night, and he said to himself: 'I'll watch who throws out my water'.

(97) *Ammantammi ilalang ri katinroang accado'.*

amm–   antang   =mo   =i   i=   lalang   ri   ka⟩   tinro   ⟨ang aC–
MV–   stay   =PFV   =3   PREP=   inside   PREP   NR⟩   sleep   ⟨NR   MV–
cado'
sit.doing.nothing
He stayed inside on his bed doing nothing.

(98) *Sannang ngasengi taua tinrona, a'garumbammi bembea ri bokona pakke'buka ampasulu' karungkunna, nampa mange a'je'ne'.*

sannang	*ngaseng*	*=i*	*tau*	*≡a*	*tinro*	*≡na*	*aC- garumbang =mo =i*
content	all	=3	person	≡DEF	sleep	≡3.POSS	MV- thump =PFV =3

bembe	*≡a*	*ri*	*boko*	*≡na*	*pakke'bu'*	*≡a*	*aN- pa- sulu'*
goat	≡DEF	PREP	back	≡3.POSS	door	≡DEF	AF- CAUS- exit

karungkung	*≡na*	*nampa*	*mange*	*aC- je'ne'*
disguise	≡3.POSS	then	go	MV- water

Everyone was sound asleep, the goat behind the door thudded out from under her costume, then went to bathe.

(99) *Nicini'mi ri bura'nenna anjo le'baka ambuntíngi, nakanamo pa'mai'na: "Anne paleng bembea, teáiji bembe tojeng, tauji".*

ni-	*cini'*	*=mo*	*=i*	*ri*	*bura'ne*	*≡nna*	*anjo le'ba' ≡a aN- bunting*
PASS-	see	=PFV	=3	PREP	man	≡3.POSS	that finished ≡DEF AF- bride

–i	*na=*	*kana*	*=mo*	*pa'mai'*	*≡na*	*anne paleng bembe ≡a*
–APPL	3=	word	=PFV	heart	≡3.POSS	this what.then goat ≡DEF

teái	*=ja*	*=i*	*bembe*	*tojeng*	*tau*	*=ja =i*
not.be	=LIM	=3	goat	true	person	=LIM =3

She was seen by the man she had married, and he said to himself: 'That goat, she's not a goat, she's a human!'

(100) *A'di'di'–di'di'mi assulu' ri kulambuna, akkadangkang nampa mange angngasala' ri bokona pakke'buka.*

aC-	*di'di'–*	*di'di'*	*=mo*	*=i*	*aC- sulu' ri*	*kulambu ≡na aC-*
MV-	RDP-	tiptoe	=PFV	=3	MV- exit PREP	mosquito.net ≡3.POSS MV-

kadangkang	*nampa*	*mange*	*aN(N)- asal*	*=a'*	*ri boko ≡na*
crawl	then	go	BV- feel	=EC	PREP back ≡3.POSS

pakke'bu'	*≡a*
door	≡DEF

He tiptoed out from his mosquito net, crawled along and then felt behind the door (in the dark).

(101) *Nagappami najama karungkunna bembea.*

na=	*gappa*	*=mo*	*=i*	*na=*	*jama*	*karungkung*	*≡na bembe ≡a*
3=	result	=PFV	=3	3=	work	disguise	≡3.POSS goat ≡DEF

He managed to get the goat's disguise.

(102) *Nabuammi naung ri buttaya, battu– tommi kongkonga ampasire'bokangi angkanrei.*

na=	buang	=mo	=i	naung	ri	butta	≡a	battu	tong	=mo	=i
3=	fall	=PFV	=3	go.down	PREP	land	≡DEF	come	also	=PFV	=3

kongkong	≡a	aN–	pa–	si–	re'bo'	–ang	=i	aN–	kanre	=i
dog	≡DEF	AF–	CAUS–	MUT–	fight.over.s.t	–BEN	=3	AF–	food	=3

He threw it down to the ground, the dogs came and fought over it, ate it.

(103) *Ta'bangka– tomminjo patanna karungkung.*

taC–	bangka	tong	=mo	=i	(a)njo	pata	≡nna	karungkung
NVOL–	be.shocked	also	=PFV	=3	that	owner	≡3.POSS	disguise

The owner of the disguise was shocked.

(104) *Larimi mange amboyai karungkunna, tenami.*

lari	=mo	=i	mange	aN–	boya	=i	karungkung	≡na	tena	=mo	=i
run	=PFV	=3	go	AF–	search	=3	disguise	≡3.POSS	NEG	=PFV	=3

She ran to look for her disguise, it wasn't anymore.

(105) *Ammantammi angngarru', angkarruki karungkunna.*

amm–	antang	=mo	=i	aN(N)–	karru'	aN–	karru'	=i	karungkung
MV–	stay	=PFV	=3	BV–	cry	AF–	cry	=3	disguise

≡na
≡3.POSS

She stayed still, crying, crying for her disguise.

(106) *Mangemi bura'nenna anynyonyoki, ampiasóri lipa'.*

mange	=mo	=i	bura'ne	≡nna	aN(N)–	nyonyo'	=i	aN–	pi–
go	=PFV	=3	man	≡3.POSS	BV–	comfort.s.o	=3	AF–	EXP–

asor	–i	lipa'
wrap.head	–APPL	sarong

Her husband came, comforted her, wrapped her with a sarong.

(107) *Pila' sanna'ji pole batena angngarru'.*

pila'	sanna'	=ja	=i	pole	bate	≡na	aN(N)–	karru'
the.more	extremely	=LIM	=3	still, yet	method	≡3.POSS	BV–	cry

Then she cried even more.

KARAENG AMMANAKA BEMBE   413

(108)   *Nakanamo bura'nenna: "Angngapai na nuballa'–ballási kamma kalennu angn-*
garru', a'jari bembe, angnganre ruku'".

na= kana =mo bura'ne ≡nna   angngapa =i na   nu= ballas–
3=   word =PFV man   ≡3.POSS why   =3 COMP 2f= RDP–
ballas –i kamma kale ≡nnu   aN(N)– karru' aC– jari   bembe
troubles –TRS thus   self ≡2f.POSS BV–   cry   MV– become goat
aN(N)– kanre ruku'
BV–   food grass
Her husband said: 'Why do you trouble yourself so, crying, becoming a goat,
eating grass?'

(109)   *Pila' sannaki batena angngarru'.*

pila'   sanna'   =i bate   ≡na   aN(N)– karru'
the.more extremely =3 method ≡3.POSS BV–   cry
She cried even more.

(110)   *Ta'bangka ngasemmi taua; karaenga ta'bangka– tommi siagáng bainenna.*

taC–   bangka   ngaseng =mo =i tau   ≡a   karaeng ≡a   taC–
NVOL– be.shocked all   =PFV =3 person ≡DEF karaeng ≡DEF NVOL–
bangka   tong =mo =i siagáng baine   ≡nna
be.shocked also =PFV =3 with   female ≡3.POSS
All the people were shocked; the karaeng was shocked too, and his wife.

(111)   *Turung ngasemmi assulukang mae.*

turung   ngaseng =mo =i aC– sulu' –ang mae
descend all   =PFV =3 MV– exit –BEN be.in.a.place
They all went down and out.

(112)   *Battu assulu' mae, nakanamo Karaeng ri Massere': "Inainjo angngarru'".*

battu aC– sulu' mae   na= kana =mo karaeng ri   Massere'
come MV– exit be.in.a.place 3=   word =PFV karaeng PREP Massere'
inai (a)njo aN(N)– karru'
who that BV–   cry
They came out, Karaeng Massere' said: 'who's crying?'

(113)   *Nakanamo ana'na Karaeng ri Roong: "Bembea Karaeng mange a'je'ne' kudikki'–*
dikki' mange ambuangi karungkunna naung ri buttaya napasire'bokang kong-
kong".

na= kana =mo ana' ≡na   karaeng ri   Roong bembe ≡a
3=   word =PFV child ≡3.POSS karaeng PREP Roong goat   ≡DEF

karaeng mange aC– je'ne' ku= dikki'– dikki' mange aN– buang =i
karaeng go   MV– water 1=   RDP– creep go   AF– fall   =3
karungkung ≡na   naung ri   butta ≡a   na= pa– si–
disguise   ≡3.POSS go.down PREP land ≡DEF 3= CAUS– MUT–
re'bo'   –ang kongkong
fight.over.s.t –BEN dog
The child of Karaeng Roong said: 'The goat Karaeng, went to bathe, I crept to throw her disguise down to the ground, it was torn apart by dogs'.

(114)   *Na anjo Karaeng ri Massere' tenamo niissengi nikana–kana rannunna.*
       na anjo karaeng ri   Massere' tena =mo ni–   isseng =i ni–
       and that karaeng PREP Massere' NEG =PFV PASS– know =3 PASS–
       kana– kana rannu ≡nna
       RDP– word happy ≡3.POSS
       And that Karaeng Massere', her happiness couldn't be expressed.

(115)   *Nabakkáimi ana'na nabau nampa nariwa.*
       na= bakka –i   =mo =i ana' ≡na   na= bau nampa na= riwa
       3= rush –APPL =PFV =3 child ≡3.POSS 3= kiss then   3= sit.on.lap
       She rushed to her daughter, kissed her and put her on her lap.

(116)   *Tenamo natinro nasingara' taua siagáng Karaenga ri Massere'.*
       tena =mo na= tinro na= singar =a' tau   ≡a   siagáng karaeng
       NEG =PFV 3= sleep 3= light =EC person ≡DEF with   karaeng
       ≡a   ri   Massere'
       ≡DEF PREP Massere'
       They didn't sleep any more until dawn, the people and Karaeng Massere'.

(117)   *Baji'i singaraka nasuro ngasemmi apparuru bone balla'na Karaeng ri Massere'*
       baji' =i singar =a' ≡a   na= suro ngaseng =mo =i aC– paruru
       good =3 light =EC ≡DEF 3= order all   =PFV =3 MV– get.ready
       bone   balla' ≡na   karaeng ri   Massere'
       contents house ≡3.POSS karaeng PREP Massere'
       The sun was well up and Karaeng Massere's household was sent to prepare.

(118)   *Le'ba' ngasemmi apparuru, nia'– tommo mange nasuro ampauangi paranna kara'–karaeng.*
       le'ba'   ngaseng =mo =i aC– paruru   nia' tong =mo mange na=
       finished all   =PFV =3 MV– get.ready be also =PFV go   3=

KARAENG AMMANAKA BEMBE   415

suro   aN- pau   -ang =i para ≡nna   karaeng- karaeng
order AF- story –BEN =3 both ≡3.POSS RDP-   karaeng

When they were all ready, there was also (someone) sent to tell all the karaengs.

(119) *Nia'- tommi nasuro ampauangi Karaeng ri Roong, angkana: "kalau'ko ka anjo bembea anjari taumi".*

nia' tong =mo =i na= suro aN- pau -ang =i karaeng ri   Roong
be   also =PFV =3 3= order AF- story –BEN =3 karaeng PREP Roong

aN- kana kalau' =ko ka   anjo bembe ≡a   aN- jari   tau
AF- word go.west =2f because that goat ≡DEF AF- become person

=mo =i
=PFV =3

There was also (someone) sent to tell Karaeng Roong, saying: 'Go west, because that goat became a human'.

(120) *Anjo paranna kara'–karaeng nasuro pauammi angkana, "apparuruki' ka nampa– tommi ero' nalekka' ana'na Karaeng ri Massere', ka a'jari taumi".*

anjo para ≡nna   kara'- karaeng na= suro pau -ang =mo =i aN-
that both ≡3.POSS RDP-   karaeng 3= order story –NR =PFV =3 AF-

kana aC- paruru   =ki' ka   nampa tong =mo =i ero' na=
word MV- get.ready =2p because then also =PFV =3 want 3=

lekka'   ana' ≡na   karaeng ri   Massere'
bring.newlyweds.to.groom's.house child ≡3.POSS karaeng PREP Massere'

ka   aC- jari   tau   =mo =i
because MV- become person =PFV =3

All the karaengs sent a message, saying: 'get ready because soon we should bring the daughter of Karaeng Massere' to her husband's home, because she became a person'.

(121) *Nia' ngasemminjo battu paranna kara'–karaeng, Karaeng ri Roong nia'– tommi battu.*

nia' ngaseng =mo =i (a)njo battu para ≡nna   karaeng- karaeng
be   all   =PFV =3 that come both ≡3.POSS RDP-   karaeng

karaeng ri   Roong nia' tong =mo =i battu
karaeng PREP Roong be   also =PFV =3 come

All the karaengs came, Karaeng Roong also came.

(122) *Tenamo kamma rannunna Karaeng ri Roong siagáng Karaeng ri Massere'*

    tena =mo kamma rannu ≡nna   karaeng ri   Roong siagáng karaeng

    NEG =PFV thus   happy ≡3.POSS karaeng PREP Roong with   karaeng

    ri   Massere'

    PREP Massere'

    There was nothing like the happiness of Karaeng Roong and Karaeng Massere'.

(123) *Atte'ne–te'ne pa'mai'mi tuju allo tuju bangngi.*

    aC– te'ne– te'ne pa'mai' =mo =i tuju   allo tuju   bangngi

    MV– RDP– sweet heart   =PFV =3 seven day seven night

    There was sweetness in their hearts for seven days and seven nights.

(124) *Nalekka'mi ana'na mange ri balla'na Karaeng ri Roong.*

    na= lekka'   =mo =i ana' ≡na   mange ri

    3= newlyweds.to.groom's.house =PFV =3 child ≡3.POSS go   PREP

    balla' ≡na   karaeng ri   Roong

    house ≡3.POSS karaeng PREP Roong

    The children were brought as newlyweds to Karaeng Roong's house.

(125) *Battui anrai' nakanamo Karaeng ri Roong ri ana'na: "Baji'na na kupisangkaiko*
    ammantang ammotere'nu anrai' mae; ka'de' tena nupilangngéri kanangku,
    darami bainennu, na tusanna'– dudu baji'–baji'na".

    battu =i anrai' na= kana =mo karaeng ri   Roong ri   ana'

    come =3 go.east 3=   word =PFV karaeng PREP Roong PREP child

    ≡na   baji' ≡na   na   ku= pi– sangka =i =ko amm– antang

    ≡3.POSS good ≡3.POSS COMP 1=   EXP– forbid =3 =2f MV–   stay

    amm– oter   =e' ≡nu   anrai' mae   ka'de' tena nu= pi–

    MV–   return =EC ≡2f.POSS go.east be.in.a.place if.only NEG 2f= EXP–

    langnger –i   kana ≡ngku dara =mo =i baine   ≡nnu   na

    listen   –APPL word ≡1.POSS a.pity =PFV =3 female ≡2f.POSS and

    tu–   sanna'   dudu baji'– baji' ≡na

    person– extremely very RDP– good ≡3.POSS

    Coming eastwards Karaeng Roong said to his son: 'It was good that I forbade
    you to stay back in the east, if you hadn't heeded my words, what a shame for
    your wife, and she is really very beautiful'.

(126) *Atte'ne–te'ne pa'mai'mi Karaeng ri Roong tallung– allo tallum– bangngi.*

    aC– te'ne– te'ne pa'mai' =mo =i karaeng ri   Roong tallu –N allo

    MV– RDP– sweet heart   =PFV =3 karaeng PREP Roong three –LK day

tallu −N bangngi
three −LK night
Karaeng Roong felt sweetness in his heart for three days, three nights.

(127) *Gannaki tallung− allo tallum− bangngi ammotere'mi karaeng ri Massere'*
       mange ri balla'na.
       ganna'   =i tallu −N allo tallu −N bangngi amm− oter   =e' =mo
       complete =3 three −LK day three −LK night   MV− return =EC =PFV
       =i karaeng ri   Massere' mange ri   balla' ≡na
       =3 karaeng PREP Massere' go   PREP house ≡3.POSS
       After three days and three nights Karaeng Massere' went back to her house.

(128) *Kammaminjo pau−pauanna karaenga ammanaka bembe.*
       kamma =mo =i (a)njo pau− pau −ang ≡na   karaeng ≡a   amm−
       thus   =PFV =3 that RDP− story −NR ≡3.POSS karaeng ≡DEF MV−
       ana' ≡a   bembe
       child ≡DEF goat
       That was the story of the karaeng who gave birth to a goat.

APPENDIX C

A'jappa–jappa ri Bulukumba: A Trip to Bulukumba

This narrative recounting a shared experience was told to me by Alimuddin, a native of Bontonompo in his early 20s. It was recorded in July 1997. It is unusual for the way in which the proclitic *ku=* has been *en*cliticised onto the conjunction/complementiser *na* in (1) and (22), and also for the variant form *siagadang* of the prepositional verb *siagáng*.

(1) *Ri allonna arabaia tette' sampulo–asse're naku a'lampa ammekang ri Bulukumba.*
ri   allo ≡nna   arabaia   tette'   sampulo aN– se're na   =ku aC–
PREP day ≡3.POSS Wednesday o'clock ten   LK– one COMP =1 MV–
lampa aN(N)– pekang ri   Bulukumba
go   BV–   hook   PREP Bulukumba
On Wednesday at 11 o'clock I went fishing at Bulukumba

(2) *Anjo alloa assiagánga' i Antoni mange ammekang nia' podeng aganna battu ri Anggarisi', niareng Brus.*
anjo allo ≡a   aC– siagáng =a' i   Antoni   mange aN(N)– pekang nia'
that day ≡DEF MV– with   =1 PREP Anthony go   BV–   hook   be
podeng agang ≡na   battu ri   Anggarisi' ni–   areng Brus
also   friend ≡3.POSS come PREP England   PASS– name Bruce
That day I accompanied Anthony to go fishing, there was also his friend from England called Bruce.

(3) *Jari i rate ri biseanga na nia' cari–caritamo siagadang i Brus, Antoni, inakke, accari–caritatonga' siagadang i Arsyad.*
jari i   rate   ri   biseang ≡a   na   nia' cari– carita =mo
SO PREP above PREP boat   ≡DEF COMP be RDP– story =PFV
siagadang i   Brus Antoni   inakke aC– cari– carita tong =a'
with   PREP Bruce Anthony 1PRO MV– RDP– story also =1
siagadang i   Arsyad
with   PERS Arsyad
So up on the ship, there was talking with Bruce, Anthony, me, I also talked with Arsyad.

A'JAPPA–JAPPA RI BULUKUMBA: A TRIP TO BULUKUMBA

(4) *Na ... narapi'mo birinna anjo puloa, nikana pulo liukang, ammantammi biseanga*
   naku ammekangmo anjoreng.

na	*na= rapi'*	*=mo biring*	*≡na*	*anjo pulo*	*≡a*	*ni–*	*kana pulo*
and	3= achieve	=PFV edge	≡3.POSS	that island	≡DEF	PASS–	word island

liukang	*amm– antang*	*=mo*	*=i*	*biseang*	*≡a*	*na*	*≡ku*	*aN(N)–*
island	MV– stay	=PFV	=3	boat	≡DEF	COMP	≡1.POSS	BV–

pekang	*=mo*	*anjoreng*
hook	=PFV	there

   And ... getting to that island, they say 'liukang' for island, the boat stopped and
   we fished there.

(5) *Mingka tena na kummantung, jari naungi taua a'je'ne'–je'ne' ri tamparanga, nasa-*
   ba' tenaja juku' nipekang.

mingka	*tena*	*na*	*ku=*	*aN(N)–*	*bantung*	*jari*	*naung*	*=i*	*tau*	*≡a*
but	NEG	COMP	1=	BV–	hoist	so	go.down	=3	person	≡DEF

aC–	*je'ne'– je'ne'*	*ri*	*tamparang*	*≡a*	*na=*	*saba'*	*tena*	*=ja*	*juku'*
MV–	RDP– water	PREP	sea	≡DEF	3=	reason	NEG	=LIM	fish

ni–	*pekang*
PASS–	hook

   But I didn't catch any, so the people went down to swim in the sea, because the
   fish weren't getting caught.

(6) *Inakke naung a'lange, i Antoni naung todonga' siagadang i Brus naung todonga'*
   a'lange.

inakke	*naung*	*aC–*	*lange*	*i*	*Antoni*	*naung*	*todong*	*=a'*	*siagadang*
1PRO	go.down	MV–	swim	PERS	Anthony	go.down	also	=1	with

i	*Brus*	*naung*	*todong*	*=a'*	*aC–*	*lange*
PERS	Bruce	go.down	also	=1	MV–	swim

   I went down to swim, Anthony also went down, with Bruce also we went down
   to swim.

(7) *Inakke a'lange na kuselang ka ... nasaba' tassambangi pekangku anjoreng ri batua,*
   jari naunga' anselángi.

inakke	*aC–*	*lange*	*na*	*ku=*	*selang*	*ka*	*na=*	*saba'*	*taC–*	*sambang*	*=i*
1PRO	MV–	swim	and	1=	dive	because	3=	reason	NVOL–	snag	=3

pekang	*≡ku*	*anjoreng*	*ri*	*batu*	*≡a*	*jari*	*naung*	*=a'*	*aN–*	*selang*
hook	≡1.POSS	there	PREP	stone	≡DEF	so	go.down	=1	AF–	dive

–i
–APPL

   I swam and dived because ... because my hook was snagged there on the rocks so
   I went down to dive to it.

(8) *I Brus tulimo langena i rawa ri tamparanga siagadang i Antoni.*

I	*Brus*	*tuli*	*=mo*	*lange*	*≡na*	*i*	*rawa*	*ri*	*tamparang*
PERS	Bruce	constant	=PFV	swim	≡3.POSS	PREP	beneath	PREP	sea

≡a	*siagadang*	*i*	*Antoni*
≡DEF	with	PREP	Anthony

Bruce swam the whole time in the sea together with Anthony.

(9) *I Arsyad i rateji ri biseanga accini'–cini' tau a'lange.*

I	*Arsyad*	*i*	*rate*	*=ja*	*=i*	*ri*	*biseang*	*≡a*	*aC–*	*cini'–*	*cini'*
PERS	Arsyad	PREP	above	=LIM	=3	PREP	boat	≡DEF	MV–	RDP–	see

tau	*aC–*	*lange*
person	MV–	swim

Arsyad just (stayed) up on the boat watching the people swimming.

(10) *Nia' poenga tau maraengang na inakke sipa'agangang naung todonga' a'je'ne'–je'ne'.*

nia'	*pole*	*–ang*	*≡a*	*tau*	*maraeng*	*–ang*	*na*	*i–*	*nakke*	*si–*
be	yet	–COMPR	≡DEF	person	other	–COMPR	and	PERS–	1PRO	MUT–

pa⟩	*aC–*	*agang*	*⟨ang*	*naung*	*todong*	*=a'*	*aC–*	*je'ne'–*	*je'ne'*
NR⟩	MV–	friend	⟨NR	go.down	also	=1	MV–	RDP–	water

There were still more other people and me and my friends also went down to swim.

(11) *I Arsyad tena naung a'je'ne'–je'ne' nasaba' tangngissengai a'lange.*

I	*Arsyad*	*tena*	*naung*	*aC–*	*je'ne'–*	*je'ne'*	*na=*	*saba'*	*ta=*	*aN(N)–*
PERS	Arsyad	NEG	go.down	MV–	RDP–	water	3=	reason	NEG=	BV–

isseng	*–a*	*=i*	*aC–*	*lange*
know	–SBJV	=3	MV–	swim

Arsyad didn't go down to bathe because he didn't know how to swim.

(12) *Sallo– salloi a'lange Antoni ero'mi nai' ri biseanga natepo' anjo tuka'na biseanga.*

sallo	*sallo*	*=i*	*aC–*	*lange*	*Antoni*	*ero'*	*=mo*	*=i*	*nai'*	*ri*	*biseang*	*≡a*
long	long	=3	MV–	swim	Anthony	want	=PFV	=3	go.up	PREP	boat	≡DEF

na=	*tepo'*	*anjo*	*tuka'*	*≡na*	*bise*	*–ang*	*≡a*
3=	broken	that	ladder	≡3.POSS	paddle	–NR	≡DEF

After swimming for a while Anthony wanted to come up on the boat, the boat's ladder was broken.

A'JAPPA–JAPPA RI BULUKUMBA: A TRIP TO BULUKUMBA 421

(13) *Jari, I Brus nai'i nanibeso'– mamo nai', nasaba' tena nakulle angngambi', nasaba'*
anjo pakalianna sanna' ca'dina nampa roso'.

jari	*I*	*Brus*	*nai'*	*=i*	*na=*	*ni–*	*beso'*	*mamo*	*nai'*	*na=*	*saba'*	*tena*
so	PERS	Bruce	go.up	=3	3=	PASS–	pull	only	go.up	3=	reason	NEG

na=	*kulle*	*aN(N)–*	*ambi'*	*na=*	*saba'*	*anjo*	*pakaliang*	*≡na*	*sanna'*
3=	can	BV–	climb	3=	reason	that	arm	≡3.POSS	extremely

ca'di	*≡na*	*nampa*	*roso'*
small	≡3.POSS	then	thin

So, Bruce had to be pulled up, because he couldn't climb up, because his arms
were too small and thin.

(14) *Le'baki a'lange, iareka le'baki taua a'je'ne'–je'ne', nai'mi taua ri puloa ero' mae*
attunu– tunu juku'.

le'ba'	*=i*	*aC–*	*lange*	*iareka*	*le'ba'*	*=i*	*tau*	*≡a*	*aC–*	*je'ne'–*	*je'ne'*
finished	=3	MV–	swim	or	finished	=3	person	≡DEF	MV–	RDP–	water

nai'	*=mo*	*=i*	*tau*	*≡a*	*ri*	*pulo*	*≡a*	*ero'*	*mae*	*aC–*
go.up	=PFV	=3	person	≡DEF	PREP	island	≡DEF	want	be.in.a.place	MV–

tunu–	*tunu*	*juku'*
RDP–	grill	fish

After swimming, or after the people had swum, the people went up on the island,
wanting to go and roast some fish.

(15) *Mingka tena pabalu'– juku', jari kaluku– loloji nikanre anjoreng anjo ri puloa.*

mingka	*tena*	*pa–*	*balu'*	*juku'*	*jari*	*kaluku*	*lolo*	*=ja*	*=i*	*ni–*	*kanre*
but	NEG	NR–	sell	fish	so	coconut	young	=LIM	=3	PASS–	food

anjoreng	*anjo*	*ri*	*pulo*	*≡a*
there	that	PREP	island	≡DEF

But there was no fishseller, so young coconut was all we ate there on the island.

(16) *Uru naikku ri puloa nia' podeng tau battu ri Perancis, limai siagadang.*

uru	*nai'*	*≡ku*	*ri*	*pulo*	*≡a*	*nia'*	*podeng*	*tau*	*battu*	*ri*
beginning	go.up	≡1.POSS	PREP	island	≡DEF	be	also	person	come	PREP

Perancis	*lima*	*=i*	*siagadang*
France	five	=3	with

At first when we went up on the island there were also people from France, 5
together.

(17) *mingka I Antoniji cari–carita siagadang I Brus siagáng anjo tau battua ri Perancis.*

mingka	*I*	*Antoni*	*=ja*	*=i*	*cari–*	*carita*	*siagadang*	*I*	*Brus*
but	PERS	Anthony	=LIM	=3	RDP–	story	with	PERS	Bruce

422 APPENDIX C

siagáng anjo tau   battu ≡a   ri   Perancis
with   that person come ≡DEF PREP France
But only Anthony talked together with Bruce with those people from France.

(18) *Inakke na I Arsyad a'lampa mae ri olo, mae a'boya kaluku.*
inakke na   I   Arsyad aC– lampa mae   ri   olo   mae
1PRO and PERS Arsyad MV– go   be.in.a.place PREP front be.in.a.place
aC– boya   kaluku
MV– search coconut
Me and Arsyad were ahead, looking for coconuts.

(19) *Wattu mange anjoreng nai'mi anjo agangku angngambi' kaluku na panaung annam– batu.*
wattu mange anjoreng nai' =mo =i anjo agang ≡ku   aN(N)– ambi'
time go   there   go.up =PFV =3 that friend ≡1.POSS BV–   climb
kaluku   na   pa–   naung   annang batu
coconut and CAUS– go.down six   CLF.misc
when we went there my friend climbed up a coconut and threw down six

(20) *Jari anjoremminjo angnganre kaluku ri puloa.*
jari anjoreng =mo =i (a)njo aN(N)– kanre kaluku   ri   pulo ≡a
so there   =PFV =3 that BV–   food coconut PREP island ≡DEF
so (we) ate coconut on the island

(21) *Sikalinna I Brus nisakkoki ri je'ne' kaluku nasaba' tena nabiasa angnginung punna tena nammake pipet iareka silang.*
si–   kali ≡nna   I   Brus ni–   sakko' =i ri   je'ne' kaluku na=
one– time ≡3.POSS PERS Bruce PASS– choke =3 PREP water coconut 3=
saba' tena na= biasa aN(N)– inung punna   tena na= aN(N)– pake pipet
reason NEG 3= usual BV–   drink if/when NEG 3= BV–   use straw
iareka silang
or   straw?
One time Bruce choked on the coconut water because he wasn't used to drinking without using a straw.

(22) *Jari, le'ba'namonjo angnganre kaluku, ammotere'ma' mange ri biseanga naku a'lampamo mange ri Tanjung Bira ri anjo tampa' kupammantang nia'.*
jari le'ba'   ≡na   =mo anjo aN(N)– kanre kaluku   amm– oter   =e'
so finished ≡3.POSS =PFV that BV–   food coconut MV–   return =EC

A'JAPPA–JAPPA RI BULUKUMBA: A TRIP TO BULUKUMBA   423

=mo =a' mange ri   biseang ≡a   na   =ku aC– lampa =mo mange
=PFV =1 go   PREP boat   ≡DEF and =1   MV– go   =PFV go
ri   Tanjung   Bira ri   anjo tampa' ku= pa– amm– antang nia'
PREP peninsula Bira PREP that place   1=   NR– MV–   stay   exist

So, when we'd finished eating coconuts, we went back to the boat and went to Tanjung Bira where the place we were staying was.

Bibliography

Abdul Azis Syarif, Djirong Basang Daeng Ngewa, A.M. Junus, Alimuddin, Rasdina, Aburaerah Arief, Arah Suyuthi. (1979) *Sistem morfologi kata kerja bahasa Makassar*. Proyek Penelitian Bahasa dan Sastra Indonesia dan Daerah Sulawesi Selatan, Ujung Pandang.

Abdul Kadir Manyambeang, Abdul Azis Syarif, Abdul Rahim Hamid, Djirong Basang Daeng Ngewa, Aburaerah Arief. (1979) *Morfologi dan sintaksis bahasa Makassar*. Pusat Bahasa, Jakarta.

Abdul Kadir Manyambeang, Abdul Kadir Mulya, Nasruddin. (1996) *Tata bahasa Makassar*. Pusat Pembinaan dan Pengembangan Bahasa, Jakarta.

Abdul Kadir Manyambeang & Abdul Rahim Daeng Mone. (1979) *Lontarak patturioloanga ri tutalloka*. Departemen Pendidikan dan Kebudayaan Proyek Penerbitan Buku Bacaan dan Sastra Indonesia dan Daerah, Jakarta.

Abdul Muthalib, Aburaerah Arief, Adnan Usmar, Syahril. (1995) *Sistem pemajemukan bahasa Makassar*. Pusat Pembinaan dan Pengembangan Bahasa, Jakarta.

Aburaerah Arief. (1995) *Kamus Makassar–Indonesia*. Yayasan YAPIK DDI, Ujung Pandang.

Aburaerah Arief. (2001) *Kamus bahasa Melayu Makasar–Indonesia*. Balai Pustaka, Jakarta.

Aburaerah Arief & Zainuddin Hakim. (1993) *Sinrilikna Kappalak Tallumbatua*. Yayasan Obor Indonesia, Jakarta.

Adelaar, K.A. (1994) The classification of the Tamanic languages (West Kalimantan). In *Language contact and change in the Austronesian world*, (Eds, Dutton, T.E. & Tryon, D.T.) Mouton de Gruyter, Berlin, pp. 1–41.

Adelaar, K.A. (2005) A historical perspective. In *The Austronesian Languages of Asia and Madagascar*, (Eds, Adelaar, K.A. & Himmelmann, N.) Routledge, London.

Aissen, J. (1992) Topic and Focus in Mayan. *Language*, 68, 43–80.

Andaya, L. (1976) Arung Palakka and Kahar Muzakkar: A study of the hero figure in Bugis–Makassar society. In *People and society in Indonesia: a biographical approach*, (Eds, Andaya, L., Coppel, C. & Suzuki, Y.) Monash University, Melbourne.

Andaya, L. (1980) A village perception of Arung Palakka and the Makassar War of 1666–1669. In *Perceptions of the Past in South-East Asia*, (Eds, Reid, A. & Marr, D.) Heinemann, Singapore, pp. 360–378.

Andaya, L. (1981) *The heritage of Arung Palakka: a history of South Sulawesi (Celebes) in the seventeenth century*. Nijhoff, The Hague.

Aronoff, M., Arsyad, A., Basri, H., Broselow, E. (1987) Tier configuration in Makasar reduplication. In *Papers from the 23rd Annual Regional Meeting of the Chicago Linguistic Society*, (Ed, Need, B.) Chicago Linguistic Society, Chicago, pp. 1–15.

BIBLIOGRAPHY

Asmah Haji Omar. (1979) *Pengimbuhan dalam Bahasa Makassar*. Dewan Bahasa dan Pustaka, Kuala Lumpur.

Aubert, M., Brumm, A., Ramli, M., Sutikna, T., Saptomo, E.W., Hakim, B., Morwood, M.J., van den Bergh, G.D., Kinsley, L. & Dosseto, A. Pleistocene cave art from Sulawesi, Indonesia. *Nature* 514 (7521), 223–227.

Austin, P. & Bresnan, J. (1996) Non-configurationality in Australian Aboriginal languages. *Natural Language and Linguistic Theory*, **14**: 215–268.

Bellwood, P.S. (1997) *Prehistory of the Indo-Malaysian Archipelago*. University of Hawaii Press, Honolulu.

Bhandari, R. (1997) Alignment and nasal substitution strategies in Austronesian languages. Paper from the fourth meeting of the Austronesian Formal Linguistics Association.

Blok, R. (1817) *History of the island of Celebes*. Calcutta Gazette Press, Calcutta.

Blust, R.A. (1977) The Proto-Austronesian pronouns and Austronesian subgrouping: a preliminary report. *Working Papers in Linguistics of the University of Hawai'i*, **9**, 1–15.

Blust, R.A. (1999) Subgrouping, circularity and extinction: some issues in Austronesian comparative linguistics. In *Selected papers from the Eighth International Conference on Austronesian Linguistics*, (Eds, Zeitoun, E. & Li, P.J.) Academica Sinica, Taipei,

Blust, R.A. (2003) Three Notes on Early Austronesian Morphology. *Oceanic Linguistics*, **42:2**, 438–478.

Blust, R.A. (2004) Austronesian Nasal Substitution: A Survey. *Oceanic Linguistics*, **43:1**, 73–148.

Brotchie, A. (1992) *Verbal agreement and constituent order in Bugis*. Honours thesis, University of Melbourne.

Bulbeck, F.D. (1992) *A tale of two kingdoms: the historical archaeology of Gowa and Tallok, South Sulawesi, Indonesia*. Ph.D. thesis, Australian National University.

Bulbeck, F.D. & Caldwell, I. (2000) *Land of Iron: The historical archaeology of Luwu and the Cenrana valley*. Centre for South-East Asian Studies, University of Hull, Hull.

Bulbeck, F.D., Pasqua, M., Di Lello, A. (2000) Culture History of the Toalean of South Sulawesi, Indonesia. *Asian Perspectives*, **39**, 71–108.

Caldwell, I. (1988) *South Sulawesi A.D. 1300–1600: ten Bugis texts*. Ph.D. thesis, Australian National University, Canberra.

Caldwell, I. (1998) The chronology of the king list of Luwu' to AD 1611. In *Living through histories: culture, history and social life in South Sulawesi*, (Eds, Robinson, K. & Paeni, M.) Research School of Pacific and Asian Studies, Australian National University, Canberra.

Caldwell, I. & Lillie, M. (2004) Manuel Pinto's inland sea: Using palaeoenvironmental techniques to assess historical evidence from South Sulawesi. *Modern Quaternary Research in Southeast Asia*, **18**, 259–272.

Cense, A.A. (1966) Old Buginese and Macassarese diaries. *Bijdragen tot de Taal-, Land- en Volkenkunde*, 122, 416–428.

Cense, A.A. (1978) Maleise Invloeden in het Ooostelijk Deel van de Indonesische Archipel. *Bijdragen tot de Taal-, Land- en Volkenkunde*, 134, 415–432.

Cense, A.A. & Abdoerrahim. (1979) *Makassaars–Nederlands woordenboek*. Nijhoff, 's-Gravenhage.

Ceria, V. (1993) Verb morphology and valence change in Selayarese. *University of Pittsburgh Working Papers in Linguistics*, 11, 76–185.

Chabot, H.T. (1950) *Verwantschap, stand en sexe in Zuid-Celebes*. J.B. Wolters, Groningen.

Chabot, H.T. (1996) *Kinship, status and gender in South Celebes*. KITLV, Leiden.

Corbett, G.G. (2003) Agreement: The range of the phenomenon and the principles of the Surrey Database of Agreement. *Transactions of the Philological Society*, 101, 155–202.

Crawfurd, J. (1820) *History of the Indian Archipelago*. Constable, Edinburgh.

Cummings, W. (1999) "Only one people but two rulers"; Hiding the past in seventeenth-century Makasarese chronicles. *Bijdragen tot de Taal-, Land- en Volkenkunde*, 155, 97–120.

Cummings, W. (2000) Reading the histories of a Maros chronicle. *Bijdragen tot de Taal-, Land- en Volkenkunde*, 156, 1–31.

Cummings, W. (2001a) The dynamics of resistance and emulation in Makasar history. *Journal of Southeast Asian Studies*, 32, 423–435.

Cummings, W. (2001b) Scripting Islamization: Arabic Texts in Early Modern Makassar. *Ethnohistory*, 48, 559–586.

Cummings, W. (2002) *Making blood white: historical transformations in early modern Makassar*. University of Hawai'i Press, Honolulu.

Cummings, W. (2003) Rethinking the imbrication of orality and literacy. *The Journal of Asian Studies*, 62, 531–551.

Cummings, W. (2007) *A chain of kings: the Makasar Chronicles of Gowa and Talloq*. KITLV Press, Leiden.

Daniels, P.T. (1990) Fundamentals of grammatology. *Journal of the American Oriental Society*, 110, 727–731.

Daniels, P.T. & Bright, W. (1996) *The world's writing systems*. Oxford University Press, New York.

Dijk, C.v. (1981) *Rebellion under the banner of Islam: the Darul Islam in Indonesia*. M. Nijhoff, The Hague.

Djirong Basang Daeng Ngewa. (1997) *Tata Bahasa Makassar Bidang Morfologi*. Departemen Pendidikan dan Kebudayaan, Ujung Pandang.

Donohue, M. (1999) *A grammar of Tukang Besi*. Mouton de Gruyter, Berlin.

Donohue, M. (2002) Voice in Tukang Besi and the Austronesian voice system. In *The his-*

BIBLIOGRAPHY

tory and typology of Western Austronesian voice systems, (Eds, Wouk, F. & Ross, M.) Pacific Linguistics, Canberra, pp. 81–99.

Dryer, M. (to appear) Clause Types. In *Clause Structure. Language Typology and Syntactic Description: Volume 1*, (Ed, Shopen, T.) Cambridge University Press, Cambridge.

Durie, M. (1985) *A grammar of Acehnese*. Foris, Dordrecht.

Errington, S. (1989) *Meaning and power in a Southeast Asian realm*. Princeton University Press, Princeton, N.J.

Esser, S.J. (1938) Talen. In *Atlas van tropisch Nederland*, Koninklijk Nederlandsch Aardrijkskundig Genootschap, Amsterdam.

Evans, N. (1992) Macassan loanwords in Top End languages. *Australian Journal of Linguistics*, 12, 45–91.

Evans, N. (1997) Macassan loans and linguistic stratification in Western Arnhem Land. In *Archaeology and linguistics: aboriginal Australia in global perspective*, (Eds, McConvell, P. & Evans, N.) Oxford University Press, Melbourne, pp. 237–260.

Evans, N. (2000) Word classes in the world's languages. In *Morphology: a Handbook on Inflection and Word Formation*, (Eds, Booij, G.E., Lehmann, C. & Mugdan, J.) Mouton de Gruyter, Berlin, pp. 708–732.

Everson, M. (2003) Revised final proposal for encoding the Lontara (Buginese) script in the UCS.

Fernández–Armesto, F. (1995) *Millennium: a history of the last thousand years*. Scribner, New York.

Finer, D. (1994) On the nature of two A' positions in Selayarese. In *Studies on scrambling*, (Eds, Corver, N. & Riemsdijk, H.C.v.) Mouton de Gruyter, Berlin, pp. 153–183.

Finer, D. (1996) Covert movement in Selayarese and the distribution of the absolutive marker. Ms at SUNY Buffalo.

Finer, D. (1997a) V to D raising in Sulawesi relatives. Paper from the fourth meeting of the Austronesian Formal Linguistics Association (AFLA4).

Finer, D. (1997b) Contrasting A-bar dependencies in Selayarese. *Natural Language and Linguistic Theory*, 15, 677–728.

Finer, D. (1998) Sulawesi Relatives, V-Raising, and the CP-Complement Hypothesis. *Canadian Journal of Linguistics*, 43, 283–306.

Finer, D. (1999) Cyclic clitics in Selayarese. *Toronto Working Papers in Linguistics: Proceedings of AFLA VI (The sixth meeting of the Austronesian Formal Linguistics Association)*.

Foley, W.A. (1991) *The Yimas language of New Guinea*. Stanford University Press, Stanford.

Forbes, D. (1979) *The Pedlars of Ujung Pandang*. Department of Geography, Monash University, Melbourne.

Friberg, B. (1988) Ergativity, focus and verb morphology in several South Sulawesi languages. *VICAL 2: Western Austronesian and contact languages: papers from the Fifth*

International Conference on Austronesian Linguistics, (Eds, Harlow, R. & Clark, R.). Auckland: Linguistic Society of New Zealand. 103–130.

Friberg, B. (1996) Konjo's peripatetic person markers. In *Papers in Austronesian Linguistics No. 3*, (Ed, Steinhauer, H.) Pacific Linguistics, Canberra, pp. 137–171.

Friberg, B. (2002) Grammatical construction differences between Makasar and Konjo. Handout from 9ICAL (the Ninth International Conference on Austronesian Linguistics).

Friberg, B. & Karda, M. (1987) *Pa'bicaraang bicara Konjo*. Publikasi UNHAS–SIL, Ujung Pandang.

Friberg, T. & Friberg, B. (1991a) Notes on Konjo phonology. *NUSA*, **33**, 71–115.

Friberg, T. & Friberg, B. (1991b) Excerpts from the complete do-it-yourself Konjo generation kit: a statement of Konjo morphology.

Friberg, T. & Laskowske, T.V. (1989) South Sulawesi languages. In *NUSA*, **31**, 1–17.

Friedericy, H.J. (1933) De standen bij de Boegineezen en Makassaren. *Bijdragen tot de Taal-, Land- en Volkenkunde*, 80, 447–602.

Gani, A., Husnah, G., Baco, B., Baddarudin. (1987) *Pengungkapan Isi Dan Latar Belakang Nilai Budaya Kelong Makassar (Puisi Makassar Dalam Naskah Kuno)*. Departemen Pendidikan Dan Kebudayaan, Jakarta.

Goldsmith, J.A. (1990) *Autosegmental and metrical phonology*. Basil Blackwell, Oxford.

Grimes, C.E. & Grimes, B.D. (1987) *Languages of South Sulawesi*. Dept. of Linguistics, Research School of Pacific Studies, Australian National University, Canberra.

Hall, R. (2001) Cenozoic reconstructions of SE Asia and the SW Pacific: changing patterns of land and sea. In *Faunal and floral migrations and evolution in SE Asia–Australasia*, (Eds, Metcalfe, I., Smith, J.M.B., Morwood, M. & Davidson, I.D.) Swets & Zeitlinger Publishers, Lisse, pp. 35–56.

Hanson, C. (2001) A description of basic clause structure in Bugis. *La Trobe Papers in Linguistics*, **11**, 143–160.

Hanson, C. (2003) *A grammar of Bugis based on the Soppeng dialect*. Ph.D. thesis, La Trobe University.

Hasan Basri. (1998) Number marking in Selayarese. In *Recent Papers in Austronesian Linguistics: Third and Fourth meetings of the Austronesian Formal Linguistics Association*, (Ed, Pearson, M.) UCLA, pp. 45–59.

Hasan Basri. (1999) *Phonological and syntactic reflections of the morphological structure of Selayarese*. Ph.D. thesis, SUNY Stony Brook.

Hasan Basri, Broselow, E., Finer, D. (1999) Clitics and crisp edges in Makasar. *Toronto Working Papers in Linguistics: Proceedings of AFLA VI (The sixth meeting of the Austronesian Formal Linguistics Association)*.

Hasan Basri & Chen, Y. (1999) When harmony meets reduplication in Selayarese. *Toronto Working Papers in Linguistics: Proceedings of AFLA VI (The sixth meeting of the Austronesian Formal Linguistics Association)*.

BIBLIOGRAPHY 429

Himmelmann, N. (1996) Person marking and grammatical relations in Sulawesi. In *Papers in Austronesian Linguistics No. 3*, (Ed, Steinhauer, H.) Pacific Linguistics, Canberra, pp. 115–136.

Himmelmann, N. (2002) Voice in western Austronesian: an update. In *The history and typology of western Austronesian voice systems*, (Eds, Wouk, F. & Ross, M.) Pacific Linguistics, Canberra, pp. 7–16.

Himmelmann, N. (2005) Typological characteristics. In *The Austronesian Languages Of Asia And Madagascar*, (Eds, Adelaar, K.A. & Himmelmann, N.) Routledge, London, pp. 110–181.

Hunter, T.M. (1996) Ancient beginnings: The spread of Indic scripts. In *Illuminations: the writing traditions of Indonesia*, (Eds, Kumar, A. & McGlynn, J.H.) Weatherhill, New York, pp. 3–12.

Ide Said DM, M. (1977) *Kamus bahasa Bugis–Indonesia*. Pusat Pembinaan dan Pengembangan Bahasa, Departemen Pendidikan dan Kebudayaan, Jakarta.

Indiyah Imran (1976) The morphology of the prefixes aN– and aK– in Makasar. Indonésie vol. 2. Actes du XXIXe Congrès international des Orientalistes, section organiséé par Denys Lombard. 86–93.

Indiyah Imran (1984) *Proses morfologi dalam kelas kata bahasa Makassar*. Ph.D. thesis, Universitas Hasanuddin.

Intje Nanggong Siradjoedin. (1940) *Pau–pauanna I Kukang*. Landsdrukkerij, Batavia.

Jacobs, H. (1966) The first locally demonstrable Christianity in Celebes, 1544. *Studia*, 17, 251–305.

Jelinek, E. (1984) Empty categories, case, and configurationality. *Natural Language and Linguistic Theory*, 2, 39–76.

Jukes, A. (1998) *The phonology and verbal morphology of Makassar*. M.A. thesis, University of Melbourne.

Jukes, A. (2005) Makassar. In *The Austronesian Languages of Asia and Madagascar*, (Eds, Adelaar, K.A. & Himmelmann, N.) Routledge, London, pp. 649–682.

Kaseng, S. (1978) *Kedudukan dan fungsi bahasa Makassar di Sulawesi Selatan*. Pusat Pembinaan dan Pengembangan Bahasa, Jakarta.

Klamer, M.A.F. (1998) *A grammar of Kambera*. Mouton de Gruyter, Berlin.

Koolhof, S. (1999) The "La Galigo"; A Bugis encyclopedia and its growth. *Bijdragen tot de Taal-, Land- en Volkenkunde*, 155, 362–387.

Kozok, U. (1996) Bark, bones and bamboo: Batak traditions of Sumatra. In *Illuminations: the writing traditions of Indonesia*, Weatherhill, New York, pp. 231–246.

Kroeger, P.R. (2005) Analyzing Grammar: An Introduction. Cambridge University Press, Cambridge.

Ladefoged, P. & Maddieson, I. (1996) *The sounds of the world's languages*. Blackwell, Oxford.

Lee, J.K.L. (2006) Transitivity, Valence and Voice in Mandar. Paper presented at the Tenth International Conference on Austronesian Linguistics.

Ligtvoet, A. (1880) Transcriptie van het dagboek der vorsten van Gowa en Tello met vertaling en aanteekeningen. *Bijdragen tot de Taal-, Land- en Volkenkunde*, 28, 1–259.

Macknight, C.C. (1976) *The voyage to Marege': Macassan trepangers in northern Australia*. Melbourne University Press, Carlton.

Macknight, C.C. (1984) The concept of a 'work' in Bugis manuscripts. *Review of Indonesian and Malaysian Affairs*, 17, 92–116.

Macknight, C.C. (1993) *The early history of South Sulawesi: some recent advances*. Monash University Centre of Southeast Asian Studies, Melbourne.

Macknight, C.C. (ed. and transl.) 2012. *Bugis and Makasar. Two short grammars*. Canberra: Karuda Press.

Macknight, C.C. & Caldwell, I. (2001) Variation in Bugis manuscripts. *Archipel*, 61, 139–154.

Manning, C.D. (1996) *Ergativity: Argument Structure and Grammatical Relations*. CSLI, Stanford.

Matthes, B.F. (1858) *Makassaarsche spraakkunst*. F. Muller, Amsterdam.

Matthes, B.F. (1859) *Makassaarsch–Hollandsch woordenboek: met Hollandsch–Makassaarsche woordenlijst, opgave van Makassaarsche plantennamen, en verklaring van een tot opheldering bijgevoegden ethnographischen atlas: uitgegeve voor rekening van het Nederlandsch Bijbelgenootschap*. Frederik Muller; Gedrukt bij C.A. Spin & Zoon, Amsterdam.

Matthes, B.F. (1860) *Makassaarsche chrestomathie*. M. Nijhoff, 's Gravenhage.

Matthes, B.F. (1874) *Boegineesch–Hollandsch woordenboek, met Hollandsch–Boegineesch woordenlijst en verklaring van een tot opheldering bijgevoegden ethnographischen atlas*. M. Nijhoff, 's-Gravenhage.

Matthes, B.F. (1883) *Makassaarsche chrestomathie*. M. Nijhoff, 's Gravenhage.

Matthes, B.F. (1885) *Makassaarsch–Hollandsch woordenboek: met Hollandsch–Makassaarsche woordenlijst, en verklaring van een tot opheldering bijgevoegden ethnographischen atlas: uitgegeve voor rekening van het Nederlandsch gouvernement*. M. Nijhoff, 's-Gravenhage.

Matthes, B.F. (1985) *Beberapa Etika dalam Sastra Makassar*. Departemen Pendidikan dan Kebudayaan, Jakarta.

McCarthy, J.J. (1998) Morpheme structure constraints and paradigm occultation. In *CLS 32, Part 2: The Panels*, (Eds, Gruber, C., Higgins, D., Olson, K. & Wysocki, T.) Chicago Linguistic Society, Chicago, pp. 123–150.

McCarthy, J.J. & Prince, A. (1994) The Emergence of the Unmarked: Optimality in Prosodic Morphology. In *Proceedings of the North-East Linguistics Society 24*, (Ed, Gonzalez, M.) Graduate Linguistic Student Association, Amherst, MA, pp. 333–379.

Mead, D. (2003) Evidence for a Celebic supergroup. In *Issues in Austronesian phonology*, (Ed, Lynch, J.) Pacific Linguistics, Canberra,

Miller, Christopher. (2011) Indonesian and Philippine Scripts and extensions not yet

BIBLIOGRAPHY 431

encoded or proposed for encoding in Unicode as of version 6.0. http://www.unicode
.org/notes/tn35/indonesian-philippine.pdf

Mills, R.F. (1975a) *Proto South Sulawesi and Proto Austronesian Phonology*. Ph.D. thesis, University of Michigan.

Mills, R.F. (1975b) The reconstruction of Proto South Sulawesi. *Archipel*, 10, 205–224.

Mithun, M. & Basri, H. (1987) The phonology of Selayarese. *Oceanic Linguistics*, 25, 210–254.

Morrell, E. (2005) Redrawing Sulawesi's map. *Inside Indonesia*, 82, 18–19.

Muhammad Mustofa (1992) The Sociocultural Approach in Controlling Violent Crime: a case study of 'Siri' Phenomenon in Buginese–Makasar Community, South Sulawesi, Indonesia. In *International Trends in Crime: East Meets West*, (Eds, Strang, H. & Vernon, J.) Australian Institute of Criminology, Canberra, pp. 25–29.

Nelson, N.A. (2003) *Assymetric Anchoring*. Ph.D. thesis, State University of New Jersey.

Niemann, G.K. (1863) Mededeelingen over Makassaarsche Taal- en Letterkunde. *Bijdragen tot de Taal-, Land- en Volkenkunde*, 6, 58–88.

Noorduyn, J. (1955) Een achttiende-eeuwse kroniek van wadjos: Buginese historiografie. H.L. Smits, 's-Gravenhage.

Noorduyn, J. (1961) Some aspects of Macassar–Buginese historiography. In *Historians of South-East Asia*, (Ed, Hall, D.G.E.) Oxford University Press, London, pp. 29–36.

Noorduyn, J. (1965) Origins of South Celebes historical writing. In *An introduction to Indonesian historiography*, (Ed, Soedjatmoko) Cornell University Press, Ithaca, pp. 137–155.

Noorduyn, J. (1991a) A critical survey of studies on the languages of Sulawesi. KITLV Press, Leiden.

Noorduyn, J. (1991b) The manuscripts of the Makasarese chronicle of Goa and Talloq; An evaluation. *Bijdragen tot de Taal-, Land- en Volkenkunde*, 147, 454–484.

Noorduyn, J. (1993) Variation in the Bugis/Makasarese script. *Bijdragen tot de Taal-, Land- en Volkenkunde*, 149, 533–570.

Nursiah Tupa (1995) *Leksem penanda waktu dalam bahasa Makassar*. Balai Penelitian Bahasa, Ujung Pandang.

Parewansa, P., Wahid, S., Ngewa, D.B.D., Johari, A.R. (1992) *Sastra sinrilik Makassar*. Pusat Bahasa, Jakarta.

Pater, J. (2001) Austronesian nasal substitution revisited. In *Segmental phonology in optimality theory: constraints and representations*, (Ed, Lombardi, L.) Cambridge University Press, New York, pp. 159–182.

Pelras, C. (1979) L'oral et l'écrit dans la tradition Bugis. *Asie du Sud-Est et Monde insulindien*, 10, 271–297.

Pelras, C. (1996) *The Bugis*. Blackwell, Oxford.

Pelras, C. (2000) Patron–client ties among the Bugis and Makasar of South Sulawesi. *Bijdragen tot de Taal-, Land- en Volkenkunde*, 156, 393–432.

Pires, T. & Rodrigues, F. (1944) The suma oriental of Tome Pires: an account of the East, from the Red Sea to Japan, written in Malacca and India in 1512–1515; and, The book of Francisco Rodrigues: rutter of a voyage in the Red Sea, nautical rules, almanack and maps, written and drawn in the East before 1815. Hakluyt Society, London.

Prapañca, M. (1995) *Deśawarṇana: (Nāgarakṛtāgama)*. KITLV, Leiden.

Raffles, T.S. (1817) *The History of Java*. Oxford University Press, Oxford.

Reid, A. (1981) A Great Seventeenth Century Indonesian Family: Matoaya and Pattingalloang of Makassar. *Masyarakat Indonesia*, 8, 1–28.

Reid, A. (1988) *Southeast Asia in the age of commerce, 1450–1680*. Yale University Press, New Haven.

Reid, A. (1993) Southeast Asia in the early modern era: trade, power, and belief. Cornell University Press, Ithaca.

Reid, A. (2000) *Charting the shape of early modern Southeast Asia*. Institute of Southeast Asian Studies, Singapore.

Ricklefs, M.C. (2001) *A history of modern Indonesia since c. 1200*. Stanford University Press, Stanford.

Rössler, M. (1987) Die soziale Realität des Rituals; Kontinuität und Wandel bei den Makassar von Gowa. Reimer, Berlin.

Rössler, M. (1990) Striving for modesty; Fundamentals of the religion and social organization of the Makasar Patuntung. *Bijdragen tot de Taal-, Land- en Volkenkunde*, 146, 289–324.

Rössler, M. (2000) From divine descent to administration; Sacred heirlooms and political change in highland Goa. *Bijdragen tot de Taal-, Land- en Volkenkunde*, 156, 539–560.

Röttger–Rössler, B. (1988) Rang und Ansehen bei den Makassar von Gowa (Süd-Sulawesi/Indonesien). D. Reimer, Berlin.

Röttger–Rössler, B. (2000) Shared responsibility; Some aspects of gender and authority in Makassar society. *Bijdragen tot de Taal-, Land- en Volkenkunde*, 156, 521–538.

Saenger, P.H. (1997) *Space between words: the origins of silent reading*. Stanford University Press, Stanford.

Sahabuddin Nappu. (1986) *Kelong dalam Sastra Makassar*. Departemen Pendidikan dan Kebudayaan, Jakarta.

Sahabuddin Nappu & Sande, J.S. (1991) *Pantun–Pantun Makassar*. Departemen Pendidikan dan Kebudayaan, Jakarta.

Said Mursalin. (1984) *Sistem perulangan bahasa Makassar*. Pusat Pembinaan dan Pengembangan Bahasa, Jakarta.

Sirk, Ü. (1988) Towards the historical grammar of the South Sulawesi languages: possessive enclitics in the postvocalic position. In *Papers in Western Austronesian linguistics No. 4*, (Ed, Steinhauer, H.) Pacific Linguistics, Canberra, pp. 283–302.

Sirk, Ü. (1989) On the evidential basis for the South Sulawesi language group. *NUSA*, 31, 55–82.

BIBLIOGRAPHY

Sirk, Ü. (1994) The South Sulawesi languages: Indigenes of Sulawesi. Paper at the 7th International Conference on Austronesian Linguistics (ICAL-7).

Sirk, Ü. (1996) The Buginese language of traditional literature. Self-published, Moscow.

Sneddon, J.N. (1993) The drift towards final open syllables in Sulawesi languages. *Oceanic Linguistics*, **32**, 1–44.

Sneddon, J.N. (1996) *Indonesian reference grammar*. Allen & Unwin, St Leonards.

Steinhauer, H. (1988) Malay in East Indonesia: The case of Macassarese Malay. In *Rekonstruksi dan cabang-cabang bahasa Melayu induk*, (Eds, Mohd Thani Ahmad, Zaini Mohamed Zain) Dewan Bahasa dan Pustaka, Kuala Lumpur, pp. 108–151.

Sutherland, H. (2001) The Makassar Malays: Adaptation and Identity, c. 1660–1790. *Journal of Southeast Asian Studies*, **32**, 397–421.

Sutton, R.A. (1995) Performing arts and cultural politics in South Sulawesi. *Bijdragen tot de Taal-, Land- en Volkenkunde*, **151**, 672–699.

Sutton, R.A. (2002) Calling back the spirit: music, dance, and cultural politics in lowland South Sulawesi. Oxford University Press, Oxford.

Syamsul Rizal & Sahabuddin Nappu. (1993) *Sastra Makassar Klasik*. Departemen Pendidikan dan Kebudayaan, Jakarta.

Tadmor, U. (2003) Makasar Malay. http://email.eva.mpg.de/~gil/jakarta/Makasar_malay.php

Thomsen, C.H. (1832) A code of Bugis maritime laws, with a translation and vocabulary. Mission Press, Singapore.

Tol, R. (1990) *Een Haan in oorlog*. Foris, Dordrecht.

Tol, R. (1992) Fish food on a tree branch; Hidden meanings in Bugis poetry. *Bijdragen tot de Taal-, Land- en Volkenkunde*, **148**, 82–102.

Tol, R. (1993) A royal collection of Bugis manuscripts. *Bijdragen tot de Taal-, Land- en Volkenkunde*, **149**, 612–629.

Tol, R. (1996) A separate empire: Writings of South Sulawesi. In *Illuminations: the writing traditions of Indonesia*, (Eds, Kumar, A. & McGlynn, J.H.) Weatherhill, New York, pp. 213–230.

Tol, R. (2000) Textual authority; The Toloq Rumpaqna Boné by I Mallaq Daéng Mabéla, Arung Manajéng. *Bijdragen tot de Taal-, Land- en Volkenkunde*, **156**, 499–520.

van den Berg, R. (1996) The demise of focus and the spread of conjugated verbs in Sulawesi. In *Papers in Austronesian Linguistics No. 3*, (Ed, Steinhauer, H.) Pacific Linguistics, Canberra, pp. 89–114.

van der Veen, H. (1940) Tae' (Zuid-Toradjasch)–Nederlandsch woordenboek: met register Nederlandsch–Tae'. Martinus Nijhoff, 's-Gravenhage.

Van Valin, R.D. (1993) A synopsis of Role and Reference Grammar. In *Advances in Role and Reference Grammar*, (Ed, Van Valin, R.D.) John Benjamins, Philadelphia, 1–164.

Van Valin, R.D. (1999) A Typology of the Interaction of Focus Structure and Syntax. In

Typology and the Theory of Language: From Description to Explanation, (Eds, Raxilina, E. & Testelec, J.), Languages of Russian Culture, Moscow, pp. 511–524.

Volkman, T.A. & Caldwell, I. (1995) *Sulawesi: the Celebes*. Periplus Editions, Berkeley.

Walker, A. & Zorc, D. (1981) Austronesian loanwords in Yolngu-Matha of northeast Arnhem Land. *Aboriginal History*, 5, 109–134.

Wolhoff, G.J. & Abdurrahim. (1959) *Sedjarah Goa*. Makassar.

Zainab. (1996) Konstruksi oblik bahasa Makassar (suatu analisis Transformasi Generatif). Balai Penelitian Bahasa, Ujung Pandang.

Zainuddin Hakim. (1991) *Rupama: cerita rakyat Makassar*. Departemen Pendidikan dan Kebudayaan, Jakarta.

Zainuddin Hakim. (1995) *Peribahasa Makassar*. Pusat Pembinaan dan Pengembangan Bahasa, Departemen Pendidikan dan Kebudayaan, Jakarta.

Index

absolutive 126, 238
active voice 283
actor 250
actor focus 232
addition of subjunctive 354
adjectival modifier 197, 225
adjectival predicates 321
adjectival roots 153
adjective phrases 152
adjectives 144
adjunct 311
admonition 328
Advanced Tongue Root (ATR) 91
adverbial particles 97
affixal clitics 118, 122
affixes 55
affricated stops 65
agentless passive 275, 281
agent-like argument (A) 330
alveolar fricative 75
alveolar lateral approximant 76
alveolar stop 71
alveolar trill 77
ambitransitive 250
anaphoric argument 290
animacy hierarchy 336
aphesis 86
apico-alveolar nasal 73
apico-dental aspirated stop 70
applicatives 101, 155
argument structure 289
aspectual distinctions 129
aspirated velar stop 73
attitudinal modifier 166
attributive 152, 345
Austronesian 1
Austronesians 7

Bantaeng 4, 8
benefactive 315, 342
bi-directional 31
bilabial nasal 73
bilabial stop 69, 70
bivalent 257
Bone, kingdom 13
Borneo 2

Bugis literature 60
Bugis printing types 51
Bugis settlement 3
Bugis-Makasar 17
Bulukumba 4

causative comparatives 294
causative derivation 181, 287
causative passive 294, 304
causative prefix 150
causative reciprocals 294
causative transitive verb 296
causative verb 155, 192, 288, 297
cave paintings 6
Cense's dictionary 55
chanted performance 63
clausal modifiers 226
clause interrogation 338
clause nucleus 310
clause-external 334
clause-final 194
clause-initial 236, 334
clitic behaviours 112
clitic fronting 130
clitic pronouns 55, 169, 240–242
clitics 97, 115, 119
clitic-stem boundaries 103
coda position 68
coda specification 94
coda, standed 111
coda, underspecified 69
code-switching 30
collocations 118
comitative 321
comparative 156
comparative, doubly 168
complementiser/conjunction 240
compounds 102
confixes 121
contingency 328
continuants 67
core arguments 231, 232
cross-referencing clitic 231, 245
customary law 62

INDEX

definite marking   223, 329
definite secondary object   227, 302
degemination   89, 101
deixis, adverbial   172
deixis, spatial   177
deletion   111
demonstratives   135
deontic modality   128, 344
derivation   119, 120, 144, 187, 289, 290, 299, 304
determiners   133
dialect chain   20
digraphs   55
diminution   112, 208
directional terms   177
discourse connectives   239
discourse particle   344
distributive meaning   187
ditransitive imperative   342
ditransitive verb   254
Dutch East India Company (VOC)   13
Dutch occupation   14

echo syllables   107
emphatic   170, 172
enclitics   1, 59, 101, 124
epenthesis   112
epistemic marker   167
equational clauses   361
ergative   126, 232, 236
etymostatistics   24
event nominals   320
existential   360
experiencer-orientation   299
extra-clausal   194
extrametrical   109

focus   232, 284, 337
folk tales   65
fricatives   65
fronting for focus   285
functor statistics   25

geminate   1, 67, 68, 69, 74, 79, 95, 112
gender neutral address   201
genetic affiliation   19
glides   66
glottal fricative   76
glottal nasalisation   267

glottal stop   68, 84
Gowa Chronicle   10
Gowa dialect   20
Gowa   4, 7, 10

Habibie, B.J.   16
habitual nominals   210
head predicates   185
head, morphological   119
head-marking   1
historical linguistics   24
homorganic sequence   84

imitation   208
immutability   117
imperative   340
imperfective clitic   163
incorporated locatives   118
incorporated nominals   247
indefinite   225, 301, 332, 346
Indic script   44
indicative clauses   340
Indonesia   2, 16
infinitival analysis   211
infixes   121
inflectional morphology   120
instrument nominalisation   212
intensifier   163
interrogative   164, 344
intonation   92, 342–343
intransitive   149, 186, 243, 246, 340, 346
intransitivisers   257, 280
irrealis   355
irregular derivation   321
irregular verbal forms   179
Islam   12, 32

Japanese invasion   15
Jawi script   54
Jeneponto   4

Kahar Muzakkar   16
Karaeng Bayo   10
Karaeng Matoaya   12
Karaeng Pattingalloang   12
Katalog Naskah Buton   41
kin terms   197
Koninklijk Instituut voor de Tropen (KIT)   48

INDEX

Koninklijk Instituut voor Taal-, Land- en
   Volkenkunde (KITLV) 35, 36

labial-velar glide 78
lamino-palatal nasal 74
lamino-palatal stop 71, 72
left-dislocation 285
legal perspective 63
length contrast 69
lexical roots 119
lexical valence 257
lexicalised prepositional phrases 192
lexically bivalent verbs 251
lexically divergent 23
lexicostatistical 22
liquids 65
literacy 30, 59
loan consonants 83

Makasar noble signatories 47
Makasar poetry (kelong) 37
Makasar proverbs 42
Makasar script 49
Makasar-Dutch dictionary 40
Makasar-Indonesian dictionary 37
Makasar-Indonesian 56
Makassar Malay 31
Makassar newspaper 40
Makassar war 14, 18
Malacca 8
Mandar 4, 26
manner modifiers 247
Maros Chronicle 42
Maros 4
Matthes foundation 35
measure noun 204
metaphorical extension 209
minimal NP 222
missionary grammarians 35
Moluccas 1, 2
monophthongs 87
monosyllabic affixes 121
monosyllabic root 99
monosyllabic words 101
Muhammad Jusuf Kalla 16

nasal coda 73
nasal substitution 263
nasal, syllable-final 51

nasalisation 90
nasalising prefixes 39
negative imperatives 342
negator, free 236
negator, nominals 357
nominal bases 208
nominal classifiers 189
nominal derivation 143
nominal modifier 171, 197
nominal predicate 144, 320
nominal properties 147
nominalisation, place/time 297
nominalising morphology 154
non-dependent lexical units 119
non-intimates 199
non-nasal continuants 108
non-specificity 112
noun phrase internal modifiers 186
noun root 143
nouns denoting substance 309
nouns, common 196
number marking 39, 312
numeral classifiers 148
numeral interrogative 351
numeral linker 352
numeral predicates 360
numerals, complex 182
numerals, compound 181
numerals, ordinal 186

Obligatory Contour Principle 95
oblique 272, 310
onset 65, 107
onsets, complex 84
Optimality Theory 38, 105, 109
oral genre/composition 61, 62
orthography, Dutch based 55

palatal glide 80
Pangkajene Kepulauan 4
Pangkep 5
Pare-pare 4
particle 119, 139
passimbang 50
passive causative benefactive 293
passive clauses 270–271
passive marker 275–276
passive verbal base 120
passive voice 283

INDEX

patient-like argument (P)   330
perfective enclitic   128
personal prefix   200
Phillipines   2
phonological independence   99
phonological unity   117
phonological word   97, 100
phonology   1
phrasal affix   133n
pitch   100
places of articulation   68
PMP affix forms   312
poems, sung   64
polymorphemic forms   97
polysyllabic affixes   121
Portugeuse   7
possessed adjectives   154
possessed reduplicated bases   157
possessive affixal clitic   220
possessive functions   360
possessive suffix   136, 326
post-lexical gemination   114
post-verbal position   180
predicate head   231
predicate possession   360
predicate, verbal   256
predicative functions   152
predictable assimilation   56
prefixes   121
preposed particles   193
pre-predicate position   334
presentative   169, 172
pre-verbal position   180
principles and parameters   38
proclitics   124
prohibitive   358
pronominal cross-referencing   122
pronominal enclitic   126
pronouns, free   169
proper nouns   196
prosodic break   338
prosodic characteristics   93
prosodic unit   99
prosodic word   91, 97
proto-Bugis   26
proto-Makasar   26
proto-South Sulawesi   22
proto-South Sulawesi   7, 87

recursive combining   120
reduplication   88, 100, 218
reduplicative prefix   113
reflexive pronoun   254
relative clauses   175
repetition   112
restricted indefinite pronoun   174
rhetorical questions   164
romanisation   54
rounded vowel   85, 86
rupama (folktale)   42

Sa'dan   4, 27
script, Brahmi   46
script, Bugis   46, 49
script, Bugis-Makassar   44
script, indigienous   44
secondary argument   304
Selayar   4
Selayarese   20, 38
semi-ditransitive   254
semi-transitive   243, 252
sentences, complex   337
Sinjai   4
sinrili' (epic poems)   42
Siri'   18
Soppeng dialect   40
South Sulawesi   1, 2, 4
specificity   244
spreading, VCV   110
stops   69
stress contour   111
stress   55, 97, 100, 101
subjunctive suffix   136
subordinate clause   138
suffixes   101, 112, 121
Sulawesi   2
Summer Institute of Linguistics   38
Sunni Muslim   17
superlative   156, 160
syllabic roles   116
syllable boundaries   50, 84, 111
syllable   44
syntactic operations   251
syntactic units   100

Tae'   4
Takalar   4
Tallo' chronicle   47

INDEX

Tallo' 7
TAM 126, 356
temporal adjuncts 203
temporal nominals 197
three-participant constructions 314
three-way deictic 172
Timor 1
Toalean 6
topic position 232
transitional language 1
transitive clause 149, 252, 253, 340
transitivised forms 307, 308
Treaty of Bungaya 41, 47
trisyllabic roots 97
trochee 97, 119
Tumapa'risi' Kallonna 11
Tunipalangga 11
Tunipasulu 12

undergoer 232, 250, 251, 269

valence 148, 286, 305
velar nasal 75
verb phrases 118

verb prefixes 86
verb root 143
verb stems 270
verbal agreement 240
verbal complements 228
verbhood 257
verbs, basic 258
vetative marker 359
V-initial roots 104
voice marker 255
voice velar stop 73
vowel harmony 91
vowel laxing 91
vowel sequences 89
vowel-initial roots 264
vowel-killer (virama) 51

Wallacea 2
West Austronesian Superstock (WMP) 22
Western-Malayo-Polynesian 1
word class 120
word formation 93
word order 231
word-level compounds 142